Juvenile Law
Cases and Comments
Second Edition

Juvenile Law
Cases and Comments
Second Edition

Joseph J. Senna
Northeastern University

Larry J. Siegel
University of Massachusetts-Lowell

West Publishing Company
St. Paul   New York   Los Angeles   San Francisco

Composition: Parkwood Composition
Copy editor: Marilyn Taylor
Cover image: Joe Lasker, "Valley Forge II," 1984.
West/Art and the Law Exhibition, 1988.
Reproduced with permission from Kraushaar Galleries, New York.
Production, Prepress, Printing, and Binding by West Publishing Company.

Library of Congress Cataloging-in-Publication Data

Senna, Joseph J.
    Juvenile law: cases and comments / Joseph J. Senna, Larry J. Siegel.—2nd ed.
        p.   cm.
    ISBN 0-314-93376-X (soft)
    1. Juvenile courts—United States—Cases.   2. Juvenile justice,
Administration of—United States—Cases.   I. Siegel, Larry J.
II. Title.
KF9794.S45   1992
345.73'08—dc20   91-30728
[347.3058]
                                                      CIP

To my wife Therese J. Libby and my children, Julie, Andrew, Eric, and Rachel.

L.J.S.

To my wife Janet and my children, Joseph, Stephen, Christian, and Peter.

J.J.S.

CONTENTS

PREFACE

There is a great national concern over the evolution of juvenile law. One reason is the enduring problem of juvenile crime. More than 1.5 million adolescents are arrested each year, and over half a million are tried in juvenile courts. While the juvenile crime rate has not skyrocketed, young people are committing serious violent crime at a steadily rising rate. Juvenile gangs and groups have become a fixture in many metropolitan areas. Some gangs contain more than five thousand members and have branch chapters around the nation. Adolescent gangs are believed to control the drug trade in inner-city areas and are quite willing to use their automatic weapons to protect and expand their markets.

Concern about adolescent misbehavior is not the only reason that the nature of juvenile law has taken on greater importance. There is significant concern about the problems of all youth in modern society. Many U.S. teenagers are approaching adulthood unable to adequately meet the requirements and responsibilities of the workplace, the family, and the neighborhood. They suffer from health problems, are educational underachievers, and are already skeptical about their ability to enter the social mainstream. Too often, these at-risk youths live in neighborhoods where they fear walking to school in the morning and where it is common to begin experimenting with drugs and alcohol at an early age. The number of teenage pregnancies has increased sharply, and many children born to underage mothers are extremely vulnerable to health problems.

U.S. youths also live in families undergoing tremendous strain. About half of all new marriages end up in divorce; many family members sacrifice time with each other in order to afford better housing and life-styles. More than 1 million youths suffer physical, emotional, and sexual abuse at the hands of their parents, guardians, or relatives.

Considering the social problems faced by U.S. youth, the law that controls their activities and defines their legal rights is an important area of study. The need to summarize new juvenile case law and related legal issues has prompted us to update our juvenile law text book, which was first published fifteen years ago. This new edition provides a survey of the changes in juvenile case law that have evolved since the first edition was published. The book now includes cases that define the legal rights of youth within the juvenile justice process and also the most critical cases defining the rights of minors within the family and at school. These new legal areas have been added because the critical role of the family and school in influencing adolescent behavior is unquestioned.

ORGANIZATION OF THE TEXT

Juvenile Law contains eight chapters that cover the legal rights of juveniles from arrest through incarceration and their rights within the family and school.

Chapter I, Juvenile Court Jurisdiction, contains cases that help define the concept of delinquency and the purpose of the juvenile court.

Chapter II, Police Processing of the Juvenile Offender, includes cases defining the rights of juveniles who are suspected of crimes. It covers search and seizure, arrest, interrogation, and pretrial identification.

Chapter III, Early Court Processing, contains cases on the pretrial stage of juvenile justice. Topics include preventive detention, the detention of youths in adult jails, and the right to bail.

Chapter IV, Transfer of Jurisdiction to the Criminal Court, covers the waiver process, including the hearing, transfer criteria, and double jeopardy.

Chapter V, The Adjudicatory Process, contains cases that define adolescents' rights during the juvenile trial. Topics include the right to a hearing, standard of proof, juries, speedy trial, and public trial.

Chapter VI, The Disposition of the Juvenile Offender, covers the dispositional process, including the dispositional hearing, institutional commitment of delinquents and status offenders, and conditions of probation.

Chapter VII, Postdispositional Processing, covers the rights of juveniles who are found to be delinquent. Case topics include the right to treatment, appeals, aftercare, and the death penalty.

Chapter VIII, Special Problems of Minors, covers the rights of minors in the home and school. Topics include removing children from abusive families, free speech in schools, school discipline, and the child as a witness in abuse cases.

SPECIAL FEATURES

Hundreds of cases were reviewed in the preparation of this book. Those chosen were the most significant in their subject area and are important teaching tools. Every effort was made to provide up-to-date and readable case presentations.

Each chapter begins with an introduction to the subject matter. Case comments within each section are used to facilitate the learning process by providing a summary of the key issues within individual cases.

A number of people helped with the preparation of this text by reviewing material and making case suggestions. They include:

- Kathleen Block
- Joseph Faltemier
- J. Robert Lilly
- Harold Schramm
- Henry Sontheimer

In addition, the authors would like to thank our colleagues at Northeastern University and the University of Lowell for their helpful comments. We would also like to thank Mary Schiller, our editor at West Publishing. Without her help and support, we would not have been able to publish this book.

Joseph J. Senna
Larry J. Siegel

ONE

Juvenile Court Jurisdiction

INTRODUCTION

The modern juvenile court is a specialized court for children.[1] It may be organized as an independent statewide court system, as a special session of a lower court, or even as part of a broader family court. Juvenile courts are normally established by state legislation and exercise jurisdiction over "delinquent" and "incorrigible" children. Delinquent children are those who reach a jurisdictional age, which may vary from state to state, and who commit a violation of the penal code. Incorrigible children include truants and habitually disobedient and ungovernable children. They are characterized in state statutes as either children, minors, persons, youths, or juveniles in need of supervision (CHINS, MINS, PINS, YINS, and JINS, respectively), and their actions are often classified as status offenses. Most states distinguish such behavior from delinquent conduct so as to lessen the effect of any stigma on the children as a result of their involvement with the juvenile court. Some juvenile courts may also have jurisdiction over adoption, neglect, and custody proceedings.

Today's juvenile court system operates on both a rehabilitation and a legal philosophy.[2] This means that the purpose of the court is traditionally therapeutic, rather than punitive, and that children under its jurisdiction must be accorded their constitutional rights. The administrative structure of the court revolves mainly around a juvenile court judge, probation staff, government prosecutors, and defense attorneys. Thus, the juvenile court functions in a socio-legal manner. It seeks to promote the rehabilitation of the child within a framework of procedural due process. In recent years, crime control advocates have initiated tougher sentencing provisions with respect to youth in the juvenile justice system.[3]

This philosophy of rehabilitation, due process, and accountability has developed primarily over the last twenty-five years. For approximately the first sixty years of the juvenile court movement, or since the establishment of the original court in Illinois in 1899, children were denied constitutional protections.[4] The juvenile court operated in a benevolent, paternalistic, and informal manner. Children were arrested, tried, convicted, and sentenced on the basis of *parens patriae*—the power of the state to act in behalf of the child and to provide care and protection equivalent to that of a parent. The application of this principle led to arbitrary treatment for many juvenile offenders. However, this philosophy has changed completely since the U.S. Supreme Court ruled that children have constitutional due process rights in juvenile proceedings.[5]

Juvenile court jurisdiction is established by state statute and based on age classifications. The states have differed in determining what age brings children under the juvenile court. Many state statutes include all children under eighteen, others set the upper limit at under seventeen, and still other states include children under sixteen. There are also jurisdictions that have a lower age limit, as well as some that provide different age categories for males and females. This latter gender-based distinction has been held to be violative of the equal protection clause of the U.S. Constitution.

Juvenile court jurisdiction is also based on the child's actions. If such action is a crime, this conduct normally falls into the category of delinquency. Definitions of delinquency vary from state to state, but most are based on the common element that delinquency is an intentional violation of the criminal law. On the other hand, the juvenile courts also have jurisdiction over status offenders or children without parental supervision. Here, the states differ markedly on defining conduct. Some states provide comprehensive definitions of a status offender, such as are found in the statement "a child who habitually disobeys the orders of his parents or guardian, or who is truant, or who may be in danger of boding an idle, dissolute, lurid or immoral life is within the jurisdiction of the court." Other states define a status offender as "one who is beyond the control of his parents."[6]

The jurisdiction of any juvenile court is also affected by state statutes that exclude certain offenses from the court's consideration, as well as by the use of transfer provisions. Some states may exclude capital offenses, such as murder, from the jurisdiction of the juvenile court. Almost all states, however, allow the juvenile court to waive, transfer, or bindover jurisdiction to the criminal court.[7]

Having once obtained jurisdiction of a child, however, the court ordinarily retains it until the child reaches a specified age, usually the age of majority (eighteen). Jurisdiction terminates in most states when the child is placed in a public child-care agency.

PURPOSE OF JUVENILE COURT

Case Comment

The traditional purpose of the juvenile court has been to rehabilitate juvenile offenders. The "best" interests of the child was the byword for policymakers in the juvenile justice system. Punishing children was unacceptable. In the last decade or so, there has been a shift from the rehabilitative ideal to a more conservative, punishment-oriented approach. The case of *In re Michael D.* explores whether an order

of the juvenile court committing a minor to the California Youth Authority may be based on punishment and public safety, as well as on rehabilitative goals. In dealing with this issue, the court recognized the rights of the legislature to adjust the fundamental philosophy and purpose of the state juvenile code from one of complete rehabilitation to punishment and accountability.[8]

IN RE MICHAEL D.

Cite as 234 Cal.Rptr. 103 (Cal.App. 1 Dist. 1987)

Low, Presiding Justice.

We hold that an order of the juvenile court committing a minor to the California Youth Authority may be validly based on punishment and public safety grounds so long as it will also provide rehabilitative benefit to the minor.

The minor, Michael D., appeals from an order of wardship (Welf. & Inst. Code, § 602)[1] committing him to the California Youth Authority (CYA) after he admitted to one count of sexual battery. (Pen.Code, § 243.4, subd. (a).) The minor contends that the juvenile court judge abused his discretion in committing him to CYA. We affirm.

On January 12, 1986, officers responded to a report that a rape was in progress in the Day Street Park playground. They found a woman being raped by a minor; appellant was observed leaning over the victim near her head and appeared to be holding her down. The minor was leaning over the neck of the victim with his hands out in front, but there was no conclusive evidence he was choking the victim. However, it was clear from the medical evidence that the victim had lacerations and bruises consistent with attempted strangulation. After the incident, the minor showed little remorse for the incident nor any concern for the victim. The minor eventually admitted to one count of sexual battery.

At the dispositional hearing, the minor introduced letters from various people in support of his request to be placed on probation and assigned to the care and custody of his parents. Dr. Paul Walker, a psychologist retained by the minor, reported that Michael did not have a propensity towards violence or sexual sadism. Paul Gibson, an instructor on adolescent sexuality for the Department of Youth Authority, recommended that the minor be placed with his parents and be given therapy as a condition of probation. Gibson communicated his concern that the minor would only increase his involvement and identification with delinquent groups if placed in CYA. In addition, Hillel Maisel, a counselor at juvenile hall who worked in the unit where the minor was housed, testified that the minor was a "young man [of] tremendous potential" whose placement in CYA "would not be for his benefit" because of his high intelligence level and the level of schooling available from CYA.

However, the court-appointed psychologist, Dr. Korpi, found the minor to possess poor judgment and to be "long . . . beyond the control of a reasonable authority," requiring a program to "slow him down [and] provide firm limits" on his behavior. Further, Dr. Walker expressed doubts about the ability of the minor's parents to place strict limits on the minor's behavior. The minor also admitted that he had a history of alcohol and hallucinogen abuse.

The probation report concluded that "[t]he magnitude and outrageousness of the conduct alone warrants a commitment to the [CYA]." The report concluded that an out-of-home placement (§ 202, subd. (e)(4)) would not be suitable and, "[w]eighing all the factors objectively, . . . in order to afford adaquate [sic] protection of the community and to have this minor atone for his participation in this most 'vicious crime,' " recommended CYA placement.

The juvenile court found the minor "guilty" of a "very brutal, heinous and vicious crime, and the conduct in this matter [was] outrageous." The judge also stated that the minor's history of drug and alcohol abuse was a significant factor, and found him "to be a threat and danger to society . . . . [H]is own interests and the interests of society would be best served by his being at this time in the California Youth Authority." He also stated that the minor would benefit from the reformatory educational discipline provided by the CYA.

I

The minor contends that his commitment to CYA was an abuse of discretion by the juvenile court in that (1) the minor was improperly committed to CYA for purposes of retribution rather than rehabilitation; (2) the juvenile court did not properly consider less restrictive alternatives; and (3) the minor could not be benefited by commitment to CYA.

The decision of the juvenile court may be reversed on appeal only upon a showing that the court abused its discretion in committing a minor to CYA. (In re Eugene R. (1980) 107 Cal.App.3d 605, 617, 166 Cal.Rptr. 219; In re Todd W. (1979) 96 Cal.App.3d 408, 416, 157 Cal.Rptr. 802.) An appellate court will not lightly substitute its decision for that rendered by the juvenile court. We must indulge all reasonable inferences to support the decision of the juvenile court and will not disturb its findings when there is substantial evidence to support them. (In re Eugene R., supra, 107 Cal.App.3d at p. 617, 166 Cal.Rptr. 219; In re Michael R. (1977) 73 Cal.App.3d 327, 332–333, 140 Cal.Rptr. 716.) In determining whether there was substantial evidence to support the commitment, we must examine the record presented at the disposition hearing in light of the purposes of the Juvenile Court Law. (§ 200 et seq.; In re Todd W., supra, 96 Cal.App.3d at pp. 416–417, 157 Cal.Rptr. 802.)

At the core of the dispute before us is a fundamental disagreement over the purposes of the Juvenile Court Law. Prior to the amending of section 202, California courts have consistently held that "[j]uvenile commitment proceedings are designed for the purposes of rehabilitation and treatment, not punishment." (In re Aline D. (1975) 14 Cal.3d 557, 567, 121 Cal.Rptr. 816, 536 P.2d 65.) The Aline court derived its conclusion from the terms of former section 502 (now § 202): "to secure for each minor . . . such care and guidance, preferably in the minor's own home, as will serve the spiritual, emotional, mental, and physical welfare of the minor. . . ." (Id., at p. 562, 121 Cal.Rptr. 816, 536 P.2d 65.) Commitment to CYA was treated as the placement of last resort "only in the most serious cases after all else has failed." (In re Eugene R., supra, 107 Cal.App.3d at p. 617, 166 Cal.Rptr. 219.) A commitment to CYA had to be supported by a determination based upon substantial evidence in the record of (1) probable benefit to the minor (In re Aline D., supra, 14 Cal.3d at p. 566, 121 Cal.Rptr. 816, 536 P.2d 65; In re John H. (1978) 21 Cal.3d 18, 27, 145 Cal.Rptr. 357, 577 P.2d 177), and (2) that a less restrictive alternative would have been ineffective or inappropriate. (In re Ricky H. (1981) 30 Cal.3d 176, 183, 178 Cal.Rptr. 324, 636 P.2d 13.)

In 1984, the Legislature replaced the provisions of section 202 with new language which emphasized different priorities for the juvenile justice system. (Stats. 1984, ch. 756, §§ 1, 2, No. 5 Deering's Adv. Legis. Service, pp. 440–441.) The new provisions recognized punishment as a rehabilitative tool. (§ 202, subd. (b).) Section 202 also shifted its emphasis from a primarily less restrictive alternative approach oriented towards the benefit of the minor to the express "protection and safety of the public" (§ 202, subd. (a); *In re Lawanda L.* (1986) 178 Cal.App.3d, 423, 433, 223 Cal.Rptr. 685; review den.), where care, treatment, and guidance shall conform to the interests of public safety and protection. (§ 202, subd. (b).)

[1] Thus, it is clear that the Legislature intended to place greater emphasis on punishment for rehabilitative purposes and on a restrictive commitment as a means of protecting the public safety. This interpretation by means loses sight of the "rehabilitative objectives" of the Juvenile Court Law. (§ 202, subd. (b).) Because commitment to CYA cannot be based solely on retribution grounds (§ 202, subd. (e)(5)), there must continue to be evidence demonstrating (1) probable benefit to the minor and (2) that less restrictive alternatives are ineffective or inappropriate. However, these must be taken together with the Legislature's purposes in amending the Juvenile Court Law. Consistent with these new objectives, we turn to the record before us.

II

[2] The crime committed was brutal and violent. The victim has been repeatedly raped with the admitted assistance of the minor. Further, even if we accepted the minor's representations that he merely aided the commission of the crime, by not offering help or aid to the victim exhibits a shocking callousness which requires appropriate treatment and guidance. This conclusion is strengthened when one considers the minor's unrepentant and cavalier attitude following his detention and arrest.

Moreover, the court-appointed psychologist concluded that the minor was "beyond parental control" and the psychologist retained by the minor also seriously questioned whether his parents could place the strict limits on his behavior necessary for rehabilitation. The minor had poor social and moral judgment that required firm guidance. The minor also admitted that he has a problem with drugs and alcohol, which the psychologists agree requires substantial help. From all these facts, the trial court could have inferred (1) that the minor's best interests required an environment providing firm, strict dis-

cipline for his "out of control" behavior, evidenced by his participation in a violent crime, (2) without such discipline and realignment of his social and moral structure he poses a demonstrated threat to public safety, and (3) that the minor required intensive rehabilitative treatment for his substance abuse, and (4) the minor's parents were demonstrably incapable of caring for the minor consistent with the minor's best interests in treatment and guidance and the objective of the protection of the public. The minor may not have been suitable for Log Cabin Ranch placement due to his age, nor suitable for an out-of-home placement. In its discretion, the juvenile court chose commitment to CYA over the obviously unsuitable alternative of release to parental custody. There was substantial evidence supporting the trial court's exercise of discretion.

The order of wardship is affirmed.

DEFINITION OF DELINQUENCY
Case Comment

The case of *In re Edwin R.* presents an analysis of a state statute that rules that a minor cannot be found delinquent unless he or she requires "supervision, treatment or confinement." In the present case, delinquency petitions against Edwin R. and his associates were dismissed because the youths seemed to have made a successful adjustment to the community while awaiting trial. The court ruled that the accused delinquents, despite the fact that their petition charged homicide, could not legally be held for treatment or confinement. Thus, the issue of deciding whether the accused was delinquent or nondelinquent became moot due to the statutory definition of the term *delinquent*.[9]

IN RE EDWIN R.

Family Court, City of New York, New York County, 1971.
67 Misc.2d 452, 323 N.Y.S.2d 909.

DECISION AND ORDER

Manuel G. Guerreiro, Judge.

This proceeding was initiated on April 28, 1969. The petition alleges that the respondents, acting in concert, fatally stabbed one Francisco Sanchez, an act which if performed by an adult would constitute the crime of murder. After the homicide was discovered on April 26, 1969, the respondents were immediately taken into custody. The youths first were questioned at their neighborhood police precinct, then they were taken to Youth House where they remained until their release in December, 1969. After the passage of two years, the entertaining of time-consuming pre-trial motions and an omnibus pre-trial hearing both on the issues of probable cause and suppression, the case is now ready for trial.

Counsel for the respondent move to dismiss the petition on the ground that there is no longer need for court intervention. The passage of time, notably two years in the prime of youth has given the respondents the opportunity to begin their development into mature and law abiding members of the community. No question of right to speedy trial has been raised, and, indeed, would be inappropriate considering the nature and source of much of the delay.

In support of their position respondents' attorneys cite Section 731 of the Family Court Act which requires that a petition to adjudicate a person a juvenile delinquent must allege that "the respondent requires supervision, treatment, or confinement."

If a fact-finding hearing is held, and if a fact-finding is made, the court must then hold a dispositional hearing "to determine whether the respondent requires supervision, treatment or confinement". (F.C.A. Sec. 743)

> * * * [T]he finding of fact as to conduct alone may not support an adjudication * * * of "delinquency." * * * This petition will be dismissed without any adjudication of "delinquency" * * * if the probation and psychiatric reports indicate that the boy is not in need of supervision, treatment or confinement under court order. (Family Court Act, §§ 743, 745, 752).
>
> In this respect, a finding of delinquency * * * requires a [sic] basis of a finding of a *condition* showing need for the attention of the court, in addition to the mere *conduct* alleged, and in this respect differs from the criminal court procedures for older persons. The Family Court does not find a child "delinquent" * * * unless there is need for its rehabilitative or protective functions. (Qu.Co.Fam.Ct.1963) (*Matter of Ronny*, 40 Misc.2d 194, 197, 242 N.Y.S.2d 844.)

In such case, both because of limited judicial resources and the potential effects of a rehashing of the events in question at a fact-finding hearing, it would be inadvisable to proceed with a fact-finding

hearing if there would be an inevitable dismissal of the petition after the dispositional hearing.

Furthermore, the Family Court is not a Criminal Court with punitive objectives. The purpose of this Court is to rehabilitate children and to make services available to them, not to vindicate private wrongs. The legislative committee which drafted the Family Court Act stated:

> The Committee concluded that it would be unwise, at this time, to give the Family Court the extensive powers given the criminal courts under the Penal Law of the State of New York.
>
> * * * In the Committee's view, while a due process of law should be used in the Family Court, criminal powers and procedures would be inconsistent with the proper development of the Family Court, during its formative period, as a special agency for the care and protection of the young and the preservation of the family.
>
> * * *
>
> Early in the history of the juvenile court movement, there was agreement that juvenile delinquency proceedings should be "civil", not "criminal." This agreement was based on a sense of a child's exuberance and vitality and the stress of the early years of life. The restraints and disciplines of adulthood have not yet been established. The possibilities of change are seemingly great. And so the decision was made to avoid a criminal conviction for the young and to shape the law and provide a court to guide and supervise, rather than punish, children in trouble. The Committee adheres to that decision.* * *" (Report of the Joint Legislative Committee on Court Reorganization, 1962 McKinney's Session Laws (Vol. 2) 3428, 3433–34.)

It is, of course, not often that the lack of need for the court's "supervision, treatment or confinement" will be evident before a dispositional hearing, which, in the normal course of events, would follow a fact-finding. However, under the exceptional circumstances of cases such as this, consideration of the probability of section 731(c) jurisdiction should be given prior to a fact-finding hearing for all the aforementioned reasons. (The Office of the Corporation Counsel assents to this view.)

The form of this consideration will necessarily vary from case to case. The special facts and circumstances of this case were presented at an adversary hearing at which all parties were permitted to present evidence. In addition, the Court Liaison Officer of the Probation Department was directed to have the files searched and to ascertain for the court if any of the respondents were known to this Court subsequent to the filing of the petition in question and the status of any pending litigation.

Given the extraordinary nature of a procedure such as this, the burden of going forward at least, must necessarily be on the respondents.

On the basis of the Liaison Officer's report and the evidence presented at the hearing, it appears:

Edwin R. was re-arrested following the Family Court action, tried before the Criminal Court and is presently incarcerated in the Riker's Island Detention Center. He no longer requires the intervention of the Family Court.

The remaining respondents have had a comparably fine adjustment. This adjustment is due in great measure to the assistance and fine direction they received from their respective attorneys. These young attorneys were counselors in every sense of the word, ably serving their clients diversified needs and encouraging their clients to more suitable objectives and goal oriented lives. The efforts of these lawyers notably were combined with those of Marilyn Shafer, a social worker at MFY Legal Services, Inc., who has worked with all the respondents from January 1970 until the present time and in addition, with regard to Edwin M.'s social workers, Mr. Kojo Odo, of Boys Harbor, and Toni Nagel of Bellevue Hospital, Dr. Chess, a psychiatrist at Bellevue Hospital and Mr. Cecil Bruckman, a specialist in education. Miss Shafer has prepared innumerable detailed studies of the boys and their adjustment. She also testified before this Court. Letters and reports have been contributed by the aforementioned individuals and others who have come into direct contact with the boys.

Edwin M., at the inception of the case possessed a cognitive (reasoning and knowledge) defect making him incapable of exercising independent judgment and reasoning beyond a superficial level. Edwin became very involved initially in the program at Bellevue Hospital attending classes there and seeing the social worker on a regular basis. Edwin was subsequently referred to Boys Harbor by his lawyer, Richard Asche, who felt that the educational and recreational program offered would benefit his client. A close relationship developed between Edwin and his social worker at the Harbor, Kojo M. Odo. Mr. Odo found the boy's development so good that he recommended him for the leadership program which trains junior summer camp counselors to which Ed-

win has been accepted. The Executive Director of Boys Harbor, Richard L. Williams, in a letter to this Court dated April 2, 1971, reported that Edwin has adjusted quite well and is a contributing member of the Boys Harbor environment. He also recommends that Edwin continue at the Phoenix School. The response of Adele Martin, a Special Teacher at the Phoenix School, in a letter dated March 20, 1971, reported that Edwin's progress has been uneven, but they will still consider him in their program.

William S. is the only respondent who has had a later encounter with Family Court. A petition was filed against William on June 30, 1970, and dismissed on August 7, 1970. The basis of the allegation of the petition was an assault by William upon his girlfriend while inebriated. According to the most recent reports of Miss Shafer, William can presently be said to have made the most dramatic behavioral adjustment in school and in the community. He now communicates better and shows no evidence of retardation. Drinking has been eliminated from William's life. William attends the Manhattan School for Boys. Mr. Blacksher, the guidance counselor, confirmed that William is not a behavior or academic problem. He felt that improvement could be shown in the areas of attendance and lateness.

Anthony H. also attends the Manhattan School for Boys where his behavior and school work are satisfactory. Anthony was described by Mr. Blacksher as "a pleasant and personable young man." The guidance counselor stated however that as in William's case a problem existed with regard to habitual absences and tardiness.

The last respondent, Victor H., is currently enrolled in the cooperative work-study program at Seward Park High School whereby he alternates weekly between school and a position as a maintenance worker with the New York City Parks Department. Prior to his transfer to the work program this semester Victor was absent approximately one-third of the fall term. Victor was admitted to the cooperative program because his poor academic and behavioral problems indicated that he was receiving no benefit from the normal academic program although he was only a tenth grader and the program is normally only opened to juniors and seniors. School personnel with personal knowledge of Victor agreed that the work program was the only chance of reaching him, but that it was still too early to offer a prognosis for future progress.

William, Anthony and Victor have all been attending Tompkins Square Community Center in the evening. Corporation Counsel's investigator spoke to the police in the respondents' neighborhood who reported that the youths now have a pacific reputation in the community.

Now, the appropriate inquiry into the facts and circumstances of the case having been made, it is

Adjudged, that none of the respondents have demonstrated any anti-social behavior except for truancy; that the omnibus hearing having consumed numerous court hours and continued use of court time serves little worthwhile purpose in that, should a fact-finding and dispositional hearing be held, the best result would be the continued supervision of the respondents which is not being adequately performed; and it is further

Ordered, that the petitions be and hereby are dismissed.

STATUS OFFENDERS

Case Comment

Juveniles often come into contact with the law for noncriminal reasons vís-a-vís PINS, CHINS, MINS or other status offense categories. In some jurisdictions, these youths, believed to be incorrigible by parents or teachers, receive substantially identical treatment to delinquents, though they have actually broken no law or ordinance. In *Martarella v. Kelley*, a juvenile found to be a PINS under a New York statute, appeals from a detention order placing him in joint custody with delinquents. In reviewing the case, the appellate court used a substantial amount of social material, expert witness testimony, and other factual evidence. In making its judgments, the court pointed out that the social and psychological forces that drive and motivate an incorrigible youth may also affect the delinquent. Therefore, it was not a

violation of due process rights to treat both categories of offenders in the same institution or environment.

The position of the status offender within the juvenile justice system remains controversial. The removal of such children, for example, from secure lockups with delinquent youths has been one of the more successful justice-related programs in the United States. Today, almost all states have legally prohibited incarcerating status offenders with delinquents.[10]

MARTARELLA v. KELLEY

United States District Court, Southern District of New York, 1972.
349 F.Supp. 575.

Lasker, District Judge.

The rapid urbanization of the United States in this century and the heavy influx of the poor to the cities in the last two decades have produced a numerous class of children whose conduct, although not criminal in character or legal designation, results in their incarceration.

Robert Martarella and his fellow plaintiffs[1] are members of that group—alleged or adjudicated to be "Persons in Need of Supervision" (PINS) pursuant to § 732 of the Family Court Act of New York (the Act). They bring this civil rights action for a declaration that their temporary detention in the "maximum security" facilities—Spofford, Manida and Zerega, juvenile centers operated by the City of New York—deprives them of due process and equal protection and constitutes cruel and unusual punishment under the conditions prevailing at those institutions.

The plaintiffs moved for preliminary injunctive relief. Pursuant to Rule 65(a) (2), Fed.R.Civ.Pr., the trial of the action was consolidated with the hearing of the application.

---

1. At the time the complaint was filed, Martarella had been confined at Spofford because he had run away from home on seven occasions for periods up to ten days in the prior nine months and refused to go to school. At first, he was paroled for investigation. His mother, however, reported that he ran away again and a warrant was issued. On the return of the warrant, he was remanded for full study and report so that a placement other than a training school could be explored. However, his mother refused to take him home and remand was continued for several weeks. He was again placed on probation but a week later ran away from home and was found unconscious in a school hallway. His probation was revoked and he was remanded for about six weeks with weekend parole privileges. A full study and psychiatric report were ordered. He was paroled again and ran away. On his return, on a warrant, the court ordered placement at Lincoln Hall, a privately operated institution. Martarella's case is not unique. Although no precise facts are in evidence as to the rate of recidivism among children in the centers, the witnesses agreed that recidivism was significant. A case like Martarella's presents difficult problems of final disposition and these difficulties may explain in part the number of cases of long stays at the centers. The details of the cases of the other plaintiffs are set forth in the pleadings * * * . None of the other plaintiffs testified at the trial and the particular facts of their cases have no determining influence in regard to the issues before us.

A "Person In Need of Supervision" is defined in § 712(b) of the Act as "a male less than sixteen years of age and a female less than eighteen years of age who does not attend school in accordance with the provisions of part one of article sixty-five of the education law or who is incorrigible, ungovernable or habitually disobedient and beyond the lawful control of parent or other lawful authority."

The boys at Spofford range in age from 7 through 15; the girls at Manida and Zerega from 7 through 17.

The Family Court Judges are authorized, by § 739 of the Act, to direct that a PINS be detained if "(a) there is a substantial probability that he will not appear in court on the return date; or (b) there is a serious risk that he may before the return date do an act which if committed by an adult would constitute a crime."

The Presiding Justices of the Appellate Division are responsible for the designation of appropriate detention centers for PINS.

The Director of the Office of Probation was, at the time this suit was instituted, responsible for the administration and operation of the centers. In November 1971, the supervision of the centers was transferred to the Department of Social Services of the City of New York, and Jule M. Sugarman, Commissioner of Social Services, has been added as a defendant.

The injunctive relief sought by the plaintiffs is to prevent the Family Court Judges from remanding PINS to the centers, to order the Presiding Justices of the Appellate Division to designate non-secure facilities which comply with New York law and the Federal Constitution as to the care and treatment of children in custody, and to order the administrator of the centers to close Manida and Zerega permanently, and Spofford until it is made "safe, sanitary and decent for its inmates."

They also move for determination of the case as a class action.

Spofford, Manida and Zerega ("the centers," except where reference is made to a specific facility) are institutions at which PINS *and* juvenile delinquents are, (on what is theoretically termed a "temporaroy" basis), detained together pending the permanent disposition of their cases by long term custody or otherwise. The term "theoretically" must be emphasized because in a significant number of cases, as we shall see below, the "temporary" nature of the detection is lengthened to as much as 100 days or more.

Generally speaking, children who have been adjudicated as PINS are truants, or runaways, or have been ungovernable at home. The acts for which they may be brought before a court, detained at the centers and thereafter held in custody for a term would not constitute crimes if committed by an adult.

The acts committed by juvenile delinquents (JDs) are criminal in character (in contrast to the acts in PINS). A JD is defined by § 712(a) of the Act as "a person over seven and less than sixteen years of age who does any act which, if done by an adult, would constitute a crime".

Plaintiffs' major contentions may be summarized as follows:

(1) The incarceration of non-criminal children in maximum security detention under conditions which plaintiffs describe as punitive, hazardous and unhealthy, and in the absence of rehabilitative treatment constitutes cruel and unusual punishment and a violation of due process under the Eighth and Fourteenth Amendments respectively.

(2) Classifying and housing PINS together with juvenile delinquents (JDs) (rather than with neglected children) for purposes of temporary detention is arbitrary and capricious and violates the equal protection clause.

The defendants deny that the conditions at the centers are punitive or (with exceptions) hazardous or unhealthy, and assert that the program provided for the plaintiff class provides treatment and rehabilitation to the extent possible in the context of temporary detention. Consequently, they assert that no cruel and unusual punishment or deprivation of due process exists. As to the issue of equal protection, they claim that housing of PINS with JDs is a rational and professionally accepted method of classification for temporary detention, so that no constitutional violation exists.

*   *   *

Before we commence an exploration of the facts and the questions of law which they present, it is essential that the issues be focused. The plaintiffs do not challenge the constitutionality of the Family Court Act or the authority of Family Court judges to remove a nondelinquent child from his home on proper grounds. They do not contest the propriety of confining non-delinquent children in *any* secure setting. The issue they raise is limited to whether PINS may constitutionally be confined in the three named detention centers: Mania, Zerega, and Spofford, and whether they may be held in custody in the same facilities as juvenile delinquents.

* * *

PHYSICAL FACILITIES AND RESTRAINTS

Spofford: Spofford is "secure" not only from the outside world, but internally as well. The building is surrounded by a high wall. Although individual sleeping rooms are left open at night unless the particular child poses a risk to himself or others, the children (boys) are otherwise locked in their dormitories, recreation rooms or classrooms * * *. Each corridor of the building that leads to the dormitories, classrooms, dining halls or offices has metal doors at each end that are locked at all times. An electronically locked metal door controls movement in and out of the buildings. The windows are secured from inside by a screen made of institutional netting. Each screen is secured to the window by a frame which is hooked to the window frame, (Stipulation No. 2).

When boys arrive at Spofford their personal clothing is taken from them and they are issued uniforms of blue jeans and T-shirts on whose fronts is an institutional legend (admitted allegations of Par. 20A(6) of the complaint).

Manida: Manida is also surrounded by a high wall. The girls there are under lock and key: specifically the doors to each unit, which contains an "open" dormitory, day room and bathroom, are locked; the doors to each corridor of the building and the doors to the stairway are locked at all times.* * *

Zerega: The girls at Zerega are confined to prefabricated metal buildings.* * * Like the other centers, Zerega is surrounded by a high wall. The buildings contain a dormitory and a room that serves as a schoolroom and recreation center.

The most comprehensive description of the physical characteristics of the centers is found in the Stone Report.[4]

Spofford is located on a four-acre tract in the Southeast Bronx. Completed in 1958, it includes

dormitories, schoolrooms, gymnasium, swimming pool, conference rooms and a room for religious purposes, infirmary, cafeteria, library and other miscellaneous supporting facilities. There are outdoor play areas for softball, shuffleboard, paddle tennis, basketball, handball and volleyball. In spite of these virtues, the Stone Report states that the facility is "fraught with problems related both to architectural layout and to maintenance." For example, it is $\frac{1}{7}$ of a mile from one end of the structure to the other; the building is "poorly designed for its functional purpose"; space for receiving children is inadequate so that searching is often conducted in the toilet facilities; there is lack of sufficient area for visitation; the school is divided among three separate floors, creating "traffic problems"; lighting is "generally inadequate," the rooms are often cold in winter, and the fire alarm system—at least at the date of the report—was in disrepair.

Manida: This center is situated on a two-acre tract in the Southeast Bronx. There are three buildings: a main three-story structure, a two-story cottage, and a one-story attached residence. There is an outdoor volleyball court and baseball diamond. The main building was constructed in 1904 as a monastery, and was renovated in 1954. The dining room in the basement and dormitories on the second and third floors were not renovated and, as the Stone Report picturesquely describes them, "survive as remnants of the monastic era." The gym is "dilapidated." The cottage is no longer in use. As far back as 1963, the Federal Department of H.E.W. reported to the director that Manida was, as the Stone Commission reports the findings, "unsuitable for the detention care of children, that no remodelling or repair could make it suitable, and that it should be replaced * * *" and "because of lack of space and general layout, a detention program could not be provided." The Stone Commission found that "since 1963 the situation has not improved" and that its serious state of disrepair was such that "Physically, Manida is depressing." To compound the situation, "The deplorable condition of Manida was exacerbated by a fire on November 14th, 1970 which destroyed two dormitories. All of the children are now being hou-

---

4. The Stone Report was submitted by plaintiffs as an exhibit to their memorandum in support of the motion for a preliminary injunction. Although the testimony at trial consisted primarily of evidence as to the conditions of life at the centers (and of the validity or invalidity of the programs there as "treatment"), such testimony as did refer to physical conditions was consistent with the findings of the Stone Report. The defendants have not contested the report's description of the physical arrangements at the centers, and we find the facts in accordance with that catalogue which was made upon an objective and detailed study by experts.

sed in the remaining dormitories which adds to the problems of the institution."

The defendants have stipulated that Manida "is inappropriate for the detention of children." (Stipulation No. 6 and admitted allegations of Par. 25B(4) of the complaint).

Zerega: Zerega was constructed in 1962 as a temporary facility and is located on a two-acre "marshy" tract in the Central East Bronx. It consists of eight buildings, which the Stone Report (and the complaint) describe as "Quonset huts," and the defendants call "prefabricated metal structures." There is an outdoor skating rink, basketball court and shuffleboard court. The Stone Report states (p. 30):

> The buildings are sinking. This becomes particularly apparent after periods of heavy rainfall. The settling of the buildings causes cracks in the hot water pipes suspended from the ceilings, which could result in serious injury if a pipe should burst. Leaks in the roof are common*   *   *.

The buildings are "hot in the summer and cold in the winter" and "there are insufficient waiting room facilities for visitors which discourages visiting during inclement weather."

As of the date of the Report (January 1971) it was "contemplated that the facility will have to be abandoned." This was still the case at the time of trial.

It will be noted that all of the centers are located in the East Bronx. Since they are the only detention centers in the city for PINS, their location in one corner of the metropolis makes it a long journey for many family visitors who come from Queens, Brooklyn and Staten Island, and acts to limit the actual number of visits which the children receive.

*   *   *

The number of boys in custody at Spofford or of girls at Manida and Zerega has varied substantially at different times, but seems to show a declining trend as plans for new or substitute facilities, which we describe below, come into fruition.

Spofford has a capacity of 300, and there were times in the past when it was seriously overcrowded. Those days seem to be over. In May of 1971 the population ranged from a low of 183 to a high of 221; while in May 1972, the spread was between 110 and 173. (Monthly Population Report May 1972, by Director of Detention Services; Human Resources Administration, Institutional Services).

The centers' total capacity for girls is 170 (*idem*). In May of 1971, 93 were at Manida and Zerega, as compared to 83 in May of 1972 (*idem*).

Although the centers were established and are conducted solely for temporary detention until final disposition of a child's case, the agonizing difficulty of permanently placing some children elsewhere results in many stays which are anything but temporary.

The average time spent at the centers as of the time of trial was only 12.06 days for girls and 16.81 for boys; for unhappily, many remain much longer. For example, plaintiff Martarella was at Spofford for six months and William Ocean, a defense witness, for seven months. John Wallace, Director of New York City Probation Department, testified that in 1969, when the total population of the centers was clearly larger than it is today—due to creditable efforts since then by the Family Court to reduce the number of children remanded to secure detention and to speed up the permanent placement of those at the centers—there were 142 children at one time who had been in custody for more than 30 days, and 30 or 40 of those had been in custody for over 100 days. In May of 1972, 44 children had been detained over 30 days, and in May of 1972 the number was still 34, of whom one had been in custody for 115 days, three more than 90 days, seven 80 days or more, four over 60 days, nine more than 50 days, three more than 40 days, and the remainder over 30.

*   *   *

RESTRAINTS AND DISCIPLINE

In addition to being locked institutions (internally and externally) whose male "inmates" must wear uniform clothing, there are other characteristics which the centers share with penal institutions. For example, according to Robert Martarella's uncontested testimony, children are required to walk in line from place to place without talking, and are "hit" or have a smoking break taken away if they get out of line. Knives are not generally furnished at meals. Homosexuality, both forced and consensual, exists in both girls' and boys' centers as what all parties appear to agree is an inevitable concomitant of incarceration.

The testimony of Mel Rivers, President of The Fortune Society, an organization dedicated to prison reform and the assistance of released prisoners, compared conditions in prison and Spofford. Rivers, who was once in custody at Spofford for a week in 1958, has also been confined in a State training school, a county jail, and for three years at Comstock Prison, his last term ending nine years ago. A year ago he visited Spofford as a consultant once a week for seven to ten weeks for "rap sessions" with the boys in custody, and made other visits as a member of a committee of the Stone Commission. When asked:

"In what way did you find that Spofford Juvenile Center is like, say, a county jail for adults or prison for adults?"

he replied:

A. Well, it is operated predominantly under the same type of a system, a count system, a march system. The counting probably in Spofford is done more silently than it is done in an adult facility. It is probably done by bed-checks, but it is still a count.

THE COURT: You mean to be sure everybody is there?

THE WITNESS: Yes, to be sure everybody is there.

The type of regimentation, to do this, to do that, that type of situation, the locking in, the inability to be really part of what is going on outside.

In juvenile institutions I realize you get out in the yard to play some ball, whereas in an adult facility you don't. But in the final analysis, you are back inside that enclosure. The windows are thick. There is a locked-in type of a situation.

In juvenile institutions, you have like a dormitory attached to a day room, and a good portion of your time is spent in the day room playing cards or looking at TV.

Q. Is this how it is up at Spofford?

A. At Spofford. And in county jails you have a day room that is attached to a prison corridor, like cells, and predominantly you spend your day in the day room playing cards and watching TV. So it is really somewhat the same system that is governed by and run by. It is just labelled different, juvenile institutions or adolescent or adult facilities.

Dr. Esther Rothman, a psychologist, is the principal of the Livingston School for Girls, a special school run by the New York City Board of Education for very aggressive girls. She was a visiting member of the detention committee of the Stone Commission and of the task force of the Citizens' Committee for Children's committee on probation, which prepared the 1971 report on the centers referred to earlier. She has visited all the centers on a number of occasions over a period of thirteen years, the last time only a few months before the trial. She testified (Tr. p. 71):

*   *   * the tone of all the facilities is one of punishment and getting even with kids and teaching them a lesson, and I never felt that there was any real treatment or any real approach to helping children.

Q. How would you describe Spofford?

A. In just that way, as a penal institution.

(Tr. p. 72)

Q. In your professional opinion what would you say were some of the effects of secure detention on nondelinquent children?

A. It is like asking me what is the effect of a concentration camp.

In Dr. Rothman's view a child does not see running away from home or truancy as harming any one else, and "*   *   * it is punitive when you are locked up some place having done nothing."

*   *   *

The punitive nature of custody at the centers is almost necessarily effected by the fact that it houses and mixes juvenile delinquents and PINS. While, as we shall see, the defendants assert that it is professionally and legally justified to treat the two classes in groups based upon their individual needs rather than their labels, nevertheless the necessities of the situation seem to require the enforcement of greater discipline when juvenile delinquents are included than would otherwise be the case. The JDs are, it must be remembered, charged with acts which would, except for the age of the actors, be crimes. The delinquencies range from the most minor to homicide and rape. While it is true that even a child who has committed one of these grievous acts may behave properly at the center, and although many PINS are by definition "ungovernable," yet it is a reasonable inference that the presence of serious offenders within a group intensifies the imposition of discipline and restraint—if for no other reasons than those of security and of safety to staff personnel and other children. The result is that the most difficult child easily becomes the lowest common denominator for disciplinary purposes. In addition, as the defendants admit, "*   *   * discipline is often enforced against many in a group for the transgressions of only one child." *   *   *

The Stone Commission found that "many children who did not require secure detention were being detained in the completely locked, prison-like (sic) maximum-security facility at Spofford. This practice is particularly shocking and offensive in the case of younger children. But since adequate facilities were not available for all children who simply needed a place to live pending disposition by the court, there was no alternative but to remand them to secure detention facility."

TREATMENT—GENERAL OBSERVATIONS

What we have said, although the record would justify more, is sufficient to establish that, however benign the purposes for which members of the plaintiff cases are held in custody, and whatever the sad necessities which prompt their detention, they are held in penal condition. Where the State, as *parens patriae*, imposes such detention, it can meet the Constitution's requirement of due process and prohibition of cruel and unusual punishment if, and only if, it furnishes adequate treatment to the detainee.

None of the defendants quarrel[s] with that proposition. The sole issue is whether the program for children at the centers measures up to constitutional standards of treatment.

We turn, therefore, to the facts relating to this critical subject: a subject as to which conclusions are more difficult to draw than as to those we have so far discussed. For one thing, the constitutional standards themselves are particularly difficult to assay. While decisions which we shall shortly review clearly pronounce the constitutional requirement of "treatment" as a quid pro quo for the exercise of the State's rights as *parens patriae*, they offer little guidance as to standards for determining the *adequacy* of treatment. Furthermore, as is perhaps to be expected in cases such as this, and in relation to a subject in which the outline of professional, like legal, standards is just emerging, the opinions of experts for the respective parties differ sharply as to the psychological and rehabilitative effect of the actual program at the centers. Finally, there are understandable limitations on the nature of the treatment that can be afforded—at least on an economically justifiable basis—at facilities established and intended for temporary detainees. These limitations may be constitutionally acceptable for those who are in fact temporarily detained but not for those who are actually held for long periods.

TREATMENT—THE PROGRAM

Expert witnesses for the plaintiffs differed sharply with defense witnesses as to the therapeutic productivity of secure detention, and as to the adequacy of the actual treatment program at the centers; but all of the experts agreed that the beginning of treatment can be provided in temporary detention facilities if the tone of the institution is such as to make a child feel that a staff member is concerned about him, and that the prerequisites for instilling such an attitude in the child are a staff (1) sufficient in numbers (2) adequately trained (3) having good relations with the children and (4) knowledgeable about the child's problems.

Judged by these standards, children detained for long terms cannot be said to receive treatment from the staff in the constitutional sense. Treatment from the staff of children detained for short terms is at best minimally acceptable. The phrase "from the staff" is deliberately used to emphasize the sociomedical nature of the treatment under discussion, differing as it does from the ordinary concept of "treating" a person kindly, indifferently or meanly. The concept of treatment as a constitutional quid pro quo for the state's right to detain those not guilty (or accused) of crime—children, the mentally ill, for example—involves the delivery of therapeutic services—services which must emanate *from* the staff. Treatment in this sense goes beyond good will and kindness, although those virtues may be indispensable to the success of the therapy. While there have been some episodes of physical mistreatment or abuse of children by staff members at the centers, they appear to be atypical, and the conclusions as to inadequacy of treatment "from the staff" do not imply any lack of good will or effort on the part of staff members in what is clearly a most difficult and demanding assignment. *   *   *

Staff Training: Through no fault of their own, the training of staff members—at least for counsellors, who work most closely with the children, and with whom the children spend markedly more time than with other staff members—appears seriously inadequate for the difficult and specialized assignment of dealing with problem children: Persons in need of supervision.

While counsellors must have had prior experience working "with people", this need not include experience working with children. The holding of a college degree is not required. The Stone Commission reported that no minimum educational requirement existed and that there was no formalized training procedure for new counsellors (except an orientation program concerned with the facility) prior to their permanent assignment, normally to supervise a dormitory of 24 children. To remedy this deficiency the Commission recommended the creation of a position of training officer who would develop and supervise programs for pre-service and in-service training, and The Citizens' Committee Study also recommended that in-service training be instituted.

*　　*　　*

COMMON CUSTODY OF PINS AND JDS

As we have earlier indicated persons in need of supervision—the class of plaintiffs in this case—are not charged with committing crimes. Normally their offenses consist of truancy or running away from home. In contrast, Juvenile Delinquents are charged with acts (ranging from minor offenses such as petty larceny to major offenses such as rape and murder) which, if committed by an adult, would be criminal. Yet when a PINS is held in temporary secure detention, he is held in the same institution as a JD. While there is no dispute as to this fundamental fact, there is sharp dispute as to the effect on the child of such common custody, and as to whether the common custody is rationally justified and professionally acceptable.

The statute (Family Court Act § 739), of course, authorizes such custody; but by regulation, neglected, abandoned and destitute children may not be confined in secure detention with JDs. The plaintiffs contend that this distinction between the custodial treatment of a PINS and a neglected child, neither of whom is accused of crime, is an arbitrary classification which violates the Equal Protection clause. The defendants respond that the distinction between the custody arrangements for PINS and neglected children is reasonable, and that the Equal Protection clause does not require that PINS and neglected children be treated identically.

The divergence of the expert testimony and what conclusions are to be drawn from it are illustrated by the following recapitulation:

Dr. Rothman testified that it was "very damaging" for girl PINS to be housed with girl JDs, because the atmosphere causes girls to boast about their criminal exploits so that such acts become a matter of "honor, prestige, and it gives them a whole set of values going in another direction, of course, of which we disapprove." This view was shared by Mel Rivers, who stated:

> Well, based on my own experience, if I can use that as a design, in most institutions, one of the ways of surviving, be it a juvenile or an adult, is the politics

called for, talking about the crimes that you committed is part of this life-style. You boast about these things because it is almost like a badge of honor to be able to say that you stole a car or to be able to say that you snatched a pocketbook or you shoplifted, and to take this and just blow it up to its highest point. *　*　*

Martarella himself testified that while at Spofford "[t]hey tried to teach me how to rob a pocketbook. They tried to teach me how to rob a car."

Rivers pointed out another danger of mixed PINS and JDs in custody:

> The other thing is that survival belongs to the fittest in institutions, juvenile or adult, and for a person to survive in an institution, regardless of what crime he is there for, he must acclimate himself to being violent. He must know how to fight.

and Dr. Rothman felt that the result of mixing PINS and JDs was that the children generally begin to "like" and "see as a way of life" an "aggressive bullying pattern".

Even defendants' witness, Dr. Greenwood agreed that it would be "desirable" to provide a facility for PINS separate from JDs. Dr. Greenwood agreed, also, that at least in some cases, as a result of the so-called "labelling" process, PINS would begin to think of themselves as JDs because of being detained in the same institution as JDs.

On the other hand, from the testimony of Judge Florence Kelley, Administrative Judge of the Family Court, a defense witness, and Dr. Weiner, for the plaintiffs, it is plain that private institutions regularly co-mingle PINS and JDs in custody.

It was Judge Kelley's view that the children should be separated "in terms of what treatment they needed, not on the basis of PINS and delinquency, but in terms of their problem and the treatment that is required by their problem." As she put it:

> I mean, some people think a person in need of supervision is somebody just staying away from school. Well, this simply does not describe a person in need of supervision. I think some of our most seriously disturbed children are the ones who come in as alleged persons in need of supervision.

Furthermore, it is important to note that the distinction between a PINS and JD is often factually less clear cut than the labels would suggest. Petitions alleging juvenile delinquency are quite regularly changed to petitions alleging a need of supervision by the Family Court judges on motion of the child's law guardian. The process appears analogous to reducing charges in an adult criminal court. Judge Kelley explained the reasons for such a procedure which, she said, "happens every day," and her testimony illustrated the interchangeable character of PINS and JDs in at least a significant number of cases:

> There are times when in certain situations it seems meaningless. If a child is brought in on an allegation of juvenile delinquent, really what you are talking about is one specific act on the part of the child. A person in need of supervision you are generally talking about a kind of behavior which must involve more than one incident.
>
> Now, when you get further into the case and know more about the child you as the judge may realize that the basic problem that will have to be dealt with in treating the child will be behavior rather than what motivated him to do that one exact act.
>
> But also you may find that the behavioral thing will yield to treatment rather than just dealing with one act, and you would change it then.

Dr. Rothman, a witness on whom the defendants relied heavily, agreed that there are not "significant personality differences between people who are adjudged PINS and people who are adjudged JDs." Indeed, the named plaintiff Martarella, for example, had stolen money from his parents more than once before he was sent to Spofford as a PINS (Tr. 39).

Dr. Greenwood (for the defense) supported the view that the labels PINS and JDs are not the basis upon which it should be determined whether children should be held in common custody. Although, as earlier indicated he felt it would be "desirable" to have a separate PINS facility, he, nevertheless, controverted the view that PINS would be "contaminated" by being housed with JDs, observing that "all kids select the things they want to imitate".
* * *

Plaintiffs' Equal Protection argument that PINS should not be housed with JDs is based on the rationale that since the law prohibits the common custody of neglected children (who have committed no crimes) with JDs, it must similarly prohibit the common custody of PINS (who have committed no crimes) with JDs. Defense witnesses disagreed with the underlying assumption that the same rule should apply to PINS as neglected children merely because neither category involves criminal activity.

Judge Kelley pointed out that in the case of a PINS the child himself is charged with misbehavior, albeit non-criminal, while in the case of a neglect petition the charge is against the parent, and the parent is alleged to be the cause of the child's misbehavior, if any.

While the housing arrangements and program for a child at the center are not determined on the basis of whether the child is a PINS or a JD, the authorities are in the process of developing standards of classification by which it will be determined how the child is to be placed and treated within the institution.

* * *

Presently no distinction is made between PINS and JDs with respect to treatment afforded, sleeping arrangements, recreation or schooling. However, the Bureau is "just now" developing a system of classification based on the nature of the child's problem rather than his status as a PINS or JD. A team of social worker, counsellor, teacher, psychiatrist and physician will observe and evaluate each child for placement. Thereafter, the child will be housed on the basis of age, maturity, emotional development, emotional and psychiatric history (when available), the charge against him or her, and evidence, if any, of drug use, but without regard to whether the child is charged as a PINS or JD * * *. Children who are charged with committing rape or murder will be separated from other children "whenever necessary", the criteria for such separation again including, in addition to the charge itself, age, maturity and psychiatric history and evaluation. * * * A separate dormitory and program for treatment has been set up for drug users for boys at Spofford, although entry into the dormitory is on a voluntary basis. * * *

In sum, the evidence establishes that PINS and JDs are not separately treated or housed on the basis of their "labels," but on a set of criteria which relate to the problems, offense and personality of each child.

* * *

At the end of a long journey we come to the legal questions raised on the merits of the case.

The Constitutionality of Common Custody of PINS and JDs:[16a] In arguing that the New York regulations violate the equal protection clause because they prohibit neglected children from being housed with JDs but do not give the same "protection" to PINS, plaintiffs rely on the rationale of *Baxstrom v. Herold,* 383 U.S. 107, 86 S.Ct. 760, 15 L.Ed.2d 620 (1969).

In *Baxstrom,* the Court held that it was arbitrary and capricious to deny to a mentally ill prisoner whose sentence was about to expire, but who was held for further custody in a hospital under the jurisdiction of the Department of Correction, the procedural protection granted all other persons civilly committed to mental hospitals. "Equal protection," the court stated (at 111, 86 S.Ct. at 763) "does not require that all persons be dealt with identically, but it does require that a distinction made have some relevance to the purpose for which the classification is made."

The question before us is whether the distinction between PINS and neglected children which allows the former, but not the latter, to be held in common custody with JDs has some relevance to the purpose for which the classification is made. We believe that it does.

It is true, of course, that a PINS and a neglected child—as distinct from a JD—have in common that neither is charged with acts of a criminal nature; but this fact alone does not require the state to treat PINS and neglected children identically if a rational basis exists for some other mode of action. The rationality demanded by the Equal Protection clause is not to be found in legal designations or labels, but must derive from the facts.

From the evidence before us we conclude that the distinction made in the custody and treatment of PINS and neglected children bears a reasonable relation to the purpose for which the classification is made.

A neglected child is defined by § 312 of The Family Court Act:

A 'neglected child' means a male less than sixteen years of age or a female less than eighteen years of age.

(a) whose parent or other person legally responsible for his care does not adequately supply the child with food, clothing, shelter, education, or medical or surgical care, though financially able or offered financial means to do so; or

(b) who suffers or is likely to suffer serious harm from the improper guardianship, including lack of moral supervision or guidance, or his parents or other person legally responsible for his care and requires the aid of the court; or

(c) who has been abandoned or deserted by his parents or other person legally responsible for his care.

A person in need of supervision is defined by § 712 of the Act: "Person in need of supervision" means a male less than sixteen years of age and a female less than eighteen years of age who is an habitual truant or who is incorrigible, ungovernable or habitually disobedient and beyond the lawful control of parent or other lawful authority.

The distinction drawn by the definitions, and the consequent factual difference in the membership of the two classes of children, is evident and forms a clearly rational basis for differences in their conditions of custody. Judge Kelley articulated the distinction clearly: a PINS is himself charged with misbehavior; in the case of a neglected child, the parent is the "defendant." Neglected children are victims, PINS are (non-criminal) offenders, or at least socially maladjusted. The neglected child is sinned against rather than sinning. On the other hand, a PINS' personal behavior is the cause of his subjection to legal authority.

While realism compels acknowledgement that the lines are often blurred, and that the PINS' maladjustment is frequently caused by misguidance or mistreatment by parents or other authority (as may be equally true of JDs) the acknowledgement does not vitiate the rationality of the distinction. For these reasons we find no violation of the equal protection clause.

16a. The Family Court Act itself as originally enacted in 1962 did not authorize placement of PINS in a maximum security institution (Laws of New York 1962, Chapter 686, § 756(a), at 2301). In 1964, 1965 and 1966, temporary amendments to the Act authorized institutionalization of PINS in the same facilities as JDs—primarily because there was no place else to send them. It was only in 1968 that the Act was permanently amended to permit such common custody. The Commonwealth of Massachusetts has recently eliminated all secure custodial institutions and substituted community-oriented programs and other alternative treatment methods that do not involve confinement. For a general discussion of the views supporting the elimination of secure detention see "Non-Delinquent Children in New York: The Need for Alternatives to Institutional Treatment", 8 Columbia Journal of Law and Social Problems 251, 1972.

We also find the purposes and criteria of the classification system at the centers to be rational and justifiable. While even defense witnesses agreed that it would be "desirable" to establish separate facilities for PINS and JDs, the conflict among experts as to whether joint custody is damaging to PINS is too sharp to sustain a finding of unconstitutionality either as a matter of due process or cruel and unusual punishment. Clearly the system of classification in effect at the time of trial, and its improved sequel, do not violate professional standards for the care of PINS and JDs. Of course, there is considerable debate within the child care profession as to whether PINS should be held in secure detention under *any* circumstances, and clearly they may not be so detained unless treatment is provided, but those questions are separate.

It is significant that among the otherwise divided experts there was virtual unanimity that no child—PINS or otherwise—should be treated according to his label, but rather according to his personal need. As Dr. Rothman, defendants' key witness and the witness most knowledgeable about the actualities at the centers, stated: "There are no significant personality differences between people who are adjudged PINS and people who are adjudged JDs."

The system in effect which classifies the child according to his age, maturity, emotional development, emotional and psychiatric history, the charge against him or her, and evidence if any, of drug use* * *, assuming that each factor is given a professionally acceptable weight, is rationally calculated to accomplish the objective approved by all the experts: treatment of the child according to his need rather than his label.

The rationality of the system assures its constitutionality. However, even were this not so and even though we may find more persuasive the view of the experts who strongly favor separation of PINS and JDs, we are bound by the rule, most recently explicated in *Sostre v. McGinnis*, 442 F.2d 178, 191 (2d. Cir.1971), that:

> Even a lifetime of study in prison administration and several advanced degrees in the field would not qualify us *as a federal court* to command state officials to shun a policy that they have decided is suitable because to us the choice may seem unsound or *personally* repugnant. As judges, we are obliged to school ourselves in such objective sources as historical usage, see *Wilkerson v. Utah*, 99 U.S. 130, 25 L.Ed. 345 (1870), practices in other jurisdictions, see *Weems v. United States*, 217 U.S. 349, 30 S.Ct. 544, 54 L.Ed. 793

(1910), and public opinion, see *Robinson v. California*, 370 U.S. 660, 666, 82 S.Ct. 1417, 8 L.Ed.2d 758 (1962), before we may responsibly exercise the power of judicial review to declare a punishment unconstitutional under the Eighth Amendment.

Nor do we find that common custody of PINS and JDs is unconstitutional on the analogy of those cases such as *White v. Reid*, 125 F.Supp. 647 (D.D.C.1954), *Kautter v. Reid*, 183 F.Supp. 352 (D.D.C.1960), and *United States ex rel. Stinnett v. Hegstrom*, 178 F.Supp. 17 (D.Conn.1959), which hold common custody of juvenile offenders and adult criminals to be impermissible. While the analogy is relevant, it is not compelling. *All* experts agree that common custody of juveniles and those who are usually described—whether accurately or not—as "hardened" criminals is damaging to the juvenile, whereas here the schools are sharply divided. Beyond that, however, the *legal* rationale as to the impermissibility of common custody of juveniles and adults is normally that the young offender is not classified as a criminal, and, therefore, may not be held in a penal institution jointly with criminals. In the case before us, however, neither a JD (though he has committed an offense which would be criminal if committed by an adult) nor, of course, a PINS is so classified.

Indeed the Court of Appeals of this Circuit appears recently, at least by implication, to have found that custody of juvenile offenders together with adult criminals does not offend the constitution. *United States ex rel. Murray v. Owens, et al.*, 2d Cir., 465 F.2d 289, 1972.

For the reasons stated, we hold that common custody of PINS and JDs does not violate the equal protection clause, due process or the Eighth Amendment.

*   *   *

REMEDY

We conclude that plaintiffs are entitled to a declaration that the conditions existing at Manida violate the Eighth Amendment, and that the program at the centers does not furnish adequate treatment for children who are not true temporary detainees, and thereby violated their right to due process. There remains for determination the sensitive and complex matter of the scope of injunctive relief.

In a case of public import involving novel and delicate issues, in which developments in the very subject matter have occurred in the period between trial and decision, injunctive relief should be fashioned with deliberation. The timing of the closing of public facilities, the alteration of the programs for long-termers, and determination of an acceptable definition distinguishing short- and long-termers are matters on which the court should not issue a decree without the considered guidance of the parties.

To conclude: The court has jurisdiction of the subject matter and of the person as to all defendants; the case is properly maintained as a class action; plaintiffs' prayer for a declaration that the physical conditions at the centers violates the constitutional rights of the class is granted as to Manida, but denied as to Spofford, and denied as to Zerega as moot; plaintiffs' claim that holding them and their class in joint custody with juvenile delinquents violates the constitution is denied; plaintiffs' claim that their rights and the rights of the members of the class are violated because they are held in secure detention without effective treatment is granted as to those members of the class actually held in long-term detention at the centers, and is otherwise denied. The parties are instructed to prepare for a conference to determine the scope and contents of injunctive relief.

It is so ordered.

PROBLEM OF VAGUENESS

Case Comment

A number of appeals have centered around the issue of vagueness in the construction of delinquency and status-offender statutes. Such questionable statutes may prohibit children from engaging in hazily defined behaviors, such as "growing up in idleness," "deportment endangering the morals of the child," or "immorality." Nonetheless, trial and appellate courts have upheld these conditions, as illustrated in the following case, *District of Columbia v. B.J.R.*

Because juvenile court jurisdiction regarding conduct is often quite broad, the issue of "vagueness" is a common legislative problem.[11] However, most courts that have addressed this issue have upheld the breadth of the statutes in view of their overall concern for the welfare of the child.

DISTRICT OF COLUMBIA v. B. J. R.

District of Columbia Court of Appeals, 1975.
332 A.2d 58.

Yeagley, Associate Judge:

This is an appeal from an order of the Family Di-

vision dismissing a petition, as amended, filed under D.C.Code 1973, § 16-2301(8)(A)(iii) and 16-2301(8)(B), on the ground that the definition of "children in need of supervision" in that statute (hereinafter CINS) is "unconstitutionally vague" and cannot be saved by reasonable construction. The amended petition alleged that the appellee was a child "in need of supervision in that she is habitually disobedient of the reasonable and lawful commands of her parent and is ungovernable." Appellee was specifically charged with absconding from home in April and October of 1969, in June and August of 1972, and on February 26, 1973. The last three abscondances were within the nine months preceding the March 6, 1973, filing of the CINS petition in the trial court.

The pertinent portion of § 16-2301 reads as follows:

> (8) The term "child in need of supervision" means a child who—
> (A) *   *   *
> (iii) is habitually disobedient of the reasonable and lawful commands of his parent, guardian, or other custodian and is ungovernable; and
> (B) is in need of care or rehabilitation.

The sole issue on appeal is whether or not this language under attack for vagueness passes constitutional muster. We find that it does.

The Supreme Court in *Parker v. Levy*, 417 U.S. 733, 752, 94 S.Ct. 2547, 2560, 41 L.Ed.2d 439 (1974), recently summarized the due process elements of the "void-for-vagueness" doctrine:

> "The doctrine incorporates notions of fair notice or warning. Moreover, it requires legislatures to set reasonably clear guidelines for law enforcement officials and triers of fact in order to prevent "arbitrary and discriminatory enforcement." Where a statute's literal scope, unaided by narrowing state court interpretation, is capable of reaching expression sheltered by the First Amendment, the doctrine demands a greater degree of specificity than in other contexts." *Smith v. Goguen*, 415 U.S. 566, 572–573, 94 S.Ct. 1242, 39 L.Ed.2d 605 (1974).

It is difficult to perceive how our CINS statute could violate these requirements when considered in regard to the conduct of the appellee.

Children of ordinary understanding know that to repeatedly abscond from home in defiance of the lawful commands of one's parent is a rather drastic form of disobedience that may well precipitate some disciplinary or punitive action. The statute here gave the appellee adequate warning that to abscond from home five times in four years, three of those times within the nine months preceding the instant petition, would subject her to the sanctions provided for a child who "is habitually disobedient of the reasonable and lawful commands of [her] parent * * *." Such conduct establishes the "frequent practice or habit acquired over a period of time" required to satisfy the "habitually" element as that term was authoritatively construed under an earlier version of our juvenile statute in *In re Elmore*, D.C.App., 222 A.2d 255, 258–259 (1966), *rev'd on other grounds*, 127 U.S.App.D.C. 176, 382 F.2d 125 (1967).

When a child's conduct clearly falls within the common understanding of the statutory language, the officials charged with enforcing the CINS statute are not compelled to make arbitrary decisions in applying it to juveniles such as the appellee. If a parent makes reasonable efforts to control a child but is unable to keep the child from running away, it seems clear that the child is "ungovernable" in his present home situation and may be in need of closer supervision than is available at home. Section 16-2301(8) was explicitly designed to provide such supervision.

*   *   *

Our juvenile code, particularly the CINS section, is not a criminal statute in the ordinary sense. Further, language limitatons are particularly acute for the draftsmen of juvenile laws designed to implement the broad social policy of reinforcing parents in carrying out their responsibility to support and promote the welfare of their children. To enable parents to carry out this legal obligation, the law gives them the authority to control their children through the giving of reasonable and lawful commands. The CINS statute reinforces this authority and may be invoked when children repeatedly refuse to recognize their obligation to obey such commands. See *Commonwealth v. Brasher*, 359 Mass. 550, 270 N.E.2d 389 (1971).

The court is also mindful that our present CINS statute, adopted in 1970, is the product of highly competent, contemporaneous legal expertise in the drafting of juvenile court statutes. The definition of "children in need of supervision" is substantially identical to those proposed in the Uniform Juvenile Court Act (U.L.A.) § 2(4) (1973) and the *Legislative Guide for Drafting Family and Juvenile Court Acts* § 2(p) (Dept. of H.E.W., Children's Bureau Pub.

No. 472-1969). The 1970 statute eliminated, *inter alia*, troublesome language from D.C.Code 1967, §§ 11-1551(a)(1)(H) and (I), which gave the juvenile court jurisdiction over children who engaged in "immoral" activities. Neither the lower court nor the appellee has provided us with convincing suggestions for further improvement in our present act. A statute passes constitutional muster

> *   *   * if the general class of offenses to which the statute is directed is plainly within its terms[.] [T]he statute will not be struck down as vague even though marginal cases could be put where doubts might arise. [*United States v. Harriss, supra*, 347 U.S. at 618, 74 S.Ct. at 812.]

Our conclusion that the CINS statute is not unconstitutionally vague is supported by the overwhelming weight of authority from other jurisdictions which have considered the validity of juvenile statutes with similar language. Most closely in point is *A. v. City of New York*, 31 N.Y.2d 83, 286 N.E.2d 432 (1972), which upheld a statute defining a "person in need of supervision" to be, *inter alia*, one who is "incorrigible, ungovernable or habitually disobedient and beyond the lawful control of parent or lawful authority." 31 N.Y.2d at 87, 286 N.E.2d at 433. In accord, in validating similar statutes, are *In re Jackson*, 6 Wash.App. 962, 497 P.2d 259 (1972); *In re Walker*, 14 N.C.App. 356, 188 S.E.2d 731, *aff'd*, 282 N.C. 28, 191 S.E.2d 702 (1972). Interpretations by sister jurisdictions of statutory language so strikingly parallel to our own cannot be dismissed, as the trial court attempted to do, merely because the language is not "identical" or is a "less-than-perfect fit."

The trial court, in finding the CINS statute unconstitutionally vague, limited itself to an examination of the statute's facial validity without consideration of whether its language gave one such as the appellee fair warning that to repeatedly abscond from home would subject her to CINS sanctions. Appellee attempts to continue this line of reasoning on appeal by anticipating potentially abusive applications of the statue in a variety of hypothetical situations, particularly emphasizing possible infringements upon First Amendment rights of children. But the Supreme Court in *Parker v. Levy, supra*, 417 U.S., at 759, 94 S.Ct. at 2563, rejected that approach when it said:

> *   *   * [e]mbedded in the traditional rules governing constitutional adjudication is the principle that

a person to whom a statute may constitutionally be applied will not be heard to challenge that statute on the ground that it may conceivably be applied unconstitutionally to others, in other situations not before the court. [*Broadrick v. Oklahoma*, 413 U.S. 601, 610, 93 S.Ct. 2908, 37 L.Ed.2d 830 (1973).] *   *   * [T]he Court has recognized some limited exceptions to these principles, but only because of the most 'weighty countervailing policies.' " *Id.*, at 611, 93 S.Ct. at 2915. One of those exceptions "has been carved out in the area of the First Amendment. Ibid. *   *   *

We find no "weighty countervailing policies" in this case to justify allowing an attack on the facial validity of the CINS statute by one whose conduct clearly falls within its parameters.

*   *   *

Neither the plainly legitimate sweep of the language of the CINS statute nor the facts of this case suggest a substantial infringement upon the constitutionally protected conduct of children so as to merit facial invalidation. The statute reinforces parents as they attempt to discipline their children in the broad ambit of family life. We conclude that the sort of activity that would establish a child as "habitually disobedient of the reasonable and lawful commands of his parent" would seldom directly and principally involve First Amendment activity such as expressive conduct or pure speech.

*   *   *

Reversed and remanded for further proceedings not inconsistent with this opinion.

CHILDREN'S INCAPACITY

Case Comment

Juvenile court statutes distinguish between being a child and being an adult by age. A maximum statutory age often establishes the upper limit of juvenile court jurisdiction, while some states also use a lower age to define delinquency.[12] "Criminal incapacity," therefore, was ordinarily not applicable in juvenile proceedings because the concept of "age" dealt with the issue of the child's legal capacity to commit a crime. Normally, what operates as a guide is the common law understanding of the responsibility of children. Under the age of seven, children are deemed incapable of committing crimes. There is a rebuttable presumption that children between seven and

fourteen do not have the capacity for criminal behavior. Over the age of fourteen, children are believed to be responsible for their actions.

In the case of *In re William A.*, the Maryland Court of Appeals concluded that the criminal law infancy defense was applicable in juvenile delinquency proceedings where *mens rea*, or the mental intent, was required for an act to constitute a crime. This theory, however, did not pertain to petitions alleging that the child was in need of supervision (status offenders).

IN RE WILLIAM A.

Cite as 548 A.2d 130 (Md. 1988)

Eldridge, Judge.

This case presents the question of whether the common law infancy defense is applicable in juvenile delinquency proceedings.

On July 6, 1984, the defendant, William A., accompanied his father and uncle to a food warehouse in Baltimore City. There, his father and uncle cut and removed copper piping from the premises. William assisted by carrying various materials from the storage facility. When the police arrived, they observed William's father and uncle carrying copper piping from the premises and William carrying a box of paper for a copying machine.

A second incident occurred on September 25, 1984. On that date, William A. accompanied his uncle to the premises of a car wash. When police arrived at the scene, they found that the car wash had been broken into, and they found William in a van nearby. His uncle had apparently fled the scene. When the police questioned William, he explained that he was "junking" with his uncle "as he always did." He also stated that he had been paid to accompany his uncle. At the time of both incidents, William was 13 years old.

On October 4, 1984, the State filed two petitions alleging that William A. had committed acts which, if committed by an adult, would be crimes, and that, therefore, William was delinquent. See Maryland Code (1974, 1984 Repl. Vol.), § 3-801(k) and (*l*) of the Courts and Judicial Proceedings Article. The petitions alleged that the acts, if they had been committed by an adult, would constitute the crimes of storehouse breaking, felony theft, and malicious destruction of property.

On February 27, 1985, William was found delinquent by a juvenile master. William filed exceptions to the Master's recommended findings and conclusions, and a hearing was held in the Circuit Court for Baltimore City. At the hearing, the defendant argued, *inter alia*, that because juvenile delinquency adjudications are based upon acts constituting crimes if committed by adults, the infancy defense should be available to children in delinquency proceedings. The defendant argued that children between ages 7 and 14 were entitled to a presumption of incapacity in juvenile delinquency proceedings and that the State in the instant cases had failed to rebut the presumption.

The circuit court overruled the defendant's exceptions, concluding that the infancy defense was inapplicable in juvenile delinquency proceedings. At a later disposition hearing, William was committed to the Juvenile Services Administration.

William appealed to the Court of Special Appeals. In an unreported opinion, the appellate court affirmed the circuit court's judgment. The court held that the infancy defense does not apply in delinquency proceedings, relying on an earlier Court of Special Appeals decision to the same effect, *In re Davis*, 17 Md.App. 98, 299 A.2d 856 (1973). Thereafter, we granted William's petition for a writ of certiorari.

[1] The common law defense of infancy or *doli incapax* as it was otherwise known, was explained by the Court of Special Appeals in *Adams v. State*, 8 Md.App. 684, 687–689, 262 A.2d 69, *cert. denied*, 258 Md. 725, *cert. denied*, 400 U.S. 928, S.Ct. 193, 27 L.Ed.2d 188 (1970), as follows (footnotes omitted):

> Since the Code of Hammurabi (*circa* 2250 B.C.) and down through the ages, society, under the law, has viewed and treated offenders of tender years in a light differently and more favorably than that accorded adults accused of breaching the law. Over the centuries and during the evolution of the common law of England, there emerged a rule of law governing 'the responsibility of infants' under which an individual below the age of seven years cannot be found guilty of committing a crime; an individual above fourteen years charged with a crime is to be adjudged as an adult; and between the ages of seven and fourteen there is a rebuttable presumption that such individual is incapable of committing a crime. In the absence of any pertinent legislative enactment in this State, the common law principles, as stated above, would appear to govern in Maryland and we so hold.

In the case at bar, the appellant was shown to be thirteen years, ten and a half months of age at the time the crime was committed. It was, therefore, incumbent upon the State to produce sufficient evidence to overcome the presumption that the appellant was *doli incapax*, an expression ordinarily employed by the text writers. The proof necessary to meet this burden has been variously phrased: It must be shown that the individual "had discretion to judge between good and evil"; "knew right from wrong"; had "a guilty knowledge of wrong-doing"; was "competent to know the nature and consequences of his conduct and to appreciate that it was wrong." Perhaps the most modern definition of the test is simply that the surrounding circumstances must demonstrate, beyond a reasonable doubt, that the individual knew what he was doing and that it was wrong.

It is generally held that the presumption of *doli incapax* is "extremely strong at the age of seven and diminishes gradually until it disappears entirely at the age of fourteen * * *." Since the strength of the presumption of incapacity decreases with the increase in the years of the accused, the quantum of proof necessary to overcome the presumption would diminish in substantially the same ratio.

See L. Hochheimer, A *Manual of Criminal Law as Established in the State of Maryland*, § 16 (1889); I *Bishop on Criminal Law* §§ 368–370, at 260–272 (9th ed. 1923); W. LaFave, A. Scott, *Criminal Law* § 4.11, at 398–403 (2d ed. 1986); R. Perkins, "Criminal Law 837–840 (2d ed. 1969); Ludwig, *Rationale of Responsibility for Young Offenders*, 29 Neb.L.Rev. 521, 526–529 (1950). See also, e.g., *Godfrey v. State*, 31 Ala. 323 (1858); *State v. Fowler*, 52 Iowa 103, 2 N.W. 983 (1879); *Angelo v. People*, 96 Ill. 209 (1880); *Heilman v. Commonwealth*, 84 Ky. 457, 1 S.W. 731 (1886); *State v. Guild*, 10 N.J.L. 163 (1828); *State v. Pugh*, 7 Jones (52 N.C.) 61 (1859); *State v. Toney*, 15 S.C. 409 (1881); *Juvenile Court of Shelby County v. State*, 139 Tenn. 549, 201 S.W. 771 (1918); *Gardiner v. State*, 33 Tex. 692 (1871); *State v. Learnard*, 41 Vt. 585 (1869); *Law v. Commonwealth*, 75 Va. 885 (1881).

With the advent of juvenile delinquency proceedings in lieu of criminal prosecutions, the issue arose in a number of jurisdictions as to whether, absent express statutory language, the infancy defense remained applicable in the delinquency proceedings. Some courts, like the Court of Special Appeals in *In re Davis*, *supra*, took the position that the defense was inapplicable. See, e.g., *Jennings v. State*, 384 So.2d 104 (Ala. 1980); *Gammons v. Ber-*

lat, 144 Ariz. 148, 696 P.2d 700 (1985); *State v. D.H.*, 340 So.2d 1163 (Fla.1976); *In Interest of Dow*, 75 Ill.App.3d 1002, 31 Ill.Dec. 39, 393 N.E.2d 1346 (1979); *In the Matter of Skinner*, 272 S.C. 135, 249 S.E.2d 746 (1978). The rationale of these cases is essentially the same, and was expressed by the Court of Special Appeals in *Davis* as follows (17 Md.App. at 104, 299 A.2d at 860):

> Under the [juvenile] statute, by its purpose and the very principles it advances, the child under the jurisdiction of a juvenile court is conclusively presumed *doli incapax*. The child is delinquent, not because he committed a crime, but because he committed an *act* which would be a crime if committed by a person who is not a child, and because he requires supervision, treatment or rehabilitation. He must be *doli capax* to commit a crime, but not to commit a delinquent act. The *raison d'etre* of the Juvenile Causes Act is that a child does not commit a crime when he commits a delinquent act and therefore is not a criminal. He is not to be punished but afforded supervision and treatment to be made aware of what is right and what is wrong so as to be amenable to the criminal laws.

Or, as another writer expressed it (Walkover, *The Infancy Defense in the New Juvenile Court*, 31 UCLA L.Rev. 503, 516–517 (1984)),

> [b]ecause *parens patriae* theory depends on the notion that the child is being helped and thus is not being tried for a crime and punished as a criminal, there was no need to determine whether the child had the capacity to act in a culpable fashion. Indeed, assertion of the defense could be viewed as wrongfully precluding treatment for those very children most susceptible to the benefits of intervention, children who had committed wrongs without a clear sense of the wrongfulness of their acts.

In the instant case the State, essentially reflecting the above view, argues that the mental state of the defendant is irrelevant in a juvenile delinquency adjudicatory proceeding and that, therefore, the infancy defense has no place. The State asserts (brief, p. 4):

> In effect, a juvenile proceeding is an acknowledgment that the person before the court is *doli incapax* and therefore subject to treatment, not punishment. As a result, the question of mental state is irrelevant to the question of whether a "delinquent act" has been committed. The mental awareness of wrongdoing is relevant only to the question of whether a child needs guidance, treatment, or rehabilitation, and, if so, the nature of the remedy.

Other courts, however, have reached the contrary conclusion, holding that the defense of infancy is fully applicable in juvenile delinquency proceedings. See, e.g., *In re R.*, 1 Cal.3d 855, 464 P.2d 127, 83 Cal. Rptr. 671 (1970); *Matter of Andrew M.*, 91 Misc.2d 813, 398 N.Y.S.2d 824 (1977); *Com. v. Durham*, 255 Pa.Super. 539, 389 A.2d 108 (1978); *State v. Q.D.*, 102 Wash.2d 19, 685 P.2d 557 (1984). See also *Walkover, supra*, 31 UCLA L.Rev. at 562.

A principal reason supporting the applicability of the defense is that juvenile statutes typically require, for a delinquency adjudication, that the child commit an act which constitutes a crime if committed by an adult, and if the child lacks capacity to have the requisite *mens rea* for a particular crime, he has not committed an act amounting to a crime. Another reason often given is that the pertinent statutes do not expressly render inapplicable the infancy defense, and that, to presume a repeal by implication, would largely eradicate the defense. These considerations were set forth by Justice Tobriner for the Supreme Court of California as follows (*In re R., supra*, 464 P.2d at 132–134):

> As we have stated, section 602 provides that any minor who violates "any law of this State" that defines crime, comes under the jurisdiction of the juvenile court. We shall point out that in order to become a ward of the court under that section, clear proof must show that a child under the age of 14 years at the time of committing the act appreciated its wrongfulness. This conclusion follows from the statutory postulate that the jurisdiction of the court must rest upon a violation of a law that defines crime and from the further statutory requirement of Penal Code section 26, subdivision One, that, by definition, a child under the age of 14 years does not commit a crime in the absence of clear proof that he "knew its wrongfulness."
>
> A ruling that a child could be committed to the juvenile court under section 602, in the absence of such clear proof, would compel the disregard of section 26 or the assumption of its repeal. Indeed, the Welfare and Institutions Code provides that the juvenile courts exercise exclusive jurisdiction over all minors under the age of 16; these children cannot otherwise be tried as criminal offenders. (See Welf. & Inst.Code, § 707; 40 Ops. Cal.Atty.Gen. 83 (1962).) Hence, if section 26 pertains at all to a definition of criminal conduct it must apply to proceedings under section 602 which, in turn, covers "[a]ny person under the age of 21 years who violates any law of this State *   *   *.*"
>
> We cannot presume the repeal of section 26 by implication; the decisions clearly establish the contrary presumption.

* * *

Section 26 accords with the historical treatment of juveniles, deriving from the early common law that children under the age of seven could not be held responsible for criminal conduct. (See *In re Gault* (1967) 387 U.S. 1, 16, 87 S.Ct. 1428 [1437–38] 18 L.Ed.2d 527.) Between the ages of seven and fourteen the common law rebuttably presumed children incapable of criminal acts, unless the particular child possessed the requisite age and experience to understand the wrongfulness of his act. (R. Perkins, Criminal Law (2d ed. 1969) p. 837.) California likewise rebuttably presumes all minors under the age of 14 incapable of committing a crime, but does not totally exclude any child from criminal responsibility. Section 26 embodies a venerable truth, which is no less true for its extreme age, that a young child cannot be held to the same standard of criminal responsibility as his more experienced elders. A juvenile court must therefore consider a child's age, experience, and understanding in determining whether he would be capable of committing conduct proscribed by section 602.

An additional reason given by the cases upholding the applicability of the infancy defense in juvenile delinquency proceedings, relates to the evolving nature of those proceedings. As explained by the Supreme Court of Washington in *State v. Q.D.*, *supra*, 102 Wash.2d at 23, 685 P.2d at 560:

> The juvenile justice system in recent years has evolved from parens patriae scheme to one more akin to adult criminal proceedings. The United States Supreme Court has been critical of the parens patriae scheme as failing to provide safeguards due an adult criminal defendant, while subjecting the juvenile defendant to similar stigma, and possible loss of liberty. See *In re Gault*, 387 U.S. 1, 87 S.Ct. 1428, 18 L.Ed.2d 527 (1966); and *In re Winship*, 397 U.S. 358, 90 S.Ct. 1068, 25 L.Ed.2d 368 (1977). . . . Being a criminal defense, [the infancy defense] should be available to juvenile proceedings that are criminal in nature.

One commentator, in urging that the infancy defense remain applicable in juvenile delinquency proceedings, has stated (*Walkover, supra*, 31 UCLA L.Rev. at 562):

> Careful review of the recent history of the juvenile court reveals that the juvenile justice system has turned from rehabilitation to principles of accountability in dealing with youthful offenders. In light of this, continued reliance on the rehabilitative ideal to undercut key protections against sanctioning the innocent in the justice process, such as the infancy defense, is intellectually and institutionally problematic. . . .

Nonculpable children faced with the criminal process must be protected, not by the state, but from the state. There is nothing unique in the juvenile process, including the concept of lesser culpability, that excludes it from this conclusion. This, in sum, is the received wisdom of the last twenty-five years of juvenile sociological and jurisprudential study.

We agree with those courts which have held that the infancy defense applies in juvenile delinquency adjudicatory hearings. The defense is a firmly established principle of our common law; the General Assembly is undoubtedly cognizant of it, but the Legislature has neither repealed it, nor modified it, nor stated that it is inapplicable to juvenile delinquency proceedings. Repeals by implication are, of course, disfavored.

[2,3] As previously discussed, Maryland law defines a "delinquent act" as "an act which would be a crime if committed by an adult." § 3-801(k) of the Courts and Judicial Proceedings Article. Most crimes require some mens rea characteristics; they are elements of the crimes. If, when one commits an act, the requisite mens rea for a crime does not exist, the act does not constitute a crime. See generally, e.g., *Hoey v. State*, 311 Md. 473, 490–495, 536 A.2d 622 (1988); *Shell v. State*, 307 Md. 46, 59–65, 512 A.2d 358 (1986). The defense of infancy relates to the presence or absence of the mens rea required for an act to constitute a crime. See *Adams v. State, supra*, 8 Md.App. at 688, 262 A.2d at 72. Consequently, the infancy defense relates to whether the act committed by a juvenile "would be a crime if committed by an adult," as prescribed in § 3-801(d) of the juvenile causes subtitle of the Courts and Judicial Proceedings Article. To hold otherwise would be judicially creating an exception to the legislative definition.

We cannot accept the State's position that, under the juvenile causes subtitle, "mental state is irrelevant to the question of whether a 'delinquent act' has been committed." (Brief, p. 4). Such a holding would render a great deal of nonculpable conduct subject to delinquency proceedings.

[4] The States points out that rejection of its position will mean that delinquency proceedings can never be brought against children six years old and younger, because their presumption of incapacity is irrebuttable. This may be. Nevertheless, we have no indication that the General Assembly intended that *delinquency* petitions be brought against children between one day and six years old. We point

out, however, that our holding is limited to *delinquency* actions. With respect to a child under seven years of age, the state may file a child in need of supervision petition (CINS), *see* § 3-801(f) of the Courts and Judicial Proceedings Article,[1] or a child in need of assistance petition (CINA), *see* § 3-801(e).[2] As these proceedings are not necessarily based on the commission of acts constituting crimes, the infancy defense obviously has no relevance to them. This option was also noted by the California Supreme Court in *In re R.*, *supra*, 464 P.2d at 135–136.

Judgment of the court of special appeals reversed, and case remanded to that court with directions to reverse the judgment of the circuit court for Baltimore City and remand the case to that court for further proceedings not inconsistent with this opinion. Respondent to pay costs.

END NOTES—CHAPTER I

1. See, generally, Larry J. Siegel and Joseph J. Senna, *Juvenile Delinquency Theory, Practice and Law* (St. Paul: West Publishing, 1990).

2. Sanford J. Fox, "Juvenile Justice Reform: A Historical Perspective," *Stanford Law Review* 22:1187 (1970).

3. See Ira M. Schwartz, *(In) Justice for Juveniles: Rethinking the Best Interests of the Child* (Lexington, Mass.: D.C. Heath, 1989).

4. Douglas R. Rendleman, "*Parens Patriae:* From Chancery to the Juvenile Court," *South Carolina Law Review* 23:205 (1971).

5. See Samuel Davis, *The Rights of Juveniles*, 2d ed. (New York: Clark Boardman, 1980), update 1989.

6. Lindsay, Arthur, "Status Offenders Need a Court of Last Resort," *Boston University Law Review* 57:631–44 (1977).

7. Barry Feld, "The Juvenile Court Meets the Principle of the Offense: Legislative Changes in Juvenile Waiver Statutes," *Journal of Criminal Law and Criminology* 78: 471–534 (1987).

8. See, for example, the early-twentieth century case of *Commonwealth v. Fisher*, where the doctrine of *parens patriae* was used to deny children due process of law and the right to a trial by jury. 213 Pa. 48 (1905).

9. At one time, some jurisdictions established age ranges that varied according to the sex of the juvenile, but statutes implying these distinctions have been held to be in violation of the equal protection clause of the Constitution (see *Lamb v. Brown*, 456 F.2d 18 (1972).

10. In *State ex rel Harris v. Calendine*, 333 S.E.2d 318 (1977), a West Virginia court prohibited housing status offenders in secure facilities that also housed children guilty of criminal conduct.

11. Another example of a statute dealing with vagueness, such as "unmanageable," "unruly," or "incorrigible" children can be found in case of *Commonwealth v. Brasher*, 359 Mass. 550 (1971).

12. See Linda A. Szymanski, *Upper Age of Juvenile Court Jurisdiction—Statutory Analysis* (Pittsburgh: National Center for Juvenile Justice, March 1987).

---

1. Section 3-801(f) provides:

"(f) *Child in need of supervision*—'Child in need of supervision' is a child who requires guidance, treatment, or rehabilitation and

(1) He is required by law to attend school and is habitually truant; or

(2) He is habitually disobedient, ungovernable, and beyond the control of the person having custody of him; or

(3) He deports himself so as to injure or endanger himself or others; or

Police Processing of the Juvenile Offender

INTRODUCTION

This chapter deals with the preadjudicatory stage of the juvenile process. Topical areas include police investigation and arrest, search and seizure, custodial interrogation, and pretrial identification procedures.

Throughout the 1960s, many U.S. Supreme Court decisions significantly increased constitutional safeguards for the adult offender.[1] During this period, nearly all the provisions of the Bill of Rights were made applicable to the states through the due process clause of the Fourteenth Amendment. Many of these decisions affected the defendant's pretrial rights. *Mapp v. Ohio* (1981), for example, extended the exclusionary rule to state court proceedings.[2] The case of *Escobedo v. Illinois* (1964) held that a state must afford an accused the right to counsel in a police station.[3] In *Miranda v. Arizona* (1966), the Court defined a defendant's Fifth Amendment privilege against self-incrimination when taken into custody.[4]

As a result of these decisions, children have also been granted pretrial protections similar to those of adults. In addition, the landmark juvenile decision of *In re Gault* (1964), although specifically applicable to the trial process, served to extend constitutional guarantees of due process to juveniles at preadjudication proceedings.[5]

When a juvenile engages in delinquent or incorrigible behavior, the police must make a decision to release the child or refer him or her to the juvenile court. This discretionary decision—to release or re-fer—is based on a police investigation of the total circumstances of a particular offense. The following partial list of factors is generally taken into consideration in making such a decision: (1) type and seriousness of the child's offense; (2) ability of the parents to be of assistance in disciplining the child; (3) history of the child's past contacts with police; (4) the degree of cooperation obtained from the child and the parents; and (5) whether the child denies the allegations in the petition and insists upon a court hearing. Cases generally involving person-oriented crimes, as well as serious property offenses, are often referred to court. On the other hand, minor disputes between juveniles, school and neighborhood complaints, petty shoplifting cases, runaways, and ungovernable children are diverted from court action. The police may consult with the juvenile probation staff in making this decision. In adjusting a case, the police may simply release the child at the point of contact on the street, give an official warning and release him or her to the child's parents at the station house or the child's home, or seek to refer the child to a social service program. It is an accepted practice for police today to establish formal alternatives to arrest and to screen out cases from juvenile court action.[6]

When a child is taken into custody by the police, the law of arrest for adults is normally applied. This requires that the police officer make a determination that probable cause exists to believe that a crime has been committed and that the child may have committed it. Most states do not have specific statutory provisions distinguishing the arrest process for children from that for adults. Some jurisdictions, however, give broad arrest powers to the police in juvenile cases by authorizing officers to make an arrest whenever it is believed that the child falls within the jurisdiction of the juvenile court. Similarly, many states give the police authority to take a child into custody if his or her welfare requires it. Because of the state's interest in the child, the police generally have more discretion in the investigatory and arrest stages of the juvenile process than in dealing with adult offenders.[7]

Once a juvenile has been taken into custody, he or she has the same constitutional right to be free from unreasonable searches and seizures as an adult. This means that the Fourth Amendment is generally held to be applicable to juvenile proceedings and that illegally seized evidence is inadmissible in a juvenile trial. The legal procedure used to exclude any incriminating evidence is for the child's attorney to make a pretrial motion to suppress the evidence, as is done in the adult criminal process. The courts have held that illegally seized evidence can be excluded on the basis of traditional due process, as exemplified in *Gault*, as well as on Fourth Amendment grounds.

One of the most difficult search and seizure problems peculiar to juveniles is whether a search of a child's possessions—or of the child—by a school official on school grounds is constitutionally valid.[8] The U.S. Supreme Court case of *New Jersey v. T.L.O.* decided that the search of a student, without permission by a school official acting as a governmental agent, was valid where the student was suspected of violating the law. Future court decisions regarding the validity of school searches will probably be decided on the basis of the reasonableness of the search, who conducts it, whether the search is of a person, place, or possession, and whether any statutes or school regulations govern such actions.

Normally, a child's parents are contacted immediately after he or she is taken into custody. In years past, the police often questioned juveniles without their parents or even an attorney present. Any incriminatory statements or confessions made by juveniles could be placed in evidence at their trial. In 1966, the U.S. Supreme Court, in *Miranda v. Arizona*, placed constitutional limitations on police interrogation procedures with adult offenders. *Miranda* held that an accused in police custody must be given the following warning: (1) that he or she

has a right to remain silent; (2) that any statements made can be used against him or her; (3) that he or she has a right to counsel; (4) and that if he or she cannot afford counsel, one will be furnished at public expense. This warning, which represents the adult defendant's Fifth Amendment privilege against self-incrimination in dealing with the police, has been made applicable to children taken into custody.[9] The landmark *Gault* decision further reinforced *Miranda* by giving juveniles similar procedural safeguards at trial proceedings, including the right to counsel, the right to confront witnesses, and the privilege against self-incrimination. These decisions would seem to require that *Miranda* warnings be given to all juvenile offenders who are questioned in custody, if the police intend to admit their statements in a subsequent proceeding. Most states have since incorporated the *Miranda* decision into their juvenile statutes.

One of the most difficult problems involving self-incrimination is whether a juvenile can waive his or her *Miranda* rights.[10] This issue has resulted in considerable litigation. Some courts have concluded that it is not essential for the parent or attorney to be present for the child to effectively waive his or her rights. The validity of the waiver in this respect is based on the totality of the circumstances of a given case. This means that the court must determine if the child has the ability to make a knowing, intelligent, and voluntary waiver. In the case of *Fare v. Michael C.*, the Court ruled that a child's asking to speak to a probation officer was not the equivalent of asking for an attorney; consequently, statements made to the police absent legal counsel were held to be admissable in court.[11] However, some jurisdictions will not accept a waiver of the juvenile's *Miranda* rights unless it is made in the presence of the child's parents or attorney.

Another issue in the early police processing of juvenile offenders is whether the constitutional safeguards established for adult offenders in lineups and other forms of identifications are applicable to juvenile proceedings. This problem has been dealt with in the adult case of *United States v. Wade*, where the Supreme Court held that the accused has a right to have counsel present at postindictment lineup procedures.[12] Where right to counsel is violated, the pretrial identification is inadmissible. The Supreme Court further clarified this issue in *Kirby v. Illinois* by holding that the defendant's right to counsel at pretrial identification proceedings attaches only after the complaint or indictment has been issued.[13] Based on these decisions, juveniles have the same constitutional protections from tainted lineup and identification procedures as adults. This means that once charged with a delinquent act, the juvenile has a right to counsel at a police lineup, and if this right is violated, the pretrial identification is to be excluded. Furthermore, the Court in *Stovall v. Denno* has developed a totality-of-the-circumstances test in analyzing the legality of any identification procedure.[14] In *Stovall*, the Court held that a lineup or showup that is unnecessarily suggestive and may lead to misidentification is a denial of the defendant's due process rights. This test is also applicable to juvenile cases.

INVESTIGATION

Case Comment

Often, judicial limitations are placed on police and prosecutorial discretion in the investigation of offenses involving children. In the case of *State v. Chavez*, the Superior Court of the state of Washington was faced with determining whether a rule permitting the dismissal of action against a juvenile if there is a delay of more than thirty days between completion of a police investigation and the filing of an information (charge) was an infringement upon the prosecutorial function. In *Chavez*, four months elapsed before the prosecutor formally charged four youths with second-degree burglary. The Superior Court concluded: (1) that the local juvenile court rule was properly adopted and, therefore, constitutional and (2) that the delay must result in actual prejudice to the children's ability to defend against the charges when the remedy is dismissal. Therefore, the trial court should not have dismissed the charges against the children without a specific determination that the delay resulted in actual harm to the juvenile's defense.

STATE v. CHAVEZ

Cite as 761 P.2d 607 (Wash. 1988)

Andersen, Justice.

FACTS OF CASE

At issue in these four consolidated cases is the validity of a local court rule providing that an action

brought against a juvenile may be dismissed if there is a delay of more than 30 days between the completion of the police investigation and the filing of an information by the prosecuting attorney.

LJuCR 7.14(b), as written by a Benton/Franklin County Superior Court judge, was circulated among the Benton/Franklin County Superior Court judges for comment, approval or disapproval in January 1986. No objective being made to the rule, it was deemed adopted. The rule provided:

> To Dismiss for Delay in Referral of Offense, the Court may dismiss an information if it is established that there has been an unreasonable delay in referral of the offense to the Court. For purposes of this rule, a delay of more than thirty (30) days from the date of completion of the police investigation of the offense to the time of filing of the charge shall be deemed *prima facie* evidence of an unreasonable delay. Upon a *prima facie* showing of unreasonable delay, the Court shall then determine whether or not dismissal or other appropriate sanctions will be imposed. Among those factors otherwise considered, the Court shall consider the following: (1) the length of the delay; (2) the reason for the delay; (3) the impact of the delay on ability to defend against the charge; and (4) the seriousness of the alleged offense. Unreasonable delay shall constitute an affirmative defense which must be raised by motion not less than one (1) week before trial. Such motion may be considered by affidavit.

LJuCR 7.14(b).

Following its approval by the judges, the rule was submitted to the Office of the Administrator for the Courts for filing. This procedure was consistent with that regularly followed by the Benton/Franklin County Superior Court judges when adopting or amending local rules. The rule was filed and became effective on April 28, 1986.

The January 1986 adoption of LJuCR 7.14(b) was nowhere documented. Neither a filed action nor a court order was entered in the county clerk's records for Franklin or Benton Counties following the rule's January 1986 adoption. Nor was LJuCR 7.14(b) submitted to the local bar for comment prior to adoption. Adoption of the rule was, however, announced at the April 24, 1986 Legal Process Quarterly Review Meeting held at the Benton/Franklin County Juvenile Justice Center. The rule was read to those present, including local attorneys and court officials.

Unable to find a court order or filed action in the county clerk's office documenting majority approval, the Franklin County Prosecuting Attorney challenged whether LJuCR 7.14(b) had been adopted by proper majority procedure. The Benton/Franklin County Superior Court judges addressed the lack of documentation at a June 9, 1986 meeting. All judges present ratified LJuCR 7.14(b) as previously adopted.[1]

Following adoption of LJuCR 7.14(b), the cases against four juvenile defendants were dismissed pursuant to a superior court finding that the delay between completion of the police investigation and filing of the information by the prosecuting attorney was unreasonable under the four LJuCR 7.14(b) factors.[2]

The relevant facts and dates resulting in dismissal of each of these four cases are as follows.

MANUEL RUELAS CHAVEZ

2-12-86 Date of alleged criminal activity
2-19-86 Completion of police investigation and submittal to prosecutor
6-11-86 Filing of information charging second degree burglary

A period of approximately 4 months elapsed between the completion of the police investigation and the filing of the information. The former prosecuting attorney, the Honorable C.J. Rabideau, who filed the appellate brief in the *Chavez* and *Rotter* cases, concedes that he purposefully delayed filing charges after the motions to dismiss were filed "in order to insure a set of facts guaranteeing [that] the rule would be squarely tested on appeal."[3] In its order of dismissal, the court determined that LJuCR 7.14(b) was not *prima facie* unreasonable and that this court's guidelines in CR 83 and GR 7 had been followed in adopting the local rule. Of the four factors to be considered, the court held that the length of delay and reason for delay were the most important considerations. The court acknowledged that burglary was a serious offense. It made no specific findings regarding prejudice to the defendant's ability to defend due to the delay. However, because of the length of and reason for delay, the court dismissed the charges.

RICHARD JAMES ROTTER

2-12-86 Date of alleged criminal activity
2-19-86 Completion of police investigation and submittal to prosecutor
6-9-86   Filing of information charging second degree burglary

A period of approximately 4 months elapsed between the police investigation and the filing of the information. After reviewing the LJuCR 7.14(b) factors, the court dismissed the second degree burglary charge against the defendant. Again, as indicated above, the former prosecuting attorney stated that he had purposefully delayed filing charges in order to challenge LJuCR 7.14(b) on appeal. The court determined that CR 83 and GR 7 had been complied with and that LJuCR 7.14(b) was not *prima facie* unreasonable. The court stated that in reviewing the LJuCR 7.14(b) factors, the length of delay and reason for the delay were the most important considerations. The court observed that the offense was serious but made no specific findings regarding prejudice to the defendant's ability to defend due to the delay. The court concluded, however, that the seriousness of the offense and the lack of actual prejudice were outweighed by the length of and reason for the delay.

TIMOTHY BLACKMAN

1-1-86   Date of alleged criminal activity
1-6-86   Completion of police report and submittal to prosecutor
2-25-87 Filing of information charging second degree burglary

A period of over 1 year elapsed between the completion of the police investigation and the filing of the information. After considering the LJuCR 7.14(b) factors, the Superior Court dismissed the second degree burglary charge against the defendant. The prosecutor had given no reasons for the delay. The court concluded that while the offense was serious, the delay caused by the prosecutor would damage

---

1. As of April 1, 1988, this local juvenile court rule was redesignated IJuCR 7.15(B) by the Superior Court judges of Benton/Franklin County.

2. At this point, we note parenthetically that the prosecuting attorney presently handling these consolidated cases took office on January 1, 1987. Thus, all of the cases herein arose during his predecessor's term of office and many of the actions and nonactions involved herein are those of his predecessor.

3. Brief of Appellant (in *Chavez* and *Rotter* cases), at 2.

the defendant's ability to defend himself, even if only slightly.

SHAMEEKA AVERY

5-21-86 Date of alleged criminal activity

7-15-86 Completion of police report and submittal to prosecutor

1-17-87 Filing of information charging third degree assault

A period of over 6 months elapsed between the completion of the police report and the filing of the information. No excuse was given for the delay. The court dismissed the third degree assault charges against the defendant after determining that although the assault charge was serious, the delay caused by the prosecutor would damage the defendant's ability to defend herself, even if only slightly.

The State then sought review of the four dismissals in the Court of Appeals. The Court of Appeals, in turn, certified the cases to this court.[4] We accepted certification on October 15, 1987.

Three issues are presented.

ISSUES

Issue One

Did the Superior Court for Benton and Franklin Counties lawfully adopt the local rule in question, LJuCR 7.14(b)?

Issue Two

Does the local rule, LJuCR 7.14(b), violate the separation of powers doctrine?

Issue Three

Was the local rule, LJuCR 7.14(b), properly applied when the court dismissed the four defendants in this case?

DECISION

Issue One

[1] Conclusion. The Benton/Franklin County Superior Court local juvenile court rule (LJuCR 7.14(b)) was not improperly adopted pursuant to this court's guidelines in CR 83 and GR 7 and is consistent with the policy of prompt adjudication that underlies the juvenile justice system.

In promulgating and amending local court rules governing practice and procedure, superior courts must follow the guidelines set forth by this court in CR 83 and GR 7. CR 83 contains three requirements. First, the adoption or amendment of a local rule must be made by action of the majority of the court. Second, the local rule must not be inconsistent with the general rules of procedure as established in the Official Rules of Court that govern all superior courts in this state. Third, the local rule or amendment becomes effective only after being filed with the state Administrator for the Courts in accordance with GR 7.

Like CR 83, GR 7 requires local rules to be consistent with those promulgated by the Supreme Court, and adds that they also should conform to those rules in numbering and format. GR 7 also states that adoptions and amendments are effective only after they have been filed with the state Administrator for the Courts.

The Benton/Franklin County Superior Court judges satisfied the first requirement of CR 83 by adopting LJuCR 7.14(b) by majority action in January 1986. CR. 83(a) does not state that a formal action must be filed or that a court order must be entered in the records of the county clerk to prove majority action. However advisable such a course might be, these words not being included in the plain language of the rule will not be read into it.[5] Moreover, while documentation of majority approval is not specifically required by CR 83, the Benton/Franklin County Superior Court judges addressed their earlier lack of documentation by ratifying LJuCR 7.14(b) (as previously approved) at their June 9, 1986 meeting. Following the January 1986

---

4. RCW 2.06.030(2)(d).

5. *State v. McIntyre*, 92 Wash.2d 620, 622–23, 600 P.2d 1009 (1979); *Detwiler v. Gall, Landau & Young Constr. Co.*, 42 Wash.App. 567, 569, 712 P.2d 316 (1986).

approval of LJuCR 7.14(b), the rule was filed with the state Administrator for the Courts, as required by both CR 83 and GR 7.

The judges also satisfied the requirement of CR 83 and GR 7 that a local rule must be consistent with the general rules of procedure in the Official Rules of Court.

[2] "Inconsistent" when involving court rules means "court rules so antithetical that it is impossible as a matter of law that they can both be effective."[6] Nothing suggests that LJuCR 7.14(b) is inconsistent with other court rules governing juvenile practice and procedure. Indeed, LJuCR 7.14(b) appears to be aimed at promoting the juvenile justice system's goal of prompt adjudication and is consistent with other rules that establish shorter time limitations for processing juvenile cases. For example, LJuCR 7.14(b) is consistent with JuCR 7.3's time restraint for filing an information when a juvenile is in custody. JuCR 7.3 provides that a juvenile who is taken into custody before an information is filed must be released unless an information is filed within 72 hours. If taken into custody and held in detention after an information is filed, the juvenile must be released if determination of the necessity of continued detention is not made within 72 hours.

Other court rules also demonstrate the goal of prompt adjudication of juvenile cases. This goal is reflected in the shorter "speedy trial" rule for juveniles pursuant to JuCR 7.8(b) (30–60 days instead of 60–90 days for an adult under CrR 3.3(c)) and the shorter period between conviction and sentencing for juveniles pursuant to JuCR 7.12(a) (14–21 days instead of 40 days for an adult under RCW 9.94A.110).

[3] While the method of adopting LJuCR 7.14(b) was informal, such informality does not affect its validity in this case. Unlike this court, superior courts are not bound by formal procedures in promulgating local court rules.[7] There is, for example, no express requirement for notification, commentary and publication. Steps surrounding promulgation and amendment of local rules are left to the discretion

of the counties concerned. In some counties the courts by local rule have very properly established requirements for promulgation, publication, and bar comment before adoption of local rules.[8] We conclude, however, that such requirements are not mandatory, and that LJuCR 7.14(b) was lawfully adopted.

Issue Two

[4] Conclusion. The local rule (LJuCR 7.14(b)) does not infringe upon the prosecutorial function in violation of the separation of powers doctrine because it is a proper exercise of the court's inherent power of review over procedural aspects of cases before it.

It is well established that the promulgation of rules governing practice and procedure is part of a court's inherent power.[9] The issue of a court's authority to adopt a rule affecting preinformation or prearrest procedures, however, is one of first impression in this state. The local juvenile court rule in this case, LJuCR 7.14(b), clearly applies before a court has jurisdiction over a juvenile case. Our own juvenile court rule, JuCR 7.1, states that "juvenile court jurisdiction is invoked over a juvenile offense proceeding by filing an information." In addition, this court has concluded that "jurisdiction over offenses committed by a juvenile is to be determined at the time proceedings are instituted against the offender."[10] LJuCR 7.14(b), the local rule here under scrutiny, examines the validity of prosecutorial delay *before* proceedings are instituted against a juvenile.

The State argues that courts have no authority to make such an examination and that the timing as well as the content of charging decisions should be left totally to the prosecutor's discretion. The juvenile defendants respond that prefiling delays can prejudice a juvenile defendant's ability to obtain a fair trial and that a juvenile ought to be able to bring such delays to a trial court's attention. " '[A] pre-prosecution delay can result in the loss of physical evidence, the unavailability of potential witnesses, and the impairment of the ability of the prospective

---

6. *Heaney v. Seattle Mun. Court*, 35 Wash.App. 150, 155, 665 P.2d 918 (1983).

7. See GR 7 and CR 83.

8. See King County Superior Court Local Rule 83(a); Yakima County Superior Court Local Rule GLR 9.0; Kitsap County Superior Court Local Rule 2.

9. *State v. Edwards*, 94 Wash.2d 208, 212, 616 P.2d 620 (1980); *State v. Smith*, 84 Wash.2d 498, 501, 527 P.2d 674 (1974).

10. *State v. Calderon*, 102 Wash.2d 348, 351–52, 684 P.2d 1293 (1984).

defendant and his witnesses to remember the events in question. . . . ' "[11]

The juvenile defendants contend that a court may review prefiling delays pursuant to state and federal speedy trial provisions.[12] The United States Supreme Court has concluded, however, that either a formal indictment or information, or else the actual restraints imposed by arrest and holding to answer to a criminal charge, are necessary to engage the protection of the Sixth Amendment speedy trial provisions.[13] This court has similarly determined that the right to a speedy trial attaches with the formal filing of an information or indictment under both the federal and state constitutions.[14] Thus, constitutional speedy trial provisions provide no support for court rules affecting preprosecution aspects of a case.

[5–7] Washington courts do, however, have authority to review prejurisdictional events pursuant to due process provisions. While statutes of limitations are the " 'primary guarantee against bringing overly stale criminal charges',"[15] such statutes do not fully define a defendant's rights with respect to events occurring prior to charging.[16] Instead, due process requires dismissal of a charge if it is shown at trial that precharging delay caused substantial prejudice to a defendant's rights to a fair trial.[17] We have framed a 3-prong test for determining when preaccusatorial delay violates due process.[18] Under that test, "(1) The defendant must show he was prejudiced by the delay; (2) the court must consider the reasons for the delay; and (3) if the State is able to justify the delay, the court must undertake a further balancing of the State's interest and the prejudice to the accused."[19]

The juvenile court rule here in question (LJuCR 7.14(b)) appears consistent with due process in that it requires the court to consider similar factors in determining whether to dismiss a case against a juvenile defendant because of prefiling delay.

[8] The State incorrectly asserts that the rule before us changes substantive law by shifting the burden to the State to disprove prejudice. Initially, the burden is on the juvenile defendant to bring a pretrial motion challenging the preprosecution delay. Under the local rule, a delay of more than 30 days between the completion of the police investigation and the filing of the information is only *prima facie* evidence of unreasonable delay. It is not evidence in itself of harm to a juvenile's defense, or prejudice. We deem it implicit under factor three of LJuCR 7.14(b) that a juvenile defendant must make a showing of prejudice to his or her ability to defend in order to justify dismissal of the charge against the juvenile. However, as with the due process analysis, the inquiry does not stop with a showing of prejudice. Rather, the court must consider the State's reasons for delay. The State is not required to disprove prejudice, but it must explain its reasons for delaying beyond 30 days in filing an information once the police investigation is complete.

[9] The State contends that any such explanation is inconsistent with the concept of broad prosecutorial discretion recognized by the Court of Appeals in *State v. Boseck*, 45 Wash.App. 62, 723 P.2d 1182 (1986). In *Boseck*, the court determined that the federal constitution does not require charges to be filed immediately after the State has sufficient evidence to prove guilt. Broad prosecutorial discretion in matters of charging was recognized as the policy reason against formulating strict rules regarding the proper time to bring a charge.[20] We do not, however, perceive such a policy as being inconsistent with a rule of court for juvenile cases that presents reasonable time limits within which the prosecutor's office should act or, if it chooses not to act, to offer an

---

11. *United States v. Marion*, 404 U.S. 307, 332 n. 4, 92 S.Ct. 455, 469 n. 4, 30 L.Ed.2d 468 (1971) (Douglas, J., concurring), quoting Note, *The Right to a Speedy Trial*, 20 Stan.L.Rev. 476, 489 (1968).

12. Const. art. 1, § 22 (amend. 10); U.S. Const. Sixth Amendment.

13. *Marion*, 404 U.S. at 320, 92 S.Ct. at 463; see also *United States v. Loud Hawk*, 474 U.S. 302, 310, 106 S.Ct. 648, 653–54, 88 L.Ed.2d 640, *reh'g denied*, 475 U.S. 1061, 106 S.Ct. 1289, 89 L.Ed.2d 596 (1986).

14. *State v. Jestes*, 75 Wash.2d 47, 51, 448 P.2d 917 (1968).

15. *State v. Haga*, 8 Wash.App. 481, 483, 507 P.2d 159, *review denied*, 82 Wash.2d 1006 (1973), quoting *United States v. Ewell*, 383 U.S. 116, 122, 86 S.Ct. 773, 777, 15 L.Ed.2d 627 (1966).

16. *Haga*, 8 Wash.App. at 484, 507 P.2d 159, citing *Marion*, 404 U.S. at 322, 92 S.Ct. at 464.

17. See *Marion*, 404 U.S. at 322–25, 92 S.Ct. at 464–66; *Haga*, 8 Wash.App. at 485, 507 P.2d 159.

18. *Calderon*, 102 Wash.2d at 352–53, 684 P.2d 1293.

19. *State v. Alvin*, 109 Wash.2d 602, 604, 746 P.2d 807 (1987) citing *Calderon*, 102 Wn.2d at 352–53, 684 P.2d 1293.

20. *State v. Boseck*, 45 Wash.App. 62, 68, 723 P.2d 1182 (1986).

explanation for its inaction. Broad prosecutorial discretion is not equivalent to completely unlimited prosecutorial authority.[21]

[10,11] The State maintains, however, that statutes of limitation are the only restraint placed on prosecutors in bringing charges and that courts may not fix lesser times before such statutes expire. Statutes of limitations specify the limit beyond which there is an irrebuttable presumption that the defendant's right to a fair trial is prejudiced.[22] However, while statutes of limitations continue as the primary guaranty against bringing stale charges, they do not preclude courts from raising a rebuttable presumption of prejudice where as here there is a prearrest delay short of the period set by the statute of limitations.[23] Nor do statutes of limitations automatically excuse unreasonable delay or failure to prosecute at an earlier time.[24] Indeed, statutes of limitations do not preclude judicial inquiry into the reasonableness or constitutionality of delays within that period.[25] This conclusion is supported by the court's ability to review prearrest delays to determine whether a defendant's due process rights have been violated.[26]

The State further contends that LJuCR 7.14(b) is an unconstitutional impingement on prosecutorial, or executive, authority because it is a judicially imposed statute of limitations more restrictive than that created by the Legislature. This court discussed a similar argument in *State v. Edwards*, 94 Wash.2d 208, 616 P.2d 620 (1980) in which the State challenged the constitutionality of the CrR 3.3 requirement that the charging decision be made within a certain time following arrest. Similar to the State's argument regarding LJuCR 7.14(b) herein, the State contended in *Edwards* that the rule interfered with the prosecutor's discretion in charging and infringed on the legislative function because it constitutes a judicial creation of substantive law. Dismissing the State's contention that the rule created a substantive statute of limitations, this court stated that "[t]he

time limits are triggered by the *State's* actions and are not an attempt to limit the time for prosecution of a specific crime. The State need neither arrest nor charge; only by beginning an action does it invoke the provisions of CrR 3.3."[27] Similarly, the time restraint placed upon the State pursuant to LJuCR 7.14(b) is initially triggered by the State's own action—here, by police referral of a juvenile case to the prosecutor.

We emphasize, however, that this local rule cannot be read to impose a duty on the prosecuting attorney to file an information against a juvenile before the police investigation is complete. It would benefit no one to have a prosecuting attorney pressured into prematurely filing charges.[28] The decision of whether or not to file a charge is too solemn and important a decision to be made in haste. In the State of Washington, a prosecuting attorney depends upon law enforcement agencies to conduct the factual investigation which must precede the decision to prosecute and, as a consequence, the prosecuting attorney has the right to see that a thorough factual investigation has been conducted before deciding whether to prosecute.[29] LJuCR 7.14(b) is not inconsistent with this right since, as we interpret the rule, it does not require a prosecutor to file an information before a thorough factual investigation has been completed. Moreover, expiration of the 30-day time limit provided for in the rule is only "prima facie evidence of unreasonable delay". The rule merely places the burden on the prosecuting attorney to explain the reasons for delay. Exceeding the LJuCR 7.14(b) time restraint is permissible if the State has legitimate reasons for delay. Only by unjustifiable delay does the State risk invocation of the dismissal sanctions of the rule.

Although we understand the prosecuting attorneys'[30] justifiable concern lest their lawful authority be infringed upon, we do not perceive this juvenile court rule as constituting an unlawful infringement upon

---

21. See *United States v. Lovasco*, 431 U.S. 783, 795, 97 S.Ct. 2044, 2051, 52 L.Ed.2d 752, *reh'g denied*, 434 U.S. 881, 98 S.Ct. 242, 54 L.Ed.2d 164 (1977).

22. *State v. Haga*, 13 Wash.App. 630, 632, 536 P.2d 648 (1975), *cert. denied*, 425 U.S. 959, 96 S.Ct. 1740, 48 L.Ed.2d 204 (1976), citing *Marion*, 404 U.S. at 322, 92 S.Ct. at 464.

23. See *Jackson v. United States*, 351 F.2d 821, 822 (D.C.Cir.1965).

24. See *Woody v. United States*, 370 F.2d 214, 216–17 (D.C.Cir.1966); *Ross v. United States*, 349 F.2d 210, 211 (D.C.Cir.1965).

25. See *Marion*, 404 U.S. at 324, 92 S.Ct. at 465; see also *Ewell*, 383 U.S. at 122, 86 S.Ct. at 777.

26. See *Marion*, 404 U.S. at 324, 92 S.Ct. at 465; *Ross*, 349 F.2d at 211–12.

27. *State v. Edwards*, 94 Wash.2d 208, 212, 616 P.2d 620 (1980).

28. See *Boseck*, 45 Wash.App. at 68–69, 723 P.2d 1182; *Lovasco*, 431 U.S. at 791–92, 97 S.Ct. at 2049–50.

29. See RCW 9.94A.440 (Guideline/Commentary).

30. See footnote 2.

prosecutorial authority. Rather, as we view it, it is a reasonable procedural rule designed to guard against unjustifiable delays in the process of charging juvenile offenders. As such, we hold that it is a valid rule that does not violate the separation of powers doctrine.

Issue Three

Conclusion. A dismissal pursuant to LJuCR 7.14(b) is unwarranted unless the court makes a finding of actual prejudice resulting from the filing delays.

[12] Under LJuCR 7.14(b) the trial court "may" dismiss an information against a juvenile defendant if the court determines that there has been an unreasonable delay. "The word 'may' gives the trial court discretion in determining whether or not to dismiss a criminal prosecution."[31] Exercise of the court's discretion in dismissal is reviewable only for a manifest abuse of discretion.[32] However, "dismissal of charges remains an extraordinary remedy", and is appropriate only if the defendant's right to a fair trial has been prejudiced.[33]

[13] The courts dismissed two defendants herein after determining that they were only "slightly" prejudiced in their abilities to defend against the charges. The other two defendants were dismissed without any specific findings of prejudice. Dismissal without specific determinations that prosecutorial delay resulted in actual harm to the four defendants' defense was improper under the standards set forth in LJuCR 7.14(b).

Having decided that the Benton/Franklin County local juvenile court rule, LJuCR 7.14(b), was properly adopted and is constitutional, we conclude that the trial courts still must determine whether the delays in any of the four cases resulted in actual prejudice to the defendant's ability to defend against the charges.

Reversed and remanded.

ARREST

Case Comment

In re Moten examines the issue of procedural due process during arrest. Moten was taken into custody after an altercation with police officers who had entered her home to investigate and locate a runaway. Upon encountering the runaway, the officers attempted to take her into custody. Moten protested and was in turn arrested herself. The arrest was overturned on appeal when the court found that the police had entered Moten's home without sufficient authority or provocation. On rehearing, the resisting arrest charge was upheld on the grounds of "reasonableness." Since the officers had good reason to believe illegal activity was occurring, they were within the boundaries of the law to enter Moten's home; therefore, the arrest was legal.

IN RE MOTEN

Court of Appeal of Louisiana, 1970.
242 So.2d 849.

Chasez, Judge.

This is an appeal from a Juvenile Court proceeding in which the three appellants, Vanessa Randall, Ramona Williams and Eloise Moten were adjudged to be delinquent and released to the custody of their parents on probation.

After an analysis of the testimony and briefs of both counsel we find the facts to be as follows: The matter originated when the mother of Vanessa Randall reported to the Juvenile Bureau of the New Orleans Police Department that her daughter was a runaway and was absenting herself from home without parental consent. Mrs. Randall furnished the authorities with the address at which she believed her daughter to be. Two officers were dispatched to apprehend the child and deliver her to the Juvenile Court for appropriate action. On arriving at the address furnished by Mrs. Randall, the two officers inquired as to whether the runaway girl was there. Eloise Moten, another juvenile, who allegedly lived at that address, asked the officers if they had a warrant. When the officers stated that they had no warrant they were refused admittance to the home. The officers then went to the home of Vanessa Randall to speak to her mother in order to ascertain whether they had been given the correct address. Mrs. Randall confirmed the address and showed the officers

---

31. *State v. Burri*, 87 Wash.2d 175, 183, 550 P.2d 507 (1976).

32. *State v. Dailey*, 93 Wash.2d 454, 456, 610 P.2d 357 (1980); *State v. Sulgrove*, 19 Wash.App. 860, 863, 578 P.2d 74 (1978).

33. *State v. Laureano*, 101 Wash.2d 745, 762, 682 P.2d 889 (1984); *State v. Cantrell*, 49 Wash.App. 917, 920, 745 P.2d 1314 (1987), *aff'd*, 111 Wash.2d 385, 758 P.2d 1 (1988).

a photograph of her daughter to assist in the identification.

The officers then returned to the address, without getting either a search or arrest warrant. They went to the backdoor and entered the home without permission, alleging to have seen the runaway, Vanessa Randall, through the kitchen door.

The testimony as to what actually took place after that is somewhat in conflict. The girls testified that when the two policemen entered the house they mistook Eloise Moten for Vanessa Randall and told her to "get ready to come with them." The girls were attired in gym suits, which necessitated a change of clothing. At this point, Vanessa Randall entered the room where the policemen and Eloise Moten were and identified herself. The girls testified that Vanessa Randall was then told to get ready too. The police officers, on the other hand, claim to have arrested Vanessa Randall immediately. In either event, Vanessa Randall was directed to change her clothing in order to make the trip to the juvenile detention facility for further action as might be directed by the Juvenile Court.

After the Randall girl had changed her clothes and was being escorted through the house, Eloise Moten, according to the police officer, became violent in that she began cursing the officer and went into the kitchen where she removed a kitchen knife from a drawer and advanced toward the policeman. At this point, the officer drew his service revolver as a defensive measure and managed to subdue the girl and placed her under arrest.

Eloise Moten and Vanessa Randall were handcuffed together and then Ramona Williams began cursing the officers. The officer then advised her that she too would be taken to the Juvenile Bureau for using obscene language to which she replied, "You're not taking my friends to jail and not taking me neither." A struggle ensued between one of the officers and the Williams girl. He called to the other officer to aid him in subduing the child. As the second officer came to the aid of the first, the two girls who were handcuffed together attempted to escape by running from the house. They were caught by one of the officers and all three were placed in the patrol car and taken to the Juvenile Bureau.

* * *

ON REHEARING

The present case, up for rehearing by this court, centers on the question of whether or not police officers may legally enter a private residence without a warrant or permission from its occupants to pick up a runaway juvenile who can be seen inside and whose parents have requested her return. In our original disposition of the case, in which we answered this question negatively, we made, after a careful analysis of the testimony and briefs of both counsel, a finding of facts which need not be restated here. However, our holding at that time did not require a determination of the truthfulness of the officer's testimony that he saw the runaway child through the kitchen door upon returning to the home. Upon reconsideration of the case, this allegation has become relevant, and we now accept it as fact. With this single exception we affirm our original factual findings.

This court, in reversing a finding of delinquency on the charge of resisting arrest, did not find fault with the warrantless arrest of a juvenile, per se. It held that R.S. 13:1570, subd. A(3) and article 213 of the Louisiana Code of Criminal Procedure clearly authorize an officer to apprehend the child in such a case.[1] It noted that the statutes covering this situation are peculiar to juveniles and analogized a child's absenting himself from home to a misdemeanor being committed by an adult in the presence of an officer who may make an arrest without first obtaining a warrant. What the court did fault, however, was the unauthorized entrance by police into a private residence to make the arrest without proper authority of the court, or a sufficient showing of emergency or the child's need of protection to justify such intrusion. Therefore, it held that the Fourth Amendment of the Federal Constitution and Article 1, Section 7 of the Louisiana Constitution had been violated. It is this holding which is now being reconsidered.

---

1. Article 13:1570 provides in part that the court (referring to the Juvenile Court) shall have exclusive original jurisdiction concerning any child whose domicile is within the Parish, or who is found within the Parish, and who has absented himself from home or usual place of abode without the consent of his parents or other custodian. Art. 213 provides, also in part that an officer may arrest without a warrant a person who has committed an offense in his presence, providing further that if it is for a misdemeanor it must be made immediately or in close pursuit.

The above-mentioned constitutional provisions protect the right of the people to be secure against unreasonable searches and seizures providing that no warrants for such searches and seizures shall be issued but upon probable cause. At the heart of this court's original decision were pronouncements of the United States Supreme Court, noted particularly in *McDonald v. United States*, 335 U.S. 451, 69 S.Ct. 191, 93 L.Ed. 153 (1948), that due process and the Fourth Amendment require that when police authorities enter a house to search for and arrest a person they must have a warrant unless "exigent circumstances" require their immediate entry. For this reason, it will be helpful to reexamine the rationale of these decisions to determine if they do, in fact, prohibit the warrantless arrest which took place in the instant case.

McDonald involved a suspected illegal lottery operation which had been under surveillance for several months. Thinking that they had detected from the outside the sound of an adding machine, the police forced their way, without a warrant for search or arrest, into a rooming house in which the defendant had rented a room. They proceeded to his room, looked through the transom and observed the defendants engaged in the operation of a lottery. They demanded and obtained entrance, arrested the defendants, and seized evidence which was in plain view. Although the Supreme Court reversed their subsequent conviction, it did not do so on the ground that the police were not justified in arresting without a warrant persons observed in the act of committing a crime in the "privacy" of their home. In fact, in his concurring opinion Justice Jackson specifically stated that had police had lawful entrance to the building they would, after observing the crime in progress, have been justified in making the arrest:

> Doubtless a tenant's quarters in a rooming or apartment house are legally as well as practically exposed to lawful approach by a good many persons without his consent or control. Had the police been admitted as guests of another tenant or had the approaches been thrown open by an obliging landlady or doorman, they would have been legally in the hallways. Like any other stranger, they could then spy or eavesdrop on others without being trespassers. If they peeped through the keyhole or climbed on a chair or on one another's shoulders to look through the transom, I should see no grounds on which the defendant could complain. If in this manner they, or any private citizen, saw a crime in the course of commission, an arrest would be permissible. 335 U.S. at 458, 69 S.Ct. at 194.

What the court did hold in *McDonald* was that the circumstances surrounding the suspected lottery operation were neither so urgent nor pressing as to justify police in foregoing a warrant and breaking and entering the landlady's bedroom in order to permit them to observe the crime in operation. Noting that there was sufficient time and adequate grounds for seeking a search warrant, the court refused to allow the constitutional barrier that protects the privacy of the individual to be hurdled so easily. In the course of its decision it elaborated on the purpose of the Fourth Amendment:

> We are not dealing with formalities. The presence of a search warrant serves a high function. Absent some grave emergency, the Fourth Amendment has interposed a magistrate between the citizen and the police. This was done not to shield criminals nor to make the home a safe haven for illegal activities. It was done so that an objective mind might weigh the need to invade that privacy in order to enforce the law. The right of privacy was deemed too precious to entrust to the discretion of those whose job is the detection of crime, and the arrest of criminals. 335 U.S. at 455, 69 S.Ct. at 193.

It can clearly be seen from the above quotation and the previously cited remarks by Justice Jackson that what the Court was contemplating was a situation where an impartial magistrate should determine if there was sufficient evidence to warrant entering to determine whether a crime was being committed and not one where a crime was actually being committed in his presence.

*   *   *

In light of the foregoing discussion it seems clear that a warrantless arrest of an individual in his private quarters under certain circumstances is proper and would be violative of neither the Fourth Amendment to the U.S. Constitution, nor Art. 1 Sec. 7 of Louisiana's Constitution. It must now be determined whether the arrest in the instant case falls within constitutionally permissible bounds.

From the outset, this case is complicated by the fact that there is no actual "crime" being committed in the technical sense of the word, this being due to the peculiar nature of the laws relating to juveniles. Nevertheless, when a child absents himself from home without parental permission he is, in fact, guilty of unlawful activity. Thus, as noted above there is no problem with his arrest. The problem is whether his "offense" warrants his being arrested prior to any type of warrant having been obtained when he is observed taking refuge in the home of another. We hold that it does.

Although this is not strictly speaking, a case involving a search or seizure, the constitutional protections of the Fourth Amendment and Art. 1 Sec. 7 of Louisiana's Constitution nevertheless come into play as the officers were required to make, without permission, an entrance into a private residence to effect the arrests. These provisions do not prohibit all intrusions into private homes, but only those which are unreasonable. As has been shown in the above cited Supreme Court decisions "reasonableness" in the case of *suspected* illegal activity is dependent upon probable cause as determined by an impartial magistrate. This is subject to the exception of "exigent circumstances," in which case the requirement of a warrant is suspended.

These decisions also clearly indicate that the above stated constitutional protections were not designed to provide a "base" on which citizens can safely flaunt violations of the law in full view of officers of the peace. Thus, an immediate arrest in such a case is not unreasonable, and the fact that it is made in a private residence, and that there may have been time to obtain a warrant is of no consequence.

In addition to the inapplicability of a search warrant an arrest warrant was equally unnecessary as well as inappropriate. Warrants of arrest * * * are designed to meet the dangers of unlimited and unreasonable arrests of persons who are not at the moment committing any crime. Even conceding *arguendo*, that being a runaway is not a "crime," the reasons for this protection are obviously not present under these circumstances.

It has been suggested to this court that a distinction be drawn between a felony and a misdemeanor regarding the officer's right to arrest for a violation of the latter committed in a private residence, but in the full view of an officer.* * * There is no question that Louisiana's authorization under art. 213(1) of the Code of Criminal Procedure is sufficiently broad to sustain the arrest in this case,[2] and the only question is whether the Fourth Amendment to the Federal Constitution and Art. 1 § 7 of Louisiana's Constitution render it illegal.

This is a novel issue and has not yet been answered by the courts. Without holding that any misdemeanor would justify such an intrusion, we hold that the arrest in this case, under these conditions violates neither the spirit nor the letter of these con-

stitutional safeguards. Just as society has a valid interest in protecting itself from dangerous felons it has an equally valid interest in the protection of its juveniles. We do not accept the argument that these children were "safe" in the home of a friend, particularly since there was no adult supervision at the time of the arrests. No child who has run away from his parent's supervision and who has taken refuge with another juvenile in the latter's home can be considered "safe"; that such action is fraught with danger is self-evident and requires no elaboration. To sustain our original holding reversing the adjudication of delinquency would defeat the purpose of laws designed for the protection of these juveniles, needlessly tieing the hands of police authorities in the process, and would pervert the very constitutional safeguards behind which they so righteously hide.

Appellant also contends that article 224 of the Code of Criminal Procedure requiring the peace officer to announce his authority and purpose before entering to make an arrest was not complied with. This argument is based on the failure of the officer to make any statements before walking into the home to make the arrest. We find this inconsequential since only a short while before, on their first visit to the residence, the officers had made clear their purpose and authority and going through the ritual of restating it was simply unnecessary. The requirement of article 224 had been satisfied.

For the foregoing reasons the original judgment of this Court, dated June 1, 1970, is vacated and the Juvenile Court's adjudication of delinquency of Eloise Moten, Ramona Williams and Vanessa Lee Randall, releasing them to the custody of their parents is reinstated and affirmed.

Original judgment vacated, adjudication of delinquency of minors affirmed.

APPLICATION OF THE FOURTH AMENDMENT TO JUVENILES

Case Comment

Do juveniles maintain the Fourth Amendment right to be free from illegal search and seizure? Should illegally seized evidence be barred from trials in juvenile court? Generally speaking, the state courts that have dealt with the issue have concluded that the provisions and protections of the Fourth Amendment apply to juvenile proceedings.[15] Therefore, evidence that is seized in an illegal search is inadmissible in a state or federal court. The Fourth Amendment prohibits unreasonable searches and requires the use of a search warrant unless the search is one of many exceptions, such as: (1) search incident to a lawful arrest, (2) stop and frisk, (3) consent, or (4) an automobile search.

In *State v. Lowry*, the Superior Court of New Jersey adapted the well-accepted view that the right of privacy, security, and liberty against unreasonable searches and seizures is applicable to juveniles in accordance with due process of law. This case explores the historical development of the search and seizure law as well as the exclusionary rule, and supports the proposition that the right to privacy is basic to all persons, regardless of age.

STATE v. LOWRY

95 N.J. Super. 307, 230 A.2d 907 (1967)

Schapira, J. C. C. (temporarily assigned).

Alan Lowry and Benjamin Ferguson, adults, and B, a juvenile aged 17, move to suppress evidence, R.R. 3:2A-6, seized as the result of an allegedly illegal search of a parked car in which they were seated.

Defendants Lowry and Ferguson are charged with unlawful possession of a narcotic drug, to wit, marijuana, N.J.S.A. 24:18-4. Juvenile B is charged with an offense under the Juvenile Delinquency Act, N.J.S. 2A:4-14(1)(a) N.J.S.A., in the Essex County Juvenile Court, the disposition of which is awaiting the outcome of this motion.

All defendants urge the court to suppress the evidence—marijuana cigarettes and a handkerchief filled with pieces of chopped tobacco leaves, identified as marijuana—because the search of their person and the car was warrantless and not incident to a valid arrest.

The issues presented are (a) whether the Fourth Amendment right is applicable to a juvenile, and (b) if the answer is in the affirmative, is the motion to suppress rule, R.R. 3:2A-6, the proper method of implementing that right.

No authority has been cited by counsel nor has research disclosed any officially reported precedent dealing precisely with these issues in this State.

The State did not oppose the procedural aspect of the juvenile's motion to suppress, and it agreed with the court (also with the express consent of coun-

sel for both adult defendants) to hear the entire matter *in camera* to insure privacy for the juvenile, R.R. 6:9-1, and to avoid hearing any promotion of a juvenile matter in a courtroom regularly used for adult criminal cases, R.R. 6:2-6.

I

The Fourth Amendment to the United States Constitution provides:

> The right of the people to be secure in their persons, houses, papers, and effects, against unreasonable searches and seizures, shall not be violated, and no Warrants shall issue, but upon probable cause, supported by Oath or affirmation, and particularly describing the place to be searched, and the persons or things to be seized.

[1,2] This constitutional mandate is a fundamental right of all *persons*, regardless of age. *Urbasek v. People*, 76 Ill.App.2d 375, 222 N.E.2d 233, 238 (App.Ct.1966). The reason some basic constitutional rights, such as indictment by grand jury, right to speedy and public trial and right to trial by jury, were not applied with respect to juveniles was on the basis that the juvenile court was established as a civil court under a guardianship philosophy, the theory being that the interests of society and the minor would be served by a solicitous attitude in the juvenile's care and training. The State assumes the position as *parens patriae*, and under its protective and rehabilitative ideals, informal and confidential procedures developed, vouchsafing constitutional safeguards only when required by the concept of due process and fair treatment—not by direct application of the constitutional clauses. *Pee v. United States*, 107 U.S.App. D.C. 47, 274 F.2d 556 (D.C.Ct.App.1959). It is noteworthy that *Pee* decision referred to rights guaranteed by the Fifth, Sixth, and Eighth Amendments, constitutional protections afforded persons involved in criminal prosecutions, thereby necessitating their application to a juvenile proceeding (noncriminal in nature) through the concept of due process. But the Fourth Amendment, not limited to persons accused of crime, should be interpreted to be applicable to all persons in accord with its terms, thereby rendering the media of due process unnecessary in granting that right to a juvenile.

Even adopting the view that a juvenile will realize constitutional rights only if required under due process of law and fair treatment, it appears that the evolution of the Fourth Amendment right leads to the same result.

The beginning concepts of illegal search and seizure were dealt with in *Body v. United States*, 116 U.S. 616, 6 S.Ct. 524, 29 L.Ed. 746 (1886), wherein the court stated:

> It is not the breaking of his doors, and the rummaging of his drawers, that constitutes the essence of the offense; * * * it is the invasion of his *indefeasible right* of personal security, personal liberty, and private property * * *. (at p. 630, 6 S.Ct. at p. 532, emphasis added)

Less than 30 years later the exclusionary rule was born in *Weeks v. United States*, 232 U.S. 383, 34 S.Ct. 341, 58 L.Ed. 652 (1914), applicable only to the federal courts, wherein the court stated that the protection of the Fourth Amendment "reaches all alike, whether accused of crime or not * * *." (at p. 392, 34 S.Ct. at p. 344) The rule subsequently became applicable to the states through the due process clause of the Fourteenth Amendment. *Wolf v. People of State of Colorado*, 338 U.S. 25, 69 S.Ct. 1359, 93 L.Ed. 1782 (1949).

> The security of one's privacy against arbitrary intrusion by the police—which is at the core of the Fourth Amendment—is basic to a free society. It is therefore implicit in 'the concept of ordered liberty' and as such enforceable against the States through the Due Process Clause. (at p. 27, 69 S.Ct. at p. 136)

To the extent *Wolf* refused to extend the Fourth Amendment right to state prosecutions wherein the evidence was illegally obtained by state officials, *Mapp v. Ohio*, 367 U.S. 643, 81 S.Ct. 1684, 6 L.Ed.2d 1081 (1961), overruled it, applying the whole of the Fourth Amendment to the States through the Due Process Clause.

> Today we once again examine *Wolf's* constitutional documentation of the *right to privacy* free from unreasonable state intrusion, and * * * are led by it to close the only courtroom door remaining open to evidence secured by official lawlessness in flagrant abuse of that *basic right*, reserved to *all persons* as a specific guarantee against that very same unlawful conduct. We hold that all evidence obtained by searches and seizures in violation of the Constitution is, by that same authority, inadmissible in a state court. (at pp. 654–655, 81 S.Ct. at p. 1691, emphasis added)

[3] The historical development clearly indicates that the rule is not only a basic right to *all* persons

to privacy, security and liberty, whether accused of a crime or not, but is fundamental to the concept of due process, a principle precluding adjudications based on methods that offend a sense of justice and one that must endure if our society is to remain free. To insure a factfinding process which at least measures up to the essentials of fair treatment, *State v. Carlo*, 48 N.J. 224, 236, 225 A.2d 110 (1966), the constitutional safeguard enunciated in the Fourth Amendment must be applicable to juveniles.

[4] The exclusionary rule of *Mapp* has become recognized as emphasizing a philosophy of governmental deterrence—a protection against official abuses—absenting from the limelight the basic right, itself. Such emphasis yields to theories espoused by some authorities that a juvenile hearing is only concerned with seeking the truth, and evidence, whether obtained lawfully or not, must be admissible for the avowed purpose of rehabilitating the youthful offender. The exclusionary rule, however, is the "correlative duty" of the government to the "constitutional right" of the individual to be secure from unreasonable searches and seizures. It is the essential ingredient of the constitutional guarantee of the right of privacy, providing a remedy for a preexisting constitutional right, *State v. Johnson*, 43 N.J. 572, 589, 206 A.2d 737 (1965), and it would best serve understanding to state that the exclusionary rule is a "deterrent safeguard," indicating it is more than a discouragement to improper police procedure; it is the force safeguarding the true substance of the rule—the individual's right as embodied in the Fourth Amendment.

[5,6] This constitutional provision perpetuates principles of humanity and liberty implanted in our mores and institutions. It is a basic right given to all persons which should not be undermined by the rehabilitative philosophy adopted by our Legislature and courts. Praiseworthy as that philosophy may be, the court is sensitive to the historical development of this constitutional mandate and the present trend toward granting a juvenile more of his basic freedoms, ever alert to prevent infringement of constitutional rights so bound up in order and society by well-meaning efforts of the Legislature and judiciary. Good intentions are not enough to deprive a juvenile of due process. Application of *Gault*, 99 Ariz. 181, 189, 407 P.2d 760, 766 (Sup.Ct.1965), probable jurisdiction noted 384 U.S. 997, 86 S.Ct. 1922, 16 L.Ed.2d 1013 (1966), Kansas Association of Probate and Juvenile Judges granted leave to join

appellee's brief, 385 U.S. 965, 87 S.Ct. 498, 17 L.Ed.2d 431 (1966).*

[7–9] It appears more reasonable that the Juvenile Court Act was promulgated, not to deprive a juvenile of his rights but to ameliorate the harshness of the criminal law. True, all the niceties of the evidentiary rules and technicalities of procedure may be relaxed in ascertaining the "truth" in a juvenile hearing, yet substantial rights cannot be so disregarded. As stated in *In Re Contreras*, 109 Cal.App.2d 787, 241 P.2d 631 (D.Ct.App.1952):

> * * * it cannot seriously be contended that the constitutional guarantee of due process of law does not extend to minors as well as to adults. (109 Cal.App.2d, at p. 791, 241 P.2d, at p. 634)

Is it not more outrageous for the police to treat children more harshly than adult offenders, especially when such is violative of due process and fair treatment? Can a court countenance a system where, as here, an adult may suppress evidence with the usual effect of having the charges dropped for lack of proof, and on the other hand, a juvenile can be institutionalized—lose the most sacred possession a human being has, his freedom—for "rehabilitative" purposes because the Fourth Amendment right is unavailable to him?

[10,11] The constitutional right of privacy should be applicable to the young and old alike. This is especially true when the juvenile is accused of an act which, as here, is equivalent to criminal conduct had it been committed by an adult.[1]

> After much reflection I am persuaded that 'the requirements of due process and fair treatment' demand that the constitutional guarantee against unreasonable searches and seizures be extended to children charged with the doing of an act which if done by an adult would be a crime * * *. *In Re Williams*, 49 Misc.2d 154, 169, 267 N.Y.S.2d 91, 109 (Family Ct.1966).[2]

[12] Difficulty arises by not differentiating procedures adequate with respect to acts of juvenile delinquency noncriminal in nature, such as truancy or incorrigibility, from procedures dealing with conduct that would be criminal had it been committed by an adult. The court is limiting its decision to the specific factual pattern presented, namely, that the juvenile is 17 years of age and has committed an act that is indictable and would be characterized as criminal had he been an adult or had he requested a presentment to the grand jury R.R. 6:9-6; N.J.S. 2A:4-15, N.J.S.A. The problem not presently passed upon, i.e., what rights, procedures and rules are applicable to children of more tender years who have engaged in "noncriminal" behavioral patterns, invites further research, analysis, discussion and promulgation of legislation and court rules which would redefine rights of a juvenile and outline a procedure whereby they could be protected. This is especially propitious in light of the present. *Proposed Revision of the Rules Governing the Courts of the State of New Jersey* (1966). In accord with the concurring opinion of Chief Justice Weintraub, *State v. Carlo*, *supra*, a method must be designed to uphold the rehabilitative objectives of the Juvenile Court system and, at the same time and in certain well-defined cases, preserve the constitutional rights of the juvenile without placing him on the same plane as an adult offender in all respects.

A final justification in granting the Fourth Amendment right to a juvenile is not so much founded in constitutional or legal principles, but, ironically, rests in the *parens patriae* philosophy, that in order to better rehabilitate the juvenile, official misbehavior must not go undeterred; for development toward responsible adult citizenship depends on behavioral patterns set for the young, especially by those displaying governmental authority.

> Our Government is the potent, the omnipresent teacher. For good or for ill, it teaches the whole people by its example. * * * If the government becomes a lawbreaker, it breeds contempt for law. *Olmstead v. United States*, 277 U.S. 438, 485, 48 S.Ct. 564, 72 L.Ed. 944 (1928) (Justice Brandeis dissenting)

---

* Decided May 15, 1967, after the handing down of this opinion, 387 U.S. 1, 87 S.Ct. 1428, 18 L.Ed.2d 527.

1. "When the jurisdiction of a court is being invoked for a criminal offense basic constitutional rights should be available to all—adults or juveniles. When the charge is the commission of a crime, rights should be identical, be the accused 16 or 60. * * * Gardner, 'The *Kent* Case and The Juvenile Court: A Challenge to Lawyers,' 52 A.B.A.J. 923, 924 (1966)" *State v. Carlo*, *supra*, 48 N.J. at p. 235, footnote 2, 225 A.2d, at p. 116.

2. New York has somewhat stronger procedural safeguards for the juvenile, as indicated by specific provisions of their Family Court Act, § 711 (purpose to provide due process of law in juvenile proceedings); § 735 (statement given during preliminary conference inadmissible at fact-finding hearing); § 741(a) (advised of right to remain silent, which has been interpreted to be the equivalent of the privilege against self-incrimination, [Committee Comments] and *Williams*, *supra*, at p. 168, 267 N.Y.S.2d 91).

[13] More specifically, as regards the juvenile and the rehabilitative process.[3] The rehabilitative goal of the Juvenile Court is to instill respect for law and order. Such a goal is best realized if the police are required to deal fairly and legally with juveniles.

[14] Although the Juvenile Court Act is intended to be salutary, and every effort should be made to further its purposes, it should not be made an instrument denying to a juvenile constitutional guarantees afforded to all persons, whether accused of crime or not. Our State and Federal Constitutions cannot be nullified by mere nomenclature, the end and substance being the same.

As the Appellate Court of Illinois indicated, the protection against unlawful search and seizure is a fundamental right and should be available to the juvenile, especially when viewed in the spirit of the "laudable purposes of Juvenile Courts." *Urbasek v. People, supra*, 222 N.E.2d at p. 238.

[15] This court, therefore, charged with the support of our Constitution and ever watchful of its fundamental guarantees afforded to all persons, holds that the right of privacy, security and liberty against unreasonable searches and seizures is applicable to a juvenile in accordance with reason and due process of law.

II

[16] The next issue presented is the manner in which the juvenile can implement his Fourth Amendment right. By order of the assignment judge of the Superior Court of Essex County, this court has been empowered to sit as a Juvenile Court, if necessary; but to do so would, in effect, allow it to create rules of procedure which are nonexistent in the Juvenile and Domestic Relations Court, a function which is the sole responsibility of the Supreme Court, N.J.Const., Art. VI, Sec. II, ¶ 3 (1947).

Further, it is the opinion of this court that a rule presently exists, namely, R.R. 3:2A-6, which would enable the juvenile, as it does an adult, to move to suppress evidence illegally seized. The pertinent part of the rule, indicating its applicability to this situation, provides:

* * * a *person* claiming to be aggrieved by an unlawful search and seizure, and having reasonable grounds to believe that the evidence obtained may be used against him in a *penal* proceeding, may apply *only* to the Superior Court or County Court for the county in which the evidence was obtained for the return of property seized and to suppress the evidence obtained, even though the offense charged or to be charged may be within the jurisdiction of a municipal court." (Emphasis added.)

[17] The rule clearly applies to the extent that a juvenile is a person and to the extent that any person claiming to be aggrieved may apply *only* to the Superior or County Court where the evidence was seized. The difficulty arises from R.R. 3:1-1 governing the scope of the criminal practice rules, of which R.R. 3:2A-6 is a part, wherein it is stated that the criminal rules of procedure are broadly applicable except in Juvenile and Domestic Relations Court. This implies that a minor within the jurisdiction of the Juvenile Court may not utilize any of the rules of criminal procedure, at the hearing or prehearing stage. Initially, it is noted that the suppression rule, adopted in December 1962, became effective January 2, 1963, more than 14 years after R.R. 3:1-1 was adopted, indicating that R.R. 3:1-1 does not strictly limit the subsequent rule. See *State v. Swiderski*, 94 N.J.Super. 14, 19, 226 A.2d 728 (App.Div.1967). In support of that thesis and more controlling is the fact that R.R. 3:2A-6 is broader in scope and goes beyond the language of R.R. 3:1-1. The latter rule limits the criminal practice rules to "criminal proceedings," whereas the suppression rule applies to a person who believes the evidence will be used against him in a "penal proceeding." "Penal" is inherently a much broader term than "criminal," since it pertains to any punishment or penalty and relates to acts which are not necessarily delineated as criminal. *Marter v. Repp*, 80 N.J.L. 530, 77 A. 1030 (Sup.Ct.1910), *affirmed* 82 N.J.L. 531, 81 A. 1134 (E. & A. 1911); *Silberman v. Skouras Theatres Corp.*, 11 N.J.Misc. 907, 169 A. 170 (C.P.1933). A juvenile between the ages of 16 and 18 years (Juvenile B is 17 years old) is subject to incarceration, N.J.S. 2A:4-37, N.J.S.A., and noth-

---

3. This view was also adopted by Chief Justice Weintraub, concurring in *State v. Carlo, supra*, wherein he stated: "If the State would rehabilitate a youngster, its officers of course should set the good example. The police should not use tactics which are palpably wrong." 48 N.J., at p. 245, 225 A.2d, at p. 122. And see *In Re Ronny*, 40 Misc.2d 194, 242 N.Y.S.2d 844 (Family Ct. 1963): "I can think of few worse examples to set for our children than to visit upon children what would be, if they were older, unreasonable and unconstitutional invasions of their all-too-limited privacy and rights, merely because they are young." 40 Misc.2d, at p. 210, 242 N.Y.S.2d, at p. 860.

ing can be more penal in nature than denying a person his freedom, even if such confinement is for rehabilitation.

On this basis, it appears that R.R. 3:2A-6 is broad enough to permit a juvenile to enforce his constitutional right, but for the language in the rule stating that even if the offense is within the jurisdiction of the municipal court, the motion must be brought in the Superior Court or County Court. This might imply that if evidence seized is the basis of an offense within the jurisdiction of any other court, the rule becomes unavailable to the movant.

Such procedure was adopted to avoid having the municipal magistrate, who issues search warrants in cases generally of the type likely to be within the jurisdiction of the County or Superior Court, hear the matter. It was also felt in the early stages of the law of search and seizure that for purposes of uniformity of decision it would be preferable to have only the Superior and County Court hear the motions to suppress. Proceedings of the Fourteenth Annual Judicial Conference (May 1962) (Report of the Supreme Court's Committee on Criminal Procedure, Morning Session, pages 5–6).

Most important is that the drafters of R.R. 3:2A-6, being in a different social context, did not consider the problem presently raised. Therefore, their expression of "municipal court" in the suppression rule should not be read as the expression of one court to the exclusion of another, but rather involves all courts dealing with penal behavior, indicating their intent that the Superior or County Court shall hear all motions to suppress no matter from which jurisdiction the offense arose.

Further, the recent trend of granting juveniles more constitutional safeguards, thereby necessitating utilization of the criminal rules of procedure by juveniles, has been recognized by the Committee on Revision of Rules of Criminal Procedure, for it has modified the scope of the criminal rules in an attempt to conform the practice and procedure of the Juvenile and Domestic Relations Court as closely as possible to the practice in the Superior and County Court. Proposed Revision of the Rules Governing the Courts of the State of New Jersey—Part III, "Rules Governing Criminal Practice," Proposed Rule 3:1-1 and comments, p. 185 (1966). If adopted, this would enable a juvenile to avail himself of the criminal rules of procedure unless otherwise expressly provided for in Part V (Juvenile and Domestic Relations Court rules).

Varying problems still exist, springing from the already entrenched differences between juvenile and adult procedures, such as R.R. 3:2A-6 requiring a hearing in open court whereas the juvenile must be given a confidential hearing, and a possible dichotomy of what constitutes probable cause, there being a lesser standard indicated for juveniles under R.R. 6:8-3(a). Neither problem need be passed upon at this time since all the motions were heard in chambers (consented to by all the parties), and the determination of the substance of the motion, infra, avoids the necessity of differentiating degrees of probable cause.

[18] Based on the foregoing the court holds that as with any person claiming to be aggrieved by an unlawful search and seizure a juvenile, charged with an act of juvenile delinquency that would otherwise be a high misdemeanor, misdemeanor or other offense, or violation of a penal law or municipal ordinance, or an offense which could be prosecuted in a method partaking of the nature of a criminal proceeding, or being a disorderly person may move to suppress evidence pursuant to R.R. 3:2A-6.[4] See *State v. Swiderski, supra.*

III

The final issue to be resolved in this case is whether the evidence—marijuana cigarettes, a handkerchief filled with chopped up greenish-brown leaves, and a box of paper used for rolling cigarettes—was seized as the result of an unlawful search.

The following testimony was adduced at the hearing of the motion. Two Newark police officers, Donald A. Janowski and Alfred Pepe, both in uniform, while patrolling in a marked police car on the evening of January 3, 1967, observed a new Mustang automobile with three occupants parked on the right-hand side of 6th Avenue, facing east, near Ridge Street, in the City of Newark. This is an open and deserted location, with Branch Brook Park on one side, a church on the other side, and no residences. Both officers testified that this area is known as "Lov-

---

4. Having concluded that the juvenile is entitled to his Fourth Amendment right, it might appear that the court is "reaching" to utilize R.R. 3:2A-6 as the implementation of that right; but since no other logical remedy is available, the court is willing to so "reach." Even if there were no remedy of this kind, on the principle of fundamental fairness the court would devise a procedure. Such, however, is not necessary in light of R.R. 3:2A-6. See R.R. 1:27A ("Relaxation of Rules").

ers Lane" and is also a known area where stolen cars are "dropped." They became suspicious and decided to investigate. Officer Pepe drove the patrol car to the rear but parallel to the Mustang, and both officers exited from their car. Patrolman Janowski approached the Mustang automobile from the passenger's side and Patrolman Pepe from the driver's side. Before reaching the other car Patrolman Janowski stated that the passenger's door opened revealing a figure of a man about to exit with something in his hand, which he could not identify. The patrolman told him to stop, and the man closed the door and resumed his position in the car. Upon reaching the right-hand side of the car, Officer Janowski observed, through a closed window, the passenger in the front seat, Benjamin Ferguson, attempt to hide cigarettes, first under his legs, then under his seat. Still looking through the window, Officer Janowski saw two or three cigarettes on the floor in front of Ferguson, a couple of cigarettes on Ferguson's lap, and a handkerchief with what looked like small pieces of tobacco lying open on the console. When Ferguson rolled down the window at his request the officer detected the sweet smell of marijuana, an odor with which he was familiar from previous investigations and arrests. The passenger in the right rear seat, Juvenile B, informed the patrolman that he was 16 years old, whereupon he was asked to leave the car. To permit this the upper portion of the front seat and defendant Ferguson had to move forward, causing several more cigarettes in the front of the car to be exposed to the view of Officer Janowski. The police officer then testified that he removed the cigarettes, at which time he did not recall if anyone was still in the car. He stated that he used a flashlight but did not recall whether he flashed it through the window or inserted part of his body in the car to look around. According to Patrolman Janowski, the arrests were made a few moments later.

Patrolman Pepe corroborated the testimony of his partner for the most part. He stated that he arrived at the driver's side of the car at the same time his partner reached the other side, and he observed, through the window, Ferguson's attempt to hide something under his person and then under his seat. When the window was rolled down, upon his request for the driver's license and registration, he too smelled the sweet aroma of marijuana. Officer Pepe further testified that he observed through the window

three or four rolled cigarettes, crimped at the ends "like marijuana is usually rolled" and at that point he placed the occupants under arrest. When the driver, Alan Lowry, was placed up against the car, Officer Pepe stated he saw on the console an open handkerchief containing chopped up leaves of brownish-green color and a box filled with paper to roll cigarettes. The entire car was then searched, revealing nothing more.

Only Benjamin Ferguson testified for the defense. He stated someone yelled "cops" and the next moment Patrolman Janowski was right alongside of him shining a flashlight in his face. He denied ever trying to leave the car and stated that Officer Janowski opened the car door, told Juvenile B and himself to get out, and searched them both, taking from his person a fingernail file, keys, matches, and Winston cigarettes. He stated that the officer put the cigarettes on the front seat and then took them out, apparently, although it was not made clear, as if he just found them. Defendant stated nothing was on the console and that both patrolmen searched the entire car. He said Patrolman Pepe took the handkerchief and box of cigarette rolling paper from the car but he could not see where the patrolman got it from.

Defense counsel contend that the arrest or apprehension of these individuals was based not on probable cause, but at most, on suspicion, which would not justify the search and seizure without a warrant. No moment of arrest was pinpointed except by counsel for defendant Lowry, who contended that when Officer Janowski saw defendant Ferguson try to leave the car and yelled "Stop," such constituted an arrest at which time no probable cause existed.

Defense counsel most accurately state the law regarding warrantless searches, but they overlook the very nature of the factual circumstances leading to the seizure of the evidence, which clearly indicates no search was involved at all.

[19] The testimony adduced was uncontradicted that there were three males sitting in a new Mustang automobile in a deserted area known to the police officers as a drop area for stolen cars, as Lovers Lane, and an area known for criminal activity. It cannot seriously be contended that these officers had no right to investigate this situation and even request the driver's license and registration. R.S. 39:3-29, N.J.S.A.

A law enforcement officer has the right to stop and question a person found in circumstances suggestive of the possibility of violation of criminal law. [Citations omitted.] Such investigatory detention is not an arrest, '[a]nd the evidence needed to make the inquiry is not of the same degree or conclusiveness as that required for an arrest.' *State v. Hope*, 85 N.J.Super. 551, 554, 205 A.2d 457, 459 (App.Div.1964)

[20] Not only did the police officers have a right to investigate under the aforementioned circumstances, but they had a *duty* to investigate, *State v. Smith*, 37 N.J. 481, 496, 181 A.2d 761 (1962); *State v. Taylor*, 81 N.J.Super. 296, 313, 195 A.2d 485 (App.Div.1963); and in the proper exercise of their responsibility these officers observed through the car windows the crimped cigarettes on the floor of the car and on the lap of defendant Ferguson. Officer Janowski also observed through the window from the passenger's side the handkerchief lying open on the console with the chopped up leaves inside of it. (This was not observed by Officer Pepe until Lowry got out of the car, at which time he also saw a box containing paper to roll cigarettes.) Defendant's story, uncorroborated by the other passenger or by the driver, that there was no handkerchief on the console is totally unbelievable.

[21,22] In the absence of any physical entry into the automobile there is no unreasonable search, for in fact there was no search. Observing this evidence, fully disclosed and in plain view of the police officers, whether or not in artificial light, is not a search. *State v. Griffin*, 84 N.J.Super. 508, 517, 202 A.2d 856 (App.Div.1964); *State v. Murphy*, 85 N.J.Super. 391, 397, 204 A.2d 888 (App.Div.1964), *affirmed* 45 N.J. 36, 211 A.2d 193 (1965). A search implies some exploratory investigation and a prying into hidden places for that which is concealed. *State v. Griffin*, *supra*, 84 N.J.Super. at p. 517, 202 A.2d 856; *People v. Elmore*, 28 Ill.2d 263, 265, 192 N.E.2d 219, 220 (Sup.Ct.1963). No such prying or investigating into hidden and concealed places was revealed at this hearing. This was observation of objects in open view to Officers Janowski and Pepe, who were conscientiously performing their duty.

[23] Briefly passing on defendants' contention that no probable cause existed, this court finds that the common and work-a-day knowledge of these police officers, their familiarity with the nature of this area, their observation of a new car parked there with three male occupants, coupled with their proper detention and investigation of the suspicious occupants, all of which led to direct perception without a search of incriminating objects within the car, constituted probable cause, and a search of the vehicle without a warrant was proper. *State v. Taylor*, *supra*, 81 N.J.Super. at p. 313, 195 A.2d 485.

If defense counsel's argument is interpreted to mean that no probable cause existed prior to the observations, it lacks merit, for such was, as indicated above, proper and responsible police procedure. Such is the answer to counsel for Lowry, who contended that Officer Janowski's order to defendant Ferguson to "stop" constituted an arrest. Not only was it proper police detention and investigation, but defendant Ferguson denied ever trying to leave the car; and further, even if it were considered such a restraint of liberty as to constitute an arrest, nothing flowed therefrom—the evidence would have been discovered nothwithstanding the alleged arrest.

Defendants' motion for suppression is denied. Submit appropriate order providing, among other things, that the matter before the Juvenile Court proceed in its normal course.

STOP INCIDENT TO LAWFUL ARREST

Case Comment

Generally, law enforcement officers have broad statutory authority to take juveniles into custody. With adult offenders, the police are required to adhere to the legal standard of "probable cause to commit a crime." In the case of *In re D.J.*, the District of Columbia Court of Appeals concluded that the investigative stop of a juvenile fleeing from authority was not warranted by the totality of the suspicious circumstances of the case. Even though the youth was subsequently found to be in possession of illegal drugs, a mere attempt to evade the police is insufficient grounds to justify a stop and cursory search or frisk under *Terry v. Ohio*.[16] Limited police intrusions, particularly with juveniles and in areas with a high incidence of narcotics trafficking, are often controversial situations and may be the basis for an abuse of police power.

IN RE D.J.

532 A.2d 138 (D.C. 1987)

Before Newman, Belson, and Terry,* Associate Judges.

Newman, Associate Judge:

Appellant D.J., a juvenile, was adjudged delinquent for possession with intent to distribute phencyclidine (PCP) and marijuana (D.C. Code § 33-541(a)(1986 Supp.)). Before trial, D.J. moved to suppress evidence and statements on the ground that both were obtained by police subsequent to an unconstitutional search and seizure. After an evidentiary hearing, the motion was denied. The evidence adduced at the hearing became the basis for a stipulated trial; D.J. was found guilty of the charged offenses. D.J. appeals the denial of his motion to suppress evidence. We reverse.

I

On a rainy evening in March, 1985, D.J. stood near the curb in the 300 block of 53rd St., N.E., Washington, D.C. He was two and one-half blocks from his home. An unmarked police car approached. The officers inside, Sergeant Miller and Lieutenant Andes, were on narcotics detail and had just monitored a lookout broadcast. D.J. did not match the description given in the broadcast. Neither Miller nor Andes had ever seen him before. As the car drew closer, D.J. made eye contact with Sergeant Miller. D.J. turned, placing his hands in his pockets, and began walking in the direction opposite to that in which the car was headed. Miller told Lieutenant Andes, driver of the car, to back up. Andes tracked D.J. in reverse gear at a pace of 15–20 miles per hour. When the car came abreast of D.J., he turned again and proceeded back in the direction from which he had come, still walking. The car again pursued him. When the car met him, D.J. once again reversed direction, and the police car again followed. At this point, Miller radioed to a second police car carrying Officer Joe Gray and his partner. He informed Gray that D.J. was walking in his direction, intending by this communication to have Gray stop D.J.

As the unmarked car approached D.J. for the third time, Lieutenant Andes stopped the car. Miller got out and started walking toward D.J. D.J. began to run; Miller ran after him. When D.J. reached the corner, he encountered Officer Gray, who had just pulled up and gotten out of his cruiser. D.J. turned around, only to find himself face to face with Sergeant Miller, five or six feet in front of him.

At this point, Miller, according to his account, saw D.J.'s hand emerge from his pocket holding a brown vial of the type often used to store packets of PCP. Miller ordered D.J. to freeze. D.J. dodged Miller and ran past him, still holding the brown vial. Miller gave chase on foot. D.J. was finally stopped by a third pair of officers, Campbell and Ortiz. D.J. exclaimed, "Okay, you got me. I'm dirty." He was placed on the ground and searched. Police confiscated a brown vial holding 11 foil packets of marijuana laced with PCP, a manila envelope containing marijuana, and $63 in currency.

D.J. testified to essentially the same facts as did Sergeant Miller, with one exception: he denied ever having pulled the brown vial containing PCP out of his pocket, maintaining that it had remained in the inside pocket of his jacket throughout the incident until his capture and the ensuing search.

The motions judge did not resolve the factual dispute as to whether or not the brown vial had become visible before the search. He ruled that a *Terry* stop occurred at the point when Sergeant Miller first began to chase D.J. on foot. He also held that at that point, D.J. had given police articulable cause for suspicion, partly by putting his hands in his pockets upon first seeing the police, but primarily by repeatedly attempting to evade them. Though troubled by the implications of his holding upon the citizen's right to avoid contact with the police, the motions judge nevertheless denied the motion to suppress, remarking that it was a close case upon which he "could have gone both ways." We hold that he went the wrong way.

II

[1] Before reaching the question of whether, in appellant, D.J.'s encounter with the police, his Fourth Amendment right "to be secure * * * against unreasonable searches and seizures" was violated, "[o]ur first task is to establish at what point in this encounter the Fourth Amendment becomes rele-

---

* Hubert B. Pair, Senior Judge, was originally a member of this division. Judge Terry was drawn to replace him pursuant to the Internal Operating Procedures of this court.

vant." *Terry v. Ohio*, 392 U.S. 1, 16, 88 S.Ct. 1868, 1877, 20 L.Ed.2d 889 (1968). The Supreme Court has made clear that a seizure has occurred when a police officer, "by means of physical force or show of authority, has in some way restrained the liberty of a citizen." *Id.* at 19 n. 16, 88 S.Ct. at 1879 n. 16. The police violate no constitutional rights by merely making inquiries.

> As long as the person to whom questions are put remains free to disregard the questions and walk away, there has been no intrusion upon that person's liberty or privacy as would under the Constitution require some particularized and objective justification. . . . [A] person has been "seized" within the meaning of the Fourth Amendment only if, in view of all of the circumstances surrounding the incident, a reasonable person would have believed that he was not free to leave.

United States v. Mendenhall, 446 U.S. 544, 554, 100 S.Ct. 1870, 1877, 64 L.Ed.2d 497 (1980) (footnote omitted).

Reviewing the facts of this case, we conclude that a seizure occurred, at the latest, when Sergeant Miller began to chase D.J. on foot.[1] "A police pursuit is a show of authority . . ." *United States v. Bennett*, 514 A.2d 414, 418 (D.C. 1986) (Mack, J., dissenting). By taking up pursuit, the police communicated emphatically to D.J. that he was not free to leave. This was a communication that no reasonable person could have misinterpreted. A person pursued by the police knows, or reasonably should know, that the object of chase is capture. He knows also that in effecting his capture, the police will resort to physical force if necessary. When the chase commences, the stop has begun.

Courts in other jurisdictions have considered the commencement of a police pursuit to be a seizure under the Fourth Amendment. See *Commonwealth v. Thibeau*, 384 Mass. 762, 764, 429 N.E.2d 1009, 1010 (1981) ("Pursuit that appears designed to effect a stop is no less intrusive than a stop itself . . . [A] stop starts when pursuit begins."); *People v. Thomas*,

660 P.2d 1272, 1275 (Colo. 1983) (en banc) (officers must have reasonable suspicion at the inception of the pursuit, and may not rely on facts observed during the chase to justify seizure); *People v. Terrell*, 77 Mich.App. 676, 680, 259 N.W.2d 187, 189 (1977); *State v. Saia*, 302 So.2d 869, 873 (La. 1974), *cert. denied*, 420 U.S. 1008, 95 S.Ct. 1454, 43 L.Ed.2d 767 (1975). We follow their lead, and hold that the initiation of a police chase such as occurred here constitutes a "seizure" for Fourth Amendment purposes.[2] In this case, seizure occurred, at the latest, when Sergeant Miller began to chase D.J. on foot.

III

To justify a particular intrusion upon a citizen's constitutionally protected interests, "the police officer must be able to point to specific and articulable facts which, taken together with rational inferences from those facts, reasonably warrant that intrusion." *Terry, supra*, 392 U.S. at 21, 88 S.Ct. at 1880 (footnote omitted). The motions judge ruled that the police intrusion in this case was justified by suspicions engendered by D.J.'s attempts to avoid the police officers, as well as by his putting his hands in his pockets. On appeal, the government offers additional articulable facts, citing D.J.'s presence in a "high narcotics area" and Sergeant Miller's experience in narcotics enforcement. We will examine these facts individually.

[2] We have recognized, "as a general proposition, that flight from authority—*implying consciousness of guilt*—may be considered *among other factors* justifying a *Terry* seizure." *United States v. Johnson*, 496 A.2d 592, 597 (D.C. 1985) (emphasis added), citing *Stephenson v. United States*, 296 A.2d 606, 609–10 (D.C. 1972), *cert. denied*, 411 U.S. 907, 93 S.Ct. 1535, 36 L.Ed.2d 197 (1973). However, the circumstances of the suspect's efforts to avoid the police must be such as "permit[ ] a rational conclusion that flight indicated a consciousness of guilt,"

---

1. The motions judge found, and the government has conceded at oral argument on appeal, that the *Terry* stop occurred at the commencement of the footrace. D.J. contends that the stop occurred at some unspecified point earlier in the encounter, when, by continually "stalking" his movements in their car, the police led him to reasonably believe that he was not free to leave. It might be difficult to pinpoint exactly when, if ever, during this gradually escalating encounter, a reasonable person would feel he was no longer free to decline contact with the police. Fortunately, we find it unnecessary to do so in order to decide this case. We leave the question open, deciding only that the seizure occurred, *at the latest*, when Sergeant Miller began to give chase on foot.

2. This issue has not heretofore been decided in this jurisdiction. In *Bennett, supra*, we left this question open, since we did not need to reach it in order to decide that case. 514 A.2d at 415 n. 2.

Lawrence v. United States, 509 A.2d 614, 618 (D.C.1986) (Newman, J., dissenting), and the evasive action must be accompanied by other factors warranting an intrusion.

To begin with, we doubt that D.J.'s behavior was of the sort which could give rise to a rational inference of consciousness of guilt. Assuming, without deciding, that he knew Miller and Andes were police officers,[3] his conduct, in itself, was not the kind of flight from authority which we have typically found to create an "articulable suspicion." In cases in this jurisdiction in which flight has been considered an indication of guilty conscience, the accused reacted by immediately running from the police. See *Bennett, supra,* 514 A.2d at 414 (appellant and companion "bolted" when police car arrived); *Lawrence, supra,* 509 A.2d at 615 (appellant ran at sight of police car emergency lights); *Tobias v. United States,* 375 A.2d 491, 492 (D.C.1977) (appellant began to run when police officer identified himself); *Franklin v. United States,* 382 A.2d 20, 21 (D.C.1978) (appellants fled in car after officer identified himself), *vacated in part on other grounds,* 392 A.2d 516 (D.C.1978), *cert. denied sub nom. Dickerson v. United States,* 440 U.S. 948, 99 S.Ct. 1428, 59 L.Ed.2d 637 (1979); *Hinton v. United States,* 137 U.S.App.D.C. 388, 391, 424 F.2d 876, 879 (1969) (appellant "bolted" when police searched his companion).

[3] D.J.'s reaction to the presence of the police was different. He did not break into a sprint upon the first approach of the police car. Instead, he merely attempted to walk away, behavior indicative simply of a desire not to talk to the police. No adverse inference may be drawn from such a desire. *Brown v. Texas,* 443 U.S. 47, 99 S.Ct. 2637, 61 L.Ed.2d 357 (1979).

[4,5] Citizens have no legal duty to talk to the police. See *Cobb v. Standard Drug Co.,* 453 A.2d 110, 112 (D.C.1982). Law enforcement officers, like anybody else, may approach an individual in a public place and put questions to him if he is willing to listen. "The person approached, however, need not answer any question put to him; indeed, he may decline to listen to the questions at all and may go on his way. . . . He may not be detained even momentarily without reasonable, objective grounds for doing so; and his refusal to listen or answer does not, without more, furnish those grounds." *Florida v. Royer,* 460 U.S. 491, 497–98, 103 S.Ct. 1319, 1324, 75 L.Ed.2d 229 (1983) (plurality opinion) (citations omitted); *Brown v. Texas, supra,* 443 U.S. at 52, 99 S.Ct. at 2641; *United States v. Barnes,* 496 A.2d 1040, 1044 n. 9 (D.C.1985). A refusal to listen or answer may take verbal form, or, it may, as in the present case, take the form of physical departure. See *People v. Howard,* 50 N.Y.2d 583, 586, 430 N.Y.S.2d 578, 581, 408 N.E.2d 908, 910 (person questioned by police may remain silent or walk or run away), *cert. denied,* 449 U.S. 1023, 101 S.Ct. 590, 66 L.Ed.2d 484 (1980). In either case, it may be inspired by any number of innocent reasons.[4] Such ambiguous conduct may not serve, of itself, as a basis for seizure. See *Wong Sun, supra* note 4, 371 U.S. at 484, 83 S.Ct. at 415; *People v. Aldridge,* 35 Cal.3d 473, 479, 198 Cal.Rptr. 538, 541, 674 P.2d 240, 243 (1984) en banc ("departure . . . from an imminent intrusion cannot bootstrap an illegal detention into one that is legal"). To permit such justification would be effectively to create a duty to respond to the police, and would seriously intrude upon the liberty and privacy interests which the Fourth Amendment was designed to protect.

For these reasons, courts in this jurisdiction have long adhered to the principle that flight is not "a reliable indicator of guilt without other circumstances to make its import less ambiguous." *Hinton, supra,* 137 U.S.App.D.C. at 391, 424 F.2d at 879. In accordance with this principle, we have sustained findings of reasonable suspicion based upon flight

---

3. Whether there was sufficient basis for a *Terry* stop is in each case an inquiry based on an objective view of the facts as the police officer knew them at the time of the seizure. *Coleman v. United States,* 337 A.2d 767, 769 (D.C.1975). At the time they were pursuing D.J., Sergeant Miller and Lieutenant Gray were in plainclothes and were driving an unmarked car. See *United States v. Jones,* 619 F.2d 494, 498 (5th Cir.1980) (plainclothes police officer could not reasonably have concluded that the accused knew he was being pursued by a policeman, and therefore, was unjustified in treating the flight as a suspicious circumstance supporting a *Terry* stop).

4. An individual may be motivated to avoid the police by a natural fear or dislike of authority, a distaste for police officers based upon past experience, an exaggerated fear of police brutality or harassment, a fear of being apprehended as the guilty party, or other legitimate personal reasons. See *Wong Sun v. United States,* 371 U.S. 471, 483 n. 10, 83 S.Ct. 407, 415 n. 10, 9 L.Ed.2d 441 (1963); *Alberty v. United States,* 162 U.S. 499, 511, 16 S.Ct. 864, 868, 40 L.Ed. 1051 (1896).

only when other circumstances were present to justify an inference that criminal activity was afoot.[5]

[6] We hold, as our past cases have indicated, that an attempt to evade the police, without more, is insufficient grounds to justify a *Terry* stop. Such conduct on the part of a suspect must be "corroborated by other suspicious circumstances. . . ." *Watkins v. State*, 288 Md. 597, 603–04, 420 A.2d 270, 273 (1980). We are in agreement with courts in other jurisdictions which, faced with facts similar to those presented in this case, have reached the same conclusion.[6]

[7] The government claims that other circumstances were present which, when combined with D.J.'s evasive maneuvers, raised sufficient cause for suspicion to justify a *Terry* stop. We find these other circumstances of no significance. Putting one's hands in one's pockets, for example, is a universal action which could hardly be called suspicious, especially on a rainy evening in March.

The experience of a police officer with the modus operandi of narcotics transactions is sometimes relevant to whether he made a reasonable conclusion that criminal activity was afoot. *Bennett, supra*, 514 A.2d at 416 (where police sighted four men in alley, saw money change hands, and saw one man putting hand in waistband, officer's suspicion aroused because he knew from experience that drug traffickers often work in pairs, one holding the money, the other holding the drugs—sometimes in his pants). However, none of D.J.'s actions—neither his putting his hands in his pockets, nor his walking away from the police—can be deemed sufficiently sinister in character, even to an experienced police officer, to transform this stop into a valid one.

Similarly, although the fact that a stop occurred in a "high narcotics area" has sometimes been con-sidered along with other factors in determining the reasonableness of the officer's suspicion, see, e.g., *Price v. United States*, 429 A.2d 514, 518 (D.C.1981), we have emphasized that "[t]his familiar talismanic litany, without a great deal more, cannot support an inference that appellant was engaged in criminal conduct." *Curtis v. United States*, 349 A.2d 469, 472 (D.C.1975). D.J. lived less than three blocks from the place where he was stopped. Thousands of persons live and go about their legitimate business in areas which are denoted "high narcotics areas" by police. Innocent activities do not become sinister by the mere fact that they take place in one of these areas. See *Brown, supra*, 443 U.S. at 52, 99 S.Ct. at 2641 ("The fact that appellant was in a neighborhood frequented by drug users, standing alone, is not a basis for concluding that appellant himself was engaged in criminal conduct.").

We conclude that the investigative stop in this case was not warranted by the totality of the facts articulated by the government. The trial court therefore erred in denying D.J.'s motion to suppress; its judgment must be reversed.

SEARCH AND SEIZURE IN PUBLIC SCHOOLS

Case Comment

Education officials often assume quasi-police powers over children in school. School officials may search students in order to determine whether they are in possession of contraband such as drugs or weapons, search their lockers and desks, and question them about illegal activities. Such actions are comparable to the acts of the regular police. In *New*

---

5. See, e.g., *Bennett, supra*, 514 A.2d at 414–15 (in addition to flight, police observed what appeared to be drug transaction); *Lawrence, supra*, 509 A.2d at 615 (two men appeared to be casing a liquor store, and partially matched police lookout description); *Johnson, supra*, 496 A.2d at 594 (type of car, number of men in it, lateness of the hour, location were factors heightened by flight of driver); *Tobias, supra*, 375 A.2d at 494 (appellant seen selling objects to several persons on street, then fled at sight of police); see also *Hinton, supra*, 137 U.S.App.D.C. at 390, 424 F.2d at 878 (appellant, en route to narcotics "pad" with companion, fled when search of companion revealed drugs).

6. See *People v. Shabaz*, 424 Mich. 42, 64, 378 N.W.2d 451, 461 (1985), *cert. granted*, 475 U.S. 1094, 106 S.Ct. 1489, 89 L.Ed.2d 733, *cert. dismissed*, ___ U.S. ___ , 106 S.Ct. 3326, 92 L.Ed.2d 733 (1986); *People v. Tebedo*, 81 Mich.App. 535, 539, 265 N.W.2d 406, 408–09 (1978); *Thibeau, supra*, 384 Mass. at 764–65, 429 N.E.2d at 1010; *Commonwealth v. Barnett*, 484 Pa. 211, 214–15, 398 A.2d 1019, 1021 (1979); *Commonwealth v. Jeffries*, 454 Pa. 320, 325, 311 A.2d 914, 917 (1973); *McClain v. State*, 408 So.2d 721, 722 (Fla.Dist.Ct.App.), *petition for review dismissed*, 415 So.2d 1361 (Fla.1982); *People v. Howard, supra*, 50 N.Y.2d at 592, 430 N.Y.S.2d at 585, 408 N.E.2d at 914; *People v. Fox*, 97 Ill.App.3d 58, 64, 421 N.E.2d 1082, 1086 (1981); *Thomas, supra*, 660 P.2d at 1276; *Jones, supra* note 3, 619 F.2d at 498; see also *Watkins, supra*, 288 Md. at 603–04, 420 A.2d at 273–74, and cases cited therein.

Jersey v. T.L.O. (1985), the U.S. Supreme Court held that a school official had the authority to search the purse of a student, even though no warrant was issued nor was there probable cause that a crime had been committed; there was only the suspicion that T.L.O. had violated school rules.

This important case involves an assistant principal's search of the purse of a fourteen-year-old student observed smoking a cigarette in a school lavatory. The search was prompted when the principal found cigarette rolling papers as the pack of cigarettes was removed from the purse. A further search revealed marijuana and several items indicating marijuana selling; as a result, T.L.O. was adjudicated as a delinquent. The Supreme Court held that the Fourth Amendment protections against unreasonable searches and seizures apply to students but said that the need to maintain an orderly educational environment modified the usual Fourth Amendment requirements of warrants and probable cause. The Court relaxed the usual probable cause standard and found the search to be reasonable. It declared that the school's right to maintain discipline on school grounds allowed it to search a student and his or her possessions as a safety precaution. Thus the Court, which had guarded the warrant requirement and its exceptions in the past, now permits warrantless searches in schools, based on the lesser standard of "reasonable suspicion," and established the concept of "reasonableness" in dealing with school searches.[17]

NEW JERSEY v. T. L. O.

469 U.S. 325, 83 L.Ed.2d 720, 105 S.Ct. 733

Justice White delivered the opinion of the Court.

[1a, 2a] We granted certiorari in this case to examine the appropriateness of the exclusionary rule as a remedy for searches carried out in violation of the Fourth Amendment by public school authorities. Our consideration of the proper application of the Fourth Amendment to the public schools, however, has led us to conclude that the search that gave rise to the case now before us did not violate the Fourth Amendment. Accordingly, we here address only the questions of the proper standard for assessing the

legality of searches conducted by public school officials and the application of that standard to the facts of this case.

I

On March 7, 1980, a teacher at Piscataway High School in Middlesex County, N.J., discovered two girls smoking in a lavatory. One of the two girls was the respondent T. L. O., who at that time was a 14-year-old high school freshman. Because smoking in the lavatory was a violation of a school rule, the teacher took the two girls to the principal's office, where they met with Assistant Vice Principal Theodore Choplick. In response to questioning by Mr. Choplick, T. L. O.'s companion admitted that she had violated the rule. T. L. O., however, denied that she had been smoking in the lavatory and claimed that she did not smoke at all.

Mr. Choplick asked T. L. O. to come into his private office and demanded to see her purse. Opening the purse, he found a pack of cigarettes, which he removed from the purse and held before T. L. O. as he accused her of having lied to him. As he reached into the purse for the cigarettes, Mr. Choplick also noticed a package of cigarette rolling papers. In his experience, possession of rolling papers by high school students was closely associated with the use of marijuana. Suspecting that a closer examination of the purse might yield further evidence of drug use, Mr. Choplick proceeded to search the purse thoroughly. The search revealed a small amount of marijuana, a pipe, a number of empty plastic bags, a substantial quantity of money in one-dollar bills, an index card that appeared to be a list of students who owed T. L. O. money, and two letters that implicated T. L. O. in marijuana dealing.

Mr. Choplick notified T. L. O's mother and the police, and turned the evidence of drug dealing over to the police. At the request of the police, T. L. O.'s mother took her daughter to police headquarters, where T. L. O. confessed that she had been selling marijuana at the high school. On the basis of the confession and the evidence seized by Mr. Choplick, the State brought delinquency charges against T. L. O. in the Juvenile and Domestic Relations Court of Middlesex County.[1] Contending that Mr.

---

1. T. L. O. also received a 3-day suspension from school for smoking cigarettes in a nonsmoking area and a 7-day suspension for possession of marijuana. On T. L. O.'s motion, the Superior Court of New Jersey, Chancery Division, set aside the 7-day suspension on the ground that it was based on evidence seized in violation of the Fourth Amendment (*T. L. O.*) v. *Piscataway Bd. of Ed.* No. C.2865-79 (Super.Ct.N.J., Ch.Div., Mar. 31, 1980). The Board of Education apparently did not appeal the decision of the Chancery Division.

Choplick's search of her purse violated the Fourth Amendment, T. L. O. moved to suppress the evidence found in her purse as well as her confession, which, she argued, was tainted by the allegedly unlawful search. The Juvenile Court denied the motion to suppress. *State ex rel T. L. O.*, 178 N.J.Super. 329, 428 A.2d 1327 (1980). Although the court concluded that the Fourth Amendment did apply to searches carried out by school officials, it held that

> a school official may properly conduct a search of a student's person if the official has a reasonable suspicion that a crime has been or is in the process of being committed, or reasonable cause to believe that the search is necessary to maintain school discipline or enforce school policies. *Id.*, at 341, 428 A.2d, at 1333 (emphasis in original).

Applying this standard, the court concluded that the search conducted by Mr. Choplick was a reasonable one. The initial decision to open the purse was justified by Mr. Choplick's well-founded suspicion that T. L. O. had violated the rule forbidding smoking in the lavatory. Once the purse was open, evidence of marijuana violations was in plain view, and Mr. Choplick was entitled to conduct a thorough search to determine the nature and extent of T. L. O.'s drug-related activities. *Id.*, at 343, 428 A.2d, at 1334. Having denied the motion to suppress, the court on March 23, 1981, found T. L. O. to be a delinquent and on January 8, 1982, sentenced her to a year's probation.

On appeal from the final judgment of the Juvenile Court, a divided Appellate Division affirmed that the trial court's finding that there had been no Fourth Amendment violation but vacated the adjudication of delinquency and remanded for a determination whether T. L. O. had knowingly and voluntarily waived her Fifth Amendment rights before confessing. *State ex rel T. L. O.*, 185 N.J.Super. 279, 448 A.2d 493 (1982). T. L. O. appealed the Fourth Amendment ruling, and the Supreme Court of New Jersey reversed the judgment of the Appellante Division and ordered the suppression of the evidence found in T. L. O.'s purse. *State ex rel T. L. O.*, 94 N.J. 331, 463 A.2d 934 (1983).

The New Jersey Supreme Court agreed with the lower courts that the Fourth Amendment applies to searches conducted by school officials. The court also rejected the State of New Jersey's argument that the exclusionary rule should not be employed to prevent the use in juvenile proceedings of evidence

unlawfully seized by school officials. Declining to consider whether applying the rule to the fruits of searches by school officials would have any deterrent value, the court held simply that the precedents of this Court establish that "if an official search violates constitutional rights, the evidence is not admissible in criminal proceedings." *Id.*, at 341, 463 A.2d, at 939 (footnote omitted).

With respect to the question of the legality of the search before it, the court agreed with the Juvenile Court that a warrantless search by a school official does not violate the Fourth Amendment so long as the official "has reasonable grounds to believe that a student possesses evidence of illegal activity or activity that would interfere with school discipline and order." *Id.*, at 346, 463 A.2d, at 941–942. However, the court, with two justices dissenting, sharply disagreed with the Juvenile Court's conclusion that the search of the purse was reasonable. According to the majority, the contents of T. L. O.'s purse had no bearing on the accusation against T. L. O., for possession of cigarettes (as opposed to smoking them in the lavatory) did not violate school rules, and a mere desire for evidence that would impeach T. L. O.'s claim that she did not smoke cigarettes could not justify the search. Moreover, even if a reasonable suspicion that T. L. O. had cigarettes in her purse would justify a search, Mr. Choplick had no such suspicion, as no one had furnished him with any specific information that there were cigarettes in the purse. Finally, leaving aside the question whether Mr. Choplick was justified in opening the purse, the court held that the evidence of drug use that he saw inside did not justify the extensive "rummaging" through T. L. O.'s papers and effects that followed. *Id.*, at 347, 463 A.2d, at 942–943.

We granted the State of New Jersey's petition for certiorari. 464 U.S. 991, 78 L.Ed.2d 678, 104 S.Ct. 480 (1983). Although the State had argued in the Supreme Court of New Jersey that the search of T. L. O.'s purse did not violate the Fourth Amendment, the petition for certiorari raised only the question whether the exclusionary rule should operate to bar consideration in juvenile delinquency proceedings of evidence unlawfully seized by a school official without the involvement of law enforcement officers. When this case was first argued last term, the State conceded for the purpose of argument that the standard devised by the New Jersey Supreme Court for determining the legality of school searches was appropriate and that the court had correctly applied that standard; the State contended only that the remedial purposes of the exclusionary rule were not well served by applying it to searches conducted by public authorities not primarily engaged in law enforcement.

Although we originally granted certiorari to decide the issue of the appropriate remedy in juvenile court proceedings for unlawful school searches, our doubts regarding the wisdom of deciding that question in isolation from the broader question of what limits, if any, the Fourth Amendment places on the activities of school authorities prompted us to order reargument on that question.[2]

Having heard argument on the legality of the search of T. L. O.'s purse, we are satisfied that the search did not violate the Fourth Amendment.[3]

II

[3] In determining whether the search at issue in this case violated the Fourth Amendment, we are faced initially with the question whether that Amendment's prohibition on unreasonable searches and seizures applies to searches conducted by public school officials. We hold that it does.

It is now beyond dispute that "the Federal Constitution, by virtue of the Fourteenth Amendment, prohibits its unreasonable searches and seizures by state officers." *Elkins v. United States*, 364 U.S. 206, 213, 4 L.Ed.2d 1669, 80 S.Ct. 1437 (1960); accord, *Mapp v. Ohio*, 367 U.S. 643, 6 L.Ed.2d 1081, 81 S.Ct. 1684, 16 Ohio Ops.2d 384, 86 Ohio L.Abs., 513, 84 A.L.R.2d 933 (1961); *Wolf v. Col-*

---

2. State and federal courts considering these questions have struggled to accommodate the interests protected by the Fourth Amendment and the interest of the States in providing a safe environment conducive to education in the public schools. Some courts have resolved the tension between these interests by giving full force to one or the other side of the balance. Thus, in a number of cases courts have held that school officials conducting in-school searches of students are private parties acting in loco parentis and are therefore not subject to the constraints of the Fourth Amendment. See, e.g., *D. R. C. v. State*, 646 P.2d 252 (Alaska Ct. App. 1982); *In re G.*, 11 Cal.App.3d 1193, 90 Cal.Rptr. 361 (1970); *In re Donaldson*, 269 Cal.App.2d 509, 75 Cal.Rptr. 220 (1969); *R. C. M. v. State*, 660 S.W.2d 552 (Tex.App. 1983); *Mercer v. State*, 450 S.W.2d 715 (Tex.Civ.App. 1970). At least one court has held, on the other hand, that the Fourth Amendment applies in full to in-school searches by school officials and that a search conducted without probable cause is unreasonable, see *State v. Mora*, 307 So.2d 317 (La.), vacated, 423 U.S. 809, 46 L.Ed.2d 29, 96 S.Ct. 20 (1975), *on remand*, 330 So.2d 900 (La. 1976); others have held or suggested that the probable-cause standard is applicable at least where the police are involved in a search, see *M. v. Board of Ed. Ball-Chatham Community Unit School Dist. No. 5*, 429 F.Supp. 288, 292 (S.D. Ill. 1977); *Picha v. Wielgos*, 410 F.Supp. 1214, 1219–1221 (N.D. Ill. 1976); *State v. Young*, 234 Ga. 488, 498, 216 S.E.2d 586, 594 (1975); or where the search is highly intrusive, see *M. M. v. Anker*, 607 F.2d 588, 589 (2d Cir. 1979).

The majority of courts that have addressed the issue of the Fourth Amendment in the schools have, like the Supreme Court of New Jersey in this case, reached a middle position: the Fourth Amendment applies to searches conducted by school authorities, but the special needs of the school environment require assessment of the legality of such searches against a standard less exacting than that of probable cause. These courts have, by and large, upheld warrantless searches by school authorities provided that they are supported by a reasonable suspicion that the search will uncover evidence of an infraction of school disciplinary rules or a violation of the law. See, e.g., *Tarter v. Raybuck*, No. 83-3174 (6th Cir., Aug. 31, 1984); *Bilbrey v. Brown*, 738 F.2d 1462 (9th Cir. 1984); *Horton v. Goose Creek Independent School Dist.*, 690 F.2d 470 (5th Cir. 1982); *Bellnier v. Lund*, 438 F.Supp. 47 (N.D.N.Y. 1977); *M. v. Board of Ed. Ball-Chatham Community Unit School Dist. No. 5, supra*; *In re W.*, 29 Cal.App.3d 777, 105 Cal.Rptr. 775 (1973); *State v. Baccino*, 282 A.2d 869 (Del.Super. 1971); *State v. D. T. W.*, 425 So.2d 1383 (Fla.App. 1983); *State v. Young, supra*; *In re J. A.*, 85 Ill.App.3d 567, 406 N.E.2d 958 (1980); *People v. Ward*, 62 Mich.App. 46, 233 N.W.2d 180 (1975); *Doe v. State*, 88 N.M. 347, 540 P.2d 827 (App. 1975); *People v. D.* 34 N.Y.2d 483, 315 N.E.2d 466 (1974); *State v. McKinnon*, 88 Wash.2d 75, 558 P.2d 781 (1977); *In re L. L.*, 90 Wis.2d 585, 280 N.W.2d 343 (App. 1979).

Although few have considered the matter, courts have also split over whether the exclusionary rule is an appropriate remedy for Fourth Amendment violations committed by school authorities. The Georgia courts have held that although the Fourth Amendment applies to the schools, the exclusionary rule does not. See, e.g., *State v. Young, supra*; *State v. Lamb*, 137 Ga.App. 437, 224 S.E.2d 51 (1976). Other jurisdictions have applied the rule to exclude the fruits of unlawful school searches from criminal trails and delinquency proceedings. See *State v. Mora, supra*; *People v. D., supra*.

3. In holding that the search of T. L. O.'s purse did not violate the Fourth Amendment, we do not implicitly determine that the exclusionary rule applies to the fruits of unlawful searches conducted by school authorities. The question whether evidence should be excluded from a criminal proceeding involves two discrete inquiries: whether the evidence was seized in violation of the Fourth Amendment, and whether the exclusionary rule is the appropriate remedy for the violation. Neither question is logically antecedent to the other, for a negative answer to either question is sufficient to dispose of the case. Thus, our determination that the search at issue in this case did not violate the Fourth Amendment implies no particular resolution of the question of the applicability of the exclusionary rule.

orado, 338 U.S. 25, 93 L.Ed. 1782, 69 S.Ct. 1359 (1949). Equally indisputable is the proposition that the Fourteenth Amendment protects the rights of students against encroachment by public school officials:

> The Fourteenth Amendment, as now applied to the States, protects the citizen against the State itself and all of its creatures—Boards of Education not excepted. These have, of course, delicate, and highly discretionary functions, but none that they may not perform within the limits of the Bill of Rights. That they are educating the young for citizenship is reason for scrupulous protection of Constitutional freedoms of the individual, if we are not to strangle the free mind at its source and teach youth to discount important principles of our government as mere platitudes. *West Virginia State Bd. of Ed. v. Barnette,* 319 U.S. 624, 637, 87 L.Ed. 1628, 63 S.Ct. 1178, 147 A.L.R. 674 (1943).

These two propositions—that the Fourth Amendment applies to the States through the Fourteenth Amendment, and that the actions of public school officials are subject to the limits placed on state action by the Fourteenth Amendment—might appear sufficient to answer the suggestion that the Fourth Amendment does not proscribe unreasonable searches by school officials. On reargument, however, the State of New Jersey has argued that the history of the Fourth Amendment indicates that the Amendment was intended to regulate only searches and seizures carried out by law enforcement officers; accordingly, although public school officials are concededly state agents for purposes of the Fourteenth Amendment, the Fourth Amendment creates no rights enforceable against them.[4]

It may well be true that the evil toward which the Fourth Amendment was primarily directed was the resurrection of the pre-Revolutionary practice of using general warrants or "writs of assistance" to authorized searches for contraband by officers of the Crown. See *United States v. Chadwick,* 433 U.S. 1, 7–8, 53 L.Ed.2d 538, 97 S.Ct. 2476 (1977); *Boyd v. United States,* 116 U.S. 616, 624–629, 29 L.Ed. 746, 6 S.Ct. 524 (1886). But this Court has never limited the Amendment's prohibition on unreasonable searches and seizures to operations conducted by the police. Rather, the Court has long spoken of the Fourth Amendment's strictures as restraints imposed upon "governmental action"—that is, "upon the activities of sovereign authority." *Burdeau v. McDowell,* 256 U.S. 465, 475, 65 L.Ed. 1048, 41 S.Ct. 574, 13 A.L.R. 1159 (1921). Accordingly, we have held the Fourth Amendment applicable to the activities of civil as well as criminal authorities: building inspectors, see *Camara v. Municipal Court,* 387 U.S. 523, 528, 18 L.Ed.2d 930, 87 S.Ct. 1727 (1967), Occupational Safety and Health Act inspectors, see *Marshall v. Barlow's, Inc.,* 436 U.S. 307, 312–313, 56 L.Ed.2d 305, 98 S.Ct. 1816 (1978), and even firemen entering privately owned premises to battle a fire, see *Michigan v. Tyler,* 436 U.S. 499, 506, 56 L.Ed.2d 486, 98 S.Ct. 1942 (1978), are all subject to the restraints imposed by the Fourth Amendment. As we observed in *Camara v. Municipal Court, supra,* "[t]he basic purpose of this Amendment, as recognized in countless decisions of this Court, is to safeguard the privacy and security of individuals against arbitrary invasions by governmental officials." 387 U.S. at 528, 18 L.Ed.2d 930, 87 S.Ct. 1727. Because the individual's interest in privacy and personal security "suffers whether the government's motivation is to investigate violations of criminal laws or breaches of other statutory or regulatory standards," *Marshall v. Barlow's, Inc., supra,* at 312–313, 56 L.Ed.2d 305, 98 S.Ct. 1816, it would be "anomalous to say that the individual and his private property are fully protected by the Fourth Amendment only when the individual is suspected of criminal behavior." *Camara v. Municipal Court, supra,* at 530, 18 L.Ed.2d 930, 87 S.Ct. 1727.

Notwithstanding the general applicability of the Fourth Amendment to the activities of civil authorities, a few courts have concluded that school officials are exempt from the dictates of the Fourth Amendment by virtue of the special nature of their authority over schoolchildren. See, e.g., *R. C. M. v. State,* 660 S.W.2d 552 (Tex.App.1983). Teachers and school administrators, it is said, act in loco parentis in their dealings with students: their authority is that of the parent, not the State, and is

---

4. Cf. *Ingraham v. Wright,* 430 U.S. 651, 51 L.Ed.2d 711, 97 S.Ct. 1401 (1977) (holding that the Eighth Amendment's prohibition of cruel and unusual punishment applies only to punishments imposed after criminal convictions and hence does not apply to the punishment of schoolchildren by public school officials).

therefore not subject to the limits of the Fourth Amendment. Ibid.

[4] Such reasoning is in tension with contemporary reality and the teachings of this Court. We have held school officials subject to the commands of the First Amendment, see *Tinker v. Des Moines Independent Community School District*, 393 U.S. 503, 21 L.Ed.2d 731, 89 S.Ct. 733, 49 Ohio.Ops.2d 222 (1969), and the Due Process Clause of the Fourteenth Amendment, see *Goss v. Lopez*, 419 U.S. 565, 42 L.Ed.2d 725, 95 S.Ct. 729 (1975). If school authorities are state actors for purposes of the constitutional guarantees of freedom of expression and due process, it is difficult to understand why they should be deemed to be exercising parental rather than public authority when conducting searches of their students. More generally, the Court has recognized that "the concept of parental delegation" as a source of school authority is not entirely "constant with compulsory education laws." *Ingraham v. Wright*, 430 U.S. 651, 662, 51 L.Ed.2d 711, 97 S.Ct. 1401 (1977). Today's public school officials do not merely exercise authority voluntarily conferred on them by individual parents; rather, they act in furtherance of publicly mandated educational and disciplinary policies. See, e.g., the opinion in *State ex rel. T. L. O.*, 94 N.J., at 343, 463 A.2d, at 934, 940, describing the New Jersey statutes regulating school disciplinary policies and establishing the authority of school officials over their students. In carrying out searches and other disciplinary functions pursuant to such policies, school officials act as representatives of the State, not merely as surrogates for the parents, and they cannot claim the parents' immunity from the strictures of the Fourth Amendment.

III

To hold that the Fourth Amendment applies to searches conducted by school authorities is only to begin the inquiry into the standards governing such searches. Although the underlying command of the Fourth Amendment is always that searches and seizures be reasonable, what is reasonable depends on the context within which a search takes place. The determination of the standard of reasonableness governing any specific class of searches requires "balancing the need to search against the invasion which the search entails." *Camara v. Municipal Court, supra*, at 536–537, 18 L.Ed.2d 930, 87 S.Ct. 1727. On one side of the balance are arrayed the individual's legitimate expectations of privacy and personal security; on the other, the government's need for effective methods to deal with breaches of public order.

We have recognized that even a limited search of the person is a substantial invasion of privacy. *Terry v. Ohio*, 392 U.S. 1, 24–25, 20 L.Ed.2d 889, 88 S.Ct. 1868, 44 Ohio Ops.2d 383 (1968). We have also recognized that searches of closed items of personal luggage are intrusions on protected privacy interests, for "the Fourth Amendment provides protection to the owner of every container that conceals its contents from plain view." *United States v. Ross*, 456 U.S. 798, 822–823, 72 L.Ed.2d 572, 102 S.Ct. 2157 (1982). A search of a child's person or of a closed purse or other bag carried on her person,[5] no less than a similar search carried out on an adult, is undoubtedly a severe violation of subjective expectations of privacy.

Of course, the Fourth Amendment does not protect subjective expectations of privacy that are unreasonable or otherwise "illegitimate." See, e.g., *Hudson v. Palmer*, 468 U.S. 517, 82 L.Ed.2d 393, 104 S.Ct. 3194 (1984); *Rawlings v. Kentucky*, 448 U.S. 98, 65 L.Ed.2d 633, 100 S.Ct. 2556 (1980). To receive the protection of the Fourth Amendment, an expectation of privacy must be one that society is "prepared to recognize as legitimate." *Hudson v. Palmer, supra*, at 526, 82 L.Ed.2d 393, 104 S.Ct. 3194. The State of New Jersey has argued that because of the pervasive supervision to which chil-

---

5. We do not address the question, not presented by this case, whether a schoolchild has a legitimate expectation of privacy in lockers, desks, or other school property provided for the storage of school supplies. Nor do we express any opinion on the standards (if any) governing searches of such areas by school officials or by other public authorities acting at the request of school officials. Compare *Zamora v. Pomeroy*, 639 F.2d 662, 670 (10th Cr. 1981) ("Inasmuch as the school had assumed joint control of the locker it cannot be successfully maintained that the school did not have a right to inspect it"), and *People v. Overton*, 24 N.Y.2d 522, 249 N.E.2d 366 (1969) (school administrators have power to consent to search of a student's locker), with *State v. Engerud*, 94 N.J. 331, 348, 463 A.2d 934, 943 (1983) ("We are satisfied that in the context of this case the student had an expectation of privacy in the contents of his locker. . . . For the four years of high school, the school locker is a home away from home. In it the student stores the kind of personal 'effects' protected by the Fourth Amendment").

dren in the schools are necessarily subject, a child has virtually no legitimate expectation of privacy in articles of personal property "unnecessarily" carried into a school. This argument has two factual premises: (1) the fundamental incompatibility of expectations of privacy with the maintenance of a sound educational environment; and (2) the minimal interest of the child in bringing any items of personal property into the school. Both premises are severely flawed.

Although this Court may take notice of the difficulty of maintaining discipline in the public schools today, the situation is not so dire that students in the schools may claim no legitimate expectations of privacy. We have recently recognized that the need to maintain order in a prison is such that prisoners retain no legitimate expectations of privacy in their cells, but it goes almost without saying that "[t]he prisoner and the schoolchild stand in wholly different circumstances, separated by the harsh facts of criminal conviction and incarceration." *Ingraham v. Wright, supra,* at 669, 51 L.Ed.2d 711, 97 S.Ct. 1401. We are not yet ready to hold that the schools and the prisons need be equated for purposes of the Fourth Amendment.

Nor does the State's suggestion that children have no legitimate need to bring personal property into the schools seem well anchored in reality. Students at a minimum must bring to school not only the supplies needed for their studies, but also keys, money, and the necessaries of personal hygiene and grooming. In addition, students may carry on their persons or in purses or wallets such nondisruptive yet highly personal items as photographs, letters, and diaries. Finally, students may have perfectly legitimate reasons to carry with them articles of property needed in connection with extracurricular or recreational activities. In short, schoolchildren may find it necessary to carry with them a variety of legitimate, noncontraband items, and there is no reason to conclude that they have necessarily waived all rights to privacy in such items merely by bringing them onto school grounds.

Against the child's interest in privacy must be set the substantial interest of teachers and administrators in maintaining discipline in the classroom and on school grounds. Maintaining order in the classroom has never been easy, but in recent years, school disorder has often taken particularly ugly forms: drug use and violent crime in the schools have become major social problems. See, generally, 1 NIE, U.S.

Dept. of Health, Education and Welfare, Violent Schools—Safe Schools: The Safe School Study Report to the Congress (1978). Even in schools that have been spared the most severe disciplinary problems, the preservation of order and a proper educational environment requires close supervision of schoolchildren, as well as the enforcement of rules against conduct that would be perfectly permissible if undertaken by an adult. "Events calling for discipline are frequent occurrences and sometimes require immediate, effective action." *Goss v. Lopez,* 419 U.S. at 580, 42 L.Ed.2d 725, 95 S.Ct. 729. Accordingly, we have recognized that maintaining security and order in the schools requires a certain degree of flexibility in school disciplinary procedures, and we have respected the value of preserving the informality of the student-teacher relationship. See *id.,* at 582–583, 42 L.Ed.2d 725, 95 S.Ct. 729; *Ingraham v. Wright,* 430 U.S. at 680–682, 51 L.Ed.2d 711, 97 S.Ct. 1401.

[5] How, then, should we strike the balance between the schoolchild's legitimate expectations of privacy and the school's equally legitimate need to maintain an environment in which learning can take place? It is evident that the school setting requires some easing of the restrictions to which searches by public authorities are ordinarily subject. The warrant requirement, in particular, is unsuited to the school environment: requiring a teacher to obtain a warrant before searching a child suspected of an infraction of school rules (or of the criminal law) would unduly interfere with the maintenance of the swift and informal disciplinary procedures needed in the schools. Just as we have in other cases dispensed with the warrant requirement when "the burden of obtaining a warrant is likely to frustrate the governmental purpose behind the search," *Camara v. Municipal Court,* 387 U.S. at 532–533, 18 L.Ed.2d 930, 87 S.Ct. 1727, we hold today that school officials need not obtain a warrant before searching a student who is under their authority.

[6] The school setting also requires some modification of the level of suspicion of illicit activity needed to justify a search. Ordinarily, a search—even one that may permissibly be carried out without a warrant—must be based upon "probable cause" to believe that a violation of the law has occurred. See, e.g., *Almeida-Sanchez v. United States,* 413 U.S. 266, 273, 37 L.Ed.2d 596, 93 S.Ct. 2535 (1973); *Sibron v. New York,* 392 U.S. 40, 62–66, 20 L.Ed.2d 917, 88 S.Ct. 1889, 44 Ohio Ops.2d

402 (1968). However, "probable cause" is not an irreducible requirement of a valid search. The fundamental command of the Fourth Amendment is that searches and seizures be reasonable, and although "both the concept of probable cause and the requirement of a warrant bear on the reasonableness of a search, . . . in certain limited circumstances neither is required." *Almeida-Sanchez v. United States, supra,* at 277, 37 L.Ed.2d 596, 93 S.Ct. 2535 (Powell, J., concurring). Thus, we have in a number of cases recognized the legality of searches and seizures based on suspicions that, although "reasonable," do not rise to the level of probable cause. See, e.g., *Terry v. Ohio,* 392 U.S. 1, 20 L.Ed.2d 889, 88 S.Ct. 1868, 44 Ohio Ops.2d 383 (1968); *United States v. Brignoni-Ponce,* 422 U.S. 873, 881, 45 L.Ed.2d 607, 95 S.Ct. 2574 (1975); *Delaware v. Prouse,* 440 U.S. 648, 654–655, 59 L.Ed.2d 660, 99 S.Ct. 1391 (1979); *United States v. Martinez-Fuerte,* 428 U.S. 543, 49 L.Ed.2d 1116, 96 S.Ct. 3074 (1976); cf. *Camara v. Municipal Court, supra,* at 534–539, 18 L.Ed.2d 930, 87 S.Ct. 1727. Where a careful balancing of governmental and private interests suggests that the public interest is best served by a Fourth Amendment standard of reasonableness that stops short of probable cause, we have not hesitated to adopt such a standard.

[1b,7] We join the majority of courts that have examined this issue[6] in concluding that the accom-

modation of the privacy interests of schoolchildren with the substantial need of teachers and administrators for freedom to maintain order in the schools does not require strict adherence to the requirement that searches be based on probable cause to believe that the subject of the search has violated or is violating the law. Rather, the legality of a search of a student should depend simply on the reasonableness, under all the circumstances, of the search. Determining the reasonableness of any search involves a twofold inquiry: first, one must consider "whether the . . . action was justified at its inception." *Terry v. Ohio,* 392 U.S. at 20, 20 L.Ed.2d 889, 88 S.Ct. 1868, 44 Ohio Ops.2d 383; second, one must determine whether the search as actually conducted "was reasonably related in scope to the circumstances which justified the interference in the first place," ibid. Under ordinary circumstances, a search of a student by a teacher or other school official[7] will be "justified at its inception" when there are reasonable grounds for suspecting that the search will turn up evidence that the student has violated or is violating either the law or the rules of the school.[8] Such a search will be permissible in its scope when the measures adopted are reasonably related to the objectives of the search and not excessively intrusive in light of the age and sex of the student and the nature of the infraction.[9]

---

7. We here consider only searches carried out by school authorities acting alone and on their own authority. This case does not present the question of the appropriate standard for assessing the legality of searches conducted by school officials in conjunction with or at the behest of law enforcement agencies, and we express no opinion on that question. Cf. *Picha v. Wielgos,* 410 F.Supp. 1214, 1219–1221 (N.D. Ill. 1976) (holding probable-cause standard applicable to searches involving the police).

8. We do not decide whether individualized suspicion is an essential element of the reasonableness standard we adopt for searches by school authorities. In other contexts, however, we have held that although "some quantum of individualized suspicion is usually a prerequisite to a constitutional search or seizure[,] . . . the Fourth Amendment imposes no irreducible requirement of such suspicion." *United States v. Martinez-Fuerte,* 428 U.S. 543, 560–561, 49 L.Ed.2d 1116, 96 S.Ct. 3074 (1976). See also *Camara v. Municipal Court,* 387 U.S. 523, 18 L.Ed.2d 930, 87 S.Ct. 1727 (1967). Exceptions to the requirement of individualized suspicion are generally appropriate only where the privacy interests implicated by a search are minimal and where "other safeguards" are available "to assure that the individual's reasonable expectation of privacy is not 'subject to the discretion of the official in the field.' " *Delaware v. Prouse,* 440 U.S. 648, 654–655, 59 L.Ed.2d 660, 99 S.Ct. 1391 (1979) (citation omitted). Because the search of T. L. O.'s purse was based upon an individualized suspicion that she had violated school rules, see *infra,* at 343–347 83 L.Ed.2d, at 736–738, we need not consider the circumstances that might justify school authorities in conducting searches unsupported by individualized suspicion.

9. Our reference to the nature of the infraction is not intended as an endorsement of Justice Stevens' suggestion that some rules regarding student conduct are by nature too "trivial" to justify a search based upon reasonable suspicion. See post, 377–382, 83 L.Ed.2d, at 758–761. We are unwilling to adopt a standard under which the legality of a search is dependent upon a judge's evaluation of the relative importance of various school rules. The maintenance of discipline in the schools requires not only that students be restrained from assaulting one another, abusing drugs and alcohol, and committing other crimes, but also that students conform themselves to the standards of conduct prescribed by school authorities. We have "repeatedly emphasized the need for affirming the comprehensive authority of the States and of school officials, consistent with fundamental constitutional safeguards, to prescribe and control conduct in the schools." *Tinker v. Des Moines Independent Community School District,* 393 U.S. 503, 507, 21 L.Ed.2d 731, 89 S.Ct. 733, 49 Ohio Ops.2d 222 (1969). The promulgation of a rule forbidding specified conduct presumably reflects a judgment on the part of school officials that such conduct is destructive of school order or of a proper educational environment. Absent any suggestion that the rule violates some substantive constitutional guarantee, the courts should, as a general matter, defer to that judgment and refrain from attempting to distinguish between rules that are important to the preservation of order in the schools and rules that are not.

This standard will, we trust, neither unduly burden the efforts of school authorities to maintain order in their schools nor authorize unrestrained intrusions upon the privacy of schoolchildren. By focusing attention on the question of reasonableness, the standard will spare teachers and school administrators the necessity of schooling themselves in the niceties of probable cause and permit them to regulate their conduct according to the dictates of reason and common sense. At the same time, the reasonableness standard should ensure that the interests of students will be invaded no more than is necessary to achieve the legitimate end of preserving order in the schools.

IV

[2b, 8a] There remains the question of the legality of the search in this case. We recognize that the "reasonable grounds" standard applied by the New Jersey Supreme Court in its consideration of this question is not substantially different from the standard that we have adopted today. Nonetheless, we believe that the New Jersey court's application of that standard to strike down the search of T. L. O.'s purse reflects a somewhat crabbed notion of reasonableness. Our review of the facts surrounding the search leads us to conclude that the search was in no sense unreasonable for Fourth Amendment purposes.[10]

The incident that gave rise to this case actually involved two separate searches, with the first—the search for cigarettes—providing the suspicion that gave rise to the second—the search for marijuana. Although it is the fruits of the second search that are at issue here, the validity of the search for marihuana must depend on the reasonableness of the initial search for cigarettes, as there would have been no reason to suspect that T. L. O. possessed marijuana had the first search not taken place. Accordingly, it is to the search for cigarettes that we first turn our attention.

The New Jersey Supreme Court pointed to two grounds for its holding that the search for cigarettes was unreasonable. First, the court observed that possession of cigarettes was not in itself illegal or a violation of school rules. Because the contents of T. L. O.'s purse would therefore have "no direct bearing on the infraction" of which she was accused (smoking in a lavatory where smoking was prohibited), there was no reason to search her purse.[11] Second, even assuming that a search of T. L. O.'s purse might under some circumstances be reasonable in light of the accusation made against T. L. O., the New Jersey court concluded that Mr. Choplick in this particular case had no reasonable grounds to suspect that T. L. O. had cigarettes in her purse. At best, according to the court, Mr. Choplick had "a good hunch." 94 N.J., at 347, 463 A.2d, at 942.

Both these conclusions are implausible. T. L. O. had been accused of smoking, and had denied the accusation in the strongest possible terms when she stated that she did not smoke at all. Surely it cannot be said that under these circumstances, T. L. O.'s possession of cigarettes would be irrelevant to the charges against her or to her response to those charges. T. L. O.'s possession of cigarettes, once it was discovered, would both corroborate the report that she had been smoking and undermine the credibility of her defense to the charge of smoking. To be sure, the discovery of the cigarettes would not prove that T. L. O. had been smoking in the lavatory; nor would it, strictly speaking, necessarily be inconsistent with her claim that she did not smoke at all. But it is universally recognized that evidence, to be relevant to an inquiry, need not conclusively prove the ultimate fact in issue, but only have "any tendency to make the existence of any fact that is of consequence to the determination of the action more probable or less probable than it would be without

---

10. [8b] Of course, New Jersey may insist on a more demanding standard under its own Constitution or statutes. In that case, its courts would not purport to be applying the Fourth Amendment when they invalidate a search.

11. Justice Stevens interprets these statements as a holding that enforcement of the school's smoking regulations was not sufficiently related to the goal of maintaining discipline or order in the school to justify a search under the standard adopted by the New Jersey court. See post, at 382–384, 83 L.Ed.2d, at 761–763. We do not agree that this is an accurate characterization of the New Jersey Supreme Court's opinion. The New Jersey court did not hold that the school's smoking rules were unrelated to the goal of maintaining discipline or order, nor did it suggest that a search that would produce evidence bearing directly on an accusation that a student had violated the smoking rules would be impermissible under the court's reasonable-suspicion standard; rather, the court concluded that any evidence a search of T. L. O.'s purse was likely to produce would not have a sufficiently direct bearing on the infraction to justify a search—a conclusion with which we cannot agree for the reasons set forth *infra*, at 345, 83 L.Ed.2d, at 737. Justice Stevens' suggestion that the New Jersey Supreme Court's decision rested on the perceived triviality of the smoking infraction appears to be a reflection of his own views rather than those of the New Jersey court.

the evidence." Fed. Rule Evid. 401. The relevance of T. L. O.'s possession of cigarettes to the question whether she had been smoking and to the credibility of her denial that she smoked supplied the necessary "nexus" between the item searched for and the infraction under investigation. See *Warden v. Hayden*, 387 U.S. 294, 306–307, 18 L.Ed.2d 782, 87 S.Ct. 1642 (1967). Thus, if Mr. Choplick in fact had a reasonable suspicion that T. L. O. had cigarettes in her purse, the search was justified despite the fact that the cigarettes, if found, would constitute "mere evidence" of a violation. *Ibid.*

Of course, the New Jersey Supreme Court also held that Mr. Choplick had no reasonable suspicion that the purse would contain cigarettes. This conclusion is puzzling. A teacher had reported that T. L. O. was smoking in the lavatory. Certainly this report gave Mr. Choplick reason to suspect that T. L. O. was carrying cigarettes with her; and if she did have cigarettes, her purse was the obvious place in which to find them. Mr. Choplick's suspicion that there were cigarettes in the purse was not an "inchoate and unparticularized suspicion or 'hunch,' " *Terry v. Ohio*, 392 U.S. at 27, 20 L.Ed.2d 889, 88 S.Ct. 1868, 44 Ohio Ops. 2d 383; rather, it was the sort of "common-sense conclusio[n] about human behavior" upon which "practical people"—including government officials—are entitled to rely. *United States v. Cortez*, 449 U.S. 411, 418, 66 L.Ed.2d 621, 101 S.Ct. 690 (1981). Of course, even if the teacher's report were true, T. L. O. *might* not have had a pack with her; she might have borrowed a cigarette from someone else or have been sharing a cigarette with another student. But the requirement of reasonable suspicion is not a requirement of absolute certainty: "sufficient probability, not certainty, is the touchstone of reasonableness under the Fourth Amendment. . . ." *Hill v. California*, 401 U.S. 797, 804, 28 L.Ed.2d 484, 91 S.Ct. 1106 (1971). Because the hypothesis that T. L. O. was carrying cigarettes in her purse was itself not unreasonable, it is irrelevant that other hypotheses were also consistent with the teacher's accusation. Accordingly, it cannot be said that Mr. Choplick acted unreasonably when he examined T. L. O.'s purse to see if it contained cigarettes.[12]

[2c] Our conclusion that Mr. Choplick's decision to open T. L. O.'s purse was reasonable brings us to the question of the further search for marijuana once the pack of cigarettes was located. The suspicion upon which the search for marijuana was founded was provided when Mr. Choplick observed a package of rolling papers in the purse as he removed the pack of cigarettes. Although T. L. O. does not dispute the reasonableness of Mr. Choplick's belief that the rolling papers indicated the presence of marijuana, she does contend that the scope of the search Mr. Choplick conducted exceeded permissible bounds when he seized and read certain letters that implicated T. L. O. in drug dealing. This argument, too, is unpersuasive. The discovery of the rolling papers concededly gave rise to a reasonable suspicion that T. L. O. was carrying marijuana as well as cigarettes in her purse. This suspicion justified further exploration of T. L. O.'s purse, which turned up more evidence of drug-related activities: a pipe, a number of plastic bags of the type commonly used to store marijuana, a small quantity of marihuana, and a fairly substantial amount of money. Under these circumstances, it was not unreasonable to extend the search to a separate zippered compartment of the purse; and when a search of that compartment revealed an index card containing a list of "people who owe me money" as well as two letters, the inference that T. L. O. was involved in marijuana trafficking was substantial enough to justify Mr. Choplick in examining the letters to determine whether they contained any further evidence. In short, we cannot conclude that the search for marijuana was unreasonable in any respect.

---

12. T. L. O. contends that even if it was reasonable for Mr. Choplick to open her purse to look for cigarettes, it was not reasonable for him to reach in and take the cigarettes out of her purse once he found them. Had he not removed the cigarettes from the purse, she asserts, he would not have observed the rolling papers that suggested the presence of marijuana, and the search for marijuana could not have taken place. T. L. O.'s argument is based on the fact that the cigarettes were not "contraband," as no school rule forbade her to have them. Thus, according to T. L. O., the cigarettes were not subject to seizure or confiscation by school authorities, and Mr. Choplick was not entitled to take them out of T. L. O.'s purse regardless of whether he was entitled to peer into the purse to see if they were there. Such hairsplitting argumentation has no place in an inquiry addressed to the issue of reasonableness. If Mr. Choplick could permissibly search T. L. O.'s purse for cigarettes, it hardly seems reasonable to suggest that his natural reaction to finding them—picking them up—could be a constitutional violation. We find that neither in opening the purse nor in reaching into it to remove the cigarettes did Mr. Choplick violate the Fourth Amendment.

Because the search resulting in the discovery of the evidence of marihuana dealing by T. L. O. was reasonable, the New Jersey Supreme Court's decision to exclude that evidence from T. L. O.'s juvenile delinquency proceedings on Fourth Amendment grounds was erroneous. Accordingly, the judgment of the Supreme Court of New Jersey is reversed.

APPLICATION OF MIRANDA RIGHTS TO JUVENILE PROCEEDINGS

Case Comment

One of the most difficult problems associated with the custodial interrogation of children has to do with their waiver of *Miranda* rights. Under what circumstances can juveniles knowingly and willingly waive the rights given them by *Miranda v. Arizona* and discuss their actions with police without benefit of a lawyer? Is it possible for a youngster, acting alone, to be mature enough to appreciate the right to remain silent? These are difficult questions.

In *Fare v. Michael C.*, the U.S. Supreme Court ruled that a juvenile's request to speak to his probation officer was not a *per se* request to remain silent nor was it tantamount to a request for an attorney. As a result, the Court concluded that the child voluntarily and knowingly waived his Fifth Amendment rights and consented to interrogation.

The Supreme Court also sought to clarify children's rights when they are interrogated by the police in the case of *California v. Prysock*.[18] Here, the Court was asked to rule on the adequacy of a *Miranda* warning given Randall Prysock, a youthful murder suspect. After reviewing the taped exchange between the police interrogator and the boy, the Court upheld Prysock's conviction when it ruled that even though the *Miranda* warning was given in slightly different terms and out of exact context, its meaning was plain and easily understandable, even to a juvenile.

Taken together, the *Fare* and *Prysock* cases make it seem indisputable that juveniles are entitled to receive at least the same *Miranda* rights as adults and ought to be entitled to even greater consideration to ensure that they understand their legal rights.

FARE v. MICHAEL C.

442 U.S. 707 (1979)

Mr. Justice Blackmun delivered the opinion of the Court.

In *Miranda v. Arizona*, 384 U.S. 436 (1966), this Court established certain procedural safeguards designed to protect the rights of an accused, under the Fifth and Fourteenth Amendments, to be free from compelled self-incrimination during custodial interrogation. The Court specified, among other things, that if the accused indicates in any manner that he wishes to remain silent or to consult an attorney, interrogation must cease, and any statement obtained from him during interrogation thereafter may not be admitted against him at his trial. *Id.*, at 444–445, 473–474.

In this case, the State of California, in the person of its acting chief probation officer, attacks the conclusion of the Supreme Court of California that a juvenile's request, made while undergoing custodial interrogation, to see his *probation officer* is *per se* an invocation of the juvenile's Fifth Amendment rights as pronounced in *Miranda*.

I

Respondent Michael C. was implicated in the murder of Robert Yeager. The murder occurred during a robbery of the victim's home on January 19, 1976. A small truck registered in the name of respondent's mother was identified as having been near the Yeager home at the time of the killing, and a young man answering respondent's description was seen by witnesses near the truck and near the home shortly before Yeager was murdered.

On the basis of this information, Van Nuys, Cal., police took respondent into custody at approximately 6:30 p.m. on February 4. Respondent then was 16½ years old and on probation to the Juvenile Court. He had been on probation since the age of 12. Approximately one year earlier he had served a term in a youth corrections camp under the supervision of the Juvenile Court. He had a record of several previous offenses, including burglary of guns and purse snatching, stretching back over several years.

Upon respondent's arrival at the Van Nuys station house two police officers began to interrogate him. The officers and respondent were the only persons in the room during the interrogation. The conversation was tape-recorded. One of the officers initiated the interview by informing respondent that he had been brought in for questioning in relation to a murder. The officer fully advised respondent of his *Miranda* rights. The following exchange then occurred, as set out in the opinion of the California Supreme Court, *In re Michael C.*, 21 Cal. 3d 471, 473–474, 579 P. 2d 7, 8 (1978) (emphasis added by that court):

Q. . . . Do you understand all of these rights as I have explained them to you?

A. Yeah.

Q. Okay, do you wish to give up your right to remain silent and talk to us about this murder?

A. What murder? I don't know about no murder.

Q. I'll explain to you which one it is if you want to talk to us about it.

A. Yeah, I might talk to you.

Q. Do you want to give up your right to have an attorney present here while we talk about it?

A. *Can I have my probation officer here?*

Q. Well I can't get a hold of your probation officer right now. You have the right to an attorney.

A. How I know you guys won't pull no police officer in and tell me he's an attorney?

Q. Huh?

A. [How I know you guys won't pull no police officer in and tell me he's an attorney?]

Q. Your probation officer is Mr. Christiansen.

A. Yeah.

Q. Well I'm not going to call Mr. Christiansen tonight. There's a good chance we can talk to him later, but I'm not going to call him right now. If you want to talk to us without an attorney present, you can. If you don't want to, you don't have to. But if you want to say something, you can, and if you don't want to say something you don't have to. That's your right. You understand that right?

A. Yeah.

Q. Okay, will you talk to us without an attorney present?

A. Yeah I want to talk to you."

Respondent thereupon proceeded to answer questions put to him by the officers. He made statements and drew sketches that incriminated him in the Yeager murder.

Largely on the basis of respondent's incriminating statements, probation authorities filed a petition in

Juvenile Court alleging that respondent had murdered Robert Yeager, in violation of Cal. Penal Code Ann. § 187 (West Supp. 1979), and that respondent therefore should be adjudged a ward of the Juvenile Court, pursuant to Cal. Welf. & Inst. Code Ann. § 602 (West Sup. 1979).[1] App. 4–5. Respondent thereupon moved to suppress the statements and sketches he gave the police during the interrogation. He alleged that the statements had been obtained in violation of *Miranda* in that his request to see his probation officer at the outset of the questioning constituted an invocation of his Fifth Amendment right to remain silent, just as if he had requested the assistance of an attorney. Accordingly, respondent argued that since the interrogation did not cease until he had a chance to confer with his probation officer, the statements and sketches could not be admitted against him in the Juvenile Court proceedings. In so arguing, respondent relied by analogy on the decision in *People v. Burton*, 6 Cal. 3d 375, 491 P. 2d 793 (1971), where the Supreme Court of California had held that a minor's request, made during custodial interrogation, to see his parents constituted an invocation of the minor's Fifth Amendment rights.

In support of his suppression motion, respondent called his probation officer, Charles P. Christiansen, as a witness. Christiansen testified that he had instructed respondent that if at any time he had "a concern with his family," or ever had "a police contact," App. 27, he should get in touch with his probation officer immediately. The witness stated that, on a previous occasion, when respondent had had a police contact and had failed to communicate with Christiansen, the probation officer had reprimanded him. *Id.*, at 28. This testimony, respondent argued, indicated that when he asked for his probation officer, he was in fact asserting his right to remain silent in the face of further questioning.

In a ruling from the bench, the court denied the motion to suppress. *Id.*, at 41–42. It held that the question whether respondent had waived his right to remain silent was one of fact to be determined on a case-by-case basis, and that the facts of this case showed a "clear waiver" by respondent of that right. *Id.*, at 42. The court observed that the tran-

---

1. The petition also alleged that respondent had participated in an attempted armed robbery earlier on the same evening Yeager was murdered. The Juvenile Court, however, held that the evidence was insufficient to support this charge and it was dismissed. App. 6. No issue relating to this second charge is before the Court.

script of the interrogation revealed that respondent specifically had told the officers that he would talk with them, and that this waiver had come at the outset of the interrogation and not after prolonged questioning. The court noted that respondent was a "16 and a half year old minor who has been through the court system before, has been to [probation] camp, has a probation officer, [and is not] a young, naive minor with no experience with the courts." *Ibid.* Accordingly, it found that on the facts of the case respondent had waived his Fifth Amendment rights, notwithstanding the request to see his probation officer.[2]

On appeal, the Supreme Court of California took the case by transfer from the California Court of Appeal and, by a divided vote, reversed. *In re Michael C.*, 21 Cal.3d 471, 579 P.2d 7 (1978). The court held that respondent's "request to see his probation officer at the commencement of interrogation negated any possible willingness on his part to discuss his case with the police [and] thereby invoked his Fifth Amendment privilege." *Id.*, at 474, 579 P.2d, at 8. The court based this conclusion on its view that, because of the juvenile court system's emphasis on the relationship between a probation officer and the probationer, the officer was "a trusted guardian figure who exercises the authority of the state as *parens patriae* and whose duty it is to implement the protective and rehabilitative powers of the juvenile court." *Id.*, at 476, 579 P.2d, at 10. As a consequence, the court found that a minor's request for his probation officer was the same as a request to see his parents during interrogation, and thus under the rule of *Burton* constituted an invocation of the minor's Fifth Amendment rights.

The fact that the probation officer also served as a peace officer, and, whenever a proceeding against a juvenile was contemplated, was charged with a duty to file a petition alleging that the minor had committed an offense, did not alter, in the court's view, the fact that the officer in the eyes of the juvenile was a trusted guardian figure to whom the minor normally would turn for help when in trouble with the police. 21 Cal.3d, at 476, 579 P.2d, at 10. Relying on *Burton*, the court ruled that it would unduly restrict *Miranda* to limit its reach in a case involving a minor to a request by the minor for an attorney, since it would be "'fatuous to assume that a minor in custody will be in a position to call an attorney for assistance and it is unrealistic to attribute no significance to his call for help from the only person to whom he normally looks—a parent or guardian.'" 21 Cal.3d, at 475–476, 579 P.2d, at 9, quoting *People v. Burton*, 6 Cal.3d, at 382, 491 P.2d, at 797–798. The court dismissed the concern expressed by the State that a request for a probation officer could not be distinguished from a request for one's football coach, music teacher, or clergyman on the ground that the probation officer, unlike those other figures in the juvenile's life, was charged by statute to represent the interests of the juvenile. 21 Cal.3d, at 477, 579 P.2d, at 10.

The court accordingly held that the probation officer would act to protect the minor's Fifth Amendment rights in precisely the way an attorney would act if called for by the accused. In so holding, the court found the request for a probation officer to be a *per se* invocation of Fifth Amendment rights in the same way the request for an attorney was found in *Miranda* to be, regardless of what the interrogation otherwise might reveal. In rejecting a totality-of-the-circumstances inquiry, the court stated:

"Here, however, we face conduct which, regardless of considerations of capacity, coercion or voluntariness, per se invokes the privilege against self-incrimination. Thus our question turns not on whether the [respondent] had the ability, capacity or willingness to give a knowledgeable waiver, and hence whether he acted voluntarily, but whether, when he called for his probation officer, he exercised his Fifth Amendment privilege. We hold that in doing so he no less invoked the protection against self-incrimination than if he asked for the presence of an attorney." *Ibid.*, 579 P.2d, at 10–11.

2. The California Court of Appeal, in an opinion reported and then vacated, affirmed. *In re Michael C.*, 135 Cal.Rptr. 762 (1977). That court noted that since the Juvenile Court's findings of fact resolved against respondent his contention that the confession had been coerced from him by threats and promises, it would have to "conclude that there was a knowing and intelligent waiver of the minor's *Miranda* rights unless it can be said that the request to speak to a probation officer was in and of itself sufficient to invoke" respondent's Fifth Amendment privilege. *Id.*, at 765–766 (footnote omitted). It refused to extend the rule of *People v. Burton*, 6 Cal.3d 375, 491 P.2d 793 (1971), to include a request for a probation officer, finding it difficult to distinguish such a request from a request to see "one's football coach, music teacher or clergyman." 135 Cal.Rptr., at 766. Even if the *Burton* rule were applicable, the court held, there was sufficient evidence of an affirmative waiver of his rights by respondent to distinguish *Burton*, where the California Supreme Court had noted that there was "nothing in the way of affirmative proof that defendant did not intend to assert his privilege." 6 Cal.3d, at 383, 491 P.2d, at 798.

See also *id.*, at 478 n. 4, 579 P.2d, at 11 n. 4. The court went on to conclude that since the State had not met its "burden of proving that a minor who requests to see his probation officer does not intend to assert his Fifth Amendment privilege," *id.*, at 478, 579 P.2d, at 11, the trial court should not have admitted the confessions obtained after respondent had requested his probation officer.[3]

The State of California petitioned this Court for a writ of certiorari. Mr. Justice Rehnquist, as Circuit Justice, stayed the execution of the mandate of the Supreme Court of California. 439 U.S. 1310 (1978). Because the California judgment extending the *per se* aspects of *Miranda* presents an important question about the reach of that case, we thereafter issued the writ. 439 U.S. 925 (1978).

II

We note at the outset that it is clear that the judgment of the California Supreme Court rests firmly on that court's interpretation of federal law. This Court, however, has not heretofore extended the *per se* aspects of the *Miranda* safeguards beyond the scope of the holding in the *Miranda* case itself.[4] We therefore must examine the California court's decision to determine whether that court's conclusion so to extend *Miranda* is in harmony with *Miranda's* underlying principles. For it is clear that "a State may not impose . . . greater restrictions as a matter of *federal constitutional law* when this Court specifically refrains from imposing them." *Oregon v. Hass*, 420 U.S. 714, 719 (1975) (emphasis in original). See *North Carolina v. Butler*, 441 U.S. 369 (1979).

The rule the Court established in *Miranda* is clear. In order to be able to use statements obtained during custodial interrogation of the accused, the State must warn the accused prior to such questioning of his right to remain silent and of his right to have counsel, retained or appointed, present during interrogation. 384 U.S., at 473. "Once [such] warnings have been given, the subsequent procedure is clear." *Ibid.*

"If the individual indicates in any manner, at any time prior to or during questioning, that he wishes to remain silent, the interrogation must cease. At this point he has shown that he intends to exercise his Fifth Amend-

---

3. Two justices concurred in the court's opinion and judgment. 21 Cal.3d, at 478, 579 P.2d, at 11. They expressed concern that a probation officer's public responsibilities would make it difficult for him to offer legal advice to a minor implicated in a crime, and that a minor advised to cooperate with the police, perhaps even to confess, justifiably could complain later "that he had been subjected to a variation of the Mutt-and-Jeff technique criticized in *Miranda*: initial interrogating by overbearing officers, then comforting by a presumably friendly and gentle peace officer in the guise of a probation officer." *Id.*, at 479, 579 P.2d, at 12.

Two justices dissented. *Id.*, at 480, 579 P.2d, at 12. They would have affirmed respondent's conviction on the basis of the finding of the Juvenile Court that, in light of all the circumstances surrounding the interrogation of respondent, there was sufficient affirmative proof that respondent had waived his privilege.

The dissenters pointed out that the opinion of the court was confusing in holding, on the one hand, that the request for a probation officer was *per se* an invocation of the minor's Fifth Amendment rights, and, on the other, that reversal was required because the State had not carried its burden of proving that respondent, by requesting his probation officer, did not intend thereby to assert his Fifth Amendment privilege. *Ibid.*, 579 P.2d, at 12–13.

There may well be ambiguity in this regard. See *id.*, at 477–478, 579 P.2d, at 11. On the basis of that ambiguity, respondent argues that the California court did not establish a *per se* rule, but held only that on the facts here respondent's request to see his probation officer constituted an invocation of his Fifth Amendment rights. The decision in *People v. Randall*, 1 Cal.3d 948, 464 P.2d 114 (1970), upon which the California court relied in both *Burton* and the present case, however, indicates that the court did indeed establish a *per se* rule in this case. In *Randall*, the court stated that even though a suspect might have invoked his Fifth Amendment rights by asking for counsel or by stating he wished to remain silent, it might be possible that subsequent voluntary statements of the accused, not prompted by custodial interrogation, would be admissible if the State could show that they were the product of the voluntary decision of the accused to waive the rights he had asserted. *People v. Randall*, 1 Cal.3d, at 956, and n. 7, 464 P.2d, at 119, and n. 7.

Randall thus indicates that the *per se* language employed by the California Supreme Court in this case is compatible with the finding that the State could have negated the *per se* effect of the request for a probation officer by showing that, notwithstanding his *per se* invocation of his rights, respondent later voluntarily decided to waive those rights and volunteer statements. In light of *Randall*, and in light of the strong *per se* language used by the California Supreme Court in its opinion in this case, see, *e.g.*, 21 Cal.3d, at 477, 579 P.2d, at 10–11, we think that any ambiguity in that opinion must be resolved in favor of a conclusion that the court did in fact establish a *per se* rule.

4. Indeed, this Court has not yet held that *Miranda* applies with full force to exclude evidence obtained in violation of its proscriptions from consideration in juvenile proceedings, which for certain purposes have been distinguished from formal criminal prosecutions. See *McKeiver v. Pennsylvania*, 403 U.S. 528, 540–541 (1971) (plurality opinion). We do not decide that issue today. In view of our disposition of this case, we assume without deciding that the *Miranda* principles were fully applicable to the present proceedings.

ment privilege; any statement taken after the person invokes his privilege cannot be other than the product of compulsion, subtle or otherwise. . . . If the individual states that he wants an attorney, the interrogation must cease until an attorney is present. At that time, the individual must have an opportunity to confer with the attorney and to have him present during any subsequent questioning. If the individual cannot obtain an attorney and he indicates that he wants one before speaking to police, they must respect his decision to remain silent." *Id.*, at 473–474 (footnote omitted).

Any statements obtained during custodial interrogation conducted in violation of these rules may not be admitted against the accused, at least during the State's case in chief. *Id.*, at 479. Cf. *Harris v. New York,* 401 U.S. 222, 224 (1971).

Whatever the defects, if any, of this relatively rigid requirement that interrogation must cease upon the accused's request for an attorney, *Miranda's* holding has the virtue of informing police and prosecutors with specificity as to what they may do in conducting custodial interrogation, and of informing courts under what circumstances statements obtained during such interrogation are not admissible. This gain in specificity, which benefits the accused and the State alike, has been thought to outweigh the burdens that the decision in *Miranda* imposes on law enforcement agencies and the courts by requiring the suppression of trustworthy and highly probative evidence even though the confession might be voluntary under traditional Fifth Amendment analysis. See *Michigan v. Tucker,* 417 U.S. 433, 443–446 (1974).

The California court in this case, however, significantly has extended this rule by providing that a request by a juvenile for his probation officer has the same effect as a request for an attorney. Based on the court's belief that the probation officer occupies a position as a trusted guardian figure in the minor's life that would make it normal for the minor to turn to the officer when apprehended by the police, and based as well on the state-law requirement that the officer represent the interests of the juvenile, the California decision found that consultation with a probation officer fulfilled the role for the juvenile that consultation with an attorney does in general, acting as a ' "protective [device] . . . to dispel the compulsion inherent in custodial surroundings.' " 21 Cal.3d, at 477, 579 P.2d, at 10, quoting *Miranda v. Arizona,* 384 U.S., at 458.

The rule in *Miranda,* however, was based on this Court's perception that the lawyer occupies a critical position in our legal system because of his unique ability to protect the Fifth Amendment rights of a client undergoing custodial interrogation. Because of this special ability of the lawyer to help the client preserve his Fifth Amendment rights once the client becomes enmeshed in the adversary process, the Court found that "the right to have counsel present at the interrogation is indispensable to the protection of the Fifth Amendment privilege under the system" established by the Court. *Id.*, at 469. Moreover, the lawyer's presence helps guard against overreaching by the police and ensures that any statements actually obtained are accurately transcribed for presentation into evidence. *Id.*, at 470.

The *per se* aspect of *Miranda* was thus based on the unique role the lawyer plays in the adversary system of criminal justice in this country. Whether it is a minor or an adult who stands accused, the lawyer is the one person to whom society as a whole looks as the protector of the legal rights of that person in his dealings with the police and the courts. For this reason, the Court fashioned in *Miranda* the rigid rule that an accused's request for an attorney is *per se* an invocation of his Fifth Amendment rights, requiring that all interrogation cease.

A probation officer is not in the same posture with regard to either the accused or the system of justice as a whole. Often he is not trained in the law, and so is not in a position to advise the accused as to his legal rights. Neither is he a trained advocate, skilled in the representation of the interests of his client before both police and courts. He does not assume the power to act on behalf of his client by virtue of his status as adviser, nor are the communications of the accused to the probation officer shielded by the lawyer-client privilege.

Moreover, the probation officer is the employee of the State which seeks to prosecute the alleged offender. He is a peace officer, and as such is allied, to a greater or lesser extent, with his fellow peace officers. He owes an obligation to the State, notwithstanding the obligation he may also owe the juvenile under his supervision. In most cases, the probation officer is duty bound to report wrongdoing by the juvenile when it comes to his attention, even if by communication from the juvenile himself. Indeed, when this case arose, the probation officer had the responsibility for filing the petition alleging wrongdoing by the juvenile and seeking to have him taken into the custody of the Juvenile Court. It was respondent's probation officer who filed the petition against him, and it is the acting chief of probation for the State of California, a probation officer, who is petitioner in this Court today.[5]

In these circumstances, it cannot be said that the probation officer is able to offer the type of independent advice that an accused would expect from a lawyer retained or assigned to assist him during questioning. Indeed, the probation officer's duty to his employer in many, if not most, cases would conflict sharply with the interests of the juvenile. For where an attorney might well advise his client to remain silent in the face of interrogation by the police, and in doing so would be "exercising [his] good professional judgment . . . to protect to the extent of his ability the rights of his client," *Miranda v. Arizona*, 384 U.S., at 480–481, a probation officer would be bound to advise his charge to cooperate with the police. The justices who concurred in the opinion of the California Supreme Court in this case aptly noted: "Where a conflict between the minor and the law arises, the probation officer can be neither neutral nor in the minor's corner." 21 Cal. 3d, at 479, 579 P.2d, at 12. It thus is doubtful that a general rule can be established that a juvenile, in every case, looks to his probation officer as a "trusted guardian figure" rather than as an officer of the court system that imposes punishment.

By the same token, a lawyer is able to protect his client's rights by learning the extent, if any, of the client's involvement in the crime under investigation, and advising his client acccordingly. To facilitate this, the law rightly protects the communications between clients and attorney from discovery. We doubt, however, that similar protection will be afforded the communications between the probation officer and the minor. Indeed, we doubt that a probation officer, consistent with his responsibilities to the public and his profession, could withhold from the police or the courts facts made known to him by the juvenile implicating the juvenile in the crime under investigation.

We thus believe it clear that the probation officer is not in a position to offer the type of legal assistance necessary to protect the Fifth Amendment rights of an accused undergoing custodial interrogation that a lawyer can offer. The Court in *Miranda* recognized that "the attorney plays a vital role in the administration of criminal justice under our Constitution." 384 U.S., at 481. It is this pivotal role of legal counsel that justifies the *per se* rule established in *Miranda*, and that distinguishes the request for counsel from the request for a probation officer, a clergyman, or a close friend. A probation officer simply is not necessary, in the way an attorney is, for the protection of the legal rights of the accused, juvenile or adult. He is significantly handicapped by the position he occupies in the juvenile system from serving as an effective protector of the rights of a juvenile suspected of a crime.

The California Supreme Court, however, found that the close relationship between juveniles and their probation officers compelled the conclusion that a probation officer, for purposes of *Miranda*,

---

5. When this case arose, a California statute provided that a proceeding in juvenile court to declare a minor a ward of the court was to be commenced by the filing of a petition by a probation officer. Cal. Welf. & Inst. Code Ann. § 650 (West 1972). This provision since has been amended to provide that most such petitions are to be filed by the prosecuting attorney. 1976 Cal. Stats., ch. 1071, § 20. Respondent argues that, whatever the status of the probation officer as a peace officer at the time this case arose, the amendment of § 650 indicates that in the future a probation officer is not to be viewed as a legal adversary of the accused juvenile. Consequently, respondent believes that any holding of this Court with regard to respondent's 1976 request for a probation officer will be mere dictum with regard to a juvenile's similar request today. Brief for Respondent 9–10, and n. 4.

We disagree. The fact that a California probation officer in 1976 was responsible for initiating a complaint is only one factor in our analysis. The fact remains that a probation officer does not fulfill the role in our system of criminal justice that an attorney does, regardless of whether he acts merely as a counselor or has significant law enforcement duties. And in California, as in many States, the other duties of a probation officer are incompatible with the view that he may act as a counselor to a juvenile accused of crime. The very California statute that imposes upon the probation officer the duty to represent the interests of the juvenile also provides: "It shall be the duty of the probation officer to prepare for every hearing [of criminal charges against a juvenile] a social study of the minor, containing such matters as may be relevant to a proper disposition of the case." Cal. Welf. & Inst. Code Ann. § 280 (West Supp. 1979).

Similarly, a probation officer is required, upon the order of the juvenile court of the Youth Authority, to investigate the circumstances surrounding the charge against the minor and to file written reports and recommendations. §§ 281, 284. And a probation officer in California continues to have the powers and authority of a peace officer in connection with any violation of a criminal statute that is discovered by the probation officer in the course of his probation activities. § 283; Cal. Penal Code Ann. § 830.5 (West 1970). The duties of a peace officer, like the investigative and reporting duties of probation officers, are incompatible with the role of legal adviser to a juvenile accused of crime.

was sufficiently like a lawyer to justify extension of the *per se* rule. 21 Cal. 3d, at 476, 579 P. 2d, at 10. The fact that a relationship of trust and cooperation between a probation officer and a juvenile might exist, however, does not indicate that the probation officer is capable of rendering effective legal advice sufficient to protect the juvenile's rights during interrogation by the police, or of providing the other services rendered by a lawyer. To find otherwise would be "an extension of the *Miranda* requirements [that] would cut this Court's holding in that case completely loose from its own explicitly stated rationale." *Beckwith v. United States*, 425 U.S. 341, 345 (1976). Such an extension would impose the burdens associated with the rule of *Miranda* on the juvenile justice system and the police without serving the interests that rule was designed simultaneously to protect. If it were otherwise, a juvenile's request for almost anyone he considered trustworthy enough to give him reliable advice would trigger the rigid rule of *Miranda*.

Similarly, the fact that the State has created a statutory duty on the part of the probation officer to protect the interests of the juvenile does not render the probation officer any more capable of rendering legal assistance to the juvenile or of protecting his legal rights, especially in light of the fact that the State has also legislated a duty on the part of the officer to report wrongdoing by the juvenile and serve the ends of the juvenile court system. The State cannot transmute the relationship between probation officer and juvenile offender into the type of relationship between attorney and client that was essential to the holding of *Miranda* simply by legislating an amorphous "duty to advise and care for the juvenile defendant." 21 Cal. 3d, at 477, 579 P. 2d, at 10. Though such a statutory duty might serve to distinguish to some degree the probation officer from the coach and the clergyman, it does not justify the extension of *Miranda* to requests to see probation officers. If it did, the State could expand the class of persons covered by the *Miranda per se* rule simply by creating a duty to care for the juvenile on the part of other persons, regardless of whether the logic of *Miranda* would justify that extension.

Nor do we believe that a request by a juvenile to speak with his probation officer constitutes a *per se* request to remain silent. As indicated, since a probation officer does not fulfill the important role in protecting the rights of the accused juvenile that an attorney plays, we decline to find that the request for the probation officer is tantamount to the request for an attorney. And there is nothing inherent in the request for a probation officer that requires us to find that a juvenile's request to see one necessarily constitutes an expression of the juvenile's right to remain silent. As discussed below, courts may take into account such a request in evaluating whether a juvenile in fact had waived his Fifth Amendment rights before confessing. But in other circumstances such a request might well be consistent with a desire to speak with the police. In the absence of further evidence that the minor intended in the circumstances to invoke his Fifth Amendment rights by such a request, we decline to attach such overwhelming significance to this request.

We hold, therefore, that it was error to find that the request by respondent to speak with his probation officer *per se* constituted an invocation of respondent's Fifth Amendment right to be free from compelled self-incrimination. It therefore was also error to hold that because the police did not then cease interrogating respondent the statements he made during interrogation should have been suppressed.

III

Miranda further recognized that after the required warnings are given the accused, "[i]f the interrogation continues without the presence of an attorney and a statement is taken, a heavy burden rests on the government to demonstrate that the defendant knowingly and intelligently waived his privilege against self-incrimination and his right to retained or appointed counsel." 384 U.S., at 475. We noted in *North Carolina v. Butler*, 441 U.S., at 373, that the question whether the accused waived his rights "is not one of form, but rather whether the defendant in fact knowingly and voluntarily waived the rights delineated in the *Miranda* case." Thus, the determination whether statements obtained during custodial interrogation are admissible against the accused is to be made upon an inquiry into the totality of the circumstances surrounding the interrogation, to ascertain whether the accused in fact knowingly and voluntarily decided to forgo his rights to remain silent and to have the assistance of counsel. *Miranda v. Arizona*, 384 U.S., at 475–477.

This totality-of-the-circumstances approach is adequate to determine whether there has been a waiver even where interrogation of juveniles is involved. We discern no persuasive reasons why any other approach is required where the question is whether a juvenile has waived his rights, as opposed to whether an adult has done so. The totality approach permits—indeed, it mandates—inquiry into all the circumstances surrounding the interrogation. This includes evaluation of the juvenile's age, experience, education, background, and intelligence, and into whether he has the capacity to understand the warnings given him, the nature of his Fifth Amendment rights, and the consequences of waiving those rights. See *North Carolina v. Butler, supra.*

Courts repeatedly must deal with these issues of waiver with regard to a broad variety of constitutional rights. There is no reason to assume that such courts—especially juvenile courts, with their special expertise in this area—will be unable to apply the totality-of-the-circumstances analysis so as to take into account those special concerns that are present when young persons, often with limited experience and education and with immature judgment, are involved. Where the age and experience of a juvenile indicate that his request for his probation officer or his parents is, in fact, an invocation of his right to remain silent, the totality approach will allow the court the necessary flexibility to take this into account in making a waiver determination. At the same time, that approach remains from imposing rigid restraints on police and courts in dealing with an experienced older juvenile with an extensive prior record who knowingly and intelligently waives his Fifth Amendment rights and voluntarily consents to interrogation.

In this case, we conclude that the California Supreme Court should have determined the issue of waiver on the basis of all the circumstances surrounding the interrogation of respondent. The Juvenile Court found that under this approach, respondent in fact had waived his Fifth Amendment rights and consented to interrogation by the police after his request to see his probation officer was denied. Given its view of the case, of course, the California Supreme Court did not consider this issue, though it did hold that the State had failed to prove that, notwithstanding respondent's request to see his probation officer, respondent had not intended to invoke his Fifth Amendment rights.

We feel that the conclusion of the Juvenile Court was correct. The transcript of the interrogation reveals that the police officers conducting the interrogation took care to ensure that respondent understood his rights. They fully explained to respondent

that he was being questioned in connection with a murder. They then informed him of all the rights delineated in *Miranda*, and ascertained that respondent understood those rights. There is no indication in the record that respondent failed to understand what the officers told him. Moreover, after his request to see his probation officer had been denied, and after the police officer once more had explained his rights to him, respondent clearly expressed his willingness to waive his rights and continue the interrogation.

Further, no special factors indicate that respondent was unable to understand the nature of his actions. He was a 16½-year-old juvenile with considerable experience with the police. He had a record of several arrests. He had served time in a youth camp, and he had been on probation for several years. He was under the full-time supervision of probation authorities. There is no indication that he was of insufficient intelligence to understand the rights he was waiving, or what the consequences of that waiver would be. He was not worn down by improper interrogation tactics or lengthy questioning or by trickery or deceit.

On these facts, we think it clear that respondent voluntarily and knowingly waived his Fifth Amendment rights. Respondent argues, however, that any statements he made during interrogation were coerced. Specifically, respondent alleges that the police made threats and promises during the interrogation to pressure him into cooperating in the hope of obtaining leniency for his cooperative attitude. He notes also that he repeatedly told the officers during his interrogation that he wished to stop answering their questions, but that the officers ignored his pleas. He argues further that the record reveals that he was afraid that the police would coerce him, and that this fear caused him to cooperate. He points out that at one point the transcript revealed that he wept during the interrogation.

Review of the entire transcript reveals that respondent's claims of coercion are without merit. As noted, the police took care to inform respondent of his rights and to ensure that he understood them. The officers did not intimidate or threaten respondent in any way. Their questioning was restrained and free from the abuses that so concerned the Court in *Miranda*. See 384 U.S., at 445–455. The police did indeed indicate that a cooperative attitude would be to respondent's benefit, but their remarks in this regard were far from threatening or coercive. And respondent's allegation that he repeatedly asked that the interrogation cease goes too far: at some points he did state that he did not know the answer to a question put to him or that he could not, or would not, answer the question, but these statements were not assertions of his right to remain silent.

IV

We hold, in short, that the California Supreme Court erred in finding that a juvenile's request for his probation officer was a *per se* invocation of that juvenile's Fifth Amendment rights under *Miranda*. We conclude, rather, that whether the statements obtained during subsequent interrogation of a juvenile who has asked to see his probation officer, but who has not asked to consult an attorney or expressly asserted his right to remain silent, are admissible on the basis of waiver remains a question to be resolved on the totality of the circumstances surrounding the interrogation. On the basis of the record in this case, we hold that the Juvenile Court's findings that respondent voluntarily and knowingly waived his rights and consented to continued interrogation, and that the statements obtained from him were voluntary, were proper, and that the admission of those statements in the proceeding against respondent in Juvenile Court was correct.

The judgment of the Supreme Court of California is reversed, and the case is remanded for further proceedings not inconsistent with this opinion.

It is so ordered.

PRETRIAL IDENTIFICATION

Case Comment

Three leading constitutional cases, *United States v. Wade* (1967), *Gilbert v. California* (1967), and *Stovall v. Denno* (1967), have set limitations on the use of pretrial identification of persons accused of crime. How do these limits apply to juveniles?

In *United States v. Wade* and *Gilbert v. California*, the Supreme Court held that the accused has a right to have counsel present at postindictment lineup procedures and that pretrial identification is inadmissible when the right to counsel is violated. In the Stovall case, the court declared that a pretrial identification of the accused in a one-on-one confrontation may be so suggestive as to constitute a

demand of the accused of due process of law under the Fourteenth Amendment. The Court further clarified this issue in *Kirby v. Illinois*, holding that the defendant's right to counsel at pretrial identification proceedings goes into effect only after the complaint or the indictment has been issued. Based on these decisions, courts have ruled that juveniles also have constitutional protection during lineup and identification procedures. They have a right to counsel at a police lineup once they are charged with a delinquent act, and if this right is violated, the pretrial identification is excluded.[19]

In re Holley is a case concerning a youth accused of rape who is identified in a prehearing lineup by the victim. In reversing Holley's conviction, the appellate court argued that a juvenile retains all the rights of the *Gilbert* and *Wade* decisions and that absence of counsel during Holley's lineup precluded the petitioner from having a fair trial.

IN RE HOLLEY

Supreme Court of Rhode Island, 1970.
107 R.I. 615, 268 A.2d 723.

Kelleher, Justice.

This is an appeal taken by a juvenile from a decision of a justice of the Family Court adjudicating him to be a delinquent because of his alleged rape of a widow in Providence. Following the delinquency adjudication, the juvenile was committed to the Rhode Island Training School for Boys until he has attained the age of 21.

The prosecutrix testified that at about 4:20 A.M. on July 19, 1968, she was awakened from her sleep by a noise in the kitchen of her first-floor tenement. She went to the kitchen where she encountered Holley and another "boy." Holley, she said, threatened her with a knife and forced her into the bedroom where he raped her. While we see no necessity to set forth all the sordid details of what occurred thereafter, the record shows that the other intruder also raped the prosecutrix and robbed her of $22. The rapists told the widow that they would kill her if she reported this incident to the police. The police, however, were called and an investigation began.

The widow was summoned to police headquarters on two different occasions to view suspects who were placed in a lineup. She recognized no one in the first lineup. However, on August 8, 1968, she viewed a second lineup[1] by means of a one-way mirror and identified Holley as the knife wielder and the one who first raped her. Holley at this time was 16 years old. At the time of his appearance in the Family Court, he had turned 17.

Holley's defense was that at the time in question, he was in Baltimore, Maryland, visiting his aunt. The trial justice * * * stated that he was convinced "even beyond a reasonable doubt" that the juvenile had raped the widow.

* * * The decisive issue in this appeal is whether a juvenile, who is suspected of committing an act that would constitute a crime if he were an adult, is entitled to the benefit of rules laid down by the Supreme Court in *United States v. Wade*, 388 U.S. 218, 87 S.Ct. 1926, 18 L.Ed.2d 1149, and *Gilbert v. California*, 388 U.S. 263, 87 S.Ct. 1951, 18 L.Ed.2d 1178. The basic principle delineated in these two cases is that a lineup is a critical stage of a prosecution and denial of the right of counsel at a lineup renders the identification made at that time inadmissible.

* * *

The issue in the case at bar has two facets: (1) Does the right to the presence of counsel at a lineup embrace a pre- as well as a post-indictment lineup? And, assuming the answer to this question is in the affirmative, (2) is a juvenile to be afforded the benefit of this rule?

While *Wade* and *Gilbert* speak of the right to counsel at a *post-indictment lineup*, we believe that the Supreme Court intended the rule laid down in those cases to be applicable to other pretrial confrontations. It is also our belief that this right to counsel belongs to juveniles as well as adults.

In holding that the right to counsel enunciated in the *Wade* and *Gilbert* cases is not limited to a lineup held after the return of an indictment, we find the following language in *People v. Fowler*, 1 Cal.3d 335, 82 Cal.Rptr. 363, 461 P.2d 643, to be sound and most persuasive:

Our reasons [for concluding that the *Wade* and *Gilbert* rules are not restricted in their application to a postindictment lineup] are several. First, and perhaps most importantly, we find nothing in the reasoning of those

opinions, and have ourselves been able to conceive of no reason, requiring that the rules should be so limited. * * * A lineup which occurs prior to the point in question may be fraught with the same risks of suggestion as one occurring after that point, and may result in the same far-reaching consequences for the defendant.

Second, we consider that the review of authorities and concluding language contained in part II of the *Wade* opinion manifests an intention to state principles governing *any* confrontation by one suspected of crime with the witnesses against him at trial. It is there indicated that the right at issue in all such confrontations—and therefore the right to be protected—is the defendant's 'most basic right as a criminal defendant— his right to a fair trial at which the witnesses against him might be meaningfully cross-examined.' (388 U.S. at p. 224, 87 S.Ct. at p. 1930). * * *

We think that once the right to counsel at a lineup has attached, the suspect is entitled to be informed of this and also be told that counsel will be appointed if necessary. Only if he is so informed can a suspect's election to proceed in the absence of counsel be deemed to be an intelligent waiver of his Sixth Amendment right.

Having determined that the right to counsel is applicable to all lineups, we now reach the issue of whether this right should be afforded a juvenile. The answer we suggest is patent. This past spring, Mr. Justice Brennan, in *In re Winship, supra*, said the same considerations which demand extreme caution in fact finding to protect the innocent adult apply as well to the innocent child. Earlier in *In re Gault*, 387 U.S. 1, 87 S.Ct. 1428, 18 L.Ed.2d 527, the United States Supreme Court held that although the Fourteenth Amendment did not require that the hearing conform with all the requirements of a criminal trial, an adjudicatory hearing must measure up to the "essentials of due process and fair treatment." One of the essentials of due process and fair treatment that *Gault* guaranteed at the adjudicatory stage was the right to counsel. We think that the reasons advanced for the right to counsel at the adjudicatory stage are equally applicable to a pretrial lineup in a case where the juvenile may be charged with an act which would constitute a crime if he were an adult. * * *

---

1. The lineup consisted of Holley and another youth. The second youth was described by the widow as being darker, heavier, taller, and older than Holley. Mrs. Holley was present when her son was identified; however, neither mother nor son were informed of the right to counsel.

Here, Holley has been found to be "delinquent" and as a result thereof, he faces the possibility of being confined at the Training School for close to four years. The boy's loss of liberty is just as serious to him as such a loss is to a convicted felon who is serving time at the Adult Correctional Institutions. In fact, there is a suggestion in the record that Holley, since his arrival at the Training School, has been administratively transferred to the state prison. As was so well pointed out in *Wade, supra* 388 U.S. at 235–236, 87 S.Ct. at 1937, 18 L.Ed.2d at 1162:

> The trial which might determine the accused's fate may well not be that in the courtroom but that at the pretrial confrontation, with the State aligned against the accused, the witness the sole jury, and the accused unprotected against the overreaching, intentional or unintentional, and with little or no effective appeal from the judgment there rendered by the witness— "that's the man."

Clearly, a juvenile suspected of an act that would constitute a crime, if he were an adult and facing several years of incarceration, should he be found to have committed the alleged act, has no lesser need for the assistance of effective counsel at the lineup than that of an adult charged with a similar act. If we were to deny the juvenile the right to counsel at this stage of such a proceeding, the right to counsel granted a juvenile by the United States Supreme Court in *Gault* would be rendered meaningless. There is no age limitation contained in the constitutional guarantee of due process.

All the grave potential for prejudice that a pretrial lineup without counsel may engender for an adult is no less grave for a juvenile. Clearly, the juvenile is as much entitled to the aid of counsel, and certainly in as much need of the aid of counsel, at this stage of the proceedings, as an adult.

Therefore, we now hold that, a juvenile who is suspected of doing an act that would constitute a crime if he were an adult has a right to counsel at a pretrial lineup that he is part of and, as an adjunct to this right, the juvenile and his parents are entitled to be informed that the juvenile has this right to counsel and, further, that one will be appointed if necessary. If the juvenile and his parents are not informed that such right has attached, the election to proceed in the absence of counsel cannot be deemed an intelligent waiver of the accrued right.

* * *

Because of the inconclusive state of the record, we believe the ends of justice will be best served by vacating the adjudication of delinquency and remitting the case to the Family Court for a new hearing at which the state may have an opportunity to show that the victim's in-court identification of her assailant had a source independent of the improper lineup.

The appeal is sustained, and the case is remitted to the Family Court.

JUVENILE RECORDS
Case Comment

For most of the twentieth century, juvenile records were kept confidential by case law or statute. Today, juvenile records can often be opened by court order, by law enforcement agencies, and by other public officials and bodies, such as the military. Some states also allow a juvenile adjudication for a criminal act such as rape to be used as evidence in a subsequent adult criminal proceeding for the same act, in order to show predisposition or criminal nature. In addition, a juvenile's record may be used during the disposition or sentencing stage of an adult criminal trial.

Davis v. Alaska presents a somewhat unusual situation involving the revelation of a juvenile's record in court. In this case, a youth's testimony during an adult's burglary trial is suspect because of his prior juvenile record. However, in order to protect him, this record was not allowed to be brought out in open court. On appeal, the Supreme Court reversed the adult's conviction, stating that the basic right of cross-examining witnesses cannot be superseded by the state's desire to protect juveniles. If the state had wished to protect the child, it could have simply done so by refraining to call him as a witness.

The problem of confidentiality of juvenile records will become more acute in the future as juvenile delinquency proceedings are opened to the public and children are held more accountable for their actions.[20]

DAVIS v. ALASKA

Certiorari to the Supreme Court of Alaska, 1974.
415 U.S. 308, 94 S.Ct. 1105, 39 L.Ed.2d 1105.

Mr. Chief Justice Burger delivered the opinion of the Court.

We granted certiorari in this case to consider whether the Confrontation Clause requires that a defendant in a criminal case be allowed to impeach the credibility of a prosecution witness by cross-examination directed at possible bias deriving from the witness' probationary status as a juvenile delinquent when such an impeachment would conflict with a State's asserted interest in preserving the confidentiality of juvenile adjudications of delinquency.

When the Polar Bar in Anchorage closed in the early morning hours of February 16, 1970, well over a thousand dollars in cash and checks was in the bar's Mosler safe. About midday, February 16, it was discovered that the bar had been broken into and the safe, about two feet square and weighing several hundred pounds, had been removed from the premises.

Later that afternoon the Alaska State Troopers received word that a safe had been discovered about 26 miles outside Anchorage near the home of Jess Straight and his family. The safe, which was subsequently determined to be the one stolen from the Polar Bar, had been pried open and the contents removed. Richard Green, Jess Straight's stepson, told investigating troopers on the scene that at about noon on February 16 he had seen and spoken with two Negro men standing alongside a late-model metallic blue Chevrolet sedan near where the safe was later discovered. The next day Anchorage police investigators brought him to the police station where Green was given six photographs of adult Negro males. After examining the photographs for 30 seconds to a minute, Green identified the photograph of petitioner as that of one of the men he had encountered the day before and described to the police. Petitioner was arrested the next day, February 18. On February 19, Green picked petitioner out of a lineup of seven Negro males.

At trial, evidence was introduced to the effect that paint chips found in the trunk of petitioner's rented blue Chevrolet could have originated from the surface of the stolen safe. Further, the trunk of the car contained particles which were identified as safe insulation characteristic of that found in Mosler safes. The insulation found in the truck matched that of the stolen safe.

Richard Green was a crucial witness for the prosecution. He testified at trial that while on an errand for his mother he confronted two men standing beside a late-model metallic blue Chevrolet, parked on a road near his family's house. The man standing at the rear of the car spoke to Green asking if Green lived nearby and if his father was home. Green offered the men help, but his offer was rejected. On his return from the errand Green again passed the two men and he saw the man with whom he had had the conversation standing at the rear of the car with "something like a crowbar" in his hands. Green identified petitioner at the trial as the man with the "crowbar." The safe was discovered later that afternoon at the point, according to Green, where the Chevrolet had been parked.

Before testimony was taken at the trial of petitioner, the prosecutor moved for a protective order to prevent any reference to Green's juvenile record by the defense in the course of cross-examination. At the time of the trial and at the time of the events Green testified to, Green was on probation by order of a juvenile court after having been adjudicated a delinquent for burglarizing two cabins. Green was 16 years of age at the time of the Polar Bar burglary, but had turned 17 prior to trial.

In opposing the protective order, petitioner's counsel made it clear that he would not introduce Green's juvenile adjudication as a general impeachment of Green's character as a truthful person but, rather, to show specifically that at the same time Green was assisting the police in identifying petitioner he was on probation for burglary. From this petitioner would seek to show—or at least argue—that Green acted out of fear or concern of possible jeopardy to his probation. Not only might Green have made a hasty and faulty identification of petitioner to shift suspicions away from himself as one who robbed the Polar Bar, but Green might have been subject to undue pressure from the police and made his identifications under fear of possible probation revocation. Green's record would be revealed only as necessary to probe Green for bias and prejudice and not generally to call Green's good character into question.

The trial court granted the motion for a protective order, relying on Alaska Rule of Children's Procedure 23,[1] and Alaska Stat. § 47.10-080(g) (1971).[2]

Although prevented from revealing that Green had been on probation for the juvenile delinquency

---

1. Rule 23 provides: "No adjudication, order, or disposition of a juvenile case shall be admissible in a court not acting in the exercise of juvenile jurisdiction except for use in a presentencing procedure in a criminal case where the superior court, in its discretion, determines that such use is appropriate."

adjudication for burglary at the same time that he originally identified petitioner, counsel for petitioner did his best to expose Green's state of mind at the time Green discovered that a stolen safe had been discovered near his home. Green denied that he was upset or uncomfortable about the discovery of the safe. He claimed not to have been worried about any suspicions the police might have been expected to harbor against him, though Green did admit that it crossed his mind that the police might have thought he had something to do with the crime.

*   *   *

Since defense counsel was prohibited from making inquiry as to the witness' being on probation under a juvenile court adjudication, Green's protestations of unconcern over possible police suspicion that he might have had a part in the Polar Bar burglary and his categorical denial of ever having been the subject of any similar law-enforcement interrogation went unchallenged. The tension between the right of confrontation and the State's policy of protecting the witness with a juvenile record is particularly evident in the final answer given by the witness. Since it is probable that Green underwent some questioning by police when he was arrested for the burglaries on which his juvenile adjudication of delinquency rested, the answer can be regarded as highly suspect at the very least. The witness was in effect asserting, under protection of the trial court's ruling, a right to give a questionably truthful answer to a cross-examiner pursuing a relevant line of inquiry; it is doubtful whether the bold "No" answer would have been given by Green absent a belief that he was shielded from traditional cross-examination. It would be difficult to conceive of a situation more clearly illustrating the need for cross-examination. The remainder of the cross-examination was devoted to an attempt to prove that Green was making his identification at trial on the basis of what he remembered from his earlier identifications at the photographic display and lineup, and not on the basis of his February 16 confrontation with the two men on the road.

The Alaska Supreme Court affirmed petitioner's conviction,[3] concluding that it did not have to re-solve the potential conflict in this case between a defendant's right to a meaningful confrontation with adverse witnesses and the State's interest in protecting the anonymity of a juvenile offender since "our reading of the trial transcript convinces us that counsel for the defendant was able adequately to question the youth in considerable detail concerning the possibility of bias or motive." 499 P.2d 1025, 1036 (1972). Although the court admitted that Green's denials of any sense of anxiety or apprehension upon the safe's being found close to his home were possibly self-serving "the suggestion was nonetheless brought to the attention of the jury, and that body was afforded the opportunity to observe the demeanor of the youth and pass on his credibility." *Ibid.* The court concluded that, in light of the indirect references permitted, there was no error.

Since we granted certiorari limited to the question of whether petitioner was denied his right under the Confrontation Clause to adequately cross-examine Green, 410 U.S. 925 (1973), the essential question turns on the correctness of the Alaska court's evaluation of the "adequacy" of the scope of cross-examination permitted. We disagree with that court's interpretation of the Confrontation Clause and we reverse.

The claim is made that the State has an important interest in protecting the anonymity of juvenile offenders and that this interest outweighs any competing interest this petitioner might have in cross-examining Green about his being on probation. The State argues that exposure of a juvenile's record of delinquency would likely cause impairment of rehabilitative goals of the juvenile correctional procedures. This exposure, it is argued, might encourage the juvenile offender to commit further acts of delinquency, or cause the juvenile offender to lose employment opportunities or otherwise suffer unnecessarily for his youthful transgression.

We do not and need not challenge the State's interest as a matter of its own policy in the administration of criminal justice to seek to preserve the anonymity of a juvenile offender. Cf. *In re Gault*, 387 U.S. 1, 25 (1967). Here, however, petitioner sought to introduce evidence of Green's probation for the purpose of suggesting that Green was biased and, therefore, that his testimony was either not to

---

2. Section 47.10.080(g) provides in pertinent part: "The commitment and placement of a child and evidence given in the court are not admissible as evidence against the minor in a subsequent case or proceedings in any other court *   *   *."

3. In the same opinion the Alaska Supreme Court also affirmed petitioner's conviction, following a separate trial, for being a felon in possession of a concealable firearm. That conviction is not in issue before this Court.

be believed in his identification of petitioner or at least very carefully considered in that light. Serious damage to the strength of the State's case would have been a real possibility had petitioner been allowed to pursue this line of inquiry. In this setting we conclude that the right of confrontation is paramount to the State's policy of protecting a juvenile offender. Whatever temporary embarrassment might result to Green or his family by disclosure of his juvenile record—if the prosecution insisted on using him to make its case—is outweighed by petitioner's right to probe into the influence of possible bias in the testimony of a crucial identification witness.

In *Alford v. United States, supra*, we upheld the right of defense counsel to impeach a witness by showing that because of the witness' incarceration in federal prison at the time of trial, the witness' testimony was biased as "given under promise or expectation of immunity, or under the coercive effect of his detention by officers of the United States." 282 U.S., at 693. In response to the argument that the witness had a right to be protected from exposure of his criminal record, the Court stated:

> [N]o obligation is imposed on the court, such as that suggested below, to protect a witness from being discredited on cross-examination, short of an attempted invasion of his constitutional protection from self incrimination, properly invoked. There is a duty to protect him from questions which go beyond the bounds of proper cross-examination merely to harass, annoy or humiliate him. *Id.*, at 694.

As in *Alford*, we conclude that the State's desire that Green fulfill his public duty to testify free from embarrassment and with his reputation unblemished must fall before the right of petitioner to seek out the truth in the process of defending himself.

The State's policy interest in protecting the confidentiality of a juvenile offender's record cannot require yielding of so vital a constitutional right as the effective cross-examination for bias of an adverse witness. The State could have protected Green from exposure of his juvenile adjudication in these circumstances by refraining from using him to make out its case; the State cannot, consistent with the right of confrontation, require the petitioner to bear the full burden of vindicating the State's interest in the secrecy of juvenile criminal records. The judg-

ment affirming petitioner's convictions of burglary and grand larceny is reversed and the case is remanded for further proceedings not inconsistent with this opinion.

It is so ordered.

END NOTES—CHAPTER II

1. See, generally, Joseph J. Senna and Larry J. Siegel, *Introduction to Criminal Justice*, 5th ed. (St. Paul: West Publishing, 1990), Chapter 9.
2. 367 U.S. 643 (1961).
3. 378 U.S. 478 (1964).
4. 385 U.S. 436 (1966).
5. 387 U.S. 1 (1967).
6. For an excellent review of early police practices with juveniles, see Donald Black and Albert J. Reiss, Jr., "Police Control of Juveniles," *American Sociological Review* 35:64 (1970).
7. See American Bar Association–Institute of Judicial Administration, *Standards Relating to Police Handling of Juvenile Problems* (Cambridge, Mass.: Ballinger Press, 1977).
8. There is a wealth of material on search and seizure in public schools. For the recent articles evaluating the T.L.O. decision, see Michael Meyers, "*T.L.O. v. New Jersey*—Officially Conducted School Searches and a New Balancing Test," *Juvenile Family Law Journal* 37:27–37 (1986); and J. Bruerman, "Public School Drug Searches," *Fordham Urban Law Journal* 14:629–84 (1986).
9. See *Haley v. Ohio*, 33265.596 (1948); and *West v. United States*, 39 F.2d 467 (1968).
10. In a frequently cited California case, *People v. Lara*, 432 P.2d 202 (1967), the court said that the question of a child's waiver is to be determined by the totality of the circumstances doctrine.
11. 442 U.S. 23 (1979).
12. 388 U.S. 218 (1967).
13. 406 U.S. 682 (1972).
14. 388 U.S. 293 (1967).
15. Without any need to apply constitutional concepts of due process, courts have generally held the Fourth Amendment applicable to juvenile delinquency proceedings. See also *Ciulla v. State*, 434 S.W.2d 948 (1968).
16. 329 U.S. 1 (1968).
17. In *T.L.O.*, of considerable importance is the fact that school searches were found justified if a student were suspected of violating the law or school rules.
18. 453 U.S. 355 (1981).
19. For a current review of the law in this area, see Robert E. Shepard, Jr., "Juvenile Identification Practices and Procedures," *American Bar Association Journal of Criminal Justice* 5:44–46 (1991).
20. Two other important cases that seek to balance juvenile privacy with freedom of the press are *Oklahoma Publishing Co. v. District Court*, 430 U.S. 97 (1977), and *Smith v. Daily Mail Publishing Co.*, 443 U.S. 97 (1977).

THREE

Early Court Processing

INTRODUCTION

This chapter deals with juvenile detention, bail, and the guilty plea. The U.S. Supreme Court has not examined constitutional issues in the prejudicial stage of the juvenile process except for the preventive detention case of *Schall v. Martin* in 1984.[1] All the states provide for such procedures by virtue of their own appellate decisions and statutes. But the case law and statutes vary widely regarding rights and procedures for juveniles in this area.

After a child is taken into custody, either as a delinquent or a status offender, it is necessary to determine whether the child should be released to the parent or guardian or detained in shelter care.[2] In the past, far too many children were routinely placed in detention to await court appearances. At the same time, detention facilities were inadequate, and in many parts of the country, jails were used to detain juvenile offenders. Although this situation may continue to some degree, the thrust in recent years has been to reduce the number of children placed in detention.[3] In practice, upon arrest and after being detained, the child is usually released to the parent or guardian. It is important to note that most jurisdictions require immediate notice to the parents after the child has been arrested. The statutes ordinarily also require a hearing on detention if the initial decision is to keep the child in custody. At a detention hearing, the child has a right to counsel and is generally given other procedural due process safeguards, notably the privilege against self-incrimination and the right to confront and cross-examine witnesses.

Most state juvenile court acts provide criteria that support a decision not to release the child. These criteria include (1) the need to protect the child, (2) whether the child presents a serious danger to the public, and (3) the likelihood of whether the juvenile will return to court for adjudication. Unlike the adult system, where the sole criteria for pretrial release is availability for trial, the juvenile may be detained for other reasons, including his or her own protection.[4] Normally, the finding of the judge that the child be detained should be supported by evidence.

---

1. "Pending the final disposition of any case, the child shall be subject to the order of the court, and may be permitted by the court to remain in the control of his or her parents or the person having him or her in charge, or in charge of a probation officer, or the child may be placed by the court in the custody of any association or society having for one of its objects the care of dependent, delinquent or neglected children, or may be ordered by the court to be kept and maintained in some place provided by the county for such purposes * * *." Act of June 2, 1933, §§ 6–8, P.L. 1433, as amended, 11 P.S. §§ 248–250. This clear legislative policy is in harmony with the protective and rehabilitative objectives of the juvenile court proceedings. See *Terry Appeal*, Pa., 265 A.2d 350 (1970); *Wilson Appeal*, Pa., 264 A.2d 614 (1970).

2. For example, detention for the purpose of administering tests would be impermissible if there were some other way to insure that the juvenile would be available for the testing.

If the child is to be detained, the question of bail arises. Here, the statutes and cases vary widely. Some states' statutes allow release on bail for juveniles, while others provide no such statutory procedure. Many states have juvenile code provisions that emphasize the release of the child to the parents as an acceptable substitute to bail. The law is also unclear as to whether juveniles have a state or federal constitutional right to bail. Some courts have found it unnecessary to rule on this issue because liberal statutory release provisions act as an appropriate alternative to the bail process.

With regard to the plea, the child may plead guilty or not guilty to a juvenile delinquency petition. Some jurisdictions seek to minimize the use of adult criminal standards by using other terminology, such as "agree to a finding" or "deny the petition." If the child pleads not guilty, the court ordinarily sets a date for trial. On the other hand, many juveniles admit to the charges against them. When the child makes an admission, juvenile court acts and rules of procedure in numerous jurisdictions require the following procedural safeguards: (1) that the child know of his or her right to a trial, (2) that the plea or admission be made voluntarily, and (3) that the child has an understanding of the charges and consequences of the plea. The same requirements have been established by the U.S. Supreme Court for adult offenders in a series of cases. Although such standards have not been set by constitutional law for juveniles, they are equally important here because the guilty plea constitutes a waiver of the juveniles' Fifth Amendment privilege against self-incrimination and the Sixth Amendment right to trial by jury.

With respect to plea bargaining, the majority of juvenile court cases that are not adjudicated seem to be the result of open admissions, rather than plea bargaining.[5] Unlike the adult system, where almost 90 percent of all charged offenders are involved in some plea bargaining, it is widely believed that there is little plea bargaining in the juvenile court. Most juvenile court legislation and rules of procedure do not provide rules governing the plea bargaining process. The *parens patriae* philosophy of the juvenile court, as well as the general availability of pretrial social services and flexibility in the disposition of cases, acts against the use of plea bargaining.

.Plea bargaining remains a hotly contested issue. As the term implies, the plea bargain represents the defendant's offer to exchange a guilty plea for some prosecutorial concession, generally a charge reduction to some lesser offense or a recommendation by the government for leniency in the sentence.

The practical application of plea bargaining in the juvenile court exists when the government, represented by the prosecutor or probation officer, negotiates a guilty plea from the defense attorney in exchange for a disposition generally involving community supervision.[6] Both parties may seek the judge's guidance in reaching an agreement and obtain his or her consent to the bargain. Although this process of negotiation is often informal, the child is generally represented by counsel. Efficient disposition of the case after plea bargaining is also an essential element of the process because it reduces the juvenile court caseload and enhances the rehabilitative prospects of the child.

DETENTION—ITS PURPOSE

Case Comment

Pretrial detention is considered a critical area of juvenile justice since it often means the incarceration of youths who have not yet been found delinquent. In *Sprowal v. Hendrick*, a boy sought release from a detention center via a habeas corpus petition. The trial judge had claimed that during the detention hearing, the youth's friends had threatened the court and had based the detention on that fact. The appellate court, in reversing the decision, argued that the detention of a child must be based on a lack of parental supervision, a threat of running away, or a need for treatment. In other words, detention cannot be used capriciously.

COMMONWEALTH ex rel. SPROWAL v. HENDRICK

Supreme Court of Pennsylvania, 1976.
438 Pa. 435, 265 A.2d 348.

Roberts, Justice.

Donald Sprowal and four other youths were arrested on March 21, 1970, and charged with assault with intent to kill and lesser related crimes. Two of the five were over eighteen years of age and, therefore, charged as adults. These two received preliminary hearings and were released on $500 bail. The two other juveniles and Donald were ordered held in custody by a juvenile probation officer pending their intake interview. All three were interviewed on March 23, and identical delinquency petitions were filed against them. The next day the three appeared in juvenile court for a detention hearing, at which time the judge ordered all three detained, appointed the Voluntary Defender to represent them, and scheduled a certification hearing for April 6.

At the certification hearing only Donald and one of the other juveniles were present, the third having been quarantined at the Youth Study Center. The two were told that the Commonwealth's witnesses were not available and that the case would be continued. Donald's counsel then requested a "probable cause hearing," which request was granted.

At the "probable cause hearing," held two days later, there was testimony introduced which the judge found sufficient to sustain the proceedings. At the conclusion of the hearing, the judge released the other two juveniles into the custody of their parents but ordered Donald held, stating that he did not want to countermand the determination of the judge who had ordered Donald's detention at the March 24 hearing. The following day, April 9, the judge who had ordered Donald detained on March 24 told Donald's counsel that he had no objection to Donald's release. Counsel then appeared before the judge who conducted the probable cause hearing and requested Donald's release. The request was denied, apparently because the judge had reason to believe that some other juveniles, including Donald's released co-defendant, had been in the vicinity of the courthouse the day before and had threatened retaliation for the court's failure to release Donald. This reason, however, does not appear of record, but was presented to the Court at oral argument.

An appeal from the refusal to release and a petition for habeas corpus were then filed in the Superior Court, which dismissed the appeal as interlocutory and denied the habeas corpus petition on its merits. On the day of the denial an original petition for habeas corpus was filed in this Court. We have taken jurisdiction in order to clarify the procedures which govern the preadjudicatory release of juvenile defendants. *Commonwealth ex rel. Paylor v. Claudy*, 366 Pa. 282, 77 A.2d 350 (1951). The case is remanded to the Court of Common Pleas, Family Court Division, for a hearing and determination of the reasons for the continued custody of the petitioner.

In the normal course of events, a juvenile who has not yet had an adjudicatory hearing is released into the custody of a responsible party, usually his or her parents.[1] This is no doubt attributable at least in part to the fact that juveniles normally have only limited mobility, and we fully expect that there will be no reduction in the high percentage of juveniles who are currently so released. As with adult, however, certain restrictive or coercive measures may be proper if they are necessary to insure the appearance of the juvenile at subsequent proceedings. Such measures should be utilized, however, only when the hearing court reasonably determines that there is no other less coercive method whereby future attendance can be reasonably assured and places the reasons for this finding on the record.

Unlike an adult, however, a juvenile may be detained by the juvenile court for reasons other than the necessity of guaranteeing his presence at future proceedings. If a juvenile does not have a home with his parents or other responsible party, or is in need of protective custody, or is in need of psychiatric help or should have psychological testing and evaluation, he or she may be detained for such protective purposes before there is an adjudication of delinquency. The judge who orders such detention must, however, specifically find that the detention is necessary and must have support for the order in the record developed at the preadjudicatory hearing. Additionally, the detention must be tailored to the justification.[2]

In the instant case, the reason for Donald's detention does not appear on the record. Since we cannot be certain Donald's continued detention is proper under the principles set forth above, we herewith vacate the detention order and remand the matter to the juvenile court for further proceedings consistent with this opinion.

PREVENTION DETENTION

Case Comment

Preventive detention refers to the practice of keeping a person in custody before trial because of his or her suspected danger to the community.

Most state jurisdictions allow judges to deny bail to adult offenders only in cases involving murder (capital crimes), when the offenders have jumped bail in the past, or when they have committed another crime while on bail. However, every state allows preventive detention of juveniles. The reason for this discrepancy hinges on the legal principle that while adults have the right to liberty, juveniles have a right to custody. Therefore, it is not unreasonable to detain youths for their own protection.

In *Schall v. Martin*, the U.S. Supreme Court upheld the state's right to place juveniles in preventive detention. It held that preventive detention serves the legitimate objective of protecting both the juvenile and society from pretrial crime. Pretrial detention need not be considered punishment merely because the juvenile is eventually released or put on probation.

Schall v. Martin establishes the right of juvenile court judges to deny youths pretrial release if they perceive them to be "dangerous." However, the case establishes a due process standard for detention hearings that includes notice and a statement of substantial reasons for the detention.[7]

SCHALL v. MARTIN

467 U.S. 253 (1984)

Justice Rehnquist delivered the opinion of the Court.

Section 320.5(3)(b) of the New York Family Court Act authorizes pretrial detention of an accused juvenile delinquent based on a finding that there is a "serious risk" that the child "may before the return date commit an act which if committed by an adult would constitute a crime."[1] Appellees brought suit on behalf of a class of all juveniles detained pursuant to that provision.[2] The District Court struck down § 320.5(3)(b) as permitting detention without due process of law and ordered the immediate release of all class members. *United States ex rel. Martin v. Strasburg*, 513 F.Supp. 691 (SDNY 1981). The Court of Appeals for the Second Circuit affirmed, holding the provision "unconstitutional as to all juveniles" because the statute is administered in such a way that "the detention period serves as punishment imposed without proof of guilt established according to the requisite constitutional standard." *Martin v. Strasburg*, 689 F.2d 365, 373–374 (1982). We noted probable jurisdiction, 460 U.S. 1079 (1983),[3] and now reverse. We conclude that preventive detention under the FCA serves a legitimate state objective, and that the procedural protections afforded pretrial detainees by the New York statute satisfy the requirements of the Due Process Clause of the Fourteenth Amendment to the United States Constitution.

---

1. New York Jud. Law § 320.5 (McKinney 1983) (Family Court Act (hereinafter FCA)) provides, in relevant part:
    "1. At the initial appearance, the court in its discretion may release the respondent or direct his detention.

*   *   *

    "3. The court shall not direct detention unless it finds and states the facts and reasons for so finding that unless the respondent is detained;
    "(a) there is a substantial probability that he will not appear in court on the return date; or
    "(b) there is a serious risk that he may before the return date commit an act which if committed by an adult would constitute a crime."
    Appellees have only challenged pretrial detention under § 320.5(3)(b). Thus, the propriety of detention to ensure that a juvenile appears in court on the return date, pursuant to § 320.5(3)(a), is not before the Court.

2. The original challenge was to § 739(a)(ii) of the FCA, which, at the time of the commencement of this suit, governed pretrial release or detention of both alleged juvenile delinquents and persons in need of supervision. Effective July 1, 1983, a new Article 3 to the Act governs, *inter alia*, "all juvenile delinquency actions and proceedings commenced upon or after the effective date thereof and all appeals and other post-judgment proceedings relating or attaching thereto." FCA § 301.3(1). Article 7 now applies only to proceedings concerning persons in need of supervision.

    Obviously, this Court must "review the judgment below in light of the . . . statute as it now stands, not as it once did." *Hall v. Beals*, 396 U.S. 45, 48 (1969). But since new Article 3 contains a preventive detention section identical to former § 739(a)(ii), see FCA § 320.5(3), the appeal is not moot. *Brockington v. Rhodes*, 396 U.S. 41, 43 (1969).

3. Although the pretrial detention of the class representatives has long since ended, see *infra*, at 257–261, this case is not moot for the same reason that the class action in *Gerstein v. Pugh*, 420 U.S. 103, 110, n. 11 (1975), was not mooted by the termination of the claims of the named plaintiffs. "Pretrial detention is by nature temporary, and it is most unlikely that any given individual could have his constitutional claim decided on appeal before he is either released or convicted. The individual could nonetheless suffer repeated deprivations, and it is certain that other persons similarly situated will be detained under the allegedly unconstitutional procedures. The claim, in short, is one that is distinctly 'capable of repetition, yet evading review.' "
    See also *People ex rel. Wayburn v. Schupf*, 39 N.Y.2d 682, 686–687, 350 N.E.2d 906, 907–908 (1976).

I

Appellee Gregory Martin was arrested on December 13, 1977, and charged with first-degree robbery, second-degree assault, and criminal possession of a weapon based on an incident in which he, with two others, allegedly hit a youth on the head with a loaded gun and stole his jacket and sneakers. See Petitioners' Exhibit 1b. Martin had possession of the gun when he was arrested. He was 14 years old at the time and, therefore, came within the jurisdiction of New York's Family Court.[4] The incident occurred at 11:30 at night, and Martin lied to the police about where and with whom he lived. He was consequently detained overnight.[5]

A petition of delinquency was filed,[6] and Martin made his "initial appearance" in Family Court on December 14th, accompanied by his grandmother.[7] The Family Court Judge, citing the possession of the loaded weapon, the false address given to the police, and the lateness of the hour, as evidencing a lack of supervision, ordered Martin detained under § 320.5(3)(b) (at that time § 739(a)(ii); see n. 2, *supra*). A probable-cause hearing was held five days later, on December 19th, and probable cause was found to exist for all the crimes charged. At the factfinding hearing held December 27–29, Martin was found guilty on the robbery and criminal possession charges. He was adjudicated a delinquent and placed on two years' probation.[8] He had been

---

4. In New York, a child over the age of 7 but less than 16 is not considered criminally responsible for his conduct. FCA § 301.2(1). If he commits an act that would constitute a crime if committed by an adult, he comes under the exclusive jurisdiction of the Family Court. § 302.1(1). That court is charged not with finding guilt and affixing punishment, *In re Bogart*, 45 Misc.2d 1075, 259 N.Y.S.2d 351 (1963), but rather with determining and pursuing the needs and best interests of the child insofar as those are consistent with the need for the protection of the community. FCA § 301.1. See *In re Craig S.*, 57 App.Div.2d 761, 394 N.Y.S.2d 200 (1977). Juvenile proceedings are, thus, civil rather than criminal, although because of the restrictions that may be placed on a juvenile adjudged delinquent, some of the same protections afforded accused adult criminals are also applicable in this context. Cf. FCA § 303.1.

5. When a juvenile is arrested, the arresting officer must immediately notify the parent or other person legally responsible for the child's care. FCA § 305.2(3). Ordinarily, the child will be released into the custody of his parent or guardian after being issued an "appearance ticket" requiring him to meet with the probation service on a specified day. § 307.1(1). See no. 9, *infra*. If, however, he is charged with a serious crime, one of several designated felonies, see § 301.2(8), or if his parent or guardian cannot be reached, the juvenile may be taken directly before the Family Court. § 305.2. The Family Court judge will make a preliminary determination as to the jurisdiction of the court, appoint a law guardian for the child, and advise the child of his or her rights, including the right to counsel and the right to remain silent.

Only if, as in Martin's case, the Family Court is not in session and special circumstances exist, such as an inability to notify the parents, will the child be taken directly by the arresting officer to a juvenile detention facility. § 305.2(4)(c). If the juvenile is so detained, he must be brought before the Family Court within 72 hours or the next day the court is in session, whichever is sooner. § 307.3(4). The propriety of such detention, prior to a juvenile's trial appearance in Family Court, is not at issue in this case. Appellees challenged only judicially ordered detention pursuant to § 320.5(3)(b).

6. A delinquency petition, prepared by the "presentment agency," originates delinquency proceedings. FCA § 310.1. The petition must contain, *inter alia*, a precise statement of each crime charged and factual allegations which "clearly apprise" the juvenile of the conduct which is the subject of the accusation. § 311.1. A petition is not deemed sufficient unless the allegations of the factual part of the petition, together with those of any supporting depositions which may accompany it, provide reasonable cause to believe that the juvenile committed the crime or crimes charged. § 311.2(2). Also, nonhearsay allegations in the petition and supporting deposition must establish, if true, every element of each crime charged and the juvenile's commission thereof. § 311.2(3). The sufficiency of a petition may be tested by filing a motion to dismiss under § 315.1.

7. The first proceeding in Family Court following the filing of the petition is known as the initial appearance even if the juvenile has already been brought before the court immediately following his arrest. FCA § 320.2.

8. The "fact-finding" is the juvenile's analogue of a trial. As in the earlier proceedings, the juvenile has a right to counsel at this hearing. § 341.2. See *In re Gault*, 387 U.S. 1 (1967). Evidence may be suppressed on the same grounds as in criminal cases, FCA § 330.2, and proof of guilt, based on the record evidence, must be beyond a reasonable doubt, § 342.2. See *In re Winship*, 397 U.S. 358 (1970). If guilt is established, the court enters an appropriate order and schedules a dispositional hearing. § 345.1.

The dispositional hearing is the final and most important proceeding in the Family Court. If the juvenile has committed a designated felony, the court must order a probation investigation and a diagnostic assessment. § 351.1. Any other material and relevant evidence may be offered by the probation agency or the juvenile. Both sides may call and cross-examine witnesses and recommend specific dispositional alternatives. § 350.4. The court must find, based on a preponderance of the evidence, § 350.3(2), that the juvenile is delinquent and requires supervision, treatment, or confinement. § 352.1. Otherwise, the petition is dismissed. *Ibid.*

If the juvenile is found to be delinquent, then the court enters an order of disposition. Possible alternatives include a conditional discharge; probation for up to two years; nonsecure placement with, perhaps, a relative or the Division for Youth; transfer to the Commissioner of Mental Health; or secure placement. §§ 353.1–353.5. Unless the juvenile committed one of the designated felonies, the court must order the least restrictive available alternative consistent with the needs and best interests of the juvenile and the need for protection of the community. § 352.2(2).

detained pursuant to § 320.5(3)(b), between the initial appearance and the completion of the factfinding hearing, for a total of 15 days.

Appellees Luis Rosario and Kenneth Morgan, both age 14, were also ordered detained pending their factfinding hearings. Rosario was charged with attempted first-degree robbery and second-degree assault for an incident in which he, with four others, allegedly tried to rob two men, putting a gun to the head of one of them and beating both about the head with sticks. See Petitioners' Exhibit 2b. At the time of his initial appearance, on March 15, 1978, Rosario had another delinquency petition pending for knifing a student, and two prior petitions had been adjusted.[9] Probable cause was found on March 21. On April 11, Rosario was released to his father, and the case was terminated without adjustment on September 25, 1978.

Kenneth Morgan was charged with attempted robbery and attempted grand larceny for an incident in which he and another boy allegedly tried to steal money from a 14-year-old girl and her brother by threatening to blow their heads off and grabbing them to search their pockets. See Petitioners' Exhibit 3b. Morgan, like Rosario, was on release status on another petition (for robbery and criminal possession of stolen property) at the time of his initial appearance on March 27, 1978. He had been arrested four previous times, and his mother refused to come to court because he had been in trouble so often she did not want him home. A probable-cause hearing was set for March 30, but was continued until April 4, when it was combined with a factfinding hearing. Morgan was found guilty of harassment and petit larceny and was ordered placed

with the Department of Social Services for 18 months. He was detained a total of eight days between his initial appearance and the factfinding hearing.

On December 21, 1977, while still in preventive detention pending his factfinding hearing, Gregory Martin instituted a habeas corpus class action on behalf of "those persons who are, or during the pendency of this action will be, preventively detained pursuant to" § 320.5(3)(b) of the FCA. Rosario and Morgan were subsequently added as additional named plaintiffs. These three class representatives sought a declaratory judgment that § 320.5(3)(b) violates the Due Process and Equal Protection Clauses of the Fourteenth Amendment.

In an unpublished opinion, the District Court certified the class. App. 20–32.[10] The court also held that appellees were not required to exhaust their state remedies before resorting to federal habeas because the highest state court had already rejected an identical challenge to the juvenile preventive detention statute. See People ex rel. Wayburn v. Schupf, 39 N.Y. 2d 682, 350 N.E. 2d 906 (1976). Exhaustion of state remedies, therefore, would be "an exercise in futility." App. 26.

At trial, appellees offered in evidence the case histories of 34 members of the class, including the three named petitioners. Both parties presented some general statistics on the relation between pretrial detention and ultimate disposition. In addition, there was testimony concerning juvenile proceedings from a number of witnesses, including a legal aid attorney specializing in juvenile cases, a probation supervisor, a child psychologist, and a Family Court Judge. On the basis of this evidence, the District Court rejected the equal protection challenge as "insub-

---

9. Every accused juvenile is interviewed by a member of the staff of the Probation Department. This process is known as "probation intake." See Testimony of Mr. Benjamin (Supervisor, New York Dept. of Probation), App. 142. In the course of the interview, which lasts an average of 45 minutes, the probation officer will gather what information he can about the nature of the case, the attitudes of the parties involved, and the child's past history and current family circumstances. Id., at 144, 153. His sources of information are the child, his parent or guardian, the arresting officer, and any records of past contacts between the child and the Family Court. On the basis of this interview, the probation officer may attempt to "adjust," or informally resolve, the case. FCA § 308.1(2). Adjustment is a purely voluntary process in which the complaining witness agrees not to press the case further, while the juvenile is given a warning or agrees to counseling sessions or, perhaps, referral to a community agency. § 308.1 (Practice Commentary). In cases involving designated felonies or other serious crimes, adjustment is not permitted without written approval of the Family Court. § 308.1(4). If a case is not informally adjusted, it is referred to the "presentment agency." See n. 6, supra.

10. We have never decided whether Federal Rule of Civil Procedure 23, providing for class actions, is applicable to petitions for habeas corpus relief. See Bell v. Wolfish, 441 U.S. 520, 527, n. 6 (1979); Middendorf v. Henry, 425 U.S. 25, 30 (1976). Although appellants contested the class certification in the District Court, they did not raise the issue on appeal; nor do they urge it here. Again, therefore, we have no occasion to reach the question.

stantial,"[11] but agreed with appellees that pretrial detention under the FCA violates due process.[12] The court ordered that "all class members in custody pursuant to Family Court Act Section [320.5(3)(b)] shall be released forthwith." *Id.*, at 93.

The Court of Appeals affirmed. After reviewing the trial record, the court opined that "the vast majority of juveniles detained under [§ 320.5(3)(b)] either have their petitions dismissed before an adjudication of delinquency or are released after adjudication." 689 F.2d, at 369. The court concluded from the fact that § 320.5(3)(b) "is utilized principally, not for preventive purposes, but to impose punishment for unadjudicated criminal acts." *Id.*, at 372. The early release of so many of those detained contradicts any asserted need for pretrial confinement to protect the community. The court therefore concluded that § 320.5(3)(b) must be declared unconstitutional as to all juveniles. Individual litigation would be a practical impossibility because the periods of detention are so short that the litigation is mooted before the merits are determined.[13]

II

There is no doubt that the Due Process Clause is applicable in juvenile proceedings. "The problem," we have stressed, "is to ascertain the precise impact of the due process requirement upon such proceedings." *In re Gault*, 387 U.S. 1, 13–14 (1967). We have held that certain basic constitutional protections enjoyed by adults accused of crimes also apply to juveniles. See *id.*, at 31–57 (notice of charges, right to counsel, privilege against self-incrimination,

right to confrontation and cross-examination); *In re Winship*, 397 U.S. 358 (1970) (proof beyond a reasonable doubt); *Breed v. Jones*, 421 U.S. 519 (1975) (double jeopardy). But the Constitution does not mandate elimination of all differences in the treatment of juveniles. See, e.g., *McKeiver v. Pennsylvania*, 403 U.S. 528 (1971) (no right to jury trial). The State has "a *parens patriae* interest in preserving and promoting the welfare of the child," *Santosky v. Kramer*, 455 U.S. 745, 766 (1982), which makes a juvenile proceeding fundamentally different from an adult criminal trial. We have tried, therefore, to strike a balance—to respect the "informality" and "flexibility" that characterize juvenile proceedings, *In re Winship*, *supra*, at 366, and yet to ensure that such proceedings comport with the "fundamental fairness" demanded by the Due Process Clause. *Breed v. Jones*, *supra*, at 531; *McKeiver*, *supra*, at 543 (plurality opinion).

The statutory provision at issue in these cases, § 320.5(3)(b), permits a brief pretrial detention based on a finding of a "serious risk" that an arrested juvenile may commit a crime before his return date. The question before us is whether preventive detention of juveniles pursuant to § 320.5(3)(b) is compatible with the "fundamental fairness" required by due process. Two separate inquiries are necessary to answer this question. First, does preventive detention under the New York statute serve a legitimate state objective? See *Bell v. Wolfish*, 441 U.S. 520, 534, n. 15 (1979); *Kennedy v. Mendoza-Martinez*, 372 U.S. 144, 168–169 (1963). And, second, are the procedural safeguards contained in the FCA adequate to authorize the pretrial detention of at least

---

11. The equal protection claim, which was neither raised on appeal nor decided by the Second Circuit, is not before us.

12. The District Court gave three reasons for this conclusion. First, under the FCA, a juvenile may be held in pretrial detention for up to five days without any judicial determination of probable cause. Relying on *Gerstein v. Pugh*, 420 U.S., at 114, the District Court concluded that pretrial detention without a prior adjudication of probable cause is, itself, a *per se* violation of due process. *United States ex rel. Martin v. Strasburg*, 513 F.Supp. 691, 717 (S.D.N.Y. 1981).

Second, after a review of the pertinent scholarly literature, the court noted that "no diagnostic tools have as yet been devised which enable even the most highly trained criminologists to predict reliably which juveniles will engage in violent crime." *Id.*, at 708. A *fortiori*, the court concluded, a Family Court judge cannot make a reliable prediction based on the limited information available to him at the initial appearance. *Id.*, at 712. Moreover, the court felt that the trial record was "replete" with examples of arbitrary and capricious detentions. *Id.*, at 713.

Finally, the court concluded that preventive detention is merely a euphemism for punishment imposed without an adjudication of guilt. The alleged purpose of the detention—to protect society from the juvenile's criminal conduct—is indistinguishable from the purpose of post-trial detention. And given "the inability of trial judges to predict which juveniles will commit crimes," there is no rational connection between the decision to detain and the alleged purpose, even if that purpose were legitimate. *Id.*, at 716.

13. Judge Newman concurred separately. He was not convinced that the record supported the majority's statistical conclusions. But he thought that the statute was procedurally infirm because it granted unbridled discretion to Family Court judges to make an inherently uncertain prediction of future criminal behavior. 689 F.2d, at 377.

some juveniles charged with crimes? See *Mathews v. Eldridge*, 424 U.S. 319, 335 (1976); *Gerstein v. Pugh*, 420 U.S. 103, 114 (1975).

A

Preventive detention under the FCA is purportedly designed to protect the child and society from the potential consequences of his criminal acts. *People ex rel. Wayburn v. Schupf*, 39 N.Y.2d, at 689–690, 350 N.E.2d, at 910. When making any detention decision, the Family Court judge is specifically directed to consider the needs and best interests of the juvenile as well as the need for the protection of the community. FCA § 301.1; *In re Craig S.*, 57 App.Div.2d 761, 394 N.Y.S.2d 200 (1977). In *Bell v. Wolfish, supra*, at 534, n. 15, we left open the question whether any governmental objective other than ensuring a detainee's presence at trial may constitutionally justify pretrial detention. As an initial matter, therefore, we must decide whether, in the context of the juvenile system, the combined interest in protecting both the community and the juvenile himself from the consequences of future criminal conduct is sufficient to justify such detention.

The "legitimate and compelling state interest" in protecting the community from crime cannot be doubted. *De Veau v. Braisted*, 363 U.S. 144, 155 (1960). See also *Terry v. Ohio*, 392 U.S. 1, 22 (1968). We have stressed before that crime prevention is "a weighty social objective," *Brown v. Texas*, 443 U.S. 47, 52 (1979), and this interest persists undiluted in the juvenile context. See *In re Gault, supra*, at 20, n. 26. The harm suffered by the victim

of a crime is not dependent upon the age of the perpetrator.[14] And the harm to society generally may even be greater in this context given the high rate of recidivism among juveniles. *In re Gault, supra*, at 22.

The juvenile's countervailing interest in freedom from institutional restraints, even for the brief time involved here, is undoubtedly substantial as well. See *In re Gault, supra*, at 27. But that interest must be qualified by the recognition that juveniles, unlike adults, are always in some form of custody. *Lehman v. Lycoming County Children's Services*, 458 U.S. 502, 510–511 (1982); *In re Gault, supra*, at 17. Children, by definition, are not assumed to have the capacity to take care of themselves. They are assumed to be subject to the control of their parents, and if parental control falters, the State must play its part as *parens patriae*. See *State v. Gleason*, 404 A.2d 573, 580 (Me. 1979); *People ex rel. Wayburn v. Schupf, supra*, at 690, 350 N.E.2d, at 910; *Baker v. Smith*, 477 S.W.2d 149, 150–151 (Ky.App. 1971). In this respect, the juvenile's liberty interest may, in appropriate circumstances, be subordinated to the State's "*parens patriae* interest in preserving and promoting the welfare of the child." *Santosky v. Kramer, supra*, at 766.

The New York Court of Appeals, in upholding the statute at issue here, stressed at some length "the desirability of protecting the juvenile from his own folly." *People ex rel. Wayburn v. Schupf, supra*, at 688–689, 350 N.E.2d, at 909.[15] Society has a legitimate interest in protecting a juvenile from the consequences of his criminal activity—both from potential physical injury which may be suffered when

---

14. In 1982, juveniles under 16 accounted for 7.5 percent of all arrests for violent crimes, 19.9 percent of all arrests for serious property crimes, and 17.3 percent of all arrests for violent and serious property crimes combined. U.S. Dept. of Justice, Federal Bureau of Investigation, Crime in the United States 176–177 (1982) ("violent crimes" include murder, nonnegligent manslaughter, forcible rape, robbery, and aggravated assault; "serious property crimes" include burglary, larceny-theft, motor vehicle theft, and arson).

15. "Our society recognizes that juveniles in general are in the earlier stages of their emotional growth, that their intellectual development is incomplete, that they have had only limited practical experience, and that their value systems have not yet been clearly identified or firmly adopted. . . .

"For the same reasons that our society does not hold juveniles to an adult standard of responsibility for their conduct, our society may also conclude that there is a greater likelihood that a juvenile charged with delinquency, if released, will commit another criminal act than that an adult charged with crime will do so. To the extent that self-restraint may be expected to contrain adults, it may not be expected to operate with equal force as to juveniles. Because of the possibility of juvenile delinquency treatment and the absence of second-offender sentencing, there will not be the deterrent for the juvenile which confronts the adult. Perhaps more significant is the fact that in consequence of lack of experience and comprehension the juvenile does not view the commission of what are criminal acts in the same perspective as an adult. . . . There is the element of gamesmanship and the excitement of 'getting away' with something and the powerful inducement of peer pressures. All of these commonly acknowledged factors make the commission of criminal conduct on the part of juveniles in general more likely than in the case of adults." *People ex rel. Wayburn v. Schupf*, 39 N.Y.2d, at 687–688, 350 N.E.2d, at 908–909.

a victim fights back or a policeman attempts to make an arrest and from the downward spiral of criminal activity into which peer pressure may lead the child. See *L. O. W. v. District Court of Arapahoe*, 623 P.2d 1253, 1258–1259 (Colo. 1981); *Morris v. D'Amario*, 416 A.2d 137, 140 (R. I. 1980). See also *Eddings v. Oklahoma*, 455 U.S. 104, 115 (1982) (minority "is a time and condition of life when a person may be most susceptible to influence and to psychological damage"); *Bellotti v. Baird*, 443 U.S. 622, 635 (1979) (juveniles "often lack the experience, perspective, and judgment to recognize and avoid choices that could be detrimental to them").

The substantiality and legitimacy of the state interests underlying this statute are confirmed by the widespread use and judicial acceptance of preventive detention for juveniles. Every State, as well as the United States in the District of Columbia, permits preventive detention of juveniles accused of crime.[16] A number of model juvenile justice Acts also contain provisions permitting preventive detention.[17] And the courts of eight States, including the New York Court of Appeals, have upheld their statutes with specific reference to protecting the juvenile and the community from harmful pretrial conduct, including pretrial crime. *L. O. W. v. District of Court of Arapahoe, supra*, at 1258–1259; *Morris v. D'Amario, supra*, at 139–140; *State v. Gleason*, 404 A.2d, at 583, *Pauley v. Gross*, 1 Kan.App.2d 736, 738–740, 574 P.2d 234, 237–238 (1977); *People ex rel. Wayburn v. Schupf*, 39 N.Y.2d, at 688–689, 350 N.E.2d, at 909–910; *Aubrey v. Gadbois*, 50 Cal.App.3d 470, 472, 123 Cal.Rptr. 365, 366 (1975); *Baker v. Smith*, 477 S.W.2d, at 150–151; *Commonwealth ex rel. Sprowal v. Hendrick*, 438 Pa. 435, 438–439, 265 A.2d 348, 349–350 (1970).

"The fact that a practice is followed by a large number of states is not conclusive in a decision as to whether that practice accords with due process, but it is plainly worth considering in determining whether the practice 'offends some principle of justice so rooted in the tradition and conscience of our people as to be ranked as fundamental.' *Snyder v. Massachusetts*, 291 U.S. 97, 105 (1934)." *Leland v. Oregon*, 343 U.S. 790, 798 (1952). In light of the uniform legislative judgment that pretrial detention of juveniles properly promotes the interests both of society and the juvenile, we conclude that the practice serves a legitimate regulatory purpose compatible with the "fundamental fairness" demanded

16. Ala. Code § 12–15–59 (1975); Alaska Stat. Ann. § 47.10.140 (1979); Rule 3, Ariz. Juv. Ct. Rules of Proc., Ariz. Rev. Stat. Ann. (Supp. 1983–1984 to vol. 17A); Ark. Stat. Ann. § 45–421 (Supp. 1983); Cal. Welf. & Inst. Code Ann. § 628 (West Supp. 1984); Colo. Rev. Stat. § 19–2–102 (Supp. 1983); Conn. Gen. Stat. § 46b–131 (Supp. 1984); Del. Fam. Ct. Rule 60 (1981); D.C. Code § 16–2310 (1981); Fla. Stat. § 39.032 (Supp. 1984); Ga. Code Ann. § 15–11–19 (1982); Haw. Rev. Stat. § 571–31.1 (Supp. 1984); Idaho Code § 16–1811 (Supp. 1983); Ill. Rev. Stat., ch. 37, § 703–4 (1983); Ind. Code § 31–6–4–5 (1982); Iowa Code § 232.22 (1983); Kan Stat. Ann. § 38–1632 (Supp. 1983); Ky. Rev. Stat. § 208.192 (1982); L. Code Juv. Proc. Ann., Art. 40 (West 1983 Pamphlet); Me. Rev. Stat. Ann., Tit. 15, § 3203 (1964 and Supp. 1983–1984); Md. Cts. & Jud. Proc. Code Ann. § 3–815 (1984); Mass. Gen. Laws Ann., ch. 119, § 66 (West Supp. 1983–1984); Mich. Comp. Laws § 712A.15 (1979); Minn. Stat. § 260.171 (1982); Miss. Code Ann. § 43–23–11 (1972); Mo. Juv. Ct. Rule 111.02 (1981); Mont. Code Ann. § 41–5–305 (1983); Neb. Rev. Stat. § 43–255 (Supp. 1982); Nev. Rev. Stat. § 62.140 (1983); N. H. Rev. Stat. Ann. § 169B:14 (Supp. 1983); N. J. Stat. Ann. § 2A:4–56 (Supp. 1983–1984); N. M. Stat. Ann. § 32–1–24 (1981); N. Y. FCA § 320.5(3) (McKinney 1983); N. C. Gen. Stat. § 7A–574 (Supp. 1983); N. D. Cent. Code § 27–20–14 (1974); Ohio Rev. Code Ann. § 2151.311 (1976); Okla. Stat., Tit. 10, § 1107 (Supp. 1983); Ore. Rev. Stat. § 419.573 (1983); 42 Pa. Cons. Stat. § 6325 (1982); R. I. Gen. Laws §§ 14–1–20, 14–1–21 (1981); S. C. Code § 20–7–600 (Supp. 1983); S. D. Codified Laws § 26–8–19.2 (Supp. 1983); Tenn. Code Ann. § 37–1–114 (1984); Tex. Fam. Code Ann. § 53.02 (1975 and Supp. 1984); Utah Code Ann. § 78–3a–30 (Supp. 1983); Vt. Stat. Ann., Tit. 33, § 643 (1981); Va. Code § 16.1–248 (1982); Wash. Rev. Code § 13.40.040 (1983); W. Va. Code § 49–5–8 (Supp. 1983); Wis. Stat. § 48.208 (1981–1982); Wyo. Stat. § 14–6–206 (1977).

17. See U.S. Dept of Justice, Office of Juvenile Justice and Delinquency Prevention, Standards for the Administration of Juvenile Justice, Report of the National Advisory Committee for Juvenile Justice and Delinquency Prevention 294–296 (July 1980); Uniform Juvenile Court Act § 14, 9A U.L.A. 22 (1979); Standard Juvenile Court Act, Art. IV, § 16, proposed by the National Council on Crime and Delinquency (1959); W. Sheridan, Legislative Guide for Drafting Family and Juvenile Court Acts § 20(a)(1) (Dept. of HEW, Children's Bureau, Pub. No. 472–1969); see also Standards for Juvenile and Family Courts 62–63 (Dept. of HEW, Children's Bureau, Pub. No. 437–1966). Cf. Institute of Judicial Administration/American Bar Association Project on Juvenile Justice Standards Relating to Interim Status: The Release, Control, and Detention of Accused Juvenile Offenders Between Arrest and Disposition § 3.2(B) (Tent. Draft 1977) (detention limited to "reducing the likelihood that the juvenile may inflict serious bodily harm on others during the interim").

by the Due Process Clause in juvenile proceedings. Cf. *McKeiver v. Pennsylvania*, 403 U.S., at 548 (plurality opinion).[18]

Of course, the mere invocation of a legitimate purpose will not justify particular restrictions and conditions of confinement amounting to punishment. It is axiomatic that "[d]ue process requires that a pretrial detainee not be punished." *Bell v. Wolfish*, 441 U.S., at 535, n. 16. Even given, therefore, that pretrial detention may serve legitimate regulatory purposes, it is still necessary to determine whether the terms and conditions of confinement under § 320.5(3)(b) are in fact compatible with those purposes. *Kennedy v. Mendoza-Martinez*, 372 U.S., at 168–169. "A court must decide whether the disability is imposed for the purpose of punishment or whether it is but an incident of some other legitimate governmental purpose." *Bell v. Wolfish, supra*, at 538. Absent a showing of an express intent to punish on the part of the State, that determination generally will turn on "whether an alternative purpose to which [the restriction] may rationally be connected is assignable for it, and whether it appears excessive in relation to the alternative purpose assigned [to it]." *Kennedy v. Mendoza-Martinez, supra*, at 168–189. See *Bell v. Wolfish, supra*, at 538; *Flemming v. Nestor*, 363 U.S. 603, 613–614 (1960).

There is no indication in the statute itself that preventive detention is used or intended as a punishment. First of all, the detention is strictly limited in time. If a juvenile is detained in his initial appearance and has denied the charges against him, he is entitled to a probable-cause hearing to be held not more than three days after the conclusion of the initial appearance or four days after the filing of the petition, whichever is sooner. FCA § 325.1(2).[19] If the Family Court judge finds probable cause, he must also determine whether continued detention is necessary pursuant to § 320.5(3)(b). § 325.3(3).

Detained juveniles are also entitled to an expedited factfinding hearing. If the juvenile is charged with one of a limited number of designated felonies, the factfinding hearing must be scheduled to commence not more than 14 days after the conclusion of the initial appearance. § 340.1. If the juvenile is charged with a lesser offense, then the factfinding hearing must be held not more than three days after the initial appearance.[20] In the latter case, since the time for the probable-cause hearing and the factfinding hearing coincide, the two hearings are merged.

Thus, the maximum possible detention under § 320.5(3)(b) of a youth accused of a serious crime, assuming a 3-day extension of the factfinding hearing for good cause shown, is 17 days. The maximum detention for less serious crimes, again assuming a 3-day extension for good cause shown, is six days. These time frames seem suited to the limited purpose of providing the youth with a controlled environment and separating him from improper influences pending the speedy disposition of his case.

The conditions of confinement also appear to reflect the regulatory purposes relied upon by the State. When a juvenile is remanded after his initial appearance, he cannot, absent exceptional circumstances, be sent to a prison or lockup where he would be exposed to adult criminals. FCA § 304.1(2). Instead, the child is screened by an "assessment unit" of the Department of Juvenile Justice. Testimony of Mr. Kelly (Deputy Commissioner of Operations, New York City Department of Juvenile Justice), App. 286–287. The assessment unit places the child in either nonsecure or secure detention. Nonsecure detention involves an open facility in the community, a sort of "halfway house," without locks, bars, or security officers where the child receives schooling and counseling and has access to recreational facilities. *Id.*, at 285; Testimony of Mr. Benjamin, *id.*, at 149–150.

---

18. Appellees argue that some limit must be placed on the categories of crimes that detained juveniles must be accused of having committed or being likely to commit. But the discretion to delimit the categories of crimes justifying detention, like the discretion to define criminal offenses and prescribe punishments, resides wholly with the state legislatures. *Whalen v. United States*, 445 U.S. 684, 689 (1980); *Rochin v. California*, 342 U.S. 165, 168 (1952). See also *Rummel v. Estelle*, 445 U.S. 263, 275 (1980) ("the presence or absence of violence does not always affect the strength of society's interest in determining a particular crime").

    More fundamentally, this sort of attack on a criminal statute must be made on a case-by-case basis. *United States v. Raines*, 362 U.S. 17, 21 (1960). The Court will not sift through the entire class to determine whether the statute was constitutionally applied in each case. And, outside the limited First Amendment context, a criminal statute may not be attacked as overbroad. See *New York v. Ferber*, 458 U.S. 747 (1982).

19. For good cause shown, the court may adjourn the hearing, but for no more than three additional court days. FCA § 325.1(3).

20. In either case, the court may adjourn the hearing for not more than three days for good cause shown. FCA § 340.1(3). The court must state on the record the reason for any adjournment. § 340.1(4).

Secure detention is more restrictive, but it is still consistent with the regulatory and *parens patriae* objectives relied upon by the State. Children are assigned to separate dorms based on age, size, and behavior. They wear street clothes provided by the institution and partake in educational and recreational programs and counseling sessions run by trained social workers. Misbehavior is punished by confinement to one's room. See Testimony of Mr. Kelly, *id.*, at 292–297. We cannot conclude from this record that the controlled environment briefly imposed by the State on juveniles in secure pretrial detention "is imposed for the purpose of punishment" rather than as "an incident of some other legitimate governmental purpose." *Bell v. Wolfish*, 441 U.S., at 538.

The Court of Appeals, of course, did conclude that the underlying purpose of § 320.5(3)(b) is punitive rather than regulatory. But the court did not dispute that preventive detention might serve legitimate regulatory purposes or that the terms and conditions of pretrial confinement in New York are compatible with those purposes. Rather, the court invalidated a significant aspect of New York's juvenile justice system based solely on some case histories and a statistical study which appeared to show that "the vast majority of juveniles detained under [§ 320.5(3)(b)] either have their petitions dismissed before an adjudication of delinquency or are released after adjudication." 689 F.2d, at 369. The court assumed that dismissal of a petition or failure to confine a juvenile at the dispositional hearing belied the need to detain him prior to factfinding and that, therefore, the pretrial detention constituted punishment. *Id.*, at 373. Since punishment imposed without a prior adjudication of guilt is *per se* illegitimate, the Court of Appeals concluded that no juveniles could be held pursuant to § 320.5(3)(b).

There are some obvious flaws in the statistics and case histories relied upon by the lower court.[21] But

even assuming it to be the case that "by far the greater number of juveniles incarcerated under [§ 320.5(3)(b)] will never be confined as a consequence of a disposition imposed after an adjudication of delinquency," 689 F.2d, at 371–372, we find that to be an insufficient ground for upsetting the widely shared legislative judgment that preventive detention serves an important and legitimate function in the juvenile justice system. We are unpersuaded by the Court of Appeals'[s] rather cavalier equation of detentions that do not lead to continued confinement after an adjudication of guilt and "wrongful" or "punitive" pretrial detentions.

Pretrial detention need not be considered punitive merely because a juvenile is subsequently discharged subject to conditions or put on probation. In fact, such actions reinforce the original finding that close supervision of the juvenile is required. Lenient but supervised disposition is in keeping with the Act's purpose to promote the welfare and development of the child.[22] As the New York Court of Appeals noted:

> It should surprise no one that caution and concern for both the juvenile and society may indicate the more conservative decision to detain at the very outset, whereas the later development of very much more relevant information may prove that while a finding of delinquency was warranted, placement may not be indicated. *People ex rel. Wayburn v. Schupf,* 39 N.Y.2d, at 690, 350 N.E.2d, at 910.

Even when a case is terminated prior to factfinding, it does not follow that the decision to detain the juvenile pursuant to § 320.5(3)(b) amounted to a due process violation. A delinquency petition may be dismissed for any number of reasons collateral to its merits, such as the failure of a witness to testify. The Family Court judge cannot be expected to anticipate such developments at the initial hearing. He makes his decision based on the information available to him at that time, and the propriety of the decision must be judged in that light. Consequently,

---

21. For example, as the Court of Appeals itself admits, 689 F.2d, at 369, n. 18, the statistical study on which it relied mingles indiscriminately detentions under § 320.5(3)(b) with detentions under § 320.5(3)(a). The latter provision applies only to juveniles who are likely not to appear on the return date if not detained, and appellees concede that such juveniles may be lawfully detained. Brief for Appellees 93. Furthermore, the 34 case histories on which the court relied were handpicked by appellees' counsel from over a 3-year period. Compare Petitioners' Exhibit 19a (detention of Geraldo Delgado on March 5, 1976) with Petitioners' Exhibit 35a (detention of James Ancrum on August 19, 1979). The Court of Appeals stated that appellants did not contest the representativeness of these case histories. 689 F.2d, at 369, n. 19. Appellants argue, however, that there was no occasion to contest their representativeness because the case histories were not even offered by appellees as a representative sample, and were not evaluated by appellees' expert statistician or the District Court in that light. See Brief for Appellant in No. 82–1278, pp. 24–25, n.**. We need not resolve this controversy.

22. Judge Quinones testified that detention at disposition is considered a "harsh solution." At the dispositional hearing, the Family Court judge usually has "a much more complete picture of the youngster" and tries to tailor the least restrictive dispositional order compatible with that picture. Testimony of Judge Quinones, App. 279–281.

the final disposition of a case is "largely irrelevant" to the legality of a pretrial detention. *Baker v. McCollan*, 443 U.S. 137, 145 (1979).

It may be, of course, that in some circumstances detention of a juvenile would not pass constitutional muster. But the validity of those detentions must be determined on a case-by-case basis. Section 320.5(3)(b) is not invalid "on its face" by reason of the ambiguous statistics and case histories relied upon by the court below.[23] We find no justification for the conclusion that, contrary to the express language of the statute and the judgment of the highest state court, § 320.5(3)(b) is a punitive rather than a regulatory measure. Preventive detention under the FCA serves the legitimate state objective, held in common with every State in the country, of protecting both the juvenile and society from the hazards of pretrial crime.

B

Given the legitimacy of the State's interest in preventive detention, and the nonpunitive nature of that detention, the remaining question is whether the procedures afforded juveniles detained prior to factfinding provide sufficient protection against erroneous and unnecessary deprivations of liberty. See *Mathews v. Eldridge*, 424 U.S., at 335.[24] In *Gerstein v. Pugh*, 420 U.S., at 114, we held that a judicial determination of probable cause is a prerequisite to any extended restraint on the liberty of an adult accused of crime. We did not, however, mandate a specific timetable. Nor did we require the "full panoply of adversary safeguards—counsel, confrontation, cross-examination, and compulsory process for witnesses." *Id.*, at 119. Instead, we recognized "the

desirability of flexibility and experimentation by the States." *Id.*, at 123. *Gerstein* arose under the Fourth Amendment, but the same concern with "flexibility" and "informality," while yet ensuring adequate predetention procedures, is present in this context. *In re Winship*, 397 U.S., at 366; *Kent v. United States*, 383 U.S. 541, 554 (1966).

In many respects, the FCA provides far more predetention protection for juveniles than we found to be constitutionally required for a probable-cause determination for adults in *Gerstein*. The initial appearance is informal, but the accused juvenile is given full notice of the charges against him and a complete stenographic record is kept of the hearing. See 513 F.Supp., at 702. The juvenile appears accompanied by his parent or guardian.[25] He is first informed of his rights, including the right to remain silent and the right to be represented by counsel chosen by him or by a law guardian assigned by the court. FCA § 320.3. The initial appearance may be adjourned for no longer than 72 hours or until the next court day, whichever is sooner, to enable an appointed law guardian or other counsel to appear before the court. § 320.2(3). When his counsel is present, the juvenile is informed of the charges against him and furnished with a copy of the delinquency petition. § 320.4(1). A representative from the presentment agency appears in support of the petition.

The nonhearsay allegations in the delinquency petition and supporting depositions must establish probable cause to believe the juvenile committed the offense. Although the Family Court judge is not required to make a finding of probable cause at the initial appearance, the youth may challenge the sufficiency of the petition on that ground. FCA § 315.1. Thus, the juvenile may oppose any recommended

---

23. Several *amici* argue that similar statistics obtain throughout the country. See, e.g., Brief for American Bar Association as *Amicus Curiae* 23; Brief for Association for Children of New Jersey as *Amicus Curiae* 8, 11; Brief for Youth Law Center et al. as *Amici Curiae* 13–14. But even if New York's experience were duplicated on a national scale, that fact would not lead us, as *amici* urge, to conclude that every State and the United States are illicitly punishing juveniles prior to their trial. On the contrary, if such statistics obtain nationwide, our conclusion is strengthened that the existence of the statistics in these cases is not a sufficient ground for striking down New York's statute. As already noted: "The fact that a practice is followed by a large number of states is not conclusive in a decision as to whether that practice accords with due process, but it is plainly worth considering in determining whether the practice 'offends some principle of justice so rooted in the traditions and conscience of our people as to be ranked as fundamental.' *Snyder v. Massachusetts*, 291 U.S. 97, 105 (1934)." *Leland v. Oregon*, 343 U.S. 790, 798 (1952).

24. Appellees urge the alleged lack of procedural safeguards as an alternative ground for upholding the judgment of the Court of Appeals. Brief for Appellees 62–75. The court itself intimated that it would reach the same result on that ground, 689 F.2d, at 373–374, and Judge Newman, in his concurrence, relied expressly on perceived procedural flaws in the statute. Accordingly, we deem it necessary to consider the question.

25. If the juvenile's parent or guardian fails to appear after reasonable and substantial efforts have been made to notify such person, the court must appoint a law guardian for the child. FCA § 320.3.

detention by arguing that there is not probable cause to believe he committed the offense or offenses with which he is charged. If the petition is not dismissed, the juvenile is given an opportunity to admit or deny the charges. § 321.1.[26]

At the conclusion of the initial appearance, the presentment agency makes a recommendation regarding detention. A probation officer reports on the juvenile's record, including other prior and current Family Court and probation contacts, as well as relevant information concerning home life, school attendance, and any special medical or developmental problems. He concludes by offering his agency's recommendation on detention. Opposing counsel, the juvenile's parents, and the juvenile himself may all speak on his behalf and challenge any information or recommendation. If the judge does decide to detain the juvenile under § 320.5(3)(b), he must state on the record the facts and reasons for the detention.[27]

As noted, a detained juvenile is entitled to a formal, adversarial probable-cause hearing within three days of his initial appearance, with one 3-day extension possible for good cause shown.[28] The burden at this hearing is on the presentment agency to call witnesses and offer evidence in support of the charges. § 325.2. Testimony is under oath and subject to cross-examination. *Ibid.* The accused juvenile may call witnesses and offer evidence in his own behalf. If the court finds probable cause, the court must again decide whether continued detention is nec-

essary under § 320.5(3)(b). Again, the facts and reasons for the detention must be stated on the record.

In sum, notice, a hearing, and a statement of facts and reasons are given prior to any detention under § 320.5(3)(b). A formal probable-cause hearing is then held within a short while thereafter, if the factfinding hearing is not itself scheduled within three days. These flexible procedures have been found constitutionally adequate under the Fourth Amendment, see *Gerstein v. Pugh*, and under the Due Process Clause, see *Kent v. United States, supra,* at 557. Appellees have failed to note any additional procedures that would significantly improve the accuracy of the determination without unduly impinging on the achievement of legitimate state purposes.[29]

Appellees argue, however, that the risk of erroneous and unnecessary detentions is too high despite these procedures because the standard for detention is fatally vague. Detention under § 320.5(3)(b) is based on a finding that there is a "serious risk" that the juvenile, if released, would commit a crime prior to his next court appearance. We have already seen that detention of juveniles on the ground serves legitimate regulatory purposes. But appellees claim, and the District Court agreed, that it is virtually impossible to predict future criminal conduct with any degree of accuracy. Moreover, they say, the statutory standard fails to channel the discretion of the Family Court judge by specifying the factors on which he should rely in making that prediction. The

---

26. If the child chooses to remain silent, he is assumed to deny the charges. FCA § 321.1. With the consent of the court and of the presentment agency, the child may admit to a lesser charge. If he wishes to admit to the charges or to a lesser charge, the court must, before accepting the admission, advise the child of his right to a factfinding hearing and of the possible specific dispositional orders that may result from the admission. *Ibid.* The court must also satisfy itself that the child actually did commit the acts to which he admits. *Ibid.*

With the consent of the victim or complainant and the juvenile, the court may also refer a case to the probation service for adjustment. If the case is subsequently adjusted, the petition is then dismissed. § 320.6.

27. Given that under *Gerstein*, 420 U.S., at 119–123, a probable-cause hearing may be informal and nonadversarial, a Family Court judge could make a finding of probable cause at the initial appearance. That he is not required to do so does not, under the circumstances, amount to a deprivation of due process. Appellees fail to point to a single example where probable cause was not found after a decision was made to detain the child.

28. The Court in *Gerstein* indicated approval of pretrial detention procedures that supplied a probable-cause hearing within five days of the initial detention. *Id.,* at 124, n. 25. The brief delay in the probable-cause hearing may actually work to the advantage of the juvenile since it gives his counsel, usually appointed at the initial appearance pursuant to FCA § 320.2(2), time to prepare.

29. Judge Newman, in his concurrence below, offered a list of statutory improvements. These suggested changes included: limitations on the crimes for which the juvenile has been arrested or which he is likely to commit if released; a determination of the likelihood that the juvenile committed the crime; an assessment of the juvenile's background; and a more specific standard of proof. The first and second of these suggestions have already been considered. See nn. 18 and 27, *supra.* We need only add to the discussion in n. 18 that there is no indication that delimiting the category of crimes justifying detention would improve the accuracy of the § 320.5(3)(b) determination in any respect. The third and fourth suggestions are discussed in text, *infra.*

procedural protections noted above are thus, in their view, unavailing because the ultimate decision is intrinsically arbitrary and uncontrolled.

Our cases indicate, however, that from a legal point of view there is nothing inherently unattainable about a prediction of future criminal conduct. Such a judgment forms an important element in many decisions,[30] and we have specifically rejected the contention, based on the same sort of sociological data relied upon by appellees and the District Court, "that it is impossible to predict future behavior and that the question is so vague as to be meaningless." *Jurek v. Texas,* 428 U.S. 262, 274 (1976) (opinion of Stewart, Powell, and Stevens, JJ.); *id.* at 279 (White, J., concurring in judgment).

We have also recognized that a prediction of future criminal conduct is "an experienced prediction based on a host of variables" which cannot be readily codified. *Greenholtz v. Nebraska Penal Inmates,* 442 U.S. 1, 16 (1979). Judge Quinones of the Family Court testified at trial that he and his colleagues make a determination under § 320.5(3)(b) based on numerous factors including the nature and seriousness of the charges; whether the charges are likely to be proved at trial; the juvenile's prior record; the adequacy and effectiveness of his home supervision; his school situation, if known; the time of day of the alleged crime as evidence of its seriousness and a possible lack of parental control; and any special circumstances that might be brought to his attention by the probation officer, the child's attorney, or any parents, relatives, or other responsible persons accompanying the child. Testimony of Judge Quinones, App. 254–267. The decision is based on as much information as can reasonably be obtained at the initial appearance. *Ibid.*

Given the right to a hearing, to counsel, and to a statement of reasons, there is no reason that the specific factors upon which the Family Court judge might rely must be specified in the statute. As the New York Court of Appeals concluded, *People ex rel. Wayburn v. Schupf,* 39 N.Y.2d, at 690, 350 N.E.2d, at 910, "to a very real extent Family Court must exercise a substitute parental control for which there can be no particularized criteria." There is also no reason, we should add, for a federal court to assume that a state court judge will not strive to apply state law as conscientiously as possible. *Sumner v. Mata,* 449 U.S. 539, 549 (1981).

It is worth adding that the Court of Appeals for the Second Circuit was mistaken in its conclusion that "[i]ndividual litigation . . . is a practical impossibility because the periods of detention are so short that the litigation is mooted before the merits are determined." 689 F.2d, at 373. In fact, one of the juveniles in the very case histories upon which the court relied was released from pretrial detention on a writ of habeas corpus issued by the State Supreme Court. New York courts also have adopted a liberal view of the doctrine of "capable of repetition, yet evading review" precisely in order to ensure that pretrial detention orders are not unreviewable. In *People ex rel. Wayburn v. Schupf, supra,* at 686, 350 N.E.2d, at 908, the court declined to dismiss an appeal from the grant of a writ of habeas corpus despite the technical mootness of the case.

> Because the situation is likely to recur . . . and the substantial issue may otherwise never be reached (in view of the predictably recurring happenstance that, however expeditiously an appeal might be prosecuted, fact-finding and dispositional hearings normally will have been held and a disposition made before the appeal could reach us), . . . we decline to dismiss [the appeal] on the ground of mootness.

The required statement of facts and reasons justifying the detention and the stenographic record of the initial appearance will provide a basis for the review of individual cases. Pretrial detention orders

---

30. See *Jurek v. Texas,* 428 U.S. 262, 274–275 (1976) (death sentence imposed by jury); *Greenholtz v. Nebraska Penal Inmates,* 442 U.S. 1, 9–10 (1979) (grant of parole); *Morrissey v. Brewer,* 408 U.S. 471, 480 (1972) (parole revocation).

A prediction of future criminal conduct may also form the basis for an increased sentence under the "dangerous special offender" statute, 18 U.S.C. § 3575. Under § 3575(f), a "dangerous" offender is defined as an individual for whom "a period of confinement longer than that provided for such [underlying] felony is required for the protection of the public from further criminal conduct by the defendant." The statute has been challenged numerous times on the grounds that the standard is unconstitutionally vague. Every Court of Appeals considering the question has rejected that claim. *United States v. Davis,* 710 F.2d 104, 108–109 (3rd Cir.), *cert. denied,* 464 U.S. 1001 (1983); *United States v. Schell,* 692 F.2d 672, 675–676 (10th Cir. 1982); *United States v. Williamson,* 567 F.2d 610, 613 (4th Cir. 1977); *United States v. Bowdach,* 561 F.2d 1160, 1175 (5th Cir. 1977); *United States v. Neary,* 552 F.2d 1184, 1194 (7th Cir), *cert. denied,* 434 U.S. 864 (1977); *United States v. Stewart,* 531 F.2d 326, 336–337 (6th Cir.), *cert. denied,* 426 U.S. 922 (1976).

in New York may be reviewed by writ of habeas corpus brought in State Supreme Court. And the judgment of that court is appealable as of right and may be taken directly to the Court of Appeals if a constitutional question is presented. N.Y.Civ.Prac.Law § 5601(b)(2) (McKinney 1978). Permissive appeal from a Family Court order may be had to the Appellate Division. FCA § 365.2. Or a motion for reconsideration may be directed to the Family Court judge. § 355.1(1)(b). These postdetention procedures provide a sufficient mechanism for correcting on a case-by-case basis any erroneous detentions ordered under § 320.5(3). Such procedures may well flesh out the standards specified in the statute.

III

The dissent would apparently have us strike down New York's preventive detention statute on two grounds: first, because the preventive detention of juveniles constitutes poor public policy, with the balance of harms outweighing any positive benefits either to society or to the juveniles themselves, *post*, at 290–291, 308, and, second, because the statute could have been better drafted to improve the quality of the decisionmaking process, *post*, at 304–306. But it is worth recalling that we are neither a legislature charged with formulating public policy nor an American Bar Association committee charged with drafting a model statute. The question before us today is solely whether the preventive detention system chosen by the State of New York and applied by the New York Family Court comports with constitutional standards. Given the regulatory purpose for the detention and the procedural protections that precede its imposition, we conclude that § 320.5(3)(b) of the New York FCA is not invalid under the Due Process Clause of the Fourteenth Amendment.

The judgment of the Court of Appeals is reversed.

JUVENILES IN ADULT JAILS

Case Comments

One of the most significant problems with detention is placing juveniles in adult jails. Under the Juvenile Justice and Delinquency Prevention (JJDP) Act of 1974, states obtaining federal funds under the act were compelled to revise their jail practices and sep-

arate juveniles from adults. Further amendments to the JJDP Act mandate the removal of juveniles from adult jails. [8]

In the federal court case of *Hendrickson v. Griggs*, the court found that the state of Iowa had not complied with the mandate of the JJDP Act to remove juveniles from jails and ordered local officials to develop a plan for bringing the state into conformity with the law.

Whether the initiative to remove juveniles from adult jails has succeeded has been the subject of much debate. It is still not known how many youths are being held in adult facilities. Today, federal agencies estimate that about fifteen hundred juveniles are being held in adult jails on any given day and about fifty thousand are held in adult jails or lockups sometime during the year. [9] Ira Schwartz, a noted expert on juvenile justice, suggests that: (1) the government enact legislation prohibiting confinement of juveniles in jails; (2) appropriate juvenile detention facilities be established; (3) funds be allocated for such programs; and (4) the responsibility for monitoring conditions of confinement be fixed by statutes and court decisions. [10]

HENDRICKSON v. GRIGGS

Cite as 672 F.Supp. 1126 (N.D.Iowa 1987)

Donald E. O'Brien, Chief Judge.

The Court has before it:

■ motions for dismissal under Rule 12(b)(6) and 12(b)(7), appointment of a guardian ad litem under Rule 17, and summary judgment filed by Defendants Griggs, Hansch, Pliner, Cunningham, Messerly, Groat, and Webster County (hereinafter the "County Defendants");

■ a motion for summary judgment and a motion for a temporary restraining order filed by the plaintiffs; and

■ a motion for summary judgment filed by Defendants Branstad and Ramsey (hereinafter the "State Defendants").

Because the motion for a temporary restraining order [TRO] was considered at a hearing at which all defendants were represented, the Court will treat that motion as a motion for a preliminary injunction. *Walker v. O'Bannon*, 487 F.Supp. 1151, 1153

(W.D.Pa.1980). The plaintiffs have filed a motion to recertify the plaintiff class and create a defendant class, although this motion will be held in abeyance by the Court. While all motions for summary judgment were filed before the plaintiffs' motion for a TRO, the Court will address the motions for summary judgment today only to the degree necessary to determine whether the plaintiffs' request for a TRO must be denied as a matter of law. For the reasons given below, the Court denies the defendants' motions for summary judgment insofar as they involve the following assertions:

1. The plaintiffs' § 1983 claims are barred by *res judicata* and collateral estoppel.
2. The plaintiffs must exhaust administrative remedies.
3. The Office of Juvenile Justice and Delinquency Prevention ("OJJDP") has primary jurisdiction over the defendant's statutory § 1983 claim.
4. The plaintiffs' statutory § 1983 claim is not ripe for adjudication.
5. The plaintiffs must proceed through a guardian ad litem.
6. The plaintiffs' JJDPA claim must be dismissed because a necessary and indispensable party has not been sued.
7. Section 1983 does not provide a cause of action to seek redress for violations of rights created by § 5633 of the Juvenile Justice and Delinquency Prevention Act, 42 U.S.C. § 5601, *et seq.* ("JJDPA").

The Court grants the state defendants' motion for summary judgment against the plaintiffs' prayer for an order compelling the state to return OJJDP funds already received and stop receiving such funds. The Court postpones consideration of the plaintiffs' motion for summary judgment and the remaining portions of the defendants' motions for summary judgment, and grants a substantially modified version of the plaintiffs' motion for a preliminary injunction.

All defendants have moved for dismissal or summary judgment on plaintiffs' claim that they are entitled to relief because several jailing practices of the county defendants violate the JJDPA. The plaintiffs claim that the state plan requirements in § 5633 of the JJDPA create rights enforceable under § 1983, or in the alternative, give rise to an implied cause of action under the four-step analysis of *Cort v. Ash*, 422 U.S. 66, 95 S.Ct. 2080, 45 L.Ed.2d 26 (1976).[1]

The Juvenile Justice and Delinquency Prevention Act was enacted in 1974, with relevant amendments in 1977, 1980 and 1984. Title II of the original Act established a formula grant program under which states and local governments could seek funds from the OJJDP for projects and programs related to juvenile justice and delinquency. Pub.L. No. 93–415, Title II, § 221, 88 Stat. 1119 (1974) (codified as amended at 42 U.S.C. § 5631 (1982)). Section 223 of the Act required states seeking formula grants to submit a plan for carrying out the purposes of the Act and established a list of state plan requirements. Section 223, *supra* (codified at § 5633). Under a 1980 amendment, participating states have been required to submit annual performance reports to "describe the status of compliance with state plan requirements." Pub.L. No. 96–509, § 11(a)(1) (codified at § 5633(a)).

This case involves the defendants' compliance with three such requirements:

1. *The deinstitutionalization of status offenders.* Section 5633(1)(12)(A), as amended in 1977 and 1980, requires each plan to "provide within three years after submission of the initial plan that juveniles who are charged with or who have committed offenses that would not be criminal if committed by an adult or offenses which do not constitute violations of valid court orders, or such nonoffenders as dependent or neglected children, shall not be placed in secure detention facilities or secure correctional facilities."[2] (Hereinafter "subsection 12.)"

---

1. Two federal courts have previously addressed this question. One summarily found a cause of action, *Kentucky Association of Retarded Citizens v. Conn*, 510 F.Supp. 1233, 1247–48 (W.D.Ky.1980), *aff'd*, 674 F.2d 582 (6th Cir.1982), *cert. denied*, 459 U.S. 1041, 103 S.Ct. 457, 74 L.Ed.2d 609 (1983). Another court summarily found no cause of action, *Doe v. McFaul*, 599 F.Supp. 1421, 1430 (S.D.Ohio 1984). Because of the brevity of the analysis in each of these decisions, this is akin to a case of first impression.

2. 1980 and 1984 amendments produced the following proviso:

Failure to achieve compliance with the requirement of subsection (a)(12)(A) of this section within the three-year time limitation shall terminate any state's eligibility for funding under this subpart unless the Administrator determines the state is in substantial compliance with the requirement, through achievement of deinstitutionalization of not less than seventy-five percentum of such juveniles or through removal of one hundred percent of such juveniles from secure correctional facilities, and has made, through appropriate executive or legislative action, an unequivocal commitment to achieving full compliance within a reasonable time not exceeding two years. Section 5633(c).

2. *The ban on regular contact between juveniles and incarcerated adults.* Section 5633(a)(13) of the original Act requires the plan to "provide that juveniles alleged to be or found to be delinquent and youth within the purview of paragraph 12 shall not be detained or confined in any institution in which they have regular contact with adult persons incarcerated because they have been convicted of a crime or are awaiting trial or criminal charges." (Hereinafter "subsection 13.")

3. *The jail removal mandate.* Finding that "the time has come to go farther," Congress added subsection (1)(14) in 1980. H.Rep. No. 946, 96th Cong., 2d Sess. 24 (1980), U.S. Code Cong. & Admin.News 1980, pp. 6098, 6111. As amended in 1984, it states that a plan must "provide that, beginning after the five-year period following December 8, 1980, no juvenile shall be detained or confined in any jail or lockup for adults, except that the Administrator shall, through 1989, promulgate regulations which make exceptions with regard to the detention of juveniles accused of nonstatus offenses who are awaiting an initial court appearance pursuant to an enforceable State law requiring such appearances within 24 hours after being taken into custody (excluding weekends and holidays) provided that such exceptions are limited to areas which—(i) are outside a Standard Metropolitan Statistical Area, (ii) have no existing acceptable alternative placement available, and (iii) are in compliance with the provisions of paragraph 13."[3] (Hereinafter "subsection 14.")

Claiming that Webster County fails to comply with each of these requirements and that the state is not substantially complying with subsections 12 and 14, the plaintiffs seek declaratory, compensatory and equitable relief under § 5633 alone and in combination with § 1983.[4]

I. PRELIMINARY ISSUES

As the plaintiff class is presently certified, its members have been or will be placed in the Webster County Jail by a juvenile court. The county defendants argue that the plaintiffs' § 1983 claims are precluded under the doctrines of res judicata (claim preclusion) and collateral estoppel (issue preclusion) because they could raise these issues in juvenile court.[5] This argument can only pertain to those plaintiffs who have already been placed in the jail, because with the exception of those now in jail, the plaintiffs who would be protected by the injunction have not had their day in court.

[1,2] The Court finds that neither issue nor claim preclusion can bar the claims of the previously jailed plaintiffs. Issue preclusion is unavailable because the defendants have produced no evidence that these issues were actually litigated or necessarily decided in any juvenile court proceedings. *Ideal Mutual Insurance Co. v. Winker*, 319 N.W.2d 289, 296 (Iowa 1982). Iowa law governs the claim preclusive effect of an Iowa juvenile court's judgment, and the Court cannot find an Iowa case in which claim preclusion was successfully asserted against a civil plaintiff because he was a defendant in a prior criminal case, let alone a juvenile court defendant. The *Restatement (Second) of Judgments* does not give prior criminal judgments a claim preclusive effect. See *id.* at § 85 comment (a) (1980). Although a § 1983 plaintiff can be precluded from raising issues which she could have raised in a prior civil action which she initiated, *Migra v. Warren City District Board of Education*, 465 U.S. 75, 104 S.Ct. 892, 79 L.Ed.2d 56 (1984), a footnote in *Migra* suggested that former state court *defendants* should be treated differently because they do not voluntarily go to state court first. *Id.* at 85 n. 7, 104 S.Ct. at 898 n. 7. In

---

3. The 1980 amendment contained a "substantial compliance" provision for subsection 14 which is very similar to the (12)(A) provision quoted in note 2, *supra*. As amended in 1984, it permits the state to retain eligibility after the December 5, 1985 deadline for compliance if the Administrator determines the state has achieved 75% removal and the state has made an unequivocal commitment to achieving compliance by 1988. Section 5633(c).

4. Because the Court finds that a cause of action is available under § 1983 to protect rights created by § 5633, the Court need not decide whether § 5633 itself gives rise to an implied cause of action.

5. The county defendants have raised a related claim that the Court must defer to the state juvenile courts under *Railroad Commission v. Pullman, Co.*, 312 U.S. 496, 61 S.Ct. 643, 85 L.Ed. 971 (1941), or *Younger v. Harris*, 401 U.S. 37, 91 S.Ct. 746, 27 L.Ed.2d 669 (1970). However, a federal court may not use *Pullman* abstention to avoid a purely statutory question, and the *Younger* doctrine is really a form of the irreparable injury equipment. Because the Court finds, *infra*, that the plaintiffs commonly suffer an irreparable injury prior to juvenile court proceedings, the Court cannot defer under *Younger*.

a very important case, the Second Circuit recently held that *Migra* does not apply to federal plaintiffs who were the defendants in a prior state court action. *Texaco v. Pennzoil*, 784 F.2d 1133, 1144 (2d Cir. 1986), *reversed on other grounds*, __ U.S. __, 107 S.Ct. 1519, 95 L.Ed.2d 1 (1987). In light of this authority, the Court finds that an Iowa court would not give a juvenile judge's placement decision a claim preclusive effect. The county defendant's motion to dismiss on this ground is denied.

[3] The defendants assert that the plaintiffs must first file a complaint with the OJJDP, as permitted in 28 C.F.R. § 18.5(j) (1986).[6] They contend that § 18.5(j) is a remedy which must be exhausted and that only the OJJDP has primary jurisdiction to decide whether states have complied with § 5633. If the plaintiffs can proceed under § 1983, no exhaustion requirement applies. *Patsy v. Board of Regents*, 457 U.S. 496, 102 S.Ct. 2557, 73 L.Ed.2d 172 (1982). The doctrine of primary jurisdiction[7] presumes that the plaintiffs can "get relief" administratively, see *Rosado v. Wyman*, 397 U.S. 397, 406 n. 8, 90 S.Ct. 1207, 1214 n. 8, 25 L.Ed.2d 442 (1970); *Chowdhury v. Reading Hospital and Medical Center*, 677 F.2d 317, 320 (3d Cir. 1982). However, the most important form of relief the plaintiffs seek—an order *requiring* compliance—is not available from the OJJDP. See § 18.5(a). The OJJDP can only cut off funding. The doctrine of primary jurisdiction therefore does not bar the plaintiffs' claim.[8]

In briefs filed prior to subsection 14's compliance deadline of December 5, 1985, the defendants argued that plaintiffs' claim under that subsection was not ripe. Following that date, they argued that the claim was not ripe because the Administrator had not yet decided whether the defendants had complied or substantially complied. To the extent that this argument implies that only the OJJDP had jurisdiction to decide whether the defendants satisfy § 5633, the argument merely restates their primary jurisdiction argument which the Court has already rejected. Ripeness depends upon whether the plaintiffs' injuries have occurred or are about to occur, not whether the illegality of that injury has already been established. That question is properly before the Court at this time.

[4] The county defendants have argued that Fed.R.Civ.P. 17 requires a plaintiff class of minors to proceed through a guardian ad litem and have asked the Court to appoint one. Plaintiffs' counsel respond that one of them can represent the class as "next friend." Under standards set out in *Child v. Beame*, 412 F.Supp. 593, 599 (S.D.N.Y. 1976), the Court concludes that the class can be adequately represented by the plaintiffs' counsel, so that a guardian ad litem need not be appointed at this time.

[5] Finally, the Court must decide whether the plaintiffs' JJDPA claim must be dismissed for failure to name an indispensable party. The county defendants argue that the plaintiffs must sue the juvenile judges who order the sheriff to place class members in jail, and that their failure to do so warrants dismissal under Rule 12(b)(7). The Eighth Circuit's decision in *R.W.T. v. Dalton*, 712 F.2d 1225, 1233 (8th Cir. 1983), indicates that juvenile judges are not indispensable parties to actions of this sort. The motion is therefore denied.

---

6. Section 18.5(j) states:

Any person may request the responsible agency official to determine whether a grantee has failed to comply with the terms or the statute under which the grant was awarded, agency regulations or the terms and conditions of the grant. The responsible agency may, in its discretion, conduct an investigation into the matter and, if warranted, make a determination of noncompliance. Only a grantee determined to be in noncompliance may request a compliance hearing.

7. In arguing that the OJJDP has primary jurisdiction, the county defendants rely in part upon deposition testimony from former OJJDP Administrator Alfred Regnery that he "would argue" that the plaintiffs must first use § 18.5(j). Although courts can sometimes defer to allow a nonjudicial resolution of a legal question, the separate question of whether the Court *can* defer is for the Court alone to decide. Cf. *AT & T Technologies, Inc. v. Communication Workers of America*, 475 U.S. 643, 648, 106 S.Ct. 1415, 1418, 89 L.Ed.2d 648 (1986).

8. The Court also believes the OJJDP lacks primary jurisdiction to determine the defendants' compliance with the JJDPA because the issue does not involve "technical questions of fact uniquely within the expertise and experience of an agency." *Nader v. Allegheny Airlines*, 426 U.S. 290, 304, 96 S.Ct. 1978, 1987, 48 L.Ed.2d 643 (1976). The task of applying law to fact is not unusually complex, the standards require little interpretation, and the Court can rely upon the same fact-gathering system of performance reports upon which the OJJDP would rely.

II. THE PLAINTIFFS' § 1983 CAUSE OF ACTION FOR RIGHTS CREATED BY § 5633

Prior to 1980, citizens could only enforce federal statutory rights if a cause of action was expressly provided for in the statute or if one could be implied under general principles stated in *Cort v. Ash*, 422 U.S. 66, 78, 95 S.Ct. 2080, 2087, 45 L.Ed.2d 26 (1975). Under these principles, a cause of action could only be implied if the plaintiff was one of the class for whose especial benefit the statute was enacted, a congressional intent to create a remedy could be found, such a remedy would be consistent with legislative purposes, and it would not inappropriately interfere with a traditionally state area. *Id*. In effect, these requirements placed the burden on the plaintiff to find a specific intent to permit this particular form of a remedy.

Since 1874, § 1983 has expressly provided a private cause of action for claims arising from "the deprivation of any rights, privileges or immunities secured by the Constitution *and laws*" by individuals acting under color of state law. Until *Maine v. Thiboutot*, 448 U.S. 1, 100 S.Ct. 2502, 65 L.Ed.2d 555 (1980), the "and laws" phrase was generally ignored. In *Thiboutot*, the court formally recognized that § 1983 provided a private cause of action for "claims based on purely statutory violations of federal law" by state actors. Now plaintiffs suing state actors who cannot satisfy *Cort v. Ash* by showing that the same Congress which created a statutory right also intended to give them a civil remedy may rely upon the general purpose of § 1983—"to provide a remedy, to be broadly construed, against all forms of official violations of federally protected rights." *Monell v. New York City Department of Social Services*, 436 U.S. 658, 700–701, 98 S.Ct. 2018, 2041, 56 L.Ed.2d 611 (1978).

[6] Two requirements persist. A separate federal statute must create enforceable rights, privileges or immunities. *Pennhurst State School and Hospital v. Halderman*, 451 U.S. 1, 19, 101 S.Ct. 1531, 1540, 67 L.Ed.2d 694 (1981) (hereinafter "*Pennhurst I*"), and Congress must not have specifically foreclosed the § 1983 remedy, *Middlesex County Sewerage Authority v. National Sea Clammers Association*, 453 U.S. 1, 20, 101 S.Ct. 2615, 2626, 69 L.Ed.2d 435 (1981).

A. *Does § 5633 Create Enforceable Rights?*

[7] The easy part of answering this question is deciding where to look; "the key to the inquiry is the intent of the legislature." See *Clammers Association*, 453 U.S. at 13, 101 S.Ct. at 2622; *Hill v. Group Three Housing Development Corp.*, 799 F.2d 385, 394 n. 10 (8th Cir. 1986). The difficult part is deciding what reflects an intent to create a right. As usual, Congress "has voiced its wishes in muted strains and left it to the courts to discern the theme" indirectly. *Rosado v. Wyman*, 390 U.S. at 412, 90 S.Ct. at 1218. If the Court were to define the term "right" so narrowly that no right would exist unless the Court could find an intent to permit a private suit, nothing would be left of *Thiboutot*.[9] On the other hand, the purpose behind the quiet inclusion in § 1983 of the phrase "and laws" is too uncertain to permit that statute to give rise to a remedy against any state official who has violated any federal law. See *Consolidated Freightways Corp. v. Kassel*, 730 F.2d 1139 (8th Cir.1984); *First National Bank of Omaha v. Marquette National Bank*, 636 F.2d 195, 198–99 (8th Cir.1980).

A right was easily found in *Thibotot* because the case involved an entitlement program. The existence of a right was easily rejected in *Pennhurst I*, when plaintiffs sought to enforce a provision labeled as a bill of rights for persons with developmental disabilities, but which created no separate obligation upon those states receiving funds under the law to respect those rights. The Supreme Court found that because the law "does no more than express a congressional preference for certain kinds of treatment," the "rights" described were not rights enforceable under § 1983. 451 U.S. at 19, 101 S.Ct. at 1541.

However, in so finding, the court emphasized that the language in question was too informal to even condition the state's eligibility for funding upon

---

9. For this reason, the Court must reject the urge to analogize § 1983 rights to the rights of third-party beneficiaries in contract law, because in most states third-party beneficiary rights exist only where both contracting parties intended to create a remedy enforceable in court by third parties. *Martinez v. Socoma Companies, Inc.*, 11 Cal.3d 394, 113 Cal.Rptr. 585, 521 P.2d 841 (1974): *Restatement (Second) of Contracts* §§ 304 and 313.

compliance therewith. *Id.* at 13, 19, 20 n. 15, 21–22, 101 S.Ct. at 1537, 1540, 1541 n. 14, 1542. For that reason, it did not fully consider the Solicitor General's position that a § 1983 right would exist if the law created conditions upon the state's eligibility for grants. *Id.* at 22, 101 S.Ct. at 1542.

The Supreme Court recently decided a case presenting that issue. In *Wright v. Roanoke Redevelopment and Housing Authority,* __ U.S. __, 107 S.Ct. 766, 93 L.Ed.2d 781 (1987), tenants in federally subsidized low-income housing sued their public housing authority, alleging that it overbilled them for their utilities and thereby violated a federal rent ceiling. The ceiling was an express funding condition; if a housing authority violated the standard, the agency could have cut off funds. *Id.* at ___, 107 S.Ct. at 773. The Fourth Circuit Court of Appeals had ruled that the rent ceiling did not create § 1983 rights because it was "highly unlikely that Congress intended federal courts to make the necessary computations regarding utility allowances that would be required to adjudicate individual claims of right." 771 F.2d 833, 836–37 (4th Cir.1985). The Fourth Circuit had also reasoned that "the existence of such a right is essentially negatived by the provisions of the annual contributions contract" between the defendants and HUD permitting HUD to sue local authorities which violated the ceiling. *Id.* at 837–38 n. 9.

The Supreme Court reversed the Fourth Circuit, finding "little substance" to the claim that the amendment created no rights. The Supreme Court merely noted that the utility rule was a "mandatory" limitation, and that "the intent to benefit tenants is undeniable." __ U.S. at __, 107 S.Ct. at 774.

The reasoning of the Fourth Circuit in that case and the defendants in this case—that an agency's right to cut off funds forecloses recognition of a § 1983 right of beneficiaries—is inconsistent with the Supreme Court's decision in *Wright.* Furthermore, the Supreme Court did not decide this issue as the Fourth Circuit had and the defendants would, by asking whether Congress would have intended federal courts to decide whether the obligations were violated; it merely looked to the mandatory nature of the defendant's obligation and the clarity of the intent to benefit the tenants.

The Court finds that the same indices of an intent to create a right are present in this case. In enacting subsections 12 through 14, Congress clearly intended to confer a special benefit upon a distinct class—detained juveniles.[10] The county defendants would characterize the subsections as an attempt to solve a societal problem, and the Court does not necessarily disagree. But if the public at large also benefits from these requirements, it is only because juveniles benefit. *Compare California v. Sierra Club,* 451 U.S. 287, 295, 101 S.Ct. 1775, 1780, 68 L.Ed.2d 101 (1981).

This conclusion is supported by the phrasing of subsection 14, a factor which the Supreme Court has considered important in other cases. In *Universities Research Association v. Coutu,* 450 U.S. 754, 772, 101 S.Ct. 1451, 1462, 67 L.Ed.2d 662 (1981), the court held that no private cause of action would be implied from § 1 of the Davis-Bacon Act in part because it was "simply phrased as a directive to federal agencies engaged in the disbursement of funds," and was not drafted with an unmistakable focus on a benefited class. *Id.* The case the *Coutu* court sought to distinguish, *Cannon v. University of Chicago,* 441 U.S. 677, 99 S.Ct. 1946, 60 L.Ed.2d 560 (1979), involved a statute phrased much like subdivision 14's ("no juvenile shall be detained . . .") requirement.[11] In *Cannon,* the court found an unmistakable focus on a benefited class from the phrasing of Title IX, 20 U.S.C. § 1681, which provides that "no person in the United States shall, on the basis of sex . . . be subject to discrimination under any educational program or activity receiving federal financial assistance."[12]

---

10. The House Report accompanying the 1980 amendment which added subsection (14) stated:
   Witnesses during the hearing pointed to potential physical and sexual abuse encountered by juveniles incarcerated in adult jails. It was pointed out that in 1978, the suicide rate for juveniles incarcerated in adult jails was approximately seven times the rate of children held in secure juvenile detention facilities. One Department of Justice official termed this a "national catastrophe." H.Rep. No. 946 at 24, U.S.Code Cong. & Admin.News 1980 at 6111.

11. Of course, subsection 14 has an exception. But as Fourth Amendment case law shows, rights can have many exceptions and still be considered "rights."

12. As a test for the existence of a right, this semantic distinction has its limitations. See, e.g., U.S. Const. Amend. 1 (Congress shall make no law. . . .). Thus, the fact that subsections 12 and 13 are not phrased like Title IX is not enough reason to find that they do not create rights, when juveniles are the primary beneficiaries of their enactment.

Furthermore, unlike the preferences in *Pennhurst I* but like the utility regulations in *Wright*, subsections 12 through 14 create mandatory funding eligibility conditions to which states such as Iowa subject themselves by receiving JJDPA funds. If Iowa has not satisfied the mandates, either through full compliance or substantial compliance and an unequivocal commitment to comply, the state loses its eligibility. Section 5633(c). For this reason, the subsections are not simply a "nudge in a preferred direction," as the defendants argue.

It is also very significant that these subsections are more than funding conditions; they have given rise to duties. In order to receive funds, the state has been required to describe its plans, procedures and timetables for "assuring" that the requirements of subsections 12 through 14 have been met or would be met by the proper deadline. 28 C.F.R. §§ 31.303(c)(1), 31.303(d)(i) and 31.303(e)(1) (1986). This language of "assurance" leaves little doubt that by receiving funds, the state has assumed responsibility for seeing that the eligibility conditions would occur.[13]

The state defendants have argued that the mandates of subsections 12 and 14 are too generalized to give rise to an individual right because substantial compliance provisions permit the state to temporarily comply while only reducing jailing of juveniles and status offenders by 75%. This is an attractive argument, but the Eighth Circuit Court of Appeals has impliedly rejected a similar theory. In *Crawford v. Janklow*, 710 F.2d 1321 (8th Cir. 1983), the plaintiffs were low-income persons who had been excluded from eligibility for assistance under South Dakota's implementation plan for the Low Income Home Energy Assistance Act. The court recognized that the responsible federal agency could only enforce the grant conditions by withholding funds, and that this could only be done in cases of substantial noncompliance. *Id.* at 1325, 1326, *citing* 42 U.S.C. § 8626(a)(1) (1982). Nevertheless, the court viewed this provision as another reason to recognize a cause of action, as a sign that "such a private remedy is

virtually a necessity to complete the legislative scheme of effective and efficient distribution of benefits." *Id.* at 1325. Furthermore, the substantial compliance exception to subsection 14 is not presently available to Iowa because it has not demonstrated an unequivocal commitment through legislative or executive action to achieving full compliance by 1988.

After looking at § 5633 for the factors which the Supreme Court and the Eighth Circuit have considered as reflective of an intent to create a right, the Court finds that subsections 12 through 14 create enforceable rights.

B. Have the Defendants Demonstrated that Congress Has Foreclosed Enforcement of These Rights in a § 1983 Action?

[8] Once the plaintiffs demonstrate that the statute creates enforceable rights, the burden shifts to the defendants to demonstrate that Congress intended to foreclose their enforcement through § 1983. *Wright* at __, 107 S.Ct. at 771. This burden is particularly heavy because the Supreme Court has limited the sources from which such an intent may be inferred to "an express provision[14] or other specific evidence in the statute itself." *Id.* Even if the statute provides its own remedial mechanism, it must be "sufficiently comprehensive and effective to raise a clear inference that Congress intended to foreclose a § 1983 cause of action." *Id.*

The defendants have argued that the OJJDP's power to terminate funding is a sufficiently comprehensive remedy for violations of any rights created by § 5633. However, the Court cannot confuse remedies with mere sanctions. If the OJJDP cuts off funding for Iowa's failure to live up to its obligations, none of the juveniles whose rights were violated by improper placement in jails will be helped in the least bit. Because the power to cut off funds is "woefully inadequate as to persons in dire need" of the statute's benefits, *Crawford*, 710 F.2d at 1326, it cannot be termed a remedy in the proper sense of that term.

---

13. For reasons best stated by Judge Cardozo, the Court finds a duty without asking whether Iowa formally promised to comply with these requirements:

> The law has outgrown its primitive stage of formalism where the precise word was the sovereign talisman, and every slip was fatal. It takes a broader view today. A promise may be lacking but yet the whole writing may be "instinct with an obligation," imperfectly expressed.

Wood v. Lucy, Lady Duff-Gordon, 222 N.Y. 88, 118 N.E. 214 (N.Y.1917). As administered by the OJJDP, § 5633 is instinct with an obligation by any reasonable reading of the statute and its regulations.

14. The defendants do not argue that an express provision in the JJDPA forecloses private enforcement.

Cf. *Wright*, ___ U.S. at ___, 107 S.Ct. at 773; *Cannon*, 441 U.S. at 704–05, 99 S.Ct. at 1961–62; *Rosado*, 397 U.S. at 420, 90 S.Ct. at 1221.

The remaining arguments of the defendants involving the statute itself presume that its provisions must be read exclusively. Under this theory, provisions showing a congressional intent to assist states constitute evidence of an intent to only assist, and provisions showing a congressional intent to cut off funds from noncomplying states show an intent to only cut off funds. However, the Supreme Court has discouraged this type of " 'excursion into extrapolation of legislative intent', *Cort v. Ash*, 422 U.S. at 83 n. 14 [95 S.Ct. at 2090 n. 14], unless there is other, more convincing, evidence that Congress meant to exclude the remedy." *Cannon*, 441 U.S. at 711, 99 S.Ct. at 1965.

Having failed to satisfy the tests in *Wright*, the county defendants attempt to distinguish *Wright* on its facts. In *Wright*, the Supreme Court noted that a comment section accompanying relevant regulations indicated that the responsible agency believed that a private cause of action was not foreclosed. In this case, former Administrator Regnery of the OJJDP made statements in a deposition which the county defendants believe show an opposite belief.

The Court recognizes that "some deference" is often due to agency interpretations of the laws they are charged with applying. *NLRB v. Hearst Publications, Inc.*, 322 U.S. 111, 64 S.Ct. 851, 88 L.Ed. 1170 (1944). But in deciding pure questions of law, the Court is reluctant to give equal respect to responses in a deposition given by a single administrator and the more formal agency statements involved in *Wright*.[15] Furthermore, Regnery's testimony shows that he never addressed the question now before the Court—whether the statute shows that Congress wished to foreclose enforcement through § 1983. His most meaningful deposition testimony merely shows that he would require the plaintiffs to

exhaust the procedures provided by 28 C.F.R. § 18. (Deposition of Alfred Regnery at 125).[16]

The defendants also contend that the failure of two bills which would have given juveniles an express cause of action to prevent the jailing of status offenders and the placement of juveniles in adult jails indicates that Congress intended to foreclose a § 1983 action to enforce similar rights created by the JJDPA and its amendments. S. 520 and S. 522, 98th Cong., 1st Sess. (1983). While this is not evidence "from the statute itself," as *Wright* requires, it is relevant under separate principles described in *Heckler v. Day*, 467 U.S. 104, 104 S.Ct. 2249, 81 L.Ed.2d 88 (1984). In *Day*, a federal court improperly granted a form of class-wide injunctive relief for agency violations of law after Congress had specifically considered, rejected and criticized that particular form of relief. The court noted that "our decision in this case is limited to the question of whether, in view of the *unequivocally clear intent of Congress to the contrary*, it is nevertheless appropriate for a federal court" to enter such relief. *Id.* at 104 n. 33, 104 S.Ct. at 2257 n. 33 (emphasis added).

The failure of these bills to progress does not show "the unequivocally clear intent of Congress" to foreclose a private cause of action to enforce the JJDPA. Unlike the JJDPA, these bills would have banned jailing practices, in every state, regardless of whether the state accepted JJDPA funds. Furthermore, the text of each bill included an unqualified declaration that the jailing of status offenders and the placement of juveniles in adult jails is unconstitutional. As the hearing record shows, these provisions were more controversial than the private cause of action provisions. *Public Welfare of Juveniles*, *supra*, at 1–36. Thus, the Court cannot attribute the failure of these bills to any particular section contained therein.

For the reasons stated above, the Court finds that Congress did not foreclose a § 1983 remedy, and such a remedy is therefore available.

---

15. The marginal value of Mr. Regnery's deposition testimony is apparent from one of the excerpts upon which the county defendants rely most heavily:

Q. You don't think [juveniles are] third-party beneficiaries to an arrangement between the government and the state?

A. I suppose the citizens of the state, all of the citizens. I'm not sure any of them have any better rights than any others. But I really don't know the answer to the question. (Deposition of Alfred Regnery at 72).

16. The county defendants also rely on Mr. Regnery's testimony before a Senate committee in opposition to S. 520 and S. 522. Upon review of this testimony, it is again apparent that Mr. Regnery did not address the question of whether the Congresses which passed the JJDPA and its amendments intended to foreclose a remedy. At most, it shows his own general hostility to civil rights suits and his belief that the JJDPA "is still working." *Public Welfare of Juveniles: Hearing Before the Subcommittee on the Constitution of the Senate Judiciary Committee*, 98th Cong., 2d Sess. 15 (1984).

III. ARE THE PLAINTIFFS ENTITLED TO A PRELIMINARY INJUNCTION?

[9] The plaintiffs seek an order which would (1) forbid the defendants from permitting certain jailing practices, (2) prohibit the defendants from receiving or spending OJJDP funds until compliance with the JJDPA is achieved, and (3) require the State to pay back funds already received from the OJJDP if compliance is not achieved. Because the plaintiffs have failed to demonstrate that they have standing or a cause of action to seek the second or third types of relief, that part of their motion must be denied. See *Linda R. S. v. Richard D.*, 410 U.S. 614, 93 S.Ct. 1146, 35 L.Ed.2d 536 (1973).[17]

[10] The plaintiffs seek to restrain three jailing practices as violative of the JJDPA and the Constitution, and have moved to restrain two other practices which they contend are prohibited by state law. However, they have not amended their complaints to state any state law claims, and even under liberal notice pleading rules, the Court cannot read state law claims into the plaintiffs' pleadings.[18] Thus, the only relief the Court can properly consider granting at this time is a preliminary injunction order requiring the defendants to comply with the Constitution or federal law. The Court must consider the statutory claims first.

Whether a preliminary injunction should issue involves consideration of

1. The threat of irreparable harm to the movant;
2. The state of the balance between this harm and the injury that granting the injunction will inflict upon the other parties litigant;
3. The probability that the movant will succeed on the merits; and
4. The public interest.

Dataphase Systems, Inc. v. C.L. Systems, 640 F.2d 109, 113 (8th Cir. 1981).

1. Probability of Success on the Merits

The plaintiffs have already demonstrated that subsections 12–14 of § 5633 create rights enforceable under § 1983. The critical question is whether the plaintiffs are likely to show that the defendants are violating each of those rights. For the reasons below, the Court finds that the plaintiffs are unlikely to show violations of subsections 12 and 13, but are very likely to prove that subsection 14 is being violated.

Neither Congress nor the OJJDP have demanded perfect compliance with plan requirements by states receiving funds under the JJDPA.[19] Thus, the OJJDP has created provisions which excuse minor failures to comply with subsections 12 through 14, see 46 Fed.Reg. 2566 (Jan. 9, 1981) (policy and criteria for de minimis exceptions to subsection (a)(12)(A)) and 28 C.F.R. § 31.303(f)(6)(ii) and (iii) (1986) (regulations creating *de minimis* exceptions to subsections 13 and 14). Thus, if a state's failure to comply is considered *de minimis* under these regulations, the state is technically not out of compliance.[20]

[11] The state's failure to completely satisfy subsection 12 by deinstitutionalizing all status offenders must be considered a *de minimis* failure. Under the 1981 *de minimis* regulations, the state must report the number of accused status offenders and nonoffenders held in secure detention facilities or secure correctional facilities in excess of 24 hours and the number of adjudicated status offenders and nonoffenders held in such facilities; if the sum is less than

---

17. The state defendants' motion for summary judgment is granted insofar as it challenges these two types of relief although the Court does not reach the Eleventh Amendment issues raised by the state in opposition to this relief.

18. The only references to state law in the Second Amended Complaint are an assertion that the Court has pendent jurisdiction over the plaintiffs' state law claims and a statement that the plaintiffs have rights under state and federal contract law. Because these conclusory statements fail to provide notice to the defendants of what the plaintiffs' state claims would be, the plaintiffs have failed to satisfy Fed.R.Civ.P. 8. *Rotolo v. Borough of Charleroi*, 532 F.2d 920, 922–23 (3d Cir. 1976).

19. The House Committee Report accompanying the 1980 amendment states that "the committee expects a 'rule of reason' to be followed in the implementation of § 223(a)(14)." H.Rep. 946 at 26, 1980 U.S.Cong. & Admin.News 1980 at 6113.

20. The *de minimis* exceptions should not be confused with the substantial compliance provisions of § 5633(c). The *de minimis* exceptions excuse minor deviations from full compliance once the statute requires full compliance, and the substantial compliance provisions permit a state to delay compliance with *de minimis* deviations by demonstrating substantial progress toward achieving full compliance, as demonstrated by a 75% reduction and an unequivocal commitment through executive or legislative action toward achieving full compliance by 1988. There are no *de minimis* exceptions to the substantial compliance provisions.

5.8 persons for every 100,000 juveniles in Iowa (or 47.9[21]), the failure is *de minimis*. 46 Fed.Reg. at 2567. The most recent monitoring report indicates that only 23 status offenders and nonoffenders were jailed in Iowa during the last reporting period for the requisite length of time (State Monitoring Report at 4). This is well within the regulations. Thus, the plaintiffs are not entitled to an order compelling compliance with subsection 12.

[12] The state's failure to achieve complete separation of juveniles and adult offenders under subsection 13 also appears to be a *de minimis* failure. While the state report indicates that 50 juveniles were incarcerated in circumstances that would be violative of subsection 13, that constitutes a *de minimis* failure if Iowa law clearly prohibited each instance, such instances were isolated, and existing state mechanisms make repetition unlikely. 28 C.F.R. § 31.303(f)(6)(ii)(B). Iowa was found to have satisfied these requirements in 1984 (Exhibit A), and the plaintiffs have not shown that the state would fail to meet these requirements this year. For these reasons, the plaintiffs' request for an order requiring compliance with subsection 13 must be denied.

[13] The jail removal mandate of subsection 14 is a different story. The state has all but conceded that it has not either substantially complied or fully complied with this provision. (Transcript of Oral Arguments at 30).[22] Using the state's own data in a formula for analyzing it which puts the state in the most favorable light,[23] the Court finds that the state has achieved no better than a 44% reduction in the jailing of juveniles. Moreover, there is every indication that the jailing of juveniles will continue at an impermissibly high rate. For these reasons, the plaintiffs have shown a very high probability of success on the merits of their claim that the defendants have violated subsection 14 and will violate it in the future.

2. *Irreparable Injury*

The plaintiffs must also show that without an injunction, they will suffer an immediate and irreparable injury. *Fenner v. Boykin*, 271 U.S. 240, 243, 46 S.Ct. 492, 493, 70 L.Ed. 927 (1926). A deprivation of the plaintiffs' rights not to be placed in an adult jail or lockup would fulfill the injury requirement, *Henry v. Greenville Airport Commission*, 284 F.2d 631, 633 (4th Cir. 1960), and without an order, those who become class members would by the nature of their membership in the class suffer this injury. In light of the number of such placements during the previous reporting period, the Court finds that the threat of future placement of class members in adult jails or lockups is sufficiently immediate to ripen the plaintiffs' claim and to satisfy the immediacy requirement. See *Kolender v. Lawson*, 461 U.S. 352, 355 n. 3, 103 S.Ct. 1855, 1857 n. 3, 75 L.Ed.2d 903 (1983). Because placement in jail often precedes the only formal adjudication at which their right not to be placed there could conceivably be asserted, see Iowa Code § 232.22(4), the injury will commonly occur before any remedy at law is available. Compare *Trucke v. Erlemeier*, 657 F.Supp. 1382 (N.D.Iowa 1987). Therefore, the irreparability requirement has been satisfied. *Gerstein v. Pugh*, 420 U.S. 103, 108 n. 9, 95 S.Ct. 854, 860 n. 9, 43 L.Ed.2d 54 (1975); *R.W.T. v. Dalton*, 712 F.2d 1225, 1234 (8th Cir.1983).

3. *Balancing the Hardships and the Public Interest*

Each party vigorously argues that the balancing of hardships and the public interest tip[s] in their favor. The county defendants argue that the injury to the plaintiffs which would occur through placement in adult jail or lockup is too small to outweigh the "compelling interest of the state of Iowa in protecting Iowa citizens from the crimes which might be committed upon it by juvenile perpetrators." The plaintiffs argue that the jailing of juveniles merely serves the convenience of judges and law officers. They contend that the defendants cannot rely upon the objective of protecting society because their own statistics indicate that the majority of juvenile jailings only last for twelve hours or less, and conclude

---

21. There were 825,573 juveniles in Iowa in 1980 according to the most recent census. (State Monitoring Report for 1986 at 4).

22. In 1984 Congress created an exception to subsection 14, so that in theory the state might satisfy this subsection if every juvenile placed in Iowa jails beyond the de minimis level fit within this exception. However, that exception does not apply to juveniles jailed in Iowa's eight largest metropolitan areas, and the testimony of Tim Buzzell indicates that the number of juvenile jailings in Iowa's metropolitan areas alone might place the state out of compliance with subsection 14.

23. Where x equals the total number of juvenile-type offenders held in adult jails and lockups and y equals the total number of accused and adjudicated status offenders and nonoffenders held in adult jails and lockups: [x for 1980 (or 4031) plus y for 1977 (or 2159)] minus [x for 1986 (or 3232) plus y for 1986 (or 230)] equals a reduction of 2728, or 44%.

that even with a "wholesale release of all juveniles, there is simply no risk of harm or injury to any other parties litigant."

The Court must evaluate the hardships and the public interest by reference to some set of values and priorities. However, the Supreme Court has consistently held that when balancing the hardships of enforcing federal law, a court cannot substitute its own values for the discernible values of Congress. "When Congress itself has struck the balance, and has defined the weight to be given the competing interests, a court of equity is not justified in ignoring that pronouncement under the guise of exercising equitable discretion." *Youngstown Sheet and Tube Co. v. Sawyer*, 343 U.S. 579, 609–10, 72 S.Ct. 863, 897, 96 L.Ed. 1153 (1952) (Frankfurter, J., concurring). As the Supreme Court noted in affirming a district court which enforced a federal law protecting the snail darter as an endangered species by enjoining the completion of a dam, "once Congress, exercising its delegated powers, has decided the order of priorities in a given area, it is for the executive to administer the laws and for the courts to enforce them when enforcement is sought." *Tennessee Valley Authority v. Hill*, 437 U.S. 153, 194, 98 S.Ct. 2279, 2302, 57 L.Ed.2d 117 (1978).

Whether this Court likes it or not, Congress has consistently valued the removal of juveniles from adult jails over the administrative, protective and penological advantages of placing them there. It makes little difference at this stage that these values were embodied in a funding program rather than a nationwide prohibition. If the state did not share Congress' priorities or did not wish to implement them, it could have merely refused to seek OJJDP funding.

The greatest difficulty arises from the fact that the state and its subdivisions have failed to build an adequate "safety net" of juvenile detention centers and foster homes which might lessen the immediate risk to society of compliance with the jail removal mandate. Hearing testimony indicated that while many counties have risen to the occasion by constructing juvenile detention center of sufficient size to absorb the effects of jail removal, the facilities in many of Iowa's most populous counties can only accommodate a small fraction of the juveniles incarcerated in that county's jails. (Testimony of Tim Buzzell at 51–54). Thus, the court must acknowledge that if it enters the order requested, in the short run juvenile authorities will probably release more accused and adjudged juvenile offenders back into society, and those authorities may send away to re-

formatories a greater number of the most dangerous delinquents who would have been kept closer to their families in county jails. However, the Court has no legitimate basis to conclude that Congress would find this result so objectionable that it would prefer to have the Court tolerate the regular deprivation of congressionally created rights.

Furthermore, it would be a mistake to view this issue as a choice between protecting criminals and protecting society from crime. Many supporters of the JJDPA and the jail removal mandate believe that placing juveniles in adult jails fosters more serious criminal conduct. Senator Arlen Specter—no coddler of criminals—stated that "the consequence of mixing juveniles and adults is simply to teach juveniles how to commit more crimes. They are training schools, and I have seen that again and again and again with the experience I have had as a prosecuting attorney." *Public Welfare of Juveniles: Hearing Before the Subcommittee on the Constitution of the Senate Judiciary Committee*, 98th Cong., 2d Sess. 10 (1984).

The defendants have argued that a compliance order would effectively compel the state and its subdivisions to spend hundreds of thousands of tax dollars to build separate juvenile facilities. It is significant for Eleventh Amendment purposes that the plaintiffs have not asked the Court to order such expenditures; they have asked the Court to enjoin the defendants from violating federally created rights. However likely it is that those officials would react to such an order by spending tax money, that discretion "rests entirely with the state, its agencies, [its subdivisions,] and legislature, not with the federal court." *Quern v. Jordan*, 440 U.S. 332, 348, 99 S.Ct. 1139, 1149, 59 L.Ed.2d 358 (1979). In considering this cost as a legitimate hardship to be balanced, the Court must remember that if jail removal was politically and economically cheap, the need for congressional action might never have arisen. For this reason, such costs must be kept in perspective.

The Court finds that the balance of hardships, as evaluated with congressional priorities in mind, tips in favor of the plaintiffs, and that the public interest, as defined by Congress, would be served by some type of compliance order. The Court must now decide what type of order shall issue.

IV. TAILORING THE REMEDY

Before the Court can decide what kind of order should issue, it must decide whether it has the authority to bind each defendant plaintiffs have named. The greatest limitation on that authority is § 1983 itself. As the Supreme Court held in *Rizzo v. Goode*, 423 U.S. 362, 370–71, 96 S.Ct. 598, 603–04, 46 L.Ed.2d 561 (1975), "the plain words of the statute impose liability—whether in the form of payment of redressive damages or being placed under an injunction—only for conduct which 'subjects, or causes to be subjected' the complainant to the deprivation of a right secured by the Constitution and laws." *Rizzo* requires a link between the affirmative conduct of liable defendants and the deprivation of the plaintiffs' rights. *Id.* at 377, 96 S.Ct. at 607.

[14] The Court has the authority to bind Sheriff Griggs because the placement of juveniles in the Webster County Jail is the relevant deprivation, and he is involved, however involuntarily, in the task of placing juveniles in the jail. See Iowa Code § 256.2. It makes no difference that the Sheriff has played no role in Iowa's participation in the JJDPA program; that participation merely gave rise to the plaintiffs' rights, and those rights can be deprived by individuals with no connection to the program.[24]

[15] While the state defendants' connection to each deprivation is less direct, the logic of the Eighth Circuit's decision in *Messimer v. Lockhart*, 702 F.2d 729 (8th Cir. 1983), leads the Court to conclude that they may be bound.[25] In *Messimer*, a prisoner sued the director of a State Department of Corrections, complaining of administrative decisions made by his subordinates at one of the state's prisons. Even though the director could not be liable for their actions under the common law doctrine of *respondeat superior*, the court found the "affirmative link" required by *Rizzo*:

> The plaintiffs are not complaining about isolated instances of alleged mistreatment; they are complaining about policy decisions made by those in charge of the prison. Lockhart has a statutory duty to administer the

Department of Corrections and supervise the administration of all institutions, facilities, and services under the Department's jurisdiction. [Statutory citations omitted]. The state conceded at oral argument that Lockhart has the authority to change policies instituted by the warden of the Cummins Unit. Thus, Lockhart may be responsible for his own failure to act.

Messimer, 702 F.2d at 732.

In this case, the state defendants did not concede that they have the authority to prevent the jailing of juveniles. It is the state itself which made a policy decision to authorize the jailing of juveniles, see Iowa Code § 232.22, and the state defendants have argued that the separation of powers in Iowa government limits the authority of Governor Branstad and Mr. Crandall to unilaterally change the course of county and municipal jailing practices. However, Congress evidently foresaw this problem and took an important step to solve it. Subsection 2 of the JJDPA's state plan requirements requires state plans to "contain satisfactory evidence that the state agency designated in accordance with paragraph 1 . . . has or will have the authority, by legislation if necessary, to implement such plan in conformity with this part." § 5633(a)(2). The Court does not know how the state fulfilled this requirement, but it does know that the state has received funds in every year since this provision was enacted. (Exhibit A). The Court infers from this that the state's plan contained assurances of agency authority upon which the OJJDP relied in extending funds. The Court has examined that the legislature need not act before the state defendants or agencies accountable to Defendant Branstad can take meaningful steps to comply with the jail removal mandate. The Iowa Department of Corrections is authorized under Iowa Code § 356.36 to "draw up minimum standards for the regulation of jails . . . and municipal holding facilities."[26] While a moratorium was adopted in 1981 which prevented

---

24. Contrary to Defendant Griggs' argument that he should not be bound because he would be immune under principles of qualified immunity or derivative judicial immunity, the fact that an official is immune from liability for damages does not preclude injunctive or declaratory relief against him. *Gross v. Tazewell County Jail*, 533 F.Supp. 413, 419 (W.D.Va.1982).

25. When the plaintiffs' second amended complaint was filed, Defendant Richard Ramsey was executive director of Iowa's Criminal and Juvenile Justice Planning Agency. At the hearing, Agency Employee Tim Buzzell testified that Mr. Jack Crandall has replaced Defendant Ramsey in that position. Although Defendant Ramsey was sued in both his official and individual capacities, the Court finds no basis to bind him in his individual capacity. Because Mr. Crandall appears to have taken over Defendant Ramsey's official capacities, he will be substituted for Ramsey for purposes of this order under Rule 25(d)(1). Plaintiffs' counsel should notify the Court if they contend Mr. Ramsey should remain a party to this action.

26. The state defendants object that the Department of Corrections has not been named as a defendant and cannot be named under *Alabama v. Pugh*, 438 U.S. 781, 98 S.Ct. 3057, 57 L.Ed.2d 1114 (1978), because it is an agency of the state. The state defendants do not contend that Governor Branstad cannot be named and enjoined in his official capacity, however. See *Ex parte Young*, 209

the implementation of enforcement of such administrative rules, that moratorium is to terminate when a "needs assessment of the individual county jails" has been completed, which presumably has occurred in the six years since the moratorium began or can occur by the end of the year. While the most direct solution may be to amend the statute authorizing judges to place juveniles in jail, see § 232.22, the Court recognizes that this is only one of several ways to meet the state's federal obligations. Thus, the Court finds that the "authority" element of the *Messimer* logic is satisfied. The Court finds that the state defendants' special duty to use this authority arises from the state's assurances that subsection 14 would be satisfied.[27]

[16] The Webster County Board of Supervisors cannot be bound, however. Unlike the state defendants, none of the supervisors appear[s] to have made assurances which would give rise to a duty to keep juveniles out of jail. The only relevant "affirmative conduct" which the Court can attribute to them is their decision well before the December 1985 deadline for compliance to construct a section for juveniles in their jail. This is not sufficient to create the "affirmative link" to each deprivation which *Rizzo* requires. Moreover, they do not appear to be liable in their official capacities under a "official policy or custom" theory because the plaintiffs have not yet demonstrated a county policy to place juveniles in jail after December 1985, and the supervisors do not appear to be the "officials responsible for establishing final policy with respect to the subject matter in question." *Williams v. Butler*, 802 F.2d 296 (8th Cir.1986) (quoting the plurality opinion in *Pembaur v. Cincinnati*, 475 U.S. 469, 106 S.Ct. 1292, 1300, 89 L.Ed.2d 452 (1986)). For the same reasons, the Court finds that the county itself cannot be bound.

[17] Whether the sheriff and the two state defendants *should* be bound is a different question, and the answer will depend upon the form of relief that the Court deems appropriate. The plaintiffs have asked the Court to forbid "the defendants, their officers, agents, employees, attorneys, successors in office and other persons acting in concert or participation with them from confining plaintiffs and any members of the plaintiff class in any Iowa adult jail or municipal lockups. . . ." For the reasons below, the Court finds that even if this kind of absolute prohibition is authorized by the JJDPA, considerations of equity and comity require the Court to adopt a less intrusive and more flexible approach.

Not every instance of juvenile jailing after December 1985 constitutes a violation of § 5633. A *de minimis* exception to subsection 14 has been created. See 28 C.F.R. § 31.303(f)(6)(iii). Furthermore, if Iowa were to satisfy the substantial compliance provisions of § 5633(c), hundreds of juveniles could be jailed this year without preventing the state from showing the 75% reduction needed to preserve its eligibility for funding.

The state does not presently qualify for either the *de minimis* exception or the substantial compliance provision. It cannot qualify for the *de minimis* exception without a "state law, court rule, or other statewide executive or judicial policy" which clearly prohibits detentions in violation of subsection 14, see 28 C.F.R. § 31.303(f)(6)(iii)(A)(1); and cannot qualify for the substantial compliance provision without "legislative or executive action" showing an unequivocal commitment to achieving full compliance by 1988. See § 5633(c). Thus, a strict interpretation of the JJDPA and its regulations suggests that until these kinds of legal changes are made, the state can only comply by totally complying with the jail removal mandate.

However, federal courts should avoid entering unworkable and excessively intrusive injunctive relief. *O'Shea v. Littleton*, 414 U.S. 488, 500, 94 S.Ct. 669, 678, 38 L.Ed.2d 674 (1974). Under a total compliance order, each juvenile arrest or detention would present an opportunity for contempt. As the inevitable instances of juvenile jailing occur, the Court's docket could fill with requests for emergency relief, and its duty to enforce obedience to its own decrees could degenerate into day-to-day intervention into juvenile justice proceedings. As anything

---

U.S. 123, 28 S.Ct. 441, 52 L.Ed. 714 (1908). Because the Department of Corrections is accountable to the governor, the Court finds that the plaintiffs' failure to name corrections officials as separate defendants is not a fatal omission. See Fed.R.Civ.P. 65(d).

27. If actual knowledge that deprivations are occurring is a third prerequisite to the state defendants' liability—compare *Tatum v. Houser*, 642 F.2d 253, 254 (8th Cir.1981), with *Villaneuva v. George*, 659 F.2d 851, 854–55 (8th Cir.1981), the Court finds that the plaintiffs are likely to show that Branstad and Crandall have such knowledge as a result of the December 1986 report. The Court emphasizes that the state defendants are not considered liable simply because they have the authority to prevent known deprivations from occurring. In this case, an additional factor is present—the state's *duty* to prevent them from occurring—which will seldom be present in other § 1983 cases.

but a last resort, such an order would disturb "the special delicacy of the adjustment to be preserved between federal equitable power and State administration of its own law." *City of Los Angeles v. Lyons*, 461 U.S. 95, 112, 103 S.Ct. 1660, 1670, 75 L.Ed.2d 675 (1983); *Stefanelli v. Minard*, 342 U.S. 117, 120, 72 S.Ct. 118, 120, 96 L.Ed. 138 (1951).

At the same time, the Court is aware that other states have achieved remarkable progress toward full compliance within very short periods of time. Appendix B of the OJJDP's most recent summary of state compliance, which is attached to Exhibit A, compares the number of juveniles held in adult jails and lockups in 1985 with the number reported only one year before. In twelve states, juvenile jailings declined over 75% that year, and in Texas, juvenile jailings declined from 12,353 to 45. This data suggests that Iowa could achieve substantial compliance or full compliance with *de minimis* exceptions by the end of this year by modeling its policy after any of a number of other states.

The state will be permitted to submit a plan for achieving a combination of policy changes and reductions in the rate of juvenile jailing which would place the state in compliance with the JJDPA by the end of this year. The choice of whether to achieve substantial compliance, or total compliance will be up to the state. Any particular decision to place a juvenile in jail will not constitute contempt and will not cause the Court to intervene. It will be the primary responsibility of the state defendants and not the Court to reduce juvenile jailings to a legal rate. However, a failure to do so will constitute contempt, and in this respect, the plan the state submits must be fundamentally different from the plans it has submitted to the OJJDP.[28] The plan should be submitted by April 30, 1987.

Whether Defendant Griggs should be bound will depend upon the nature of the plan submitted; if the state defendants present an effective plan which does not rely upon the Court's power to enjoin Griggs, the Court has no reason to do so. For the same reason, the Court will hold the plaintiffs' motion

for certification of a defendant class in abeyance pending receipt of the plan. The plaintiffs have moved for recertification of the plaintiff class to include "all juveniles who are currently or will in the future be confined in any county jail or municipal lockup within the state of Iowa." The Court will take this matter up at its next hearing, but the state should prepare its plan under the assumption that the Court will either recertify the plaintiff class as requested, or refuse to recertify it for the sole reason that an expansion of the class would be superfluous, as the county defendants argue.[29]

CONCLUSION

This Court recognizes that some might contend that it is acting outside of its normal scope of authority in entering this order, or that the order borders on "lawmaking." This Court has carefully weighed this matter and is persuaded that such contentions would be incorrect. While performing its constitutional duty to decide a case which it did not ask to be brought, the Court has found that two congressional enactments—42 U.S.C. §§ 5633 and 1983—combine to give these plaintiffs a remedy to prevent the deprivation of congressionally created rights. If this Court has departed in any degree from the wishes of Congress as expressed in these statutes, it has done so to accommodate the defendants by tempering the statutory remedy.

Accordingly,

It is hereby ordered that the defendants' motions are denied insofar as they involve the following conclusions of the Court:

1) The plaintiffs' § 1983 claims are not barred by *res judicata* and collateral estoppel.
2) The plaintiffs need not exhaust administrative remedies.
3) The Office of Juvenile Justice and Delinquency Prevention does not have primary jurisdiction over the defendant's statutory § 1983 claim.
4) The plaintiffs' statutory § 1983 claim is ripe for adjudication.

---

28. As the reapportionment cases adequately demonstrate, it is occasionally necessary for federal courts to issue orders which will require a legislative or quasi-legislative act to insure compliance. See, e.g., *Reynolds v. Sims*, 377 U.S. 533, 84 S.Ct. 1362, 12 L.Ed.2d 506 (1964).

29. Because the county defendants' 12(b)(7) motion was denied and their 12(b)(6) motion was treated as a motion for summary judgment and denied, they should file an answer within fifteen days of the receipt of this order.

5) The plaintiffs need not proceed through a guardian *ad litem*.
6) The plaintiffs' JJDPA claim need not be dismissed because a necessary and indispensable party has not been sued.
7) Section 1983 provides a cause of action to seek redress for violations of rights created by § 5633 of the Juvenile Justice and Delinquency Prevention Act.

It is further ordered that the state defendants shall submit for the Court's approval a plan for achieving a combination of policy changes and reductions in the rate of juvenile jailing which would place the state in compliance with the JJDPA by the end of this year. This plan shall be filed by April 30, 1987.

It is further ordered that the Court will rule on the remaining grounds for summary judgment, including the defendant's assertions of immunity from damage awards and the cross-motions for summary judgment on the plaintiffs' constitutional claims.

It is further ordered that a hearing shall take place soon after the Court receives the state's plan at which the Court will consider the plaintiff's motions for class certification.

RIGHT TO BAIL

Case Comment

Pretrial release is often a discretionary decision left to state courts and legislatures. The appellate courts recognize the need for due process of law at every stage of the juvenile justice system where incarceration is a possibility. Bail, they argue, is a central feature of due process of law and is a key element in the presumption of innocence. Nonetheless, the uniqueness of juvenile law makes a bail system unworkable—what happens, for example, if a parent refuses to take a child back? The Court relies on the doctrine that in lieu of a bail system, every effort must be made to release the child to his or her parents or a reasonable alternative; only if this is impossible should a child be held in detention. Thus, the right to bail is often a moot issue.

These sentiments are reiterated in *Baldwin v. Lewis*, where the state's system of parental release is held to be an adequate substitute for a constitutional right to money bail.

BALDWIN v. LEWIS

United States District Court, E.D. Wisconsin, 1969.
300 F.Supp. 1220.

* * *

DOES THE PETITIONER HAVE A CONSTITUTIONAL RIGHT TO BAIL?

Petitioner contends that the refusal of the State courts to admit him to bail is a violation of his rights under the Eighth Amendment to the United States Constitution. I find it unnecessary to reach the question of whether there is a "constitutional right to bail" in juvenile proceedings, because I believe that the Wisconsin Children's Code, when applied consistent with the aforementioned requirements of due process, provides an adequate substitute for bail.

The Wisconsin Children's Code, specifically § 48.29, requires that a juvenile *shall* be released to the custody of his parents unless there is a finding that because of the circumstances, including the gravity of the alleged crime, the nature of the juvenile's home life, and the juvenile's previous contacts with the court, the parents or guardian of the juvenile are incapable under the circumstances to care for him. Only if such a finding is made may the juvenile be detained pending trial of the accusations against him. As I have already held, the hearing at which the question of detention of the juvenile is determined must satisfy the requirements of due process of law. When this is done, the interest of the juvenile is protected, and he is not subjected to the arbitrary confinement which the Eighth Amendment is designed to prohibit.

In so holding, my decision is in accord with the ruling of the Court of Appeals for the District of Columbia in *Fulwood v. Stone*, 129 U.S.App.D.C. 314, 394 F.2d 939 (1967). Faced with initial detention provisions very similar to those found in the Wisconsin Statutes, the court held that the D.C.Code, "if faithfully observed in practice," is "more than an adequate substitute for bail." Likewise, the Wisconsin Children's Code, when applied in a manner consistent with due process, affords a juvenile an adequate substitute for bail.

For the foregoing reasons, the petitioner, Richard Lee Baldwin, was ordered released to the custody of his mother pending further disposition of the charges pending against him in the State courts.

END NOTES—CHAPTER III

1. James Brown, Robert Shepherd, and Andrew Shookhoff, *Preventive Detention after Schall v. Martin* (Washington, D.C.: American Bar Association, 1985).

2. Charles Frazier and Donna Bishop, "The Pretrial Detention of Juveniles and Its Impact on Case Dispositions," *Journal of Criminal Law and Criminology* 76:112–52 (1986).

3. See, generally, Ira Schwartz, ed., "Children in Jails," *Crime and Delinquency* 34:131–228 (1988).

4. American Bar Association, *Standards Relating to Interim Status of Juveniles* (Cambridge, Mass.: Ballinger Publishing, 1977).

5. Albert W. Alschuler, "The Prosecutor's Role in Plea Bargaining," *University of Chicago Law Review* 36:50–112 (1968);

see also Darlene Ewing, "Juvenile Plea Bargaining: A Case Study," *American Journal of Criminal Law* 6:167 (1978).

6. Joyce Dougherty, "A Comparison of Adult Plea Bargaining and Juvenile Intake," *Federal Probation* (June 1988):72–79.

7. Samuel Davis, *Rights of Juveniles: The Juvenile Justice System* (New York: Clark Boardman, 1980, Supplement 1988).

8. See Henry Swanger, "*Hendrickson v. Griggs*—A Review of Legal and Policy Implications for Juvenile Justice Policymakers," *Crime and Delinquency* 34:209 (1988).

9. "Plans for Jail Removal Described," *Criminal Justice Newsletter*, 15 April 1987.

10. See Ira Schwartz, Linda Harris, and Lauri Levi, "The Jailing of Juveniles in Minnesota," *Crime and Delinquency* 34:131 (1988).

Transfer of Juvenile Jurisdiction to the Criminal Court

INTRODUCTION

Prior to the development of the first modern juvenile court in Illinois in 1899, juveniles were tried for violations of the law in adult criminal courts. The consequences of such a procedure were devastating, since many children were treated as criminal offenders and often sentenced to adult prisons. The subsequent passage of state legislation creating juvenile courts eliminated this problem. However, the juvenile justice system did recognize that certain forms of conduct require children to be tried as adults. Today, most jurisdictions provide by statute for "waiver" or "transfer" of juvenile offenders to the criminal courts.[1]

The transfer of a juvenile to the criminal court is often based on statutory criteria established by the states' juvenile court acts, and waiver provisions are generally quite varied among the jurisdictions. Such criteria include the age of the child and the type of offense alleged in the petition. For example, some jurisdictions require that the child be over a certain age and be charged with a felony. Others permit waiver of jurisdiction to the criminal court above a certain age, without regard to the offense. There are also some jurisdictions that permit waiver not only on the basis of age and type of offense but also on consideration of the child's prior criminal record and probability of further juvenile conduct.[2]

Because of the nature and effect of the waiver decision on the child in terms of status and disposition, the U.S. Supreme Court has sought to impose procedural protections for juveniles in the waiver process (see *Kent v. United States* [1966]).[3] The Supreme Court held that the waiver proceeding was a "critically important" stage in the juvenile process and that juveniles must be afforded minimum requirements of due process of law at such proceedings. *Kent* concluded that the following conditions must be observed for a valid waiver: (1) a hearing must be held on the motion of waiver; (2) the child is entitled to be represented by counsel; (3) the defense attorney must be given access to all records and reports relied upon to reach a waiver decision; and (4) the court must provide a written statement of the reasons for the waiver decision.

Many jurisdictions have established specific rules of practice for the waiver of a juvenile to the criminal court as a result of the *Kent* case. Most jurisdictions that have waiver proceedings require by statute or court rule a hearing, right to counsel, an investigation by the probation staff into whether the juvenile is amenable to treatment, evidence that reasonable ground exists to believe the child committed the delinquent act, and a statement of reasons for the waiver.

One of the most difficult issues in the waiver process is to decide what standards should be used to support a waiver decision. The appendix in the *Kent* case lists eight objective criteria to be used in determining whether to transfer a child to criminal court. These criteria generally include such factors as (1) the type of offense; (2) the child's prior record; (3) nature of past treatment efforts; (4) the availability of rehabilitative services; and (5) the reasonable likelihood of the child being rehabilitated in the juvenile court.

The most recent opinion by the Supreme Court on juvenile waiver proceedings is the case of *Breed v. Jones* (1975).[4] *Breed* held that the prosecution of a juvenile as an adult in the California Superior Court after an adjudicatory proceeding in juvenile court violated the double jeopardy clause of the Fifth Amendment, as applied to the states through the Fourteenth Amendment. The Court concluded that jeopardy attached when the juvenile court began to hear evidence at the adjudicatory hearing. This holding basically requires that the waiver hearing take place prior to any adjudicatory hearing. *Breed v. Jones* is significant because it is another example of the Supreme Court applying criminal procedural standards to the juvenile justice system.

WAIVER HEARING— CONSTITUTIONAL REQUIREMENTS

Case Comment

In *Kent v. United States*, the Supreme Court formulated procedural guidelines to be followed in the waiver of a delinquent from juvenile to adult courts. Kent claimed that his waiver from the juvenile court violated his statutory and constitutional right to due process of law.

In granting the petition, the Supreme Court argued that the difference between the juvenile and adult courts is so vast that the relief requested by petitioner is necessary to ensure equal protection of law. In its decision, the Court reviewed the purpose of waiver and the procedures to be followed for its just application. The Court's conclusion reflects the belief that although latitude and discretion are important functions of the juvenile court system, its procedures must also satisfy a fundamental fairness doctrine.

KENT v. UNITED STATES

Supreme Court of the United States, 1966.
383 U.S. 541, 86 S.Ct. 1045, 16 L.Ed.2d 84.

Mr. Justice Fortas delivered the opinion of the Court.

This case is here on certiorari to the United States Court of Appeals for the District of Columbia Circuit. The facts and the contentions of counsel raise a number of disturbing questions concerning the administration by the police and the Juvenile Court authorities of the District of Columbia laws relating to juveniles. Apart from raising questions as to the adequacy of custodial and treatment facilities and policies, some of which are not within judicial competence, the case presents important challenges to the procedure of the police and Juvenile Court officials upon apprehension of a juvenile suspected of serious offenses. Because we conclude that the Juvenile Court's order waiving jurisdiction of petitioner was entered without compliance with required procedures, we remand the case to the trial court.

Morris A. Kent, Jr., first came under the authority of the Juvenile Court of the District of Columbia in 1959. He was then aged 14. He was apprehended as a result of several housebreakings and an attempted purse snatching. He was placed on probation, in the custody of his mother who had been separated from her husband since Kent was two years old. Juvenile Court officials interviewed Kent from time to time during the probation period and accumulated a "Social Service" file.

On September 2, 1961, an intruder entered the apartment of a woman in the District of Columbia. He took her wallet. He raped her. The police found in the apartment latent fingerprints. They were developed and processed. They matched the fingerprints of Morris Kent, taken when he was 14 years old and under the jurisdiction of the Juvenile Court. At about 3 P.M. on September 5, 1961, Kent was taken into custody by the police. Kent was then 16 and therefore subject to the "exclusive jurisdiction" of the Juvenile Court. D.C.Code § 11–907 (1961), now § 11–1551 (Supp. IV, 1965). He was still on probation to that court as a result of the 1959 proceedings.

Upon being apprehended, Kent was taken to police headquarters where he was interrogated by police officers. It appears that he admitted his involvement in the offense which led to his apprehension and volunteered information as to similar offenses involving housebreaking, robbery, and rape. His interrogation proceeded from about 3 P.M. to 10 P.M. the same evening.[1]

Some time after 10 P.M. petitioner was taken to the Receiving Home for Children. The next morning he was released to the police for further interrogation at police headquarters, which lasted until 5 P.M.[2]

The record does not show when his mother became aware that the boy was in custody but shortly after 2 P.M. on September 6, 1961, the day following petitioner's apprehension, she retained counsel.

Counsel, together with petitioner's mother, promptly conferred with the Social Service Director of the Juvenile Court. In a brief interview, they discussed the possibility that the Juvenile Court might waive jurisdiction under D.C.Code § 11–914 (1961), now § 11–1553 (Supp. IV, 1965) and remit Kent to trial by the District Court. Counsel made known his intention to oppose waiver.

Petitioner was detained at the Receiving Home for almost a week. There was no arraignment during this time, no determination by a judicial officer of probable cause for petitioner's apprehension.[3]

During this period of detention and interrogation, petitioner's counsel arranged for examination of petitioner by two psychiatrists and a psychologist. He thereafter filed with the Juvenile Court a motion for a hearing on the question of waiver of Juvenile Court jurisdiction, together with an affidavit of a psychiatrist certifying that petitioner "is a victim of severe psychopathology" and recommending hospitalization for psychiatric observation. Petitioner's counsel, in support of his motion to the effect that the Juvenile Court should retain jurisdiction of petitioner, offered to prove that if petitioner were given adequate treatment in a hospital under the aegis of the Juvenile Court, he would be a suitable subject for rehabilitation.

At the same time, petitioner's counsel moved that the Juvenile Court should give him access to the Social Service file relating to petitioner which had been accumulated by the staff of the Juvenile Court during petitioner's probation period, and which would be available to the Juvenile Court judge in considering the question whether it should retain or waive jurisdiction. Petitioner's counsel represented that access to this file was essential to his providing petitioner with effective assistance of counsel.

The Juvenile Court judge did not rule on these motions. He held no hearing. He did not confer with petitioner or petitioner's parents or petitioner's counsel. He entered an order reciting that after "full investigation, I do hereby waive" jurisdiction of petitioner and directing that he be "held for trial for [the alleged] offenses under the regular procedure of the U.S. District Court for the District of Co-

---

1. There is no indication in the file that the police complied with the requirement of the District Code that a child taken into custody, unless released to his parent, guardian or custodian, "shall be placed in the custody of a probation officer or other person designated by the court, or taken immediately to the court or to a place of detention provided by the Board of Public Welfare, and the officer taking him shall immediately notify the court and shall file a petition when directed to do so by the court." D.C. Code § 11–912 (1961), now § 16–2306 (Supp.IV, 1965).

2. The elicited statements were not used in the subsequent trial before the United States District Court. Since the statements were made while petitioner was subject to the jurisdiction of the Juvenile Court, they were inadmissible in a subsequent criminal prosecution under the rule of *Harling v. United States*, 111 U.S.App.D.C. 174, 295 F.2d 161 (1961).

3. In the case of adults, arraignment before a magistrate for determination of probable cause and advice to the arrested person as to his rights, etc., are provided by law and are regarded as fundamental. Cf. Fed.Rules Crim. Proc. 5(a), (b); *Mallory v. United States*, 354 U.S. 449, 77 S.Ct. 1356, 1 L.Ed.2d 1479. In *Harling v. United States*, supra, the Court of Appeals for the District of Columbia has stated the basis for this distinction between juveniles and adults as follows: "It is, of course, because children are, generally speaking, exempt from criminal penalties that safeguards of the criminal law, such as Rule 5 and the exclusionary *Mallory* rule, have no general application in juvenile proceedings." 111 U.S.App.D.C., at 176, 295 F.2d, at 163.

In *Edwards v. United States*, 117 U.S. App.D.C. 383, 384, 330 F.2d 849, 850 (1964) it was said that: "* * * special practices * * * follow the apprehension of a juvenile. He may be held in custody by the juvenile authorities—and is available to investigating officers—for five days before any formal action need be taken. There is no duty to take him before a magistrate, and no responsibility to inform him of his rights. He is not booked. The statutory intent is to establish a non-punitive, non-criminal atmosphere."

We indicate no view as to the legality of these practices. Cf. *Harling v. United States*, supra, 111 U.S.App.D.C., at 176, 295 F.2d, at 163, n. 12.

lumbia." He made no findings. He did not recite any reason for the waiver.[4] He made no reference to the motions filed by petitioner's counsel. We must assume that he denied, *sub silentio*, the motions for a hearing, the recommendation for hospitalization for psychiatric observation, the request for access to the Social Service file, and the offer to prove that petitioner was a fit subject for rehabilitation under the Juvenile Court's jurisdiction.[5]

Presumably, prior to entry of his order, the Juvenile Court judge received and considered recommendations of the Juvenile Court staff, the Social Service file relating to petitioner, and a report dated September 8, 1961 (three days following petitioner's apprehension), submitted to him by the Juvenile Probation Section. The Social Service file and the September 8 report were later sent to the District Court and it appears that both of them referred to petitioner's mental condition. The September 8 report spoke of "a rapid deterioration of [petitioner's] personality structure and the possibility of mental illness." As stated, neither this report nor the Social Service file was made available to petitioner's counsel.

The provision of the Juvenile Court Act governing waiver expressly provides only for "full investigation." It states the circumstances in which jurisdiction may be waived and the child held for trial under adult procedures, but it does not state standards to govern the Juvenile Court's decision as to waiver. The provision reads as follows:

> If a child sixteen years of age or older is charged with an offense which would amount to a felony in the case of an adult, or any child charged with an offense which if committed by an adult is punishable by death of life imprisonment, the judge may, after full investigation, waive jurisdiction and order such child held for trial under the regular procedure of the court which would

have jurisdiction of such offense if committed by an adult; or such other court may exercise the powers conferred upon the juvenile court in this subchapter in conducting and disposing of such cases.[6]

Petitioner appealed from the Juvenile Court's waiver order to the Municipal Court of Appeals, which affirmed, and also applied to the United States District Court for a writ of habeas corpus, which was denied. On appeal from these judgments, the United States Court of Appeals held on January 22, 1963, that neither appeal to the Municipal Court of Appeals nor habeas corpus was available. In the Court of Appeals' view, the exclusive method of reviewing the Juvenile Court's waiver order was a motion to dismiss the indictment in the District Court. *Kent v. Reid*, 114 U.S.App.D.C. 330, 316 F.2d 331 (1963).

Meanwhile, on September 25, 1961, shortly after the Juvenile Court order waiving its jurisdiction, petitioner was indicted by a grand jury of the United States District Court for the District of Columbia. The indictment contained eight counts alleging two instances of housebreaking, robbery, and rape, and one of housebreaking and robbery. On November 16, 1961, petitioner moved the District Court to dismiss the indictment on the grounds that the waiver was invalid. He also moved the District Court to constitute itself a Juvenile Court as authorized by D.C.Code § 11–914 (1961), now § 11–1553 (Supp. IV, 1965). After substantial delay occasioned by petitioner's appeal and habeas corpus proceedings, the District Court addressed itself to the motion to dismiss on February 8, 1963.[7]

The District Court denied the motion to dismiss the indictment. The District Court ruled that it would not "go behind" the Juvenile Court judge's recital that his order was entered "after full investigation."

---

4. At the time of these events, there was in effect Policy Memorandum No. 7 of November 30, 1959, promulgated by the judge of the Juvenile Court to set forth the criteria to govern disposition of waiver requests. It is set forth in the Appendix. This Memorandum has since been rescinded. See *United States. v. Caviness*, 239 F.Supp. 545, 550 (D.C.D.C.1965).

5. It should be noted that at this time the statute provided for only one Juvenile Court judge. Congressional hearings and reports attest the impossibility of the burden which he was supposed to carry. See Amending the Juvenile Court Act of the District of Columbia, Hearings before Subcommittee No. 3 of the House Committee on the District of Columbia, 87th Cong., 1st Sess. (1961); Juvenile Delinquency, Hearings before the Subcommittee to Investigate Juvenile Delinquency of the Senate Committee on the Judiciary, 86th Cong., 1st Sess. (1959–1960); Additional Judges for Juvenile Court, Hearing before the House Committee on the District of Columbia, 86th Cong., 1st Sess. (1959); H.R.Rep.No.1041, 87th Cong., 1st Sess. (1961); S.Rep.No.841, 87th Cong., 1st Sess. (1961); S.Rep.No.116, 86th Cong., 1st Sess. (1959). The statute was amended in 1962 to provide for three judges for the court. 76 Stat. 21; D.C.Code § 11–1502 (Supp. IV, 1965).

6. D.C.Code § 11–914 (1961), now § 11–1553 (Supp. IV, 1965).

7. On February 5, 1963, the motion to the District Court to constitute itself a Juvenile Court was denied. The motion was renewed orally and denied on February 8, 1963, after the District Court's decision that the indictment should not be dismissed.

It held that "[t]he only matter before me is as to whether or not the statutory provisions were complied with and the Courts have held * * * with reference to full investigation, that that does not mean a quasi judicial or judicial hearing. No hearing is required."

On March 7, 1963, the District Court held a hearing on petitioner's motion to determine his competency to stand trial. The court determined that petitioner was competent.[8]

At trial, petitioner's defense was wholly directed toward proving that he was not criminally responsible because "his unlawful act was the product of mental disease or mental defect." *Durham v. United States*, 94 U.S.App.D.C. 228, 241, 214 F.2d 862, 875, 45 A.L.R.2d 1430 (1954). Extensive evidence, including expert testimony, was presented to support this defense. The jury found as to the counts alleging rape that petitioner was "not guilty by reason of insanity." Under District of Columbia law, this made it mandatory that petitioner be transferred to St. Elizabeths Hospital, a mental institution, until his sanity is restored.[9] On the six counts of housebreaking and robbery, the jury found that petitioner was guilty.[10]

Kent was sentenced to serve five to 15 years on each count as to which he was found guilty, or a total of 30 to 90 years in prison. The District Court ordered that the time to be spent at St. Elizabeths on the mandatory commitment after the insanity acquittal be counted as part of the 30- to 90-year sentence. Petitioner appealed to the United States Court of Appeals for the District of Columbia Circuit. That court affirmed. 119 U.S.App.D.C. 378, 343 F.2d 247 (1964).[11]

Before the Court of Appeals and in this Court, petitioner's counsel has urged a number of grounds for reversal. He argues that petitioner's detention and interrogation, described above, were unlawful. He contends that the police failed to follow the procedure prescribed by the Juvenile Court Act in that they failed to notify the parents of the child and the Juvenile Court itself, note 1, *supra*; that petitioner was deprived of his liberty for about a week without a determination of probable cause which would have been required in the case of an adult, see note 3, *supra*; that he was interrogated by the police in the absence of counsel or a parent, cf. *Harling v. United States*, 111 U.S.App.D.C. 174, 176, 295 F.2d 161, 163, n. 12 (1961), without warning of his right to remain silent or advice as to his right to counsel, in asserted violation of the Juvenile Court Act and in violation of rights that he would have if he were an adult; and that petitioner was fingerprinted in violation of the asserted intent of the Juvenile Court Act and while unlawfully detained and that the fingerprints were unlawfully used in the District Court proceeding.[12]

---

8. The District Court had before it extensive information as to petitioner's mental condition, bearing upon both competence to stand trial and the defense of insanity. The court had obtained the Social Service file from the Juvenile Court and had made it available to petitioner's counsel. On October 13, 1961, the District Court had granted petitioner's motion of October 6 for commitment to the Psychiatric Division of the General Hospital for 60 days. On December 20, 1961, the hospital reported that "[i]t is the concensus [sic] of the staff that Morris is emotionally ill and severely so* * * we feel that he is incompetent to stand trial and to participate in a mature way in his own defense. His illness has interfered with his judgment and reasoning ability* * *." The prosecutor opposed a finding of incompetence to stand trial, and at the prosecutor's request, the District Court referred petitioner to St. Elizabeths Hospital for psychiatric observation. According to a letter from the Superintendent of St. Elizabeths of April 5, 1962, the hospital's staff found that petitioner was "suffering from mental disease at the present time, Schizophrenic Reaction, Chronic Undifferentiated Type," that he had been suffering from this disease at the time of the charged offenses, and that "if committed by him [those criminal acts] were the product of this disease." They stated, however, that petitioner was "mentally competent to understand the nature of the proceedings against him and to consult properly with counsel in his own defense."

9. D.C.Code § 24–301 (1961).

10. The basis for this distinction—that petitioner was "sane" for purposes of the housebreaking and robbery but "insane" for the purposes of the rape—apparently was the hypothesis, for which there is some support in the record, that the jury might find that the robberies had anteceded the rapes, and in that event, it might conclude that the housebreakings and robberies were not the products of his mental disease or defect, while the rapes were produced thereby.

11. Petitioner filed a petition for rehearing *en banc*, but subsequently moved to withdraw the petition in order to prosecute his petition for certiorari to this Court. The Court of Appeals permitted withdrawal. Chief Judge Bazelon filed a dissenting opinion in which Circuit Judge Wright joined. 119 U.S.App.D.C., at 395, 343 F.2d, at 264 (1964).

12. Cf. *Harling v. United States*, 111 U.S.App.D.C. 174, 295 F.2d 161 (1961); *Bynum v. United States*, 104 U.S.App.D.C. 368, 262 F.2d 465 (1958). It is not clear from the record whether the fingerprints used were taken during the detention period or were those taken while petitioner was in custody in 1959, nor is it clear that petitioner's counsel objected to the use of the fingerprints.

These contentions raise problems of substantial concern as to the construction of and compliance with the Juvenile Court Act. They also suggest basic issues as to the justifiability of affording a juvenile less protection than is accorded to adults suspected of criminal offenses, particularly where, as here, there is an absence of any indication that the denial of rights available to adults was offset, mitigated or explained by action of the Government, as *parens patriae*, evidencing the special solicitude for juveniles commanded by the Juvenile Court Act. However, because we remand the case on account of the procedural error with respect to waiver of jurisdiction, we do not pass upon these questions.[13]

It is to petitioner's arguments as to the infirmity of the proceedings by which the Juvenile Court waived its otherwise exclusive jurisdiction that we address our attention. Petitioner attacks the waiver of jurisdiction on a number of statutory and constitutional grounds. He contends that the waiver is defective because no hearing was held; because no findings were made by the Juvenile Court; because the Juvenile Court stated no reasons for waiver; and because counsel was denied access to the Social Service file which presumably was considered by the Juvenile Court in determining to waive jurisdiction.

We agree that the order of the Juvenile Court waiving its jurisdiction and transferring petitioner for trial in the United States District Court for the District of Columbia was invalid. There is no question that the order is reviewable on motion to dismiss the indictment in the District Court, as specified by the Court of Appeals in this case. *Kent v. Reid*,

supra. The issue is the standards to be applied upon such review.

We agree with the Court of Appeals that the statute contemplates that the Juvenile Court should have considerable latitude within which to determine whether it should retain jurisdiction over a child or—subject to the statutory delimitation[14]—should waive jurisdiction. But this latitude is not complete. At the outset, it assumes procedural regularity sufficient in the particular circumstances to satisfy the basic requirements of due process and fairness, as well as compliance with the statutory requirement of a "full investigation." *Green v. United States*, 113 U.S.App.D.C. 348, 308 F.2d 303 (1962).[15] The statute gives the Juvenile Court a substantial degree of discretion as to the factual considerations to be evaluated, the weight to be given them and the conclusion to be reached. It does not confer upon the Juvenile Court a license for arbitrary procedure. The statute does not permit the Juvenile Court to determine in isolation and without the participation or any representation of the child the "critically important" question whether a child will be deprived of the special protections and provisions of the Juvenile Court Act.[16] It does not authorize the Juvenile Court, in total disregard of a motion for hearing filed by counsel, and without any hearing or statement or reasons, to decide—as in this case—that the child will be taken from the Receiving Home for Children and transferred to jail along with adults, and that he will be exposed to the possibility of a death sentence[17] instead of treatment for a maximum, in Kent's case, of five years, until he is 21.[18]

---

13. Petitioner also urges that the District Court erred in the following respects:

(1) It gave the jury a version of the "Allen" charge. See *Allen v. United States*, 164 U.S. 492, 17 S.Ct. 154, 41 L.Ed. 528.

(2) It failed to give an adequate and fair competency hearing.

(3) It denied the motion to constitute itself a juvenile court pursuant to D.C.Code § 11–914 (1961), now § 11–1553. (Supp. IV, 1965).

(4) It should have granted petitioner's motion for acquittal on all counts, *n. o. v.* on the grounds of insanity.

We decide none of these claims.

14. The statute is set out at p. 1050, *supra*.

15. "What is required before a waiver is, as we have said, 'full investigation.' * * * It prevents the waiver of jurisdiction as a matter of routine for the purpose of easing the docket. It prevents routine waiver in certain classes of alleged crimes. It requires a judgment in each case based on 'an inquiry not only into the facts of the alleged offense but also into the question whether the *parens patriae* plan of procedure is desirable and proper in the particular case.' *Pee v. United States*, 107 U.S.App.D.C. 47, 50, 274 F.2d 556, 559 (1959)." *Green v. United States*, *supra*, at 350, 308 F.2d, at 305.

16. See *Watkins v. United States*, 119 U.S.App.D.C. 409, 413, 343 F.2d 278, 282 (1964); *Black v. United States*, 122 U.S.App.D.C. 393, 355 F.2d 104 (1965).

17. D.C.Code § 22–2801 (1961) fixes the punishment for rape at 30 years, or death if the jury so provides in its verdict. The maximum punishment for housebreaking is 15 years, D.C.Code § 22–1801 (1961); for robbery it is also 15 years, D.C.Code § 22–2901 (1961).

18. The jurisdiction of the Juvenile Court over a child ceases when he becomes 21. D.C.Code § 11–907 (1961), now § 11–1551 (Supp. IV, 1965).

We do not consider whether, on the merits, Kent should have been transferred; but there is no place in our system of law for reaching a result of such tremendous consequences without ceremony— without hearing, without effective assistance of counsel, without a statement of reasons. It is inconceivable that a court of justice dealing with adults, with respect to a similar issue, would proceed in this manner. It would be extraordinary if society's special concern for children, as reflected in the District of Columbia's Juvenile Court Act, permitted this procedure. We hold that it does not.

1. The theory of the District's Juvenile Court Act, like that of other jurisdictions,[19] is rooted in social welfare philosophy rather than in the *corpus juris*. Its proceedings are designated as civil rather than criminal. The Juvenile Court is theoretically engaged in determining the needs of the child and of society rather than adjudicating criminal conduct. The objectives are to provide measures of guidance and rehabilitation for the child and protection for society, not to fix criminal responsibility, guilt and punishment. The State is *parens patriae* rather than prosecuting attorney and judge.[20] But the admonition to function in a "parental" relationship is not an invitation to procedural arbitrariness.

2. Because the State is supposed to proceed in respect of the child as *parens patriae* and not as adversary, courts have relied on the premise that the proceedings are "civil" in nature and not criminal, and have asserted that the child cannot complain of the deprivation of important rights available in criminal cases. It has been asserted that he can claim only the fundamental due process right to fair treatment.[21] For example, it has been held that he is not entitled to bail; to indictment by grand jury; to a speedy and public trial; to trial by jury; to immunity against self-incrimination; to confrontation of his accusers; and in some jurisdictions (but not in the District of Columbia, see *Shioutakon v. District of Columbia*, 98 U.S.App.D.C. 371, 236 F.2d 666

(1956), and *Black v. United States, supra*) that he is not entitled to counsel.[22]

While there can be no doubt of the original laudable purpose of juvenile courts, studies and critiques in recent years raise serious questions as to whether actual performance measures well enough against theoretical purpose to make tolerable the immunity of the process from the reach of constitutional guaranties applicable to adults.[23] There is much evidence that some juvenile courts, including that of the District of Columbia, lack the personnel, facilities and techniques to perform adequately as representatives of the State in a *parens patriae* capacity, at least with respect to children charged with law violation. There is evidence, in fact, that there may be grounds for concern that the child receives the worst of both worlds: that he gets neither the protections accorded to adults nor the solicitous care and regenerative treatment postulated for children.[24]

This concern, however, does not induce us in this case to accept the invitation[25] to rule that constitutional guaranties which would be applicable to adults charged with the serious offenses for which Kent was tried must be applied in juvenile court proceedings concerned with allegations of law violation. The Juvenile Court Act and the decisions of the United States Court of Appeals for the District of Columbia Circuit provide an adequate basis for decision of this case, and we go no further.

3. It is clear beyond dispute that the waiver of jurisdiction is a "critically important" action determining vitally important statutory rights of the juvenile. The Court of Appeals for the District of Columbia Circuit has so held. See *Black v. United States, supra; Watkins v. United States*, 119 U.S.App.D.C. 409, 343 F.2d 278 (1964). The statutory scheme makes this plain. The Juvenile Court is vested with "original and exclusive jurisdiction" of the child. This jurisdiction confers special rights and immunities. He is, as specified by the statute, shielded from publicity. He may be confined, but

---

19. All States have juvenile court systems. A study of the actual operation of these systems is contained in Note, Juvenile Delinquents: The Police, State Courts, and Individualized Justice, 79 Harv.L.Rev. 775 (1966).

20. See Handler, The Juvenile Court and the Adversary System: Problems of Function and Form, 1965 Wis.L.Rev. 7.

21. *Pee v. United States*, 107 U.S.App.D.C. 47, 274 F.2d 556 (1959).

22. See *Pee v. United States, supra*, at 54, 274 F.2d, at 563; Paulsen, Fairness to the Juvenile Offender, 41 Minn.L.Rev. 547 (1957).

23. Cf. *Harling v. United States*, 111 U.S.App.D.C. 174, 177, 295 F.2d 161, 164 (1961).

24. See Handler, *op. cit. supra*, note 20; Note, *supra*, note 19; materials cited in note 5, *supra*.

25. See brief of *amicus curiae*. 16–2313, 11–1586 (Supp. IV, 1965).

with rare exceptions he may not be jailed along with adults. He may be detained, but only until he is 21 years of age. The court is admonished by the statute to give preference to retaining the child in the custody of his parents "unless his welfare and the safety and protection of the public can not be adequately safeguarded without * * * removal." The child is protected against consequences of adult conviction such as the loss of civil rights, the use of adjudication against him in subsequent proceedings, and disqualification for public employment. D.C.Code §§ 11–907, 11–915, 11–927, 11–929 (1961).[26]

The net, therefore, is that petitioner—then a boy of 16—was by statute entitled to certain procedures and benefits as a consequence of his statutory right to the "exclusive" jurisdiction of the Juvenile Court. In these circumstances, considering particularly that decision as to waiver of jurisdiction and transfer of the matter to the District Court was potentially as important to petitioner as the difference between five years' confinement and a death sentence, we conclude that, as a condition to a valid waiver order, petitioner was entitled to a hearing, including access by his counsel to the social records and probation or similar reports which presumably are considered by the court, and to a statement of reasons for the Juvenile Court's decision. We believe that this result is required by the statute read in the context of constitutional principles relating to due process and the assistance of counsel.[27]

The Court of Appeals in this case relied upon *Wilhite v. United States*, 108 U.S.App.D.C. 279, 281 F.2d 642 (1960). In that case, the Court of Appeals held, for purposes of a determination as to waiver of jurisdiction, that no formal hearing is required and that the "full investigation" required of the Juvenile Court need only be such "as is needed to satisfy *that* court * * * on the question of waiver."[28] (Emphasis supplied.) The authority of *Wilhite*, however, is substantially undermined by other, more recent, decisions of the Court of Appeals.

In *Black v. United States*, decided by the Court of Appeals on December 8, 1965, the court[29] held that assistance of counsel in the "critically important" determination of waiver is essential to the proper administration of juvenile proceedings. Because the juvenile was not advised of his right to retained or appointed counsel, the judgment of the District Court, following waiver of jurisdiction by the Juvenile Court, was reversed. The court relied upon its decision in *Shioutakon v. District of Columbia*, 98 U.S.App.D.C. 371, 236 F.2d 666 (1956), in which it had held that effective assistance of counsel in juvenile court proceedings is essential. See also *McDaniel v. Shea*, 108 U.S.App.D.C. 15, 278 F.2d 460 (1960). In *Black*, the court referred to the Criminal Justice Act, enacted four years after *Shioutakon*, in which Congress provided for the assistance of counsel "in proceedings before the juvenile court of the District of Columbia." D.C.Code § 2–2202 (1961). The court held that "The need is even greater in the adjudication of waiver [than in a case like *Shioutakon*] since it contemplates the imposition of criminal sanctions." 122 U.S.App.D.C., at 395, 355 F.2d, at 106.

In *Watkins v. United States*, 119 U.S.App.D.C. 409, 343 F.2d 278 (1964), decided in November 1964, the Juvenile Court had waived jurisdiction of appellant who was charged with housebreaking and larceny. In the District Court, appellant sought disclosure of the social record in order to attack the validity of the waiver. The Court of Appeals held that in a waiver proceeding a juvenile's attorney is entitled to access to such records. The court observed that

All of the social records concerning the child are usually relevant to waiver since the Juvenile Court must be deemed to consider the entire history of the child in determining waiver. The relevance of particular items must be construed generously. Since an attorney has no certain knowledge of what the social records contain, he cannot be expected to demonstrate the rele-

---

26. These are now, without substantial changes, §§ 11–1551, 16–2307, 16–2308, 16–2313, 11–1586 (Supp. IV, 1965).

27. While we "will not ordinarily review decisions of the United States Court of Appeals [for the District of Columbia Circuit], which are based upon statutes * * * limited [to the District] * * *," *Del Vecchio v. Bowers*, 296 U.S. 280, 285, 56 S.Ct. 190, 192, 80 L.Ed. 229, the position of that court, as we discuss infra, is self-contradictory. Nor have we deferred to decisions on local law where to do so would require adjudication of difficult constitutional questions. See *District of Columbia v. Little*, 339 U.S. 1, 70 S.Ct. 468, 94 L.Ed. 599.

28. The panel was composed of Circuit Judges Miller, Fahy and Burger. Judge Fahy concurred in the result. It appears that the attack on the regularity of the waiver of jurisdiction was made 17 years after the event, and that no objection to waiver had been made in the District Court.

29. Bazelon, C. J., and Fahy and Leventhal, J.J.

vance of particular items in his request.

The child's attorney must be advised of the information upon which the Juvenile Court relied in order to assist effectively in the determination of the waiver question, by insisting upon the statutory command that waiver can be ordered only after 'full investigation,' and by guarding against action of the Juvenile Court beyond its discretionary authority. 119 U.S.App.D.C., at 413, 343 F.2d, at 282.

The court remanded the record to the District Court for a determination of the extent to which the records should be disclosed.

The Court of Appeals' decision in the present case was handed down on October 26, 1964, prior to its decisions in *Black* and *Watkins*. The Court of Appeals assumed that since petitioner had been a probationer of the Juvenile Court for two years, that court had before it sufficient evidence to make an informed judgment. It therefore concluded that the statutory requirement of a "full investigation" had been met. It noted the absence of "a specification by the Juvenile Court Judge of precisely why he concluded to waive jurisdiction." 119 U.S.App.D.C., at 384, 343 F.2d at 253. While it indicated that "in some cases at least" a useful purpose might be served "by a discussion of the reasons motivating the determination," *id.*, at 384, 343 F.2d, at 253, n. 6, it did not conclude that the absence thereof invalidated the waiver.

As to the denial of access to the social records, the Court of Appeals stated that "the statute is ambiguous." It said that petitioner's claim, in essence, is "that counsel should have the opportunity to challenge them, presumably in a manner akin to cross-examination." *Id.*, at 389, 343 F.2d, at 258. It held, however, that this is "the kind of adversarial tactics which the system is designed to avoid." It characterized counsel's proper function as being merely that of bringing forward affirmative information which might help the court. His function, the Court of Appeals said, "is not to denigrate the staff's submissions and recommendations." Ibid. Accordingly, it held that the Juvenile Court had not abused its discretion in denying access to the social records.

We are of the opinion that the Court of Appeals misconceived the basic issue and the underlying values in this case. It did note, as another panel of the same court did a few months later in *Black* and *Watkins*, that the determination of whether to transfer a child from the statutory structure of the Juvenile Court to the criminal processes of the District Court

is "critically important." We hold that it is, indeed, a "critically important" proceeding. The Juvenile Court Act confers upon the child a right to avail himself of that court's "exclusive" jurisdiction. As the Court of Appeals has said, "[I]t is implicit in [the Juvenile Court] scheme that noncriminal treatment is to be the rule—and the adult criminal treatment, the exception which must be governed by the particular factors of individual cases." *Harling v. United States*, 111 U.S.App.D.C. 174, 177–178, 295 F.2d 161, 164–165 (1961).

Meaningful review requires that the reviewing court should review. It should not be remitted to assumptions. It must have before it a statement of the reasons motivating the waiver including, of course, a statement of the relevant facts. It may not "assume" that there are adequate reasons, nor may it merely assume that "full investigation" has been made. Accordingly, we hold that it is incumbent upon the Juvenile Court to accompany its waiver order with a statement of the reasons or considerations therefor. We do not read the statute as requiring that this statement must be formal or that it should necessarily include conventional findings of fact. But the statement should be sufficient to demonstrate that the statutory requirement of "full investigation" has been met; and that the question has received the careful consideration of the Juvenile Court; and it must set forth the basis for the order with sufficient specificity to permit meaningful review.

Correspondingly, we conclude that an opportunity for a hearing which may be informal, must be given the child prior to entry of a waiver order. Under *Black*, the child is entitled to counsel in connection with a waiver proceeding, and under *Watkins*, counsel is entitled to see the child's social records. These rights are meaningless—an illusion, a mockery—unless counsel is given an opportunity to function.

The right to representation by counsel is not a formality. It is not a grudging gesture to a ritualistic requirement. It is of the essence of justice. Appointment of counsel without affording an opportunity for hearing on a "critically important" decision is tantamount to denial of counsel. There is no justification for the failure of the Juvenile Court to rule on the motion for hearing filed by petitioner's counsel, and it was error to fail to grant a hearing.

We do not mean by this to indicate that the hearing to be held must conform with all of the requirements of a criminal trial or even of the usual administrative hearing; but we do hold that the hearing must measure up to the essentials of due process and fair treatment.

With respect to access by the child's counsel to the social records of the child, we deem it obvious that since these are to be considered by the Juvenile Court in making its decision to waive, they must be made available to the child's counsel. This is what the Court of Appeals itself held in *Watkins*. There is no doubt as to the statutory basis for this conclusion, as the Court of Appeals pointed out in *Watkins*. We cannot agree with the Court of Appeals in the present case that the statute is "ambiguous." The statute expressly provides that the record shall be withheld from "indiscriminate" public inspection, "except that such records or parts thereof *shall* be made available by rule of court or special order of court to such persons * * * as have a *legitimate interest* in the protection * * * of the child * * *." D.C.Code § 11–929(b) (1961), now § 11–1586(b) (Supp. IV, 1965). (Emphasis supplied.)[30] The Court of Appeals has held in *Black*, and we agree, that counsel must be afforded to the child in waiver proceedings. Counsel, therefore, have a "legitimate interest" in the protection of the child, and must be afforded access to these records.[31]

We do not agree with the Court of Appeals' statement, attempting to justify denial of access to these records, that counsel's role is limited to presenting "to the court anything on behalf of the child which might help the court in arriving at a decision; it is not to denigrate the staff's submissions and recommendations." On the contrary, if the staff's submissions include materials which are susceptible to challenge or impeachment, it is precisely the role of counsel to "denigrate" such matter. There is no irrebuttable presumption of accuracy attached to staff reports. If a decision on waiver is "critically important" it is equally of "critical importance" that the

material submitted to the judge—which is protected by the statute only against "indiscriminate" inspection—be subjected, within reasonable limits having regard to the theory of the Juvenile Court Act, to examination, criticism and refutation. While the Juvenile Court judge may, of course, receive *ex parte* analyses and recommendations from his staff, he may not, for purposes of a decision on waiver, receive and rely upon secret information, whether emanating from his staff or otherwise. The Juvenile Court is governed in this respect by the established principles which control courts and quasi-judicial agencies of the Government.

For the reasons stated, we conclude that the Court of Appeals and the District Court erred in sustaining the validity of the waiver by the Juvenile Court. The Government urges that any error committed by the Juvenile Court was cured by the proceedings before the District Court. It is true that the District Court considered and denied a motion to dismiss on the grounds of the invalidity of the waiver order of the Juvenile Court, and that it considered and denied a motion that it should itself, as authorized by statute, proceed in this case to "exercise the powers conferred upon the juvenile court." D.C.Code § 11–914 (1961), now § 11–1553 (Supp. IV, 1965). But we agree with the Court of Appeals in *Black*, that "the waiver question was primarily and initially one for the Juvenile Court to decide and its failure to do so in a valid manner cannot be said to be harmless error. It is the Juvenile Court, not the District Court, which has the facilities, personnel and expertise for a proper determination of the waiver issue." 122 U.S.App.D.C., at 396, 355 F.2d, at 107.[32]

Ordinarily we would reverse the Court of Appeals and direct the District Court to remand the case to the Juvenile Court for a new determination of waiver. If on remand the decision were against waiver, the indictment in the District Court would be dismissed.

---

30. Under the statute, the Juvenile Court has power by rule or order, to subject the examination of the social records to conditions which will prevent misuse of the information. Violation of any such rule or order, or disclosure of the information "except for purposes for which * * * released," is a misdemeanor. D.C.Code § 11–929 (1961), now, without substantial changes, § 11–1586 (Supp. IV, 1965).

31. In *Watkins*, the Court of Appeals seems to have permitted withholding of some portions of the social record from examination by petitioner's counsel. To the extent that *Watkins* is inconsistent with the standard which we state, it cannot be considered as controlling.

32. It also appears that the District Court requested and obtained the Social Service file and the probation staff's report of September 8, 1961, and that these were made available to petitioner's counsel. This did not cure the error of the Juvenile Court. Perhaps the point of it is that it again illustrates the maxim that while nondisclosure may contribute to the comfort of the staff, disclosure does not cause heaven to fall.

See *Black v. United States, supra.* However, petitioner has now passed the age of 21 and the Juvenile Court can no longer exercise jurisdiction over him. In view of the unavailability of a redetermination of the waiver question by the Juvenile Court, it is urged by petitioner that the conviction should be vacated and the indictment dismissed. In the circumstances of this case, and in light of the remedy which the Court of Appeals fashioned in *Black, supra,* we do not consider it appropriate to grant this drastic relief.[33] Accordingly, we vacate the order of the Court of Appeals and the judgment of the District Court and remand the case to the District Court for a hearing *de novo* on waiver, consistent with this opinion.[34] If that court finds that waiver was inappropriate, petitioner's conviction must be vacated. If, however, it finds that the waiver order was proper when originally made, the District Court may proceed, after consideration of such motions as counsel may make and such further proceedings, if any, as may be warranted, to enter an appropriate judgment. Cf. *Black v. United States, supra.*

Reversed and remanded.

APPENDIX TO OPINION OF THE COURT

*Policy Memorandum No. 7,
November 30, 1959.*

The authority of the Judge of the Juvenile Court of the District of Columbia to waive or transfer jurisdiction to the U.S. District Court for the District of Columbia is contained in the Juvenile Court Act (§ 11–914 D.C.Code, 1951 Ed.). This section permits the Judge to waive jurisdiction "after full investigation" in the case of any child "sixteen years of age or older [who is] charged with an offense which would amount to a felony in the case of an adult, or any child charged with an offense which if committed by an adult is punishable by death or life imprisonment."

The statute sets forth no specific standards for the exercise of this important discretionary act, but leaves the formulation of such criteria to the Judge. A knowledge of the Judge's criteria is important to the child, his parents, his attorney, to the judges of the U.S. District Court for the District of Columbia, to the United States Attorney and his assistants and to the Metropolitan Police Department, as well as to the staff of this court, especially the Juvenile Intake Section.

Therefore, the Judge has consulted with the Chief Judge and other judges of the U.S. District Court for the District of Columbia, with the United States Attorney, with representatives of the Bar, and with other groups concerned and has formulated the following criteria and principles concerning waiver of jurisdiction which are consistent with the basic aims and purpose of the Juvenile Court Act.

An offense falling within the statutory limitations (set forth above) will be waived if it has prosecutive merit and if it is heinous or of an aggravated character, or—even though less serious—if it represents a pattern of repeated offenses which indicate that the juvenile may be beyond rehabilitation under Juvenile Court procedures, or if the public needs the protection afforded by such action.

The determinative factors which will be considered by the Judge in deciding whether the Juvenile Court's jurisdiction over such offenses will be waived are the following:

1. The seriousness of the alleged offense to the community and whether the protection of the community requires waiver.
2. Whether the alleged offense was committed in an aggressive, violent, premeditated or willful manner.
3. Whether the alleged offense was against persons or against property, greater weight being given to offenses against persons especially if personal injury resulted.
4. The prosecutive merit of the complaint, i.e., whether there is evidence upon which a Grand Jury may be expected to return an indictment (to be determined by consultation with the United States Attorney).
5. The desirability of trial and disposition of the entire offense in one court when the juvenile's as-

---

33. Petitioner is in St. Elizabeths Hospital for psychiatric treatment as a result of the jury verdict on the rape charges.

34. We do not deem it appropriate merely to vacate the judgment and remand to the Court of Appeals for reconsideration of its present decision in light of its subsequent decisions in *Watkins* and *Black, supra.* Those cases were decided by different panels of the Court of Appeals from that which decided the present case, and in view of our grant of certiorari and of the importance of the issue, we consider it necessary to resolve the question presented instead of leaving it open for further consideration by the Court of Appeals.

sociates in the alleged offense are adults who will be charged with a crime in the U.S. District Court for the District of Columbia.

6. The sophistication and maturity of the juvenile as determined by consideration of his home, environmental situation, emotional attitude and pattern of living.

7. The record and previous history of the juvenile, including previous contacts with the Youth Aid Division, other law enforcement agencies, juvenile courts and other jurisdictions, prior periods of probation to this Court, or prior commitments to juvenile institutions.

8. The prospects for adequate protection of the public and the likelihood of reasonable rehabilitation of the juvenile (if he is found to have committed the alleged offense) by the use of procedures, services and facilities currently available to the Juvenile Court.

It will be the responsibility of any officer of the Court's staff assigned to make the investigation of any complaint in which waiver of jurisdiction is being considered to develop fully all available information which may bear upon the criteria and factors set forth above. Although not all such factors will be involved in an individual case, the Judge will consider the relevant factors in a specific case before reaching a conclusion to waive juvenile jurisdiction and transfer the case to the U.S. District Court for the District of Columbia for trial under the adult procedures of that Court.

STATE TRANSFER CRITERIA

Case Comment

Most jurisdictions provide statutory waiver criteria to determine if a juvenile should be waived to the adult court. The criteria is often similar to the standards established in *Kent v. United States*.

Other states address the issue of transfer by the analysis of a general question that asks "whether the public interest requires that youth be placed within the jurisdiction of the adult criminal court."

In *In the Matter of Seven Minors*, the Court reviewed the consolidated appeals of seven children and concluded that the individual juveniles should not be transferred to adult court unless it appears clear and convincing that the public safety and welfare require transfer.

This case is an example of the application of a broad transfer procedure.[5]

The waiver process is a statutory one, and the criteria that affect the decision to transfer the child to the criminal court are found in each of the state juvenile court acts. Today, forty-eight states, the District of Columbia, and the federal government have judicial waiver provisions.[6]

MATTER OF SEVEN MINORS

Cite as 664 P.2d 947 (Nev. 1983)

Springer, Justice:

The subject matter of these appeals is the practice of transferring certain serious juvenile offenders out of the juvenile division for criminal prosecution in district court. NRS 62.080[1] authorizes the juvenile court to certify[2] for adult criminal proceedings 16 and 17 year old juveniles chargeable with felony offenses. These appeals, presented by juveniles facing adult criminal prosecutions, give us occasion to examine an important and critical aspect of juvenile court law and to establish certain procedural and substantive standards for the guidance of juvenile courts in dealing with these matters.

Transfer has played an important role in juvenile court jurisprudence since its earliest days and has acted as a safety valve through which offenders who were within the statutory age of juvenile court ju-

---

1. NRS 62.080 provides as follows:

   62.080 Procedure when person 16 years or older is charged with felony. If a child 16 years of age or older is charged with an offense which would be a felony if committed by an adult, the juvenile division of the district court, after full investigation, may in its discretion retain jurisdiction or certify the child for proper criminal proceedings to any court which would have trial jurisdiction of such offense if committed by an adult; but no child under 16 years of age may be so certified. After such a child has been certified for proper criminal proceedings and his case has been transferred out of the juvenile division, original jurisdiction of the person rests with the court to which the child has been certified and the child may thereafter petition for transfer back to the juvenile division only upon a showing of exceptional circumstances.

2. Transferring or certifying juveniles to the adult criminal system has been variously referred to as "transfer," "certification," "waiver" and by other designations. We shall use the term "transfer" throughout this opinion.

risdiction could in appropriate circumstances be held accountable for their criminal acts by referral to the adult criminal justice system.

The transfer process is based upon the sound idea that there is no arbitrary age at which all youths should be held fully responsible as adults for their criminal acts and that there should be a transition period during which an offender may or may not be held criminally liable, depending on the nature of the offender and the offense.[3]

Other than the requirement of a "full investigation" the statute places no limitations on the discretion of the juvenile courts in such matters. The latitude of this discretion has been limited in some degree by our opinion in *Lewis v. State*, 86 Nev. 889, 478 P.2d 168 (1970), wherein we adopted the so-called *Kent*[4] criteria to be followed by juvenile courts in transfer matters.

Although the *Kent* criteria give some guidance to judges making transfer decisions, our adoption of these criteria in *Lewis* still did not provide a definitive, substantive rule to be applied in transfer proceedings.[5]

It is the office of this opinion, building on the Juvenile Court Act and on *Kent* and *Lewis*, to construct an understandable and usable transfer rule to be applied by juvenile court judges in making transfer decisions. We start with the Juvenile Court Act.

The Juvenile Court Act requires that juvenile courts function in a manner which is conducive to the child's welfare and to the best interests of the state. NRS 62.031(1).

Juvenile courts have traditionally been preoccupied with the interests of the child, and the interests of the state, as such, did not become a declared, joint purpose of our Juvenile Court Act until 1949.

The juvenile court from its inception in Illinois in 1899 until approximately the middle of this century was a child-centered institution based on theories taken from the positive school of criminology and especially on the deterministic principle that youthful law violators are not morally or criminally

responsible for their behavior but, rather, are victims of their environment—an environment which can be ameliorated and modified much in the way that a physician modifies the *milieu intérieur* of a sick patient.

Under such a doctrine the juvenile court tended to lose its identity as a court and became more of a social clinic than a court of law. Lost to such an institution was the moralizing and socializing influence associated with the operation of criminal courts; and, more importantly, lost too were society's ageless responses to criminal behavior: punishment, deterrence, retribution and segregation. So it was that juvenile courts in Nevada prior to 1949 were not charged with administering the criminal law for the protection of society against juvenile criminality but were required to treat the youthful law violator "not as a criminal, but as misdirected, and misguided and needing aid, encouragement and assistance." NCL § 1032.

This kind of kindly, paternalistic approach was eventually seen as being ill-suited to the task of dealing with juvenile crime. The legislative response to this realization was that toward the middle of this century a number of state legislatures, including our own, made changes in the purpose clause of juvenile court acts so that juvenile courts were required to consider the public interest as well as the child's interest. This departure from traditional juvenile justice philosophy is significant. We take it to indicate that the status of juvenile courts *as* courts is to be recognized and that protection of the public against juvenile criminal offenders may be effected by invocation of the means traditionally employed in the judicial administration of the criminal law. Juvenile courts may under such legislative direction properly consider the punitive, deterrent and other accepted adjuncts of the criminal law.

Although juvenile courts may have difficulty at times in balancing the interests of the child and the public, there is no irreconcilable opposition between the two. By formally recognizing the legitimacy of

---

3. The common law recognized a comparable transition period. A child between seven and fourteen was presumed to be *doli incapax*, incapable of distinguishing between good and evil, and therefore not criminally responsible. Although *prima facie* free from criminal liability, such a child could be proven to be *doli capax*, capable of forming criminal intent, and convicted of a crime.

4. *Kent v. United States*, 383 U.S. 541, 86 S.Ct. 1045, 16 L.Ed.2d 84 (1966).

5. The *Kent* case dealt only with procedural rights and was not a decision on the merits as to whether a transfer should take place. The *Kent* criteria were offered somewhat gratuitously in the form of an appendix which set forth the terms of a "policy memorandum" issued by a judge of the juvenile court of the District of Columbia. These criteria are not consolidated into a substantive rule, but they do present useful material out of which a substantive rule can be derived.

punitive and deterrent sanctions for criminal offenses juvenile courts will be properly and somewhat belatedly expressing society's firm disapproval of juvenile crime and will be clearly issuing a threat of punishment for criminal acts to the juvenile population.

Juvenile delinquents are brought before the court for committing crimes. They should be made to recognize that they have done something wrong and be prepared to accept unpleasant consequences together with the treatment and rehabilitation normally forthcoming in juvenile court proceedings. The two are related, and punishment has in many cases a rehabilitative effect on the child and consequently will serve the child's best interests as well as the state's.

Enforcing the state's interests in a manner designed to hold juveniles responsible for their violations of the criminal laws need not by any means dilute the strength of educative and rehabilitative measures properly taken by the juvenile courts in attempting to socialize and civilize errant youth. Guidance, understanding and care still have the same place in juvenile court proceedings. Even youths who commit more serious crimes can profit from a separation from adult offenders and from the special treatment and special programs which are available in juvenile courts; this does not mean that they should go unpunished.

[1] While juvenile courts must balance these sometimes conflicting interests, the court's duty to the public is paramount. The primary purpose of juvenile court intervention in delinquency cases is social control; and when one interest must predominate, it should be that of the public.

Generally speaking, in the juvenile court's weighing of the treatment and rehabilitative aspects of the juvenile process against the public protection aspects (accountability, punishment, deterrence and the like), the less serious and repetitive the criminal acts and the younger and more immature the child, the more can *parens patriae* be invoked for the care, rehabilitation and advancement of the best interest of the child. By the same token, the older and more mature the child and the more serious and repetitive the offenses, the more emphasis must be placed on public protection. We reach the extreme of this spectrum when we come to the matter of transfer. Here we have an all-or-none situation, one in which the basic decision is whether the public interest and safety will permit the youth before the court to be treated as a child. The public interest and safety require that some youths be held accountable as adults for their criminal misconduct, and be subjected to controls, punishment, deterrence and retribution found only in the adult criminal justice system. This is the reason for transfer.

Once transfer is justified on the basis of public interest and safety, there is no need to consider the "best interests of the child" or the youth's amenability to treatment in the juvenile court system except insofar as such considerations bear on the public interest. Once in a given case transfer is decided upon on this basis, the youth is no longer presumed to be a child in the eyes of the law and no longer entitled to the grace provided by the Juvenile Court Act in that particular case. Accordingly, the juvenile court need not consider the youth's best interests (and comfort) as such; although, in weighing the public necessity for transfer, the court may consider, for example, that the probability of a given youth's becoming a productive and law abiding citizen is much greater under juvenile court cognizance and that retention in the juvenile system may therefore be more in the longterm public interest than would be transfer for adult prosecution. As mentioned below, such subjective factors may be properly considered in determining which youths should *not* be transferred to adult court in those cases where the public interest does not clearly demand transfer.

Adoption of a rule for transfer based primarily on public safety interests is not in harmony with the rules commonly seen in operation throughout the juvenile justice system. As a general rule when substantive standards for transfer have been articulated either legislatively or judicially, they have been based on what was best for the child and on whether the youth subject to transfer proceedings appeared to be "unlikely to benefit from any disposition available to the juvenile court."[6] Under this view a youth who can establish a likelihood of benefit from juvenile court handling is immunized from transfer no mat-

---

6. ABA Institute of Judicial Administration, Juvenile Justice Standards, *Standards Relating to Transfer Between Courts*, § 2.2C, Commentary (1980). Hereinafter, referred to as ABA-IJA, *Standards Relating to Transfer Between Courts*.

ter how serious the crime committed or how extensive past criminal behavior has been. This is totally unacceptable.

With community protection as the guiding principle to be considered in transfer proceedings, subjective evaluations and prognostications as to whether a given youth is or is not likely to respond favorably to juvenile court treatment will no longer be the court's primary focus in transfer proceedings; rather, the dispositive question to be addressed by the court is whether the public interest requires that the youth be placed within the jurisdiction of the adult criminal courts. The juvenile court must make a rational discrimination, based upon the best interests of the state, between youths who should properly be kept in the juvenile court system and youths who should be sent to adult court.

[2] With public protection established as the general controlling principle upon which the transfer decision is to be based, we are able to formulate guidelines to be applied by the transfer decision maker. The *Kent* memorandum mentions two specific factors which should be taken into account, namely, whether the charged offense is of a heinous or aggravated character and whether there has been a pattern of repeated past offenses. These two factors together with a third, the personal qualities and background of the offender, are the factors ordinarily considered by a sentencing judge in a criminal case; they are also the factors which should be considered in determining whether or not the public interest requires that a particular youth be transferred to adult court. In transfer matters, then, we hold that the juvenile court should consider a decisional matrix comprised of the following three categories: first, nature and seriousness of the charged offense or offenses; second, persistency and seriousness of past adjudicated or admitted criminal offenses; and third, what we will refer to as the subjective factors, namely, such personal factors as age, maturity, character, personality, and family relationships and controls.

As in the sentencing process, primary and most weighty consideration will be given to the first two of these categories.[7] By focusing on the youth's crim-

inal activity, past and present, the court is in a better position to make objective judgments in differentiating between the hardcore offender and the majority of 16 and 17 year old youths who do not, in the public interest, necessarily have to suffer the consequences of adult prosecution. By stressing objective records rather than subjective clinical factors, the court will be adopting much safer and fairer criteria for transfer decisions.

It follows, then, that the transfer decision may be based on either or both of the first two categories. For example, the nature and seriousness of the crime upon which the transfer proceedings are based may be such that transfer should be based on this factor alone. Only the most heinous and egregious offenses would fall into this category, however. Similarly, a persistent record of past serious offenses may alone justify transfer even if the supporting, present charge were of relatively less seriousness.

The third category, the subjective factors, must be considered with greater caution; and transfer should not be based on this category alone. For example, a judge's conclusion that the youth in court is relatively sophisticated, uncontrite or rebellious does not justify a decision to transfer, absent a finding that one or both of the first two categories call for adult treatment. This third category, involving subjective evaluation of the youth, will come into play principally in close cases in which neither of the other two categories clearly impels transfer to adult court. In such cases, even given fairly serious criminal activity, a decision *not* to transfer may be properly and wisely made because such individual considerations as mental attitude, maturity level, emotional stability, family support and positive psychological and social evaluation require a finding that the public interest and safety are best served by retaining the youth in the juvenile system.

Once punishment and deterrence are accepted as standard fare on the juvenile court menu, there should be a greater tendency to retain youths in the juvenile system rather than to send them off to the dire consequences of the adult system. Juvenile courts should be able to fashion reasonable punitive sanctions as

---

7. A survey of some 207 juvenile court judges disclosed that the two factors which were weighed most heavily in making the decision to transfer to adult court were the past delinquency record of the juvenile and the seriousness of the charged offense. President's Commission on Law Enforcement and the Administration of Justice, *Task Force Report: Juvenile Delinquency and Youth Crime* (Washington, D.C., U.S. Government Printing Office, 1967), Appendix B, Table 5, p. 78.

part of dispositional programs in delinquency cases.[8] Such programs can provide acceptable levels of punishment and personal accountability for the offender and provide protection to the community in such a manner that it will not be necessary in most cases to consider having to resort to the adult criminal justice system. This might very well not be the case if the juvenile court were restricted to nonpunitive types of rehabilitative and therapeutic measures alone. Premature transfer to adult court of young and immature youths would frequently be contrary to the interests of society, as well as being contrary to the interests of the youth. The harsher treatment and association with hardened criminals may increase the incipient criminal tendencies of the youthful offender. Another consideration militating against premature transfer is the nullification process whereby transferred youths may avoid punishment altogether by reason of a sentencing judge's understandable reluctance to commit a 16 or 17 year old to the miseries of an adult prison.

PROCEDURAL CONSIDERATIONS

To complete the elaboration of a community safety standard applicable in transfer proceedings it is necessary to deal with two procedural considerations, namely, burden of proof and prosecutive merit.

[3] The legislature has set the upper limit of original juvenile court jurisdiction at age 18. Persons under 18 years of age are presumed to come within the jurisdiction of the juvenile court; they should not be transferred from the juvenile court to adult court unless it is made to appear clearly and convincingly that the public safety and welfare require transfer.

[4] "Prosecutive merit" is a term referring to the necessity for establishing the merit of the prosecution's case as a condition for proceeding with the transfer process. According to the *Kent* memorandum, prosecutive merit exists if there is evidence upon which a grand jury would be expected to return an indictment. To say that there is prosecutive merit is to say that there is probable cause to believe that the subject minor committed the charged crime.

Judicial economy requires that a preliminary determination be made as to the prosecutive merit of the charge before going ahead with the transfer process. If there is no *prima facie* case to support the charge, there is no point in the court's involving itself further in the process. Thus, the only reasonable way to proceed is for the court to make an initial determination of prosecutive merit. Unless probable cause is conceded by the minor, the court should proceed to hear and determine this issue before proceeding further.

THE TRANSFER CASES

A. *Thomas R. (Case No. 12966)*

Thomas R. was 17 years old at the time of his certification hearing. He was charged with residential burglary.

The minor has a number of previous felony offenses. In November, 1975 when he was only ten years old, he was adjudicated a delinquent on felony charges of burglary and arson. On February 2, 1977, he was adjudicated a delinquent on a burglary charge.

[5] The minor's record of past adjudicated offenses is of the kind that would support transfer; however, we note that in making the decision to transfer Thomas the juvenile judge also considered past offenses which were neither admitted by the juvenile nor adjudicated as delinquencies.[9] This is error. See *Marvin v. State*, 95 Nev. 836, 603 P.2d 1056 (1979) (requiring reliance upon "accurate and reliable information"). To be considered by the court past offenses should be either adjudicated or properly admitted by the youth.

---

8. This opinion is intended to have the effect of affording considerable added breadth to the juvenile dispositional process. By expressly approving punishment and community protection as legitimate concerns of the juvenile court process we allow for a whole spectrum of sanctions by which youthful offenders can be held accountable for their criminal acts. These sanctions can include community service, deprivation of driving and other privileges, house detention, restitution to victims in the form of actual indemnity and additional compensation for intangible injuries suffered by crime victims, temporary detention in detention homes and detention of 16 and 17 years olds for brief periods in jail facilities apart from adult inmates. Obviously, punishment is not restricted to confinement and incarceration. Since the legislature has not set determinate sentences in training centers for commission of criminal offenses by juveniles, we would not undertake to do so judicially. We do not think it would be unreasonable, however, for juvenile judges to order periods of punitive detention in juvenile detention facilities, not to exceed 60 days.

9. "[T]his youngster is charged with having committed a number of offenses in the past . . . which he has denied and they have not been proven."

[6] The question, then, is whether, absent the improperly considered criminal offenses, there is still support in the record for the transfer decision. When the seriousness of the present offense, residential burglary, is viewed in conjunction with the previous felony delinquency adjudications, a quantum of culpability is reached which precludes appellate interference in the juvenile judge's decision.

We consider burglary to be a very serious crime. Intentional and trespassory invasion of the home of another, especially in the nighttime, can arguably be considered as a form of violence. It is an offense which conduces towards violence and may cause serious and permanent psychological harm to the victim. It is the type of crime which may, when considered with other factors, justify the imposition of the punitive and deterrent consequences found only in the adult criminal justice system.

In examining the third category, the personal attributes of this youth, we find no cause to question the trial judge's decision. Although he was only 16 years old at the time of the charged burglary, the record shows that the minor has spent time in the restrictive environment of the Spring Mountain Youth Camp, apparently to no avail. The record further shows an admission by the youth that he discharged a firearm during the previous burglary. There is nothing that we can find concerning the personal character and attributes of this youth which would cast any doubt on the juvenile judge's decision to transfer. The juvenile judge did not abuse his discretion in ordering the transfer, and his decision is, in our opinion, supported by clear and convincing evidence. We affirm.

B. Michael S. (Case No. 13296)

[7] Michael is charged with participating in two residential burglaries which occurred on the same day. He was 17 years old at the time the charged offense was committed; he was 18 at the time of his hearing. Michael's past record is that in June, 1979 he and a companion stole two bicycles.

The primary factors discussed above, seriousness of the charged offense and past record, are not of such weight in this instance as to require the invocation of the heavy sanctions available in the adult criminal justice system. We have here a boy who had previously stolen a couple of bicycles and who was involved with three other youths in the daytime burglary of two homes.

Although burglary is a serious crime which can, when combined with other factors, support a transfer decision, we do not think the charges in this case support a decision which calls for adult prosecution and possible prison sentence. We most certainly are neither diminishing the seriousness of the charges nor suggesting that this minor should not be punished for his criminality. We say only that this case does not rise to the level or degree that calls for removal to the adult system. This 17 year old minor can be and should be punished, but this may be accomplished in the juvenile court system.

There is evidence in the record that Michael's mother, a policewoman, and his stepfather are supportive of him and that his problem seems to turn around the use of marijuana and "peer pressure." The subjective category appears to weigh in favor of Michael's retention in juvenile court.

The interests of the state and the interests of the child will be best served by Michael's retention in the juvenile court. A one-time bicycle thief charged with burglary need not be sent off to the adult criminal justice system. The transfer order will be reversed.

C. Terry M. (Case No. 13483)

[8] This 17 year old juvenile appeared on a petition for transfer on a charge of residential burglary. He was found hiding in the burglarized victim's house, and there appears to be little question concerning his complicity in the charged offense. Although we agree with appellant that the mere filing of a juvenile petition by the district attorney would not by itself support a challenged finding of prosecutive merit, there is in the present record sufficient unchallenged evidence of the youth's complicity in the charged burglary to support the juvenile court judge's finding of prosecutive merit, and we will not set it aside.

This youth's record shows that he is a persistent offender. In 1977 he was adjudicated to be a delinquent child by reason of his having committed the offense of possession of stolen property. In January, 1978, Terry was committed to the Nevada Youth Training Center following adjudication of delinquency on two counts of burglary and one count of possession of a controlled substance.

Concerning the personal attributes of the youth, it is interesting to note that the record contains a qualified professional opinion of the Superintendent of the Nevada Youth Training Center that this young man is immature and would benefit from further treatment as a juvenile in juvenile court. As indicated above, we do not accept amenability to juvenile court treatment as immunizing a youth from adult transfer, and we adopt a much more objective standard which looks primarily to what the youth has done rather than to subjective evaluation as to present character or future potential.

There is clear and convincing evidence to support the transfer; we affirm.

D. Brett G. (Case No. 13488)

[9] This case presents very little difficulty. Brett G., 17 years of age, is accused of two residential burglaries. A finding of prosecutive merit will be upheld for the same reasons stated in the case of Terry M. He was adjudicated a delinquent twice in 1977 for burglary. He has been institutionalized for juvenile offenses. He is a heavy drug user, and little or no case is made for his retention in juvenile court. The case is clear and convincing, the transfer is affirmed.

E. Parris W. (Case No. 13494).

[10] This case is similar to that of Michael S. Parris, a 17 year old, has a previous adjudicated delinquency, possession of stolen property, and is presently charged with residential burglary. The case of Parris differs from Michael in that Parris was on probation at the time of the alleged commission of the residential burglaries. This certainly is indicative of incorrigibility and persistency on the minor's part and favors the transfer decision; however, the previous charge of possession of stolen property does not seem to be of great consequence, and it does not appear clear and convincing to us that the combination of this and the present charge rise to the degree of culpability which would require adult treatment in order to afford proper protection to the community.

There are a number of other considerations in this case. It is obvious from the record that the juvenile judge was strongly and improperly influenced by a number of previous arrests and referrals as opposed to felony delinquency adjudications or admissions.

Concerning personal attributes of the youth, we note that the juvenile's probation officer recommended against transfer, stating that the youth "has had very little services through the Probation Department," and had been on probation only approximately 100 days. The minor lived at home and had

close family ties. He was enrolled in high school and near graduation at the time the charged offense was committed. He has received tentative acceptance by the University of Nevada-Las Vegas.

The mentioned matrix of past offenses, present charges and personal attributes fails to bring this case to a level which would clearly and convincingly justify transfer. We reverse the transfer order.

F. Sandra C. (No. 13679)

[11] Sandra, age 17, is accused of stealing $118 worth of clothing from J.C. Penney's. The record shows two petty larceny adjudications prior to the present grand larceny charge as well as an adjudication of attempted larceny from the person.

There is very little in this record to show that community safety and the public interest can be served only by subjecting this juvenile to adult prosecution. The child has never been institutionalized by juvenile authorities. The girl's probation officer advised the judge that the juvenile court could offer a better rehabilitation program for Sandra; this could include juvenile institutionalization, an approach not yet tried with her.

The report to the court by the juvenile probation department indicates that the juvenile's degree of maturity is questionable and that she functioned "extremely well under an alternate living situation and intensive supervision in the past." It is true that she has had three adjudications relating to theft during the three years preceding the transfer hearing, but this does not mean that community safety and the best interests of the state require that she be removed from juvenile court and face adult imprisonment. Sandra is uneducated and immature. She has never been placed in a juvenile institution such as the Girl's Training Center in Caliente. There is every reason to believe that the optimal treatment of this girl from the standpoint of the community and the child is the imposition of some punitive sanction and continued training and rehabilitation in the juvenile court system. For these reasons the transfer order is reversed and the matter remanded to the juvenile division, wherein the minor will be treated in accordance with the Juvenile Court Act.

G. Amanda C. (No. 13819)

[12] Amanda C., age 17, is charged with the felonious offense of taking property from the person of another under circumstances not amounting to rob-

bery. She is accused of picking the pockets of a man with whom she was engaged in prostitution. The commission of this isolated, essentially nonviolent crime, if proven, would not by itself, absent any established record of prior criminal activity, support in a clear and convincing fashion the necessity, in the public interest, to transfer this young lady to the adult system.

Amanda has no juvenile record of any kind. The certification report indicates that Amanda had been engaged in prostitution, but there is no evidence in the record of any adjudications, convictions or admissions of any previous offenses. As a consequence, if Amanda is to be transferred, it must be on the basis of the charged offense.

Certainly there are criminal offenses which are so heinous and so outrageous that standing alone they would require transfer even absent a record of prior criminal activity. This is not such an offense. The order of transfer will be reversed in this case.

SUMMARY

By way of emphasis, we deem it advisable to summarize by enumeration the indicated procedures in transfer matters. We do so, thus:

1. Transfer proceedings are to be initiated by written motion or petition which states explicitly the charged felony offense or offenses upon which the requested transfer is based and which further states the past record of criminal conduct. The motion or petition may also include material relating to the personal background and attributes of the subject youth which are considered material to the court's decision.

2. A transfer investigation is to be ordered and a report completed and filed. The investigative report is to be served on the subject minor and his parents or guardians and should state the details of the offense or offenses charged, the specific nature of previous adjudicated or admitted criminal offenses, and elements relating to personal attributes of the youth.

3. A preliminary determination of prosecutive merit is to be made to assure that there is probable cause to believe that the subject youth committed the offense or offenses charged. This may be done on the basis of legal admissions or confessions or by voluntary waiver of probable cause. When the minor challenges the issue of prosecutive merit and probable cause, due process requires that a hearing be held and that a judicial determination be made on the basis of the hearing.

4. The hearing judge should decide for or against transfer on the basis of the mentioned matrix of categories: nature and seriousness of the charged offense or offenses, persistency and seriousness of adjudicated or voluntarily admitted past criminal offenses and the personal attributes of the offender. Either seriousness of the charged offense or past record, or a combination of the two categories, may support a decision to transfer. Transfer may not be based solely on subjective evaluation of the youth, on character, attitude or other personal attributes alone; however, such matters may be considered in conjunction with the other factors in deciding whether transfer of the youth before the court is clearly and convincingly necessary for public protection. Transfer cannot be avoided merely by a showing of amenability to treatment in juvenile court.

5. Specific written findings which support the decision to transfer are to be made in each case as part of the formal order of transfer.

Manoukian, C.J., and Mowbray, Steffen, and Gunderson, JJ., concur.

DOUBLE JEOPARDY IN WAIVER PROCEEDINGS

Case Comment

What is the rule of law governing prosecution in the adult courts after a child was originally held in jeopardy within the jurisdiction of the juvenile court? In *Breed v. Jones*, the Supreme Court found that further prosecution (after waiver) of a boy already found to be a delinquent violated his Fifth and Fourteenth Amendment rights ("tried twice for same offense"). In reaching its decision, the Court cites the recent trend in juvenile court to provide the delinquent with protection similar to that enjoyed by an adult offender. Though discretionary flexibility may be an important feature of juvenile court, the heavy burden imposed by criminal trial outweighs such consideration. In essence, the decision mandates that waiver procedures be held prior to the adjudicatory hearing.

The *Breed* case provides answers on several important waiver issues: (1) *Breed* prohibits trying a child in an adult court when there has been a prior adjudicatory juvenile proceeding; (2) probable cause may exist at a transfer hearing, and this does not violate subsequent jeopardy if the child is transferred to the adult court; and (3) because the same evidence is often used in both the transfer hearing and subsequent trial in either the juvenile or adult court, a different judge is often required for the hearing.

BREED v. JONES

United States Supreme Court, 1975.
421 U.S. 519, 95 S.Ct. 1779, 44 L.Ed.2d 346.

Mr. Chief Justice Burger delivered the opinion of the Court.

We granted certiorari to decide whether the prosecution of respondent as an adult, after juvenile court proceedings which resulted in a finding that respondent had violated a criminal statute and a subsequent finding that he was unfit for treatment as a juvenile, violated the Fifth and Fourteenth Amendments to the United States Constitution.

On February 9, 1971, a petition was filed in the Superior Court of California, County of Los Angeles Juvenile Court, alleging that respondent, then 17 years of age, was a person described by Cal.Welf. & Inst'ns Code § 602,[1] in that, on or about February 8, while armed with a deadly weapon, he had committed acts which, if committed by an adult, would constitute the crime of robbery in violation of Cal.Penal Code § 211. The following day, a detention hearing was held, at the conclusion of which respondent was ordered detained pending a hearing on the petition.[2]

The jurisdictional or adjudicatory hearing was conducted on March 1, pursuant to Cal.Welf. & Inst'ns Code § 701.[3] After taking testimony from two prosecution witnesses and respondent, the Juvenile Court found that the allegations in the petition were true and that respondent was a person described by § 602, and it sustained the petition. The proceedings were continued for a dispositional hearing,[4] pending

---

1. As of the date of filing of the petition in this case, Cal.Welf. & Inst'ns Code § 602 (West 1966) provided:

"Any person under the age of 21 years who violates any law of this State or of the United States or any ordinance of any city or county of this State defining crime or who, after having been found by the juvenile court to be a person described by Section 601, fails to obey any lawful order of the juvenile court, is within the jurisdiction of the juvenile court, which may adjudge such person to be a ward of the court."

An amendment in 1971, not relevant here, lowered the jurisdictional age from 21 to 18. C. 1748, § 66, 1971 Cal.Stats. 3766.

2. See Cal.Welf. & Inst'ns Code §§ 632, 635, 636 (West 1966). The probation officer was required to present a prima facie case that respondent had committed the offense alleged in the petition. In re William M., 3 Cal.3d 16, 89 Cal.Rptr. 33, 473 P.2d 737 (1970). Respondent was represented by court-appointed counsel at the detention hearing and thereafter.

3. At the time of the hearing, Cal.Welf. & Inst'ns Code § 701 (West 1966) provided:

"At the hearing, the court shall first consider only the question whether the minor is a person described by Sections 600, 601, or 602, and for this purpose, any matter or information relevant and material to the circumstances or acts which are alleged to bring him within the jurisdiction of the juvenile court is admissible and may be received in evidence; however, *a preponderance of evidence*, legally admissible in the trial of criminal cases, must be adduced to support a finding that the minor is a person described by Section 602, and a preponderance of evidence, legally admissible in the trial of civil cases must be adduced to support a finding that the minor is a person described by Sections 600 or 601. When it appears that the minor has made an extra judicial admission or confession and denies the same at the hearing, the court may continue the hearing for not to exceed seven days to enable the probation officer to subpoena witnesses to attend the hearing to prove the allegations of the petition. If the minor is not represented by counsel at the hearing, it shall be deemed that objections that could have been made to the evidence were made." (Emphasis added.)

A 1971 amendment substituted "proof beyond a reasonable doubt supported by evidence" for the language in italics. C. 934, § 1, 1971 Cal.Stats. 1832. Respondent does not claim that the standard of proof at the hearing failed to satisfy due process. See In re Winship, 397 U.S. 358, 90 S.Ct. 1068, 25 L.Ed.2d 368 (1970); DeBacker v. Brainard, 396 U.S. 28, 31, 90 S.Ct. 163, 165, 24 L.Ed.2d 148 (1969).

Hereafter, the § 701 hearing will be referred to as the adjudicatory hearing.

4. At the time, Cal.Welf. & Inst'ns Code § 702 (West Supp.1968) provided:

"After hearing such evidence, the court shall make a finding, noted in the minutes of the court, whether or not the minor is a person described by Sections 600, 601, or 602. If it finds that the minor is not such a person, it shall order that the petition be dismissed and the minor be discharged from any detention or restriction theretofore ordered. If the court finds that the minor is such a person, it shall make and enter its findings and order accordingly and shall then proceed to hear evidence on the question of the proper disposition to be made of the minor. Prior to doing so, it may continue the hearing, if necessary, to receive the social study of the probation officer or to receive other evidence on its own motion or the motion of a parent or guardian for not to exceed 10 judicial days if the minor is detained during such continuance, and if the minor is not detained, it may continue the hearing to a date not later than 30 days after the date of filing of the petition. The court may, for good cause shown continue the hearing for an additional 15 days, if the minor is not detained. The court may make such order for detention of the minor or his release from detention, during the period of the continuance, as is appropriate."

which the court ordered that respondent remain detained.

At a hearing conducted on March 15, the Juvenile Court indicated its intention to find respondent "not * * * amenable to the care, treatment and training program available through the facilities of the juvenile court" under Cal. Welf. & Inst'ns Code § 707.[5] Respondent's counsel orally moved "to continue the matter on the ground of surprise," contending that respondent "was not informed that it was going to be a fitness hearing." The court continued the matter for one week, at which time, having considered the report of the probation officer assigned to the case and having heard her testimony, it declared respondent "unfit for treatment as a juvenile,"[6] and ordered that he be prosecuted as an adult.[7]

Thereafter, respondent filed a petition for a writ of habeas corpus in Juvenile Court, raising the same double jeopardy claim now presented. Upon the denial of that petition, respondent sought habeas corpus relief in the California Court of Appeal, Second Appellate District. Although it initially stayed the criminal prosecution pending against respondent, that court denied the petition. *In re Gary Steven J.*, 17 Cal. App. 3d 704, 95 Cal. Rptr. 185 (1971). The Supreme Court of California denied respondent's petition for hearing.

After a preliminary hearing respondent was ordered held for trial in Superior Court, where an information was subsequently filed accusing him of having committed robbery, in violation of Cal. Penal Code § 211, while armed with a deadly weapon, on or about February 8, 1971. Respondent entered a plea of not guilty, and he also pleaded that he had "already been placed once in jeopardy and convicted of the offense charged, by the judgment of the Superior Court of the County of Los Angeles, Juvenile Court, rendered * * * on the 1st day of March, 1971." App. 47. By stipulation, the case was submitted to the court on the transcript of the preliminary hearing. The court found respondent guilty of robbery in the first degree under Cal. Penal Code § 211a and ordered that he be committed to the California Youth Authority.[8] No appeal was taken from the judgment of conviction.

---

5. At the time, Cal. Welf. & Inst'ns Code § 707 (West Supp. 1967) provided:

"At any time during a hearing upon a petition alleging that a minor is, by reason of violation of any criminal statute or ordinance, a person described in Section 602, when substantial evidence has been adduced to support a finding that the minor was 16 years of age or older at the time of the alleged commission of such offense and that the minor would not be amenable to the care, treatment and training program available through the facilities of the juvenile court, or if, at any time after such hearing, a minor who was 16 years of age or older at the time of the commission of an offense and who was committed therefor by the court to the Youth Authority, is returned to the court by the Youth Authority pursuant to Section 780 or 1737.1, the court may make a finding noted in the minutes of the court that the minor is not a fit and proper subject to be dealt with under this chapter, and the court shall direct the district attorney or other appropriate prosecuting officer to prosecute the person under the applicable criminal statute or ordinance and thereafter dismiss the petition or, if a prosecution has been commenced in another court but has been suspended while juvenile court proceedings are held, shall dismiss the petition and issue its order directing that the other court proceedings resume.

"In determining whether the minor is a fit and proper subject to be dealt with under this chapter, the offense, in itself, shall not be sufficient to support a finding that such minor is not a fit and proper subject to be dealt with under the provisions of the Juvenile Court Law.

"A denial by the person on whose behalf the petition is brought of any or all of the facts or conclusions set forth therein or of any inference to be drawn therefrom is not, of itself, sufficient to support a finding that such person is not a fit and proper subject to be dealt with under the provisions of the Juvenile Court Law.

"The court shall cause the probation officer to investigate and submit a report on the behavioral patterns of the person being considered for unfitness."

6. The Juvenile Court noted:

"This record I have read is one of the most threatening records I have read about any Minor who has come before me.

"We have, as a matter of simple fact, no less than three armed robberies, each with a loaded weapon. The degree of delinquency which that represents, the degree of sophistication which that represents and the degree of impossibility of assistance as a juvenile which that represents, I think is overwhelming * * * " App. 33.

7. In doing so, the Juvenile Court implicitly rejected respondent's double jeopardy argument, made at both the original § 702 hearing and in a memorandum submitted by counsel prior to the resumption of that hearing after the continuance.

8. The authority for the order of commitment derived from Cal. Welf. & Inst'ns Code § 1731.5 (West Supp. 1970). At the time of the order, Cal. Welf. & Inst'ns Code § 1771 (West 1966) provided:

"Every person convicted of a felony and committed to the authority shall be discharged when such person reaches his 25th birthday, unless an order for further detention has been made by the committing court pursuant to Article 6 (commencing with Section 1800) or unless a petition is filed under Article 5 of this chapter. In the event such a petition under Article 5 is filed, the authority shall retain control until the final disposition of the proceeding under Article 5."

On December 10, 1971, respondent, through his mother as guardian *ad litem*, filed the instant petition for a writ of habeas corpus in the United States District Court for the Central District of California. In his petition he alleged that his transfer to adult court pursuant to Cal.Welf. & Inst'ns Code § 707 and subsequent trial there "placed him in double jeopardy." App. 13. The District Court denied the petition, rejecting respondent's contention that jeopardy attached at his adjudicatory hearing. It concluded that the "distinctions between the preliminary procedures and hearings provided by California law for juveniles and a criminal trial are many and apparent and the effort of [respondent] to relate them is unconvincing," and that "even assuming jeopardy attached during the preliminary juvenile proceedings * * * it is clear that no new jeopardy arose by the juvenile proceeding sending the case to the criminal court." 343 F.Supp. 690, 692 (CD Cal. 1972).

The Court of Appeals reversed, concluding that applying double jeopardy protection to juvenile proceedings would not "impede the juvenile courts in carrying out their basic goal of rehabilitating the erring youth," and that the contrary result might "do irreparable harm to or destroy their confidence in our judicial system." The court therefore held that the Double Jeopardy Clause "is fully applicable to juvenile court proceedings." 497 F.2d 1160, 1165 (CA9 1974).

Turning to the question whether there had been a constitutional violation in this case, the Court of Appeals pointed to the power of the Juvenile Court to "impose severe restrictions upon the juvenile's liberty," *ibid.*, in support of its conclusion that jeopardy attached in respondent's adjudicatory hearing.[9] It rejected petitioner's contention that no new jeopardy attached when respondent was referred to Superior Court and subsequently tried and convicted, finding "continuing jeopardy" principles advanced by petitioner inapplicable. Finally, the Court of Appeals observed that acceptance of petitioner's position would "allow the prosecution to review in advance the accused's defense and, as here, hear him testify about the crime charged," a procedure it found offensive to "our concepts of basic, even-handed fairness." The court therefore held that once jeopardy attached at the adjudicatory hearing, a minor could not be retried as an adult or a juvenile "absent some exception to the double jeopardy prohibition," and that there "was none here." 497 F.2d, at 1168.

We granted certiorari because of a conflict between courts of appeals and the highest courts of a number of States on the issue presented in this case and similar issues and because of the importance of final resolution of the issue to the administration of the juvenile court system.

I

The parties agree that, following his transfer from Juvenile Court, and as a defendant to a felony information, respondent was entitled to the full protection of the Double Jeopardy Clause of the Fifth Amendment, as applied to the States through the Fourteentn Amendment. See *Benton v. Maryland*, 395 U.S. 784, 89 S.Ct. 2056, 23 L.Ed.2d 707 (1969). In addition, they agree that respondent was put in jeopardy by the proceedings on that information, which resulted in an adjudication that he was guilty of robbery in the first degree and in a sentence of commitment. Finally, there is no dispute that the petition filed in Juvenile Court and the information filed in Superior Court related to the "same offence" within the meaning of the constitutional prohibition. The point of disagreement between the parties, and the question for our decision, is whether, by reason of the proceedings in Juvenile Court, respondent was "twice put in jeopardy."

II

Jeopardy denotes risk. In the constitutional sense, jeopardy describes the risk that is traditionally associated with a criminal prosecution. See *Price v. Georgia*, 398 U.S. 323, 326, 329, 90 S.Ct. 1757, 1759, 26 L.Ed.2d 300 (1970); *Serfass v. United States*, 420 U.S. 377, 95 S.Ct. 1055, 43 L.Ed.2d 265 (1975). Although the constitutional language, "jeopardy of life or limb," suggests proceedings in which only the most serious penalties can be imposed, the Clause has long been construed to mean something far broader than its literal language. See *Ex parte Lange*, 85 U.S. (18 Wall.) 163, 170–173,

---

9. In reaching this conclusion, the Court of Appeals also relied on *Fain v. Duff*, 488 F.2d 218 (CA5 1973), cert. pending, No. 73–1768, and *Richard M. v. Superior Court*, 4 Cal.3d 370, 93 Cal.Rptr. 752, 482 P.2d 664 (1971), and it noted that "California concedes that jeopardy attaches when the juvenile is adjudicated a ward of the court." 497 F.2d at 1166.

21 L.Ed. 872 (1873).[10] At the same time, however, we have held that the risk to which the Clause refers is not present in proceedings that are not "essentially criminal." *Helvering v. Mitchell*, 303 U.S. 391, 398, 58 S.Ct. 630, 632, 82 L.Ed. 917 (1938). See *United States ex rel. Marcus v. Hess*, 317 U.S. 537, 63 S.Ct. 379, 87 L.Ed. 498 (1943); *One Lot Emerald Cut Stones v. United States*, 409 U.S. 232, 93 S.Ct. 489, 34 L.Ed.2d 438 (1972). See also J. Sigler, Double Jeopardy 60–62 (1969).

Although the juvenile court system had its genesis in the desire to provide a distinctive procedure and setting to deal with the problems of youth, including those manifested by antisocial conduct, our decisions in recent years have recognized that there is a gap between the originally benign conception of the system and its realities. With the exception of *McKeiver v. Pennsylvania*, 403 U.S. 528, 91 S.Ct. 1976, 29 L.Ed.2d 647 (1971), the Court's response to that perception has been to make applicable in juvenile proceedings constitutional guarantees associated with traditional criminal prosecutions. *In re Gault*, 387 U.S. 1, 87 S.Ct. 1428, 18 L.Ed.2d 527 (1967); *In re Winship*, 397 U.S. 358, 90 S.Ct. 1068, 25 L.Ed.2d 368 (1970). In so doing the Court has evinced awareness of the threat which such a process represents to the efforts of the juvenile court system, functioning in a unique manner, to ameliorate the harshness of criminal justice when applied to youthful offenders. That the system has fallen short of the high expectations of its sponsors in no way detracts from the broad social benefits sought or from those benefits that can survive constitutional scrutiny.

We believe it is simply too late in the day to conclude, as did the District Court in this case, that a juvenile is not put in jeopardy at a proceeding whose object is to determine whether he has committed acts that violate a criminal law and whose potential consequences include both the stigma inherent in such a determination and the deprivation of liberty for many years.[11] For it is clear under our cases that determining the relevance of constitu-

tional policies, like determining the applicability of constitutional rights, in juvenile proceedings, requires that courts eschew "the 'civil' label-of-convenience which has been attached to juvenile proceedings," *In re Gault, supra*, 387 U.S. at 50, 87 S.Ct. at 1455, and that "the juvenile process * * * be candidly appraised." 387 U.S. at 21, 87 S.Ct. at 1440. See *In re Winship, supra*, 397 U.S. at 365–366, 90 S.Ct. at 1073.

As we have observed, the risk to which the term *jeopardy* refers is that traditionally associated with "actions intended to authorize criminal punishment to vindicate public justice." *United States ex rel. Marcus v. Hess, supra*, 317 U.S. at 548–549, 63 S.Ct. at 388. Because of its purpose and potential consequences, and the nature and resources of the State, such a proceeding imposes heavy pressures and burdens—psychological, physical, and financial—on a person charged. The purpose of the Double Jeopardy Clause is to require that he be subject to the experience only once "for the same offence." See *Green v. United States*, 355 U.S. 184, 187, 78 S.Ct. 221, 223, 2 L.Ed.2d 199 (1957); *Price v. Georgia*, 398 U.S. at 331, 90 S.Ct. at 1765; *United States v. Jorn*, 400 U.S. 470, 479, 91 S.Ct. 547, 554, 27 L.Ed.2d 543 (1971).

In *In re Gault, supra*, 387 U.S. at 36, 87 S.Ct. at 1448, this Court concluded that, for purposes of the right to counsel, a "proceeding where the issue is whether the child will be found to be 'delinquent' and subjected to the loss of his liberty for years is comparable in seriousness to a felony prosecution." See *In re Winship, supra*, 397 U.S. at 366, 90 S.Ct. at 1073. The Court stated that the term *delinquent* had "come to involve only slightly less stigma than the term 'criminal' applied to adults," *In re Gault, supra*, 387 U.S. at 24, 87 S.Ct. at 1441; see *In re Winship, supra*, 397 U.S. at 367, 90 S.Ct. at 1074, and that, for purposes of the privilege against self-incrimination, "commitment is a deprivation of liberty. It is incarceration against one's will, whether it is called 'criminal' or 'civil.' " *In re Gault, supra*, 387 U.S. at 50, 87 S.Ct. at 1455. See 387 U.S.,

---

10. Distinctions which in other contexts have proved determinative of the constitutional rights of those charged with offenses against public order have no similarly confined the protection of the Double Jeopardy Clause. Compare *Robinson v. Neil*, 409 U.S. 505, 93 S.Ct. 876, 35 L.Ed.2d 29 (1973), with *Baldwin v. New York*, 399 U.S. 66, 90 S.Ct. 1886, 26 L.Ed.2d 437 (1970), and *Argersinger v. Hamlin*, 407 U.S. 25, 92 S.Ct. 2006, 32 L.Ed.2d 530 (1972). For the details of Robinson's trial for violating a city ordinance, see *Robinson v. Henderson*, 268 F.Supp. 349 (E.D.Tenn.1967), *aff'd*, 391 F.2d 933 (CA6 1968).

11. At the time of respondent's dispositional hearing, permissible dispositions included commitment to the California Youth Authority until he reached the age of 21 years. See Cal.Welf. & Inst'ns Code §§ 607, 731 (West 1966). Petitioner has conceded that the "adjudicatory hearing is, in every sense, a court trial." Tr. of Oral Arg. 4.

at 27, 87 S.Ct. at 1443; *In re Winship, supra*, 397 U.S. at 367,[12] 90 S.Ct. at 1074.

Thus, in terms of potential consequences, there is little to distinguish an adjudicatory hearing such as was held in this case from a traditional criminal prosecution. For that reason, it engenders elements of "anxiety and insecurity" in a juvenile, and imposes a "heavy personal strain." See *Green v. United States, supra*, 355 U.S. at 187, 78 S.Ct. at 223; *United States v. Jorn, supra*, 400 U.S. at 479, 91 S.Ct. at 554; Snyder, The Impact of the Juvenile Court Hearing on the Child, 17 Crime & Delinquency 180 (1971). And we can expect that, since our decisions implementing fundamental fairness in the juvenile court system, hearings have been prolonged, and some of the burdens incident to a juvenile's defense increased, as the system has assimilated the process thereby imposed. See Note, Double Jeopardy and the Waiver of Jurisdiction in California's Juvenile Courts, 24 Stan.L.Rev. 874, 902 n. 138 (1972). Cf. Canon and Kolson, Rural Compliance with *Gault*; Kentucky, A Case Study, 10 J.Fam.L. 300, 320–326 (1971).

We deal here, not with "the formalities of the criminal adjudicative process," *McKeiver v. Pennsylvania*, 403 U.S., at 551, 91 S.Ct. at 1989, but with an analysis of an aspect of the juvenile court system in terms of the kind of risk to which jeopardy refers. Under our decisions we can find no persuasive distinction in that regard between the proceeding conducted in this case pursuant to Cal.Welf. & Inst'ns Code § 701 and a criminal prosecution, each of which is designed "to vindicate [the] very vital interest in enforcement of criminal laws." *United States v. Jorn, supra*, 400 U.S. at 479, 91 S.Ct. at 554. We therefore conclude that respondent was put in jeopardy at the adjudicatory hearing. Jeopardy attached when respondent was "put to trial before the trier of the facts," *ibid.*, that is, when the Juvenile Court, as the trier of the facts, began to hear evidence. See *Serfass v. United States*, 420 U.S at ___, 95 S.Ct. 1055.[13]

III

Petitioner argues that, even assuming jeopardy attached at respondent's adjudicatory hearing, the procedure by which he was transferred from Juvenile Court and tried on a felony information in Superior Court did not violate the Double Jeopardy Clause. The argument is supported by two distinct, but in this case overlapping, lines of analysis. First, petitioner reasons that the procedure violated none of the policies of the Double Jeopardy Clause or that, alternatively, it should be upheld by analogy to those cases which permit retrial of an accused who has obtained reversal of a conviction on appeal. Second, pointing to this Court's concern for "the juvenile court's assumed ability to function in a unique manner," *McKeiver v. Pennsylvania, supra*, 403 U.S. at 547, 91 S.Ct. at 1987, petitioner urges that, should we conclude traditional principles "would otherwise bar a transfer to adult court after a delinquency adjudication," we should avoid that result here because it "would diminish the flexibility and informality of juvenile court proceedings without conferring any additional due process benefits upon juveniles charged with delinquent acts."

A

We cannot agree with petitioner that the trial of respondent in Superior Court on an information charging the same offense as that for which he had been tried in Juvenile Court violated none of the policies of the Double Jeopardy Clause. For, even accepting petitioner's premise that respondent "never faced the risk of more than one punishment," we have pointed out that "the Double Jeopardy Clause * * * is written in terms of potential or risk of *trial* and conviction, not punishment." *Price v. Georgia*, 398 U.S. at 329, 90 S.Ct. at 1761. (Emphasis added.) And we have recently noted:

The policy of avoiding multiple trials has been regarded as so important that exceptions to the principle

---

12. Nor does the fact "that the purpose of the commitment is rehabilitative and not punitive * * * change its nature. * * * Regardless of the purposes for which incarceration is imposed, the fact remains that it is incarceration. The rehabilitative goals of the system are admirable, but they do not change the drastic nature of the action taken. Incarceration of adults is also intended to produce rehabilitation." *Fain v. Duff*, 488 F.2d, at 225. See President's Commission on Law Enforcement and Administration of Justice, Task Force Report: Juvenile Delinquency and Youth Crime 8–9 (1967).

13. The same conclusion was reached by the California Court of Appeal in denying respondent's petition for a writ of habeas corpus. *In re Gary Steven J.*, 17 Cal.App.3d, at 710, 95 Cal.Rptr., at 189.

have been only grudgingly allowed. Initially, a new trial was thought to be unavailable after appeal, whether requested by the prosecution or the defendant. * * * It was not until 1896 that it was made clear that a defendant could seek a new trial after conviction, even though the Government enjoyed no similar right. * * * Following the same policy, the Court has granted the Government the right to retry a defendant after a mistrial only where "there is a manifest necessity for the act, or the ends of public justice would otherwise be defeated." *United States v. Perez*, 9 Wheat. (22 U.S.) 579, 580, 6 L.Ed. 165 (1824). *United States v. Wilson*, 420 U.S. 332, ___ , 95 S.Ct. 1013, 1022, 43 L.Ed.2d 232 (1975). (Footnote omitted.)

Respondent was subjected to the burden of two trials for the same offense; he was twice put to the task of marshalling his resources against those of the State, twice, subjected to the "heavy personal strain" which such an experience represents. *United States v. Jorn*, 400 U.S., at 479, 91 S.Ct. at 554. We turn, therefore, to inquire whether either traditional principles or "the juvenile court's assumed ability to function in a unique manner," *McKeiver v. Pennsylvania, supra*, 403 U.S. at 547, 91 S.Ct. at 1987, support an exception to the "constitutional policy of finality" to which respondent would otherwise be entitled. *United States v. Jorn, supra*.

B

In denying respondent's petitions for writs of habeas corpus, the California Court of Appeal first, and the United States District Court later, concluded that no new jeopardy arose as a result of his transfer from Juvenile Court and trial in Superior Court. See *In re Gary Steven J.*, 17 Cal.App.3d, at 710, 95 Cal.Rptr. at 189; 343 F.Supp., at 692. In the view of those courts, the jeopardy that attaches at an adjudicatory hearing continues until there is a final disposition of the case under the adult charge. See also *In re Juvenile, Mass.*, 306 N.E. 2d 822 (1974). Cf. *Bryan v. Superior Court*, 7 Cal.3d 575, 102 Gal. Rptr. 831, 498 P.2d 1079 (1972), *cert. denied*, 410 U.S. 944, 93 S.Ct. 1380, 35 L.Ed.2d 610 (1973).

The phrase "continuing jeopardy" describes both a concept and a conclusion. As originally articulated by Mr. Justice Holmes in his dissent in *Kepner v. United States*, 195 U.S. 100, 134–137, 24 S.Ct. 797, 806, 49 L.Ed. 114 (1904), the concept has proved an interesting model for comparison with the system of constitutional protection which the Court

has in fact derived from the rather ambiguous language and history of the Double Jeopardy Clause. See *United States v. Wilson, supra*, at ___ , 95 S.Ct. 1013. Holmes's view has "never been adopted by a majority of this Court." *United States v. Jenkins*, 420 U.S. 358, ____, 95 S.Ct. 1006, 1013, 43 L.Ed.2d 250 (1975).

The conclusion, "continuing jeopardy," as distinguished from the concept, has occasionally been used to explain why an accused who has secured the reversal of a conviction on appeal may be retried for the same offense. See *Green v. United States*, 355 U.S., at 189, 78 S.Ct. at 224; *Price v. Georgia*, 398 U.S., at 326, 90 S.Ct. at 1759; *United States v. Wilson, supra*, at ____ n. 11, 95 S.Ct. at 1022. Probably a more satisfactory explanation lies in analysis of the respective interests involved. See *United States v. Tateo*, 377 U.S. 463, 465–466, 84 S.Ct. 1587, 1589, 12 L.Ed.2d 448 (1964); *Price v. Georgia, supra*, 398 U.S. at 329 n. 4, 90 S.Ct. at 1761; *United States v. Wilson, supra*. Similarly, the fact that the proceedings against respondent had not "run their full course," *Price v. Georgia, supra*, 398 U.S. at 326, 90 S.Ct. at 1759, within the contemplation of the California Welfare and Institutions Code, at the time of transfer, does not satisfactorily explain why respondent should be deprived of the constitutional protection against a second trial. If there is to be an exception to that protection in the context of the juvenile court system, it must be justified by interests of society, reflected in that unique institution, or of juveniles themselves, of sufficient substance to render tolerable the costs and burdens, noted earlier, which the exception will entail in individual cases.

C

The possibility of transfer from Juvenile Court to a court of general criminal jurisdiction is a matter of great significance to the juvenile. See *Kent v. United States*, 383 US. 541, 86 S.Ct. 1045, 16 L.Ed.2d 84 (1966). At the same time, there appears to be widely shared agreement that not all juveniles can benefit from the special features and programs of the juvenile court system and that a procedure for transfer to an adult court should be available. See, e.g., National Advisory Commission on Criminal Justice Standards and Goals, Report on Courts, Commentary to Standard 14.3, at 300–301 (1973).

This general agreement is reflected in the fact that an overwhelming majority of jurisdictions permits transfer in certain circumstances.[14] As might be expected, the statutory provisions differ in numerous details. Whatever their differences, however, such transfer provisions represent an attempt to impart to the juvenile court system the flexibility needed to deal with youthful offenders who cannot benefit from the specialized guidance and treatment contemplated by the system.

We do not agree with petitioner that giving respondent the constitutional protection against multiple trials in this context will diminish flexibility and informality to the extent that those qualities relate uniquely to the goals of the juvenile court system.[15] We agree that such a holding will require, in most cases, that the transfer decision be made prior to an adjudicatory hearing. To the extent that evidence concerning the alleged offense is considered relevant,[16] it may be that, in those cases where transfer is considered and rejected, some added burden will be imposed on the juvenile courts by reason of duplicative proceedings. Finally, the nature of the evidence considered at a transfer hearing may in some States require that, if transfer is rejected, a different judge preside at the adjudicatory hearing.[17]

We recognize that juvenile courts, perhaps even more than most courts, suffer from the problems created by spiraling caseloads unaccompanied by enlarged resources and manpower. See President's Commission on Law Enforcement and Administration of Justice, Task Force Report: Juvenile Delinquency and Youth Crime 7–8 (1967). And courts should be reluctant to impose on the juvenile court system any additional requirements which could so strain its resources as to endanger its unique functions. However, the burdens that petitioner envisions appear to us neither qualitatively nor quantitatively sufficient to justify a departure in this context from the fundamental prohibition against double jeopardy.

A requirement that transfer hearings be held prior to adjudicatory hearings affects not at all the nature of the latter proceedings. More significant, such a requirement need not affect the quality of decision-making at transfer hearings themselves. In *Kent v. United States*, 383 U.S., at 562, 86 S.Ct. at 1057, the Court held that hearings under the statute there involved "must measure up to the essentials of due process and fair treatment." However, the Court has never attempted to prescribe criteria for, or the nature and quantum of evidence that must support a decision to transfer a juvenile for trial in adult court. We require only that, whatever the relevant criteria, and whatever the evidence demanded, a State determine whether it wants to treat a juvenile within the juvenile court system before entering upon a proceeding that may result in an adjudication that he has violated a criminal law and in a substantial deprivation of liberty, rather than subject him to the

---

14. See generally Task Force Report, *supra*, n. 12, at 24–25. See also Rudstein, Double Jeopardy in Juvenile Proceedings, 14 Wm. & Mary L.Rev. 266, 297–300 (1972); Carr, The Effect of the Double Jeopardy Clause on Juvenile Proceedings, 6 U.Tol.L.Rev. 1, 21–22 (1974).

15. That the flexibility and informality of juvenile proceedings are diminished by the application of due process standards is not open to doubt. Due process standards inevitably produce such an effect, but that tells us no more than that the Constitution imposes burdens on the functioning of government and especially of law enforcement institutions.

16. Under Cal.Welf. & Inst'ns Code § 707 (West 1972), the governing criterion with respect to transfer, assuming the juvenile is 16 years of age is charged with a violation of a criminal statute or ordinance, is amenability "to the care, treatment and training program available through the facilities of the juvenile court." The section further provides that neither "the offense, in itself" nor a denial by the juvenile of the facts or conclusions set forth in the petition shall be "sufficient to support a finding that [he] is not a fit and proper subject to be dealt with under the provisions of the Juvenile Court Law." See n. 5, *supra*. The California Supreme Court has held that the only factor a juvenile court must consider is the juvenile's "behavior pattern as described in the probation officer's report," *Jimmy H. v. Superior Court*, 3 Cal.3d 709, 714, 478 P.2d 32, 35 (1970), but that it may also consider, *inter alia*, the nature and circumstances of the alleged offense. See *id.*, at 716, 478 P.2d, at 36.

In contrast to California, which does not require any evidentiary showing with respect to the commission of the offense, a number of jurisdictions require a finding of probable cause to believe the juvenile committed the offense before transfer is permitted. See Rudstein, *supra*, n. 14, at 298–299; Carr, *supra*, n. 14, at 21–22. In addition, two jurisdictions appear presently to require a finding of delinquency before the transfer of a juvenile to adult court. Ala.Code, Tit. 13, § 364 (1958) [see *Rudolph v. State*, 286 Ala. 189, 238 So.2d 542 (1970)]; W.Va. Code Ann. § 49–5–14 (1966).

17. See, e.g., Fla.Stat.Ann. § 39.09(2)(g) (1974); Tenn.Code Ann. § 37–234(c) (Supp.1974); Wyo.Stat. § 14–115.38(c) (Supp.1973); Uniform Juvenile Court Act, § 34(e), approved in July 1968 by the National Conference of Commissioners on Uniform State Laws. See also *Donald L. v. Superior Court*, 7 Cal.3d 592, 598, 498 P.2d 1098, 1101 (1972).

expense, delay, strain and embarrassment of two such proceedings.[18]

Moreover, we are not persuaded that the burdens petitioner envisions would pose a significant problem for the administration of the juvenile court system. The large number of jurisdictions that presently require that the transfer decision be made prior to an adjudicatory hearing,[19] and the absence of any indication that the juvenile courts in those jurisdictions have not been able to perform their task within that framework, suggest the contrary. The likelihood that in many cases the lack of need or basis for a transfer hearing can be recognized promptly reduces the number of cases in which a commitment of resources is necessary. In addition, we have no reason to believe that the resources available to those who recommend transfer or participate in the process leading to transfer decisions are inadequate to enable them to gather the information relevant to informed decision prior to an adjudicatory hearing. See generally *State v. Halverson*, 192 N.W.2d 765, 769 (Iowa 1971); Rudstein, *Double Jeopardy in Juvenile Proceedings*, 14 Wm. & Mary L.Rev. 266, 305–306 (1972); Note, 24 Stan.L.Rev., at 897–899.[20]

To the extent that transfer hearings held prior to adjudication result in some duplication of evidence if transfer is rejected, the burden on juvenile courts will tend to be offset somewhat by the cases in which, because of transfer, no further proceedings in Juvenile Court are required. Moreover, when transfer has previously been rejected, juveniles may well be more likely to admit the commission of the offense charged, thereby obviating the need for adjudicatory hearings, than if transfer remains a possibility. Finally, we note that those States which presently require a different judge to preside at an adjudicatory hearing if transfer is rejected also permit waiver of that requirement.[21] Where the requirement is not waived, it is difficult to see a substantial strain on judicial resources. See Note 24, Stan.L.Rev., at 900–901.

Quite apart from our conclusions with respect to the burdens on the juvenile court system envisioned by petitioner, we are persuaded that transfer hearings prior to adjudication will aid the objectives of that system. What concerns us here is the dilemma that the possibility of transfer after an adjudicatory hearing presents for a juvenile, a dilemma to which the Court of Appeals alluded. See *supra*, at 1784. Because of that possibility, a juvenile, thought to be the beneficiary of special consideration, may in fact suffer substantial disadvantages. If he appears uncooperative, he runs the risk of an adverse adjudication, as well as of an unfavorable dispositional recommendation.[22] If, on the other hand, he is cooperative, he runs the risk of prejudicing his chances in adult court if transfer is ordered. We regard a

18. We note that nothing decided today forecloses States from requiring, as a prerequisite to the transfer of a juvenile, substantial evidence that he committed the offense charged, so long as the showing required is not made in an adjudicatory proceeding. See *Collins v. Loisel*, 262 U.S. 426, 429, 43 S.Ct. 618, 625, 67 L.Ed. 1062 (1923); *Serfass v. United States*, 420 U.S. 377, 95 S.Ct. 1055, 43 L.Ed.2d 265 (1975). The instant case is not one in which the judicial determination was simply a finding of, e.g., probable cause. Rather, it was an adjudication that respondent had violated a criminal statute.

19. See Rudstein, *supra*, n. 14, at 299–300; Carr, *supra*, n. 14, at 24, 57–58. See also Uniform Juvenile Court Act §§ 34(a), (c); Model Rules for Juvenile Courts, Rule 9 (National Council on Crime and Delinquency 1969); Legislative Guide for Drafting Family and Juvenile Court Acts §§ 27, 31(a) (Dept. of HEW, Children's Bureau Pub. No. 472–1969). In contrast, apparently only three States presently require that a hearing on the juvenile petition or complaint precede transfer. Ala. Code, Tit. 13, § 364 (1958) [see *Rudolph v. State*, 286 Ala. 189, 238 So.2d 542]; Mass.Gen.Laws Ann. c. 119, § 61 (1969) [see *In re Juvenile, Mass.*, and n. 10, 306 N.E.2d 822, 829–830 and n. 10 (1974)]; W.Va.Code Ann. § 49–5–14 (1966).

20. We intimate no views concerning the constitutional validity of transfer following the attachment of jeopardy at an adjudicatory hearing where the information which forms the predicate for the transfer decision could not, by the exercise of due diligence, reasonably have been obtained previously. Cf., e.g., *Illinois v. Somerville*, 410 U.S. 458, 93 S.Ct. 1066, 35 L.Ed.2d 425 (1973).

21. See the statutes cited in n. 16, supra.

"The reason for this waiver provision is clear. A juvenile will ordinarily not want to dismiss a judge who has refused to transfer him to a criminal court. There is a risk of having another judge assigned to the case who is not as sympathetic. Moreover, in many cases, a rapport has been established between the judge and the juvenile, and the goal or rehabilitation is well on it way to being met." Brief for National Council of Juvenile Court Judges as *amicus curiae*, at 38.

22. Although denying respondent's petition for a writ of habeas corpus, the judge of the Juvenile Court noted: "If he doesn't open up with a probation officer there is of course the danger that the probation officer will find that he is so uncooperative that he cannot make a recommendation for the kind of treatment you think he really should have and, yet, as the attorney worrying about what might happen as [sic] the disposition hearing, you have to advise him to continue to more or less stand upon his constitutional right not to incriminate himself. *   *   *" App. 38. See Note, 24 Stan.L.Rev., at 902 n. 137.

procedure that results in such a dilemma as at odds with the goal that, to the extent fundamental fairness permits, adjudicatory hearings be informal and non-adversary. See *In re Gault*, 387 U.S., at 25–27, 87 S.Ct. at 1442; *In re Winship*, 397 U.S., at 366–367, 90 S.Ct. at 1074; *McKeiver v. Pennsylvania*, 403 U.S., at 534, 550, 91 S.Ct. at 1981. Knowledge of the risk of transfer after an adjudicatory hearing can only undermine the potential for informality and cooperation which was intended to be the hallmark of the juvenile court system. Rather than concerning themselves with the matter at hand, establishing innocence or seeking a disposition best suited to individual correctional needs, the juvenile and his attorney are pressed into a posture of adversary wariness that is conducive to neither. Cf. Kay and Segal, The Role of the Attorney in Juvenile Court Proceedings: A Non-Polar Approach, 61 Geo.L.J. 1401 (1973); Carr, The Effect of the Double Jeopardy Clause on Juvenile Proceedings, 6 U.Tol.L.Rev. 1, 52–54 (1974).[23]

IV

We hold that the prosecution of respondent in Superior Court, after an adjudicatory proceeding in Juvenile Court, violated the Double Jeopardy Clause of the Fifth Amendment, as applied to the States through the Fourteenth Amendment. The mandate of the Court of Appeals, which was stayed by that court pending our decision, directs the District Court "to issue a writ of habeas corpus directing the state court, within 60 days, to vacate the adult conviction of Jones and either set him free or remand him to the juvenile court for disposition." Since respondent is no longer subject to the jurisdiction of the California Juvenile Court, we vacate the judgment and remand the case to the Court of Appeals for such further proceedings consistent with this opinion as may be appropriate in the circumstances.

So ordered.

Judgment vacated and case remanded.

END NOTES—CHAPTER IV

1. See Linda A. Szymanski, *Statutory Waiver Criteria* (Pittsburgh: National Center for Juvenile Justice, October 1989).

2. Barry Feld, "The Juvenile Court Meets the Principle of the Offense: Legislative Changes in Juvenile Waiver Statutes," *Journal of Criminal Law and Criminology* 78:471–534 (1987); see also Paul Marcotte, "Criminal Kids," *American Bar Association Journal* 76:60–66 (1990).

3. 358 U.S. 541 (1966).

4. 421 U.S. 519 (1975).

5. See the National Council of Juvenile and Family Court Judges, "The Juvenile Court and Serious Offenders," *Juvenile and Family Court Journal* 35:13 (1984).

6. See Szymanski, *Statutory Waiver Criteria*, 1989; see also Mark Soler, James Bell, Elizabeth Jameson, Carole Shauffer, Alice Shotton, and Loren Warboys, *Representing the Client Child* (New York: Matthew Bender, 1989), sec. 5.

---

23. With respect to the possibility of "making the juvenile proceedings confidential and not being able to be used against the minor," the judge of the Juvenile Court observed: "I must say that doesn't impress me because if the minor admitted something in the Juvenile Court and named his companions nobody is going to eradicate from the minds of the district attorney or other people the information they obtained." App. 41–42.

FIVE

The Adjudicatory Process

INTRODUCTION

The adjudicatory process, often called the fact-finding hearing in the juvenile court, exists to hear evidence on the allegations in the petition. In its early development, the juvenile court did not emphasize judicial rule-making similar to the criminal trial process. Such basic requirements as standard of proof, rules of evidence, and other adjudicatory formalities were generally kept out of the juvenile court. The reason for this approach was that the traditional juvenile system was designed to diagnose and rehabilitate children appearing before the court. This was consistent with the view that the court should be social-service oriented and that the proceedings be nonadversary, informal, and noncriminal in nature.[1]

Gradually, however, the juvenile court movement became the subject of much criticism and disillusionment. This growing dissatisfaction was based primarily on the inability of the court to rehabilitate the juvenile offender, while at the same time failing to safeguard his or her constitutional rights. Juvenile courts apparently were punishing many children under the pretense of being a social-service agency, while arguing that constitutional protections were not necessary because the juvenile was being "helped" in the name of the state. Because of this *parens patriae* philosophy, where the state acted in promoting the child's welfare, the adjudicatory proceeding, as well as the subsequent disposition, was conceived to be in the child's best interest. Thus,

there generally was no need for legal rules and procedures in the nature of the criminal process nor for the introduction of state prosecutors or defense attorneys, since this was inconsistent with the philosophy of the juvenile court.

But these views and practices have been severely changed by the U.S. Supreme Court as a result of the landmark case of *In re Gault*.[2] In *Gault*, the Court decided that the concept of fundamental fairness must be made applicable to juvenile delinquency proceedings. In other words, the Supreme Court ruled that the due process clause of the Fourteenth Amendment required that certain procedural guarantees were essential to the adjudication of delinquency cases. It then specified the precise nature of due process by indicating that juveniles who have violated a criminal statute and who may be committed to an institution in which their freedom may be curtailed are entitled to: (1) fair notice of charges against them; (2) right to representation by counsel; (3) right to confrontation and cross-examination; and (4) the privilege against self-incrimination.

Gault did not hold that the juvenile offender was entitled to all procedural guarantees applicable in the case of an adult charged with a crime. The Supreme Court did not rule, for instance, on such issues as whether the juvenile had a right to a transcript of the proceedings or a right to appellate review. Nor was it clear as to what extent the right to counsel should apply to nondelinquent children. *Gault* specifically ruled that a juvenile is entitled to counsel in delinquency actions that may result in institutionalization. In this regard, some states provide juveniles with a right to counsel in all kinds of cases. Other jurisdictions specify that the right to counsel is applicable in delinquency and status offenses. Still other states go beyond *Gault* and provide counsel in neglect and dependency proceedings as well.

The *Gault* decision, and particularly the constitutional right of a juvenile to the assistance of counsel, has completely altered the juvenile justice system. Instead of dealing with children in a benign and paternalistic fashion, the court must process juvenile offenders within the framework of appropriate constitutional procedures. And although *Gault* was technically limited to the adjudicatory stage, it has spurred further legal reform throughout the juvenile system. Today, the right to counsel, the privilege against self-incrimination, the right to treatment in detention and correctional facilities, and other elements of the adversary process have come to be applied at all stages of the juvenile process, from investigation through adjudication to parole.

After *Gault*, the Supreme Court continued its trend toward "legalizing" and "formalizing" the juvenile adjudication process with its decision in *In re Winship* (1970).[3] In *Winship*, the Court held that the standard in a criminal prosecution of proof beyond a reasonable doubt is also required in the adjudication of a delinquency petition. It is unsettled from the *Winship* decision whether this burden of proof is also applicable to nondelinquent forms of conduct. As a result, some state statutes require proof beyond a reasonable doubt only in delinquency matters. In these jurisdictions, such standards of proof as clear and convincing evidence or a preponderance of the evidence are used for incorrigibility, neglect, or dependency-type cases. Some jurisdictions, however, apply the reasonable-doubt standard to all types of juvenile actions. In spite of various statutory differences, *Winship* does impose the constitutional requirement of proof beyond a reasonable doubt during the adjudicatory stage of a delinquency proceeding.

Although the traditional juvenile court trial has been severely altered by *Gault* and *Winship*, this movement for increased rights for juveniles was somewhat curtailed by the Supreme Court's decision in *McKeiver v. Pennsylvania* (1971).[4] In *McKeiver*, the court held that the Fourteenth Amendment's due process clause does not require the states to provide juveniles with a jury trial. This decision,

however, does not prevent the various states from giving juveniles a trial by jury as a state constitutional right or by state statute.

Despite the impact of constitutional law in the adjudicatory stage of the juvenile process, many states retain their own standards in such areas as rules of evidence, double jeopardy, and findings of the juvenile court.

Rules of evidence represent the means by which evidentiary matters may be admitted in court to prove or disprove a particular point. Thus, for example, evidence must be relevant, which means it must shed light on the issue, or material, which means it must relate to the importance of proving the issue of the case. One of the most fundamental rules of evidence is the hearsay rule, which generally means that a witness can only testify to matters of his or her own personal knowledge.

Most states do not have a definitive statutory statement of evidentiary rules of juvenile proceedings, as they ordinarily have for the criminal process. Some states do not comply with strict rules of evidence in such major areas as opinion testimony, hearsay evidence, rules of impeachment, and so forth. Other jurisdictions apply those rules of evidence that determine admissibility in a criminal case. Still other states use the rules of evidence of civil law to apply to juvenile proceedings.

There are evidentiary problems, apart from the strict rules of evidence, that spring from constitutional law and procedure. These problem areas include oral testimony or physical evidence obtained from illegal arrests, search and seizure problems, the legality of confessions, lineups, and the rules involving custodial interrogation and right to counsel. As a result of *Gault*, many of these pretrial rights previously available only in criminal proceedings have been extended to juveniles.

In regard to the issue of double jeopardy, at trial children are protected from being tried twice for the same offense by the Fifth Amendment of the U.S. Constitution. More than one adjudicatory hearing in the juvenile court on the same delinquent act would violate the juvenile's constitutional right to be free from double jeopardy. This is unlikely to occur in light of the *Gault* decision and the increased formality in juvenile proceedings. More prevalent is the double jeopardy provision barring the juvenile from subsequent criminal prosecution after adjudication for the same act in the juvenile court.

Once an adjudicatory hearing has been completed, the court is normally required to enter a judgment against the child. This may take the form of declaring the child delinquent, adjudging him or her to be a ward of the court, or possibly even suspending judgment so as to avoid the stigma of a juvenile record. Once a judgment has been entered in accordance with the appropriate state statute, the court can begin its determination of possible dispositions for the child.

NOTICE AND HEARING

Case Comment

In re Gault, which changed the complexion of juvenile justice, is considered the leading constitutional case in juvenile law. Because of *Gault*, juvenile offenders were provided with many basic rights—counsel, notice, confrontation of witnesses, freedom from self-incrimination—that previously only adults enjoyed.

The *Gault* decision reshaped the constitutional and philosophical nature of the juvenile court system. As a result, those working in the system—judges, social workers, attorneys, and so on—are faced with the problem of reaffirming the rehabilitative ideal of the juvenile court while ensuring that juveniles receive proper procedural due process rights.[5] As Justice Hugo Black stated in the *Gault* case:

> When a person, infant or adult, can be seized by the state, charged and convicted, for violating a criminal law, and then ordered by the state to be confined for six years, I think the Constitution requires that he be tried in accordance with the guarantees of all the provisions of the Bill of Rights, made applicable to the states by the Fourteenth Amendment.[6]

IN RE GAULT

Supreme Court of the United States, 1967.
387 U.S. 1, 87 S.Ct. 1428, 18 L.Ed.2d 527.

Mr. Justice Fortas delivered the opinion of the Court.

This is an appeal under 28 U.S.C. § 1257(2) from a judgment of the Supreme Court of Arizona affirming the dismissal of a petition for a writ of habeas corpus. 99 Ariz. 181, 407 P.2d 760 (1965). The petition sought the release of Gerald Francis Gault, appellants' 15-year-old son, who had been committed as a juvenile delinquent to the State Industrial School by the Juvenile Court of Gila County, Arizona. The Supreme Court of Arizona affirmed dismissal of the writ against various arguments which included an attack upon the constitutionality of the Arizona Juvenile Code because of its alleged denial of procedural due process rights to juveniles charged with being "delinquents." The court agreed that the constitutional guarantee of due process of law is applicable in such proceedings. It held that Arizona's Juvenile Code is to be read as "impliedly" implementing the "due process concept." It then proceeded to identify and describe "the particular elements which constitute due process in a juvenile hearing." It concluded that the proceedings ending in commitment of Gerald Gault did not offend those requirements. We do not agree, and we reverse. We begin with a statement of the facts.

I

On Monday, June 8, 1964, at about 10 A.M., Gerald Francis Gault and a friend, Ronald Lewis, were taken into custody by the Sheriff of Gila County. Gerald was then still subject to a six months' probation order which had been entered on February 25, 1964, as a result of his having been in the company of another boy who had stolen a wallet from a lady's purse. The police action on June 8 was taken as the result of a verbal complaint by a neighbor of the boys, Mrs. Cook, about a telephone call made to her in which the caller or callers made lewd or indecent remarks. It will suffice for purposes of this opinion to say that the remarks or questions put to her were of the irritatingly offensive, adolescent, sex variety.

At the time Gerald was picked up, his mother and father were both at work. No notice that Gerald was being taken into custody was left at the home. No other steps were taken to advise them that their son had, in effect, been arrested. Gerald was taken to the Children's Detention Home. When his mother arrived home at about 6 o'clock, Gerald was not there. Gerald's older brother was sent to look for him at the trailer home of the Lewis family. He apparently learned then that Gerald was in custody. He so informed his mother. The two of them went to the Detention Home. The deputy probation officer, Flagg, who was also superintendent of the

Detention Home, told Mrs. Gault "why Jerry was there" and said that a hearing would be held in Juvenile Court at 3 o'clock the following day, June 9.

Officer Flagg filed a petition with the court on the hearing day, June 9, 1964. It was not served on the Gaults. Indeed, none of them saw this petition until the habeas corpus hearing on August 17, 1964. The petition was entirely formal. It made no reference to any factual basis for the judicial action which it initiated. It recited only that "said minor is under the age of eighteen years, and is in need of the protection of this Honorable Court; [and that] said minor is a delinquent minor." It prayed for a hearing and an order regarding "the care and custody of said minor." Officer Flagg executed a formal affidavit in support of the petition.

On June 9, Gerald, his mother, his older brother, and Probation Officers Flagg and Henderson appeared before the Juvenile Judge in chambers. Gerald's father was not there. He was at work out of the city. Mrs. Cook, the complainant, was not there. No one was sworn at this hearing. No transcript or recording was made. No memorandum or record of the substance of the proceedings was prepared. Our information about the proceedings and the subsequent hearing on June 15, derives entirely from the testimony of the Juvenile Court Judge,[1] Mr. and Mrs. Gault and Officer Flagg at the habeas corpus proceeding conducted two months later. From this, it appears that at the June 9 hearing Gerald was questioned by the judge about the telephone call. There was conflict as to what he said. His mother recalled that Gerald said he only dialed Mrs. Cook's number and handed the telephone to his friend, Ronald. Officer Flagg recalled that Gerald had admitted making the lewd remarks. Judge McGhee testified that Gerald "admitted making one of these [lewd] statements." At the conclusion of the hearing, the judge said he would "think about it." Gerald was taken back to the Detention Home. He was not sent to his own home with his parents. On June 11 or

12, after having been detained since June 8, Gerald was released and driven home.[2] There is no explanation in the record as to why he was kept in the Detention Home or why he was released. At 5 P.M. on the day of Gerald's release, Mrs. Gault received a note signed by Officer Flagg. It was on plain paper, not letterhead. Its entire text was as follows:

> "Mrs. Gault:
> "Judge McGhee has set Monday June 15, 1964 at 11:00 A.M. as the date and time for further Hearings on Gerald's delinquency
>
> "/s/Flagg"

At the appointed time on Monday, June 15, Gerald, his father and mother, Ronald Lewis and his father, and Officers Flagg and Henderson were present before Judge McGhee. Witnesses at the habeas corpus proceeding differed in their recollections of Gerald's testimony at the June 15 hearing. Mr. and Mrs. Gault recalled that Gerald again testified that he had only dialed the number and that the other boy had made the remarks. Officer Flagg agreed that at this hearing Gerald did not admit making the lewd remarks.[3] But Judge McGhee recalled that "there was some admission again of some of the lewd statements. He—he didn't admit any of the more serious lewd statements."[4] Again, the complainant, Mrs. Cook, was not present. Mrs. Gault asked that Mrs. Cook be present "so she could see which boy that done the talking, the dirty talking over the phone."

The Juvenile Judge said "she didn't have to be present at that hearing." The judge did not speak to Mrs. Cook or communicate with her at any time. Probation Officer Flagg had talked to her once— over the telephone on June 9.

At this June 15 hearing a "referral report" made by the probation officers was filed with the court, although not disclosed to Gerald or his parents. This listed the charge as "Lewd Phone Calls." At the conclusion of the hearing, the judge committed Gerald as a juvenile delinquent to the State Indus-

---

1. Under Arizona law, juvenile hearings are conducted by a judge of the Superior Court, designated by his colleagues on the Superior Court to serve as Juvenile Court Judge. Arizona Const., Art. 6, § 15, A.R.S.; Arizona Revised Statutes (hereinafter ARS) §§ 8–201, 8–202.

2. There is a conflict between the recollection of Mrs. Gault and that of Officer Flagg. Mrs. Gault testified that Gerald was released on Friday, June 12, Officer Flagg that it had been on Thursday, June 11. This was from memory; he had no record, and the note hereafter referred to was undated.

3. Officer Flagg also testified that Gerald had not, when questioned at the Detention Home, admitted having made any of the lewd statements, but that each boy had sought to put the blame on the other. There was conflicting testimony as to whether Ronald had accused Gerald of making the lewd statements during the June 15 hearing.

4. Judge McGhee also testified that Gerald had not denied "certain statements" made to him at the hearing by Officer Henderson.

trial School "for the period of his minority [that is, until 21], unless sooner discharged by due process of law." An order to that effect was entered. It recites that "after a full hearing and due deliberation the Court finds that said minor is a delinquent child, and that said minor is of the age of 15 years."

No appeal is permitted by Arizona law in juvenile cases. On August 3, 1964, a petition for a writ of habeas corpus was filed with the Supreme Court of Arizona and referred by it to the Superior Court for hearing.

At the habeas corpus hearing on August 17, Judge McGhee was vigorously cross-examined as to the basis for his actions. He testified that he had taken into account the fact that Gerald was on probation. He was asked "under what section of * * * the code you found the boy delinquent?"

His answer is set forth in the margin.[5] In substance, he concluded that Gerald came within ARS § 8–201, subsec. 6(a), which specifies that a "delinquent child" includes one "who has violated a law of the state or an ordinance or regulation of a political subdivision thereof." The law which Gerald was found to have violated is ARS § 13–377. This section of the Arizona Criminal Code provides that a person who "in the presence or hearing of any woman or child * * * uses vulgar, abusive or obscene language, is guilty of a misdemeanor * * * ." The penalty specified in the Criminal Code, which would apply to an adult, is $5 to $50, or imprisonment for not more than two months. The judge also testified that he acted under ARS § 8–201, subsec. 6(d) which includes the definition of a "delinquent child" one who, as the judge phrased it, is "habitually involved in immoral matters."[6]

Asked about the basis for his conclusion that Gerald was "habitually involved in immoral matters," the judge testified, somewhat vaguely, that two years earlier, on July 2, 1962, a "referral" was made con-

cerning Gerald, "where the boy had stolen a baseball glove from another boy and lied to the Police Department about it." The judge said there was "no hearing," and "no accusation" relating to this incident, "because of lack of material foundation." But it seems to have remained in his mind as a relevant factor. The judge also testified that Gerald had admitted making other nuisance phone calls in the past which, as the judge recalled the boy's testimony, were "silly calls, or funny calls, or something like that."

The Superior Court dismissed the writ, and appellants sought review in the Arizona Supreme Court. That court stated that it considered appellants' assignments of error as urging (1) that the Juvenile Code, ARS § 8–201 to § 8–239, is unconstitutional because it does not require that parents and children be apprised of the specific charges, does not require proper notice of a hearing, and does not provide for an appeal; and (2) that the proceedings and order relating to Gerald constituted a denial of due process of law because of the absence of adequate notice of the charge and the hearing; failure to notify appellants of certain constitutional rights including the rights to counsel and to confrontation, and the privilege against self-incrimination; the use of unsworn hearsay testimony; and the failure to make a record of the proceedings. Appellants further asserted that it was error for the Juvenile Court to remove Gerald from the custody of his parents without a showing and finding of their unsuitability, and alleged a miscellany of other errors under state law.

The Supreme Court handed down an elaborate and wide-ranging opinion affirming dismissal of the writ and stating the court's conclusions as to the issues raised by appellants and other aspects of the juvenile process. In their jurisdictional statement and brief in this Court, appellants do not urge upon us all of the points passed upon by the Supreme

---

5. "Q. All right. Now, judge, would you tell me under what section of the law or tell me under what section of—of the code you found the boy delinquent?

"A. Well, there is a—I think it amounts to disturbing the peace. I can't give you the section, but I can tell you the law, that when one person uses lewd language in the presence of another person, that it can amount to—and I consider that when a person makes it over the phone, that it is considered in the presence, I might be wrong, that is one section. The other section upon which I consider the boy delinquent is Section 8–201, Subsection (d), habitually involved in immoral matters."

6. ARS § 8–201, subsec. 6, the section of the Arizona Juvenile Code which defines a delinquent child, reads:

" 'Delinquent child' includes:

"(a) A child who has violated a law of the state or an ordinance or regulation of a political subdivision thereof.

"(b) A child who, by reason of being incorrigible, wayward or habitually disobedient, is uncontrolled by his parent, guardian or custodian.

"(c) A child who is habitually truant from school or home.

"(d) A child who habitually so deports himself as to injure or endanger the morals or health of himself or others."

Court of Arizona. They urge that we hold the Juvenile Code of Arizona invalid on its face or as applied in this case because, contrary to the Due Process Clause of the Fourteenth Amendment, the juvenile is taken from the custody of his parents and committed to a state institution pursuant to proceedings in which the Juvenile Court has virtually unlimited discretion, and in which the following basic rights are denied:

1. Notice of the charges;
2. Right to counsel;
3. Right to confrontation and cross-examination;
4. Privilege against self-incrimination;
5. Right to a transcript of the proceedings; and
6. Right to appellate review.

We shall not consider other issues which were passed upon by the Supreme Court of Arizona. We emphasize that we indicate no opinion as to whether the decision of that court with respect to such other issues does or does not conflict with requirements of the Federal Constitution.[7]

II

The Supreme Court of Arizona held that due process of law is requisite to the constitutional validity of proceedings in which a court reaches the conclusion that a juvenile has been at fault, has engaged in conduct prohibited by law, or has otherwise misbehaved with the consequence that he is committed to an institution in which his freedom is curtailed. This conclusion is in accord with the decisions of a number of courts under both federal and state constitutions.[8]

This Court has not heretofore decided the precise question. In *Kent v. United States*, 383 U.S. 541, 86 S.Ct. 1045, 16 L.Ed.2d 84 (1966), we considered the requirements for a valid waiver of the "exclusive" jurisdiction of the Juvenile Court of the District of Columbia so that a juvenile could be tried in the adult criminal court of the District. Although our decision turned upon the language of the statute, we emphasized the necessity that "the basic requirements of due process and fairness" be satisfied in such proceedings.[9] *Haley v. State of Ohio*, 332 U.S. 596, 68 S.Ct. 302, 92 L.Ed. 224 (1948), involved the admissibility, in a state criminal court of general jurisdiction, of a confession by a 15-year-old boy. The Court held that the Fourteenth Amendment applied to prohibit the use of the coerced confession. Mr. Justice Douglas said, "Neither man nor child can be allowed to stand condemned by methods which flout constitutional requirements of due process of law."[10] To the same effect is *Gallegos v. State of Colorado*, 370 U.S. 49, 82 S.Ct. 1209, 8 L.Ed.2d

---

7. For example, the laws of Arizona allow arrest for a misdemeanor only if a warrant is obtained or if it is committed in the presence of the officer. ARS § 13–1403. The Supreme Court of Arizona held that this is inapplicable in the case of juveniles. See ARS § 8–221 which relates specifically to juveniles. But compare *Two Brothers and a Case of Liquor*, Juv.Ct.D.C., Nos. 66–2652–J, 66–2653–J, December 28, 1966 (opinion of Judge Ketcham): Standards for Juvenile and Family Courts, Children's Bureau Pub.No. 437–1966, p. 47 (hereinafter cited as Standards); New York Family Court Act § 721 (1963) (hereinafter cited as N.Y.Family Court Act).

The court also held that the judge may consider hearsay if it is "of a kind on which reasonable men are accustomed to rely in serious affairs." But compare Note, Juvenile Delinquents: The Police, State Courts, and Individualized Justice, 79 Harv.L.Rev. 775, 794–795 (1966) (hereinafter cited as Harvard Law Review Note):

"The informality of juvenile court hearings frequently leads to the admission of hearsay and unsworn testimony. It is said that 'close adherence to the strict rules of evidence might prevent the court from obtaining important facts as to the child's character and condition which could only be to the child's detriment.' The assumption is that the judge will give normally inadmissible evidence only its proper weight. It is also declared in support of these evidentiary practices that the juvenile court is not a criminal court, that the importance of the hearsay rule has been overestimated, and that allowing an attorney to make 'technical objections' would disrupt the desired informality of the proceedings. But to the extent that the rules of evidence are not merely technical or historical, but like the hearsay rule have a sound basis in human experience, they should not be rejected in any judicial inquiry. Juvenile court judges in Los Angeles, Tucson, and Wisconsin Rapids, Wisconsin report that they are satisfied with the operation of their courts despite application of unrelaxed rules of evidence." (Footnotes omitted.)

It ruled that the correct burden of proof is that "the juvenile judge must be persuaded by clear and convincing evidence that the infant has committed the alleged delinquent act." Compare the "preponderance of the evidence" test. N.Y.Family Court Act § 744 (where maximum commitment is three years, §§ 753, 758). Cf. Harvard Law Review Note, p. 795.

8. See, e. g., *In Matters of W. and S.*, 19 N.Y.2d 55, 277 N.Y.S.2d 675, 224 N.E.2d 102 (1966); *In Interests of Carlo and Stasilowicz*, 48 N.J. 224, 225 A.2d 110 (1966); *People v. Dotson*, 46 Cal.2d 891, 299 P.2d 875 (1956); *Pee v. United States*, 107 U.S.App.D.C. 47, 274 F.2d 556 (1959); *Wissenburg v. Bradley*, 209 Iowa 813, 229 N.W. 205, 67 A.L.R. 1075 (1930); *Bryant v. Brown*, 151 Miss. 398, 118 So. 184, 60 A.L.R. 1325 (1928); *Dendy v. Wilson*, 142 Tex. 460, 179 S.W.2d 269, 151 A.L.R. 1217 (1944); *Application of Johnson*, 178 F.Supp. 155 (D.C.N.J.1957).

9. 383 U.S., at 553, 86 S.Ct., at 1053.

10. 332 U.S., at 601, 68 S.Ct., at 304 (opinion for four Justices).

325 (1962). Accordingly, while these cases relate only to restricted aspects of the subject, they unmistakably indicate that, whatever may be their precise impact, neither the Fourteenth Amendment nor the Bill of Rights is for adults alone.

We do not in this opinion consider the impact of these constitutional provisions upon the totality of the relationship of the juvenile and the state. We do not even consider the entire process relating to juvenile "delinquents." For example, we are not here concerned with the procedures or constitutional rights applicable to the pre-judicial stages of the juvenile process, nor do we direct our attention to the post-adjudicative or dispositional process. See note 48, infra. We consider only the problems presented to us by this case. These relate to the proceedings by which a determination is made as to whether a juvenile is a "delinquent" as a result of alleged misconduct on his part, with the consequence that he may be committed to a state institution. As to these proceedings, there appears to be little current dissent from the proposition that the Due Process Clause has a role to play.[11] The problem is to ascertain the precise impact of the due process requirement upon such proceedings.

From the inception of the juvenile court system, wide differences have been tolerated—indeed insisted upon—between the procedural rights accorded to adults and those of juveniles. In practically all jurisdictions, there are rights granted to adults which are withheld from juveniles. In addition to the specific problems involved in the present case, for example, it has been held that the juvenile is not entitled to bail, to indictment by grand jury, to a public trial or to trial by jury.[12] It is frequent practice that rules governing the arrest and interrogation of adults by the police are not observed in the case of juveniles.[13]

The history and theory underlying this development are well-known, but a recapitulation is necessary for purposes of this opinion. The Juvenile Court movement began in this country at the end of the last century. From the juvenile court statute adopted in Illinois in 1899, the system has spread to every State in the Union, the District of Columbia, and Puerto Rico.[14] The constitutionality of juvenile court laws has been sustained in over 40 jurisdictions against a variety of attacks.[15]

The early reformers were appalled by adult procedures and penalties, and by the fact that children could be given long prison sentences and mixed in jails with hardened criminals. They were profoundly convinced that society's duty to the child could not be confined by the concept of justice alone. They believed that society's role was not to ascertain whether the child was "guilty" or "innocent," but "What is he, how has he become what he is, and what had best be done in his interest and in the interest of the state to save him from a downward career."[16] The child—essentially good, as they saw it—was to be made "to feel that he is the object of [the state's] care and solicitude,"[17] not that he was under arrest

---

11. See Report by the President's Commission on Law Enforcement and Administration of Justice, "The Challenge of Crime in a Free Society" (1967) (hereinafter cited as Nat'l Crime Comm'n Report), pp. 81, 85–86; Standards, p. 71; Gardner, The *Kent* Case and the Juvenile Court: A Challenge to Lawyers, 52 A.B.A.J. 923 (1966); Paulsen, Fairness to the Juvenile Offender, 41 Minn.L.Rev. 547 (1957); Ketcham, The Legal Renaissance in the Juvenile Court, 60 Nw.U.L.Rev. 585 (1965); Allen, The Borderland of Criminal Justice (1964), pp. 19–23; Harvard Law Review Note, p. 791; Note, Rights and Rehabilitation in the Juvenile Courts, 67 Col.L.Rev. 281 (1967); Comment, Criminal Offenders in the Juvenile Court: More Brickbats and Another Proposal, 114 U.Pa.L.Rev. 1171 (1966).

12. See *Kent v. United States*, 383 U.S. 541, 555 86 S.Ct. 1045, 1054 and n. 22 (1966).

13. See n. 7, *supra*.

14. See National Council of Juvenile Court Judges, Directory and Manual (1964), p. 1. The number of Juvenile Judges as of 1964 is listed as 2,987, of whom 213 are full-time Juvenile Court Judges. Id., at 305. The Nat'l Crime Comm'n Report indicates that half of these judges have no undergraduate degree, a fifth have no college education at all, a fifth are not members of the bar, and three-quarters devote less than one-quarter of their time to juvenile matters. See also McCune, Profile of the Nation's Juvenile Court Judges (monograph, George Washington University, Center for the Behavioral Sciences, 1965), which is a detailed statistical study of Juvenile Court Judges, and indicates additionally that about a quarter of these judges have no law school training at all. About one-third of all judges have no probation and social work staff available to them; between eighty and ninety percent have no available psychologist or psychiatrist. Ibid. It has been observed that while "good will, compassion, and similar virtues are * * * admirably prevalent throughout the system * * * expertise, the keystone of the whole venture, is lacking." Harvard Law Review Note, p. 809. In 1965, over 697,000 delinquency cases (excluding traffic) were disposed of in these courts, involving some 601,000 children, or 2% of all children between 10 and 17. Juvenile Court Statistics—1965, Children's Bureau Statistical Series No. 85 (1966), p. 2.

15. See Paulsen, *Kent v. United States*: The Constitutional Context of Juvenile Cases, 1966 Sup.Ct.Review 167, 174.

16. Julian Mack, The Juvenile Court, 23 Harv.L.Rev. 104, 119–120 (1909).

17. Id., at 120.

or on trial. The rules of criminal procedure were therefore altogether inapplicable. The apparent rigidities, technicalities, and harshness which they observed in both substantive and procedural criminal law were therefore to be discarded. The idea of crime and punishment was to be abandoned. The child was to be "treated" and "rehabilitated" and the procedures, from apprehension through institutionalization, were to be "clinical" rather than punitive.

These results were to be achieved, without coming to conceptual and constitutional grief, by insisting that the proceedings were not adversary, but that the state was proceeding as *parens patriae.*[18] The Latin phrase proved to be a great help to those who sought to rationalize the exclusion of juveniles from the constitutional scheme; but its meaning is murky and its historic credentials are of dubious relevance. The phrase was taken from chancery practice, where, however, it was used to describe the power of the state to act *in loco parentis* for the purpose of protecting the property interests and the person of the child.[19] But there is no trace of the doctrine in the history of criminal jurisprudence. At common law, children under seven were considered incapable of possessing criminal intent. Beyond that age, they were subjected to arrest, trial, and in theory to punishment like adult offenders.[20] In these old days, the state was not deemed to have authority to

accord them fewer procedural rights than adults.

The right of the state, as *parens patriae*, to deny to the child procedural rights available to his elders was elaborated by the assertion that a child, unlike an adult, has a right "not to liberty but to custody." He can be made to attorn to his parents, to go to school, etc. If his parents default in effectively performing their custodial functions—that is, if the child is "delinquent"—the state may intervene. In doing so, it does not deprive the child of any rights, because he has none. It merely provides the "custody" to which the child is entitled.[21] On this basis, proceedings involving juveniles were described as "civil" not "criminal" and therefore not subject to the requirements which restrict the state when it seeks to deprive a person of his liberty.[22]

Accordingly, the highest motives and most enlightened impulses led to a peculiar system for juveniles, unknown to our law in any comparable context. The constitutional and theoretical basis for this peculiar system is—to say the least—debatable. And in practice, as we remarked in the *Kent* case, *supra*, the results have not been entirely satisfactory.[23] Juvenile Court history has again demonstrated that unbridled discretion, however benevolently motivated, is frequently a poor substitute for principle and procedure. In 1937, Dean Pound wrote: "The powers of the Star Chamber were a trifle

---

18. Id., at 109; Paulsen, op. cit., *supra*, n. 15, at 173–174. There seems to have been little early constitutional objection to the special procedures of juvenile courts. But see Waite, How Far Can Court Procedure Be Socialized Without Impairing Individual Rights, 12 J.Crim.L. & Criminology 339, 340 (1922): "The court which must direct its procedure even apparently to do something *to* a child because of what he *has done*, is parted from the court which is avowedly concerned only with doing something *for* a child because of what he *is* and *needs*, by a gulf too wide to be bridged by any humanity which the judge may introduce into his hearings, or by the habitual use of corrective rather than punitive methods after conviction."

19. Paulsen, op. cit. *supra*, n. 15, at 173; Hurley, Origin of the Illinois Juvenile Court Law, in The Child, The Clinic, and The Court (1925), pp. 320, 328.

20. Julian Mack, The Chancery Procedure in the Juvenile Court, in The Child, The Clinic, and The Court (1925), p. 310.

21. See, e. g., Shears, Legal Problems Peculiar to Children's Courts, 48 A.B.A.J. 719, 720 (1962) ("The basic right of a juvenile is not to liberty but to custody. He has the right to have someone take care of him, and if his parents do not afford him this custodial privilege, the law must do so."); Ex parte Crouse, 4 Whart. 9, 11 (Sup.Ct.Pa.1839); Petition of Ferrier, 103 Ill. 367, 371–373 (1882).

22. The Appendix to the opinion of Judge Prettyman in *Pee v. United States*, 107 U.S.App.D.C. 47, 274 F.2d 556 (1959), lists authority in 51 jurisdictions to this effect. Even rules required by due process in civil proceedings, however, have not generally been deemed compulsory as to proceedings affecting juveniles. For example, constitutional requirements as to notice of issues, which would commonly apply in civil cases, are commonly disregarded in juvenile proceedings, as this case illustrates.

23. "There is evidence * * * that there may be grounds for concern that the child receives the worst of both worlds: that he gets neither the protections accorded to adults nor the solicitous care and regenerative treatment postulated for children." 383 U.S., at 556, 86 S.Ct., at 1054, citing Handler, The Juvenile Court and the Adversary System: Problems of Function and Form, 1965 Wis.L.Rev. 7; Harvard Law Review Note; and various congressional materials set forth in 383 U.S., at 546, 86 S.Ct., at 1050, n. 5.

On the other hand, while this opinion and much recent writing concentrate upon the failures of the Juvenile Court system to live up to the expectations of its founders, the observation of the Nat'l Crime Comm'n Report should be kept in mind:

"Although its shortcomings are many and its results too often disappointing, the juvenile justice system in many cities is operated by people who are better educated and more highly skilled, can call on more and better facilities and services, and has more ancillary agencies to which to refer its clientele than its adult counterpart." Id., at 78.

in comparison with those of our juvenile courts * * * ."[24] The absence of substantive standards has not necessarily meant that children receive careful, compassionate, individualized treatment. The absence of procedural rules based upon constitutional principle has not always produced fair, efficient, and effective procedures. Departures from established principles of due process have frequently resulted not in enlightened procedure, but in arbitrariness. The Chairman of the Pennsylvania Council of Juvenile Court Judges has recently observed: "Unfortunately, loose procedures, high-handed methods and crowded court calendars, either singly or in combination, all too often, have resulted in

depriving some juveniles of fundamental rights that have resulted in a denial of due process."[25]

Failure to observe the fundamental requirements of due process has resulted in instances, which might have been avoided, of unfairness to individuals and inadequate or inaccurate findings of fact and unfortunate prescriptions of remedy. Due process of law is the primary and indispensable foundation of individual freedom. It is the basic and essential term in the social compact which defines the rights of the individual and delimits the powers which the state may exercise.[26] As Mr. Justice Frankfurter has said: "The history of American freedom is, in no small measure, the history of procedure."[27] But, in addi-

---

24. Foreword to Young, Social Treatment in Probation and Delinquency (1937), p. xxvii. The 1965 Report of the United States Commission on Civil Rights, "Law Enforcement—A Report on Equal Protection in the South," pp. 80–83, documents numerous instances in which "local authorities used the broad discretion afforded them by the absence of safeguards [in the juvenile process]" to punish, intimidate, and obstruct youthful participants in civil rights demonstrations. See also, Paulsen, Juvenile Courts, Family Courts, and the Poor Man, 54 Calif.L.Rev. 694, 707–709 (1966).

25. Lehman, A Juvenile's Right to Counsel in a Delinquency Hearing, 17 Juvenile Court Judges Journal 53, 54 (1966).

Compare the observation of the late Arthur T. Vanderbilt, Chief Justice of the Supreme Court of New Jersey, in a foreword to Virtue, Basic Structure for Children's Services in Michigan (1953), p. x:

"In their zeal to care for children neither juvenile judges nor welfare workers can be permitted to violate the Constitution, especially the constitutional provisions as to due process that are involved in moving a child from its home. The indispensable elements of due process are: first, a tribunal with jurisdiction; second, notice of a hearing to the proper parties; and finally, a fair hearing. All three must be present if we are to treat the child as an individual human being and not to revert, in spite of good intentions, to the more primitive days when he was treated as a chattel."

We are warned that the system must not "degenerate into a star chamber proceeding with the judge imposing his own particular brand of culture and morals on indigent people * * * ." Judge Marion G. Woodward, letter reproduced in 18 Social Service Review 366, 368 (1944). Doctor Bovet, the Swiss psychiatrist, in his monograph for the World Health Organization, Psychiatric Aspects of Juvenile Delinquency (1951), p. 79, stated that: "One of the most definite conclusions of this investigation is that few fields exist in which more serious coercive measures are applied, on such flimsy objective evidence, than in that of juvenile delinquency." We are told that "The judge as amateur psychologist, experimenting upon the unfortunate children who must appear before him, is neither an attractive nor a convincing figure." Harvard Law Review Note, at 808.

26. The impact of denying fundamental procedural due process to juveniles involved in "delinquency" charges is dramatized by the following considerations: (1) In 1965, persons under 18 accounted for about one-fifth of all arrests for serious crimes (Nat'l Crime Comm'n, Report, p. 55) and over half of all arrests for serious property offenses (id., at 56), and in the same year some 601,000 children under 18, or 2% of all children between 10 and 17, came before juvenile courts (Juvenile Court Statistics—1965, Children's Bureau Statistical Series No. 85 (1966), p. 2). About one out of nine youths will be referred to juvenile court in connection with a delinquent act (excluding traffic offenses) before he is 18 (Nat'l Crime Comm'n Report, p. 55). Cf. also Wheeler & Cottrell, Juvenile Delinquency—Its Prevention and Control (Russell Sage Foundation, 1965), p. 2; Report of the President's Commission on Crime in the District of Columbia (1966) (hereinafter cited as D.C.Crime Comm'n Report), p. 773. Furthermore, most juvenile crime apparently goes undetected or not formally punished. Wheeler & Cottrell, supra, observe that "[A]lmost all youngsters have committed at least one of the petty forms of theft and vandalism in the course of their adolescence." Id., at 28–29. See also Nat'l Crime Comm'n Report, p. 55, where it is stated that "self-report studies reveal that perhaps 90 percent of all young people have committed at least one act for which they could have been brought to juvenile court." It seems that the rate of juvenile delinquency is also steadily rising. See Nat'l Crime Comm'n Report, p. 56; Juvenile Court Statistics, supra, pp. 2–3. (2) In New York, where most juveniles are represented by counsel (see n. 69, infra) and substantial procedural rights are afforded (see, e g., nn. 80, 81, 99, infra), out of a fiscal year 1965–1966 total of 10,755 juvenile proceedings involving boys, 2,242 were dismissed for failure of proof at the fact-finding hearing; for girls, the figures were 306 out of a total of 1,051. New York Judicial Conference, Twelfth Annual Report, pp. 314, 316 (1967). (3) In about one-half of the States, a juvenile may be transferred to an adult penal institution after a juvenile court has found him "delinquent" (Delinquent Children in Penal Institutions, Children's Bureau Pub. No. 415–1964, p. 1). (4) In some jurisdictions a juvenile may be subjected to criminal prosecution for the same offense for which he has served under a juvenile court commitment. However, the Texas procedure to this effect has recently been held unconstitutional by a federal district court judge, in a habeas corpus action. Sawyer v. Hauck, 245 F.Supp. 55 (D.C.W.D.Tex1965). (5) In most of the States the juvenile may end in criminal court through waiver (Harvard Law Review Note, p. 793).

27. Malinski v. People of State of New York, 324 U.S. 401, 414, 65 S.Ct. 781, 787, 89 L.Ed. 1029 (1945) (separate opinion).

tion, the procedural rules which have been fashioned from the generality of due process are our best instruments for the distillation and evaluation of essential facts from the conflicting welter of data that life and our adversary methods present. It is these instruments of due process which enhance the possibility that truth will emerge from the confrontation of opposing versions and conflicting data. "Procedure is to law what 'scientific method' is to science."[28]

It is claimed that juveniles obtain benefits from the special procedures applicable to them which more than offset the disadvantages of denial of the substance of normal due process. As we shall discuss, the observance of due process standards, intelligently and not ruthlessly administered, will not compel the States to abandon or displace any of the substantive benefits of the juvenile process.[29] But it is important, we think, that the claimed benefits of the juvenile process should be candidly appraised. Neither sentiment nor folklore should cause us to shut our eyes, for example, to such startling findings as that reported in an exceptionally reliable study of repeaters or recidivism conducted by the Stanford Research Institute for the President's Commission on Crime in the District of Columbia. This Commission's Report states:

In fiscal 1966 approximately 66 percent of the 16- and 17-year-old juveniles referred to the court by the Youth

Aid Division had been before the court previously. In 1965, 56 percent of those in the Receiving Home were repeaters. The SRI study revealed that 61 percent of the sample Juvenile Court referrals in 1965 had been previously referred at least once and that 42 percent had been referred at least twice before. *Id.*, at 773.

Certainly, these figures and the high crime rates among juveniles to which we have referred (*supra*, n. 26), could not lead us to conclude that the absence of constitutional protections reduces crime, or that the juvenile system, functioning free of constitutional inhibitions as it has largely done, is effective to reduce crime or rehabilitate offenders. We do not mean by this to denigrate the juvenile court process or to suggest that there are not aspects of the juvenile system relating to offenders which are valuable. But the features of the juvenile system which its proponents have asserted are of unique benefit will not be impaired by constitutional domestication. For example, the commendable principles relating to the processing and treatment of juveniles separately from adults are in no way involved or affected by the procedural issues under discussion.[30] Further, we are told that one of the important benefits of the special juvenile court procedures is that they avoid classifying the juvenile as a "criminal." The juvenile offender is now classed as a "delinquent." There is, of course, no reason why this should

⋅

---

28. Foster, Social Work, the Law, and Social Action, in Social Casework, July 1964, pp. 383, 386.

29. See Note, Rights and Rehabilitation in the Juvenile Courts, 67 Col.L.Rev. 281, 321, and *passim* (1967).

30. Here again, however, there is substantial question as to whether fact and pretension, with respect to the separate handling and treatment of children, coincide. See generally infra.

While we are concerned only with procedure before the juvenile court in this case, it should be noted that to the extent that the special procedures for juveniles are thought to be justified by the special consideration and treatment afforded them, there is reason to doubt that juveniles always receive the benefits of such a *quid pro quo*. As to the problem and importance of special care at the adjudicatory stage, cf. nn. 14 and 26, *supra*.

As to treatment, see Nat'l Crime Comm'n Report, pp. 80, 87: D.C. Crime Comm'n Report, pp. 665–676, 686–687 (at p. 687 the Report refers to the District's "bankruptcy of dispositional resources"), 692–695, 700–718 (at p. 701 the Report observes that "The Department of Public Welfare currently lacks even the rudiments of esssential diagnostic and clinical services"); Wheeler & Cottrell, Juvenile Delinquency—Its Prevention and Control (Russell Sage Foundation, 1965), pp. 32–35; Harvard Law Review Note, p. 809; Paulsen, Juvenile Courts, Family Courts, and the Poor Man, 54 Calif.L.Rev. 694, 709–712 (1966); Polier, A View From the Bench (1964). Cf. also, In the Matter of the Youth House, Inc., Report of the July 1966 "A" Term of the Bronx County Grand Jury, Supreme Court of New York, County of Bronx, Trial Term, Part XII, March 21, 1967 (cf. New York Times, March 23, 1967, p. 1, col. 8). The high rate of juvenile recidivism casts some doubt upon the adequacy of treatment afforded juveniles. See D.C.Crime Comm'n Report, p. 773; Nat'l Crime Comm'n Report, pp. 55, 78.

In fact, some courts have recently indicated that appropriate treatment is essential to the validity of juvenile custody, and therefore that a juvenile may challenge the validity of his custody on the ground that he is not in fact receiving any special treatment. See *Creek v. Stone*, 379 F.2d 106 (D.C.Cir. 1967); *Kautter v. Reid*, 183 F.Supp. 352 (D.C.D.C.1960); *White v. Reid*, 125 F.Supp. 647 (D.C.D.C.1954). See also *Elmore v. Stone*, 122 U.S.App.D.C. 416, 355 F.2d 841 (1966) (separate statement of Bazelon, C. J.); *Clayton v. Stone*, 123 U.S.App.D.C. 181, 358 F.2d 548 (1966) (separate statement of Bazelon, C. J.). Cf. Wheeler & Cottrell, *supra*, pp. 32, 35; In re Rich, 125 Vt. 373, 216 A.2d 266 (1966). Cf. also *Rouse v. Cameron*, 125 U.S.App.D.C. 366, 373, F.2d 451 (1966); *Millard v. Cameron*, 125 U.S.App.D.C. 383, 373 F.2d 468 (1966).

not continue. It is disconcerting, however, that this term has come to involve only slightly less stigma than the term "criminal" applied to adults.[31] It is also emphasized that in practically all jurisdictions, statutes provide that an adjudication of the child as a delinquent shall not operate as a civil disability or disqualify him for civil service appointment.[32] There is no reason why the application of due process requirements should interfere with such provisions.

Beyond this, it is frequently said that juveniles are protected by the process from disclosure of their deviational behavior. As the Supreme Court of Arizona phrased it in the present case, the summary procedures of Juvenile Courts are sometimes defended by a statement that it is the law's policy "to hide youthful errors from the full gaze of the public and bury them in the graveyard of the forgotten past." This claim of secrecy, however, is more rhetoric than reality. Disclosure of court records is discretionary with the judge in most jurisdictions. Statutory restrictions almost invariably apply only to the court records, and even as to those the evidence is that many courts routinely furnish information to the FBI and the military, and on request to government agencies and even to private employers.[33] Of more importance are police records. In most States the police keep a complete file of juvenile "police contacts" and have complete discretion as to disclosure of juvenile records. Police departments receive requests for information from the FBI and other law-enforcement agencies, the Armed Forces, and social service agencies, and most of them generally comply.[34] Private employers word their application forms to produce information concerning juvenile arrests and court proceedings, and in some jurisdictions information concerning juvenile police contacts is furnished private employers as well as government agencies.[35]

In any event, there is no reason why, consistently with due process, a State cannot continue if it deems it appropriate, to provide and to improve provision for the confidentiality of records of police contacts and court action relating to juveniles. It is interesting to note, however, that the Arizona Supreme Court used the confidentiality argument as a justification for the type of notice which is here attacked as inadequate for due process purposes. The parents were given merely general notice that their child was charged with "delinquency." No facts were specified. The Arizona court held, however, as we shall discuss, that in addition to this general "notice," the child and his parents must be advised "of the facts involved in the case" no later than the initial hearing by the judge. Obviously, this does not "bury" the word about the child's transgressions. It merely defers the time of disclosure to a point when it is of limited use to the child or his parents in preparing his defense or explanation.

Further, it is urged that the juvenile benefits from informal proceedings in the court. The early conception of the Juvenile Court proceeding was one in which a fatherly judge touched the heart and conscience of the erring youth by talking over his problems, by paternal advice and admonition, and in which, in extreme situations, benevolent and wise institutions of the State provided guidance and help "to save him from a downward career."[36] Then, as now, goodwill and compassion were admirably prevalent. But recent studies have, with surprising unanimity, entered sharp dissent as to the validity of this gentle conception. They suggest that the appearance as well as the actuality of fairness, impartiality and orderliness—in short, the essentials of due process—may be a more impressive and more therapeutic attitude so far as the juvenile is concerned. For example, in a recent study, the sociologists Wheeler and Cottrell observe that when the procedural laxness of the "*parens patriae*" attitude is followed by stern disciplining, the contrast may have an adverse effect upon the child, who feels that

---

31. "[T]he word 'delinquent' has today developed such invidious connotations that the terminology is in the process of being altered; the new descriptive phrase is 'persons in need of supervision,' usually shortened to 'pins.' " Harvard Law Review Note, p. 799, n. 140. The N.Y.Family Court Act § 712 distinguishes between "delinquents" and "persons in need of supervision."

32. See, e. g., the Arizona provision, ARS § 8–228.

33. Harvard Law Review Note, pp. 784–785, 800. Cf. Nat'l Crime Comm'n Report, pp. 87–88; Ketcham, The Unfulfilled Promise of the Juvenile Court, 7 Crime & Delin. 97, 102–103 (1961).

34. Harvard Law Review Note, pp. 785–787.

35. Id., at 785, 800. See also, with respect to the problem of confidentiality of records, Note, Rights and Rehabilitation in the Juvenile Courts, 67 Col.L.Rev. 281, 286–289 (1967). Even the privacy of the juvenile hearing itself is not always adequately protected. Id., at 285–286.

36. Mack, The Juvenile Court, 23 Harv.L.Rev. 104, 120 (1909).

he has been deceived or enticed. They conclude as follows: "Unless appropriate due process of law is followed, even the juvenile who has violated the law may not feel that he is being fairly treated and may therefore resist the rehabilitative efforts of court personnel."[37] Of course, it is not suggested that juvenile court judges should fail appropriately to take account, in their demeanor and conduct, of the emotional and psychological attitude of the juveniles with whom they are confronted. While due process requirements will, in some instances, introduce a degree of order and regularity to Juvenile Court proceedings to determine delinquency, and in contested cases will introduce some elements of the adversary system, nothing will require that the conception of the kindly juvenile judge be replaced by its opposite, nor do we here rule upon the question whether ordinary due process requirements must be observed with respect to hearings to determine the disposition of the delinquent child.

Ultimately, however, we confront the reality of that portion of the Juvenile Court process with which we deal in this case. A boy is charged with misconduct. The boy is committed to an institution where he may be restrained of liberty for years. It is of no constitutional consequence—and of limited practical meaning—that the institution to which he is committed is called an Industrial School. The fact of the matter is that, however euphemistic the title, a "receiving home" or an "industrial school" for juveniles is an institution of confinement in which the child is incarcerated for a greater or lesser time. His world becomes "a building with whitewashed walls, regimented routine and institutional hours * * * ."[38] Instead of mother and father and sisters and brothers and friends and classmates, his world is peopled by guards, custodians, state employees, and "delinquents" confined with him for anything from waywardness[39] to rape and homicide.

In view of this, it would be extraordinary if our Constitution did not require the procedural regularity and the exercise of care implied in the phrase "due process." Under our Constitution, the condition of being a boy does not justify a kangaroo court. The traditional ideas of Juvenile Court procedure, indeed, contemplated that time would be available and care would be used to establish precisely what the juvenile did and why he did it—was it a prank of adolescence or a brutal act threatening serious consequences to himself or society unless corrected?[40] Under traditional notions, one would assume that in a case like that of Gerald Gault, where the juvenile appears to have a home, a working mother and father, and an older brother, the Juvenile Judge would have made a careful inquiry and judgment as to the possibility that the boy could be disciplined and dealt with at home, despite his previous transgressions.[41] Indeed, so far as appears in the record before us, except for some conversation with Gerald about his school work and his "wanting to go to * * * Grand Canyon with his father," the points to which the judge directed his attention were little different from those that would be involved in determining any charge of violation of a penal statute.[42] The essential difference between Gerald's case and a normal criminal case is that safeguards available to adults were discarded in Gerald's case. The summary procedure as well as the

---

37. Juvenile Delinquency—Its Prevention and Control (Russell Sage Foundation, 1966), p. 33. The conclusion of the Nat'l Crime Comm'n Report is similar: "[T]here is increasing evidence that the informal procedures, contrary to the original expectation, may themselves constitute a further obstacle to effective treatment of the delinquent to the extent that they engender in the child a sense of injustice provoked by seemingly all-powerful and challengeless exercise of authority by judges and probation officers." Id., at 85. See also Allen, The Borderland of Criminal Justice (1964), p. 19.

38. Holmes' Appeal, 379 Pa. 599, 616, 109 A.2d 523, 530 (1954) (Musmanno, J., dissenting). See also The State (Sheerin) v. Governor, [1966] I.R. 379 (Supreme Court of Ireland); Trimble v. Stone, 187 F.Supp. 483, 485–486 (D.C.D.C.1960); Allen, The Borderland of Criminal Justice (1964), pp. 18, 52–56.

39. Cf. the Juvenile Code of Arizona, ARS § 8–201, subsec. 6.

40. Cf., however, the conclusions of the D.C. Crime Comm'n Report, pp. 692–693, concerning the inadequacy of the "social study records" upon which the Juvenile Court Judge must make this determination and decide on appropriate treatment.

41. The Juvenile Judge's testimony at the habeas corpus proceeding is devoid of any meaningful discussion of this. He appears to have centered his attention upon whether Gerald made the phone call and used lewd words. He was impressed by the fact that Gerald was on six months' probation because he was with another boy who allegedly stole a purse—a different sort of offense, sharing the feature that Gerald was "along." And he even referred to a report which he said was not investigated because "there was no accusation" "because of lack of material foundation."

   With respect to the possible duty of a trial court to explore alternatives to involuntary commitment in a civil proceedings, cf. Lake v. Cameron, 124 U.S.App.D.C. 264, 364 F.2d 657 (1966), which arose under statutes relating to treatment of the mentally ill.

42. While appellee's brief suggests that the probation officer made some investigation of Gerald's home life, etc., there is not even a claim that the judge went beyond the point stated in the text.

long commitment was possible because Gerald was 15 years of age instead of over 18.

If Gerald had been over 18, he would not have been subject to Juvenile Court proceedings.[43] For the particular offense immediately involved, the maximum punishment would have been a fine of $5 to $50, or imprisonment in jail for not more than two months. Instead, he was committed to custody for a maximum of six years. If he had been over 18 and had committed an offense to which such a sentence might apply, he would have been entitled to substantial rights under the Constitution of the United States as well as under Arizona's laws and constitution. The United States Constitution would guarantee him rights and protections with respect to arrest, search, and seizure, and pretrial interrogation. It would assure him of specific notice of the charges and adequate time to decide his course of action and to prepare his defense. He would be entitled to clear advice that he could be represented by counsel, and, at least if a felony were involved, the State would be required to provide counsel if his parents were unable to afford it. If the court acted on the basis of his confession, careful procedures would be required to assure its voluntariness. If the case went to trial, confrontation and opportunity for cross-examination would be guaranteed. So wide a gulf between the State's treatment of the adult and of the child requires a bridge sturdier than mere verbiage, and reasons more persuasive than cliché can provide. As Wheeler and Cottrell have put it, "The rhetoric of the juvenile court movement has developed without any necessarily close correspondence to the realities of court and institutional routines."[44]

In *Kent v. United States, supra,* we stated that the Juvenile Court Judge's exercise of the power of the state as *parens patriae* was not unlimited. We said that "the admonition to function in a 'parental' relationship is not an invitation to procedural arbitrariness."[45] With respect to the waiver by the Juvenile Court to the adult court of jurisdiction over an offense committed by a youth, we said that "there is no place in our system of law for reaching a result of such tremendous consequences without ceremony—without hearing, without effective assistance of counsel, without a statement of reasons."[46] We announced with respect to such waiver proceedings that while "We do not mean * * * to indicate that the hearing to be held must conform with all of the requirements of a criminal trial or even of the usual administrative hearing; but we do hold that the hearing must measure up to the essentials of due process and fair treatment."[47] We reiterate this view, here in connection with a juvenile court adjudication of "delinquency," as a requirement which is part of the Due Process Clause of the Fourteenth Amendment of our Constitution.[48]

We now turn to the specific issues which are presented to us in the present case.

III

Notice of Charges

Appellants allege that the Arizona Juvenile Code is unconstitutional or alternatively that the proceedings before the Juvenile Court were constitutionally defective because of failure to provide adequate notice of the hearings. No notice was given to Gerald's parents when he was taken into custody on Monday, June 8. On that night, when Mrs. Gault went to the Detention Home, she was orally informed that there would be a hearing the next afternoon and was told the reason why Gerald was in custody. The only written notice Gerald's parents received at any time was a note on plain paper from Officer Flagg delivered on Thursday or Friday, June 11 or 12, to the

---

43. ARS §§ 8–201, 8–202.

44. Juvenile Delinquency—Its Prevention and Control (Russell Sage Foundation, 1966), p. 35. The gap between rhetoric and reality is also emphasized in the Nat'l Crime Comm'n Report, pp. 80–81.

45. 383 U.S., at 555, 86 S.Ct., at 1054.

46. 383 U.S., at 554, 86 S.Ct., at 1053. The Chief Justice stated in a recent speech to a conference of the National Council of Juvenile Court Judges, that a juvenile court "must function within the framework of law and * * * in the attainment of its objectives it cannot act with unbridled caprice." Equal Justice for Juveniles, 15 Juvenile Court Judges Journal, No. 3, pp. 14, 15 (1964).

47. 383 U.S., at 562, 86 S.Ct., at 1057.

48. The Nat'l Crime Comm'n Report recommends that "Juvenile courts should make fullest feasible use of preliminary conferences to dispose of cases short of adjudication." *Id.*, at 84. See also D.C. Crime Comm'n Report, pp. 662–665. Since this "consent decree" procedure would involve neither adjudication of delinquency nor institutionalization, nothing we say in this opinion should be construed as expressing any views with respect to such procedure. The problems of pre-adjudication treatment of juveniles, and of post-adjudication disposition, are unique to the juvenile process; hence what we hold in this opinion with regard to the procedural requirements at the adjudicatory stage has no necessary applicability to other steps of the juvenile process.

effect that the judge had set Monday, June 15, "for further Hearings on Gerald's delinquence."

A "petition" was filed with the court on June 9 by Officer Flagg, reciting only that he was informed and believed that "said minor is a delinquent minor and that it is necessary that some order be made by the Honorable Court for said minor's welfare." The applicable Arizona statute provides for a petition to be filed in Juvenile Court, alleging in general terms that the child is "neglected, dependent or delinquent." The statute explicitly states that such a general allegation is sufficient, "without alleging the facts."[49] There is no requirement that the petition be served and it was not served upon, given to, or shown to Gerald or his parents.[50]

The Supreme Court of Arizona rejected appellants' claim that due process was denied because of inadequate notice. It stated that "Mrs. Gault knew the exact nature of the charge against Gerald from the day he was taken to the detention home." The court also pointed out that the Gaults appeared at the two hearings "without objection." The court held that because "the policy of the juvenile law is to hide youthful errors from the full gaze of the public and bury them in the graveyard of the forgotten past," advance notice of the specific charges or basis for taking the juvenile into custody and for the hearing is not necessary. It held that the appropriate rule is that "the infant and his parents or guardian will receive a petition only reciting a conclusion of delinquency.[51] But no later than the initial hearing by the judge, they must be advised of the facts involved in the case. If the charges are denied, they must be given a reasonable period of time to prepare."

We cannot agree with the court's conclusion that adequate notice was given in this case. Notice, to comply with due process requirements, must be given sufficiently in advance of scheduled court proceedings so that reasonable opportunity to prepare will be afforded, and it must "set forth the alleged misconduct with particularity."[52] It is obvious, as we have discussed above, that no purpose of shielding the child from the public stigma of knowledge of his having been taken into custody and scheduled for hearing is served by the procedure approved by the court below. The "initial hearing" in the present case was a hearing on the merits. Notice at that time is not timely; and even if there were a conceivable purpose served by the deferral proposed by the court below, it would have to yield to the requirements that the child and his parents or guardian be notified, in writing, of the specific charge or factual allegations to be considered at the hearing, and that such written notice be given at the earliest practicable time, and in any event sufficiently in advance of the hearing to permit preparation. Due process of law requires notice of the sort we have described—that is, notice which would be deemed constitutionally adequate in a civil or criminal proceeding.[53] It does not allow a hearing to be held in which a youth's freedom and his parents' right to his custody are at stake without giving them timely notice, in advance of the hearing, of the specific issues that they must meet. Nor, in the circumstances of this case, can it

---

49. ARS § 8–222, subsec. B.

50. Arizona's Juvenile Code does not provide for notice of any sort to be given at the commencement of the proceedings to the child or his parents. Its only notice provision is to the effect that if a person other than the parent or guardian is cited to appear, the parent or guardian shall be notified "by personal service" of the time and place of hearing. ARS § 8–224. The procedure for initiating a proceeding, as specified by the statute, seems to require that after a preliminary inquiry by the court, a determination may be made "that formal jurisdiction should be acquired." Thereupon the court may authorize a petition to be filed. ARS § 8–222. It does not appear that this procedure was followed in the present case.

51. No such petition was served or supplied in the present case.

52. Nat'l Crime Comm'n Report, p. 87. The Commission observed that "The unfairness of too much informality is * * * reflected in the inadequacy of notice to parents and juveniles about charges and hearings." Ibid.

53. For application of the due process requirement of adequate notice in a criminal context, see, e. g., *Cole v. State of Arkansas*, 333 U.S. 196, 68 S.Ct. 514, 92 L.Ed. 644 (1948); *In re Oliver*, 333 U.S. 257, 273–278, 68 S.Ct. 499, 507–510, 92 L.Ed. 682 (1948). For application in a civil context, see, e. g., *Armstrong v. Manzo*, 380 U.S. 545, 85 S.Ct. 1187, 14 L.Ed.2d 62 (1965); *Mullane v. Central Hanover Bank & Tr. Co.*, 339 U.S. 306, 70 S.Ct. 652, 94 L.Ed. 865 (1950). Cf. also *Chaloner v. Sherman*, 242 U.S. 455, 37 S.Ct. 136, 61 L.Ed. 427 (1917). The Court's discussion in these cases of the right to timely and adequate notice forecloses any contention that the notice approved by the Arizona Supreme Court, or the notice actually given the Gaults, was constitutionally adequate. See also Antieau, Constitutional Rights in Juvenile Courts, 46 Cornell L.Q. 387, 395 (1961); Paulsen, Fairness to the Juvenile Offender, 41 Minn.L.Rev. 547, 557 (1957). Cf. Standards, pp. 63–65; Procedures and Evidence in the Juvenile Court, A Guidebook for Judges, prepared by the Advisory Council of Judges of the National Council on Crime and Delinquency (1962), pp. 9–23 (and see cases discussed therein).

reasonably be said that the requirement of notice was waived.[54]

IV

Right to Counsel

Appellants charge that the Juvenile Court proceedings were fatally defective because the court did not advise Gerald or his parents of their right to counsel, and proceeded with the hearing, the adjudication of delinquency and the order of commitment in the absence of counsel for the child and his parents or an express waiver of the right thereto. The Supreme Court of Arizona pointed out that "[t]here is disagreement [among the various jurisdictions] as to whether the court must advise the infant that he has a right to counsel."[55] It noted its own decision in *Arizona State Dept. of Public Welfare v. Barlow*, 80 Ariz. 249, 296 P.2d 298 (1956), to the effect "that *the parents* of an infant in a juvenile proceeding cannot be denied representation by counsel of their choosing." (Emphasis added.) It referred to a provision of the Juvenile Code which it characterized as requiring "that the probation officer shall look after the interests of neglected, delinquent and dependent children," including representing their interests in court.[56] The court argued that "[t]he parent and the probation officer may be relied upon to protect the infant's interests." Accordingly it re-

jected the proposition that "due process requires that an infant have a right to counsel." It said that juvenile courts have the discretion, but not the duty, to allow such representation; it referred specifically to the situation in which the Juvenile Court discerns conflict between the child and his parents as an instance in which this discretion might be exercised. We do not agree. Probation officers, in the Arizona scheme, are also arresting officers. They initiate proceedings and file petitions which they verify, as here, alleging the delinquency of the child; and they testify, as here, against the child. And here the probation officer was also superintendent of the Detention Home. The probation officer cannot act as counsel for the child. His role in the adjudicatory hearing, by statute and in fact, is as arresting officer and witness against the child. Nor can the judge represent the child. There is no material difference in this respect between adult and juvenile proceedings of the sort here involved. In adult proceedings, this contention has been foreclosed by decisions of this Court.[57] A proceeding where the issue is whether the child will be found to be "delinquent" and subjected to the loss of his liberty for years is comparable in seriousness to a felony prosecution. The juvenile needs the assistance of counsel to cope with problems of law,[58] to make skilled inquiry into the facts, to insist upon regularity of the proceedings, and to ascertain whether he has a defense and to prepare and submit it. The child "requires the guiding hand

---

54. Mrs. Gault's "knowledge" of the charge against Gerald, and/or the asserted failure to object, does not excuse the lack of adequate notice. Indeed, one of the purposes of notice is to clarify the issues to be considered, and as our discussion of the facts, supra, shows, even the Juvenile Court Judge was uncertain as to the precise issues determined at the two "hearings." Since the Gaults had no counsel and were not told of their right to counsel, we cannot consider their failure to object to the lack of constitutionally adequate notice as a waiver of their rights. Because of our conclusion that notice given only at the first hearing is inadequate, we need not reach the question whether the Gaults ever received adequately specific notice even at the June 9 hearing, in light of the fact they were never apprised of the charge of being habitually involved in immoral matters.

55. For recent cases in the District of Columbia holding that there must be advice of the right to counsel, and to have counsel appointed if necessary, see, e. g., *Shioutakon v. District of Columbia*, 98 U.S.App.D.C. 371, 236 F.2d 666, 60 A.L.R.2d 686 (1956); *Black v. United States*, 122 U.S.App.D.C. 393, 355 F.2d 104 (1965); *In re Poff*, 135 F.Supp. 224 (D.C.D.C.1955). Cf. also *In re Long*, 184 So.2d 861, 862 (Sup.Ct.Miss., 1966); *People v. Dotson*, 46 Cal.2d 891, 299 P.2d 875 (1956).

56. The section cited by the court, ARS § 8–204, subsec. C, reads as follows:
   "The probation officer shall have the authority of a peace officer. He shall:
   "1. Look after the interests of neglected, delinquent and dependent children of the county.
   "2. Make investigations and file petitions.
   "3. Be present in court when cases are heard concerning children and represent their interests.
   "4. Furnish the court information and assistance as it may require.
   "5. Assist in the collection of sums ordered paid for the support of children.
   "6. Perform other acts ordered by the court."

57. *Powell v. State of Alabama*, 287 U.S. 45, 61, 53 S.Ct. 55, 61, 77 L.Ed. 158 (1932); *Gideon v. Wainwright*, 372 U.S. 335, 83 S.Ct. 792, 9 L.Ed.2d 799 (1963).

58. In the present proceeding, for example, although the Juvenile Judge believed that Gerald's telephone conversation was within the condemnation of ARS § 13–377, he suggested some uncertainty because the statute prohibits the use of vulgar language "in the presence or hearing of" a woman or child.

of counsel at every step in the proceedings against him."[59] Just as in *Kent v. United States, supra*, 383 U.S., at 561–562, 86 S.Ct., at 1057–1058, we indicated our agreement with the United States Court of Appeals for the District of Columbia Circuit that the assistance of counsel is essential for purposes of waiver proceedings, so we hold now that it is equally essential for the determination of delinquency, carrying with it the awesome prospect of incarceration in a state institution until the juvenile reaches the age of 21.[60]

During the last decade, court decisions,[61] experts,[62] and legislatures[63] have demonstrated increas-

ing recognition of this view. In at least one-third of the States, statutes now provide for the right of representation by retained counsel in juvenile delinquency proceedings, notice of the right, or assignment of counsel, or a combination of these. In other States, court rules have similar provisions.[64]

The President's Crime Commission has recently recommended that in order to assure "procedural justice for the child," it is necessary that "Counsel * * * be appointed as a matter of course wherever coercive action is a possibility, without requiring any affirmative choice by child or parent."[65] As stated by the authoritative "Standards for Juvenile and Family

---

59. *Powell v. State of Alabama*, 287 U.S. 45, 69, 53 S.Ct. 55, 64 (1932).

60. This means that the commitment, in virtually all cases, is for a minimum of three years since jurisdiction of juvenile courts is usually limited to age 18 and under.

61. See cases cited in n. 55, *supra*.

62. See, e. g., Schinitsky, 17 The Record 10 (N.Y. City Bar Assn. 1962); Paulsen, Fairness to the Juvenile Offender, 41 Minn.L.Rev. 547, 568–573 (1957); Antieau, Constitutional Rights in Juvenile Courts, 46 Cornell L.Q. 387, 404–407 (1961); Paulsen, *Kent v. United States*: The Constitutional Context of Juvenile Cases, 1966 Sup.Ct.Rev. 167, 187–189; Ketcham, The Legal Renaissance in the Juvenile Court, 60 Nw.U.L.Rev. 585 (1965); Elson, Juvenile Courts & Due Process, in Justice for the Child (Rosenheim ed.) 95, 103–105 (1962); Note, Rights and Rehabilitation in the Juvenile Courts, 67 Col.L.Rev. 281, 321–327 (1967). See also Nat'l Probation and Parole Assn., Standard Family Court Act (1959) § 19, and Standard Juvenile Court Act (1959), § 19, in 5 NPPA Journal 99, 137, 323, 367 (1959) (hereinafter cited as Standard Family Court Act and Standard Juvenile Court Act, respectively).

63. Only a few state statutes require advice of the right to counsel and to have counsel appointed. See N. Y. Family Court Act §§ 241, 249, 728, 741; Calif.Welf. & Inst'ns Code §§ 633, 634, 659, 700 (1966) (appointment is mandatory only if conduct would be a felony in the case of an adult); Minn.Stat.Ann. § 260.155(2) (1966 Supp.) (see Comment of Legislative Commission accompanying this section); District of Columbia Legal Aid Act, D.C.Code Ann. § 2–2202 (1961) (Legal Aid Agency "shall make attorneys available to represent indigents * * * in proceedings before the juvenile court * * *." See *Black v. United States*, 122 U.S.App.D.C. 393, 395–396, 355 F.2d 104, 106–107 (1965), construing this Act as providing a right to appointed counsel and to be informed of that right). Other state statutes allow appointment on request, or in some classes of cases, or in the discretion of the court, etc. The state statutes are collected and classified in Riederer, The Role of Counsel in the Juvenile Court, 2 J.Fam.Law 16, 19–20 (1962), which, however, does not treat the statutes cited above. See also Note, Rights and Rehabilitation in the Juvenile Courts, 67 Col.L.Rev. 281, 321–322 (1967).

64. Skoler & Tenney, Attorney Representation in Juvenile Court, 4 J.Fam.Law 77, 95–96 (1964); Riederer, The Role of Counsel in the Juvenile Court, 2 J.Fam.Law 16 (1962).

Recognition of the right to counsel involves no necessary interference with the special purposes of juvenile court procedures; indeed, it seems that counsel can play an important role in the process of rehabilitation. See Note, Rights and Rehabilitation in the Juvenile Courts, 67 Col.L.Rev. 281, 324–327 (1967).

65. Nat'l Crime Comm'n Report, pp. 86–87. The Commission's statement of its position is very forceful:

"The Commission believes that no single action holds more potential for achieving procedural justice for the child in the juvenile court than provision of counsel. The presence of an independent legal representative of the child, or of his parent, is the keystone of the whole structure of guarantees that a minimum system of procedural justice requires. The rights to confront one's accusers, to cross-examine witnesses, to present evidence and testimony of one's own, to be unaffected by prejudicial and unreliable evidence, to participate meaningfully in the dispositional decision, to take an appeal have substantial meaning for the overwhelming majority of persons brought before the juvenile court only if they are provided with competent lawyers who can invoke those rights effectively. The most informal and well-intentioned of judicial proceedings are technical; few adults without legal training can influence or even understand them; certainly children cannot. Papers are drawn and charges expressed in legal language. Events follow one another in a manner that appears arbitrary and confusing to the uninitiated. Decisions, unexplained, appear too official to challenge. But with lawyers come records of proceedings; records make possible appeals which, even if they do not occur, impart by their possibility a healthy atmosphere of accountability.

"Fears have been expressed that lawyers would make juvenile court proceedings adversary. No doubt this is partly true, but it is partly desirable. Informality is often abused. The juvenile courts deal with cases in which facts are disputed and in which, therefore, rules of evidence, confrontation of witnesses, and other adversary procedures are called for. They deal with many cases involving conduct that can lead to incarceration or close supervision for long periods, and therefore juveniles often need the same safeguards that are granted to adults. And in all cases children need advocates to speak for them and guard their interests, particularly when

(continued on next page)

Courts," published by the Children's Bureau of the United States Department of Health, Education, and Welfare:

> As a component part of a fair hearing required by due process guaranteed under the 14th amendment, notice of the right to counsel should be required at all hearings and counsel provided upon request when the family is financially unable to employ counsel. Standards, p. 57.

This statement was "reviewed" by the National Council of Juvenile Court Judges at its 1965 Convention and they "found no fault" with it.[66] The New York Family Court Act contains the following statement:

> This act declares that minors have a right to the assistance of counsel of their own choosing or of law guardians[67] in neglect proceedings under article three and in proceedings to determine juvenile delinquency and whether a person is in need of supervision under article seven. This declaration is based on a finding that counsel is often indispensable to a practical re-

alization of due process of law and may be helpful in making reasoned determinations of fact and proper orders of disposition.[68]

The Act provides that "At the commencement of any hearing" under the delinquency article of the statute, the juvenile and his parent shall be advised of the juvenile's "right to be represented by counsel chosen by him or his parent * * * or by a law guardian assigned by the court * * * ."[69] The California Act (1961) also requires appointment of counsel.[70]

We conclude that the Due Process Clause of the Fourteenth Amendment requires that in respect of proceedings to determine delinquency which may result in commitment to an institution in which the juvenile's freedom is curtailed, the child and his parents must be notified of the child's right to be represented by counsel retained by them, or if they are unable to afford counsel, that counsel will be appointed to represent the child.

---

disposition decisions are made. It is the disposition stage at which the opportunity arises to offer individualized treatment plans and in which the danger inheres that the court's coercive power will be applied without adequate knowledge of the circumstances.

"Fears also have been expressed that the formality lawyers would bring into juvenile court would defeat the therapeutic aims of the court. But informality has no necessary connection with therapy; it is a device that has been used to approach therapy, and it is not the only possible device. It is quite possible that in many instances lawyers, for all their commitment to formality, could do more to further therapy for their clients than can the small, overworked social staffs of the courts.* * *

"The Commission believes it is essential that counsel be appointed by the juvenile court for those who are unable to provide their own. Experience under the prevailing systems in which children are free to seek counsel of their choice reveals how empty of meaning the right is for those typically the subjects of juvenile court proceedings. Moreover, providing counsel only when the child is sophisticated enough to be aware of his need and to ask for one or when he fails to waive his announced right [is] not enough, as experience in numerous jurisdictions reveals.

"*The Commission recommends:*

"COUNSEL SHOULD BE APPOINTED AS A MATTER OF COURSE WHEREVER COERCIVE ACTION IS A POSSIBILITY, WITHOUT REQUIRING ANY AFFIRMATIVE CHOICE BY CHILD OR PARENT."

66. Lehman, A Juvenile's Right to Counsel in a Delinquency Hearing, 17 Juvenile Court Judge's Journal 53 (1966). In an interesting review of the 1966 edition of the Children's Bureau's "Standards," Rosenheim, Standards for Juvenile and Family Courts: Old Wine in a New Bottle, 1 Fam.L.Q. 25, 29 (1967), the author observes that "The 'Standards' of 1966, just like the 'Standards' of 1954, are valuable precisely because they represent a diligent and thoughtful search for an accommodation between the aspirations of the founders of the juvenile court and the grim realities of life against which, in part, the due process of criminal and civil law offers us protection."

67. These are lawyers designated, as provided by the statute, to represent minors. N.Y.Family Court Act § 242.

68. N.Y.Family Court Act § 241.

69. N.Y.Family Court Act § 741. For accounts of New York practice under the new procedures, see Isaacs, The Role of the Lawyer in Representing Minors in the New Family Court, 12 Buffalo L.Rev. 501 (1963); Dembitz, Ferment and Experiment in New York: Juvenile Cases in the New Family Court, 48 Cornell L.Q. 499, 508–512 (1963). Since introduction of the law guardian system in September of 1962, it is stated that attorneys are present in the great majority of cases. Harvard Law Review Note, p. 796. See New York Judicial Conference, Twelfth Annual Report, pp. 288–291 (1967), for detailed statistics on representation of juveniles in New York. For the situation before 1962, see Schinitsky, The Role of the Lawyer in Children's Court, 17 The Record 10 (N.Y.City Bar Assn. 1962). In the District of Columbia, where statute and court decisions require that a lawyer be appointed if the family is unable to retain counsel, see n. 63, supra, and where the juvenile and his parents are so informed at the initial hearing, about 85% to 90% do not choose to be represented and sign a written waiver form. D.C. Crime Comm'n Report, p. 646. The Commission recommends adoption in the District of Columbia of a "law guardian" system similar to that of New York, with more effective notification of the right to appointed counsel, in order to eliminate the problems of procedural fairness, accuracy of factfinding, and appropriateness of disposition which the absence of counsel in so many juvenile court proceedings involves. Id., at 681–685.

70. See n. 63, supra.

At the habeas corpus proceeding, Mrs. Gault testified that she knew that she could have appeared with counsel at the juvenile hearing. This knowledge is not a waiver of the right to counsel which she and her juvenile son had, as we have defined it. They had a right expressly to be advised that they might retain counsel and to be confronted with the need for specific consideration of whether they did or did not choose to waive the right. If they were unable to afford to employ counsel, they were entitled in view of the seriousness of the charge and the potential commitment, to appointed counsel, unless they chose waiver. Mrs. Gault's knowledge that she could employ counsel was not an "intentional relinquishment or abandonment" of a fully known right.[71]

V

Confrontation, Self-Incrimination, Cross-Examination

Appellants urge that the writ of habeas corpus should have been granted because of the denial of the rights of confrontation and cross-examination in the Juvenile Court hearings, and because the privilege against self-incrimination was not observed. The Juvenile Court Judge testified at the habeas corpus hearing that he had proceeded on the basis of Gerald's admissions at the two hearings. Appellants attack this on the ground that the admissions were obtained in disregard of the privilege against self-incrimination.[72] If the confession is disregarded, appellants argue that the delinquency conclusion, since it was fundamentally based on a finding that Gerald had made lewd remarks during the phone call to Mrs. Cook, is fatally defective for failure to accord the rights of confrontation and cross-examination which the Due Process Clause of the Fourteenth Amendment of the Federal Constitution guarantees in state proceedings generally.[73]

Our first question, then, is whether Gerald's admission was improperly obtained and relied on as the basis of decision, in conflict with the Federal Constitution. For this purpose, it is necessary briefly to recall the relevant facts.

Mrs. Cook, the complainant, and the recipient of the alleged telephone call, was not called as a witness. Gerald's mother asked the Juvenile Court Judge why Mrs. Cook was not present and the judge replied that "she didn't have to be present." So far as appears, Mrs. Cook was spoken to only once, by Officer Flagg, and this was by telephone. The judge did not speak with her on any occasion. Gerald had been questioned by the probation officer after having been taken into custody. The exact circumstances of this questioning do not appear but any admissions Gerald may have made at this time do not appear in the record.[74] Gerald was also questioned by the Juvenile Court Judge at each of the two hearings. The judge testified in the habeas corpus proceeding that Gerald admitted making "some of the lewd statements * * * [but not] any of the more serious lewd statements." There was conflict and uncertainty among the witnesses at the habeas corpus proceeding—the Juvenile Court Judge, Mr. and Mrs. Gault, and the probation officer—as to what Gerald did or did not admit.

We shall assume that Gerald made admissions of the sort described by the Juvenile Court Judge, as quoted above. Neither Gerald nor his parents were advised that he did not have to testify or make a statement, or that an incriminating statement might result in his commitment as a "delinquent."

The Arizona Supreme Court rejected appellants' contention that Gerald had a right to be advised that he need not incriminate himself. It said: "We think the necessary flexibility for individualized treatment will be enhanced by a rule which does not require the judge to advise the infant of a privilege against self-incrimination."

In reviewing this conclusion of Arizona's Supreme Court, we emphasize again that we are here concerned only with a proceeding to determine whether a minor is a "delinquent" and which may result in commitment to a state institution. Specifically, the question is whether, in such a proceeding, an admission by the juvenile may be used against

71. *Johnson v. Zerbst,* 304 U.S. 458, 464, 58 S.Ct. 1019, 1023, 82 L.Ed. 1461 (1938); *Carnley v. Cochran,* 369 U.S. 506, 82 S.Ct. 884, 8 L.Ed.2d 70 (1962); *United States ex rel. Brown v. Fay,* 242 F.Supp. 273 (D.C.S.D.N.Y.1965).

72. The privilege is applicable to state proceedings. *Malloy v. Hogan,* 378 U.S. 1, 84 S.Ct. 1489, 12 L.Ed.2d 653 (1964).

73. *Pointer v. State of Texas,* 380 U.S. 400, 85 S.Ct. 1065, 13 L.Ed.2d 923 (1965); *Douglas v. State of Alabama,* 380 U.S. 415, 85 S.Ct. 1074, 13 L.Ed.2d 934 (1965).

74. For this reason, we cannot consider the status of Gerald's alleged admissions to the probation officers. Cf., however, Comment, Miranda Guarantees in the California Juvenile Court, 7 Santa Clara Lawyer 114 (1966).

him in the absence of clear and unequivocal evidence that the admission was made with knowledge that he was not obliged to speak and would not be penalized for remaining silent. In light of *Miranda v. State of Arizona*, 384 U.S. 436, 86 S.Ct. 1602, 16 L.Ed.2d 694 (1966), we must also consider whether, if the privilege against self-incrimination is available, it can effectively be waived unless counsel is present or the right to counsel have been waived.

It has long been recognized that the eliciting and use of confessions or admissions require careful scrutiny. Dean Wigmore states:

> The ground of distrust of confessions made in certain situations is, in a rough and indefinite way, judicial experience. There has been no careful collection of statistics of untrue confessions, nor has any great number of instances been even loosely reported * * * but enough have been verified to fortify the conclusion, based on ordinary observation of human conduct, that under certain stresses a person, especially one of defective mentality or peculiar temperament, may falsely acknowledge guilt. This possibility arises wherever the innocent person is placed in such a situation that the untrue acknowledgment of guilt is at the time the more promising of two alternatives between which he is obliged to choose; that is, he chooses any risk that may be in falsely acknowledging guilt, in preference to some worse alternative associated with silence.

> * * *

> The principle, then, upon which a confession may be excluded is that it is, under certain conditions, *testimonially untrustworthy* * * * . [T]he essential feature is that the principle of exclusion is a testimonial one, analogous to the other principles which exclude narrations as untrustworthy* * * .[75]

This Court has emphasized that admissions and confessions of juveniles require special caution. In *Haley v. State of Ohio*, 332 U.S. 596, 68 S.Ct. 302, 92 L.Ed. 224, where this Court reversed the conviction of a 15-year-old boy for murder, Mr. Justice Douglas said:

> What transpired would make us pause for careful inquiry if a mature man were involved. And when, as here, a mere child—an easy victim of the law—is before us, special care in scrutinizing the record must

be used. Age 15 is a tender and difficult age for a boy of any race. He cannot be judged by the more exacting standards of maturity. That which would leave a man cold and unimpressed can overawe and overwhelm a lad in his early teens. This is the period of great instability which the crisis of adolescence produces. A 15-year-old lad, questioned through the dead of night by relays of police, is a ready victim of the inquisition. Mature men possibly might stand the ordeal from midnight to 5 a. m. But we cannot believe that a lad of tender years is a match for the police in such a contest. He needs counsel and support if he is not to become the victim first of fear, then of panic. He needs someone on whom to lean lest the overpowering presence of the law, as he knows it, crush him. No friend stood at the side of this 15-year-old boy as the police, working in relays, questioned him hour after hour, from midnight until dawn. No lawyer stood guard to make sure that the police went so far and no farther, to see to it that they stopped short of the point where he became the victim of coercion. No counsel or friend was called during the critical hours of questioning.[76]

In *Haley*, as we have discussed, the boy was convicted in an adult court, and not a juvenile court. In notable decisions, the New York Court of Appeals and the Supreme Court of New Jersey have recently considered decisions of Juvenile Courts in which boys have been adjudged "delinquent" on the basis of confessions obtained in circumstances comparable to those in *Haley*. In both instances, the State contended before its highest tribunal that constitutional requirements governing inculpatory statements applicable in adult courts do not apply to juvenile proceedings. In each case, the State's contention was rejected, and the juvenile court's determination of delinquency was set aside on the grounds of inadmissibility of the confession. *In Matters of W. and S.*, 19 N.Y.2d 53, 277 N.Y.S.2d 675, 224 N.E.2d 102 (1966) (opinion by Keating, J.), and *In Interests of Carlo and Stasilowicz*, 48 N.J. 224, 225 A.2d 110 (1966) (opinion by Proctor, J.). The privilege against self-incrimination is, of course, related to the question of the safeguards necessary to assure that admissions or confessions are reasonably trustworthy, that they are not the mere fruits of fear or coercion, but are reliable expressions of the truth. The roots of the privilege are, however, far deeper. They tap the basic stream of religious and political

---

75. 3 Wigmore, Evidence § 822 (3d ed. 1940).

76. 332 U.S., at 599–600, 68 S.Ct., at 303 (opinion of Mr. Justice Douglas, joined by Justices Black, Murphy and Rutledge; Justice Frankfurter concurred in a separate opinion).

principle because the privilege reflect the limits of the individual's attornment to the state and—in a philosophical sense—insists upon the equality of the individual and the state.[77] In other words, the privilege has a broader and deeper thrust than the rule which prevents the use of confessions which are the product of coercion because coercion is thought to carry with it the danger of unreliability. One of its purposes is to prevent the state, whether by force or by psychological domination, from overcoming the mind and will of the person under investigation and depriving him of the freedom to decide whether to assist the state in securing his conviction.[78]

It would indeed by surprising if the privilege against self-incrimination were available to hardened criminals but not to children. The language of the Fifth Amendment, applicable to the States by operation of the Fourteenth Amendment, is unequivocal and without exception. And the scope of the privilege is comprehensive. As Mr. Justice White, concurring, stated in *Murphy v. Waterfront Commission*, 378 U.S. 52, 94, 84 S.Ct. 1594, 1611, 12 L.Ed.2d 678 (1964):

> The privilege can be claimed in *any proceeding*, be it criminal or civil, administrative or judicial, investigatory or adjudicatory. * * * it protects *any disclosures* which the witness may reasonably apprehend *could be used in a criminal prosecution or which could lead to other evidence that might be so used.*[79] (Emphasis added.)

With respect to juveniles, both common observation and expert opinion emphasize that the "distrust of confessions made in certain situations" to which Dean Wigmore referred in the passage quoted *supra*, at 1453, is imperative in the case of children from an early age through adolescence. In New York,

for example, the recently enacted Family Court Act provides that the juvenile and his parents must be advised at the start of the hearing of his right to remain silent.[80] The New York statute also provides that the police must attempt to communicate with the juvenile's parents before questioning him,[81] and that absent "special circumstances" a confession may not be obtained from a child prior to notifying his parents or relatives and releasing the child either to them or to the Family Court.[82] In *In Matters of W. and S.*, referred to above, the New York Court of Appeals held that the privilege against self-incrimination applies in juvenile delinquency cases and requires the exclusion of involuntary confessions, and that *People v. Lewis*, 260 N.Y. 171, 183 N.E. 353, 86 A.L.R. 1001 (1932), holding the contrary, had been specifically overruled by statute.

The authoritative "Standards for Juvenile and Family Courts" concludes that, "Whether or not transfer to the criminal court is a possibility, certain procedures should always be followed. Before being interviewed [by the police], the child and his parents should be informed of his right to have legal counsel present and to refuse to answer questions or be fingerprinted[83] if he should so decide."[84]

Against the application to juveniles of the right to silence, it is argued that juvenile proceedings are "civil" and not "criminal," and therefore the privilege should not apply. It is true that the statement of the privilege in the Fifth Amendment, which is applicable to the States by reason by the Fourteenth Amendment, is that no person "shall be compelled in any *criminal case* to be a witness against himself." However, it is also clear that the availability of the privilege does not turn upon the type of proceeding in which its protection is invoked, but upon the nature of the statement or admission and the ex-

---

77. See Fortas, The Fifth Amendment, 25 Cleveland Bar Assn. Journal 91 (1954).

78. See *Rogers v. Richmond*, 365 U.S. 534, 81 S.Ct. 735, 5 L.Ed.2d 760 (1961); *Culombe v. Connecticut*, 367 U.S. 568, 81 S.Ct. 1860, 6 L.Ed.2d 1037 (1961) (opinion of Mr. Justice Frankfurter, joined by Mr. Justice Stewart); *Miranda v. State of Arizona*, 384 U.S. 436, 86 S.Ct. 1602, 16 L.Ed.2d 694 (1966).

79. See also *Malloy v. Hogan*, 378 U.S. 1, 84 S.Ct. 1489, 12 L.Ed.2d 653 (1964); *McCarthy v. Arndstein*, 266 U.S. 34, 40, 45 S.Ct. 16, 17, 69 L.Ed. 158 (1924).

80. N.Y.Family Court Act § 741.

81. N.Y.Family Court Act § 724(a). In *In Matter of Williams*, 49 Misc.2d 154, 267 N.Y.S.2d 91 (1966), the New York Family Court held that "The failure of the police to notify this child's parents that he had been taken into custody, if not alone sufficient to render his confession inadmissible, is germane on the issue of its voluntary character * * * ." Id., at 165, 267 N.Y.S.2d, at 106. The confession was held involuntary and therefore inadmissible.

82. N.Y.Family Court Act § 724 (as amended 1963, see Suppl.1966). See *In Matter of Addison*, 20 A.D.2d 90, 245 N.Y.S.2d 243 (1963).

83. The issues relating to fingerprinting of juveniles are not presented here, and we express no opinion concerning them.

84. Standards, p. 49.

posure which it invites. The privilege may, for example, be claimed in a civil or administrative proceeding, if the statement is or may be inculpatory.[85]

It would be entirely unrealistic to carve out of the Fifth Amendment all statements by juveniles on the ground that these cannot lead to "criminal" involvement. In the first place, juvenile proceedings to determine "delinquency," which may lead to commitment to a state institution, must be regarded as "criminal" for purposes of the privilege against self-incrimination. To hold otherwise would be to disregard substance because of the feeble enticement of the "civil" label-of-convenience which has been attached to juvenile proceedings. Indeed, in over half of the States, there is not even assurance that the juvenile will be kept in separate institutions, apart from adult "criminals." In those States juveniles may be placed in or transferred to adult penal institutions[86] after having been found "delinquent" by a juvenile court. For this purpose, at least, commitment is a deprivation of liberty. It is incarceration against one's will, whether it is called "criminal" or "civil." And our Constitution guarantees that no person shall be "compelled" to be a witness against himself when he is threatened with deprivation of his liberty—a command which this Court has broadly applied and generously implemented in accordance with the teaching of the history of the privilege and its great office in mankind's battle for freedom.[87]

In addition, apart from the equivalence for this purpose of exposure to commitment as a juvenile delinquent and exposure to imprisonment as an adult offender, the fact of the matter is that there is little or no assurance in Arizona, as in most if not all of the States, that a juvenile apprehended and interrogated by the police or even by the Juvenile Court itself will remain outside of the reach of adult courts as a consequence of the offense for which he has been taken into custody. In Arizona, as in other States, provision is made for Juvenile Courts to relinquish or waive jurisdiction to the ordinary criminal courts.[88] In the present case, when Gerald Gault was interrogated concerning violation of a section of the Arizona Criminal Code, it could not be certain that the Juvenile Court Judge would decide to "suspend" criminal prosecution in court for adults by proceeding to an adjudication in Juvenile Court.[89]

It is also urged, as the Supreme Court of Arizona here asserted, that the juvenile and presumably his parents should not be advised of the juvenile's right to silence because confession is good for the child as the commencement of the assumed therapy of the juvenile court process, and he should be encouraged to assume an attitude of trust and confidence toward the officials of the juvenile process. This proposition has been subjected to widespread challenge on the basis of current reappraisals of the rhetoric and realities of the handling of juvenile offenders.

In fact, evidence is accumulating that confessions by juveniles do not aid in "individualized treatment," as the court below put it, and that compelling the child to answer questions, without warning or advice as to his right to remain silent, does not serve this or any other good purpose. In light of the observations of Wheeler and Cottrell,[90] and others, it seems probable that where children are induced to confess by "paternal" urgings on the part of officials and the confession is then followed by disciplinary action, the child's reaction is likely to be hostile and adverse—the child may well feel that he has been led or tricked into confession and that despite his confession, he is being punished.[91]

Further, authoritative opinion has cast formidable doubt upon the reliability and trustworthiness of "confessions" by children. This Court's observations

---

85. See n. 79, *supra*, and accompanying text.

86. Delinquent Children in Penal Institutions, Children's Bureau Pub. No. 415–1964, p. 1.

87. See, e. g., *Miranda v. State of Arizona*, 384 U.S. 436, 86 S.Ct. 1602, 16 L.Ed.2d 694 (1966); *Garrity v. State of New Jersey*, 385 U.S. 493, 87 S.Ct. 616, 17 L.Ed.2d 562 (1967); *Spevack v. Klein*, 385 U.S. 511, 87 S.Ct. 625, 636, 17 L.Ed.2d 574 (1967); *Haynes v. State of Washington*, 373 U.S. 503, 83 S.Ct. 1336, 10 L.Ed.2d 513 (1963); *Culombe v. State of Connecticut*, 367 U.S. 568, 81 S.Ct. 1860, 6 L.Ed.2d 1037 (1961); *Rogers v. Richmond*, 365 U.S. 534, 81 S.Ct. 735, 5 L.Ed.2d 760 (1961); *Malloy v. Hogan*, 378 U.S. 1, 84 S.Ct. 1489, 12 L.Ed.2d 653 (1964); *Griffin v. State of California*, 380 U.S. 609, 85 S.Ct. 1229, 14 L.Ed.2d 106 (1965).

88. Arizona Constitution, Art. 6, § 15 (as amended 1960); ARS §§ 8–223, 8–228, subsec. A; Harvard Law Review Note, p. 793. Because of this possibility that criminal jurisdiction may attach it is urged that "* * * all of the procedural safeguards in the criminal law should be followed." Standards, p. 49. Cf. *Harling v. United States*, 111 U.S.App.D.C. 174, 295 F.2d 161 (1961).

89. ARS § 8–228, subsec. A.

90. Juvenile Delinquency—Its Prevention and Control (Russell Sage Foundation, 1966).

91. *Id.*, at 33. See also the other materials cited in n. 37, *supra*.

in *Haley v. State of Ohio* are set forth above. The recent decision of the New York Court of Appeals referred to above, *In Matters of W. and S.* deals with a dramatic and, it is to be hoped, extreme example. Two 12-year-old Negro boys were taken into custody for the brutal assault and rape of two aged domestics, one of whom died as the result of the attack. One of the boys was schizophrenic and had been locked in the security ward of a mental institution at the time of the attacks. By a process that may best be described as bizarre, his confession was obtained by the police. A psychiatrist testified that the boy would admit "whatever he thought was expected so that he could get out of the immediate situation." The other 12-year-old also "confessed." Both confessions were in specific detail, albeit they contained various inconsistencies. The Court of Appeals, in an opinion by Keating, J., concluded that the confessions were products of the will of the police instead of the boys. The confessions were therefore held involuntary and the order of the Appellate Division affirming the order of the Family Court adjudging the defendants to be juvenile delinquents was reversed.

A similar and equally instructive case has recently been decided by the Supreme Court of New Jersey. *In Interests of Carlo and Stasilowicz, supra.* The body of a 10-year-old girl was found. She had been strangled. Neighborhood boys who knew the girl were questioned. The two appellants, aged 13 and 15, confessed to the police, with vivid detail and some inconsistencies. At the Juvenile Court hearing, both denied any complicity in the killing. They testified that their confessions were the product of fear and fatigue due to extensive police grilling. The Juvenile Court Judge found that the confessions were voluntary and admissible. On appeal, in an extensive opinion by Proctor, J., the Supreme Court of

New Jersey reversed. It rejected the State's argument that the constitutional safeguard of voluntariness governing the use of confessions does not apply in proceedings before the Juvenile Court. It pointed out that under New Jersey court rules, juveniles under the age of 16 accused of committing a homicide are tried in a proceeding which "has all of the appurtenances of a criminal trial," including participation by the county prosecutor, and requirements that the juvenile be provided with counsel, that a stenographic record by made, etc. It also pointed out that under New Jersey law, the confinement of the boys after reaching age 21 could be extended until they had served the maximum sentence which could have been imposed on an adult for such homicide, here found to be second-degree murder carrying up to 30 years' imprisonment.[92] The court concluded that the confessions were involuntary, stressing that the boys, contrary to statute, were placed in the police station and there interrogated,[93] that the parents of both boys were not allowed to see them while they were being interrogated;[94] that inconsistencies appeared among the various statements of the boys and with the objective evidence of the crime; and that there were protracted periods of questioning. The court noted the State's contention that both boys were advised of their constitutional rights before they made their statements, but it held that this should not be given "significant weight in our determination of voluntariness."[95] Accordingly, the judgment of the Juvenile Court was reversed.

In a recent case before the Juvenile Court of the District of Columbia, Judge Ketcham rejected the proffer of evidence as to oral statements made at police headquarters by four juveniles who had been taken into custody for alleged involvement in an assault and attempted robbery. *In the Matter of Four Youths*, Nos. 28–776–J, 28–778–J, 28–783–J, 78–

---

92. N.J.Rev.Stat. § 2A:4–37(b)(2), N.J.S.A. (Supp.1966); N.J.Rev.Stat. 2A:113–4, N.J.S.A.

93. N.J.Rev.Stat. § 2A:4–32, 33, N.J.S.A. The court emphasized that the "frightening atmosphere" of a police station is likely to have "harmful effects on the mind and will of the boy," citing *In Matter of Rutane*, 37 Misc.2d 234, 234 N.Y.S.2d 777 (Fam.Ct.Kings County, 1962).

94. The court held that this alone might be enough to show that the confessions were involuntary "even though, as the police testified, the boys did not wish to see their parents" (citing *Gallegos v. State of Colorado*, 370 U.S. 49, 82 S.Ct. 1209, 8 L.Ed.2d 325 (1962)).

95. The court quoted the following passage from *Haley v. State of Ohio*, supra, 332 U.S., at 601, 68 S.Ct., at 304:

"But we are told that this boy was advised of his constitutional rights before he signed the confession and that, knowing them, he nevertheless confessed. That assumes, however, that a boy of fifteen, without aid of counsel, would have a full appreciation of that advice and that on the facts of this record he had a freedom of choice. We cannot indulge those assumptions. Moreover, we cannot give any weight to recitals which merely formalize constitutional requirements. Formulas of respect for constitutional safeguards cannot prevail over the facts of life which contradict them. They may not become a cloak for inquisitorial practices and make an empty form of the due process of law for which free men fought and died to obtain."

859–J, Juvenile Court of the District of Columbia, April 7, 1961. The court explicitly stated that it did not rest its decision on a showing that the statements were involuntary, but because they were untrustworthy. Judge Ketcham said:

> Simply, stated, the Court's decision in this case rests upon the considered opinion—after nearly four busy years on the Juvenile Court bench during which the testimony of thousands of such juveniles has been heard—that the statements of adolescents under 18 years of age who are arrested and charged with violations of law are frequently untrustworthy and often distort the truth.

We conclude that the constitutional privilege against self-incrimination is applicable in the case of juveniles as it is with respect to adults. We appreciate that special problems may arise with respect to waiver of the privilege by or on behalf of children, and that there may well be some differences in technique—but not in principle—depending upon the age of the child and the presence and competence of parents. The participation of counsel will, of course, assist the police, Juvenile Courts and appellate tribunals in administering the privilege. If counsel was not present for some permissible reason when an admission was obtained, the greatest care must be taken to assure that the admission was voluntary, in the sense not only that it was not coerced or suggested, but also that it was not the product of ignorance of rights or of adolescent fantasy, fright or despair.[96] The "confession" of Gerald Gault was first obtained by Officer Flagg, out of the presence of Gerald's parents, without counsel and without advising him of his right to silence, as far as appears.

The judgment of the Juvenile Court was stated by the judge to be based on Gerald's admissions in court. Neither "admission" was reduced to writing, and, to say the least, the process by which the "admissions," were obtained and received must be characterized as lacking the certainty and order which are required of proceedings of such formidable consequences.[97] Apart from the "admission," there was nothing upon which a judgment or finding might be based. There was no sworn testimony. Mrs. Cook, the complainant, was not present. The Arizona Supreme Court held that "sworn testimony must be required of all witnesses including police officers, probation officers and others who are part of or officially related to the juvenile court structure." We hold that this is not enough. No reason is suggested or appears for a different rule in respect of sworn testimony in juvenile courts than in adult tribunals. Absent a valid confession adequate to support the determination of the Juvenile Court, confrontation and sworn testimony by witnesses available for cross-examination were essential for a finding of "delinquency" and an order committing Gerald to a state institution for a maximum of six years.

The recommendations in the Children's Bureau's "Standards for Juvenile and Family Courts" are in general accord with our conclusions. They state that testimony should be under oath and that only competent, material and relevant evidence under rules applicable to civil cases should be admitted in evidence.[98] The New York Family Court Act contains a similar provision.[99]

As we said in *Kent v. United States*, 383 U.S. 541, 554, 86 S.Ct. 1045, 1053, 16 L.Ed.2d 84 (1966), with respect to waiver proceedings, "there is

---

96. The N.Y. Family Court Act § 744(b) provides that "an uncorroborated confession made out of court by a respondent is not sufficient" to constitute the required "preponderance of the evidence."

See *United States v. Morales*, 233 F.Supp. 160 (D.C.Mont. 1964), holding a confession inadmissible in proceedings under the Federal Juvenile Delinquency Act (18 U.S.C.A. § 5031 et seq.) because, in the circumstances in which it was made, the District Court could not conclude that it "was freely made while Morales was afforded all of the requisites of due process required in the case of a sixteen year old boy of his experience." *Id.*, at 170.

97. Cf. *Jackson v. Denno*, 378 U.S. 368, 84 S.Ct. 1774, 12 L.Ed.2d 908 (1964); *Miranda v. State of Arizona*, 384 U.S. 436, 86 S.Ct. 1602, 16 L.Ed.2d 694 (1966).

98. Standards, pp. 72–73. The Nat'l Crime Comm'n Report concludes that "the evidence admissible at the adjudicatory hearing should be so limited that findings are not dependent upon or influenced by hearsay, gossip, rumor, and other unreliable types of information. To minimize the danger that adjudication will be affected by inappropriate considerations, social investigation reports should not be made known to the judge in advance of adjudication." Id., at 87 (bold face eliminated). See also Note, Rights and Rehabilitation in the Juvenile Courts, 67 Col.L.Rev. 281, 336 (1967): "At the adjudication stage, the use of clearly incompetent evidence in order to prove the youth's involvement in the alleged misconduct * * * is not justifiable. Particularly in delinquency cases, where the issue of fact is the commission of a crime, the introduction of hearsay—such as the report of a policeman who did not witness the events—contravenes the purposes underlying the sixth amendment right of confrontation." (Footnote omitted.)

99. N.Y. Family Court Act § 744(a). See also Harvard Law Review Note, p. 795. Cf. *Willner v. Committee on Character*, 373 U.S. 96, 83 S.Ct. 1175, 10 L.Ed.2d 224 (1963).

no place in our system of law for reaching a result of such tremendous consequences without ceremony *   *   * ." We now hold that, absent a valid confession, a determination of delinquency and an order of commitment to a state institution cannot be sustained in the absence of sworn testimony subjected to the opportunity for cross-examination in accordance with our law and constitutional requirements.

VI

Appellate Review and Transcript of Proceedings

Appellants urge that the Arizona statute is unconstitutional under the Due Process Clause because, as construed by its Supreme Court, "there is no right of appeal from a juvenile court order *   *   * ." The court held that there is no right to a transcript because there is no right to appeal and because the proceedings are confidential and any record must be destroyed after a prescribed period of time.[100] Whether a transcript or other recording is made, it held, is a matter for the discretion of the juvenile court.

This Court has not held that a State is required by the Federal Constitution "to provide appellate courts or a right to appellate review at all."[101] In view of the fact that we must reverse the Supreme Court of Arizona's affirmance of the dismissal of the writ of habeas corpus for other reasons, we need not rule on this question in the present case or upon the failure to provide a transcript or recording of the hearings—or, indeed, the failure of the Juvenile Judge to state the grounds for his conclusion. Cf. *Kent v. United States, supra,* 383 U.S., at 561, 86 S.Ct., at 1057, where we said, in the context of a decision of the juvenile court waiving jurisdiction to the adult court, which by local law, was permissible: " *   *   * it is incumbent upon the Juvenile Court to accompany its waiver order with a statement of the reasons or considerations therefor." As the present case illustrates, the consequences of failure to provide an appeal, to record the proceedings, or to make findings or state the grounds for the juvenile court's conclusion may be to throw a burden upon the machinery for habeas corpus, to saddle the reviewing process with the burden of attempting to reconstruct a record, and to impose upon the Juvenile Judge the unseemly duty of testifying under cross-examination as to the events that transpired in the hearings before him.[102]

For the reasons stated, the judgment of the Supreme Court of Arizona is reversed and the cause remanded for further proceedings not inconsistent with this opinion. It is so ordered.

Judgment reversed and cause remanded with directions.

*   *   *

Mr. Justice Stewart, dissenting.

The Court today uses an obscure Arizona case as a vehicle to impose upon thousands of juvenile courts throughout the Nation restrictions that the Constitution made applicable to adversary criminal trials.[1] I believe the Court's decision is wholly unsound as a matter of constitutional law and sadly unwise as a matter of judicial policy.

Juvenile proceedings are not criminal trials. They are not civil trials. They are simply not adversary proceedings. Whether treating with a delinquent child, a neglected child, a defective child, or a dependent child, a juvenile proceeding's whole purpose and mission is the very opposite of the mission and purpose of a prosecution in a criminal court. The object of the one is correction of a condition. The object of the other is conviction and punishment for a criminal act.

---

100. ARS § 8–238.

101. *Griffin v. People of State of Illinois,* 351 U.S. 12, 18, 76 S.Ct. 585, 590, 100 L.Ed. 891 (1956).

102. "Standards for Juvenile and Family Courts" recommends "written findings of fact, some form of record of the hearing" and the right to appeal." Standards, p. 8. It recommends verbatim recording of the hearing by stenotypist or mechanical recording (p. 76) and urges that the judge make clear to the child and family their right to appeal (p. 78). See also, Standard Family Court Act §§ 19, 24, 28; Standard Juvenile Court Act §§ 19, 24, 28. The Harvard Law Review Note, p. 799, states that "The result [of the infrequency of appeals due to absence of record, indigency, etc.] is that juvenile court proceedings are largely unsupervised." The Nat'l Crime Comm'n Report observes, p. 86, that "records make possible appeals which, even if they do not occur, impart by their possibility a healthy atmosphere of accountability."

1. I find it strange that a Court so intent upon fastening an absolute right to counsel upon nonadversary juvenile proceedings has not been willing even to consider whether the Constitution requires a lawyer's help in a criminal prosecution upon a misdemeanor charge. See *Winters v. Beck,* 385 U.S. 907, 87 S.Ct. 207, 17 L.Ed.2d 137; *DeJoseph v. Connecticut,* 385 U.S. 982, 87 S.Ct. 526, 17 L.Ed.2d 443.

In the last 70 years many dedicated men and women have devoted their professional lives to the enlightened task of bringing us out of the dark world of Charles Dickens in meeting our responsibilities to the child in our society. The result has been the creation in this century of a system of juvenile and family courts in each of the 50 States. There can be no denying that in many areas the performance of these agencies has fallen disappointingly short of the hopes and dreams of the courageous pioneers who first conceived them. For a variety of reasons, the reality has sometimes not even approached the ideal, and much remains to be accomplished in the administration of public juvenile and family agencies—in personnel, in planning, in financing, perhaps in the formulation of wholly new approaches.

I possess neither the specialized experience nor the expert knowledge to predict with any certainty where may lie the brightest hope for progress in dealing with the serious problems of juvenile delinquency. But I am certain that the answer does not lie in the Court's opinion in this case, which serves to convert a juvenile proceeding into a criminal prosecution.

The inflexible restrictions that the Constitution so wisely made applicable to adversary criminal trials have no inevitable place in the proceedings of those public social agencies known as juvenile or family courts. And to impose the Court's long catalog of requirements upon juvenile proceedings in every area of the country is to invite a long step backwards into the nineteenth century. In that era there were no juvenile proceedings, and a child was tried in a conventional criminal court with all the trappings of a conventional criminal trial. So it was that a 12-year-old boy named James Guild was tried in New Jersey for killing Catharine Beakes. A jury found him guilty of murder, and he was sentenced to death by hanging. The sentence was executed. It was all very constitutional.[2]

A State in all its dealings must, of course, accord every person due process of law. And due process may require that some of the same restrictions which the Constitution has placed upon criminal trials must be imposed upon juvenile proceedings. For example, I suppose that all would agree that a brutally coerced confession could not constitutionally be considered in a juvenile court hearing. But it surely does not follow that the testimonial privilege against self-incrimination is applicable in all juvenile proceedings.[3] Similarly, due process clearly requires timely notice of the purpose and scope of any proceedings affecting the relationship of parent and child. *Armstrong v. Manzo*, 380 U.S. 545, 85 S.Ct. 1187, 14 L.Ed.2d 62. But it certainly does not follow that notice of a juvenile hearing must be framed with all the technical niceties of a criminal indictment. See *Russell v. United States*, 369 U.S. 749, 82 S.Ct. 1038, 8 L.Ed.2d 240.

In any event, there is no reason to deal with issues such as these in the present case. The Supreme Court of Arizona found that the parents of Gerald Gault "knew of their right to counsel, to subpoena and cross examine witnesses, of the right to confront the witnesses against Gerald and the possible consequences of a finding of delinquency." 99 Ariz. 181, 185, 407 P.2d 760, 763. It further found that "Mrs. Gault knew the exact nature of the charge against Gerald from the day he was taken to the detention home." 99 Ariz., at 193, 407 P.2d, at 768. And, as Mr. Justice White correctly points out, p. 1463, ante, no issue of compulsory self-incrimination is presented by this case.

I would dismiss the appeal.

---

2. *State v. Guild*, 5 Halst. 163, 10 N.J.L. 163, 18 Am.Dec. 404.

"Thus, also, in very modern times, a boy of ten years old was convicted on his own confession of murdering his bedfellow, there appearing in his whole behavior plain tokens of a mischievous discretion; and as the sparing this boy merely on account of his tender years might be of dangerous consequence to the public, by propagating a notion that children might commit such atrocious crimes with impunity, it was unanimously agreed by all the judges that he was a proper subject of capital punishment." 4 Blackstone, Commentaries 23 (Wendell 3d. 1847).

3. Until June 13, 1966, it was clear that the Fourteenth Amendment's ban upon the use of a coerced confession is constitutionally quite a different thing from the Fifth Amendment's testimonial privilege against self-incrimination. See, for example, the Court's unanimous opinion in *Brown v. State of Mississippi*, 297 U.S. 278, at 285–286, 56 S.Ct. 461, 464–465, 80 L.Ed. 682, written by Chief Justice Hughes and joined by such distinguished members of this Court as Mr. Justice Brandeis, Mr. Justice Stone, and Mr. Justice Cardozo. See also Tehan v. United States ex rel. Shott, 382 U.S. 406, 86 S.Ct. 459, 15 L.Ed.2d 453, decided January 19, 1966, where the Court emphasized the "contrast" between "the wrongful use of a coerced confession" and "the Fifth Amendment's privilege against self-incrimination." 392 U.S., at 416, 86 S.Ct., at 465. The complete confusion of these separate constitutional doctrines in Part V of the Court's opinion today stems, no doubt, from Miranda v. State of Arizona, 384 U.S. 436, 86 S.Ct. 1602, a decision which I continue to believe was constitutionally erroneous.

STANDARD OF PROOF

Case Comment

Do the essentials of due process and equal protection require proof beyond a reasonable doubt in determining the culpability of youth in delinquency proceedings? Some states held that merely a "preponderance of evidence" was sufficient to consider a youth delinquent. However, in *In re Winship*, the U.S. Supreme Court mandated that the "beyond a reasonable doubt" doctrine must apply to minors, as well as adults. Even if juvenile court was considered by some a civil procedure, the Supreme Court found it clear that such "labels and good intentions" did not obviate the need for procedural safeguards in the trial process.

Although the standard of proof beyond a reasonable doubt is not stated in the Constitution, the U.S. Supreme Court said that *Gault* had established that due process required the essentials of fair treatment, although it did not require that the adjudication conform to all the requirements of the criminal trial. The Court further said that the due process clause recognized proof beyond a reasonable doubt as being among the essentials of fairness required when a child is charged with a delinquent act. The state of New York argued that juvenile delinquency proceedings were civil in nature, not criminal, and that the preponderance of evidence standard was therefore valid. The Supreme Court indicated that the standard of proof beyond a reasonable doubt plays a vital role in the U.S. criminal justice system and ensures a greater degree of safety for the presumption of innocence of those accused of a crime.

Thus, the *Winship* case required proof beyond a reasonable doubt as a standard for juvenile adjudication proceedings and eliminated the use of lesser standards, such as a preponderance of the evidence, clear and convincing proof, and reasonable proof.

IN RE WINSHIP

Supreme Court of the United States, 1970.
397 U.S. 358, 90 S.Ct. 1068, 25 L.Ed.2d 368.

Mr. Justice Brennan delivered the opinion of the Court.

Constitutional questions decided by this Court concerning the juvenile process have centered on the adjudicatory stage at "which a determination is made as to whether a juvenile is a 'delinquent' as a result of alleged misconduct on his part, with the consequence that he may be committed to a state institution." *In re Gault*, 387 U.S. 1, 13, 87 S.Ct. 1428, 1436, 18 L.Ed.2d 527 (1967). *Gault* decided that, although the Fourteenth Amendment does not require that the hearing at this stage conform with all the requirements of a criminal trial or even of the usual administrative proceeding, the Due Process Clause does require application during the adjudicatory hearing of " 'the essentials of due process and fair treatment.' " *Id.*, at 30, 87 S.Ct. at 1445. This case presents the single, narrow question whether proof beyond a reasonable doubt is among the "essentials of due process and fair treatment" required during the adjudicatory stage when a juvenile is charged with an act which would constitute a crime if committed by an adult.[1]

Section 712 of the New York Family Court Act defines a juvenile delinquent as "a person over seven and less than sixteen years of age who does any act which, if done by an adult, would constitute a crime." During a 1967 adjudicatory hearing, conducted pursuant to § 742 of the Act, a judge in New York Family Court found that appellant, then a 12-year-old boy, had entered a locker and stolen $112 from a woman's pocketbook. The petition which charged appellant with delinquency alleged that his act, "if done by an adult, would constitute the crime or

---

1. Thus, we do not see how it can be said in dissent that this opinion "rests entirely on the assumption that all juvenile proceedings are 'criminal prosecutions,' hence subject to constitutional limitations." As in *Gault*, "we are not here concerned with * * * the pre-judicial stages of the juvenile process, nor do we direct our attention to the post-adjudicative or dispositional process." 387 U.S., at 13, 87 S.Ct., at 1436. In New York, the adjudicatory stage of a delinquency proceeding is clearly distinct from both the preliminary phase of the juvenile process and from its dispositional stage. See N.Y. Family Court Act §§ 731–749. Similarly, we intimate no view concerning the constitutionality of the New York procedures governing children "in need of supervision." See id., at §§ 711, 712, 742–745. Nor do we consider whether there are other "essentials of due process and fair treatment" required during the adjudicatory hearing of a delinquency proceeding. Finally, we have no occasion to consider appellant's argument that § 744(b) is a violation of the Equal Protection Clause, as well as a denial of due process.

crimes of Larceny." The judge acknowledged that the proof might not establish guilt beyond a reasonable doubt, but rejected appellant's contention that such proof was required by the Fourteenth Amendment. The judge relied instead on § 744(b) of the New York Family Court Act which provides that "[a]ny determination at the conclusion of [an adjudicatory] hearing that a [juvenile] did an act or acts must be based on a preponderance of the evidence."[2] During a subsequent dispositional hearing, appellant was ordered placed in a training school for an initial period of 18 months, subject to annual extensions of his commitment until his 18th birthday—six years in appellant's case. The Appellate Division of the New York Supreme Court, First Judicial Department, affirmed without opinion, 30 A.D.2d 781, 291 N.Y.S.2d 1005 (1968). The New York Court of Appeals then affirmed by a four-to-three vote, expressly sustaining the constitutionality of § 744(b), 24 N.Y.2d 196, 299 N.Y.S.2d 414, 247 N.E.2d 253 (1969).[3] We noted probable jurisdiction, 396 U.S. 885, 90 S.Ct. 179, 24 L.Ed.2d 160 (1969). We reverse.

I

The requirement that guilt of a criminal charge be established by proof beyond a reasonable doubt dates at least from our early years as a Nation. The "demand for a higher degree of persuasion in criminal cases was recurrently expressed from ancient times, [though] its crystallization into the formula 'beyond a reasonable doubt' seems to have occurred as late as 1798. It is now accepted in common law jurisdictions as the measure of persuasion by which the prosecution must convince the trier of all the essential elements of guilt." C. McCormick, Evidence § 321, pp. 681–682 (1954); see also 9 J. Wigmore, Evidence, § 2497 (3d ed. 1940). Although virtually unanimous adherence to the reasonable-doubt standard in common-law jurisdictions may not conclusively establish it as a requirement of due process, such adherence does "reflect a profound judgment about the way in which law should be enforced and justice administered." *Duncan v. Louisiana*, 391 U.S. 145, 155, 88 S.Ct. 1444, 1451, 20 L.Ed.2d 491 (1968).

Expressions in many opinions of this Court indicate that it has long been assumed that proof of a criminal charge beyond a reasonable doubt is constitutionally required.* * * Mr. Justice Frankfurter stated that "[i]t is the duty of the Government to establish* * * guilt beyond a reasonable doubt. This notion—basic in our law and rightly one of the boasts of a free society—is a requirement and a safeguard of due process of law in the historic, procedural content of 'due process.' " *Leland v. Oregon, supra*, 343 U.S., at 802–803, 72 S.Ct., at 1009 (dissenting opinion). In a similar vein, the Court said in *Brinegar v. United States, supra*, 338 U.S., at 174, 69 S.Ct., at 1310, that "[g]uilt in a criminal case must be proved beyond a reasonable doubt and by evidence confined to that which long experience in the common-law tradition, to some extent embodied in the Constitution, has crystallized into rules of evidence consistent with that standard. These rules

---

2. The ruling appears in the following portion of the hearing transcript:

Counsel: "Your Honor is making a finding by the preponderance of the evidence."

Court: "Well, it convinces me."

Counsel: "It's not beyond a reasonable doubt, Your Honor."

Court: "That is true * * * Our statute says a preponderance and a preponderance it is."

3. Accord. *e. g.*, *In re Dennis M.*, 70 Cal.2d 444, 75 Cal.Rptr. 1, 450 P.2d 296 (1969); *In re Ellis*, 253 A.2d 789 (D.C.Ct.App.1969); *State v. Arenas*, 253 Or. 215, 453 P.2d 915 (Or.1969); *State v. Santana*, 444 S.W.2d 614 (Texas 1969). *Contra. United States v. Costanzo*, 395 F.2d 441 (C.A.4th Cir. 1968); *In re Urbasek*, 38 Ill.2d 535, 232 N.E.2d 716 (1967); *Jones v. Commonwealth*, 185 Va. 335, 28 S.E.2d 444 (1946); N.D.Cent.Code § 27–20–29(2) (Supp.1969); Colo.Rev.Stat.Ann. § 22–3–6(1) (1967); Md.Ann.Code, Art. 26, § 70–18(a) (Supp.1969); N.J.Ct.Rule 6:9(1)(f) (1967); Wash.Sup.Ct., Juv.Ct.Rule § 4.4(b) (1969); cf. In re Angler, 19 Ohio St.2d 70, 249 N.E.2d 808 (1969).

Legislative adoption of the reasonable-doubt standard has been urged by the National Conference of Commissioners on Uniform State Laws and by the Children's Bureau of the Department of Health, Education, and Welfare's Social and Rehabilitation Service. See Uniform Juvenile Court Act § 29(b) (1968): Children's Bureau, Social and Rehabilitation Service, U.S. Department of Health, Education and Welfare, Legislative Guide for Drafting Family and Juvenile Court Acts § 32(c) (1969). Cf. the proposal of the National Council on Crime and Delinquency that a "clear and convincing" standard be adopted. Model Rules for Juvenile Courts, Rule 26, p. 57 (1969). See generally Cohen, The Standard of Proof in Juvenile Proceedings; *Gault* Beyond a Reasonable Doubt, 68 Mich.L.Rev. 567 (1970).

are historically grounded rights of our system, developed to safeguard men from dubious and unjust convictions, with resulting forfeitures of life, liberty and property." *Davis v. United States, supra,* 160 U.S., at 488, 16 S.Ct., at 358 stated that the requirement is implicit in "constitutions * * * [which] recognize the fundamental principles that are deemed essential for the protection of life and liberty." In *Davis* a murder conviction was reversed because the trial judge instructed the jury that it was their duty to convict when the evidence was equally balanced regarding the sanity of the accused. This Court said: "On the contrary, he is entitled to an acquittal of the specific crime charged, if upon all the evidence, there is reasonable doubt whether he was capable in law of committing crime. * * * No man should be deprived of his life under the forms of law unless the jurors who try him are able, upon their consciences, to say that the evidence before them * * * is sufficient to show beyond a reasonable doubt the existence of every fact necessary to constitute the crime charged." *Id.,* at 484, 493, 16 S.Ct., at 357, 360.

The reasonable-doubt standard plays a vital role in the American scheme of criminal procedure. It is a prime instrument for reducing the risk of convictions resting on factual error. The standard provides concrete substance for the presumption of innocence—that bedrock "axiomatic and elementary" principle whose "enforcement lies at the foundation of the administration of our criminal law." *Coffin v. United States, supra,* 156 U.S., at 453, 15 S.Ct., at 403. As the dissenters in the New York Court of Appeals observed, and we agree, "a person accused of a crime * * * would be at a severe disadvantage, a disadvantage amounting to a lack of fundamental fairness, if he could be adjudged guilty and imprisoned for years on the strength of the same evidence as would suffice in a civil case." 24 N.Y.2d, at 205, 299 N.Y.S.2d, at 422, 247 N.E.2d, at 259.

The requirement of proof beyond a reasonable doubt has this vital role in our criminal procedure for cogent reasons. The accused during a criminal prosecution has at stake interest of immense importance, both because of the possibility that he may lose his liberty upon conviction and because of the certainty that he would be stigmatized by the conviction. Accordingly, a society that values the good name and freedom of every individual should not condemn a man for commission of a crime when there is reasonable doubt about his guilt. As we said

in *Speiser v. Randall, supra,* 357 U.S., at 525–526, 78 S.Ct., at 1342: "There is always in litigation a margin of error, representing error in factfinding, which both parties must take into account. Where one party has at stake an interest of transcending value—as a criminal defendant his liberty—this margin of error is reduced as to him by the process of placing on the other party the burden of * * * persuading the factfinder at the conclusion of the trial of his guilt beyond a reasonable doubt. Due process commands that no man shall lose his liberty unless the Government has borne the burden of * * * convincing the factfinder of his guilt." To this end, the reasonable-doubt standard is indispensable, for it "impresses on the trier of fact the necessity of reaching a subjective state of certitude of the facts in issue." Dorsen & Rezneck, *In Re Gault* and the Future of Juvenile Law, 1 Family Law Quarterly, No. 4, pp. 1, 26 (1967).

Moreover, use of the reasonable-doubt standard is indispensable to command the respect and confidence of the community in applications of the criminal law. It is critical that the moral force of the criminal law not be diluted by a standard of proof that leaves people in doubt whether innocent men are being condemned. It is also important in our free society that every individual going about his ordinary affairs have confidence that his government cannot adjudge him guilty of a criminal offense without convincing a proper factfinder of his guilt with utmost certainty.

Lest there remain any doubt about the constitutional stature of the reasonable-doubt standard, we explicitly hold that the Due Process Clause protects the accused against conviction except upon proof beyond a reasonable doubt of every fact necessary to constitute the crime with which he is charged.

II

We turn to the question whether juveniles, like adults, are constitutionally entitled to proof beyond a reasonable doubt when they are charged with violation of a criminal law. The same considerations that demand extreme caution in factfinding to protect the innocent adult apply as well to the innocent child. We do not find convincing the contrary arguments of the New York Court of Appeals, *Gault* rendered untenable much of the reasoning relied upon by that court to sustain the constitutionality of § 744(b). The Court of Appeals indicated that a delinquency adjudication "is not a 'conviction' (§ 781); that it affects no right or privilege, including the right to hold public office or to obtain a license (§ 782); and a cloak of protective confidentiality is thrown around all the proceedings (§§ 783–784)." The court said further: "The delinquency status is not made a crime; and the proceedings are not criminal. There is, hence, no deprivation of due process in the statutory provision [challenged by appellant] * * * ." In effect the Court of Appeals distinguished the proceedings in question here from a criminal prosecution by use of what *Gault* called the " 'civil' label-of-convenience which has been attached to juvenile proceedings." 387 U.S., at 50, 87 S.Ct., at 1455. But *Gault* expressly rejected that distinction as a reason for holding the Due Process Clause inapplicable to a juvenile proceeding. 387 U.S., at 50–51, 87 S.Ct., at 1455, 1456. The Court of Appeals also attempted to justify the preponderance standard on the related ground that juvenile proceedings are designed "not to punish, but to save the child." Again, however, *Gault* expressly rejected this justification. We made clear in that decision that civil labels and good intentions do not themselves obviate the need for criminal due process safeguards in juvenile courts, for "[a] proceeding where the issue is whether the child will be found to be 'delinquent' and subjected to the loss of his liberty for years is comparable in seriousness to a felony prosecution."

Nor do we perceive any merit in the argument that to afford juveniles the protection of proof beyond a reasonable doubt would risk destruction of beneficial aspects of the juvenile process.[4] Use of the reasonable-doubt standard during the adjudicatory hearing will not disturb New York's policies that a finding that a child has violated a criminal law does not constitute a criminal conviction, that such a finding does not deprive the child of his civil rights, and that juvenile proceedings are confiden-

tial. Nor will there be any effect on the informality, flexibility, or speed of the hearing at which the fact-finding takes place. And the opportunity during the post-adjudicatory or dispositional hearing for a wide-ranging review of the child's social history and for his individualized treatment will remain unimpaired. Similarly, there will be no effect on the procedures distinctive to juvenile proceedings that are employed prior to the adjudicatory hearing.

The Court of Appeals observed that "a child's best interest is not necessarily, or even probably, promoted if he wins in the particular inquiry which may bring him to the juvenile court." * * * It is true, of course, that the juvenile may be engaging in a general course of conduct inimical to his welfare that calls for judicial intervention. But that intervention cannot take the form of subjecting the child to the stigma of a finding that he violated a criminal law[5] and to the possibility of institutional confinement on proof insufficient to convict him were he an adult.

We conclude, as we concluded regarding the essential due process safeguards applied in *Gault*, that the observance of the standard of proof beyond a reasonable doubt "will not compel the States to abandon or displace any of the substantive benefits of the juvenile process." * * *

Finally, we reject the Court of Appeals' suggestion that there is, in any event, only a "tenuous difference" between the reasonable-doubt and preponderance standards. The suggestion is singularly unpersuasive. In this very case, the trial judge's ability to distinguish between the two standards enabled him to make a finding of guilt that he conceded he might not have made under the standard of proof beyond a reasonable doubt. Indeed, the trial judge's action evidences the accuracy of the observation of commentators that "the preponderance test is susceptible to the misinterpretation that it calls on the trier of fact merely to perform an abstract weighing

---

4. Appellee, New York City, apparently concedes as much in its Brief, page 8, where it states:

"A determination that the New York law unconstitutionally denies due process because it does not provide for use of the reasonable doubt standard probably would not have a serious impact if all that resulted would be a change in the quantum of proof."

And Dorsen & Rezneck, *supra*, at 27, have observed:

"[T]he reasonable doubt test is superior to all others in protecting against an unjust adjudication of guilt, and that is as much a concern of the juvenile court as of the criminal court. It is difficult to see how the distinctive objectives of the juvenile court give rise to a legitimate institutional interest in finding a juvenile to have committed a violation of the criminal law on less evidence than if he were an adult."

5. The more comprehensive and effective the procedures used to prevent public disclosure of the finding, the less the danger of stigma. As we indicated in *Gault*, however, often the "claim of secrecy * * * is more rhetoric than reality." 387 U.S., at 24, 87 S.Ct., at 1442.

of the evidence in order to determine which side has produced the greater quantum, without regard to its effect in convincing his mind of the truth of the proposition asserted."

III

In sum, the constitutional safeguard of proof beyond a reasonable doubt is as much required during the adjudicatory stage of a delinquency proceeding as are those constitutional safeguards applied in *Gault*—notice of charges, right to counsel, the rights of confrontation and examination, and the privilege against self-incrimination. We therefore hold, in agreement with Chief Judge Fuld in dissent in the Court of Appeals, "that, where a 12-year-old child is charged with an act of stealing which renders him liable to confinement for as long as six years, then, as a matter of due process * * * the case against him must be proved beyond a reasonable doubt."

Reversed.

Mr. Justice Harlan concurring.

No one, I daresay, would contend that state juvenile court trials are subject to *no* federal constitutional limitations. Differences have existed, however, among the members of this Court as to *what* constitutional protections do apply.

The present case draws in question the validity of a New York statute that permits a determination of juvenile delinquency, founded on a charge of criminal conduct, to be made on a standard of proof that is less rigorous than that which would obtain had the accused been tried for the same conduct in an ordinary criminal case. While I am in full agreement that this statutory provision offends the requirement of fundamental fairness embodied in the Due Process Clause of the Fourteenth Amendment, I am constrained to add something to what my Brother Brennan has written for the Court, lest the true nature of the constitutional problem presented become obscured or the impact on state juvenile court systems of what the Court holds today be exaggerated.

I

Professor Wigmore, in discussing the various attempts by courts to define how convinced one must be to be convinced beyond a reasonable doubt, wryly observed: "The truth is that no one has yet invented or discovered a mode of measurement for the intensity of human belief. Hence there can be yet no successful method of communicating intelligibly * * * a sound method of self-analysis for one's belief," 9 J. Wigmore, Evidence 325 (3d ed. 1940).[1]

Notwithstanding Professor Wigmore's skepticism, we have before us a case where the choice of the standard of proof has made a difference: the juvenile court judge below forthrightly acknowledged that he believed by a preponderance of the evidence, but was not convinced beyond a reasonable doubt, that appellant stole $112 from the complainant's pocketbook. Moreover, even though the labels used for alternative standards of proof are vague and not a very sure guide to decisionmaking, the choice of the standard for a particular variety of adjudication does, I think, reflect a very fundamental assessment of the comparative social costs of erroneous factual determinations.[2]

To explain why I think this so, I begin by stating two propositions, neither of which I believe can be fairly disputed. First, in a judicial proceeding in which there is a dispute about the facts of some earlier event, the factfinder cannot acquire unassailably accurate knowledge of what happened. Instead, all the factfinder can acquire is a belief of what *probably* happened. The intensity of this belief—the degree to which a factfinder is convinced that a given act actually occurred—can, of course, vary. In this regard, a standard of proof represents an attempt to instruct the factfinder concerning the degree of confidence our society thinks he should have in the correctness of factual conclusions for a particular type of adjudication. Although the phrases "preponderance of the evidence" and "proof beyond a reasonable doubt" are quantitatively imprecise, they do communicate to the finder of fact different notions concerning the degree of confidence he is expected to have in the correctness of his factual conclusions.

A second proposition, which is really nothing more than a corollary of the first, is that the trier of fact will sometimes, despite his best efforts, be wrong in his factual conclusions. In a lawsuit between two parties, a factual error can make a difference in one

---

1. See also Paulsen, Juvenile Courts and the Legacy of '67, 43 Ind.L.J. 527, 551–552 (1968).

2. For an interesting analysis of standards of proof see Kaplan, Decision Theory and the Factfinding Process, 20 Stan.L.Rev. 1065, 1071–1077 (1968).

of two ways. First, it can result in a judgment in favor of the plaintiff when the true facts warrant a judgment for the defendant. The analogue in a criminal case would be the conviction of an innocent man. On the other hand, an erroneous factual determination can result in a judgment for the defendant when the true facts justify a judgment in plaintiff's favor. The criminal analogue would be the acquittal of a guilty man.

The standard of proof influences the relative frequency of these two types of erroneous outcomes. If, for example, the standard of proof for a criminal trial were a preponderance of the evidence rather than proof beyond a reasonable doubt, there would be a smaller risk of factual errors that result in freeing guilty persons, but a far greater risk of factual errors that result in convicting the innocent. Because the standard of proof affects the comparative frequency of these two types of erroneous outcomes, the choice of the standard to be applied in a particular kind of litigation should, in a rational world, reflect an assessment of the comparative social disutility of each.

When one makes such an assessment, the reason for different standards of proof in civil as opposed to criminal litigation becomes apparent. In a civil suit between two private parties for money damages, for example, we view it as no more serious in general for there to be an erroneous verdict in the defendant's favor than for there to be an erroneous verdict in the plaintiff's favor. A preponderance of the evidence standard therefore seems peculiarly appropriate for, as explained most sensibly,[3] it simply requires the trier of fact "to believe that the existence of a fact is more probable than its nonexistence before [he] may find in favor of the party who has the burden to persuade the [judge] of the fact's existence."[4]

In a criminal case, on the other hand, we do not view the social disutility of convicting an innocent man as equivalent to the disutility of acquitting someone who is guilty. As Mr. Justice Brennan wrote for the Court in *Speiser v. Randall*, 357 U.S. 513, 525–526, 78 S.Ct. 1332, 1341–1342, 2 L.Ed.2d 1460 (1958):

> There is always in litigation a margin of error, representing error in factfinding, which both parties must take into account. Where one party has at stake an interest of transcending value—as a criminal defendant his liberty—this margin of error is reduced as to him by the process of placing on the other party the burden * * * of persuading the fact-finder at the conclusion of the trial of his guilt beyond a reasonable doubt.

In this context, I view the requirement of proof beyond a reasonable doubt in a criminal case as bottomed on a fundamental value determination of our society that it is far worse to convict an innocent man than to let a guilty man go free. It is only because of the nearly complete and long-standing acceptance of the reasonable-doubt standard by the States in criminal trials that the Court has no before today had to hold explicitly that due process, as an expression of fundamental procedural fairness,[5] re-

---

3. The preponderance test has been criticized, justifiably in my view, when it is read as asking the trier of fact to weigh in some objective sense the quantity of evidence submitted by each side rather than asking him to decide what he believes most probably happened. See J. Maguire, Evidence, Common Sense and Common Law 180 (1947).

4. F. James, Civil Procedure 250–251 (1965); see E. Morgan, Some Problems of Proof Under the Anglo-American System of Litigation 84–85 (1956).

5. In dissent my Brother Black again argues that, apart from the specific prohibitions of the first eight amendments, any procedure spelled out by a legislature—no matter how unfair—passes constitutional muster under the Due Process Clause. He bottoms his conclusion on history that he claims demonstrates (1) that due process means "law of the land"; (2) that any legislative enactment, *ipso facto*, is part of the law of the land; and (3) that the Fourteenth Amendment incorporates the prohibitions of the Bill of Rights and applies them to the States. I cannot refrain from expressing my continued bafflement at my Brother Black's insistence that due process, whether under the Fourteenth Amendment or the Fifth Amendment, does not embody a concept of fundamental fairness as part of our scheme of constitutionally ordered liberty. His thesis flies in the face of a course of judicial history reflected in an unbroken line of opinions that have interpreted due process to impose restraints on the procedures government may adopt in its dealing with its citizens, *e. g.*, the cases cited in my dissenting opinions in *Poe v. Ullman*, 367 U.S. 497, 522, 539–545, 81 S.Ct. 1752, 1765, 1774–1778, 6 L.Ed.2d 989 (1961); *Duncan v. Louisiana*, 391 U.S. 145, 171, 88 S.Ct. 1444, 1458, 1459, 20 L.Ed.2d 491 (1968); as well as the uncontroverted scholarly research (notwithstanding H. Flack, The Adoption of the Fourteenth Amendment (1908)), respecting the intendment of the Due Process Clause of the Fourteenth Amendment, see Fairman, Does the Fourteenth Amendment Incorporate the Bill of Rights? The Original Understanding, 2 Stan.L.Rev. 5 (1949). Indeed, with all respect, the very case cited in Brother Black's dissent as establishing that "due process of law" means "law of the land" rejected the argument that any statute, by the mere process of enactment, met the requirements of the Due Process Clause. In *Murray's Lessee v. Hoboken Land & Improv. Co.*, 18 How. 272, 15 L.Ed. 372 (1856), an issue was whether a "distress warrant" issued by the Solicitor of the Treasury under an act of Congress to

(continued on next page)

quires a more stringent standard for criminal trials than for ordinary civil litigation.

II

When one assesses the consequences of an erroneous factual determination in a juvenile delinquency proceeding in which a youth is accused of a crime, I think it must be concluded that, while the consequences are not identical to those in a criminal case, the differences will not support a distinction in the standard of proof. First, and of paramount importance, a factual error here, as in a criminal case, exposes the accused to a complete loss of his personal liberty through a state-imposed confinement away from his home, family, and friends. And, second, a delinquency determination, to some extent at least, stigmatizes a youth in that it is by definition bottomed on a finding that the accused committed a crime.[6] Although there are no doubt costs to society (and possibly even to the youth himself) in letting a guilty youth go free, I think here, as in a criminal case, it is far worse to declare an innocent youth a delinquent. I therefore agree that a juvenile court judge should be no less convinced of the factual conclusion that the accused committed the criminal act with which he is charged than would be required in a criminal trial.

III

I wish to emphasize, as I did in my separate opinion in *Gault* 387 U.S. 1, 65, 87 S.Ct. 1428, 1463, that

there is no automatic congruence between the procedural requirements imposed by due process in a criminal case, and those imposed by due process in juvenile cases.[7] It is of great importance, in my view, that procedural strictures not be constitutionally imposed that jeopardize "the essential elements of the State's purpose" in creating juvenile courts, *id.*, at 72, 87 S.Ct. at 1467. In this regard, I think it worth emphasizing that the requirement of proof beyond a reasonable doubt that a juvenile committed a criminal act before he is found to be a delinquent does not (1) interfere with the worthy goal of rehabilitating the juvenile, (2) make any significant difference in the extent to which a youth is stigmatized as a "criminal" because he has been found to be a delinquent, or (3) burden the juvenile courts with a procedural requirement that will make juvenile adjudications significantly more time consuming, or rigid. Today's decision simply requires a juvenile court judge to be more confident in his belief that the youth did the act with which he has been charged.

With these observations, I join the Court's opinion, subject only to the constitutional reservations expressed in my opinion in *Gault*.

Chief Justice Burger, with whom Justice Stewart joins, dissenting.

The Court's opinion today rests entirely on the assumption that all juvenile proceedings are "criminal prosecutions," hence subject to constitutional limitations. This derives from earlier holdings, which, like today's holding, were steps eroding the differences between juvenile courts and traditional crim-

collect money due for taxes offended the Due Process Clause. Justice Curtis wrote: "That the warrant now in question is legal process, is not denied. It was issued in conformity with an Act of Congress. But is it 'due process of law?' The constitution contains no description of those processes which it was intended to allow or forbid. It does not even declare what principles are to be applied to ascertain whether it be due process. *It is manifest that it was not left to the legislative power to enact any process which might be devised. The article is a restraint on the legislative as well as on the executive and judicial powers of the government, and cannot be so construed as to leave congress free to make any process 'due process of law,' by its mere will.*" *Id.*, at 276. (Emphasis supplied.)

6. The New York statute was amended to distinguish between a "juvenile delinquent," i. e., a youth "who does any act which, if done by an adult, would constitute a crime," N.Y.Family Court Act § 712 (1963), and a "[p]erson in need of supervision" [PINS] who is a person "who is an habitual truant or who is incorrigible, ungovernable or habitually disobedient and beyond the lawful control of parent or other lawful authority." The PINS category was established in order to avoid the stigma of finding someone to be a "juvenile delinquent" unless he committed a criminal act. The Legislative Committee report stated: " 'Juvenile delinquent' is now a term of disapproval. The judges of the Children's Court and the Domestic Relations Court of course are aware of this and also aware that government officials and private employers often learn of an adjudication of delinquency." N.Y.Jt. Legislative Committee on Court Reorganization, The Family Court Act, pt. 2, p. 7 (1962). Moreover, the powers of the police and courts differ in these two categories of cases. See *id.*, at 7–9. Thus, in a PINS type case, the consequences of an erroneous factual determination are by no means identical to those involved here.

7. In *Gault*, for example, I agreed with the majority that due process required (1) adequate notice of the "nature and terms" of the proceedings; (2) notice of the right to retain counsel, and an obligation on the State to provide counsel for indigents "in cases in which the child may be confined"; and (3) a written record "adequate to permit effective review." 387 U.S., at 72, 87 S.Ct., at 1467. Unlike the majority, however, I thought it unnecessary at the time of *Gault* to impose the additional requirements of the privilege against self-incrimination, confrontation, and cross-examination.

inal courts. The original concept of the juvenile court system was to provide a benevolent and less formal means than criminal courts could provide for dealing with the special and often sensitive problems of youthful offenders. Since I see no constitutional requirement of due process sufficient to overcome the legislative judgment of the States in this area, I dissent from further straitjacketing of an already overly restricted system. What the juvenile court system needs is not more but less of the trappings of legal procedure and judicial formalism; the juvenile court system requires breathing room and flexibility in order to survive, if it can survive the repeated assaults from this Court.

Much of the judicial attitude manifested by the Court's opinion today and earlier holdings in this field is really a protest against inadequate juvenile court staffs and facilities; we "burn down the stable to get rid of the mice." The lack of support and the distressing growth of juvenile crime have combined to make for a literal breakdown in many if not most juvenile courts. Constitutional problems were not seen while those courts functioned in an atmosphere where juvenile judges were not crushed with an avalanche of cases.

My hope is that today's decision will not spell the end of a generously conceived program of compassionate treatment intended to mitigate the rigors and trauma of exposing youthful offenders to a traditional criminal court; each step we take turns the clock back to the pre-juvenile-court era. I cannot regard it as a manifestation of progress to transform juvenile courts into criminal courts, which is what we are well on the way to accomplishing. We can only hope the legislative response will not reflect our own by having these courts abolished.

* * *

RIGHT TO TRIAL BY JURY

Case Comment

McKeiver v. Pennsylvania is an important case for two reasons: (1) it denied that juveniles have a constitutional right to jury trial and (2) it retreated from the previously standard practice of judicial equalization of procedure in adult and juvenile court. In deciding for the defendants, the Supreme Court recognized that while recent constitutional cases have focused on the issue of fundamental fairness in fact-finding procedures, juries are not actually an essen-

tial part of this area of justice, nor are they required for all types of trials. Fearing that the jury trial would put an end to the informal nature of the juvenile court and introduce open adversary procedures to it, the Supreme Court decreed that the states themselves must determine whether juries are an acceptable form of procedure in juvenile court.

The case of *State v. Schaaf* is an example of the state of Washington's statutory denial of jury trials to juveniles because of its interest in preserving the rehabilitative aspects of the juvenile court.[7]

On the other hand, a limited number of jurisdictions provide for a jury trial for juveniles by statute or case decision. In *People in the Interest of T.M.*, the Colorado Children's Code provided a statutory right to a jury trial in a delinquency adjudication hearing in all cases except those involving minor delinquent acts.[8]

The juvenile, a thirteen-year-old charged with mischief, claimed that the Colorado statute was unconstitutional in that it denied her the right to a trial by jury, but the appellate court disagreed and affirmed the judgment of the Denver Juvenile Court.

McKEIVER v. PENNSYLVANIA

Supreme Court of the United States, 1971.
403 U.S. 528, 91 S.Ct. 1976, 29 L.Ed.2d 647.

Mr. Justice Blackmun announced the judgments of the Court and an opinion in which the Chief Justice, Mr. Justice Stewart, and Mr. Justice White join.

These cases present the narrow but precise issue whether the Due Process Clause of the Fourteenth Amendment assures the right to trial by jury in the adjudicative phase of a state juvenile court delinquency proceeding.

I

The issue arises understandably, for the Court in a series of cases already has emphasized due process factors protective of the juvenile:

1. *Haley v. Ohio*, 332 U.S. 596, 68 S.Ct. 302, 92 L.Ed. 224 (1948), concerned the admissibility of a confession taken from a 15-year-old boy on trial for first-degree murder. It was held that upon the facts there developed, the Due Process Clause barred the use of the confession. Mr. Justice Douglas, in an opinion in which three other Justices joined, said,

"Neither man nor child can be allowed to stand condemned by methods which flout constitutional requirements of due process of law." 332 U.S., at 601, 68 S.Ct., at 304.

2. *Gallegos v. Colorado*, 370 U.S. 49, 82 S.Ct. 1209, 8 L.Ed.2d 325 (1962) where a 14-year-old was on trial, is to the same effect.

3. *Kent v. United States*, 383 U.S. 541, 86 S.Ct. 1045, 16 L.Ed.2d 84 (1966), concerned a 16-year-old charged with housebreaking, robbery, and rape in the District of Columbia. The issue was the propriety of the juvenile court's waiver of jurisdiction "after full investigation," as permitted by the applicable statute. It was emphasized that the latitude the court possessed within which to determine whether it should retain or waive jurisdiction "assumes procedural regularity sufficient in the particular circumstances to satisfy the basic requirements of due process and fairness, as well as compliance with the statutory requirement of a 'full investigation.' " 383 U.S., at 553, 86 S.Ct., at 1053.

4. *In re Gault*, 387 U.S. 1, 87 S.Ct. 1428, 18 L.Ed.2d 527 (1967), concerned a 15-year-old, already on probation, committed in Arizona as a delinquent after being apprehended upon a complaint of lewd remarks by telephone. Mr. Justice Fortas, in writing for the Court, reviewed the cases just cited and observed

> Accordingly, while these cases relate only to restricted aspects of the subject, they unmistakably indicate that, whatever may be their precise impact, neither the Fourteenth Amendment nor the Bill of Rights is for adults alone. 387 U.S., at 13, 87 S.Ct., at 1436.

The Court focused on "the proceedings by which a determination is made as to whether a juvenile is a 'delinquent' as a result of alleged misconduct on his part, with the consequence that he may be committed to a state institution" and, as to this, said that "there appears to be little current dissent from the proposition that the Due Process Clause has a role to play." Ibid. *Kent* was adhered to: "We reiterate this view, here in connection with a juvenile court adjudication of 'delinquency,' as a requirement which is part of the Due Process Clause of the Fourteenth Amendment of our Constitution." *Id.*, at 30–31, 87 S.Ct., at 1445. Due process, in that proceeding, was held to embrace adequate written notice; advice as to the right to counsel, retained or appointed; confrontation; and cross-examination. The privilege against self-incrimination was also held available to

the juvenile. The Court refrained from deciding whether a State must provide appellate review in juvenile cases or a transcript or recording of the hearings.

5. *DeBacker v. Brainard*, 396 U.S. 28, 90 S.Ct. 163, 24 L.Ed.2d 148 (1969), presented, by state habeas corpus, a challenge to a Nebraska statute providing that juvenile court hearings "shall be conducted by the judge without a jury in an informal manner." However, because that appellant's hearing had antedated the decisions in *Duncan v. Louisiana*, 391 U.S. 145, 88 S.Ct. 1444, 20 L.Ed.2d 491 (1968), and *Bloom v. Illinois*, 391 U.S. 194, 88 S.Ct. 1477, 20 L.Ed.2d 522 (1968), and because *Duncan* and *Bloom* had been given only prospective application by *DeStefano v. Woods*, 392 U.S. 631, 88 S.Ct. 2093, 20 L.Ed.2d 1308 (1968), DeBacker's case was deemed an inappropriate one for resolution of the jury trial issue. His appeal was therefore dismissed. Mr. Justice Black and Mr. Justice Douglas, in separate dissents, took the position that a juvenile is entitled to a jury trial at the adjudicative stage. Mr. Justice Black described this as "a right which is surely one of the fundamental aspects of criminal justice in the English-speaking world," 396 U.S., at 34, 90 S.Ct., at 166 and Mr. Justice Douglas described it as a right required by the Sixth and Fourteenth Amendments "where the delinquency charged is an offense that, if the person were an adult, would be a crime triable by jury." 396 U.S., at 35, 90 S.Ct., at 167.

6. *In re Winship*, 397 U.S. 358, 90 S.Ct. 1068, 25 L.Ed.2d 368 (1970), concerned a 12-year-old charged with delinquency for having taken money from a woman's purse. The Court held that "the Due Process Clause protects the accused against conviction except upon proof beyond a reasonable doubt of every fact necessary to constitute the crime with which he is charged," 397 U.S., at 364, 90 S.Ct., at 1073, and then went on to hold, at 368, 90 S.Ct., at 1075, that this standard was applicable, too, "during the adjudicatory stage of a delinquency proceeding."

From these six cases—*Haley, Gallegos, Kent, Gault, DeBacker*, and *Winship*—it is apparent that:

1. Some of the constitutional requirements attendant upon the state criminal trial have equal application to that part of the state juvenile proceeding that is adjudicative in nature. Among these are the rights to appropriate notice, to counsel, to confrontation and to cross-examination, and the privilege

against self-incrimination. Included, also, is the standard of proof beyond a reasonable doubt.

2. The Court, however, has not yet said that *all* rights constitutionally assured to an adult accused of crime also are to be enforced or made available to the juvenile in his delinquency proceeding. Indeed, the Court specifically has refrained from going that far:

> We do not mean by this to indicate that the hearing to be held must conform with all of the requirements of a criminal trial or even of the usual administrative hearing; but we do hold that the hearing must measure up to the essentials of due process and fair treatment. *Kent*, 383 U.S., at 562, 86 S.Ct., at 1057; *Gault*, 387 U.S., at 30, 87 S.Ct., at 1445.

3. The Court, although recognizing the high hopes and aspirations of Judge Julian Mack, the leaders of the Jane Addams School[1] and the other supporters of the juvenile court concept, has also noted the disappointments of the system's performance and experience and the resulting widespread disaffection. *Kent*, 383 U.S., at 555–556, 86 S.Ct., at 1054–1055; *Gault*, 387 U.S., at 17–19, 87 S.Ct., at 1438–1439. There have been, at one and the same time, both an appreciation for the juvenile court judge who is devoted, sympathetic, and conscientious, and a disturbed concern about the judge who is untrained and less than fully imbued with an understanding approach to the complex problems of childhood and adolescence. There has been praise for the system and its purposes, and there has been alarm over its defects.

4. The Court has insisted that these successive decisions do not spell the doom of the juvenile court system or even deprive it of its "informality, flexibility, or speed." *Winship*, 397 U.S., at 366, 90 S.Ct., at 1074. On the other hand, a concern precisely to the opposite effect was expressed by two dissenters in *Winship*. *Id.*, at 375–376, 90 S.Ct., at 1078–1079.

II

With this substantial background already developed, we turn to the facts of the present cases:

No. 322. Joseph McKeiver, then age 16, in May 1968 was charged with robbery, larceny, and receiving stolen goods (felonies under Pennsylvania law, Pa.Stat.Ann., Tit. 18, §§ 4704, 4807, and 4817 (1963)) as acts of juvenile delinquency. At the time of the adjudication hearing he was represented by counsel.[2] His request for a jury trial was denied and his case was heard by Judge Theodore S. Gutowicz of the Court of Common Pleas, Family Division, Juvenile Branch, of Philadelphia County, Pennsylvania. McKeiver was adjudged a delinquent upon findings that he had violated a law of the Commonwealth. Pa.Stat.Ann., Tit. 11, § 243(4)(a) (1965). On appeal, the Superior Court affirmed without opinion. *In re McKeiver*, 215 Pa.Super. 760, 255 A.2d 921 (1969).

Edward Terry, then age 15, in January 1969 was charged with assault and battery on a police officer and conspiracy (misdemeanors under Pennsylvania law, Pa.Stat.Ann., Tit. 18, §§ 4708 and 4302 (1963)) as acts of juvenile delinquency. His counsel's request for a jury trial was denied and his case was heard by Judge Joseph C. Bruno of the same Juvenile Branch of the Court of Common Pleas of Philadelphia County. Terry was adjudged a delinquent on the charges. This followed an adjudication and commitment in the preceding week for an assault on a teacher. He was committed, as he had been on the earlier charge, to the Youth Development Center at Cornwells Heights. On appeal, the Superior Court affirmed without opinion. *In re Terry*, 215 Pa.Super. 762, 255 A.2d 922 (1969).

The Supreme Court of Pennsylvania granted leave to appeal in both cases and consolidated them. The single question considered, as phrased by the court, was "whether there is a constitutional right to a jury trial in juvenile court." The answer, one justice dissenting, was in the negative. *In re Terry*, 438 Pa. 339, 265 A.2d 350 (1970). We noted probable jurisdiction. 399 U.s. 925, 90 S.Ct. 2271, 26 L.Ed.2d 791 (1970).

The details of the McKeiver and Terry offenses are set forth in Justice Roberts' opinion for the Pennsylvania court, 438 Pa., at 341–342, nn. 1 and 2, 265 A.2d, at 351 nn. 1 and 2, and need not be repeated at any length here. It suffices to say that

---

1. See Mr. Justice Fortas' article, Equal Rights—For Whom*He*, 42 N.Y.U.L.Rev. 401, 406 (1967).

2. At McKeiver's hearing his counsel advised the court that he had never seen McKeiver before and "was just in the middle of interviewing" him. The court allowed him five minutes for the interview. Counsel's office, Community Legal Services, however, had been appointed to represent McKeiver five months earlier. App. 2.

McKeiver's offense was his participating with 20 or 30 youths who pursued three young teenagers and took 25 cents from them; and McKeiver never before had been arrested and had a record of gainful employment; that the testimony of two of the victims was described by the court as somewhat inconsistent and as "weak"; and that Terry's offense consisted of hitting a police officer with his fists and with a stock when the officer broke up a boys' fight Terry and others were watching.

No. 128. Barbara Burrus and approximately 45 other black children, ranging in age from 11 to 15 years,[3] were the subjects of juvenile court summonses issued in Hyde County, North Carolina, in January 1969.

The charges arose out of a series of demonstrations in the county in late 1968 by black adults and children protesting school assignments and a school consolidation plan. Petitions were filed by North Carolina state highway patrolmen. Except for one relating to James Lambert Howard, the petitions charged the respective juveniles with wilfully impeding traffic. The charge against Howard was that he wilfully made riotous noise and was disorderly in the O. A. Peay School in Swan Quarter; interrupted and disturbed the school during its regular sessions; and defaced school furniture. The acts so charged are misdemeanors under North Carolina law. N.C.Gen.Stat. §§ 20–174.1 (1965 and Supp. 1969), 14–132(a), 14–273 (1969).

The several cases were consolidated into groups for hearing before District Judge Hallett S. Ward, sitting as a juvenile court. The same lawyer appeared for all the juveniles. Over counsel's objection, made in all except two of the cases, the general public was excluded. A request for a jury trial in each case was denied.

The evidence as to the juveniles other than Howard consisted solely of testimony of highway patrolmen. No juvenile took the stand or offered any witness. The testimony was to the effect that on various occasions the juveniles and adults were observed walking along Highway 64 singing, shouting, clapping, and playing basketball. As a result, there was interference with traffic. The marchers were asked to leave the paved portion of the highway and they were warned that they were committing a statutory offense. They either refused or left the roadway

and immediately returned. The juveniles and participating adults were taken into custody. Juvenile petitions were then filed with respect to those under the age of 16.

The evidence as to Howard was that on the morning of December 5, he was in the office of the principal of the O. A. Peay School with 15 other persons while school was in session and was moving furniture around; that the office was in disarray; that as a result the school closed before noon; and that neither he nor any of the others was a student at the school or authorized to enter the principal's office.

In each case the court found that the juvenile had committed "an act for which an adult may be punished by law." A custody order was entered declaring the juvenile a delinquent "in need of more suitable guardianship" and committing him to the custody of the County Department of Public Welfare for placement in a suitable institution "until such time as the Board of Juvenile Correction or the Superintendent of said institution may determine, not inconsistent with the laws of this State." The court, however, suspended these commitments and placed each juvenile on probation for either one or two years conditioned upon his violating none of the State's laws, upon his reporting monthly to the County Department of Welfare, upon his being home by 11 p.m. each evening, and upon his attending a school approved by the Welfare Director. None of the juveniles has been confined on these charges.

On appeal, the cases were consolidated into two groups. The North Carolina Court of Appeals affirmed. *In re Burrus*, 4 N.C.App. 523, 167 S.E.2d 454 (1969); *In re Shelton*, 5 N.C.App. 487, 168 S.E.2d 695 (1969). In its turn the Supreme Court of North Carolina deleted that portion of the order in each case relating to commitment, but otherwise affirmed. *In re Burrus*, 275 N.C. 517, 169 S.Ed.2d 879 (1969). Two justices dissented without opinion. We granted certiorari. 397 U.S. 1036, 90 S.Ct. 1379, 25 L.Ed.2d 647 (1970).

III

It is instructive to review, as an illustration, the substance of Justice Roberts' opinion for the Pennsylvania court. He observes, 438 Pa., at 343, 265 A.2d, at 352, that "[f]or over sixty-five years the

---

3. In North Carolina juvenile court procedures are provided only for persons under the age of 16. N.C.Gen.Stat. §§ 7A–277 and 7A–278(1) (1969).

Supreme Court gave no consideration at all to the constitutional problems involved in the juvenile court area"; that *Gault* "is somewhat of a paradox, being both broad and narrow at the same time"; that it "is broad in that it evidences a fundamental and far-reaching disillusionment with the anticipated benefits of the juvenile court system"; that it is narrow because the court enumerated four due process rights which it held applicable in juvenile proceedings, but declined to rule on two other claimed rights, *id.*, at 344–345, 265 A.2d at 353; that as a consequence the Pennsylvania court was "confronted with a sweeping rationale and a carefully tailored holding," *id.*, at 345, 265 A.2d, at 353; that the procedural safeguards "*Gault* specifically made applicable to juvenile courts have already caused a significant 'constitutional domestication' of juvenile court proceedings," *id.*, at 346, 265 A.2d, at 354; that those safeguards and other rights, including the reasonable-doubt standard established by *Winship*, "insure that the juvenile court will operate in an atmosphere which is orderly enough to impress the juvenile with the gravity of the situation and the impartiality of the tribunal and at the same time informal enough to permit the benefits of the juvenile system to operate" (footnote omitted), *id.*, at 347, 265 A.2d, at 354; that the "proper inquiry, then, is whether the right to a trial by jury is 'fundamental' within the meaning of *Duncan*, in the context of a juvenile court which operates with *all* of the above constitutional safeguards," *id.*, at 348, 265 A.2d, at 354; and that his court's inquiry turned "upon whether there are elements in the juvenile process which render the right to a trial by jury less essential to the protection of an accused's rights in the juvenile system than in the normal criminal process." *Ibid.*

Justice Roberts then concluded that such factors do inhere in the Pennsylvania juvenile system: (1) Although realizing that "faith in the quality of the juvenile bench is not an entirely satisfactory substitute for due process," *id.*, at 348, 265 A.2d, at 355, the judges in the juvenile courts "to take a different view of their role than that taken by their counterparts in the criminal courts." *Id.*, at 348, 265 A.2d, at 354–355. (2) While one regrets its inadequacies, "the juvenile system has available and utilizes much more fully various diagnostic and rehabilitative services" that are "far superior to those available in the regular criminal process." *Id.*, at 348–349, 265 A.2d, at 355. (3) Although conceding

that the post-adjudication process "has in many respects fallen far short of its goals, and its reality is far harsher than its theory," the end result of a declaration of delinquency "*is* significantly different from and less onerous than a finding of criminal guilt" and "we are not yet convinced that the current practices do not contain the seeds from which a truly appropriate system can be brought forth." (4) Finally, "of all the possible due process rights which could be applied in the juvenile courts, the right to trial by jury is the one which would most likely be disruptive of the unique nature of the juvenile process." It is the jury trial that "would probably require substantial alteration of the traditional practices." The other procedural rights held applicable to the juvenile process "will give the juvenile sufficient protection" and the addition of the trial by jury "might well destroy the traditional character of juvenile proceedings." *Id.*, at 349–350, 265 A.2d, at 355.

The court concluded, *id.*, at 350, 265 A.2d, at 356, that it was confident "that a properly structured and fairly administered juvenile court system can serve our present societal needs without infringing on individual freedoms."

IV

The right to an impartial jury "[i]n all criminal prosecutions" under federal law is guaranteed by the Sixth Amendment. Through the Fourteenth Amendment that requirement has now been imposed upon the States "in all criminal cases which—were they to be tried in a federal court—would come within the Sixth Amendment's guarantee." This is because the Court has said it believes "that trial by jury in criminal cases is fundamental to the American scheme of justice." *Duncan v. Louisiana*, 391 U.S. 145, 149, 88 S.Ct. 1444, 1447, 20 L.Ed.2d 491 (1968); *Bloom v. Illinois*, 391 U.S. 194, 210–211, 88 S.Ct. 1477, 1486–1487, 20 L.Ed.2d 522 (1968).

This, of course, does not automatically provide the answer to the present jury trial issue, if for no other reason than that the juvenile court proceeding has not yet been held to be a "criminal prosecution," within the meaning and reach of the Sixth Amendment, and also has not yet been regarded as devoid of criminal aspects merely because it usually has been given the civil label. *Kent*, 383 U.S., at 554, 86 S.Ct., at 1054; *Gault*, 387 U.S., at 17, 49–50,

87 S.Ct., at 1438, 1455–1456; *Winship*, 397 U.S., at 365–366, 90 S.Ct., at 1073–1074.

Little, indeed, is to be gained by any attempt simplistically to call the juvenile court proceeding either "civil" or "criminal." The Court carefully has avoided this wooden approach. Before *Gault* was decided in 1967, the Fifth Amendment's guarantee against self-incrimination had been imposed upon the state criminal trial. *Malloy v. Hogan*, 378 U.S. 1, 84 S.Ct. 1489, 12 L.Ed.2d 653 (1964). So, too, had the Sixth Amendment's rights of confrontation and self-examination. *Pointer v. Texas*, 380 U.S. 400, 85 S.Ct. 1065, 13 L.Ed.2d 923 (1965), and *Douglas v. Alabama*, 380 U.S. 415, 85 S.Ct. 1074, 13 L.Ed.2d 934 (1965). Yet the Court did not automatically and peremptorily apply those rights to the juvenile proceeding. A reading of *Gault* reveals the opposite. And the same separate approach to the standard-of-proof issue is evident from the carefully separated application of the standard, first to the criminal trial, and then to the juvenile proceeding, displayed in *Winship*. 397 U.S., at 361 and 365, 90 S.Ct., at 1071 and 1073.

Thus, accepting "the proposition that the Due Process Clause has a role to play," *Gault*, 387 U.S., at 13, 87 S.Ct., at 1436, our task here with respect to trial by jury, as it was in *Gault* with respect to other claimed rights, "is to ascertain the precise impact of the due process requirement." *Id.*, at 13–14, 87 S.Ct., at 1436.

V

The Pennsylvania juveniles' basic argument is that they were tried in proceedings "substantially similar to a criminal trial." They say that a delinquency proceeding in their State is initiated by a petition charging a penal code violation in the conclusory language of an indictment; that a juvenile detained prior to trial is held in a building substantially similar to an adult prison; that in Philadelphia juveniles over 16 are, in fact, held in the cells of a prison; that counsel and the prosecution engage in plea bargaining; that motions to suppress are routinely heard and decided; that the usual rules of evidence are applied; that the customary common-law defenses are available; that the press is generally admitted in the Philadelphia juvenile courtrooms; that members of the public enter the room; that arrest and prior record may be reported by the press (from police sources, however, rather than from the juvenile

court records); that, once adjudged delinquent, a juvenile may be confined until his majority in what amounts to a prison (see *In re Bethea*, 215 Pa.Super. 75, 76, 257 A.2d 368, 369 (1969), describing the state correctional institution at Camp Hill as a "maximum security prison for adjudged delinquents and youthful criminal offenders"); and that the stigma attached upon delinquency adjudication approximates that resulting from conviction in an adult criminal proceeding.

The North Carolina juveniles particularly urge that the requirement of a jury trial would not operate to deny the supposed benefits of the juvenile court system; that the system's primary benefits are its discretionary intake procedure permitting disposition short of adjudication, and its flexible sentencing permitting emphasis on rehabilitation; that realization of these benefits does not depend upon dispensing with the jury; that adjudication of factual issues on the one hand and disposition of the case on the other are very different matters with very different purposes; that the purpose of the former is indistinguishable from that of the criminal trial; that the jury trial provides an independent protective factor; that experience has shown that jury trials in juvenile courts are manageable; that no reason exists why protection traditionally accorded in criminal proceedings should be denied young people subject to involuntary incarceration for lengthy periods; and that the juvenile courts deserve healthy public scrutiny.

VI

All the litigants here agree that the applicable due process standard in juvenile proceedings, as developed by *Gault* and *Winship*, is fundamental fairness. As that standard was applied in those two cases, we have an emphasis on factfinding procedures. The requirements of notice, counsel, confrontation, cross-examination, and standard of proof naturally flowed from this emphasis. But one cannot say that in our legal system the jury is a necessary component of accurate factfinding. There is much to be said for it, to be sure, but we have been content to pursue other ways for determining facts. Juries are not required, and have not been, for example, in equity cases, in workmen's compensation, in probate, or in deportation cases. Neither have they been generally used in military trials. In *Duncan* the Court said, "We would not assert, however, that every criminal trial—or any particular trial—held before a judge alone is unfair or that a defendant may never be as fairly treated by a judge as he would be by a jury." 391 U.S., at 158, 88 S.Ct., at 1452. In *DeStefano*, for this reason and others, the Court refrained from retrospective application of *Duncan*, an action it surely would have not taken had it felt that the integrity of the result was seriously at issue. And in *Williams v. Florida*, 399 U.S. 78, 90 S.Ct. 1893, 26 L.Ed.2d 446 (1970), the Court saw no particular magic in a 12-man jury for a criminal case, thus revealing that even jury concepts themselves are not inflexible.

We must recognize, as the Court has recognized before, that the fond and idealistic hopes of the juvenile court proponents and early reformers of three generations ago have not been realized. The devastating commentary upon the system's failures as a whole, contained in the President's Commission on Law Enforcement and Administration of Justice, Task Force Report: Juvenile Delinquency and Youth Crime 7–9 (1967), reveals the depth of disappointment in what has been accomplished. Too often the juvenile court judge falls far short of that stalwart, protective, and communicating figure the system envisaged.[4] The community's unwillingness to provide people and facilities and to be concerned, the insufficiency of time devoted, the scarcity of professional help, the inadequacy of dispositional alternatives, and our general lack of knowledge all contribute to dissatisfaction with the experiment.[5]

The Task Force Report, however, also said, *id.*, at 7, "To say that juvenile courts have failed to achieve their goals is to say no more than what is true of criminal courts in the United States. But failure is most striking when hopes are highest."

Despite all these disappointments, all these failures, and all these shortcomings, we conclude that trial by jury in the juvenile court's adjudicative stage is not a constitutional requirement. We so conclude for a number of reasons:

1. The Court has refrained, in the cases heretofore decided, from taking the easy way with a flat holding that all rights constitutionally assured for the adult accused are to be imposed upon the state juvenile proceeding. What was done in *Gault* and in *Winship* is aptly described in *Commonwealth v. Johnson*, 211 Pa.Super. 62, 74, 234 A.2d 9, 15 (1967):

> It is clear to use that the Supreme Court has properly attempted to strike a judicious balance by injecting procedural orderliness into the juvenile court system. It is seeking to reverse the trend [pointed out in *Kent*, 383 U.S., at 556, 86 S.Ct. 1045] whereby "the child receives the worst of both worlds: *   *   * ."

2. There is a possibility, at least, that the jury trial, if required as a matter of constitutional precept, will remake the juvenile proceeding into a fully adversary process and will put an effective end to what has been the idealistic prospect of an intimate, informal protective proceeding.

3. The Task Force Report, although concededly pre-*Gault*, is notable for its not making any recommendation that the jury trial be imposed upon the juvenile court system. This is so despite its vivid description of the system's deficiencies and disappointments. Had the Commission deemed this vital to the integrity of the juvenile process, or to the handling of juveniles, surely a recommendation or suggestion to this effect would have appeared. The intimations, instead, are quite the other way. Task

---

4. "A recent study of juvenile court judges *   *   * revealed that half had not received undergraduate degrees; a fifth had received no college education at all; a fifth were not members of the bar." Task Force Report 7.

5. "What emerges, then, is this: In theory the juvenile court was to be helpful and rehabilitative rather than punitive. In fact the distinction often disappears, not only because of the absence of facilities and personnel but also because of the limits of knowledge and technique. In theory the court's action was to affix no stigmatizing label. In fact a delinquent is generally viewed by employers, schools, the armed services—by society generally—as a criminal. In theory the court was to treat children guilty of criminal acts in noncriminal ways. In fact it labels truants and runaways as junior criminals.

"In theory the court's operations could justifiably be informal, its findings and decisions made without observing ordinary procedural safeguards, because it would act only in the best interest of the child. In fact it frequently does nothing more nor less than deprive a child of liberty without due process of law—knowing not what else to do and needing, whether admittedly or not, to act in the community's interest even more imperatively than the child's. In theory it was to exercise its protective powers to bring an errant child back into the fold. In fact there is increasing reason to believe that its intervention reinforces the juvenile's unlawful impulses. In theory it was to concentrate on each case the best of current social science learning. In fact it has often become a vested interest in its turn, loathe to cooperate with innovative programs or avail itself of forward-looking methods." Task Force Report 9.

Force Report 38. Further, it expressly recommends against abandonment of the system and against the return of the juvenile to the criminal courts.[6]

4. The Court specifically has recognized by dictum that a jury is not a necessary part even of every criminal process that is fair and equitable. *Duncan v. Louisiana*, 391 U.S., at 149–150, n. 14, and 158, 88 S.Ct., at 1447, and 1452.

5. The imposition of the jury trial on the juvenile court system would not strengthen greatly, if at all, the factfinding function, and would, contrarily, provide an attrition of the juvenile court's assumed ability to function in a unique manner. It would not remedy the defects of the system. Meager as has been the hoped-for advance in the juvenile field, the alternative would be regressive, would lose what has been gained, and would tend once again to place the juvenile squarely in the routine of the criminal process.

6. The juvenile concept held high promise. We are reluctant to say that, despite disappointments of grave dimensions, it still does not hold promise, and we are particularly reluctant to say, as do the Pennsylvania appellants here, that the system cannot accomplish its rehabilitative goals. So much depends on the availability of resources, on the interest and commitment of the public, on willingness to learn, and on understanding as to cause and effect and cure. In this field, as in so many others, one perhaps learns best by doing. We are reluctant to disallow the States to experiment further and to seek in new and different ways the elusive answers to the prob-

lems of the young, and we feel that we would be impeding that experimentation by imposing the jury trial. The States, indeed, must go forward. If, in its wisdom, any State feels the jury trial is desirable in all cases, or in certain kinds, there appears to be no impediment to its installing a system embracing that feature. That, however, is the State's privilege and not its obligation.

7. Of course there have been abuses. The Task Force Report has noted them. We refrain from saying at this point that those abuses are of constitutional dimension. They relate to the lack of resources and of dedication rather than to inherent unfairness.

8. There is, of course, nothing to prevent a juvenile court judge, in a particular case where he feels the need, or when the need is demonstrated, from using an advisory jury.

9. "The fact that a practice is followed by a large number of states is not conclusive in a decision as to whether that practice accords with due process, but it is plainly worth considering in determining whether the practice 'offends some principle of justice so rooted in the traditions and conscience of our people as to be ranked as fundamental.' *Snyder v. Massachusetts*, 291 U.S. 97, 105, 54 S.Ct. 330, 332, 78 L.Ed. 674 (1934)." *Leland v. Oregon*, 343 U.S. 790, 798, 72 S.Ct. 1002, 1007, 96 L.Ed. 1302 (1952). It therefore is of more than passing interest that at least 28 States and the District of Columbia by statute deny the juvenile a right to a jury trial in cases such as these.[7] The same result is achieved in

---

6. "Nevertheless, study of the juvenile courts does not necessarily lead to the conclusion that the time has come to jettison the experiment and remand the disposition of children charged with crime to the criminal courts of the country. As trying as are the problems of the juvenile courts, the problems of the criminal courts, particularly those of the lower courts, which would fall heir to much of the juvenile court jurisdiction, are even graver; and the ideal of separate treatment of children is still worth pursuing. What is required is rather a revised philosophy of the juvenile court based on the recognition that in the past our reach exceeded our grasp. The spirit that animated the juvenile court movement was fed in part by a humanitarian compassion for offenders who were children. That willingness to understand and treat people who threaten public safety and security should be nurtured, not turned aside as hopeless sentimentality, both because it is civilized and because social protection itself demands constant search for alternatives to the crude and limited expedient of condemnation and punishment. But neither should it be allowed to outrun reality. The juvenile court is a court of law, charged like other agencies of criminal justice with protecting the community against threatening conduct. Rehabilitating offenders through individualized handling is one way of providing protection, and appropriately the primary way in dealing with children. But the guiding consideration for a court of law that deals with threatening conduct is nonetheless protection of the community. The juvenile court, like other courts, is therefore obliged to employ all the means at hand, not excluding incapacitation, for achieving that protection. What should distinguish the juvenile from the criminal courts is greater emphasis on rehabilitation, not exclusive preoccupation with it."

7. Ala.Code, Tit. 13, § 369 (1958); Alaska Stat. § 47.10.070 (Supp.1970); Ariz.Rev.Stat.Ann. § 8–229 (1956), see Ariz. Laws, c. 223 (May 19, 1970); Ark.Stat.Ann. § 45–206 (1964); Del.Code ann., Tit. 10, § 1175 (Supp.1970); Fla.Stat. § 39.09(2) (1965), F.S.A.; Ga.Code Ann. § 24–2420 (Supp.1970); Hawaii Rev.Stat. § 571–41 (1968); Idaho Code § 16–1813 (Supp.1969); Ind.Ann.Stat. § 9–3215 (Supp.1970); Iowa Code § 232.27 (1971); Ky.Rev.Stat. § 208.060 (1962); La.Rev.Stat. § 13:1579 (Supp.1962); Minn.Stat. § 260.155 subd. 1 (1969); Miss.Code Ann. § 7185–08 (1942); Mo.Rev.Stat. § 211.171(6) (1969) (equity practice controls), V.A.M.S.;

(continued on next page)

other States by judicial decision.[8] In 10 States statutes provide for a jury trial under certain circumstances.[9]

10. Since *Gault* and since *Duncan* the great majority of States, in addition to Pennsylvania and North Carolina, that have faced the issue have concluded that the considerations that led to the result in those two cases do not compel trial by jury in the juvenile court. *In re Fucini*, 44 Ill.2d 305, 255 N.E.2d 380 (1970); Bible v. State, 254 N.E.2d 319 (Ind.1970); *Dryden v. Commonwealth*, 435 S.W.2d 457 (Ky.1968); *In re Johnson*, 254 Md. 517, 255 A.2d 419 (1969); *Hopkins v. Youth Court*, 227 So.2d 282 (Miss.1969); *In re J. W.*, 106 N.J.Super. 129, 254 A.2d 334 (1969); *In re D.*, 27 N.Y.2d 90, 313 N.Y.S.2d 704, 261 N.E.2d 627 (1970); *In re Agler*, 19 Ohio St.2d 70, 249 N.E.2d 808 (1969); *State v. Turner*, 253 Or. 235, 453 P.2d 910 (1969). See *In re Estes v. Hopp*, 73 Wash.2d 263, 438 P.2d 205 (1968); *McMullen v. Geiger*, 184 Neb. 581, 169 N.W.2d 431 (1969). To the contrary are *Peyton v. Nord*, 78 N.M. 717, 437 P.2d 716 (1968), and, *semble*, *Nieves v. United States*, 280 F.Supp. 994 (SDNY 1968).

11. Stopping short of proposing the jury trial for juvenile proceedings are the Uniform Juvenile Court Act, § 24(a), approved in July 1968 by the National Conference of Commissioners on Uniform State Laws; the Standard Juvenile Court Act, Art. V, § 19, proposed by the National Council on Crime and Delinquency (see W. Sheridan, Standards for Juvenile and Family Courts 73 Dept. of H. E. W., Children's Bureau Pub. No. 437–1966); and the Legislative Guide for Drafting Family and Juvenile Court Acts § 29(a) (Dept. of H. E. W., Children's Bureau Pub. No. 472–1969).

12. If the jury trial were to be injected into the juvenile court system as a matter of right, it would bring with it into that system the traditional delay, the formality, and the clamor of the adversary system

and, possibly, the public trial. It is of interest that these very factors were stressed by the District Committee of the Senate when, through Senator Tydings, it recommended, and Congress then approved, as a provision in the District of Columbia Crime Bill, the abolition of the jury trial in the juvenile court. S.Rep.No. 91–620, pp. 13–14 (1969).

13. Finally, the arguments advanced by the juveniles here are, of course, the identical arguments that underlie the demand for the jury trial for criminal proceedings. The arguments necessarily equate the juvenile proceeding—or at least the adjudicative phase of it—with the criminal trial. Whether they should be so equated is our issue. Concern about the inapplicability of exclusionary and other rules of evidence, about the juvenile court judge's possible awareness of the juvenile's prior record and of the contents of the social file, about repeated appearances of the same familiar witnesses in the persons of juvenile and probation officers and social workers—all to the effect that this will create the likelihood of pre-judgment—chooses to ignore it seems to us, every aspect of fairness, of concern, of sympathy, and of paternal attention that the juvenile court system contemplates.

If the formalities of the criminal adjudicative process are to be superimposed upon the juvenile court system, there is little need for its separate existence. Perhaps the ultimate disillusionment will come one day, but for the moment we are disinclined to give impetus to it.

Affirmed.

SPEEDY TRIAL

Case Comment

United States v. Doe analyzes the application of the Federal Speedy Trial Act (18 U.S.C.) to juveniles proscribed in the federal court system. In *Doe*, the juvenile offender sought to have his indictment dis-

---

Neb.Rev.Stat. § 43–206.03(2) (1968); Nev.Rev.Stat. § 62.190(3) (1968); N.J.Stat.Ann. § 2A:4–35 (1952); N.Y.Family Court Act §§ 164 and 165 and Civ.Prac. Law and Rules § 4101; N.C.Gen.Stat. § 7A–285 (1969); N.D.Cent.Code § 27–16–18 (1960); Ohio Rev.Code Ann. § 2151.35 (Supp. 1970); Ore.Rev.Stat. § 419.498(1) (1968); Pa.Stat.Ann., Tit. 11, § 247 (1965); S.C.Code Ann. § 15–1095.19 (Supp.1970); Utah Code Ann. § 55–10–94 (Supp.1969); Vt. Stat.Ann., Tit. 33, § 651(a) (Supp.1970); Wash.Rev. Code Ann. § 13.04.030; D.C.Code § 16–2316(a) (Supp.1971).

8. *In re Daedler*, 194 Cal. 320, 228 P. 467 (1924); *Cinque v. Boyd*, 99 Conn. 70, 121 A. 678 (1923); *In re Fletcher*, 251 Md. 520, 248 A.2d 364 (1968); *Commonwealth v. Page*, 339 Mass. 313, 316, 159 N.E.2d 82, 85 (1959); *In re Perham*, 104 N.H. 276, 184 A.2d 449 (1962).

9. Colo.Rev.Stat.Ann. § 37–19–24 (Supp.1965); Kan.Stat.Ann. § 38–808 (Supp.1969); Mich.Comp.Laws § 712A.17 (1948); Mont.Rev.Codes Ann. § 10–604.1 (Supp.1969); Okla.Stat.Ann., Tit. 10, § 1110 (Supp.1970); S.D.Comp.Laws § 26-8-31 (1967); Tex.Civ.Stat., Art. 2338–1, § 13(b) (Supp.1970); W.Va.Code Ann. § 49–5–6 (1966); Wis.Stat.Ann. § 48.25(2) (Supp.1971); Wyo.Stat.Ann. § 14–115.24 (Supp.1971).

missed on grounds that the thirty-day speedy trial period had expired. However, the Court concluded that a one-day delay in bringing the juvenile to trial was "in the interest of justice" and that the federal government had basically complied with the statutory requirements.

UNITED STATES v. DOE

882 F.2d 926 (1988)

Before Gee, Jones, Circuit Judges, and Hunter, District Judge. Gee, Circuit Judge:

This appeal addresses a single issue: the effect of a one-day delinquency in proceedings governed by the federal juvenile speedy trial act.

On July 19, 1988, federal authorities arrested John Doe (Doe) on the bridge spanning the Rio Grande River between El Paso, Texas, and Juarez, Mexico. Doe was charged with possession of heroin with intent to distribute. Immediately after the arrest, the arresting officers began the immigration procedures necessary to bring Doe into the United States. The arresting officers then transferred Doe to the regional Drug Enforcement Agency (DEA) office, where officials determined that he was a juvenile.[1] Upon discovering that Doe was a juvenile, the federal officials complied with 18 U.S.C. Section 5032 and transferred Doe to state authorities, tendering jurisdiction to them. The state declined to prosecute Doe, thus giving federal authorities jurisdiction to do so. On July 20, the state returned Doe to federal custody and moved for a detention order. Also on the 20th, the magistrate held a detention hearing and, on the following day, entered a detention order.

On August 19, 1988, Doe was tried and convicted as a delinquent. Before the trial began, Doe moved to dismiss the indictment on the ground that the 30-day speedy trial period for federal juvenile defendants had expired on August 18. The court denied the motion, reasoning that the detention order was filed on July 20 and, thus, the 30-day period did not expire until August 19. Doe appeals.

Although the district court incorrectly interpreted the juvenile speedy trial provision, we need not reverse. If a federal juvenile is "in detention pending trial," his trial must begin 30 days from the date detention began; if the trial begins after the 30-day

period expires, the court must dismiss the information. 18 U.S.C. Section 5036. Under the District court's interpretation of Section 5036, a juvenile is not "in detention until a detention order is filed. The district court's understanding of Section 5036 is, however, inconsistent with our interpretation of that provision and with the ordinary meaning of the term detention. Moreover, the district court's holding requires us to rewrite Section 5036, adding to the statutory language. Despite the court's error, however, we need not reverse. Section 5036 permits delays that are in the interest of justice. In this case, the federal officials spent one day completing the processes necessary both to bring Doe into the United States and to exercise jurisdiction over a juvenile defendant. This one-day delay, occasioned by a good-faith and expeditious compliance with the federal statutory requirements for prosecuting Doe, is a delay that we countenance in the interest of justice.

"DETENTION"

[1] The district court erred when it concluded that the juvenile speedy trial period began to run when the detention order was filed, not when Doe was taken into physically restrictive custody. Section 5036 provides:

> [i]f an alleged delinquent who is in detention pending trial is not brought to trial within thirty days from the date upon which such detention was begun, the information shall be dismissed

Section 5036. The definition of the term "detention" is, as we noted in *United States v. Cuomo*, unclear. 525 F.2d 1285, 1290 (5th Cir.1976). In our attempt to give meaning to the term, we explained that "in the understanding of juvenile court specialists and the language of statutes, model codes, and judicial opinions, 'detention' almost invariably is used as a term of art to mean physically restrictive custody, confinement within a specific institution." *Id.* at 1291 (footnotes omitted). Thus, in *Cuomo*, the 30-day period did not run while the defendant was out on restrictive bail, but not in physically restrictive custody. *Id.* at 1292. Consistent with our analysis in *Cuomo*, we determine whether a juvenile is in "detention" by asking whether he is in physically restrictive custody—not whether the prosecu-

---

1. Doe was 16 years old at the time of his arrest.

tor has complied with the procedural requirement of filing a detention order.[2]

Furthermore, the *Cuomo* court relied, in part, on the National Council of Crime and Delinquency's definition of detention: " 'Detention is the temporary care of children in physically restricted facilities pending court disposition or transfer to another jurisdiction or agency . . .' " *Id.* at 1291 n. 12 (quoting Hammergran, *The Role of Juvenile Detention in a Changing Juvenile Justice System*, 24 Juvenile Justice No. 3, at 46 (1973)). Under this definition of detention, Doe was "in detention" from the moment he was arrested and taken into physically restrictive custody. While the arresting officers were completing the immigration process, Doe was in physically restrictive custody pending his transfer to the regional DEA office. Next, DEA officials transferred Doe to state authorities, where Doe remained in physically restrictive custody awaiting the state's decision whether to prosecute him. After the state declined to exert jurisdiction, it returned Doe to the federal authorities, who held him in physically restrictive custody until trial. Thus, according to our understanding of "detention," Doe was in detention from the moment he was first placed in physically restrictive custody.

In addition to conflicting with our understanding of detention in Cuomo, the district court's interpretation conflicts with the ordinary meaning of the term detention. In ordinary usage, the word detention means "(1) the act or fact of detaining: (a) holding in custody . . ." Webster's Third New International Dictionary 616. "Detain," as it commonly is used, means "to hold or keep in or as if in custody." *Id.* As the term detention usually is used, a person is in detention when he is in custody, and his period of detention begins when he is taken into custody. Under the district court's understanding of the word,

however, a person is not "in detention" until the person detaining him has filed the necessary papers. The district court's interpretation is at odds both with the usual meaning and with our judicial understanding of the term detention. We thus decline to adopt the district court's reasoning.

Finally, we cannot accept the district court's interpretation, as it requires us to add to the language of Section 5036. Section 5036 requires the court to dismiss an information if "an alleged delinquent who is in detention is not brought to trial within such 30 days from the date *upon which such detention was begun . . . .*" Section 5036 (emphasis added). Although the statute makes no reference to whether the prosecutor has filed a detention order, the district court concluded that the 30-day period is not triggered until the prosecutor has filed one. To reach the district court's conclusion, we would have to add to the statutory language, so that Section 5036 would read: "if an alleged delinquent who is in detention pending trial is not brought to trial within 30 days from the date *upon which such detention was begun and from the date upon which such detention order was filed*, the information shall be dismissed. . . ." If Congress had wanted to 30-day period to run from the date of filing a detention order, it could have used language that mentioned the filing. Congress chose not to refer to (or neglected to consider) the filing of the detention order and we will not amend Section 5036 to include language that does so.[3]

THE INTEREST OF JUSTICE

[2] Although the district court erred in interpreting Section 5036, we need not reverse. Measuring the 30-day period from the date upon which Doe was in physically restrictive custody, we conclude that the 30-day period expired on August 18—one day

---

2. Indeed, to define "in detention" with reference to whether a detention order was filed would be to place form above substance. A juvenile can be, as Doe was, in physically restrictive custody long before the prosecutor files a detention order.

3. Holding that the 30-day period begins when the juvenile is taken into custody puts us at odds with the Ninth Circuit. We decline to follow the Ninth Circuit's interpretation of Section 5036, however, because its interpretation is inconsistent with our analysis in *Cuomo* and with the language of Section 5036. In *United States v. Andy*, the Ninth Circuit used 18 U.S.C. Section 5032 to set the date upon which Section 5036's 30-day period begins to run. 549 F.2d 1281 (9th Cir.1977). Section 5032 requires, as a prerequisite to federal prosecution of a juvenile, that the Attorney General certify that the state court cannot or will not exert jurisdiction over the juvenile. According to the *Andy* court, the 30-day period beings to run on

(1) the date that the Attorney General certifies, or in the exercise of reasonable diligence could have certified, to the conditions stated in Section 5032, or (2) the date upon which the Government formally assumes jurisdiction over the juvenile, whichever event earlier occurs.

Id. at 1293. We decline to follow the Ninth Circuit for two reasons.

(continued on next page)

before Doe's trial began. This one-day delay does not, however, automatically warrant a reversal. Section 5036 requires a dismissal "unless the Attorney General shows that additional delay . . . would be in the interest of justice in the particular case." A federal delinquency proceeding cannot begin until the Attorney General, after investigation, certifies to the district court that (1) the state juvenile court does not have jurisdiction or will not exercise jurisdiction over the juvenile or (2) the state does not have programs or services for juveniles. 18 U.S.C. Section 5032. In other words, federal prosecutors must tender the case to state prosecutors before exerting federal jurisdiction. After placing Doe in custody, the federal authorities spent one day arranging to bring Doe into the United States and tendering the case to the state. Immediately after the state declined to exercise jurisdiction, the prosecutors started the federal procedural ball rolling. This one-day delay, during which federal prosecutors were complying with their statutory duties, is a delay that we determine to countenance in the interest of justice.

Affirmed.

OPEN VERSUS CLOSED HEARINGS

Case Comment

Generally, juvenile hearings are closed to the public and press and the names of the offenders kept secret. In *Oklahoma Publishing Co. v. District Court* and *Smith v. Daily Mail Publishing Co.*, the U.S. Supreme Court balanced the issue of juvenile privacy with freedom of the press.[9]

In the *Oklahoma* case, the Supreme Court ruled that a state court was not allowed to prohibit the publication of information obtained in an open juvenile proceeding. The case involves an eleven-year-old boy suspected of homicide who appeared at a detention hearing and of whom photographs were taken and published in local newspapers. When the local district court prohibited further disclosure, the publishing company claimed that the court order was a restraint in violation of the First Amendment, and the Supreme Court agreed. The *Smith v. Daily Mail* case involved the discovery and subsequent publication by news reporters of the identity of a juvenile suspect in violation of a state statute prohibiting publication. The Supreme Court, however, declared the statute unconstitutional because it believed that the state's interest in protecting the child's identity was not of such a magnitude as to justify the use of a crime statute.

These decisions do not give the press complete access to juvenile trials. Today, some jurisdictions still bar the press from juvenile proceedings unless they show at a hearing that their presence will not harm the youth. In other words, when states follow a *parens patriae* philosophy, ordinarily the public and press are generally excluded, but the court has discretion to permit interested parties to observe the hearings.

According to such experts as Ira Schwartz, there is far less need for confidentiality to protect juveniles than for opening up the courts to public scrutiny and accountability.[10]

OKLAHOMA PUBLISHING CO. v. DISTRICT COURT IN AND FOR OKLAHOMA COUNTY, OKLAHOMA, ET AL.

430 U.S. 306 (1977)

Per curiam.

A pretrial order entered by the District Court of Oklahoma County enjoined members of the news media from "publishing, broadcasting, or dissemi-

---

First, the Ninth Circuit's interpretation is inconsistent with our holding and analysis in *Cuomo*. In *Cuomo*, we held that detention begins when the juvenile is in custody, reaching the conclusion without reference to whether the Attorney General has filed the appropriate papers. Moreover, we arrived at our interpretation by searching for the correct meaning of the words of Section 5036. Section 5036 commands that the 30-day period begins when detention begins; defining detention as physical custody, we concluded that detention begins when physical custody begins. The Ninth Circuit, in contrast, defines detention not by reference to the meaning of the word, but by reference to the procedural requirements for prosecuting a juvenile.

Second, the *Andy* court effectively amended the language of Section 5036. Under the *Andy* court's approach, the 30-day period does not begin to run from the time detention has "begun," as the statute requires. Rather, the 30-day period begins to run when the Attorney General files a certification. Taking physical custody of a juvenile and filing a certification are two distinct and separate acts. The Ninth Circuit erased from Section 5036 the language that measures the 30-day period from the "date upon which detention was begun" and substituted in its place language that measures the 30-day period from the date of certification. We decline to follow the Ninth Circuit's efforts to rewrite Section 5036.

nating, in any manner, the name or picture of [a] minor child" in connection with a juvenile proceeding involving that child then pending in that court. On application for prohibition and mandamus challenging the order as a prior restraint on the press violative of the First and Fourteenth Amendments, the Supreme Court of the State of Oklahoma sustained the order. This Court entered a stay pending the time filing and disposition of a petition for certiorari. 429 U.S. 967 (1976). We now grant the petition for certiorari and reverse the decision below.

A railroad switchman was fatally shot on July 26, 1976. On July 29, 1976, an 11-year-old boy, Larry Donnell Brewer, appeared at a detention hearing in Oklahoma County Juvenile Court on charges filed by state juvenile authorities alleging delinquency by second-degree murder in the shooting of this switchman. Reporters, including one from petitioner's newspapers, were present in the courtroom during the hearing and learned the juvenile's name. As the boy was escorted from the courthouse to a vehicle, one of petitioner's photographers took his picture. Thereafter, a number of stories using the boy's name and photograph were printed in newspapers within the county, including petitioner's three newspapers in Oklahoma City; radio stations broadcast his name and television stations showed film footage of him and identified him by name.

On August 3, 1976, the juvenile was arraigned at a closed hearing, at which the judge entered the pretrial order involved in this case.[1] Additional news reports identifying the juvenile appeared on August 4 and 5. On August 16, the District Court denied petitioner's motion to quash the order. The Oklahoma Supreme Court then denied petitioner's writ of prohibition and mandamus, relying on Oklahoma statutes providing that juvenile proceedings are to be held in private "unless specifically ordered by the judge to be conducted in public," and that juvenile records are open to public inspection "only by order of the court to persons having a legitimate interest therein." Okla. Stat. Ann., Tit. 10, §§ 1111, 1125 (Supp. 1976).

As we noted in entering our stay of the pretrial order, petitioner does not challenge the constitu-

tionality of the Oklahoma statutes relied on by the court below. Petitioner asks us only to hold that the First and Fourteenth Amendments will not permit a state court to prohibit the publication of widely disseminated information obtained at court proceedings which were in fact open to the public. We think this result is compelled by our recent decisions in *Nebraska Press Assn. v. Stuart*, 427 U.S. 539 (1976), and *Cox Broadcasting Corp. v. Cohn*, 420 U.S. 469 (1975).

In *Cox Broadcasting* the Court held that a State could not impose sanctions on the accurate publication of the name of a rape victim "which was publicly revealed in connection with the prosecution of the crime." *Id.*, at 471. There, a reporter learned the identity of the victim from an examination of indictments made available by a clerk for his inspection in the courtroom during a recess of court proceedings against the alleged rapists. The Court expressly refrained from intimating a view on any constitutional questions arising from a state policy of denying the public or the press access to official records of juvenile proceedings, *id.*, at 496 n. 26, but made clear that the press may not be prohibited from "truthfully publishing information released to the public in official court records." *Id.*, at 496.

This principle was reaffirmed last Term in *Nebraska Press Assn. v. Stuart*, *supra*, which held unconstitutional an order prohibiting the press from publishing certain information tending to show the guilt of a defendant in an impending criminal trial. In Part VI-D of its opinion, the Court focused on the information covered by the order that had been adduced as evidence in a preliminary hearing open to the public and the press; we concluded that, to the extent the order prohibited the publication of such evidence, "it plainly violated settled principles," 427 U.S., at 568, citing *Cox Broadcasting Corp. v. Cohn, supra*; *Sheppard V. Maxwell*, 384 U.S. 333, 362–363 (1966) ("[T]here is nothing that proscribes the press from reporting events that transpire in the courtroom"); and *Craig v. Harney*, 331 U.S. 367, 374 (1947) ("Those who see and hear what transpired [in the courtroom] can report it with impunity"). The Court noted that under state law

---

1. In addition to enjoining publication of the name and picture of the juvenile, the order also enjoined law enforcement officials, juvenile authorities, and prosecution and defense counsel "from disclosing any information or making any comments concerning "the delinquency proceeding pending against the juvenile. Petitioner does not now challenge the restraints on counsel (which were rescinded in a modification of the order on August 5) or on public officials.

the trial court was permitted in certain circumstances to close pretrial proceedings to the public, but indicated that such an option did not allow the trial judge to suppress publication of information from the hearing if the public was allowed to attend: "[O]nce a public hearing had been held, what transpired there could not be subject to prior restraint." 427 U.S., at 568.

The court below found the rationale of these decisions to be inapplicable here because a state statute provided for closed juvenile hearings unless specifically opened to the public by court order and because "there is no indication that the judge distinctly and expressly ordered the hearing to be public." We think *Cox* and *Nebraska Press* are controlling nonetheless. Whether or not the trial judge expressly made such an order, members of the press were in fact present at the hearing with the full knowledge of the presiding judge, the prosecutor, and the defense counsel. No objection was made to the presence of the press in the courtroom or to the photographing of the juvenile as he left the courthouse. There is no evidence that petitioner acquired the information unlawfully or even without the State's implicit approval. The name and picture of the juvenile here were "publicly revealed in connection with the prosecution of the crime," 420 U.S., at 471, much as the name of the rape victim in *Cox Broadcasting* was placed in the public domain.[2] Under these circumstances, the District Court's order abridges the freedom of the press in violation of the First and Fourteenth Amendments.

The petition for certiorari is granted, and the judgment is reversed.

SMITH v. DAILY MAIL PUBLISHING CO.

443 U.S. 97 (1979)

Chief Justice Burger delivered the opinion of the Court.

We granted certiorari to consider whether a West Virginia statute violated the First and Fourteenth Amendments of the United States Constitution by making it a crime for a newspaper to publish, without the written approval of the juvenile court, the name of any youth charged as a juvenile offender.

(1)

The challenged West Virginia statute provides:

> [N]or shall the name of any child, in connection with any proceedings under this chapter, be published in any newspaper without a written order of the court. . . .
> W. Va. Code § 49–7–3 (1976);

and:

> A person who violates . . . a provision of this chapter for which punishment has not been specifically provided, shall be guilty of a misdemeanor, and upon conviction shall be fined not less than ten nor more than one hundred dollars, or confined in jail not less than five days nor more than six months, or both such fine and imprisonment." § 49–7–20.

On February 9, 1978, a 15-year-old student was shot and killed in Hayes Junior High School in St. Albans, W. Va., a small community located about 13 miles outside of Charleston, W. Va. The alleged assailant, a 14-year-old classmate, was identified by seven different eyewitnesses and was arrested by police soon after the incident.

The Charleston Daily Mail and the Charleston Gazette, respondents here, learned of the shooting by monitoring routinely the police band radio frequency; they immediately dispatched reporters and photographers to the junior high school. The reporters for both papers obtained the name of the alleged assailant simply by asking various witnesses, the police, and an assistant prosecuting attorney who were at the school.

The staffs of both newspapers prepared articles for publication about the incident. The Daily Mail's first article appeared in its February 9 afternoon edition. The article did not mention the alleged attacker's name. The editorial decision to omit the name was made because of the statutory prohibition against publication without prior court approval.

---

2. In *Cox Broadcasting* the Court quoted the following description by the reporter of the manner in which the name of the rape victim was revealed to him:

" '[D]uring a recess of the said trial, I approached the clerk of the court, who was sitting directly in front of the bench, and requested to see a copy of the indictments. In open court, I was handed the indictments, both the murder and the rape indictments, and was allowed to examine fully this document. . . . Moreover, no attempt was made by the clerk or anyone else to withhold the name and identity of the victim from me or from anyone else and the said indictments apparently were available for public inspection upon request.' " 420 U.S., at 473 n. 3.

The Gazette made a contrary editorial decision and published the juvenile's name and picture in an article about the shooting that appeared in the February 10 morning edition of the paper. In addition, the name of the alleged juvenile attacker was broadcast over at least three different radio stations on February 9 and 10. Since the information had become public knowledge, the Daily Mail decided to include the juvenile's name in an article in its afternoon paper on February 10.

On March 1, an indictment against the respondents was returned by a grand jury. The indictment alleged that each knowingly published the name of a youth involved in a juvenile proceeding in violation of W. Va. Code § 49–7–3 (1976). Respondents then filed an original-jurisdiction petition with the West Virginia Supreme Court of Appeals, seeking a writ or prohibition against the prosecuting attorney and the Circuit Court Judges of Kanawha County, petitioners here. Respondents alleged that the indictment was based on a statute that violated the First and Fourteenth Amendments of the United States Constitution and several provisions of the State's Constitution and requested an order prohibiting the county officials from taking any action on the indictment.

The West Virginia Supreme Court of Appeals issued the writ of prohibition. ___ W. Va. ___, 248 S.E.2d 269 (1978). Relying on holdings of this Court, it held that the statute abridged the freedom of the press. The court reasoned that the statute operated as a prior restraint on speech and that the State's interest in protecting the identity of the juvenile offender did not overcome the heavy presumption against the constitutionality of such prior restraints.

We granted certiorari. 439 U.S. 963 (1978).

(2)

Respondents urge this Court to hold that because § 49–7–3 requires court approval prior to publication of the juvenile's name it operates as a "prior restraint" on speech.[1] See *Nebraska Press Assn. v. Stuart*, 427 U.S. 539 (1976); *New York Times Co. v. United States*, 403 U.S. 713 (1971); *Organization*

for a Better Austin v. Keefe, 402 U.S. 415 (1971); *Near v. Minnesota ex rel. Olson*, 283 U.S. 697 (1931). Respondents concede that this statute is not in the classic mold of prior restraint, there being no prior injunction against publication. Nonetheless, they contend, that the prior-approval requirement acts in "operation and effect" like a licensing scheme and thus is another form of prior restraint. See *Near v. Minnesota ex rel. Olson, supra*, at 708. As such, respondents argue, the statute bears "a 'heavy presumption' against its constitutional validity." *Organization for a Better Austin v. Keefe, supra*, at 419. They claim that the State's interest in the anonymity of a juvenile offender is not sufficient to overcome that presumption.

Petitioners do not dispute that the statute amounts to a prior restraint on speech. Rather, they take the view that even if it is a prior restraint the statute is constitutional because of the significance of the State's interest in protecting the identity of juveniles.

(3)

The resolution of this case does not turn on whether the statutory grant of authority to the juvenile judge to permit publication of the juvenile's name is, in and of itself, a prior restraint. First Amendment protection reaches beyond prior restraints, *Landmark Communications, Inc. v. Virginia*, 435 U.S. 829 (1978); *Cox Broadcasting Corp. v. Cohn*, 420 U.S. 469 (1975), and respondents acknowledge that the statutory provision for court approval of disclosure actually may have a less oppressive effect on freedom of the press than a total ban on the publication of the child's name.

Whether we view the statute as a prior restraint or as a penal sanction for publishing lawfully obtained, truthful information is not dispositive because even the latter action requires the highest form of state interest to sustain its validity. Prior restraints have been accorded the most exacting scrutiny in previous cases. See *Nebraska Press Assn. v. Stuart, supra*, at 561; *Organization for a Better Austin v. Keefe, supra*, at 419; *Near v. Minnesota ex rel. Olson, supra*, at 716. See also *Southeastern Promo-*

---

1. Respondents do not argue that the statute is a prior restraint because it imposes a criminal sanction for certain types of publication. At page 11 of their brief they state: "The statute in question is, to be sure, not a prior restraint because it subjects newspapers to criminal punishments for what they print" after the event.

So far as the Daily Mail was concerned, the statute operated as a deterrent for 24 hours and became the basis for a prosecution after the delayed publication.

tions, Ltd. v. Conrad, 420 U.S. 546 (1975). However, even when a state attempts to punish publication after the event it must nevertheless demonstrate that its punitive action was necessary to further the state interests asserted. *Landmark Communications, Inc. v. Virginia, supra*, at 843. Since we conclude that this statute cannot satisfy the constitutional standards defined in *Landmark Communications, Inc.*, we need not decide whether, as argued by respondents, it operated as a prior restraint.

Our recent decisions demonstrate that state action to punish the publication of truthful information seldom can satisfy constitutional standards. In *Landmark Communications* we declared unconstitutional a Virginia statute making it a crime to publish information regarding confidential proceedings before a state judicial review commission that heard complaints about alleged disabilities and misconduct of state-court judges. In declaring that statute unconstitutional, we concluded:

> [T]he publication Virginia seeks to punish under its statute lies near the core of the First Amendment, and the Commonwealth's interests advanced by the imposition of criminal sanctions are insufficient to justify the actual and potential encroachments on freedom of speech and of the press which follow therefrom. 435 U.S., at 838.

In *Cox Broadcasting Corp. v. Cohn, supra*, we held that damages could not be recovered against a newspaper for publishing the name of a rape victim. The suit had been based on a state statute that made it a crime to publish the name of the victim; the purpose of the statute was to protect the privacy right of the individual and the family. The name of the victim had become known to the public through official court records dealing with the trial of the rapist. In declaring the statute unconstitutional, the Court, speaking through Mr. Justice White, reasoned:

> By placing the information in the public domain on official court records, the State must be presumed to have concluded that the public interest was thereby being served. . . . States may not impose sanctions on the publication of truthful information contained in official court records open to public inspection. 420 U.S., at 495.

One case that involved a classic prior restraint is particularly relevant to our inquiry. In *Oklahoma Publishing Co. v. District Court*, 430 U.S. 308 (1977), we struck down a state-court injunction prohibiting the news media from publishing the name or photograph of an 11-year-old boy who was being tried before a juvenile court. The juvenile court judge had permitted reporters and other members of the public to attend a hearing in the case, notwithstanding a state statute closing such trials to the public. The court then attempted to halt publication of the information obtained from that hearing. We held that once the truthful information was "publicly revealed" or "in the public domain" the court could not constitutionally restrain its dissemination.

None of these opinions directly controls this case; however, all suggest strongly that if a newspaper lawfully obtains truthful information about a matter of public significance then state officials may not constitutionally punish publication of the information, absent a need to further a state interest of the highest order. These cases involved situations where the government itself provided or made possible press access to the information. That factor is not controlling. Here respondent relied upon routine newspaper reporting techniques to ascertain the identity of the alleged assailant. A free press cannot be made to rely solely upon the sufferance of government to supply it with information. See *Houchins v. KQED, Inc.*, 438 U.S. 1, 11 (1978) (plurality opinion); *Branzburg v. Hayes*, 408 U.S. 665, 681 (1972). If the information is lawfully obtained, as it was here, the state may not punish its publication except when necessary to further an interest more substantial than is present here.

(4)

The sole interest advanced by the State to justify its criminal statute is to protect the anonymity of the juvenile offender. It is asserted that confidentiality will further his rehabilitation because publication of the name may encourage further antisocial conduct and also may cause the juvenile to lose future employment or suffer other consequences for this single offense. In *Davis v. Alaska*, 415 U.S. 308 (1974), similar arguments were advanced by the State to justify not permitting a criminal defendant to impeach a prosecution witness on the basis of his juvenile record. We said there that "[w]e do not and need not challenge the State's interest as a matter of its own policy in the administration of criminal justice to seek to preserve the anonymity of a juvenile offender." *Id.*, at 319. However, we concluded that the State's policy must be subordinated to the defendant's Sixth Amendment right of confrontation. *Ibid.* The important rights created by the First Amendment must be considered along with the rights of defendants guaranteed by the Sixth Amendment. See *Nebraska Press Assn. v. Stuart*, 427 U.S., at 561. Therefore, the reasoning of *Davis* that the constitutional right must prevail over the state's interest in protecting juveniles applies with equal force here.

The magnitude of the State's interest in this statute is not sufficient to justify application of a criminal penalty to respondents. Moreover, the statute's approach does not satisfy constitutional requirements. The statute does not restrict the electronic media or any form of publication, except "newspapers," from printing the names of youths charged in a juvenile proceeding. In this very case, three radio stations announced the alleged assailant's name before the Daily Mail decided to publish it. Thus, even assuming the statute served a state interest of the highest order, it does not accomplish its stated purpose.

In addition, there is no evidence to demonstrate that the imposition of criminal penalties is necessary to protect the confidentiality of juvenile proceedings. As the Brief for Respondents points out at 29 n. **, all 50 states have statutes that provide in some way for confidentiality, but only 5, including West Virginia,[2] impose criminal penalties on nonparties for publication of the identity of the juvenile. Although every state has asserted a similar interest, all but a handful have found other ways of accomplishing the objective. See *Landmark Communications, Inc. v. Virginia*, 435 U.S., at 843.[3]

(5)

Our holding in this case is narrow. There is no issue before us of unlawful press access to confidential judicial proceedings, see *Cox Broadcasting Corp. v. Cohn*, 420 U.S., at 496 n. 26; there is no issue here of privacy or prejudicial pretrial publicity. At issue is simply the power of a state to punish the truthful publication of an alleged juvenile delinquent's name lawfully obtained by a newspaper.[4] The asserted state interest cannot justify the statute's imposition of criminal sanctions on this type of publication. Accordingly, the judgment of the West Virginia Supreme Court of Appeals is affirmed.

END NOTES—CHAPTER V

1. Barry Krisberg, *The Juvenile Court: Reclaiming the Vision* (San Francisco: National Council on Crime and Delinquency, 1988).

2. 387 U.S. 1 (1967).

3. 397 U.S. 358 (1970).

4. 403 U.S. 528 (1971).

5. See Barry Feld, "The Right to Counsel in Juvenile Court: An Empirical Study of When Lawyers Appeal and the Difference They Make," *Journal of Criminal Law and Criminology* 79:1187–1346 (1989).

6. 387 U.S. 1 (1967), 19.

7. *State v. Schaaf*, 743 P.2d 240 (1987).

8. *People in Interest of T.M.*, 742 P.2d 905 (1987).

9. 430 U.S. 97 (1977); 443 U.S. 97 (1977).

10. Ira M. Schwartz, *(In) Justice for Juveniles: Rethinking the Best Interests of the Child* (Lexington, Mass.: D.C. Heath, 1989), p. 172.

---

2. Colo. Rev. Stat. § 19–1–107(6) (1973); Ga. Code § 24A–3503(g)(1) (1978); N.H.Rev.Stat.Ann. § 169:27–28 (1977); S.C. Code § 14–21–30 (1976).

3. The approach advocated by the National Council of Juvenile Court Judges is based on cooperation between juvenile court personnel and newspaper editors. It is suggested that if the courts make clear their purpose and methods then the press will exercise discretion and generally decline to publish the juvenile's name without some prior consultation with the juvenile court judge. See Conway, Publicizing the Juvenile Court: A Public Responsibility, 16 Juv. Ct. Judges J. 21, 21–22 (1965); Riederer, Secrecy or Privacy? Communication Problems in the Juvenile Court Field, 17 J. Mo. Bar 66, 69–70 (1961).

4. In light of our disposition of the First and Fourteenth Amendment issue, we need not reach respondents' claim that the statute violates equal protection by being applicable only to newspapers but not other forms of journalistic expression.

SIX

The Disposition of the Juvenile Offender

INTRODUCTION

After adjudication, the child is brought before the court for disposition. This means that the court must decide what sentence should be imposed upon the juvenile offender in light of his or her offense, prior record, and family background. Normally, the sentence is imposed by a juvenile court judge who has broad discretionary power to proscribe a range of dispositions, from dismissal to institutional commitment.[1] In theory, the dispositional decision is an effort by the court to serve the best interests of the child, his or her family, and the community. In many respects, this postadjudicative process is the most important in the juvenile court system because it represents the last opportunity for the court to influence the child and control his or her behavior.[2]

Most jurisdictions have statutes that require the court to proceed with disposition following adjudication of the child as a delinquent or status offender. This is done as part of the adjudicatory process or at a separate dispositional hearing. Statutory provisions that use the bifurcated hearing process are preferred, since different evidentiary rules apply at both hearings. The basic purpose of having two separate hearings is to ensure that only evidence appropriate to determine whether the child committed the alleged offense is considered by the court. If evidence relating to the presentence report on the child is used in the adjudicatory hearing, it would normally result in a reversal of the court's delinquency finding. On the other hand, the social history report is essential for court use in the dispositional hearing. Thus, the bifurcated process seeks to ensure that the adjudicatory hearing is used solely to determine the merits of the allegations, while the dispositional hearing determines if the child is in need of rehabilitation.

Since disposition is concerned with the treatment interests of the child, most jurisdictions remain unclear regarding what evidentiary rules apply at such a hearing. This is unlike the adjudicatory process that is governed by the *Gault* decision and is generally bound by the same formality and rules of evidence as the adult criminal system. At disposition, most jurisdictions provide the child with a statutory right to counsel. But the majority of states do not have clear-cut rules on such other issues as the admissibility of presentencing information, the application of the privilege against self-incrimination, or the use of the exclusionary rule at the dispositional stage of the proceedings. Generally, whatever evidence is relevant for the judge in making a disposition may be admissible for the purposes of that decision.

In theory, the juvenile court seeks to provide a disposition that represents an individualized treatment plan for the child. This decision is normally based to a large degree on the presentence investigation of the probation department, reports from social agencies, and possibly a psychiatric evaluation. Although the judge generally has broad discretion in dispositional matters, he or she is limited by the provisions of the state's juvenile court act. Most states have a statutory scheme that provides for the following types of alternative dispositions: (1) dismissal of the petition; (2) suspended judgment; (3) probation; (4) placement in a community treatment program; and (5) commitment to the state agency responsible for juvenile institutional care. In addition, the court may place the child with parents or relatives, make dispositional arrangements with private youth-serving agencies, or order commitment to a mental institution or adult correctional agency.[3]

The most formal dispositions used in the juvenile court include probation and commitment. Probation involves placing the child under the supervision of a probation officer for the purpose of community treatment.[4] Probation accounts for over 90 percent of all juvenile dispositions. Conditions of probation are normally imposed on the child by either statute or court order and are of two kinds. There are general conditions, such as requiring the child to "stay away from other delinquents" or demanding "that he must obey the law." These types of conditions are often vague but have been upheld by the courts. More specific conditions of probation include requiring the child to participate in a vocational training program, attend school regularly, obtain treatment at a child guidance clinic, or make restitution.

Once placed on probation, the child is ordinarily required to meet regularly with the probation officer for counseling and supervision and to adhere to the conditions of probation established by the court. This plan may continue for a period of time, possibly six months to two years, depending upon the duration of probation established in the statutes. Most states allow the child to be released early from probation if he or she is making a good adjustment; they also permit an extension of the probation period. If the child complies with the court order, his or her probation is terminated. Proceedings to revoke probation occur if the there is a violation of the conditions of probation or if the child commits a new offense. Most states provide that the child shall have notice, a hearing, right to counsel, and other due process safeguards similar to those provided to adult offenders at such proceedings.

The most severe of the statutory dispositions available to the juvenile court is committing the child to a juvenile institution.[5] This may involve sending the child to a state training school or a private residential treatment facility. Some jurisdictions distinguish in their placement procedures between delinquent and status offenders and prohibit committing incorrigible youth to training schools for delinquent children. The reason for such an approach is generally based on the theory that only children who commit crimes should be placed in state institutions.

Most states statutes vary on the length of the child's commitment. Traditionally, many jurisdictions would commit children up to their majority, which usually meant until they reached the age of twenty-one. This form of sentencing normally deprived the children of their freedom for a long period of time—sometimes longer than that imposed on an adult sentenced for the same offense. Some court decisions have argued that such an approach may be a denial of the child's due process and equal protection rights. As a result, some states have sought to avoid this problem by passing legislation committing children for periods varying from one to three years. In certain jurisdictions, the court may be authorized to extend the original period of commitment.

During the past decade, the treatment-oriented philosophy has taken a backseat to the development of more formal and punitive laws aimed at juveniles charged with serious crimes.[6] Although more than half the states still use indefinite sentencing, the trend is toward more determinate and fixed sentences. As a result, the juvenile institutional population has increased in recent years, and incarceration has become the disposition of choice, particularly for serious juvenile offenders.

DISPOSITIONAL HEARING

Case Comment

In re Roberts focuses on the dispositional stage of the juvenile justice process. Roberts, a minor, was tried and sentenced to a state training school nearly one year after an incident in which he allegedly assaulted and injured another youth. In analyzing the facts of the case, the appellate court notes the mutual culpability of both boys in the altercation. Furthermore, it acknowledges the fact that separate trial and dispositional hearings were not held. Considering these circumstances, it is suggested that the trial court probably had limited knowledge of the youth's background and therefore was not able to be consistent with the statutory objectives of keeping a youth in the community at all possible costs. This decision reflects the doctrine that disposition must incorporate the "physical, mental and moral" interest of the child and not his or her delinquency.

IN RE ROBERTS

Court of Special Appeals of Maryland, 1971.
13 Md.App. 644, 284 A.2d 621.

Moylan, Judge.

The appellant, George Roberts, at that time a twelve year old, 7th grade student at the Pimlico Junior High School, was charged on the petition of Joseph E. Maddox, the Security Officer at that school, with being a delinquent child in that on April 7, 1970, he "assaulted and beat by jumping on his back, knocking him to the ground, and choking him, David Horowitz." Significantly, the petition was not filed until November 19, 1970, seven months after the alleged assault. After a hearing on March 31, 1971, one week short of a full year after the alleged assault, before the Division for Juvenile Causes of the Circuit Court for Baltimore City, the appellant was adjudged to be a delinquent child and was committed to the custody of the Department of Juvenile Services for transfer to the Boys' Village. He contends on this appeal that the court erred by committing him to a training school.

We are constrained to agree. The very presence of his case upon the docket of the Juvenile Court, suggests some answer as to why those courts, nationally, are suffering under almost untriable caseloads. The appellant here had no record of prior experience of any sort with the courts. The incident which gave rise to this case was, under any interpretation, a "schoolboy fight." The fight occurred immediately outside the Pimlico Junior High School within minutes after the "last bell" had dismissed the pupils for the day on April 7, 1970. The appellant, who at the time of trial was thirteen years of age and weighed 93 pounds, was on the day of the fight twelve years of age and weighed between 83 and 85 pounds. The alleged victim of the assault, David Horowitz, on the day of the fight was also twelve years of age and weighed approximately 150 pounds. David was a Little League baseball player. Some three years earlier, the appellant and David had been classmates in the fourth grade at the Fallstaff Elementary School. At the time of the fight, they were, although no longer classmates, both students in the seventh grade at the Pimlico Junior High School. Their lockers were located in the same cor-

ridor but were separated from each other by the width of that corridor.

The incident that ultimately escalated into the fight occurred some few minutes before school was dismissed for the day, when the students were permitted to go to their lockers immediately before returning to their homerooms to be dismissed. David shared a locker with a fellow student. For some ill-defined reason, David and his locker partner had a disagreement about the opening of the locker. According to David, mere words were exchanged between them. According to the appellant, David pushed his locker partner. In any event, the appellant interjected himself into the dispute on the side of David's locker partner and ordered David "to stop pushing him around." At that point, it was incumbent upon all of the students to return to their respective homerooms.

As they were parting company, it is clear that there was some contact on the part of David directed toward the appellant. According to David himself, the appellant and several other persons were standing in his way as he attempted to proceed into the door of his classroom and his contact amounted to nothing more than pushing his way through. According to the appellant, as soon as he had ordered David not to push his locker partner, David immediately crossed the corridor, pushed the appellant and started laughing. Whether the contact at which the appellant took umbrage was as recited in the former version or as in the latter version, it is clear that the appellant responded to that contact with the words, "Wait until you get outside." A few minutes later, the last bell rang and the students left the school for the day. When David got outside, the appellant was waiting for him. Once the boys were outside the school building, the appellant, whether in response to a real or an imagined provocation, was clearly the aggressor. Fortuitously for David, his mother was parked a few feet away to drive him home from school. As he exited the building, there was eye contact between him and his mother. Mrs. Horowitz and David gave one version of the fight which ensued; the appellant gives another. There were no other witnesses.

According to David and his mother, the appellant approached David initially from the rear, grabbed him by the neck and "flipped" him down. David then got up and pushed the appellant out of his way. David picked up his books, which had fallen to the ground, and started walking. The appellant grabbed him a second time, by the shoulders, and pulled him down again. The appellant grabbed David around the neck and banged his head onto the concrete "four or five" times.

According to the appellant, he approached David from the front and said, "David, I told you when I get outside I was going to hit you back." He then hit David. He testified that David then saw his mother in the car and "started going wild with me." The two then wrestled each other to the ground. The appellant testified that they were on the grass and not on concrete. He asserted that they went to the ground only one time instead of twice, that they both were exchanging blows, that he was hit on the neck at least once by David, but at the moment the fight ended, it was he (the appellant) who was on top.

The fight was ended by the timely intervention of Mrs. Horowitz. It is clear that she grabbed the appellant from behind and pulled him off of her son and that she then carried him to Mr. Maddox, the school Security Officer. All versions of the intervention coincide, except for the additional detail asserted by the appellant that Mrs. Horowitz "had her fingernails down in my neck" and that, despite his protestations that he knew how to walk, "she kept them in there until we got to the office."

David and his mother both testified that he suffered a broken foot, contusions and a sprained neck. David acknowledged that his head was not cut or bleeding and that he received no stitches. He acknowledged that the contusions complained of consisted of a scrape on the inside of his wrist that required neither stitches nor bandaging. He acknowledged that he received no medical treatment for the sprained neck but that it was sore when he tried to use it. Mrs. Horowitz testified that she took her son to a Dr. Baitch, an orthopedic doctor, and that he placed a cast on David's right foot which remained on for four or five weeks. She testified that she paid a medical bill to Dr. Baitch of $125. It was David who testified that his foot had been broken and that the damage to his foot had occurred when he "fell the first time."

Mr. Maddox, the Security Officer, testified that at about 2:35 p.m. on April 7, 1970, Mrs. Horowitz brought the appellant to him, explained that he had just attacked her son, and indicated that "she wanted action taken." Mr. Maddox sent the appellant into the building and told him to wait there until his parents had been notified of the difficulty. Mr. Mad-

dox further testified that it is not his policy to file juvenile petitions in cases such as this unless there is a weapon involved or unless "parents insist that I press charges." There was clearly no weapon involved in this case. Mr. Maddox indicated that the petition here was filed because of parental insistence.

We do not question the finding of the court below that the actions of the appellant technically constituted an act of delinquency since those same actions, if committed by an adult, would technically have constituted an assault. It is rather the disposition, commitment to a training school, which gives us pause.

We think the trial court was initially in error in not holding a separate dispositional hearing distinct from the adjudicatory hearing on the question of delinquency. As Chief Judge Murphy said for this Court in the case of *Matter of Wooten*, Md.App., 284 A.2d 32, (1971):

> That a disposition hearing separate and distinct from the delinquency adjudication hearing is required subsequent to the finding of delinquency is plainly mandated by Article 26, Section 70–17 and by the provisions of Maryland Rules 912 (The Adjudicatory Hearing) and 913 (Disposition Hearing). The reason for such a bifurcated process is equally clear. The adjudicatory hearing is solely to determine the merits of the allegations of delinquency. Section 70–17. The disposition hearing is to determine whether the delinquent child is in need of 'supervision, treatment, or rehabilitation' and, if so, the nature required. Section 70–1(y). Consistent, with that determination the juvenile judge is enjoined by Section 70–19 to "make disposition as most suited to the physical, mental, and moral welfare of the child." To assist the court in making a proper disposition, Section 70–14(a) contemplates that it will direct a probation officer or other qualified agency to make a study and report to it "concerning the child, his family, his environment, and other matters relevant to the disposition of the case." Section 70–14(c) provides that as part of such study the child or his parents may be examined by a physician, psychiatrist, psychologist or other professionally qualified person.

In addition to and probably because of the procedural defect inherent in the disposition before us here for review, we hold that all of the factors were not considered that should go into a proper determination of what disposition to make of a juvenile adjudged to be delinquent. In the case of *In re Hamill*, 10 Md.App. 586, at 591, 271 A.2d 762, at 765 we said, "(T)he mere fact of delinquency, without more, ordinarily does not justify the taking of the child from his parents and his commitment to a State training school." In *Hamill*, again in the case of *In re Arnold*, 12 Md.App. 384, 278 A.2d 658, and in *Wooten*, *supra*, we pointed out that judges should, "in making dispositions in juvenile cases, think not in terms of guilt, but of the child's need for protection or rehabilitation; we said that the juvenile court is to make dispositions so as to provide for the care, protection and wholesome mental and physical development of the child by a program of treatment, training and rehabilitation consistent with the protection of the public interests." *Wooten*, *supra*.

In the instant case, the trial judge did not have the benefit of any information about the background of the appellant here, about his home life and his parents, about his school record, nor about any of those things which would aid in a determination of whether or not he was a fit candidate for rehabilitation. Nor did he, we feel, bear in mind, in making a disposition, that the Maryland law clearly contemplates the retention of a delinquent child in his home wherever possible, if that is consistent with his own as well as the public interest. *In Re Hamill*, *supra*, 10 Md.App. at 591–592, 271 A.2d 762. Two of the legislative purposes underlying enactment of the now-governing juvenile statute are set forth in Sections 70(3) and 70(4) and expressly articulate the objective as:

> (3) To place a [delinquent] child in a wholesome family environment whenever possible.
>
> (4) To separate a [delinquent] child from his parents only when necessary for his welfare or in the interest of public safety.

It appears clear, in the instant case, that the trial judge based his disposition primarily on the nature of the delinquent act itself and, seemingly to some extent at least, on conditions generally in this school and in other schools:

> I am aware of the fact that I believe that this was the first time that George has been in this court, or in a court, however, I do not subscribe to the theory that everybody is entitled to one bite out of the apple. I think it depends on what that bite is, and I don't believe anybody is entitled to the kind of bite of a brutal assault of this nature resulting in serious injuries to this boy, and which could have resulted in far more serious injuries, when a boy's head is being bashed against concrete several times, it could lead to very serious injuries. Fortunately, in that respect those injuries didn't develop here.   *   *   *

> I am aware of the testimony and I, myself, cannot treat lightly these kinds of aggressive assaults, unprovoked assaults of innocent people, and I recall the testimony also that when David looked up, there were boys surrounding him, and I think that we are unfortunately witness to, in our schools, and around our schools, are so extremely serious with violent acts, wherein, children are just innocent victims of these attacks. We are beyond the area of physical harm that is being done to the children, we have a climate of fear on the part of these children when they go to school, and they have to go there and live there in an atmosphere of fear, where they are afraid to do certain things in and around the school, where they are afraid to go to certain places in and about the school, where the parents each day are plagued with fears when the child leaves the home; what may happen to him, is he going to be safe, is he not going to be safe. This terrible atmosphere of fear that we have in our schools today is a horrible thing, and it is the kind of act which is leading directly to that, and it is leading, I might say, to a very rapid erosion of the quality of our school system, because we are seeing parents of both races, wherever they are able to, to get their children out of the public school system to get them into private schools, to get them into the counties because of the great fear of the climate in our public schools today, and this, to me, is a terrible commentary on the course that our public school system is taking now with regard to the quality of the young people who are being taken out of it.

> I don't expect anybody to be remorseful of the things he can do, but he admitted he committed an assault. I see here no remorse, or regret on the part of the Respondent. I think he is trying to lie his way out of this thing and paint an untrue picture. And for these reasons, I am going to commit him to the Department of Juvenile Services for commitment to the appropriate training school.

We feel here, as we did in *Wooten*:

> However relevant the nature of the delinquent act and the circumstances surrounding its commission may be in making a proper disposition, those factors cannot be applied without regard to, or wholly apart from, the child's best interests and those of the public viewed in light of the purposes underlying the juvenile law. In other words, to make disposition "most suited to the physical, mental and moral welfare of the child" under Section 70–19 requires that the juvenile judge consider more than the delinquent act itself, no matter how extreme or violent it may have been. On the record before us, we conclude that the court's determination to commit appellant to a training school was not reached in conformity with the procedural requirements of the

law governing juvenile dispositions, nor was it based on sufficient information or knowledge to justify it.

The record before us contains nothing to indicate or suggest that the appellant's physical, mental and moral welfare would be served from separating him from his parents and committing him to a training school. We feel that this case should be remanded without affirmance or reversal for further consideration by the juvenile judge with respect to the proper disposition to be made. In the course of such reconsideration, we think it appropriate that the court hear evidence concerning the appellant's conduct and behavior from the time of his delinquent act, in April of 1970, to the time of the hearing on remand, including his public school record, as well as evidence relating to his family background.

Judgment adjudicating appellant a delinquent child affirmed; case remanded without affirmance or reversal for further proceedings in accordance with this opinion with respect to the matter of the proper disposition to be made.

DISPOSITIONAL PROCEDURES AND COURT DISCRETION

Case Comment

In addition to substantive findings, appellate courts have also ruled on procedural matters in the juvenile court disposition process.

In re J.L.P. involves the violation of statutory rights during a dispositionary hearing. At J.L.P.'s initial hearing, the trial judge advised him that he had the option of having his case tried in the juvenile court or waived to the adult system. However, he was warned that due to the seriousness of the charges against him, the choice of juvenile court would probably result in a placement with the California Youth Authority. Although it recognized that the trial judge had attempted to shield J.L.P. from a felony conviction, the appellate court reversed the finding on the grounds that the pretrial statement of intent violated the youth's right to disposition solely on the basis of social evidence and not the seriousness of his crime.

Other examples of dispositional procedures in the juvenile court can be found in the cases of *In re Cecilia R.* and *In the Matter of D.S.F.* The case of Cecilia R. concerns a girl who was deprived of her right to be present during most of her dispositional hearing. On consideration of the case, the appellate court reversed the placement order, arguing that

absence from the hearing deprived Cecilia R. of her right to react to the testimony and advise counsel of the veracity of the evidence.[7]

In *In the Matter of D.S.F.*, the Minnesota Court of Appeals concluded that the evidence at the juvenile's trial for assault was sufficient to prove intent and that the court order of restitution and a ninety-day placement was not an abuse of its judicial discretion.[8]

IN RE J. L. P.

Court of Appeals, First District, 1972.
25 Cal. App. 3d 86, 100 Cal. Rptr. 601.

Harold C. Brown, Associate Judge.

This is an appeal from a judgment and order of the Superior Court of the County of Santa Clara, sitting as a juvenile court, declaring appellant a ward of said court and committing him to the California Youth Authority.

In April 1971, a petition was filed in the Superior Court for Santa Clara County, in session as a juvenile court, alleging that appellant, a person under the age of 21 years, came within the provisions of California Welfare & Institutions Code section 602 in that on April 7, 1971, he violated California Penal Code sections 261, subdivision 3 (Count I—rape), 236 (Count II—false imprisonment) and 207 (Count III—kidnapping).

When appellant first appeared with his attorney in superior court, in session as a juvenile court, he was informed by the court that he had two choices: he could be tried in the adult court, or, if he was tried in the juvenile court and if any court of the petition was sustained that appellant would be committed to the Youth Authority. Defense counsel, after consulting with appellant, agreed to remain in the juvenile court.

A further hearing was thereafter held and the court reiterated its earlier determination that if appellant remained in juvenile court, he would be committed to the Youth Authority. The court stated that appellant was "not amenable to the Juvenile Court services" and the only reason he was permitted to remain was to protect his record. The court also noted that appellant was "for all intents and purposes emancipated" and that an earlier term of probation had proven ineffective.

Thereafter the petition was read and appellant was informed of his constitutional rights. Appellant admitted Counts I and III, and the court dismissed Count II in the interest of justice. The court found the allegations in the petition to be true and that appellant was a minor coming within the provisions of California Welfare and Institutions Code section 602. The court declared appellant a ward of the court and ordered him committed to the California Youth Authority.

It is contended on appeal that the court committed error in refusing to hear evidence concerning the disposition to be made of appellant after he had plead guilty to two of the charges in the petition.

Preliminarily, reference is made to the pertinent sections of the Welfare and Institutions Code which disclose a sophisticated, specially designed procedure for retention of jurisdiction and the disposition of juveniles charged under sections 600, 601, and 602 of that code.

Section 650 et seq., provides that the filing of a petition commences proceedings to declare the minor a ward of the court. Section 675 et seq., provides for the hearing of this petition. At the hearing, the court must first determine whether or not it has jurisdiction. (Welf. & Inst. Code, § 701.) Appellant was charged under section 602, i. e., that the appellant was under the age of 21 years and had violated a law defining crime.

Appellant was charged with rape, false imprisonment and kidnapping. He plead guilty to rape and kidnapping and was, therefore, properly within the jurisdiction of the court.

After determining the issue of jurisdiction, the second or dispositional phase must be considered and all relevant evidence must be heard. (Welf. & Inst. Code, § 706.) In determining disposition, section 731 gives the court authority to commit the minor to the Youth Authority, but section 726 makes it mandatory prior to a commitment that *the court find* (1) the parent or guardian is incapable of caring for the minor, or (2) that the minor has been tried on probation and failed to reform, or (3) that the welfare of the minor requires that he be taken from the custody of the parent or guardian.

Section 707 further provides that in the case of individuals over 16 years of age who are charged under section 602, if, at any time during the hearing, the court finds that the minor would not be amenable to the care, treatment and training of the juvenile court facilities, the court may dismiss the petition and direct the district attorney to prosecute under the applicable criminal statutes.

In *In re R.*, 1 Cal. 3d 855, 859–860, 83 Cal. Rptr. 671, 464 P. 2d 127, the Supreme Court held that it was reversible error for the court to review the social study before determination of the issue of jurisdiction.

Likewise it is error to commit the minor merely because of the gravity of the crime. Such order would in effect be punitive. Juvenile court authorities are not designed to punish.

The court in *In re R.*, *supra*, 1 Cal. 3d 855, 859, 83 Cal. Rptr. 671, 674, 464 P. 2d 127, 130, stated: "The history of Welfare and Institutions Code sections 701 [fn. omitted], 702 [fn. omitted], and 706 [fn. omitted] clearly indicates that the Legislature intended to create a bifurcated juvenile court procedure in which the court would first determine whether the facts of the case would support the jurisdiction of the court in declaring a wardship and *thereafter* would consider the social study report at a hearing on the appropriate disposition of that ward. [fn. omitted] * * * * "

The theory underlying this legislative policy is that once the minor has been declared a fit subject for juvenile treatment, the court exists not for punishment but to help him. Thus, the considerations relative to the proper disposition of the minor are different from those that bear upon a determination that a crime has been committed.

The appellant here was given the alternative of being treated as a juvenile and committed to the Youth Authority or to be prosecuted as an adult. *The court decision to commit was made prior to a determination of the jurisdictional and dispositional phases as required under the provisions of the Welfare and Institutions Code.* The appellant accepted commitment only after these alternatives were presented to him.

The court at the time of the commitment of appellant to the Youth Authority had before it the probation officer's report which was divided into two parts: "Jurisdiction" and "Social Study," and the social study portion of the report treated the following areas: "Previous Referrals," "Additional Circumstances," "Present Whereabouts of Minor," "Probation Adjustment," "Statement of Minor," "Statement of Parents," "School Report," "Juvenile Hall Report," "Personal and Family Background," "Evaluation" and "Recommendation." As such, it was received into evidence by the trial judge and was read and considered. The court, however, denied appellant's offer to present testimony of counselors in juvenile hall, testimony of his parents, his employer and job foreman. Welfare and Institutions Code section 706 requires that such relevant testimony be received when offered. Furthermore, the court did not indicate the basis for its determination that appellant be removed from the custody of his parents; no showing was made of abuse or neglect by the parents. While Welfare and Institutions Code section 726 provides no criteria for determining when the welfare of the minor requires that he be removed from the custody of his parents, it is clear that there must be some facts and evidence to support this finding. (*In re L.*, 267 Cal.App.2d 397, 406, 73 Cal.Rptr. 76.) We recognize that the court, in prejudging the issue of disposition, had the best interests of appellant in mind. It was desirous of protecting the minor from a felony record. The court, however, by its predetermination of disposition and its refusal to hear the offered evidence, was in error. We do not imply, of course, nor should there be any inference, as to the ultimate disposition of the youth. We determine only that such decision as to disposition be made after all available evidence has been submitted.

We have concluded that the judgment and order of commitment to the Youth Authority be reversed and that the matter be remanded to the superior court sitting as the juvenile court to consider evidence as to the appropriate disposition of appellant.

Draper, P. J., and Caldecott, J., concur.

CONDITIONS AND REVOCATION OF PROBATION

Case Comment

Violation of the conditions of probation may result in a court-ordered termination of community-based correction and rehabilitation. *In re Davis* deals with the procedural rights associated with probation revocation in Pennsylvania and concludes that juveniles are entitled to due process protections similar to those available to adults in such proceedings.

In re Green is another example that illustrates the use of judicial discretion in revocation decision mak-

ing. Green had his probation revoked as a result of his participation in a demonstration that violated the condition that he "stay out of trouble." His appeal stated that the vagueness of this order violated his Fourteenth Amendment rights. In deciding for the defendant, the appellate court argued that conditions of probation are usually broad and that the admonition to stay out of trouble is no more vague than the statement "violate no laws." Moreover, the court ruled that behavior that constituted grounds for probation revocation need not actually fall within the jurisdictional boundary of the juvenile court.[9]

IN INTEREST OF DAVIS

Cite as 546 A.2d 1149 (Pa.Super. 1988)

Karl Baker, Asst. Public Defender, Philadelphia, for appellant.

Before Cirillo, President Judge, and Cavanaugh, Rowley, Wieand, McEwen, Olszewski, Beck, Tamilia and Popovich, JJ.

Wieand, Judge:

[1–5] In this proceeding to review the probationary status of a juvenile because of "problems in the home," the court revoked probation and ordered the juvenile committed based on his probation officer's testimony, over objection,[1] that "[the juvenile's] father advised me that [the juvenile] pulled a knife on him." On appeal, the juvenile contends that his probation was revoked improperly and he was deprived of his liberty on the basis of hearsay testimony without an opportunity to confront his accuser.

Harvey Davis had been adjudicated delinquent on May 6, 1985 on a charge of simple assault. At the dispositional hearing, he had been placed on probation upon the condition that he attend school, with no absences, lateness, or suspensions.

On August 28, 1985, Davis's probation officer filed a motion to review the order of probation, with a request that Davis be committed to Glen Mills Diagnostic Center, because of "problems in the home

---

1. The objection, although general, was adequate to preserve the court's evidentiary ruling for appellate review. Where only a general objection is made, the admission of the evidence is not grounds for reversal if it is proper for any purpose. *Commonwealth v. Bell*, 288 Pa. 29, 35, 135 A. 645, 647 (1927); *Commonwealth v. Marshall*, 287 Pa. 512, 521, 135 A. 301, 304 (1926); *Fischer v. Anderson*, 173 Pa.Super. 175, 179, 96 A.2d 168, 170 (1953). See also: Henry on Pennsylvania Evidence, § 724. The better practice is to state specifically the reason for the objection. When this is done, all other reasons for excluding the evidence are deemed waived. *Commonwealth ex rel. Wilkes v. Maroney*, 423 Pa. 113, 119, 222 A.2d 856, 860 (1966); *Commonwealth v. Markwich*, 178 Pa.Super. 169, 172, 113 A.2d 323, 325 (1955); *Huffman v. Simmons*, 131 Pa.Super. 370, 375, 200 A. 274, 276 (1938).

and [Davis] appears to be in need of an extensive diagnostic study."

At the revocation hearing, the following occurred:

PROBATION OFFICER: . . . I got involved with the case because of [Harvey's] father some time ago, and there was quite a bit of disturbance in the home between Harvey and his father and Harvey's father advised me that Harvey pulled a knife on him—
DEFENSE ATTORNEY: Objection, respectfully.
THE COURT: Overruled.
PROBATION OFFICER: And he protected himself, and that there were threats against Harvey and Harvey didn't want to stay home, and as a result of that, I felt it was the best thing to bring the case back to court . . . .

At the conclusion of the hearing, Davis's counsel renewed his objection to the hearsay testimony of the probation officer and argued that no basis for revocation had been presented. The court revoked probation and committed appellant to the Glen Mills Diagnostic Center.

On appeal, Davis argues that his right to confrontation under the state and federal constitutions was violated when the trial court based its decision to revoke probation solely on the hearsay testimony of the probation officer.[2] We agree and reverse.

[6] The Juvenile Act in Pennsylvania, 42 Pa.C.S. § 6301 et seq., provides specifically that in adjudicatory proceedings, extrajudicial statements which would be constitutionally inadmissible in a criminal proceeding shall not be used against a juvenile. See: 42 Pa.C.S. § 6338(b). In dispositional hearings, however, the statute provides that "all evidence helpful in determining the questions presented, including oral and written reports, may be received by the court and relied upon to the extent of its probative value even though not otherwise competent in the hearing on the petition." 42 Pa.C.S. § 6341(d). With respect to probation revocation hearings, the Act is silent. See: 42 Pa.C.S. § 6324(5). For constitutional reasons hereinafter stated, however, we hold that a juvenile's probation cannot be revoked solely on the basis of extrajudicial statements made by an accuser whom the juvenile has not been permitted to confront.

The leading decision regarding the constitutional safeguards which are applicable to juveniles is *Application of Gault*, 387 U.S. 1, 87 S.Ct. 1428, 18 L.Ed.2d 527 (1967). The Supreme Court there observed:

Juvenile Court history has again demonstrated that unbridled discretion, however benevolently motivated, is frequently a poor substitute for principle and procedure. In 1937, Dean Pound wrote: "The powers of the Star Chamber were a trifle in comparison with those of our juvenile courts. . . . The absence of substantive standards has not necessarily meant that children receive careful, compassionate, individualized treatment. The absence of procedural rules based upon constitutional principle has not always produced fair, efficient, and effective procedures. Departures from established principles of due process have frequently resulted not in enlightened procedure but in arbitrariness.

Id. at 18–19, 87 S.Ct. at 1438–1439, 18 L.Ed.2d at 541. Therefore, the Court determined that certain fundamental due process rights which had been recognized in adult criminal proceedings were applicable also in juvenile proceedings. The Court reasoned that a balance had to be struck between fundamental procedural protections and the goals of the juvenile court system to ensure that juvenile proceedings "measure[d] up to the essentials of due process and fair treatment." *Id.* at 30, 87 S.Ct. at 1445, 18 L.Ed.2d at 548. With respect to the adjudicatory phase of a juvenile proceeding, the Court held, an alleged juvenile offender is entitled to receive notice of the charges, to be represented by counsel, to confront his accuser, to cross-examine witnesses, and to be free of the constraints of self-incrimination. In addition, proof beyond a reasonable doubt has been held necessary in order to adjudicate a juvenile delinquent. *In re Winship*, 397 U.S. 358, 90 S.Ct. 1068, 25 L.Ed.2d 368 (1970). Double jeopardy principles are also applicable to juvenile proceedings. *Breed v. Jones*, 421 U.S. 519, 95 S.Ct. 1779, 44 L.Ed.2d 346 (1975). However, the Constitution does not guarantee the right to trial by jury in juvenile proceedings. *McKeiver v. Pennsylvania*, 403 U.S. 528, 91 S.Ct. 1976, 29 L.Ed.2d 647 (1971).

[7] Because a juvenile is entitled to confront his accuser, an adjudication of delinquency which is

---

2. The probation officer also testified, in response to an inquiry by the court, that Davis had been absent from school. Davis's attorney objected to this testimony on the ground that Davis had had no prior notice that he was being charged with violating probation because of absence from school. The court overruled the objection, stating, "It is additional information." Appellant argues that this was error. In its opinion, however, the juvenile court has stated that it did not consider this testimony and that it did not have any effect on its decision to revoke the juvenile's probation. Therefore, we find it unnecessary to review this aspect of appellant's hearing.

based solely on hearsay evidence will be reversed. *In Interest of LaMore*, 356 Pa.Super. 322, 514 A.2d 633 (1986); *Commonwealth v. McNaughton*, 252 Pa.Super. 302, 381 A.2d 929 (1977).

In *Morrissey v. Brewer*, 408 U.S. 471, 92 S.Ct. 2593, 33 L.Ed.2d 484 (1972), the Supreme Court held, in the context of adult proceedings, that a parolee had a substantial interest in retaining liberty until it had been determined that he had violated the conditions of his parole and that, therefore, parole could not be revoked absent due process. Although "the full panoply of rights" is not available, the Court said, a structured procedure, albeit informal, is necessary to assure that a revocation of parole will not be based on unverified facts or an inaccurate analysis of the circumstances. Thus, the Court formulated a two step procedure. The first step, similar to a preliminary hearing, is a factual inquiry to determine the existence of probable cause. The second step combines the factfinding function with the exercise of discretion to determine whether revocation of parole is necessary. In both proceedings, there exist conditional rights to confront accusers and cross-examine witnesses. In the first step, these rights must be recognized unless it is determined that disclosure of the identity of an informant will create a risk of harm to him. In the second step, the right to confront and cross-examine an accuser can be denied only upon a finding of good cause.

These rights are also accorded to an adult probationer in proceedings to revoke probation. In *Gagnon v. Scarpelli*, 411 U.S. 778, 93 S.Ct. 1756, 36 L.Ed.2d 656 (1973), the Supreme Court said, "Probation revocation is not a stage of a criminal prosecution, but does result in a loss of liberty." *Id.* at 783, 93 S.Ct. at 1760, 36 L.Ed.2d at 661–662. Therefore, "a probationer can no longer be denied due process . . . [on the ground] that probation is an 'act of grace.' " *Id.* at 783 n. 4, 93 S.Ct. at 1760 n. 4, 36 L.Ed.2d at 662 n. 4. See also: *Commonwealth v. Kavanaugh*, 334 Pa.Super. 151, 482 A.2d 1128 (1984).

The appellate courts in Pennsylvania have held unequivocally that "probation revocation proceedings entail the right to confront and cross-examine accusers." *Commonwealth v. Riley*, 253 Pa.Super. 260, 267, 384 A.2d 1333, 1336 (1978). "[B]efore hearsay testimony may be admitted, the hearing judge must make a finding that there is good cause for not allowing confrontation." *Commonwealth v. Holmes*, 268 Pa.Super. 396, 399, 408 A.2d 846, 848 (1979). See also: *In the Interest of Bonner*, 301 Pa.Super.

431, 447 A.2d 1043 (1982); *Gartner v. Comm., Penna. Bd. of Probation and Parole*, 79 Pa.Cmwlth. 141, 469 A.2d 1371 (1983).

[8,9] A juvenile has the same substantial interest in retaining his liberty as an adult. See: *State ex rel D.E. v. Dougherty*, 298 S.E.2d 834 (W.Va.1982). Similarly, society's interests in a juvenile probationer are no different than its interests in an adult probationer or parolee. It has been said that:

> [a] parolee is not the only one who has a stake in conditional liberty. Society has a stake in whatever may be the chance of restoring him to a normal and useful life within the law. Society thus has an interest in not having parole revoked because of erroneous information or because of an erroneous evaluation of the need to revoke parole, given the breach of conditions.

Morrisey v. Brewer, supra, at 484, 92 S.Ct. at 2601, 33 L.Ed.2d at 496.

[10] In view of the substantial liberty interests which exist in not having probation revoked on the basis of unverified facts or erroneous information, we conclude that due process considerations entailing the right to confront and cross-examine an accuser must extend to probation revocation proceedings for a juvenile. In *Gault*, the Supreme Court said:

> The informality of juvenile court hearings frequently leads to the admission of hearsay and unsworn testimony. It is said that "close adherence to the strict rules of evidence might prevent the court from obtaining important facts as to the child's character and condition which could only be to the child's detriment." The assumption is that the judge will give normally inadmissible evidence only its proper weight. It is also declared in support of these evidentiary practices that the juvenile court is not a criminal court, that the importance of the hearsay rule has been overestimated, and that allowing an attorney to make "technical objections" would disrupt the desired informality of the proceedings. *But to the extent that the rules of evidence are not merely technical or historical, but like the hearsay rule have a sound basis in human experience, they should not be rejected in any judicial inquiry.*

Application of Gault, supra 387 U.S. at 11 n. 7, 87 S.Ct. at 1435 n. 7, 18 L.Ed.2d at 537 n. 7, quoting, Note, *Juvenile Delinquents: The Police, State Courts, and Individualized Justice*, 79 Harv.L.Rev. 775, 794–795 (1966) (footnotes omitted) (emphasis added). By ignoring the hearsay exclusion, "[t]he great engine of cross-examination would lie unused while error and perjury would travel untrammeledly to an unreliable and often tainted judgment." *Johnson v. Peoples Cab Co.*, 386 Pa. 513, 514, 126 A.2d 720, 721 (1956).

There can be no benefit to the juvenile, to society, or to the integrity of the juvenile court system to permit Davis's probation to be revoked solely on the basis of a hearsay declaration by his father without requiring the father to appear and be cross-examined. The goals of the juvenile system will not be defeated or even threatened by wrapping probation revocation proceedings in the same safeguards which apply to adult revocation hearings in order to insure the reliability of the information upon which a court is required to act. We conclude, therefore, that it was error to base the revocation of appellant's probation solely on an extrajudicial statement made by appellant's father to appellant's probation officer.

The order revoking appellant's probation is reversed.

INSTITUTIONAL COMMITMENT OF DELINQUENCY OFFENDERS

Case Comment

Institutional commitment is often considered the most severe of all juvenile dispositions. Most state juvenile codes have adhered to the principle of the "least restrictive alternative approach" in juvenile sentencing.[10]

The case of *Scott L. v. State* deals with a punitive placement disposition. In this case, a sixteen-year-old was adjudicated delinquent for selling drugs and committed by the juvenile court to "a place of involuntary confinement and punitive incarceration." The appellate court sustained that juvenile court's decision, stating that the "public interest was served by institutionalization for the purpose of deterrence" in this case.

In the case of *In re Aline D.*, the Los Angeles County Juvenile Court placed the juvenile with the California Youth Authority, while expressing doubt that she could benefit from such commitment. On appeal, the Supreme Court indicated that commitment proceedings are designed for purposes of rehabilitation, not necessarily punishment, and if no

appropriate placement exists, proceedings against the juvenile should be dismissed.[11]

SCOTT L. v. STATE
760 P.2d 134 (1988).

Springer, Justice:

Appellant Scott L., a sixteen-year-old high school student, was heavily involved in the sale of marijuana to his fellow students. Following a sale of marijuana to an undercover drug enforcement agent the minor was adjudicated a delinquent and committed by the juvenile court to the Spring Mountain Youth Camp, a "place of involuntary confinement and punitive incarceration." See *Glenda Kay S., A Minor v. State*, 103 Nev. 53, 732 P.2d 1356 (1987). The sole reason given by the presiding juvenile court judge for such disposition was the "deterrent effect" of incarcerating a youthful drug dealer. We approve of the juvenile court's decision in this case and affirm its dispositional order.

[1] The juvenile court judge wisely and properly (see *Glenda Kay*) stated in open court his reasons for ordering this punitive disposition, namely, that "[t]here is a deterrent effect by incarcerating" a youth who engages in the sale of marijuana to other minors. Said the judge:

> When children sell [drugs] to children, the other children in the community are watching, all right. There is a deterrent effect by incarcerating. . . .
>
>   . . . .
>
> [B]y removal from the community, removing them from their friends, kids talk, they know who is gone, they know who is back in the community. . . .
>
> [I]t is in the public's interest to institutionalize this young man for at least the first semester of the school year, because I believe very strongly that it is "in order to deter them or others."

[2] The minor claims, citing *Glenda Kay*, above, that there is not in this case "sufficient reason to depart from the presumption that a child should be placed in his home" and to put him in confinement.[1]

---

1. The minor also claims that the juvenile court judge erred by acting upon a "self-imposed policy of sending all children who commit such acts to an institution, with rare exception." The judge did observe that "approximately every one of those children" who were involved in high school drug trafficking had been sent away. This observation does not show a fixed predisposition or policy on the judge's part. For this reason and because appellant has cited no authority to support this claim of error, we decline to consider the point. *Cunningham v. State*, 94 Nev. 128, 575 P.2d 936 (1978). We do note with some chagrin that appellant's counsel has misstated the record to us, saying that "the Judge stated on the record, 'I think on its own merits, he would have probably been sent home on probation by itself.'" The judge did not say this; Scott's mother did.

We deem the deterrence of others from engaging in drug sales in our schools to be "sufficient reason" to incarcerate a youth adjudged guilty of such criminal conduct, and we see the juvenile court as having acted in an eminently wise and prudent manner in deciding upon this disposition. See *Glenda Kay*.

[3] Factors other than deterrence present themselves in justification of the juvenile court's removal of Scott from the community and his commitment to Spring Mountain. In *Glenda Kay* we noted that the integrity of the criminal law is maintained by seeing to it that those who commit crimes are punished. We noted also that punitive incarceration may be justified in juvenile cases for serious criminal violations because the youthful offender deserves to be punished.

To permit Scott to remain at home and escape any appreciable punitive sanction for so serious a crime would tend to be destructive of the integrity of the criminal law.[2] When the law is broken something must be done about it. The law must be vindicated; otherwise, it loses its meaning and effect as law. Scott is described in the record as a "middleman in drug sales" among high school students. If such a person can be adjudged guilty of drug sales in the schools and escape any punitive sanction, the law and its moral force are indeed in jeopardy. To maintain the integrity of our drug laws some punishment must follow, as it did here, from the violation of these laws.

[4,5] We also mentioned in *Glenda Kay* that a criminal offender may be punished because he *deserves* it. Retribution or just desserts as a response to criminal law violation is thought by many jurists and social theorists to be archaic and inappropriate. We disagree. Although the juvenile court judge has in the present case eschewed the use of punishment *as punishment* in a juvenile court case, reason tells us that the juvenile court's decision to incarcerate could well have been grounded on the fact that Scott deserved to be punished. He has a previous juvenile record (carrying an illegal weapon). He was deeply involved in drug trafficking to minors. He was a disciplinary problem in school. It is hard to argue that Scott did not deserve to be removed from his home and school environment and confined in a

youth camp. This is little enough punishment for a crime calling for a life sentence. NRS 453.321.

[6] Finally, the record would support a conclusion by the juvenile court that the best interests of Scott would be served by this disposition. Spring Mountain has a regular high school educational program conducted by the Clark County School District and offers several treatment and rehabilitation programs likely to be of benefit to Scott. Also we must not ignore the value of punishment itself as a rehabilitative tool. Using punishment as a means for changing youthful behavior is not exactly a new phenomenon; and, punishment must be recognized as a valid and useful rehabilitative tool. This court has recognized that "punishment has in many cases a rehabilitative effect on the child and . . . will serve the child's best interests as well as the state's." *In the Matter of Seven Minors*, 99 Nev. 427, 664 P.2d 947 (1983).

> Enforcing the state's interests in a manner designed to hold juveniles responsible for their violations of the criminal laws need not by any means dilute the strength of educative and rehabilitative measures properly taken by the juvenile courts in attempting to socialize and civilize errant youth. Guidance, understanding and care still have the same place in juvenile court proceedings. Even youths who commit more serious crimes can profit from a separation from adult offenders and from the special treatment and special programs which are available in juvenile courts; this does not mean that they should go unpunished.

Seven Minors, 99 Nev. at 432, 664 P.2d at 951.

In *Seven Minors* we recognized the beneficence and utility of "educative and rehabilitative measures properly taken by the juvenile court," but noted firmly that "the court's duty to the public is paramount." The juvenile court judge in the present case was correct in declaring that it was "in the public's interest to institutionalize this young man," focusing on the deterrent effect that this disposition would have on others.

Purposes of the juvenile courts appear to have been optimally served by the juvenile court judge's decision "to institutionalize this young man" for purposes of deterrence. As stated above, other public interests are also served as are the interests of the

---

2. It used to be argued that marijuana is not a dangerous drug and should not be legally banned. In today's drug-ridden society this argument is not often heard, and Nevada's legislature has inscribed a law which attaches life imprisonment as a penalty for the sale or distribution of this drug. NRS 453.321. The people of this state have spoken through their elected representatives in such a manner as to obviate any discussion of the degree of culpability attached to this crime. The minor, in his brief, concedes that this is indeed, a "serious" crime.

delinquent. The juvenile judge in this case, the Honorable John S. McGroarty, had every justification for deciding as he did. We affirm the order of commitment.

Gunderson, C.J., and Steffen, Young and Mowbray, JJ., concur.

INSTITUTIONAL COMMITMENT OF STATUS OFFENDERS

Case Comment

In the case of *In re Michael G.*, a juvenile adjudicated a status offender for truancy brought a habeas corpus petition challenging a court order holding him in contempt for not attending school and placing him in a secure facility for forty-eight hours. On review, the Supreme Court of California found that the juvenile court had authority to exercise contempt power over a status offender. In addition, since less restrictive alternatives were considered by the court, the placement order was also found to be appropriate so long as it was consistent with barring the intermingling of status offenders with juvenile delinquents.

IN RE MICHAEL G.

Cite as 243 Cal.Rptr. 224 (Cal.1988)

Arguelles, Justice.

[1] In this case we decide whether a minor made a ward of the court pursuant to Welfare and Institutions Code section 601, subdivision (b)[1] as a result of his truancy, and later found in contempt of court for wilfully disobeying a juvenile court order to attend school, may be punished with confinement in a secure facility during nonschool hours, or whether sections 601, subdivision (b) and 207 prohibit such a disposition. Like the majority of other state courts which have addressed similar statutory schemes, we conclude that a juvenile court retains the authority,

pursuant to its contempt power, to order the secure, nonschool-hours confinement of a contemptuous section 601 ward. At the same time, in order to harmonize the juvenile court's exercise of its contempt power with the legislative determination that status offenders, including truants,[2] should not ordinarily be confined in secure facilities, we conclude—again following the lead of a number of out-of-state decisions—that before a juvenile court orders such incarceration pursuant to its contempt authority, it should make a number of specified findings establishing the necessity of such a course of action.

FACTS

Petitioner Michael G., a minor, was adjudged a ward of the Fresno County Superior Court, Juvenile Division, pursuant to section 601, subdivision (b)—truancy. As a condition of probation he was ordered, *inter alia*, to "attend school regularly and not be tardy or absent." Following numerous unexcused absences from school, the court ordered petitioner to show cause why he should not be held in contempt of court. A demurrer and alternative motion to dismiss the order to show cause were filed in which petitioner acknowledged receiving a copy of the probationary order and that "he was able to comply with each order and failed to comply with such orders."

Hearings were held on November 26 and December 3, 1984, after which the juvenile court concluded petitioner wilfully disobeyed the order of the court to attend school regularly and not be tardy or absent. Rejecting petitioner's demurrer and alternative motion to dismiss, the court ordered petitioner be delivered to the custody of the Director of Institutions of the Fresno County Probation Department for confinement for a 48-hour period. The court also ordered petitioner be held out of sight and hearing of any section 602 wards and that the 48-

---

1. All further statutory references are to the Welfare and Institutions Code unless otherwise stated.

2. "The status offender is a statutory creation, who occupies a unique position in the juvenile justice system. In contrast to the neglected, dependent or abused child, the status offender comes within the jurisdiction of the juvenile court because of his or her behavior, rather than on a finding of improper parental care or guidance. Unlike children charged with or found guilty of delinquency, alleged or adjudicated status offenders have not committed acts which would be considered criminal if done by an adult. When status offenders are incarcerated, therefore, it is not for any violation of the penal code, but for behavior which is considered unacceptable solely because of their age." (Costello & Worthington, *Incarcerating Status Offenders: Attempts to Circumvent the Juvenile Justice and Delinquency Prevention Act* (1981) 16 Harv.C.R.—C.L.L.Rev. 41, 42 [hereinafter cited as *Costello & Worthington*].) In California, juvenile court jurisdiction over status offenders is conferred by section 601. This opinion will use the terms "status offender" and "section 601 ward" interchangeably.

hour period would commence on Friday at 6 p.m., and end at 6 p.m., the following Sunday.

However, the juvenile court thereafter ordered petitioner to deliver himself into custody some 11 days hence "[t]o afford the minor the opportunity to ask review by the appellate court." Indeed, the juvenile court "earnestly" asked petitioner's counsel to seek writ review, stating: "[a]nd if it is determined that contempt proceedings or sanctions cannot be imposed against a Section 601(b) ward and that the Court cannot enforce its orders, then I certainly think that it's high time that the Court got out of the truancy business, [and] the [L]egislature place the Court in the position where it will have some dignity again. Certainly nothing is to be gained by the courts sitting here and pronouncing meaningless orders." The matter was later stayed by the Court of Appeal for the Fifth Appellate District but upon reflection, that court vacated the stay and denied a petition for a writ of habeas corpus and/or prohibition. We then granted review.

DISCUSSION

In finding petitioner in contempt for violating a valid court order, the juvenile court exercised the traditional power inherent in judicial officials. "We start with the premise that the right of courts to conduct their business in an untrammeled way lies at the foundation of our system of government and that courts necessarily must possess the means of punishing for contempt when conduct tends directly to prevent the discharge of their functions." (*Wood v. Georgia* (1962) 370 U.S. 375, 383, 82 S.Ct. 1364, 1369, 8 L.Ed.2d 569.) "It is well established that a court has inherent power to punish for contempt of court [citation]." (*In re Buckley* (1973) 10 Cal.3d 237, 247, 110 Cal.Rptr. 121, 514 P.2d 1201, cert. den. 418 U.S. 910, 94 S.Ct. 3202, 41 L.Ed.2d 1156.) The contempt power thus exists independent from legislative sanction although in this case the Legislature has specifically recognized that the juvenile court retains the ordinary contempt powers. (§ 213.)[3]

Although the petitioner concedes that the juvenile court in general retains authority to hold wards who disobey its orders in contempt, he argues that, with respect to truants and other status offenders, the Legislature has specifically proscribed the incarceration of such juveniles even as a sanction for contempt. He relies on sections 601, subdivision (b) and 207. In response, the People argue (1) that the limitations of those sections are inapplicable to the contempt setting, and (2) that if the sections were intended to limit the contempt power, they could not constitutionally do so. As we shall explain, we find that there is no need to reach the constitutional question in this case because we conclude that the applicable statutes can and should be harmonized to both preserve the trial court's contempt authority and at the same time give recognition to the legislative policy reflected in sections 601, subdivision (b) and 207.

We begin with the actual language of those sections. The relevant portion of section 601, subdivision (b) states "it is the intent of the Legislature that no minor who is adjudged a ward of the court pursuant solely to this subdivision shall be removed from the custody of the parent or guardian except during school hours." Section 207, subdivision (a) states in pertinent part: "[n]o minor shall be detained in any jail, lockup, juvenile hall, or other secure facility who is taken into custody solely upon the ground that he or she is a person described in Section 601 or adjudged to be such or made a ward of the juvenile court solely upon that ground. . . ."

While the language of the statutes clearly indicates that the Legislature has determined that no juvenile is to be detained in jail or juvenile hall" solely upon the ground that he or she is a person described in section 601," neither statute expressly indicates that it was intended to apply to the contempt setting. Although the ascertainment of legislative intent is the paramount principle of statutory interpretation (*Pollack v. Department of Motor Vehicles* (1985) 38 Cal.3d 367, 372, 211 Cal.Rptr. 748, 696 P.2d 141; see also *People v. Craft* (1986) 41 Cal.3d 554, 559, 224 Cal.Rptr. 626, 715 P.2d 585), the statutory language does not reveal whether the Legislature intended sections 601, subdivision (b) and 207 to apply to the contempt situation.

A consideration of "the legislative history of the statute as well as the historical circumstances of its enactment" (*People v. Black* (1982) 32 Cal.3d 1, 5,

---

3. Section 213 states "[a]ny willful disobedience or interference with any lawful order of the juvenile court or of a judge or referee thereof constitutes a contempt of court." While no case has yet construed the scope of this section, the penalties for violation of section 213 are apparently those set forth in Code of Civil Procedure section 1218 for contempts generally: a fine of up to $1,000, imprisonment of up to five days, or both.

184 Cal.Rptr. 454, 648 P.2d 104) is similarly unhelpful. Truancy has long been a concern of the state but section 601 was codified in largely its present form in 1961. (Stats.1961, ch. 1616, § 2, pp. 3471–3472.) Over the years, the statute was altered and renumbered several times in ways not material to our present inquiry. The most important overall change was to require referral of truants to school attendance review boards before juvenile court intervention. In 1975, the Legislature added the school hours limitation to section 601, subdivision (b). (Stats.1975, ch. 1183, § 2, pp. 2917–2918.)

The Legislature's move towards utilizing the school attendance review boards as a condition precedent to the juvenile court's intervention is understandable and in keeping with legal commentary calling for greater participation of school and social welfare professionals, even to the exclusion of the juvenile court's jurisdiction.[4] However, no legislative statement of purpose exists concerning the Legislature's imposition of a school-hours limitation. More to the point, there is no evidence suggesting the Legislature intended this new provision to either include or except juvenile contemners.

[2] The history of section 207 and its prohibition on secure detention for status offenders also fails to inform us whether the Legislature intended to affect the juvenile court's contempt power. Section 207 was first added to the code as part of the Arnold-Kennick Juvenile Court Law in 1976 (Stats.1976,

ch. 1068, § 1.5, p. 4741), and was a mirror image of former section 507, added to the code in 1961. (Stats.1961, ch. 1616, § 2, p. 3461.)[5]

This initial version of section 207 permitted the secure detention of status offenders if no other option was available. However, the Legislature amended the statute the next year to prohibit such detention of status offenders. (Stats.1977, ch. 1241, § 1, p. 4180.) Slight alterations were made in the following years but none of these amendments shed light on the applicability of section 207 to juvenile contemners. Thus, an examination of the history of sections 601, subdivision (b) and 207 yields no clue as to whether the Legislature intended these sections to limit a juvenile court's power to place a contemptuous status offender in secure surroundings during nonschool hours.

The structure of section 207 itself provides some hint as to our Legislature's intent, however. In addition to generally proscribing the secure detention of status offenders, that section permits three exceptions.[6] "Under the familiar rule of construction, *expressio unius est exclusio alterius*, where exceptions to a general rule are specified by statute, other exceptions are not to be implied or presumed. [Citations.] This rule, of course, is inapplicable where its operation would contradict a discernible and contrary legislative intent. [Citation.]" (*Wildlife Alive v. Chickering* (1976) 18 Cal.3d 190, 195, 132 Cal.Rptr. 377, 553 P.2d 537; see also *Cianci v.*

---

4. See Ketcham, *Why Jurisdiction over Status Offenders Should Be Eliminated from Juvenile Courts* (1977) 57 B.U.L.Rev. 645 (advocating the elimination of juvenile court jurisdiction over status offenders). Judge Ketcham was writing in support of the 1977 tentative draft of the Standards Relating to Noncriminal Misbehavior, written by the Institute of Judicial Administration and American Bar Association, Joint Commission or Juvenile Justice Standards. (But see Arthur, *Status Offenders Need a Court of Last Resort* (1977) 57 B.U.L.Rev. 631 [assailing the same standards].)

Others have recommended an initial referral to social welfare professionals and intervention of the court only after such a referral has proved fruitless. (See Comment, *Legislative Response to In re Ronald S.*; Cal.A.B. 958 (1978) 5 Pepperdine L.Rev. 847, 854 [proposing the same as an alternative] hereafter cited as Comment].) However, the commentators seem unanimous in calling for greater intervention of social welfare and mental health professionals. The Juvenile Court Law Revision Commission recently came to the same conclusion. In its January 1984 final report (Report), the commission concluded that the secure confinement of truants was not appropriate but instead recommended strengthening the power of the school attendance review boards. "Truancy is often a symptom of problems which may or may not be related to school, such as undiagnosed learning disabilities, misprogramming of the student by the school, problems with authority, personal problems, inner conflicts, home problems and the like. A strengthened SARB [school attendance review board] would be better able to diagnose the problem *and* prescribe a program appropriate to the student from among the many programs available through the education system and/or community programs." (*Report, supra,* at p. 66, emphasis in original.)

5. The People find the timing of the enactment of section 207—one year after the enactment of the school hours limitation in section 601, subdivision (b)—significant. They argue this timing reveals the Legislature's intent that the school-hours limitation should apply to section 601, subdivision (b) wards (i.e., truants) while the secure-confinement ban in section 207 should apply only to section 601, subdivison (a) wards (i.e., out-of-control minors). Inasmuch as section 207 was a verbatim reenactment of former section 507 which dates back to 1961, this argument is meritless.

6. The exceptions are: for up to 12 hours to determine whether there are outstanding wants, warrants, or holds against the minor where the arresting officer or the probation officer has cause to believe such holds exist (§ 207, subd. (b)(I)); for up to 24 hours to locate the minor's parents (§ 207, subd. (b)(2)); and for up to 72 hours where location of the minor's parents and his return to them cannot be reasonably accomplished within 24 hours. (§ 207, subd. (b)(3); see Stats.1978, ch. 1061, § 1, pp. 3271–3272.)

Superior Court (1985) 40 Cal.3d 903, 918, 221 Cal.Rptr. 575, 710 P.2d 375 [citing *Chickering*].) Thus, subject to a "discernible and contrary legislative intent," it is possible the Legislature, by specifying three exceptions to the general ban against secure detention for status offenders without also excepting juvenile contemners from the general rule, intended the general rule to apply to contemners.

This reasoning is arguably consistent with the timing of the enactment of the exceptions in section 207. Little more than one year prior to the enactment of the section 207 exceptions, a court confronted the instant statutory scheme for the first time. In *In re Ronald S.* (1977) 69 Cal.App.3d 866, 138 Cal.Rptr. 387, a minor was adjudged a section 601 ward and sent to a nonsecure crisis center, from which he promptly walked away. A section 602 petition was thereafter filed, alleging the minor had violated Penal Code section 166 subd. 4, making it a misdemeanor to wilfully disobey "any process or order lawfully issued by any Court." The petition was sustained and he was ordered detained in juvenile hall, a secure facility.

The minor's petition for a writ of habeas corpus was granted by Division Two of the Court of Appeal of the Fourth Appellate District. The court noted that under prior law, a juvenile could become a section 602 ward by failing to obey a lawful order of the juvenile court. Thus, by walking out of a foster home or failing to attend school, a section 601 ward was transformed into a section 602 ward, i.e., a juvenile delinquent. Observing that such express "bootstrapping" was eliminated by a 1976 amendment deleting failure to obey a court order as a basis for sustaining a section 602 petition (see Stats.1976, ch. 1071, § 12, p. 4819), the court reasoned that resort to Penal Code section 166 subd. 4 to sustain a section 602 petition and thereby justify secure incarceration was contrary to legislative intent. To permit such a procedure, the court noted, would render the "deletion of language in section 602 . . . meaningless and we would simply revert to the bootstrapping operation again. The court would be doing by indirection that which cannot be done

directly. As the law now stands, the Legislature has said that if a [section] 601 [ward] wants to run, let him run. While this may be maddening, baffling and annoying to the juvenile court judge, ours is not to question the wisdom of the Legislature." (*Ronald S., supra,* 69 Cal.App.3d at p. 874, 138 Cal.Rptr. 387.) Thus, after *Ronald S.,* it was clear that the secure detention of a status offender could not be justified by converting him into a section 602 ward via a criminal contempt citation. (See also *In re Mary D.* (1979) 95 Cal.App.3d 34, 156 Cal.Rptr. 829 [following *Ronald S.* on different facts].)

Because the section 207 exceptions were enacted just over a year later, those provisions may have been a response to the *Ronald S.* decision. (See Comment, *supra.*) However, since none of the exceptions in section 207, subdivision (b) (then numbered (c)) embrace the juvenile contemner situation, we can initially infer the Legislature intended to preserve the *Ronald S.* holding. " 'Where a statute has been construed by judicial decision, and that construction is not altered by subsequent legislation, it must be presumed that the Legislature is aware of the judicial construction and approves of it.' " (*Wilkoff v. Superior Court* (1985) 38 Cal.3d 345, 353, 211 Cal.Rptr. 742, 696 P.2d 134, quoting *People v. Hallner* (1954) 43 Cal.2d 715, 719, 277 P.2d 393.)

Although *Ronald S.* involved a contemptuous status offender, it also involved elevating a section 601 ward to delinquency status as a result of the contempt, something not done in petitioner's case. Thus, even assuming we can infer that the Legislature intended to preserve the *Ronald S.* holding (i.e., that a contempt conviction pursuant to Penal Code section 166 subd. 4 is impermissible to justify secure confinement via a section 602 wardship proceeding), that decision does not answer the question of whether a juvenile court is prohibited by sections 601, subdivision (b) and 207 from ordering the secure, nonschoolhours detention of a contemptuous status offender without conveying the youth into a section 602 ward.[7]

[3] We are similarly unable to infer legislative intent from the comparatively recent enactment of

---

7. The dissent thus read *Ronald S.* too broadly when it concludes that "[n]othing could be clearer than the [*Ronald S.*] court's conclusion that even contempt of a court's dispositional order in a section 601 wardship cannot be punished by incarceration." (*Post,* at p. 237 of 243 Cal.Rptr., at p. 1165 of 747 P.2d.) As the dissent states in an earlier passage, the "whole purpose of the 1976 amendments was to end the practice of bootstrapping a status offender *into a section 602 ward.*" (*Post,* at p. 237 of 243 Cal.Rptr., at P. 1165 of 747 P.2d, emphasis added.) Inasmuch as there was no attempt in this case to elevate petitioner's status to that of a delinquent, we reiterate that *Ronald S.* does not fully resolve the question of whether secure confinement of contemptuous truants is permissible if no attempt is made to convert them into section 602 wards.

sections 207 and 601, subdivision (b) as compared to the more general section 213. Section 213 has existed in some form for decades.[8] By contrast, sections 207 and 601, subdivision (b) were enacted comparatively recently. Thus, one could infer that the Legislature intended sections 207 and 601, subdivision (b) to limit a court's power under section 213 because later enacted statutes ordinarily control over previously enacted statutes and we should assume the Legislature was aware of section 213 when it enacted sections 207 and 601, subdivision (b). (*In re Misener* (1985) 38 Cal.3d 543, 553, 213 Cal.Rptr. 569, § 98 P.2d 637; *Fuentes v. Workers' Comp. Appeals Bd.* (1976) 16 Cal.3d 1, 7, 128 Cal.Rptr. 673, 547 P.2d 449.)

Similarly, one could argue sections 207 and 601, subdivision (b) should control because they are more specific in scope than section 213, and specific statutory provisions relating to a particular subject normally control as against more general provisions concerning the same subject. (*Bailey v. Superior Court* (1977) 19 Cal.3d 970, 976–977, fn. 8, 140 Cal.Rptr. 669, 568 P.2d 394; see also 58 Cal.Jur.3d Statutes, § 108, p. 483.)

However, these are tenuous inferences inasmuch as they require that we infer the Legislature intended to override the juvenile court's contempt power without expressly stating such a purpose. Given the fundamental nature of the contempt power (see discussion, ante), we should not presume the Legislature intended to override such long-established power "unless such intention is made clearly to appear either by express declaration or by necessary implication [citation]." (*People v. Davenport* (1985) 41 Cal.3d 247, 266, 221 Cal.Rptr. 794, 710 P.2d 861, citing *Fuentes, supra,* 16 Cal.3d at p. 7, 128 Cal.Rptr. 673, 547 P.2d 449.)

The dissent would devine legislative intent from a pilot program established by the Legislature which permits, under certain conditions, the secure confinement of section 601, subdivision (a) wards, i.e., runaways and out-of-control minors. (*Post,* at pp. 237–238 of 243 Cal.Rptr., at pp. 1165–1166 of 747 P.2d.) Because the Legislature passed a special law to permit such confinement, the dissent finds the conclusion "unavoidable" that the Legislature must understand that secure confinement is otherwise impermissible for status offenders.

However, a close reading of the legislation creating the pilot program shows the Legislature has gone much farther than merely permitting incarceration of runaways. Subject to enumerated procedural safeguards (such as a timely probable cause hearing), a section 601, subdivision (a) ward may be held in secure confinement for up to 72 hours, not including nonjudicial days, *if it is merely alleged* that he or she violated a related dispositional order. (Stats.1986, ch. 1369, § 1, p. 302, emphasis added.) Hence, the pilot program does not simply permit incarceration after a hearing, it authorizes *prehearing* confinement as a means of preventing crimes both by and against such juveniles. Therefore, even if the Legislature understood that secure confinement was a permissible sanction for a status offender's contempt of court, it would still follows that such special legislative authorization would be needed to justify the prehearing confinement permitted by the pilot program. To the extent the dissent asserts we can infer the Legislature's intent regarding incarceration of status offenders in general from its enactment of the pilot program, it is unpersuasive.

Viewing the statutory scheme as a whole, we thus conclude that while the legislative history demonstrates an intent to prohibit the juvenile court from relying on a ward's violation of a court order as a justification for elevating a section 601 ward to a delinquent (*Ronald S., supra,* 69 Cal.App.3d 866, 138 Cal.Rptr. 387), there is nothing in that history which specifically indicates that the Legislature intended to prohibit a juvenile court from enforcing obedience to a court order through a contempt sanction that does not alter the status of the ward.[9] Moreover, the Legislature's failure to expressly mention section 213 in either section 601, subdivision (b) or

---

8. The express statutory power to hold an uncooperative juvenile in contempt of court, expressed today in section 213, has long been a part of the code. It was first inserted into the code in 1915 (see Stats.1915, ch. 631, p. 1228), and existed in various versions until it was codified as former section 579 in substantially the same formulation as its present form. (See Stats.1937, ch. 369, p. 1022; see also Stats.1961, ch. 1616, p. 3462 [recodifying former § 579 as former § 512].)

9. The People argue we may infer that the Legislature intended to preserve a court's contempt powers by its use of the word "solely" in both section 601, subdivision (b) and section 207. From this, they contend petitioner was not ordered into custody "solely" because he was a section 601 ward but that it flowed from his status as a contemner. Although this interpretation of the word "solely" as used in sections 601, subdivision (b) and 207 may well be correct, we need not reach that issue in light of our conclusion that there is nothing in the legislative history demonstrating an intent to circumscribe the longstanding power of the juvenile court to punish contemners with incarceration.

207, or to amend section 213 itself, provides some evidence that it did not intend the secure detention ban or the school hours limitation to affect the scope of the juvenile court's contempt powers.

[4] By so concluding we avoid deciding whether the Legislature could constitutionally override the inherent contempt power of the courts. "[W]e do not reach constitutional questions unless absolutely required to do so to dispose of the matter before us." (*People v. Williams* (1976) 16 Cal.3d 663, 667, 128 Cal.Rptr. 888, 547 P.2d 1000; *Palermo v. Stockton Theatres, Inc.* (1948) 32 Cal.2d 53, 65–66, 195 P.2d 1; see also 13 Cal.Jur.3d Constitutional Law, § 57, pp. 106–107.)[10]

Although we conclude the limitations as stated in sections 207 and 601, subdivision (b) were not intended to affect the juvenile court's power to punish a contemptuous section 601 ward with secure detention during nonschool hours, we need not ignore the Legislature's general intent to deinstitutionalize status offenders. " '[E]very statute should be construed with reference to the whole system of law of which it is a part so that all may be harmonized and have effect. [Citations.]' " (*Landrum v. Superior Court* (1981) 30 Cal.3d 1, 14, 177 Cal.Rptr. 325, 634

P.2d 352, quoting *Stafford v. Realty Bond Service Corp.* (1952) 39 Cal.2d 797, 805, 249 P.2d 241.) Thus, although the Legislature's general prohibition on the secure detention during nonschool hours for section 601 wards does not apply to contemners, respect for the intent of our coequal branch of government demands that courts exercise caution when imposing such sanctions against contemptuous status offenders.

In mandating that courts exercise caution before ordering a status offender into secure custody for a contemptuous act, we do not paint on a wholly blank canvas. In 1974, Congress passed the Juvenile Justice and Delinquency Prevention Act (hereafter the Act) (42 U.S.C. §§ 5601–5639 (1976) & Supp.III 1979, as amended by Juvenile Justice Amendments of 1980, Pub.L. No. 96–509, 94 Stat. 2750), conditioning block grants to the states on compliance with the Act's requirement of the deinstitutionalization of status offenders.[11] As a result, nearly every state in the union passed a statute similar to section 207. (See *Costello & Worthington, supra*, at p. 53, fn. 50.)

Thus, many of our sister states have already confronted the problem of how juvenile courts can ef-

---

10. There is a serious question whether the Legislature could so severely limit the inherent contempt power of the court. While limitations are permitted, the Legislature cannot "fetter the power itself" without impinging on the constitutional powers of the court. (*In re Shortridge* (1893) 99 Cal. 526, 532, 34 P. 227.) We previously approved some limitations on a court's contempt power when we upheld the validity of Code of Civil Procedure section 1218, which then limited the punishment for contempt to five days in jail and a $500 fine. (*In re Garner* (1918) 179 Cal. 409, 177 P. 162, disapproved on another point in *In re Lynch* (1972) 8 Cal.3d 410, 424, fn. 15, 105 Cal.Rptr. 217, 503 P.2d 921.)

In *Garner*, we were careful to note, however, that while the Legislature could impose some limitations upon the contempt power, any regulation which "takes from the courts all power to punish for contempt, *or fixes a penalty wholly inadequate for the purpose*, would not be countenanced by the courts." (*Garner, supra*, 179 Cal. at pp. 411–412, 177 P. 162, emphasis added.) Stated more forthrightly, a legislative act eliminating available sanctions for contempt of court, which leaves the remaining penalties wholly inadequate to vindicate the power of the court, is unconstitutional. (See *In re San Francisco Chronicle* (1934) 1 Cal.2d 630, 634–665, 36 P.2d 369; *Shortridge, supra*.)

It is arguable that without the ability to order the secure, nonschool hours detention of a contemptuous status offender, a court's remaining sanctions are "wholly inadequate" to achieve the purpose underlying the contempt power. Under sections 207 and 601, subdivision (b), the juvenile court could punish a contemptuous minor by, among other things, ordering him or her detained in a nonsecure facility during school hours, to pay a fine, or to perform community work. However, the recalcitrant ward could refuse those directives with impunity since without the power to order secure confinement, the juvenile court's effective options would then be exhausted. As the Court of Appeals observed below, "[i]t is difficult to equate this result with punishment. In our view, such a constraint upon the court's power to punish for contempt would completely undermine the dignity and authority of the court, [and] make the court a laughing stock in the eyes of the very persons it is charged with the duty to supervise and control. . . ."

As stated above, however, we need not reach this question because we find the Legislature has not circumscribed the juvenile court's contempt powers by its enactment of sections 207 and 601, subdivision (b).

11. Interestingly, the Act initially prohibited incarcerating a status offender after elevating him to delinquency status due to his failure to comply with a court order. (Legal Opinion No. 77–25—Classification of Juveniles as Status Offenders (Mar. 15, 1977) [from the Office of the General Counsel of the Law Enforcement Assistance Administration].) However, section 5633, subdivision (a)(12)(A) of title 42 of the United States Code was amended in 1980 and now requires the states to file a plan to achieve the goal, within three years, "that juveniles who are charged with or who have committed offenses that would not be criminal if committed by an adult *or offenses which do not constitute violations of valid court orders* . . . shall not be placed in secure detention facilities or secure correctional facilities." (Emphasis added.) The amended Act would now apparently except juvenile contemners from its general requirement of abolishing the secure confinement of status offenders. (See *Costello & Worthington, supra*, at p. 55 and accompanying fns.)

fectively deal with status offenders who continually disobey the court's orders if secure incarceration is not an available option. Most states have affirmed their courts' use of the contempt power to order the secure detention of contemptuous status offenders despite an expression of legislative intent generally banning such detention (*In the Interest of D.L.D.* (1983) 110 Wis.2d 168, 327 N.W.2d 682; *Interest of Darlene C.* (1983) 278 S.C. 664, 301 S.E.2d 136; *State v. Norlund* (1982) 31 Wash.App. 725, 644 P.2d 724; *In re G.B.* (1981) 88 Ill.2d 36, 58 Ill.Dec. 845, 430 N.E.2d 1096 *cert. den.* 456 U.S. 963, 102 S.Ct. 2041, 72 L.Ed.2d 487; *State ex rel. L.E.A. v. Hammergren* (Minn.1980) 294 N.W.2d 705), although a minority of states have disapproved this practice. (*W.M. v. State of Indiana* (Ind.App.1982) 437 N.E.2d 1028; *Interest of Tasseing H.* (1980) 281 Pa.Super. 400, 422 A.2d 530 [holding an adjudication of delinquency against a status offender based on contempt was improper].)

Interest of D.L.D., supra, 110 Wis.2d 168, 827 N.W.2d 682, is perhaps most illustrative. In that case, the Supreme Court of Wisconsin was faced with a minor declared a "child in need of protection or services" (i.e., a status offender) who was not following the court's previously ordered conditions of supervision. The trial court found the minor in contempt of court, ordered the minor to serve 20 days in secure detention, and the intermediate appellate court affirmed. The high court reasoned that although the Wisconsin Children's Code generally prohibited the secure incarceration of status offenders with some exceptions,[12] the statutory limitation cannot operate to deprive the court of its inherent contempt powers to enforce its orders.

[5] However, the Wisconsin Supreme Court then stated: "[t]his court recognizes that the power of contempt is an extraordinary one that should be used sparingly and with the utmost sensitivity. This caveat is especially true since the 1977 revisions to the Children's Code adopted the general policy of deinstitutionalizing status offenders. Accordingly, we determine that a status offender may be found in contempt and incarcerated, but with the following limitations: (1) the juvenile is given sufficient notice to comply with the order and understands its provisions; (2) the violation of the court order is egre-

gious; (3) less restrictive alternatives were considered and found to be ineffective; and (4) special confinement conditions are arranged consistent with . . . [the statutory provisions barring intermingling with delinquents]." (*Interest of D.L.D., supra*, 110 Wis.2d at p. 182, 327 N.W.2d at p. 689.)

These four qualifications are sound and we hold California courts should adhere to them. Imposition of these qualifications on a juvenile court's contempt power achieves the twin goals of vindicating the inherent power of the courts while giving practical effect to the Legislature's express intent to deinstitutionalize status offenders in general. The necessity of the first requirement is self-evident; due process concerns would be implicated if the juvenile who lacked notice of the court's orders was held in contempt for violating those orders. (*Arthur v. Superior Court* (1965) 62 Cal.2d 404, 408–409, 42 Cal.Rptr. 441, 398 P.2d 777; *Rosenstock v. Municipal Court* (1976) 61 Cal.App.3d 1, 6–7, 132 Cal.Rptr. 59.)

The requirement of an egregious violation ensures that secure incarceration will not become a commonplace sanction in contravention of the Legislature's intent to comply with the federal mandate to deinstitutionalize status offenders. (Accord *Hammergren, supra*, 294 N.W.2d at p. 707.) The reservation of the nonschool hours, secure-detention sanction for the most severe cases will require the juvenile court to decide whether, based on the entire record, imposition of this harsh penalty is justified because no other sanction will suffice. Moreover, this requirement has the additional benefit of ensuring our juvenile courts will exercise this facet of their inherent contempt power to the least extent possible so as to give maximum effect to the Legislature's avowed intent to house status offenders in nonsecure surroundings.

[6] The third requirement—consideration and rejection of less restrictive sanctions—is closely akin to the second requirement that the violation of the court's order be egregious since it too has its genesis in the idea that incarceration should be the exception, not the rule. While the court need not necessarily have attempted lesser penalties before imposing secure confinement (cf. *In re John H.* (1978) 21 Cal.3d 18, 27, 145 Cal.Rptr. 357, 577 P.2d 177 [lesser dispositional alternatives need not be shown

---

12. Exceptions include where there is probable cause to believe (1) the child will injure himself or herself or others, or will be subjected to injury by others; (2) the parents or legal guardians of the child are unable or unwilling to provide adequate supervision or care of the child; or (3) the child will run away or be taken away and thus be unavailable for aftercare supervision. (See Wis.Child.Code. § 48.205, quoted in *Interest of D.L.D., supra*, 110 Wis.2d at p. 175, 327 N.W.2d at p. 686.)

to have failed in a delinquency case where the evidence shows the minor will derive a probable benefit from a Youth Authority commitment]), the record should indicate that lesser alternatives were considered by the juvenile court before ordering incarceration. (Contra *Norlund, supra,* 31 Wash.App. at p. 729, 644 P.2d at 727 [requiring a showing on the record that less restrictive alternatives have "failed"]; *Hammergren, supra,* 294 N.W.2d at pp. 707–708 [same].)

By requiring the juvenile court to memorialize its findings on the record, we again ensure the court is aware that, by ordering the secure confinement of a juvenile who has not committed a criminal offense, it is taking the extraordinary step of acting contrary to the wishes of the Legislature but is justified in doing so because it is convinced there is no other alternative which will adequately serve the purpose of the contempt citation.

We can infer the Legislature would agree with these requirements concerning the egregiousness of the violation and that less restrictive alternatives to secure detention were not feasible when we consider the Legislature's recent addition of section 1219.5 to the Code of Civil Procedure. (See Stats.1984, ch. 1643, § 1, p. 5919.) That section provides that a minor under the age of 16 who refuses to take the oath or testify when called to do so should be referred to the probation officer in charge before imposition of sanctions for contempt of court.

[7,8] This new section makes two other limitations applicable to the determination of the appropriate punishment for such a contempt of court. First, where the court is considering placing the minor outside his or her home, "the placement shall be in the least restrictive setting available." (Code Civ.Proc., § 1219.5, subd. (b).) Second, "the court shall not order the minor to be placed in a secure facility unless other placements have been made and the minor has fled the custody and control of the person under the control of whom he or she has been placed or has persistently refused to obey the reasonable and proper orders or directions of the person under the control of whom he or she has been placed." (*Ibid.*) However, less restrictive placements need not be first attempted if the court makes a finding on the record that the minor would likely flee if placed in a nonsecure facility. (Code Civ.Proc., § 1219.5, subd. (d).)

Although these requirements are applicable to a special type of juvenile contemner, they are sub-

stantially similar to those we impose on courts passing judgment on contemptuous status offenders in general. We may thus infer our requirements are consistent with the Legislature's manifested intent that if the secure detention of underage contemners is ordered, that decision is made with sensitivity for the relevant competing interests and that the court's decision be justified on the record.

Finally, the juvenile court ordering the incarceration of a status offender should also prohibit the minor from coming in contact with those minors confined due to their commission of a crime, i.e., section 602 wards. Although other states also impose this requirement, we need only turn to section 207 for a clear expression of our own Legislature's intent on this subject. Recall section 207, subdivision (b) provides three exceptions to the general prohibition on secure detention of section 601 wards. (*Ante,* fn. 6.) Subdivision (c) of that section provides "[a]ny minor detained in juvenile hall pursuant to subdivision (b) may not be permitted to come or remain in contact with any person detained on the basis that he or she has been taken into custody upon the ground that he or she is a person described in Section 602 or adjudged to be such or made a ward of the juvenile court upon that ground."

As if to emphasize the importance of the point, section 207, subdivision (d) further clarifies the matter: "[m]inors detained in juvenile hall pursuant to Sections 601 and 602 may be held in the same facility provided they are not permitted to come or remain in contact within that facility." Moreover, the clear ban on the intermingling of section 601 and 602 wards finds expression in other statutory provisions as well. (See § 601.1, subd. (b) [to the extent practically feasible, § 601 wards participating in community service programs shall not be permitted to come in contact with § 602 wards participating in the same program]; cf. § 208 [no minor under 18 years old detained in an institution where adults are confined (subd. (a)) or in a state hospital where adults are committed (subd. (b)) shall be permitted to come in contact with such adults].) It thus seems manifest that incarcerated status offenders must be segregated so as to avoid contact with section 602 wards and others confined due to their criminal conduct.

We realize our decision permits the contemptuous status offender to suffer the major disadvantage heretofore reserved for section 602 wards: secure confinement during nonschool hours. However, the nature of the confinement suffered by the contemptuous status offender differs in at least one substantial respect: he cannot come in contact with other section 602 wards who may be confined in the same facility. This limitation, as recognized by the juvenile court below, is important to ensure the status offender's problems, noncriminal at that time, are not exacerbated by mingling with delinquents. We thus avoid the unsavory situation whereby "the youngster whose only offense against society was that he could not get along with his parents, found himself cheek by jowl with the underage rapist, robber or heroin peddler." (*Ronald S.*, *supra*, 69 Cal. App. 3d at p. 870, 138 Cal. Rptr. 387.)

CONCLUSION

[9] Applying these standards here, we hold that although the juvenile court ensured petitioner had notice of and understood the court's orders, and properly ordered petitioner's confinement be arranged to prevent contact with section 602 wards, it made no express findings that petitioner's contumacious conduct was egregious or that less restrictive alternatives to incarceration were not feasible. In the present case, of course, the trial court was unaware it must make these specific findings before ordering confinement pursuant to its contempt authority. The judgment of the Court of Appeal is therefore reversed with directions to remand the cause to the trial court for further proceedings consistent with this opinion.

END NOTES—CHAPTER VI

1. See Adrienne E. Volenik, *Checklist for Use in Juvenile Delinquency Proceedings* (Washington, D.C.: American Bar Association, 1985).

2. For most of the juvenile court's history, disposition was based on the presumed needs of the child. See, for example, Joseph Goldstein, Anna French, and Albert Solnit, *Beyond the Best Interests of the Child* (New York: Free Press, 1973).

3. Criminal Justice Program of National Conference of State Legislatures, *Legal Dispositions and Confinement Policies for Delinquent Youth* (Denver: National Conference of State Legislatures, July 1988).

4. See American Bar Association, *Standards Relating to Juvenile Probation Function* (Cambridge, Mass.: Ballinger Publishing, 1977).

5. For a detailed description of children in custody in the United States, see Bureau of Justice Statistics, *Fact Sheet on Children in Custody* (Washington, D.C.: U.S. Department of Justice, 1989).

6. See, for example, Washington Juvenile Justice Act of 1977, Chapter 291 (Washington Rev. Code Ann. Title 9A-SEC 1. (1977)); also, Aaron Singer and David McDowall, "Criminalizing Delinquency: The Deterrent Effects of New York Juvenile Offender Law," *Law and Society Review* 22:21–37 (1988).

7. *In re Cecilia R.*, 327 N.E.2d 812 (1975).

8. *Matter of D.S.F.*, 416 N.W.2d 772 (1987).

9. *In re Green*, 203 So.2d 470 (1967).

10. See Stanley Fisher, "The Dispositional Process under the Juvenile Justice Standards Project," *Boston University Law Review* 57:732 (1977); also, Alan Breed, "Reforming Juvenile Justice: A Model or Ideology?" *Juvenile Justice Digest*, 15 (April 1987).

11. *In re Aline D.*, 536 P.2d 65 (1972).

Postdispositional Processing

INTRODUCTION

The postdispositional stage of the juvenile process normally covers (1) juvenile aftercare and (2) provisions for appeal of cases disposed of in the juvenile court. In addition, the question has been raised as to whether children committed to juvenile institutions have a constitutional or statutory right to treatment. This claim rests on the premise that the state must provide treatment for the juvenile offender, if it intends to exercise control over him or her.

Lastly, this chapter reviews the issue of capital punishment of minors. Because this type of sentence is very limited and often involves extensive appellate review, it is discussed here as part of the postdispositional process.

Once a juvenile is released from an institution, he or she may be placed on aftercare or parole under the supervision of a juvenile parole worker.[1] This means that the child will complete his or her period of confinement in the community where he or she will receive assistance from the parole officer in the form of counseling, referral to school and vocational training, and other services. If there is a violation of the conditions of parole, the juvenile may have his or her parole revoked and be returned to the institution. Unlike the adult postconviction process where the U.S. Supreme Court has imposed procedural safeguards in revocation of probation and parole proceedings, the Court has not constitutionally guaranteed juveniles such due process rights.

Since *In re Gault*, however, many state court decisions, statutes, and administrative regulations require juvenile agencies to incorporate such due process procedures as proper notice, hearing, and right to counsel in postconviction proceedings.[2]

After the disposition of the case in the juvenile court, the child is usually able to appeal the adjudication to a higher court. The provisions for such an appeal vary greatly within the jurisdictions. Many states authorize either the juvenile court or an intermediate court to review the original decision. The child may also appeal by virtue of collateral review, which often tests the validity of the commitment.

There is also the question of whether juveniles who are committed to institutions have a right to treatment.[3] The basis for this right originated with such cases as *Rouse v. Cameron (1966)*, and *Wyatt v. Stickney (1971)*, which dealt with the right to treatment for mentally ill persons.[4] The *Wyatt* case was particularly important since it held that involuntary commitment without rehabilitation was a violation of due process of law. Because the system of dealing with juvenile offenders is somewhat similar to the system of commitment for the mentally ill, that is, based on the *parens patriae* philosophy, juveniles have also sought a right to treatment.

The most significant appellate issue in the postdispositional area is the application of the death penalty to children. Of the thirty-seven states that have laws authorizing capital punishment, twenty-two allow the death penalty for crimes committed by juveniles under eighteen years of age.[5] Today, capital punishment is a constitutionally legal disposition for those who commit capital crimes while still in their minority.[6]

JUVENILE AFTERCARE

Case Comment

Adams v. Ross concerns the requirements of procedural due process in juvenile probation and parole. In light of *In re Gault* and the adult cases of *Morrissey v. Brewer (1972)* and *Gagnon v. Scarpelli (1973)*, juvenile authorities ordinarily grant children procedural rights similar to those of adult offenders at probation and parole revocation proceedings.[7] These generally include written notice, a hearing, presentation of evidence, and the right to confrontation and cross-examination. The use of counsel is ordinarily determined on a case-by-case basis, unless the state statute or juvenile court rules of procedure permit legal representation.

ADAMS v. ROSS

Cite as, Alaska, 551 P.2d 948

Connor, Justice.

S.L.M. was adjudicated a delinquent on February 22, 1974, and committed to the custody of the Department of Health and Welfare for an indefinite period, not to exceed his 19th birthday.[1] He was 16 years old at the time. He was released on probation from McLaughlin Youth Center in October of that year, with the knowledge of the court. S.L.M. was apprehended by Kenai police officers on January 10, 1975, for allegedly violating the law. A hearing was held five days later before Judge Hanson concerning the state's petition to modify or revoke S.L.M.'s probation because of the alleged violation. Judge Hanson dismissed the petition as unnecessary, reasoning that since S.L.M. had previously been committed to the department's custody, it was in the commissioner's discretion as to whether he should be returned to McLaughlin. He made no ruling on the merits, and disqualified himself from considering the facts because, based on knowledge outside the courtroom and on S.L.M.'s reputation in the community, he felt he "would lean over backwards to keep [S.L.M.] in an institution because I frankly feel he should be there. . . ."

S.L.M.'s attorney, Wayne Ross, brought an action for habeas corpus before Judge Butcher in Anchorage to compel the state to release S.L.M. from McLaughlin.[2] The Anchorage court ordered S.L.M. released, since no hearing had been held within two days of his arrest. See Alaska Children's Rule 7(b). The court did not order a new hearing, since Judge Hanson had dismissed the state's petition, and hence no such petition was before the court. The court declined to rule on whether the state would be barred from further proceedings, but indicated that it would not. From the release of S.L.M., the state appeals.

JURISDICTION

[1] Mr. Ross notes that the appellate jurisdiction of the supreme court is defined in AS 22.05.010. Subsection (a) provides in part:

> that the state shall have no right of appeal in criminal cases, except to test the sufficiency of the indictment or information

or to appeal a sentence under AS 22.05.010(b). See Appellate Rule 5. Thus, he argues, the state is precluded from bringing this appeal.

[2–4] Ross' technical challenge is not well taken, however. This is an appeal from a discharge granted in a habeas corpus proceeding. See AS 12.75.230.[3] "It is apparently well settled that a habeas corpus proceeding is civil in nature," not criminal. *In re Spracher*, 17 Alaska 144, 145, 150 F.Supp. 555

---

1. Unless the Department of Health and Welfare petitions for a continuance until his 20th birthday. See AS 47.10.080.
2. The action was brought in Ross' name to protect the identity of S.L.M.
3. AS 12.75.230 provides in part:
   A party to a proceeding by habeas corpus may appeal from the judgment of the court refusing to allow the writ or a final judgment therein in like manner and with like effect as in an action.
   This language does not, of its own, negate the jurisdictional language of AS 22.05.101 (a), since it only permits appeals "in like manner . . . as in an action."

(D.Alaska 1957).[4] Further, even for adults,[5] a probation revocation hearing is not a criminal proceeding in the sense that indictment, jury trial, or proof beyond a reasonable doubt are required, *Trumbly v. State*, 515 P.2d 707, 709 (Alaska 1973), *Snyder v. State*, 496 P.2d 62, 63 (Alaska 1973), although the revocation proceeding is necessarily an outgrowth of the initial criminal case.

[5] Ross also asserts that since the state is not precluded from filing its delinquency petition, the habeas corpus release is not an appealable "final judgment,"[6] and the state should only be allowed to file a petition for review rather than an appeal. It is true that because refiling is possible, further consideration of S.L.M.'s reincarceration at McLaughlin is not terminated before the appropriate court. Cf. *P.H. v. State*, 504 P.2d 837, 839 n. 1 (Alaska 1972). As to the habeas corpus proceeding, however, an order for release ends the litigation on the merits and leaves nothing for the court to do but execute that judgment. *Greater Anchorage Area Borough v. City of Anchorage*, 504 P.2d 1027, 1030 (Alaska 1972). That the state might file again seems irrelevant; *this* dispute, based on this filing, is terminated in the lower court. Thus it appears that an appealable final judgment has been entered.

The Discharge

[6] As to the habeas corpus proceeding itself, the law as it has recently developed supports the propriety of S.L.M.'s discharge. AS 47.10.080(b)(1) authorizes commitment to the department "for an indeterminate period of time not to extend past a specified date or in any event past the day the minor becomes 19" unless a one-year extension is obtained. S.L.M. was committed for an indefinite period, but this does not necessarily mean that he could not have been released from custody before his 19th birthday, only that such custody should not extend beyond it. He was released, and placed upon probation.

[7,8] Adult parolees and probationers must be allowed a hearing under the law before they can be reincarcerated. *Gagnon v. Scarpelli*, 411 U.S. 778, 782, 93 S.Ct. 1756, 36 L.Ed.2d 656 (1973); *Morrissey v. Brewer*, 408 U.S. 471, 484, 92 S.Ct. 2593, 33 L.Ed.2d 484 (1972); *Trumbly v. State, supra*; see generally, A.B.A. Standards: Probation § 5.4 (1970). Other states have held that this right is also required for juveniles despite explicit language to the contrary in the terms of release or applicable statute. *Keller v. State ex rel. Epperson*, 265 So.2d 497 (Fla.1972); *People ex rel. Silbert v. Cohen*, 29 N.Y.2d 12, 323 N.Y.S.2d 422, 271 N.E.2d 908 (1971). In Alaska, we have said:

> we believe that due process safeguards are necessary not only at the adjudicative hearing, but at any stage which may result in deprivation of the child's liberty. *Doe v. State*, 487 P.2d 47, 51 (Alaska 1971).

Accord, *In re Gault*, 387 U.S. 1, 16–18, 87 S.Ct. 1428, 18 L.Ed.2d 527 (1967). All parties before the court, including the Department of Health and Social Services, urge that a hearing be required. Finally, Children's Rule 7(b) provides that no child may be detained "prior to a first hearing of the case" unless a hearing is held within 48 hours after the child is taken into custody. Since the alleged probation violation appears to constitute a "case" separate from that involved in the original wrongdoing that produced the commitment and probation, Cf.

---

4. "Though habeas corpus is technically 'civil,' it is not automatically subject to all the rules governing ordinary civil actions." *Schlanger v. Seamans*, 401 U.S. 487, 490 n. 4, 91 S.Ct. 995, 997, 28 L.Ed.2d 251 (1971), *reh. den.*, 402 U.S. 990, 91 S.Ct. 1671, 29 L.Ed.2d 156.

5. Ross argues that juvenile probation revocation proceedings are more criminal than civil in nature. He asserts that the fact that they are juvenile proceedings should not prevent them from being considered "criminal." In *In re White*, 445 P.2d 813, 815 (Alaska 1968), in deciding that a defendant has no right to peremptorily challenge a judge in juvenile proceedings, this court held that juvenile proceedings were neither civil nor criminal. However, that holding was overruled by *In re G.K.*, 497 P.2d 914 (Alaska 1972); see also *R.L.R. v. State*, 487 P.2d 27, 33 n. 35 (Alaska 1971). Under federal law a juvenile proceeding is not a "criminal prosecution" for purposes of the federal Sixth Amendment. *McKeiver v. Pennsylvania*, 403 U.S. 528, 541, 553, 557, 91 S.Ct. 1976, 29 L.Ed.2d 647 (1971). It must be noted that Alaska Crim.R. 1 makes the Criminal Rules applicable to "all criminal proceedings," while it is clear that the procedure governing juvenile delinquency proceedings emanates from the Alaska Children's Rules. We need not decide whether an appropriate juvenile proceeding might be considered "criminal" for purposes of appellate jurisdiction under AS 22.05.010.

6. AS 12.75.230 provides for appeal of a habeas corpus proceeding from the "judgment of the court refusing to allow the writ or a final judgment therein. . . ."

Keller v. State ex rel. Epperson, supra at 498, this rule should be applied to S.L.M.

[9] Since a hearing is required, the release of S.L.M. was proper under the circumstances. Children's Rule 7 provides that no detention may "be continued" unless a hearing has been held within 48 hours after the minor has been taken into custody. Since Judge Hanson had dismissed the state's petition, nothing was before the court to support a probation revocation hearing until the state had refiled. Therefore, Judge Butcher was required to release S.L.M.[7]

Affirmed.

RIGHT TO TREATMENT

Case Comment

An individual's right to treatment has been an important and controversial topic in the juvenile justice system. On one hand, too narrow an interpretation of this issue seems to impede the rehabilitation ideal; on the other hand, extending treatment availability may outrage those who feel "convicted criminals" should not receive greater benefits than law-abiding citizens. In *Nelson v. Heyne*, the juveniles' right to treatment is analyzed. In this case, the violation of youthful inmates' Eighth and Fourteenth Amendment rights was charged by reason of their being given tranquilizing drugs to control their behavior. The appellate court declared that such practices do in fact constitute cruel and unusual punishment. Treatment must be individual and adequate to meet the needs of the child.

Other case decisions, although not used in this text, have also analyzed this concept. In *Inmates of Boy's Training School v. Affleck*, the juvenile inmates' right to due process and equal protection was violated by confinement in an ill-equipped and understaffed detention center.[8] The decision reflects a careful examination of the conditions of the center. The court argued that rehabilitation was the true purpose of the juvenile court and that without that goal, due process guarantees are violated. It condemned such devices as solitary confinement, "strip cells," and the lack of educational opportunities and

set out the minimum standards needed to rectify the situation.

In a recent case, *Gary H. v. Hegstrom*, a federal judge ruled that isolation punishments at the McClaren School for Boys in Oregon were excessive and that residents were being denied their right to treatment.[9] The appeals court affirmed the lower court's judgment regarding the existence of unconstitutional conditions at the school and ordered due process hearings prior to confinement in excess of twenty-four hours and minimum sanitary health educational and medical resources for the residents. But the wholesale adoption of various professional association standards for model institutions was not constitutionally mandated. The court also held that it was not appropriate to mandate dispositions that were so costly that other children would be deprived of services. Some experts believe that the right to treatment may eventually reach the U.S. Supreme Court and provide an avenue for a definite decision on this issue.

NELSON v. HEYNE

United States Court of Appeals, Seventh Circuit, 1974.
491 F.2d 352.

Kiley, Senior Circuit Judge.

The district court in this class civil rights action[1] enjoined defendants from implementing alleged unconstitutional practices and policies in conducting the Indiana Boys School under their administration; and declared the practices and policies unconstitutional. In Appeal No. 72-1970 defendants challenge the validity of the judgment granting the injunction, and in Appeal No. 73–1446 challenge the declaratory judgment. We affirm.

The School, located in Plainfield, Indiana, is a medium security state correctional institution for boys twelve to eighteen years of age, an estimated one-third of whom are non-criminal offenders. The boys reside in about sixteen cottages. The School also has academic and vocational school buildings, a gymnasium and an administrative building. The

---

7. Civil Rule 86(*l*) is inapplicable here. It is specifically limited by its terms to cases in which a parent, foster parent, or other relative of a child under sixteen attempts to obtain custody. S.L.M. was already sixteen when committed. Thus a show cause order was not required in place of a writ of habeas corpus by Rule 86.

1. 42 U.S.C.A. § 1983.

average length of a juvenile's stay at the School is about six and one-half months. Although the School's maximum capacity is less than 300 juveniles, its population is generally maintained at 400. The counselling staff of twenty individuals includes three psychologists with undergraduate academic degrees, and one part-time psychiatrist who spends four hours a week at the institution. The medical staff includes one part-time physician, one registered nurse, and one licensed practical nurse.

The complaint alleged that defendants' practices and policies violated the 8th and 14th Amendment rights of the juveniles under their care. Plaintiffs moved for a temporary restraining order to protect them from, inter alia, defendants' corporal punishment and use of control-tranquilizing drugs. After hearing, the district court denied the motion and set the date for hearing on the merits. Defendants' answer generally denied plaintiffs' allegations. Trial briefs were filed upon the issue whether defendants deprived plaintiffs of their alleged right to adequate rehabilitative treatment.

The court found that it had jurisdiction and that the corporal punishment and the method of administering tranquilizing drugs by defendants constituted cruel and unusual punishment in violation of plaintiffs' 8th and 14th Amendment rights. The judgment restraining the challenged practices fol-

lowed. The court thereafter, in a separate judgment, declared plaintiffs had the right to adequate rehabilitative treatment.[2]

I—CRUEL AND UNUSUAL PUNISHMENT

A

It is not disputed that the juveniles who were returned from escapes or who were accused of assaults on other students or staff members were beaten routinely by guards under defendants' supervision. There is no proof of formal procedures that governed the beatings which were administered after decision by two or more staff members. Two staff members were required to observe the beatings.

In beating the juveniles, a "fraternity paddle" between ½" and 2" thick, 12" long, with a narrow handle, was used. There is testimony that juveniles weighing about 160 pounds were struck five blows on the clothed buttocks, often by a staff member weighing 285 pounds. The beatings caused painful injuries.[3] The district court found that this disciplinary practice violated the plaintiffs' 8th and 14th Amendment rights, and ordered it stopped immediately.

We recognize that the School is a correctional, as well as an academic, institution.[4] No case pre-

2. *Nelson v. Heyne*, 355 F.Supp. 451 (N.D.Ind.1972). The district court's decision was entered as if a declaratory judgment on the right to treatment. We treat that portion of the decision, however, as an otherwise nonappealable interlocutory order and grant review pursuant to 28 U.S.C.A. § 1292(b).

3. The trial record indicates that one juvenile was struck with such force that it caused him to sleep on his face for three days, with black, blue and numb buttocks. One juvenile testified that he bled after receiving five blows on his buttocks. Another, Daniel Roberts, testified that once he pleaded, to no avail, with staff personnel not to be beaten until after certain blisters on his buttocks ceased to cause him pain.

4. (a) The law appears to be well settled in both state and federal jurisdictions that school officials do not violate 8th Amendment proscriptions against cruel and unusual punishment where the punishment is reasonable and moderate. *Ware v. Estes*, 328 F.Supp. 657 (N.D.Tex.1971); *Sims v. Board of Education*, 329 F.Supp. 678 (D.C.N.M.1971); *Tinkham v. Kole*, 252 Iowa 1303, 110 N.W.2d 258 (1961); *Carr v. Wright* (Ky.) 423 S.W.2d 521 (1968); *Houeye v. St. Helen Parish School Board*, 223 La. 966, 67 So.2d 553 (1953). In *Ware* there was evidence of beatings usually administered by hitting the student on his buttocks with a paddle. The paddle was wooden, 2" long, ¼" to ½" thick, 6" wide, used under a written rule which proscribed corporal punishment without parents' permission. The district court found that "some of the seven thousand" teachers in the public school district abused the policy, but that that fact, and nothing more, would not make the policy itself unconstitutional. In *Sims*, the court found that beatings by school officials did not constitute cruel and unusual punishment where the plaintiff student received three blows with a paddle on the buttocks and experienced slight physical harm. In our case, there is ample evidence that the beatings caused severe injury. See generally 68 Am. Jur.2d Schools § 258 (1973).

(b) The courts in recent years have frowned upon the use of corporal punishment in penal and correctional institutions. *See generally* 60 Am.Jur.2d Penal and Correctional Institutions § 43 (1972). Corporal punishment has not been used for years in federal prisons. Jackson v. Bishop, 404 F.2d 571, 575 (8th Cir. 1968). Courts have enjoined prison personnel from inflicting corporal punishment including the use of a strap for whipping. *Talley v. Stephens*, 247 F.Supp. 683 (E.D.Ark.1965); *Jackson v. Bishop, supra*. In *Talley* the court did not hold prison whippings are per se unconstitutional, but stated that they will be enjoined if excessive, and not applied under recognizable standards. In *Jackson* the 8th Circuit held that use of a strap in Arkansas penitentiaries was cruel and unusual punishment. See generally, *Holt v. Sarver*, 309 F.Supp. 362 (E.D.Ark.1970); Comment, Cruel and Unusual Punishment-Arkansas Penitentiary Violates the Eighth Amendment, 84 Harv.L.Rev. 456 (1970); M. Wheeler, Toward a Theory of Limited Punishment, 24 Stan.L.Rev. 838 (1972).

cisely in point has been cited or found which decided whether supervised beatings in a juvenile reformatory violated the "cruel and unusual" clause of the 8th Amendment.[5] However, the test of "cruel and unusual" punishment has been outlined. In his concurring opinion in *Furman v. Georgia*, 408 U.S. 238, 279, 92 S.Ct. 2726, 2747, 33 L.Ed.2d 346 (1971), Justice Brennan stated that:

> The final principle inherent in the [Cruel and Unusual Punishment] Clause is that a severe punishment must not be excessive. A punishment is excessive under this principle if it is unnecessary: The infliction of a severe punishment by the State cannot comport with human dignity when it is nothing more than the pointless infliction of suffering. If there is a significantly less severe punishment adequate to achieve the purposes for which the punishment is inflicted, the punishment inflicted is unnecessary and therefore excessive. (Citations omitted.)

Expert evidence adduced at the trial unanimously condemned the beatings. The uncontradicted authoritative evidence indicates that the practice does not serve as useful punishment or as treatment, and it actually breeds counter-hostility resulting in greater aggression by a child. For these reasons we find the beatings presently administered are unnecessary and therefore excessive. We think, under the test of *Furman*, that the district court did not err in deciding that the disciplinary beatings shown by this record constituted cruel and unusual punishment.[6]

The 8th Amendment prohibition against cruel and unusual punishment is binding on the states through the 14th Amendment. *Robinson v. California*, 370 U.S. 660, 82 S.Ct. 1417, 8 L.Ed.2d 758 (1962); *Francis v. Resweber*, 329 U.S. 459, 67 S.Ct. 374, 91 L.Ed. 422 (1947). The meaning of cruel and unusual punishment in law has varied through the course of history, and as the Court observed in *Trop v. Dulles*, 356 U.S. 86, 101, 78 S.Ct. 590, 598, 2 L.Ed.2d 630 (1958):

> The [8th Amendment] must draw its meaning from the evolving standards of decency that mark the progress of a maturing society.

The district court's decision meets tests that have been applied in decisions to determine whether the standards of decency in a maturing society have been met, i.e.: whether the punishment is disproportionate to the offense, *Weems v. United States*, 217 U.S. 349, 30 S.Ct. 544, 54 L.Ed. 793 (1910); and whether the severity or harshness of the punishment offends "broad and idealistic concepts of dignity, civilized standards, humanity, and decency." *Jackson v. Bishop*, 404 F.2d 571 (8th Cir. 1968). The record before us discloses that the beatings employed by defendants are disproportionate to the offenses for which they are used, and do not measure up to contemporary standards of decency in our contemporary society.

There is nothing in the record to show that a less severe punishment would not have accomplished the disciplinary aim. And it is likely that the beatings have aroused animosity toward the School and substantially frustrated its rehabilitative purpose. We find in the record before us, to support our holding, general considerations similar to those the court in *Jackson* found relevant: (1) corporal punishment is easily subject to abuse in the hands of the sadistic and unscrupulous, and control of the punishment is inadequate; (2) formalized School procedures governing the infliction of the corporal punishment are at a minimum; (3) the infliction of such severe punishment frustrates correctional and rehabilitative goals; and (4) the current sociological trend is toward the elimination of all corporal punishment in all correctional institutions.

The Indiana Supreme Court decision in *Indiana State Personnel Board v. Jackson*, 244 Ind. 321, 192 N.E.2d 740 (1963), cited by the defendants, is of no aid to set aside the district court decision. There the court held, inter alia, under the *parens patriae* doctrine, that a public school teacher, in proper cases and proportions, may administer corporal punishment.[7] We agree with that decision.

B

Witnesses for both the School and the juveniles testified at trial that tranquilizing drugs, specifically

---

5. The court in *Lollis v. New York*, 322 F.Supp. 473 (S.D.N.Y.1070), involving the constitutionality of solitary confinement in juvenile institutions, obliquely considered the binding and handcuffing of an inmate. *Inmates of Boys' Training School v. Affleck*, 346 F.Supp. 1354 (D.C.R.I.1972), also concerned the question of whether isolation of juvenile inmates constitutes cruel and unusual punishment.

6. We do not hold that all corporal punishment in juvenile institutions or reformatories is *per se* cruel and unusual.

7. There the dismissed teacher disciplined a fourteen-year-old girl in the classroom and in his office by striking her, in the presence of witnesses, very lightly and without anger, across the buttocks with a belt, and only after persuasion and other means had been tried and had failed.

Sparine and Thorazine, were occasionally administered to the juveniles, not as part of an ongoing psychotherapeutic program, but for the purpose of controlling excited behavior.[8] The registered nurse and licensed practical nurse prescribed intramuscular dosages of the drugs upon recommendation of the custodial staff under standing orders by the physician.[9] Neither before nor after injections were the juveniles examined by medically competent staff members to determine their tolerances.

The district court also found this practice to be cruel and unusual punishment. Accordingly the court ordered the practice stopped immediately, and further ordered that no drug could be administered intramuscularly unless specifically authorized or directed by a physician in each case, and unless oral medication was first tried, except where the staff was directed otherwise by a physician in each case.

We agree with defendants that a judge lacking expertise in medicine should be cautious when considering what are "minimal medical standards" in particular situations. However, practices and policies in the field of medicine, among other professional fields are within judicial competence when measured against requirements of the Constitution. We find no error in the competent district court's determination here that the use of tranquilizing drugs as practiced by defendants was cruel and unusual punishment.

We are not persuaded by defendants' argument that the use of tranquilizing drugs is not "punishment." Experts testified that the tranquilizing drugs administered to the juveniles can cause: the collapse of the cardiovascular system, the closing of a patient's throat with consequent asphyxiation, a de-

pressant effect on the production of bone marrow, jaundice from an affected liver, and drowsiness, hemotological disorders, sore throat and ocular changes.[10]

The interest of the juveniles, the School, and the state must be considered in determining the validity of the use of the School's tranquilizing drugs policy. The interest of the state appears to be identical more or less with the interest of the maladjusted juveniles committed to the School's care, i.e., reformation so that upon release from their confinement juveniles may enter free society as well adjusted members. The School's interest is in the attainment and maintenance of reasonable order so that the state's purpose may be pursued in a suitable environment. The School's interest, however, does not justify exposing its juveniles to the potential dangers noted above. Nor can Indiana's interest in reforming its delinquent or maladjusted juveniles be so compelling that it can use "cruel and unusual" means to accomplish its benevolent end of reformation.

We hold today only that the use of disciplinary beatings and tranquilizing drugs in the circumstances shown by this record violates plaintiffs' 14th Amendment right protecting them from cruel and unusual punishment. We do not intend that penal and reform institutional physicians cannot prescribe necessary tranquilizing drugs in appropriate cases. Our concern is with actual and potential abuses under policies where juveniles are beaten with an instrument causing serious injuries, and drugs are administered to juveniles intramuscularly by staff, without trying medication short of drugs and without adequate medical guidance and prescription.[11]

---

8. Plaintiff Steven Hegg testified that on one occasion while he was recuperating from a blow to the nose inflicted upon him by another student, his nose began to bleed profusely and he began to vomit and "holler for help." The nurse told him there was nothing seriously wrong with him: but when Steven continued to request help, she became infuriated and injected him with a tranquilizing drug. Eric Nelson testified to the effect that he was given shots of tranquilizing drugs on several occasions for the purpose of preventing him from running away from the School.

9. The standing order provided that an emotionally upset boy under 116 pounds be given a half cc or 25 milligrams of Sparine. Above that weight he was to be given one cc or 50 milligrams of Sparine.

10. Dr. James W. Worth, psychologist with the Mental Health Center of St. Joseph County, Indiana, also testified as follows:
   I think the use of major tranquilizing drugs without intelligent and informed medical observation have no place . . . in the institution. They have serious effect on the individual. . . . [I]f this is not done with a full medical understanding of this individual with a physician present, harm could occur and furthermore, I think it tends to be degrading to an individual.

11. Experts testified that the following minimum medical safeguards should be followed in the use of tranquilizing drugs:
   (1) The individual administered the drug should be observed, during the duration of the drug's effect, by trained medical personnel, familiar with the possible adverse and harmful side effects of the drug used.
   (2) The person receiving an IM (intramuscular) injection of a major tranquilizing drug should first receive a diagnosis or prescription authorizing the use of said drug by a qualified medical doctor, child psychiatrist, psychologist, or physician.

(continued on next page)

II—THE RIGHT TO REHABILITATIVE TREATMENT

The School staff-to-juvenile ratio for purposes of treatment is approximately one to thirty. The sixteen counselors are responsible for developing and implementing individualized treatment programs at the institution, but the counselors need have no specialized training or experience. Administrative tasks ("paper work") occupy more than half of the counselors' time. The duties of the staff psychiatrist are limited to crises. He has no opportunity to develop and manage individual psychotherapy programs. The three staff psychologists do not hold graduate degrees and are not certified by Indiana. They render, principally, diagnostic services, mostly directed toward supervising in-take behavior classifications.

In June, 1971, the School adopted what was described as a differential treatment program, bottomed mainly on the Quay Classification System. Under the Quay System, upon their admission to the School, juveniles are classified with respect to four personality and behavior types on the basis of standardized tests: the inadequate, the neurotic, the aggressive, and the subcultural. Each of the sixteen cottages at the School houses twenty to thirty juveniles, with common personality and behavior patterns. Each cottage is served by a staff comprising a house manager, a counselor, an educator, and a consulting psychologist. The cottage staff meets weekly for evaluation of the rehabilitation program of each inmate. Upon admission to a cottage, each juvenile agrees to improve his behavior in four areas of institutional life: "cottage," "recreation," "school," and "treatment." Correspondingly, each has responsibility for physical maintenance of the residential area, social and athletic activities, specified levels of academic or vocational skills, and improved personality goals. With success in each of the four areas, the juvenile earns additional privileges, ultimately culminating in a parole date.

The district court decided that both Indiana law and the federal Constitution secure for juvenile offenders a "right to treatment," and that the School failed to provide minimal rehabilitative treatment. Defendants contend that there exists no right to treatment under the Constitution or Indiana law, and that if there is the right, the Quay Classification System used at the School did not violate the right. We hold, with the district court, that juveniles have a right to rehabilitative treatment.

The right to rehabilitative treatment for juvenile offenders has roots in the general social reform of the late nineteenth century, was nurtured by court decisions throughout the first half of this century, and has been established in state and federal courts in recent years. *In re Gault*, 387 U.S. 1, 15–16, 87 S.Ct. 1428, 1437, 18 L.Ed.2d 527 (1967), the Court stated:

> The early reformers were appalled by adult procedures and penalties, and by the fact that children could be given long prison sentences and mixed in jails with hardened criminals* * * . The child was to be "treated and "rehabilitated" and the procedures, from apprehension through institutionalization, were to be "clinical" rather than punitive.

Since the beginning, state courts have emphasized the need for "treatment" in their Juvenile Court Acts. *Wisconsin Industrial School for Girls v. Clark County*, 103 Wis. 651, 79 N.W. 422, 427 (1899); *Commonwealth v. Fisher*, 213 Pa. 48, 62 A. 198, 199 (1905); *Ex Parte Sharp*, 15 Idaho 120, 96 P. 563, 564 (1908); *Wissenberg v. Bradley*, 209 Iowa 813, 229 N.W. 205, 207 (1929).

The United States Supreme Court has never definitely decided that a youth confined under the jurisdiction of a juvenile court has a constitutionally guaranteed right to treatment. But the Court has assumed, in passing on the validity of juvenile proceedings, that a state must provide treatment for juveniles. In *Kent v. United States*, 383 U.S. 541, 86 S.Ct. 1045, 16 L.Ed.2d 84 (1966), the Court reversed the district court's conviction of a sixteen year old after the District of Columbia Juvenile Court had waived its jurisdiction. Justice Fortas there, writ-

---

(3) IM injections should only be administered by a physician or intern and only after all attempts have failed to get the individual to take the drug orally.

(4) Major tranquilizing drugs, such as Thorazine and Sparine, should not be administered IM, unless given in a hospital where there is an intensive care unit and emergency facilities which could deal with possible adverse effects from the use of said drugs.

(5) Major tranquilizing drugs should only be used to control psychotic or pre-psychotic breakdowns or as a followup in assisting a schizophrenic patient from having a recurrence of a psychotic breakdown.

(6) Major tranquilizing drugs should not be used merely to induce sleep or unconsciousness for a period of time, but only as a part of a psychotherapeutic program of treatment.

ing for the Court, commented on the theory and practice of juvenile courts:

> There is evidence, in fact, that there may be grounds for concern that the child receives the worst of both worlds: that he gets neither the protections accorded to adults nor the solicitous care and regenerative treatment postulated for children. 383 U.S. at 556, 86 S.Ct. at 1954.

Later, in *In re Gault, supra,* Justice Fortas "reiterate[d] the view" of *Kent* that the juvenile process need not meet the constitutional requirements of an adult criminal trial, but must provide essential "due process and fair treatment." This view has been continued subsequent to *Gault* in the Supreme Court decisions involving juvenile court procedures. *In re Winship,* 397 U.S. 358, 90 S.Ct. 1068, 25 L.Ed.2d 368 (1970); *McKeiver v. Pennsylvania,* 403 U.S. 528, 91 S.Ct. 1976, 29 L.Ed.2d 647 (1971).

It is true that the Supreme Court cases discussed above deal with procedural due process and not the right to rehabilitative treatment, but several recent state and federal cases, out of concern—based upon the *parens patriae* doctrine underlying the juvenile justice system—that rehabilitative treatment was not generally accorded in the juvenile reform process, have decided that juvenile inmates have a constitutional right to that treatment. *M. v. M.,* 71 Misc.2d 396, 336 N.Y.S.2d 304 (1972); *Inmates of Boys' Training School v. Affleck,* 346 F.Supp. 1354 (D.C.R.I.1972); *Martarella v. Kelley,* 349 F.Supp. 575 (S.D.N.Y.1972).

In *Martarella* the court found a clear constitutional right to treatment for juveniles based on the 8th and 14th Amendments:

> What we have said, although the record would justify more, is sufficient to establish that, however benign the purposes for which members of the plaintiff class are held in custody, and whatever the sad necessities which prompt their detention, they are held in penal condition. Where the State, as *parens patriae,* imposes such detention, it can meet the Constitution's requirement of due process and prohibition of cruel and unusual punishment *if, and only if, it furnishes adequate treatment to the detainee.* 349 F.Supp. at 585. (Emphasis supplied, footnotes omitted.)

After an historical analysis of the development of the right, the court concluded:

> In sum, the law has developed to a point which justifies the assertion that: "A new concept of substantive due process is evolving in the therapeutic realm. This concept is founded upon a recognition of the concurrency between the state's exercise of sanctioning powers and its assumption of the duties of social responsibility. Its implication is that effective treatment must be the *quid pro quo* for society's right to exercise its *parens patriae* controls. Whether specifically recognized by statutory enactment or implicitly derived from the constitutional requirements of due process, the right to treatment exists." 349 F.Supp. at 600. (Footnotes omitted.)

In a most recent case, *Morales v. Turman,* 364 F.Supp. 166 (E.D.Tex.1973), a federal district court specifically found that juveniles at Texas' six juvenile training schools have both a statutory and constitutional right to treatment.

We hold that on the record before us the district court did not err in deciding that the plaintiff juveniles have the right under the 14th Amendment due process clause to rehabilitative treatment.[12]

III—ADEQUACY OF TREATMENT

Experts testified at the trial, and the defendants admit, that the Quay System of behavior classification is not treatment. And case histories of maladjusted juveniles show that use of the System falls far short of its improved personality goals. Mrs. Betty Levine, resident instructor in sociology at the University of Indiana, testified that the School lacks the individual treatment given in the Indiana Girls School. The record shows very little individual treatment programmed, much less implemented, at the School; and it is unclear exactly how much time is spent in individual counseling. We conclude that the district court could properly infer that the Quay System as used in the School failed to provide adequate rehabilitative treatment.

We leave to the competent district court the decision: what is the minimal treatment required to provide constitutional due process, having in mind

---

12. We note that the district court additionally determined that a right to treatment in this case has a statutory basis in view of the "custody, *care,* and discipline" language of the Indiana Juvenile Court Act, Burns Ind. Stat.Ann. § 9–3201, IC 1971, 31–5–7–1. (Emphasis supplied.) We agree with this conclusion. Since we have today determined that the federal Constitution affords juveniles a right to treatment, any interpretation of the Indiana Act which would find no such right to exist would itself be unconstitutional.

that the juvenile process has elements of both the criminal and mental health processes.[13]

In our view the "right to treatment" includes the right to minimum acceptable standards of care and treatment for juveniles and the right to *individualized* care and treatment. Because children differ in their need for rehabilitation, individual need for treatment will differ. When a state assumes the place of a juvenile's parents, it assumes as well the parental duties, and its treatment of its juveniles should, so far as can be reasonably required, be what proper parental care would provide. Without a program of individual treatment the result may be that the juveniles will not be rehabilitated, but warehoused, and that at the termination of detention they will likely be incapable of taking their proper places in free society; their interests and those of the state and the school thereby being defeated.

We therefore affirm the judgment of the district court in each appeal, and remand[14] only for limited purpose of further proceedings in No. 73–1446 with respect to the right to rehabilitative treatment.

APPEALS

Case Comment

Whether a juvenile has the right of appeal has been left to the discretion of the states. The majority of state jurisdictions allow an appeal from an order of the juvenile or family court. In many situations, juvenile court statutes limit appeals to cases where the juvenile seeks review of a "final judgment" or that end the litigation between the parties.

There are two basic methods of appellate review: the direct appeal and the collateral attack. The direct appeal normally involves a court review to determine whether the rulings of law and judgment of the lower court based on the evidence are correct. The collateral or secondary method of attacking a juvenile court judgment uses extraordinary writs to challenge the lower court position.

The case of *Murray v. Owens* illustrates the successful use of the "Great Writ," habeas corpus, as an appellate mechanism in juvenile court.

UNITED STATES ex rel. MURRAY v. OWENS

United States District Court, S.D. New York, 1972.
341 F.Supp. 722.

Gurfein, District Judge.

The petitioner, a fifteen-year-old at the time of his sentence to three years' commitment to Elmira Reception Center, brings this petition for a writ of habeas corpus. He was sentenced by the Bronx County Family Court after a juvenile delinquency proceeding in which a motion for trial by jury was denied. The commitment to Elmira is authorized by the New York Family Court Act § 758(b). That section, in pertinent part, reads as follows:

> (b) Upon an adjudication of delinquency of a person who is fifteen years of age at the time of the commission of any act which, if committed by an adult, would be a class A or class B felony as defined in the penal law, commitment may be for males to Elmira reception center * * *.

His conviction and commitment were appealed, *inter alia*, upon federal constitutional grounds. The New York Court of Appeals dismissed the appeal. He then brought an action in this Court under 42 U.S.C. § 1983 and 28 U.S.C. §§ 2201, 2202 seeking a declaratory judgment and injunctive relief. He moved in that action for the convening of a three-judge court and for a temporary restraining order against his transfer from the Spofford Juvenile Center, where he was held, to Elmira Reception Center. I held that in a civil rights action the doctrine of res judicata applied, and that the adverse decision of the New York Court of Appeals could not be relitigated in that type of action. *Murray v. Oswald*, 333 F.Supp. 490, 493 (S.D.N.Y.1971); see *Lackawanna Police Benevolent Ass'n v. Balen*, 446 F.2d 52 (2 Circ. 1971). I suggested, however, that habeas corpus might be a proper remedy, since there is no defense of *res judicata* in such a proceeding where constitutional issues are involved. *Brown v. Allen*, 344 U.S. 443, 506–08, 73 S.Ct. 397, 97 L.Ed. 469 (1953). And the petitioner's failure to seek re-

---

13. The juvenile justice process can be understood to be a hybrid between the criminal system and the mental health process.
   * * * Finally, the arguments for the right to treatment in both processes rely heavily upon the medical services, especially psychiatry and psychology.
      Note, A Right to Treatment for Juveniles, 1973 Wash.U.L.Q. 157, 160. See also N. Kittrie, Can the Right to Treatment Remedy the Ills of the Juvenile Process? 57 Geo.L.J. 848, 860–861 (1969); Note, The Courts, the Constitution and Juvenile Institutional Reform, 52 B.U.L.Rev. 33, 42–49 (1972).

14. See note 2, *supra*.

view in the United States Supreme Court would not be fatal on the question of exhaustion of remedies. See *Fay v. Noia*, 372 U.S. 391, 435–36, 83 S.Ct. 822, 9 L.Ed.2d 837 (1963).

Accordingly, the petitioner now seeks the writ and this Court is obliged to consider the constitutional issues, without benefit or need of a three-judge court. *Wilson v. Gooding*, 431 F.2d 855 (5 Cir. 1970); *United States ex rel. Laino v. Warden*, 246 F.Supp. 72, 92 n. 16 (S.D.N.Y.1965), *aff'd*, 355 F.2d 208 (2 Cir. 1966). The petitioner urges that he was denied his constitutional rights to due process and equal protection because he was committed to a penal facility without a jury trial. Habeas corpus is available not only to an applicant who claims he is entitled to be free of all restraints, but also to an applicant who protests that his confinement in a certain place vitiates the justification for confinement. See *Creek v. Stone*, 379 F.2d 106, 109 (D.C.Cir.1967).

The constitutional issue is one of narrow application, but it nevertheless must be decided. The equal protection argument runs as follows. The New York statute, as we have seen, applies only to the class of fifteen-year-olds who commit acts equivalent to serious crimes. A juvenile of fourteen, who has committed the same acts as Murray, may not be sent to the Elmira Reception Center. Youths of sixteen to nineteen (youthful offenders) may be sent to Elmira, but if the prosecution is for a serious crime, they are entitled to a jury trial. *People v. Michael A. C.*, 27 N.Y.2d 79, 86, 313 N.Y.S.2d 695, 261 N.E.2d 620 (1970). In other words, if the petitioner had been fourteen or sixteen, rather than fifteen, he could not legally have been tried and committed as he was. Singling out his small class for curtailment of rights is alleged to be violative of the principle of *Bastrom v. Herold*, 383 U.S. 107, 111–12, 86 S.Ct. 760, 15 L.Ed.2d 620 (1966).

The due process argument centers on the idea that it is fundamentally unfair to try the offender as a child, but then to imprison him as an adult. It has been noted that in certain juvenile courts "the child receives the worst of both worlds: that he gets neither the protections accorded to adults nor the solicitous care and regenerative treatment postulated for children." *Kent v. United States*, 383 U.S. 541, 556, 86 S.Ct. 1045, 1054, 16 L.Ed.2d 84 (1966). Here the incongruity between "solicitous care" and "the protections accorded to adults" does not arise from the failure of the care in fact to meet intended standards, but rather from a legislative permission to make this very incongruity a part of the judicial process.

The juvenile court system was first instituted in 1899 in Cook County, Illinois. It was assumed that the informality of the procedure would give the judge insight into available means to deal with the juvenile other than imprisonment with criminals. The purpose was not to escape the burdensome necessity of a jury trial in order to give the juvenile *less* protection than if he were adult. Rather the safeguard of jury trial was traded for a sympathetic review by the judge of the personality of the particular juvenile so that more useful *treatment* could be ordered. As was said in *Pee v. United States*, 107 U.S.App.D.C. 47, 274 F.2d 556, 558 (1959), under the juvenile court procedure "such a one" is "not punished as a criminal."

The growth of separate juvenile courts was, accordingly, accompanied in New York and many other states by the development of separate institutions for the juvenile delinquent. "The early reformers were appalled by adult procedures and penalties, and by the fact that children could be given long prison sentences and mixed in jails with hardened criminals." *In re Gault*, 387 U.S. 1, 15, 87 S.Ct. 1428, 1437, 18 L.Ed.2d 527 (1967). In New York, two systems of institutions for confinement have evolved, one for juveniles under the Division for Youth and the other for adults and youthful offenders under the Department of Correction. The State Training Schools, which take boys adjudicated to be juvenile delinquents for conduct while under the age of sixteen, are supervised by the Division for Youth; see N.Y.Laws 1971, c. 947, § 3. The Elmira Reception Center, on the other hand, normally takes only males over sixteen. It is a medium security facility which is administered by the Department of Correction, as part of the State prison system, and which functions as a way-station for the purpose of "reception, classification and program-planning." See N.Y.Correction Law, McKinney Consol. Laws c. 43, §§ 2, 70–72; 7 N.Y.C.R.R. §§ 100.75(b) & (c), 150.1(c). Any individual received at the Reception Center (and this would presumably apply to the petitioner) may be sent elsewhere within the State prison system, including a maximum security prison, under the authority of N.Y.Correction Law § 23 permitting administrative transfers.

It is clear, therefore, that the petitioner has been sentenced to imprisonment for three years in a facility in which juveniles generally are not placed and where his fellow inmates will not have been sentenced to a three year term without benefit of trial by jury. *Duncan v. Louisiana*, 391 U.S. 145, 88 S.Ct. 1444, 20 L.Ed.2d 491 (1968); *Baldwin v. New York*, 399 U.S. 66, 90 S.Ct. 1886, 26 L.Ed.2d 437 (1969); *People v. Michael A.C., supra.*

New York seeks to justify this anomaly by urging that there is a compelling State interest in fostering the juvenile court system and that the alternative disposition provided by Section 758(b) should be viewed as a legitimate and rational part of the total scheme, the coincident absence of a jury trial also being considered as an integral part of that system. It contends that it is reasonable for the Legislature to differentiate, for purposes of disposition, between older, hardened, violent delinquents and other juvenile delinquents. It notes, quite properly, that the older, hardened delinquent might corrupt those younger boys placed in a Training School and substantially reduce or destroy the School's rehabilitative function. As I indicated in my earlier opinion (333 F.Supp. at 493), "a boy of fifteen may be as precocious in the field of criminality as another might be in better fields of endeavor." So it is, indeed, rational for the New York Legislature to make provision for keeping the very bad, older youngster from corrupting the younger children.

This still leaves open the question of what procedure is to be followed as a preliminary to this prophylactic segregation. Many state courts, in upholding the constitutionality of juvenile court acts, have emphasized not only that the proceedings are non-criminal, but also that the *institution* to which the delinquent is being committed is not of a penal character. See the state cases collected in *White v. Reid*, 125 F.Supp. 647, 649–50 (D.D.C.1954). But Surrogate Midonick, formerly of the New York Family Court, has noted that:

> * * * is should be observed that non-juvenile reformatories such as the Elmira Reception Center and Westfield State Farms in New York, while they also are engaged in the quest for rehabilitation and treatment (as any decent penal institution should be), are not capable of dealing with juveniles as juveniles. The very age differential of the inmates makes treatment of a juvenile in a non-juvenile facility quite inadequate and often harmful because of the inappropriate mingling of fifteen-year-olds with inmates up to age 21 and over. M. Midonick, Children, Parents and the Courts 25 (1972).

Formerly, in New York a juvenile could be held for trial as an adult, or removed to Family Court.

N.Y.Family Court Act § 715 (1963); N.Y.Code Crim.Proc. §§ 312–c & 312–f (1958). In 1967, instead of continuing this concurrent jurisdiction over juveniles, exclusive jurisdiction of children up to age 16 was conferred upon the Family Court. N.Y.Laws 1967, c. 680, § 87; Family Court Act §§ 712–13. This was a progressive measure, but while creating the exclusive jurisdiction, the provision regarding fifteen-year-olds in § 758(b) of the Family Court Act was permitted to remain with only formal changes. In summary, the situation today in New York is that the precociously criminal fifteen-year-old can be sent to an adult penal facility after a non-jury trial in Family Court. It is this combination of procedure and disposition, not the disposition alone, which is under attack.

In recent years attention has centered upon the constitutional rights of juveniles. In *In re Gault*, juveniles were held to possess rights inherent in due process—"neither the Fourteenth Amendment nor the Bill of Rights is for adults alone" (387 U.S. at 13, 87 S.Ct. at 1436).

There was no occasion to decide in *Gault* whether, as part of the Sixth Amendment guarantee (carried over to the states by the Fourteenth) or as part of due process itself, the juvenile was entitled to a jury trial. Thereafter, the Supreme Court held in the non-juvenile field that "trial by jury in criminal cases is fundamental to the American scheme of justice," *Duncan v. Louisiana*, 391 U.S. at 149, 88 S.Ct. at 1447, and that any prosecution in which the possible confinement could exceed six months required a jury trial as a matter of due process. *Baldwin v. New York, supra.*

Thus, by the doctrine of *Gault* the juvenile appeared to have rights to due process like an adult, and by the doctrine of *Duncan* and *Baldwin* the right to due process included the right to trial by jury. * * * This apparent syllogism to the contrary notwithstanding, the juvenile was not destined to get his trial by jury. First the New York Court of Appeals, in *In re Daniel D.*, 27 N.Y.2d 90, 313 N.Y.S.2d 704, 261 N.E.2d 627 (1970), and then the Supreme Court, held that juvenile court proceedings do not require jury trials in order to conform to the Constitution. *McKeiver v. Pennsylvania*, 403 U.S. 528, 91 S.Ct. 1976, 29 L.Ed.2d 647 (1971).

The *McKeiver* plurality opinion of the Court, written by Mr. Justice Blackmun, broke the syllogism by stating that "the juvenile court proceeding has not yet been held to be a 'criminal prosecution,' within the meaning and reach of the Sixth Amendment" (403 U.S. at 541, 91 S.Ct. at 1984). Mr. Justice Harlan concurred because he did not feel constrained by *stare decisis* to follow *Duncan*, from which he had dissented, but he commented: "I do not see why, given *Duncan*, juveniles as well as adults would not be constitutionally entitled to jury trials, so long as juvenile delinquency systems are not restructured to fit their original purpose" (403 U.S. at 557, 91 S.Ct. at 1992). There is no doubt, however, that a majority of the Supreme Court did hold that, even though the juvenile court system in practice leaves much to be desired in many places, it is still of sufficient social utility to permit its basic procedure to be sustained. At the same time, all the Justices except Mr. Justice Harlan, accepted the continued validity of *Duncan*.

McKeiver represented a clash between two sets of reformers—the progeny of the Jane Addams school of reform in the handling of juveniles and the civil libertarians who, often enough, had probably been themselves supporters of juvenile courts. A contrary decision in *McKeiver* might conceivably have sounded the death knell for juvenile courts as we know them, for jury trials are alien to their essential philosophy.

Mr. Justice Blackmun emphasized in *McKeiver* the benevolence of the juvenile court system, justifying the informality of the input and adjudicative procedures by the resulting effort at rehabilitation. The effort at *rehabilitation*, in my opinion, lay at the heart of the decision and essentially justified exclusion of the juvenile from the safeguards of *Duncan* and *Baldwin*. The Court did not consider, or certainly not with any emphasis, the problem we must now consider. If the dispositional end of the procedure is to jail the child with more mature criminals, under a relatively substantial sentence, then to what avail is the destruction of constitutional safeguards? *McKeiver*, I believe, did not purport to answer this. While confinement for more than six months in a proper *juvenile* institution would not mandate a trial by jury despite *Duncan*, there was no answer given to the question that confronts us in this case. If the disposition of the fifteen-year-old juvenile is not only for a term of more than six months, but is *also* for confinement to a penal institution where the defendant may be compelled to mingle with more hardened and older prisoners, the juvenile court "proceeding" is no more than a euphemism (a "civil label of convenience") for a criminal trial. And if it is, indeed, a substitute for a criminal trial, *Duncan* becomes more apposite than *McKeiver*.

Judge J. Joseph Smith, then a District Judge, noted more than a decade ago that to permit the sending of a juvenile, subsequent to a federal juvenile proceeding, to an institution which was not for the care and custody of juveniles "would be to permit confinement for crime without a right to trial. This would be violative of the constitutional right to due process under the Fifth Amendment and to the guarantees of fair trial of the Sixth Amendment." *United States ex rel. Stinnett v. Hegstrom*, 178 F.Supp. 17, 20–21 (D.Conn.1959); see *White v. Reid*, 126 F.Supp. 867 (D.D.C.1954). Quite simply, the respondents cannot argue that denial of jury trial is offset by the protective treatment received, when the petitioner is sent to an institution which the New York courts (*People v. Michael A.C.*, *supra*) have determined to be sufficiently penal to entitle everyone else there to the right to jury trial if he was accused of a serious crime.

Nor can the respondents fall back on the argument that the difference in treatment is justified by the juveniles' protection from the stigma of criminality. The actual benefit derived by the "unstigmatized" juvenile has been repeatedly downgraded. The small benefit cannot offset the loss of an important right. Thus, in this case, the State of New York cannot point to treatment subsequent to adjudication as a legitimate validation of the informal procedures of the Family Court.

In conclusion, I believe that Murray has a valid claim, based on the denial of that fundamental fairness which had been guaranteed to him by *In re Gault*. His claim lies within the mainstream of the juvenile due process cases, and not beyond the limit erected by *McKeiver*.

While the judicial duty to vindicate constitutional rights under the Great Writ cannot be abdicated, interference with State authorities is never a task eagerly accepted. Here, however, two factors reduce my reluctance to interfere. First, this decision will have an extremely limited disruptive effect. Only a very few boys are committed each year under § 758(b). Second, it is a small imposition to make the authorities decide, before the proceeding begins, whether they wish to seek an Elmira commitment, in which case a right to jury trial should be respected, or whether they will settle for a commitment to a State Training School, in which case more informal procedures will suffice under *McKeiver*. Every day prosecuting authorities make the same kind of threshold decision under the six-month rule established by *Baldwin v. New York*; for the right to a jury trial rides on the decision of the prosecutor whether to seek a conviction which would carry a possible sentence exceeding six months.

I hold, accordingly, that the petitioner was denied due process of law under the Fourteenth Amendment to the United States Constitution when he was sentenced to a term of three years and committed to Elmira Reception Center without benefit of the right to a trial by jury. In view of this decision, it is unnecessary to pass upon the equal protection argument.

The writ is granted, but it is ordered that the petitioner is to remain in custody pending further action by the State, whether that be:

1. A commitment by the Family Court to a State Training School; or
2. A motion by the State to transfer jurisdiction from the Family Court to the Supreme Court, pursuant to N.Y.Constitution, Article 6, § 19(a), or otherwise, so as to afford the petitioner a trial by jury on the issue of whether he committed the acts charged, with remand to the Family Court for ultimate disposition in accordance with the provisions of the Family Court Act.

If the State does not so act within thirty days from this date, he is to be discharged from custody.

It is so ordered.

CAPITAL PUNISHMENT

Case Comment

The U.S. Supreme Court first confronted the issue of age and capital punishment in 1982 in *Eddings v. Oklahoma*.[10] This case involved a sixteen-year-old boy who killed a highway patrol officer. While the Court overturned his sentence, it did so on the grounds that the trial court had failed to consider his emotional state and troubled childhood when dispensing the death penalty.

In 1988, however, the Supreme Court prohibited the execution of persons below age sixteen in the narrowly interpreted case of *Thompson v. Oklahoma*.[11] Some justices endorsed the idea that less responsibility should exist when a child commits a criminal homicide. This decision left unanswered the issue of whether the Constitution prohibits the

use of the death penalty for juveniles who were sixteen or seventeen year olds when they committed their crimes.

And finally, with the following case of *Stanford v. Kentucky*, the Court confronted the constitutionality of executing juveniles again. The question was: at what age does the Eighth Amendment ban the death penalty as punishment no matter what the crime? Critics of the death penalty believed that there was a consensus against executing young people in the United States. Supporters of capital punishment argued that juveniles after age sixteen should be held fully responsible for murder. The Supreme Court concluded that states were free to impose the death penalty for murderers who committed their crimes while age sixteen or seventeen. According to the majority opinion written by Justice Antonin Scalia, society had not formed a consensus that such executions constitute a cruel and unusual punishment in violation of the Eighth Amendment.[12]

STANFORD v. KENTUCKY

Cite as 109 S.Ct. 2969 (1989)

Justice Scalia delivered the opinion of the Court with respect to Parts I, II, III, and IV-A, concluding that the imposition of capital punishment on an individual for a crime committed at 16 or 17 years of age does not constitute cruel and unusual punishment under the Eighth Amendment. Pp. 2972–2977.

(a) Whether a particular punishment violates the Eighth Amendment depends on whether it constitutes one of "those modes or acts of punishment . . . considered cruel and unusual at the time that the Bill of Rights was adopted," *Ford v. Wainwright*, 477 U.S. 399, 405, 106 S.Ct. 2595, 2600, 91 L.Ed.2d 335, or is contrary to the "evolving standards of decency that mark the progress of a maturing society," *Trop v. Dulles*, 356 U.S. 86, 101, 78 S.Ct. 590, 598, 2 L.Ed.2d 630. Petitioners have not alleged that their sentences would have been considered cruel and unusual in the 18th century, and could not support such a contention, since, at that time, the common law set the rebuttable presumption of incapacity to commit felonies (which were punishable by death) at the age of 14. In accordance with this common-law tradition, at least 281 offenders under 18, and 126 under 17, have been executed in this country. P. 2974.

(b) In determining whether a punishment violates evolving standards of decency, this Court looks not to its own subjective conceptions, but, rather, to the conceptions of modern American society as reflected by objective evidence. E.g., *Coker v. Georgia*, 433 U.S. 584, 592, 97 S.Ct. 2861, 2866, 53 L.Ed.2d 982. The primary and most reliable evidence of national consensus—the pattern of federal and State laws—fails to meet petitioner's heavy burden of proving a settled consensus against the execution of 16- and 17-year-old offenders. Of the 37 States that permit capital punishment, 15 decline to impose it on 16-year-olds and 12 on 17-year-olds. This does not establish the degree of national agreement this Court has previously thought sufficient to label a punishment cruel and unusual. See *Tison v. Arizona*, 481 U.S. 137, 154, 107 S.Ct. 1676, 1686, 95 L.Ed.2d 127. Pp. 2974–2977.

(c) Nor is there support for petitioners' argument that a demonstrable reluctance of juries to impose, and prosecutors to seek, capital sentences for 16- and 17-year-olds establishes a societal consensus that such sentences are inappropriate. Statistics showing that a far smaller number of offenders under 18 than over 18 have been sentenced to death reflect in part the fact that a far smaller percentage of capital crimes is committed by persons in the younger age group. Beyond that, it is likely that the very considerations that induce petitioners to believe death should *never* be imposed on such young offenders cause prosecutors and juries to believe it should *rarely* be imposed, so that the statistics are no proof of a categorical aversion. P. 2977.

Justice Scalia, joined by the Chief Justice, Justice White, and Justice Kennedy, concluded in Parts IV-B and V that:

1. There is no relevance to the state laws cited by petitioners which set 18 or more as the legal age for engaging in various activities, ranging from driving to drinking alcoholic beverages to voting. Those laws operate in gross, and do not conduct individualized maturity tests for each driver, drinker, or voter; an age appropriate in the vast majority of cases must therefore be selected. In the realm of capital punishment, however, individualized consideration is a constitutional requirement. Twenty-nine States, including Kentucky and Missouri, have codified this requirement in laws specifically designating age as a mitigating factor that capital sentencers must be permitted to consider. Moreover, the determinations required by transfer statutes such as Kentucky's

and Missouri's to certify a juvenile for trial as an adult ensure individualized consideration of the maturity and moral responsibility of 16- and 17-year-olds before they are even held to stand trial as adults. It is those particularized laws, rather than the generalized driving, drinking, and voting laws, that display society's views on the age at which no youthful offender should be held responsible. Pp. 2977–2979.

2. The indicia of national consensus offered by petitioner other than state and federal statutes and the behavior of prosecutors and juries cannot establish constitutional standards. Public opinion polls, the views of interest groups, and the positions of professional associations are too uncertain a foundation for constitutional law. Also insufficient is socioscientific or ethicoscientific evidence tending to show that capital punishment fails to deter 16- and 17-year-olds because they have a less highly developed fear of death, and fails to exact just retribution because juveniles, being less mature and responsible, are less morally blameworthy. The audience for such arguments is not this Court but the citizenry. Although several of the Court's cases have engaged in so-called "proportionality" analysis—which examines whether there is a disproportion between the punishment imposed, and the defendant's blameworthiness, and whether a punishment makes any measurable contribution to acceptable goals of punishment—those decisions have never invalidated a punishment on that basis alone, but have done so only when there was also objective evidence of state laws or jury determinations establishing a societal consensus against the penalty. Pp. 2979–2980.

Justice O'Connor, although agreeing that no national consensus presently forbids the imposition of capital punishment on 16- or 17-year-old murderers, concluded that this Court has a constitutional obligation to conduct proportionality analysis, see e.g., *Penry v. Lynaugh*, __ U.S. __ , 109 S.Ct. 2934, __ L.Ed.2d __ , and should consider age-based statutory classifications that are relevant to that analysis. Pp. 2980–2981.

Scalia, J., announced the judgment of the Court and delivered the opinion of the Court with respect to Parts I, II, II, and IV-A, in which Rehnquist, C.J., and White, O'Connor, and Kennedy, JJ. joined, and an opinion with respect to Parts IV-B and V, in which Rehnquist, C.J., and White and Kennedy, JJ., joined. O'Connor, J., filed an opinion concurring in part and concurring in the judgment. Brennan, J., filed a dissenting opinion in which Marshall, Blackmun and Stevens, J.J., joined.

Frank W. Heft, Jr., Louisville, Ky., for petitioner.

Frederic J. Cowan, Louisville, Ky., for respondent.

Justice Scalia announced the judgment of the Court and delivered the opinion of the Court with respect to Parts I, II, III, and IV-A, and an opinion with respect to Parts IV-B and V, in which the Chief Justice, Justice White and Justice Kennedy join.

These two consolidated cases require us to decide whether the imposition of capital punishment on an individual for a crime committed at 16 or 17 years of age constitutes cruel and unusual punishment under the Eighth Amendment.

I

The first case, No. 87–5765, involves the shooting death of 20-year-old Baerbel Poore in Jefferson County, Kentucky. Petitioner Kevin Stanford committed the murder on January 7, 1981, when he was approximately 17 years and 4 months of age. Stanford and his accomplice repeatedly raped and sodomized Poore during and after their commission of a robbery at a gas station where she worked as an attendant. They then drove her to a secluded area near the station, where Stanford shot her point-blank in the face and then in the back of her head. The proceeds from the robbery were roughly 300 cartons of cigarettes, two gallons of fuel and a small amount of cash. A corrections officer testified that petitioner explained the murder as follows: " '[H]e said, I had to shoot her, [she] lived next door to me and she would recognize me. . . . I guess we could have tied her up or something or beat [her up] . . . and tell her if she tells, we would kill her. . . . Then after he said that he started laughing.' " 734 S.W.2d 781, 788 (Ky. 1987).

After Stanford's arrest, a Kentucky juvenile court conducted hearings to determine whether he should be transferred for trial as an adult under Ky.Rev.Stat. § 208.170 (Michie 1982). That statute provided that juvenile court jurisdiction could be waived and an offender tried as an adult if he was either charged with a Class A felony or capital crime, or was over 16 years of age and charged with a felony. Stressing the seriousness of petitioner's offenses and the unsuccessful attempts of the juvenile system to treat him for numerous instances of past delinquency, the juvenile court found certification for trial as an adult to be in the best interest of petitioner and the community.

Stanford was convicted of murder, first-degree sodomy, first-degree robbery, and receiving stolen property, and was sentenced to death and 45 years in prison. The Kentucky Supreme Court affirmed the death sentence, rejecting Stanford's "deman[d] that he has a constitutional right to treatment" 734 S.W.2d, at 792. Finding that the record clearly demonstrated that "there was no program or treatment appropriate for the appellant in the juvenile justice system," the court held that the juvenile court did not err in certifying petitioner for trial as an adult. The court also stated that petitioner's "age and the possibility that he might be rehabilitated were mitigating factors appropriately left to the consideration of the jury that tried him." Ibid.

The second case before us today, No. 87–6026, involves the stabbing death of Nancy Allen, a 26-year-old mother of two who was working behind the sales counter of the convenience store she and David Allen owned and operated in Avondale, Missouri. Petitioner Heath Wilkins committed the murder on July 27, 1985, when he was approximately 16 years and 6 months of age. The record reflects that Wilkins' plan was to rob the store and murder "whoever was behind the counter" because "a dead person can't talk." While Wilkins' accomplice, Patrick Stevens, held Allen, Wilkins stabbed her, causing her to fall to the floor. When Stevens had trouble operating the cash register, Allen spoke up to assist him, leading Wilkins to stab her three more times in her chest. Two of these wounds penetrated the victim's heart. When Allen began to beg for her life, Wilkins stabbed her four more times in the neck, opening her carotid artery. After helping themselves to liquor, cigarettes, rolling papers, and approximately $450 in cash and checks, Wilkins and Stevens left Allen to die on the floor.

Because he was roughly six months short of the age of majority for purposes of criminal prosecution, Mo.Rev.Stat. § 211.021(1) (1986), Wilkins could not automatically be tried as an adult under Missouri law. Before that could happen, the juvenile court was required to terminate juvenile-court jurisdiction and certify Wilkins for trial as an adult under § 211.071, which permits individuals between 14 and 17 years of age who have committed felonies to be tried as adults. Relying on the "viciousness, force, and violence" of the alleged crime, petitioner's maturity, and the failure of the juvenile justice system to rehabilitate him after previous delinquent acts, the juvenile court made the necessary certification.

Wilkins was charged with first-degree murder, armed criminal action, and carrying a concealed weapon. After the court found him competent, petitioner entered guilty pleas to all charges. A punishment hearing was held, at which both the State and petitioner himself urged imposition of the death sentence. Evidence at the hearing revealed that petitioner had been in and out of juvenile facilities since the age of eight for various acts of burglary, theft, and arson, had attempted to kill his mother by putting insecticide into Tylenol capsules, and had killed several animals in his neighborhood. Although psychiatric testimony indicated that Wilkins had "personality disorders," the witnesses agreed that Wilkins was aware of his actions and could distinguish right from wrong.

Determining that the death penalty was appropriate, the trial court entered the following order:

> The court finds beyond reasonable doubt that the following aggravated circumstances exist:
>
> 1. The murder in the first degree was committed while the defendant was engaged in the perpetration of the felony and robbery, and
>
> 2. The murder in the first degree involved depravity of mind and that as a result thereof, it was outrageously or wantonly vile, horrible or inhuman. App. in No. 87–6026.

On mandatory review of Wilkins' death sentence, the Supreme Court of Missouri affirmed, rejecting the argument that the punishment violated the Eighth Amendment. 736 S.W.2d 409 (1987).

We granted certiorari in these cases, 488 U.S. __ , 109 S.Ct. 217, 102 L.Ed.2d 208 and 487 U.S. __ , 108 S.Ct. 2896, 101 L.Ed.2d 930 (1988), to decide whether the Eighth Amendment precludes the death penalty for individuals who commit crimes at 16 or 17 years of age.

II

The thrust of both Wilkins' and Stanford's arguments is that imposition of the death penalty on those who were juveniles when they committed their crimes falls within the Eighth Amendment's prohibition against "cruel and unusual punishments."

Wilkins would have us define juveniles as individuals 16 years of age and under. Stanford would draw the line at 17.

[1] Neither petitioner asserts that this sentence constitutes one of "those modes or acts of punishment that had been considered cruel and unusual at the time that the Bill of Rights was adopted." *Ford v. Wainwright*, 477 U.S. 399, 405, 106 S.Ct. 2595, 2600, 91 L.Ed.2d 335 (1986). Nor could they support such a contention. At that time, the common law set the rebuttable presumption of incapacity to commit any felony at the age of 14, and theoretically permitted capital punishment to be imposed on anyone over the age of 7. See 4 Blackstone, Commentaries *23–24; 1 M. Hale, Pleas of the Crown, 24–29 (1800 ed.). See also *In re Gault*, 387 U.S. 1, 16, 87 S.Ct. 1428, 1437, 18 L.Ed.2d 527 (1967); Streib, Death Penalty for Children: The American Experience with Capital Punishment for Crime Committed While Under Age Eighteen, 36 Okla.L.Rev. 613, 614–615 (1983); Kean, The History of the Criminal Liability of Children, 53 L.Q.Rev. 364, 369–370 (1937). In accordance with the standards of this common-law tradition, at least 281 offenders under the age of 18 have been executed in this country, and at least 126 under the age of 17. See V. Streib, Death Penalty for Juveniles 57 (1987).

[2] Thus petitioners are left to argue that their punishment is contrary to the "evolving standards of decency that mark the progress of a maturing society," *Trop v. Dulles*, 356 U.S. 86, 101, 78 S.Ct. 590, 598, 2 L.Ed.2d 630 (1958) (plurality opinion). They are correct in asserting that this Court has "not confined the prohibition embodied in the Eighth Amendment to 'barbarous' methods that were generally outlawed in the 18th century," but instead has interpreted the Amendment "in a flexible and dynamic manner." *Gregg v. Georgia*, 428 U.S. 153, 171, 96 S.Ct. 2909, 2924, 49 L.Ed.2d 859 (1976). In determining what standards have "evolved," however, we have looked not to our own conceptions of decency, but to those of modern American society as a whole.[1] As we have said, "Eighth Amendment judgments should not be, or appear to be, merely

---

1. We emphasize that it is *American* conceptions of decency that are dispositive, rejecting the contention of petitioners and their various *amici* (accepted by the dissent, see *post*, at 2984–2986) that the sentencing practices of other countries are relevant. While "the practices of other nations, particularly other democracies, can be relevant to determining whether a practice uniform among our people is not merely an historical accident, but rather so 'implicit in the concept of ordered liberty' that it occupies a place not merely

(continued on next page)

the subjective views of individual Justices; judgment should be informed by objective factors to the maximum possible extent." *Coker v. Georgia*, 433 U.S. 584, 592, 97 S.Ct. 2861, 2866, 53 L.Ed.2d 982 (1977) (plurality opinion). See also *Penry v. Lynaugh*, __ U.S. at __ , 109 S.Ct., at __ ; *Ford v. Wainwright, supra*, 477 U.S., at 406, 106 S.Ct., at 2600, *Enmund v. Florida*, 458 U.S. 782, 788–789, 102 S.Ct. 3368, 787–788, 73 L.Ed.2d 1140 (1982); *Furman v. Georgia*, 408 U.S. 238, 277–279, 92 S.Ct. 2726, 2746–2747, 33 L.Ed.2d 346 (1972) (Brennan, J., concurring). This approach is dictated both by the language of the Amendment—which proscribes only those punishments that are both "cruel and *unusual*"—and by the "deference we owe to the decisions of the state legislatures under our federal system," *Gregg v. Georgia, supra*, 428 U.S., at 176, 96 S.Ct., at 2926.

III

[3] "[F]irst" among the " 'objective indicia that reflect the public attitude toward a given sanction' " are statutes passed by society's elected representatives. *McCleskey v. Kemp*, 481 U.S. 279, 300, 107 S.Ct. 1756, 1770, 95 L.Ed.2d 262 (1987), quoting *Gregg v. Georgia, supra*, 428 U.S., at 173, 96 S.Ct., at 2925. Of the 37 States whose laws permit capital punishment, 15 decline to impose it upon 16-year-

old offenders and 12 decline to impose it on 17-year-old offenders.[2] This does not establish the degree of national consensus this Court has previously thought sufficient to label a particular punishment cruel and unusual. In invalidating the death penalty for rape of an adult woman, we stressed that Georgia was the *sole* jurisdiction that authorized such a punishment. See *Coker v. Georgia*, 433 U.S., at 595–596, 97 S.Ct., at 2867–2868. In striking down capital punishment for participation in a robbery in which an accomplice takes a life, we emphasized that only eight jurisdictions authorized similar punishment. *Enmund v. Florida*, 458 U.S., at 792, 102 S.Ct., at 3374. In finding that the Eighth Amendment precludes execution of the instance and thus requires an adequate hearing on the issue of sanity, we relied upon (in addition to the common-law rule) the fact that "no State in the Union" permitted such punishment. *Ford v. Wainwright*, 477 U.S., at 408, 106 S.Ct., at 2601. And in striking down a life sentence without parole under a recidivist statute, we stressed that "[i]t appears that [petitioner] was treated more severely than he would have been in any other State." *Solem v. Helm,* 463 U.S. 277, 300, 103 S.Ct. 3001, 3015, 77 L.Ed.2d 637 (1983).

[4] Since a majority of the States that permit capital punishment authorize it for crimes committed at age 16 or above,[3] petitioners' cases are more analogous to *Tison v. Arizona*, 481 U.S. 137, 107 S.Ct.

---

in our mores, but, text permitting, in our Constitution as well," see *Thompson v. Oklahoma*, 487 U.S. __ , __ __ , n. 4, 108 S.Ct. 2687, 2691–2692, n. 4, 101 L.Ed.2d 702 (1988) (Scalia, J., dissenting), quoting *Palko v. Connecticut*, 302 U.S. 319, 325, 58 S.Ct. 149, 152, 82 L.Ed. 288 (1937) (Cardozo, J.), they cannot serve to establish the first Eighth Amendment prerequisite, that the practice is accepted among our people.

2. The following States preclude capital punishment of offenders under 18: California (Cal.Penal Code Ann. § 190.5 (West 1988)); Colorado (Col.Rev.Stat. § 16–11–103(1)(a) (1986)); Connecticut (Conn.Gen.Stat.Ann. § 53a–46a(g)(1) (1985)); Illinois (Ill.Rev.Stat. ch. 38, ¶ 9–1(b) (1987)); Maryland (Md.Ann.Code, Art. 27, § 412(f) (Supp.1988)); Nebraska (Neb.Rev.Stat. § 28–105.01 (1985)); New Jersey (N.J.Stat.Ann. § 2A:4A–22(a) (1987) and 2C:11–3(g) (Supp.1988)); New Hampshire (N.H.Rev.Stat.Ann. § 630:5(XIII) (Supp.1988)); New Mexico (N.M.Stat.Ann. §§ 28–6–1(A), 31–18–14(A) (1987)); Ohio (Ohio Rev.Code Ann. § 2929.02(A) (1987)); Oregon (Ore.Rev.Stat. §§ 161.620 and 419.476(1) (1987)); Tennessee (Tenn.Code Ann. §§ 37–1–102(3), 37–1–102(4), 37–1–103, 37–1–134(a)(1) (1984 and Supp.1988)). Three more States preclude the death penalty for offenders under 17: Georgia (Ga.Code Ann. § 17–9–3 (1982)); North Carolina (N.C.Gen.Stat. § 14–17 (Supp.1988)); Texas (Tex.Penal Code Ann. § 8.07(d) Supp.1989)).

The dissent takes issue with our failure to include, among those States evidencing a consensus against executing 16- and 17-year-old offenders, the District of Columbia and the 14 States that do not authorize capital punishment. *Post*, at 2982–2983. It seems to us, however, that while the number of those jurisdictions bears upon the question whether there is a consensus against capital punishment altogether, it is quite irrelevant to the specific inquiry in this case: whether there is a settled consensus in favor of punishing offenders under 18 differently from those over 18 insofar as capital punishment is concerned. The dissent's position is rather like discerning a national consensus that wagering on cockfights is inhumane by counting within that consensus those States that bar all wagering. The issue in the present case is not whether capital punishment is thought to be desirable but whether persons under 18 are thought to be specially exempt from it. With respect to that inquiry, it is no more logical to say that the capital-punishment laws of those States which prohibit capital punishment (and thus do not address age) support the dissent's position, than it would be to say that the age-of-adult-criminal-responsibility laws of those same States (which do not address capital punishment) support our position.

3. The dissent again works its statistical magic by refusing to count among the States that authorize capital punishment of 16- and 17-year-old offenders those 18 States that set no minimum age in their death penalty statute, and specifically permit 16-and 17-year-olds to be sentenced as adults. *Post*, at 2983. We think that describing this position is adequate response.

1676, 95 L.Ed.2d 127 (1987) than *Coker, Enmund, Ford*, and *Solem*. In *Tison*, which upheld Arizona's imposition of the death penalty for major participation in a felony with reckless indifference to human life, we noted that only 11 of those jurisdictions imposing capital punishment rejected its use in such circumstances. *Id.*, at 154, 107 S.Ct. at 1686. As we noted earlier, here the number is 15 for offenders under 17, and 12 for offenders under 18. We think the same conclusion as in *Tison* is required in this case.

Petitioners make much of the recently enacted federal statute providing capital punishment for certain drug-related offenses, but limiting that punishment to offenders 18 and over. The Anti-Drug Abuse Act of 1988, Pub.L. 100–690, 102 Stat. 4390, § 7001(b). That reliance is entirely misplaced. To begin with, the statute in question does not embody a judgment by the Federal Legislature that *no* murder is heinous enough to warrant the execution of such a youthful offender, but merely that the narrow class of offense it defines is not. The congressional judgment on the broader question, if apparent at all, is to be found in the law that permits 16- and 17-year-olds (after appropriate findings) to be tried and punished as adults for *all* federal offenses, including those bearing a capital penalty that is not limited to 18-year-olds.[4] See 18 U.S.C. § 5032 (1982 ed., Supp.V). Moreover, even if it were true that no federal statute permitted the execution of persons under 18, that would not remotely establish—in the face of a substantial number of state statutes to the contrary—a national consensus that such punishment is inhumane, any more than the absence of a federal lottery establishes a national consensus that lotteries are socially harmful. To be sure, the absence of a federal death penalty for 16- or 17-year-olds (if it existed) might be evidence that there is no national consensus *in favor* of such punishment. It is not the burden of Kentucky and Missouri, however, to establish a national consensus approving what their citizens have voted to do; rather, it is the "heavy burden" of petitioners, *Gregg v. Georgia*, 428 U.S., at 175, 96 S.Ct., at 2926, to establish a national consensus *against* it. As far as the primary and most reliable indication of consensus is concerned—the pattern of enacted laws—petitioners have failed to carry that burden.

IV

A

[5] Wilkins and Stanford argue, however, that even if the laws themselves do not establish a settled consensus, the application of the laws does. That contemporary society views capital punishment of 16- and 17-year-old offenders as inappropriate is demonstrated, they say, by the reluctance of juries to impose, and prosecutors to seek, such sentences. Petitioners are quite correct that a far smaller number of offenders under 18 than over 18 have been sentenced to death in this country. From 1982 through 1988, for example, out of 2,106 total death sentences, only 15 were imposed on individuals who were 16 or under when they committed their crimes, and only 30 on individuals who were 17 at the time of the crime. See Streib, Imposition of Death Sentences For Juvenile Offenses, January 1, 1982, Through April 1, 1989, p. 2 (paper for Cleveland-Marshall College of Law, April 5, 1989). And it appears that actual executions for crimes committed under age 18 accounted for only about two percent of the total number of executions that occurred between 1642 and 1986. See Streib, Death Penalty for Juveniles, at 55, 57. As Wilkins points out, the last execution of a person who committed a crime under 17 years of age occurred in 1959. These statistics, however, carry little significance. Given the undisputed fact that a far smaller percentage of capital crimes is committed by persons under 18 than over 18, the discrepancy in treatment is much less than

---

4. See 10 U.S.C. § 906a (1982 ed., Supp. V) (peacetime espionage); 10 U.S.C. § 918 (murder by persons subject to Uniform Code of Military Justice); 18 U.S.C. §§ 32, 33, and 34 (1982 ed. and Supp. V) (destruction of aircraft, motor vehicles, or related facilities resulting in death); § 115(b)(3) (1982 ed., Supp. V) (retaliatory murder of member of immediate family of law enforcement officials) (by cross-reference to § 1111 (1982 ed. and Supp. V)); § 351 (1982 ed. and Supp. V); (murder of Member of Congress, high-ranking executive official, or Supreme Court Justice) (by cross-reference to § 1111); § 794 (1982 ed. and Supp. V) (espionage); § 844(f) (1982 ed., Supp. V) (destruction of government property resulting in death); § 1111 (first-degree murder within federal jurisdiction); § 1716 (1982 ed. and Supp. V) (mailing of injurious articles resulting in death); § 1751 (assassination or kidnapping resulting in death of President or Vice President); § 1992 (willful wrecking of train resulting in death); § 2113 (1982 ed. and Supp. V) (bank robbery-related murder or kidnapping); § 2381 (treason); 49 U.S.C.App. §§ 1472 and 1473 (1982 ed. and Supp. IV) (death resulting from aircraft hijacking).

might seem. Granted, however, that a substantial discrepancy exists, that does not establish the requisite proposition that the death sentence for offenders under 18 is categorically unacceptable to prosecutors and juries. To the contrary, it is not only possible but overwhelmingly probable that the very considerations which induce petitioners and their supporters to believe that death should *never* be imposed on offenders under 18 cause prosecutors and juries to believe that it should *rarely* be imposed.

B

[6] This last point suggests why there is also no relevance to the laws cited by petitioners and their *amici* which set 18 or more as the legal age for engaging in various activities, ranging from driving to drinking alcoholic beverages to voting. It is, to begin with, absurd to think that one must be mature enough to drive carefully, to drink responsibly, or to vote intelligently, in order to be mature enough to understand that murdering another human being is profoundly wrong, and to conform one's conduct to that most minimal of all civilized standards. But even if the requisite degrees of maturity were comparable, the age-statutes in question would still not be relevant. They do not represent a social judgment that all persons under the designated ages are not responsible enough to drive, to drink, or to vote, but at most a judgment that the vast majority are not. These laws set the appropriate ages for the operation of a system that makes its determinations in gross, and that does not conduct individualized ma-

turity tests for each driver, drinker, or voter. The criminal justice system, however, does provide individualized testing. In the realm of capital punishment in particular, "individualized consideration [is] a constitutional requirement," *Lockett v. Ohio*, 438 U.S. 586, 605, 98 S.Ct. 2954, 2965, 57 L.Ed.2d 973 (1978) (opinion of Burger, C.J.) (footnote omitted); see also *Zant v. Stephens*, 462 U.S. 862, 879, 103 S.Ct. 2733, 2743, 77 L.Ed.2d 235 (1983) (collecting cases), and one of the individualized mitigating factors that sentencers must be permitted to consider is the defendant's age. See *Eddings v. Oklahoma*, 455 U.S. 104, 115–116, 102 S.Ct. 869, 877–878, 71 L.Ed.2d 1 (1982). Twenty-nine States, including both Kentucky and Missouri, have codified this constitutional requirement in laws specifically designating the defendant's age as a mitigating factor in capital cases.[5] Moreover, the determinations required by juvenile transfer statutes to certify a juvenile for trial as an adult ensure individualized consideration of the maturity and moral responsibility of 16- and 17-year-old offenders before they are even held to stand trial as adults.[6] The application of this particularized system to the petitioners can be declared constitutionally inadequate only if there is a consensus not that 17 or 18 is the age at which most persons, or even almost all persons, achieve sufficient maturity to be held fully responsible for murder; but that 17 or 18 is the age before which *no one* can reasonably be held fully responsible. What displays society's views on this latter point are not the ages set forth in the generalized system of driving, drinking, and voting laws cited

5. See Ala.Code § 13A–5–51(7) (1982); Ariz.Rev.Stat.Ann. § 13–703(G)(5) (Supp.1988); Ark.Code Ann. § 5–4–605(4) (1987); Cal.Penal Code Ann. § 190.05(h)(9) (West 1988); Col.Rev.Stat. § 16–11–103(5)(a) (1986); Conn.Gen.Stat. § 53a–46a(g)(1) (1985); Fla.Stat. § 921.141(6)(g) (1987); Ind.Code § 35–50–2–9(c)(7) (1988); Ky.Rev.Stat.Ann. § 532.025(2)(b)(8) (Baldwin 1988); La.Code Crim.Pro.Ann., Art. 905.5(f) (West 1984); Md.Ann.Code, Art. 27, § 413(g)(5) (1988); Miss.Code Ann. § 99–19–101(6)(g) (Supp.1988); Mo.Rev.Stat. § 565.032.3(7) (1986); Mont.Code Ann. § 46–18–304(7) (1987); Neb.Rev.Stat. § 29–2523(2)(d) (1985); Nev.Rev.Stat. § 200.035(6) (1987); N.H.Rev.Stat.Ann. § 630:5(II)(b)(5) (1986); N.J.Stat.Ann. § 2C:11–3(c)(5)(c) (Supp.1988); N.M.Stat.Ann. § 31–20A–6(I) (1987); N.C.Gen.Stat. § 15A–2000(f)(7) (1988); Ohio Rev.Code Ann. § 2929.04(B)(4) (1987); Ore.Rev.Stat. § 163.150(1)(b)(B) (1987); 42 Pa.Cons.Stat. § 9711(e)(4) (1982); S.C.Code § 16–3–20(C)(b)(9) (1988); Tenn.Code Ann. § 39–2–203(j)(7) (1982); Utah Code Ann. § 76–3–207(2)(e) (Supp.1988); Va.Code § 19.2–264.4(B)(v) (1983); Wash.Rev.Code § 10.95.070(7) (Supp.1989); Wyo.Stat. § 6–2–102(j)(vii) (1988).

6. The Kentucky statute under which Stanford was certified to be tried as an adult provides in relevant part:

"(3) If the court determines that probable cause exists [to believe that a person 16 years old or older committed a felony or that a person under 16 years of age committed a Class A felony or a capital offense], it shall then determine if it is in the best interest of the child and the community to order such a transfer based upon the seriousness of the alleged offense; whether the offense was against person or property, with greater weight being given to offenses against persons; the maturity of the child as determined by his environment; the child's prior record; and the prospects for adequate protection of the public and the likelihood of reasonable rehabilitation of the child by the use of procedures, services, and facilities currently available to the juvenile justice system." Ky.Rev.Stat. § 208.170 (Michie 1982) (repealed effective July 15, 1984).

by petitioners and their *amici*, but the ages at which the States permit their particularized capital punishment systems to be applied.[7]

V

[7] Having failed to establish a consensus against capital punishment for 16- and 17-year-old offenders through state and federal statutes and the behavior of prosecutors and juries, petitioners seek to demonstrate it through other indicia, including public opinion polls, the views of interest groups and the positions adopted by various professional associations. We decline the invitation to rest constitutional law upon such uncertain foundations. A revised national consensus so broad, so clear and so enduring as to justify a permanent prohibition upon all units of democratic government must appear in the operative acts (laws and the application of laws) that the people have approved.

[8] We also reject petitioners' argument that we should invalidate capital punishment of 16- and 17-year-old offenders on the ground that it fails to serve the legitimate goals of penology. According to petitioners, it fails to deter because juveniles, possessing less developed cognitive skills than adults, are less likely to fear death; and it fails to exact just retribution because juveniles, being less mature and responsible, are also less morally blameworthy. In support of these claims, petitioners and their supporting *amici* marshall an array of socioscientific evidence concerning the psychological and emotional development of 16- and 17-year-olds.

If such evidence could conclusively establish the entire lack of deterrent effect and moral responsibility, resort to the Cruel and Unusual Punishments Clause would be unnecessary; the Equal Protection Clause of the Fourteenth Amendment would invalidate these laws for lack of rational basis. See *Dallas v. Stanglin*, 490 U.S. ___, 109 S.Ct. 1591, 104 L.Ed.2d 18 (1989). But as the adjective "socioscientific" suggests (and insofar as evaluation of moral responsibility is concerned perhaps the adjective "ethicoscientific" would be more apt), it is not demonstrable that no 16-year-old is "adequately responsible" or significantly deterred. It is rational, even if mistaken, to think the contrary. The battle must be fought, then, on the field of the Eighth Amendment; and in that struggle socioscientific, ethicoscientific, or even purely scientific evidence is not an available weapon. The punishment is either "cruel *and* unusual" (i.e., society has set its face against it) or it is not. The audience for these arguments, in other words, is not this Court but the citizenry of the United States. It is they, not we, who must be persuaded. For as we stated earlier, our job is to *identify* the "evolving standards of decency"; to determine, not what they *should* be, but what they *are*. We have no power under the Eighth Amendment to substitute our belief in the scientific evidence for the society's apparent skepticism. In short, we emphatically reject petitioner's suggestion

---

The Missouri statute under which Wilkins was certified provides that in determining whether to transfer a juvenile the court must consider

"(1) The seriousness of the offense alleged and whether the protection of the community requires transfer to the court of general jurisdiction;

"(2) Whether the offense alleged involved viciousness, force and violence;

"(3) Whether the offense alleged was against persons or property with greater weight being given to the offense against persons, especially if personal injury resulted;

"(4) Whether the offense alleged is a part of a repetitive pattern of offenses which indicates that the child may be beyond rehabilitation under the juvenile code;

"(5) The record and history of the child, including experience with the juvenile justice system, other courts, supervision, commitments to juvenile institutions and other placements;

"(6) The sophistication and maturity of the child as determined by consideration of his home and environmental situation, emotional condition and pattern of living;

"(7) The program and facilities available to the juvenile court in considering disposition; and

"(8) Whether or not the child can benefit from the treatment or rehabilitative programs available to the juvenile court." Mo.Rev.Stat. § 211.07(6) (1986).

7. The dissent believes that individualized consideration is no solution, because "the Eighth Amendment requires that a person who lacks that full degree of responsibility for his or her actions associated with adulthood not be sentenced to death," and this absolute cannot be assured if "a juvenile offender's level of responsibility [is] taken into account only along with a host of other factors that the court or jury may decide outweigh that want of responsibility." *Post*, at 2989. But it is equally true that individualized consideration will not absolutely assure immunity from the death penalty to the *non* juvenile who happens to be immature. If individualized consideration is constitutionally inadequate, then, the only logical conclusion is that *everyone* is exempt from the death penalty.

that the issues in this case permit us to apply our "own informed judgment," Brief for Petitioner in No. 87–6026, p. 23, regarding the desirability of permitting the death penalty for crimes by 16- and 17-year-olds.

We reject the dissent's contention that our approach, by "largely return[ing] the task of defining the contours of Eighth Amendment protection to political majorities," leaves " '[c]onstitutional doctrine [to] be formulated by the acts of those institutions which the Constitution is supposed to limit,' " *post*, at 2986 (citation omitted). When this Court cast loose from the historical moorings consisting of the original application of the Eighth Amendment, it did not embark rudderless upon a wide-open sea. Rather, it limited the Amendment's extension to those practices contrary to the "evolving *standards* of decency that mark the progress of a maturing *society*." *Trop v. Dulles*, 356 U.S. 86, 101, 78 S.Ct. 590, 598, 2 L.Ed.2d 630 (1958) (plurality opinion) (emphasis added). It has never been thought that this was a shorthand reference to the preferences of a majority of this Court. By reaching a decision supported neither by constitutional text nor by the demonstrable current standards of our citizens, the dissent displays a failure to appreciate that "those institutions which the Constitution is supposed to limit" include the Court itself. To say, as the dissent says, that "it is for *us* ultimately to judge whether the Eighth Amendment permits imposition of the death penalty," *post*, at 2986 (emphasis added), quoting *Enmund v. Florida*, 458 U.S. 782, 797, 102 S.Ct. 3368, 3377, 73 L.Ed.2d 1140 (1982)—and to mean that as the dissent means it, i.e., that it is for *us* to judge, not on the basis of what we perceive the Eighth Amendment originally prohibited, or on the basis of what we perceive the society through its democratic processes now overwhelmingly disapproves, but on the basis of what we think "proportionate" and "measurably contributory to acceptable goals of punishment"—to say and mean that, is to replace judges of the law with a committee of philosopher-kings.

While the dissent is correct that several of our cases have engaged in so-called "proportionality" analysis, examining whether "there is a disproportion 'between the punishment imposed and the defendant's blameworthiness,' " and whether punishment makes any "measurable contribution to acceptable goals of punishment see *post*, at 2987, we have never invalidated a punishment on this basis

alone. All of our cases condemning a punishment under this mode of analysis also found that the objective indicators of state laws or jury determinations evidenced a societal consensus against that penalty. See *Solem v. Helm*, 463 U.S. 277, 299–300, 103 S.Ct. 3001, 3014–3015, 77 L.Ed.2d 637 (1983); *Enmund v. Florida*, *supra*, 458 U.S. at 789–796, 102 S.Ct., at 3372–3376; *Coker v. Georgia*, 433 U.S. 584, 593–597, 97 S.Ct. 2861, 2866–2869, 53 L.Ed.2d 982 (1977) (plurality opinion). In fact, the two methodologies blend into one another, since "proportionality" analysis itself can only be conducted on the basis of the standards set by our own society; the only alternative, once again, would be our personal preferences.

*   *   *

We discern neither a historical nor a modern societal consensus forbidding the imposition of capital punishment on any person who murders at 16 or 17 years of age. Accordingly, we conclude that such punishment does not offend the Eighth Amendment's prohibition against cruel and unusual punishment.

The judgments of the Supreme Court of Kentucky and the Supreme Court of Missouri are therefore affirmed.

Justice O'Connor, concurring in part and concurring in the judgment.

Last Term, in *Thompson v. Oklahoma*, 487 U.S. ___ , ___ , 108 S.Ct. 2687, ___ , 101 L.Ed.2d 702 (1988) (concurring in judgment), I expressed the view that a criminal defendant who would have been tried as a juvenile under state law, but for the granting of a petition waiving juvenile court jurisdiction, may only be executed for a capital offense if the State's capital punishment statute specifies a minimum age at which the commission of a capital crime can lead to an offender's execution and the defendant had reached that minimum age at the time the crime was committed. As a threshold matter, I indicated that such specificity is not necessary to avoid constitutional problems if it is clear that no national consensus forbids the imposition of capital punishment for crimes committed at such an age. *Id.* at ___ , 108 S.Ct., at ___ . Applying this two-part standard in *Thompson*, I concluded that Oklahoma's imposition of a death sentence on an individual who was 15 years old at the time he committed a capital offense should be set aside. Applying the same standard today, I conclude that the death sentences for capital murder imposed by Missouri and Kentucky on petitioners Wilkins and Stanford respectively should not be set aside because it is sufficiently clear that no national consensus forbids the imposition of capital punishment on 16 or 17-year-old capital murderers.

In *Thompson* I noted that "[t]he most salient statistic that bears on this case is that every single American legislature that has expressly set a minimum age for capital punishment has set that age at 16 or above." *Id.*, at __, 108 S.Ct., at 2706. It is this difference between *Thompson* and these cases, more than any other, that convinces me there is no national consensus forbidding the imposition of capital punishment for crimes committed at the age of 16 and older. See *ante*, at 2975–2976. As the Court indicates, "a majority of the States that permit capital punishment authorize it for crimes committed at age 16 or above. . . ." *Ante*, at 2976. Three States, including Kentucky, have specifically set the minimum age for capital punishment at 16, see Ind. Code § 35–50–2–3(b) (1988); Ky. Rev. Stat. Ann. § 640.040(1) (Baldwin 1987); Nev. Rev. Stat. § 176.025 (1987), and a fourth, Florida, clearly contemplates the imposition of capital punishment on 16-year-olds in its juvenile transfer statute. See Fla. Stat. § 39.02(5)(c) (1987). Under these circumstances, unlike the "peculiar circumstances" at work in *Thompson*, I do not think it necessary to require a state legislature to specify that the commission of a capital crime can lead to the execution of a 16 or 17-year-old offender. Because it is sufficiently clear that today no national consensus forbids the imposition of capital punishment in these circumstances, "the implicit nature of the [Missouri] Legislature's decision [is] not . . . constitutionally problematic." 487 U.S., at __, 108 S.Ct., at 2711. This is true, *a fortiori*, in the case of Kentucky, which has specified 16 as the minimum age for the imposition of the death penalty. The day may come when there is such general legislative rejection of the execution of 16 or 17-year-old capital murderers that a clear national consensus can be said to have developed. Because I do not believe that day has yet arrived, I concur in Parts I–IV–A of the plurality's opinion and I concur in its judgment.

I am unable, however, to join the remainder of the plurality's opinion for reasons I stated in *Thompson*. Part V of the plurality's opinion "emphatically reject[s]," *ante*, at 2979, the suggestion that beyond an assessment of the specific enactments of Amer-

ican legislatures, there remains a constitutional obligation imposed upon this Court to judge whether the " 'nexus between the punishment imposed and the defendant's blameworthiness' " is proportional. *Thompson*, *supra*, at __, 108 S.Ct., at 2708, quoting *Enmund v. Florida*, 458 U.S. 782, 825, 102 S.Ct. 3368, 3391, 73 L.Ed.2d 1140 (1982) (dissenting opinion). Part IV–B of the plurality's opinion specifically rejects as irrelevant to Eighth Amendment considerations state statutes that distinguish juveniles from adults for a variety of other purposes. In my view, this Court does have a constitutional obligation to conduct proportionality analysis. See *Penry v. Lynaugh*, __ U.S. __, __, 109 S.Ct. 2934, __, __ L.Ed.2d __ (1989); *Tison v. Arizona*, 481 U.S. 137, 155–158, 107 S.Ct. 1676, 1687–1688, 95 L.Ed.2d 127 (1987); *Enmund*, 458 U.S., at 797–801, 102 S.Ct., at 3376–3379; *id.*, at 825–826, 102 S.Ct., at 3391–3392 (dissenting opinion). In *Thompson* I specifically identified age-based classifications as "relevant to Eighth Amendment proportionality analysis." 487 U.S., at __, 108 S.Ct., at 2709. Thus, although I do not believe that these particular cases can be resolved through proportionality analysis, see *Thompson*, *supra*, at __–__, 108 S.Ct., at __–__ (concurring in judgment), I reject the suggestion that the use of such analysis is improper as a matter of Eighth Amendment jurisprudence. Accordingly, I join all but Parts IV–B and V of the Court's opinion.

END NOTES—CHAPTER VII

1. See Patrick Jackson, *The Paradox of Control: Parole Supervision of Youthful Offenders* (New York: Praeger, 1983).

2. Malcolm Goddard, "Juvenile Parole Revocation Hearings: The New York State Experience," *Criminal Law Bulletin* 13:552–73 (1977).

3. See Morton Birnhaum, "The Right to Treatment," *American Bar Association Journal* 46:499 (1960).

4. Note, "Wyatt v. Stickney—A Constitutional Right to Treatment for the Mentally Ill," *University of Pittsburgh Law Review* 34:79–84 (1972).

5. Victor Streib, *Death Penalty for Juveniles* (Bloomington, Ind.: Indiana University Press, 1987); see also Paul Reiginger, "The Death Row Kids," *American Bar Association Journal* (April 1989):78.

6. Steven Gerstein, "The Constitutionality of Executing Juvenile Offenders, *Thompson v. Oklahoma*," *Criminal Law Bulletin* 24:91–98 (1988).

7. *Morrissey v. Brewer* 408 U.S. 471 (1972); *Gagnon v. Scarpelli* 411 U.S. 778 (1973).

8. 346 F. Supp. 1354 (1972).

9. 831 F.2d 1430 (1987).
10. 455 U.S. 104 (1982).
11. 108 S.Ct. 2687 (1988).

12. For a recent analysis of the *Stanford v. Kentucky* and *Wilkins v. Missouri* cases, see Note, "Juveniles, Capital Crime, and Death Penalty," *Criminal Justice Journal* 11:240–66 (1989).

Special Problems of Minors

INTRODUCTION

This chapter deals with selected issues involving the constitutional rights of minors. It focuses primarily on the relationship between the child and two important social institutions—(1) the family and (2) the school—since both exert a powerful influence on potential delinquent behavior.

The first section reviews two important new cases dealing with the role of the child witness/victim in the judicial process. Since prosecution in child abuse cases is virtually impossible without the child's testimony, the courts have been hampered in their efforts to get at the truth. Some states have adopted innovative procedures, such as using television cameras or screens, to minimize the trauma of child witness testimony in such cases.[1] As a result, the U.S. Supreme Court has been required to determine whether such procedures unduly infringe on the constitutional rights of defendants.

The next section deals with the relationship of the child to the school. Students may be suspended for breaking rules or disobeying school officials.[2] In such cases, the U.S. Supreme Court has mandated that a hearing be held before such decisions are made.

The First Amendment rights of students in a school setting is another important issue because schools are in a position to discipline children. Students are persons under the Constitution and possess the same fundamental rights as everyone else. As a result, the Supreme Court reiterated the principle that they are entitled to procedural and substantive safeguards in a school setting.

Finally, there is the question of the termination of parental rights. This occurs whenever children are being denied care and state intervention is required on the basis that they may be harmed if they remain in parental custody. Removal of children from the home is normally only authorized by state statute and under such grounds as (1) abandonment or (2) child neglect and abuse. Since removal from the home is the most drastic order that the state may impose, the Supreme Court has established guidelines for termination proceedings.

In evaluating the various issues, the Court often utilizes a balancing test to assess the impact of the proposed freedoms on the school or the parent, as the case may be. For example, in the area of child abuse, the question may be whether the well-being of the child outweighs the defendant's right to confrontation under the Sixth Amendment. Regarding constitutionally protected free speech, the question may be whether or not the student's right to express an opinion interferes with appropriate school discipline. With respect to the termination of parental rights, the balancing test may concern itself with questions of parental unfitness versus the best interest of the child. Any analysis of constitutional rights for minors proceeds against this background.

225

THE CHILD AS A WITNESS

Case Comment

In the case of *Coy v. Iowa*, the Supreme Court limited the protection available to child sex abuse victims at the trial stage. In *Coy*, two girls were allowed to be cross-examined behind a screen that separated them from the defendant. The Court ruled that the screen violated the defendant's right to confront witnesses and overturned his conviction. However, in her supporting opinion, Justice Sandra Day O'Connor made it clear that ruling out the protective screen did not bar the states from using videotapes or closed-circuit television. Although Justice O'Connor recognized that the Sixth Amendment right to confront witnesses was violated, she indicated that an exception to a literal interpretation of the confrontation clause may be appropriate.

In *Maryland v. Craig*, the second case in this section, the Supreme Court carved out an exception to the Sixth Amendment confrontation clause by deciding that alleged child abuse victims could testify by closed-circuit television if face-to-face confrontation would cause the victims trauma. In allowing the states to take testimony via closed-circuit television, the Supreme Court has found that circumstances exist in child sex abuse cases that override the defendants' right of confrontation.

COY v. IOWA

487 U.S. 1012 (1988)

Justice Scalia delivered the opinion of the Court.

Appellant was convicted of two counts of lascivious acts with a child after a jury trial in which a screen placed between him and the two complaining witnesses blocked him from their sight. Appellant contends that this procedure, authorized by state statute, violated his Sixth Amendment right to confront the witnesses against him.

I

In August 1985, appellant was arrested and charged with sexually assaulting two 13-year-old girls earlier

that month while they were camping out in the backyard of the house next door to him. According to the girls, the assailant entered their tent after they were asleep wearing a stocking over his head, shined a flashlight in their eyes, and warned them not to look at him; neither was able to describe his face. In November 1985, at the beginning of appellant's trial, the State made a motion pursuant to a recently enacted statute, Act of May 23, 1985, § 6, 1985 Iowa Acts 338, now codified at Iowa Code § 910A.14 (1987),[1] to allow the complaining witnesses to testify either via closed-circuit television or behind a screen. See App. 4–5. The trial court approved the use of a large screen to be placed between appellant and the witness stand during the girls' testimony. After certain lighting adjustments in the courtroom, the screen would enable appellant dimly to perceive the witnesses, but the witnesses to see him not at all.

Appellant objected strenuously to use of the screen, based first of all on his Sixth Amendment confrontation right. He argued that, although the device might succeed in its apparent aim of making the complaining witnesses feel less uneasy in giving their testimony, the Confrontation Clause directly addressed this issue by giving criminal defendants a right to face-to-face confrontation. He also argued that his right to due process was violated, since the procedure would make him appear guilty and thus erode the presumption of innocence. The trial court rejected both constitutional claims, though it instructed the jury to draw no inference of guilty from the screen.

The Iowa Supreme Court affirmed appellant's conviction, 397 N.W.2d 730 (1986). It rejected appellant's confrontation argument on the ground that, since the ability to cross-examine the witnesses was not impaired by the screen, there was no violation of the Confrontation Clause. It also rejected the due process argument, on the ground that the screening procedure was not inherently prejudicial. We noted probable jurisdiction, 483 U.S. __ , 107 S.Ct. 3260, 97 L.Ed.2d 760 (1987).

II

The Sixth Amendment gives a criminal defendant the right "to be confronted with the witnesses against

---

1. Section 910A.14 provides in part as follows: The court may require a party be confined [sic] to an adjacent room or behind a screen or mirror that permits the party to see and hear the child during the child's testimony, but does not allow the child to see or hear the party. However, if a party is so confined, the court shall take measures to insure that the party and counsel can confer during the testimony and shall inform the child that the party can see and hear the child during testimony.

him." This language "comes to us on faded parchment," *California v. Green*, 399 U.S. 149, 174, 90 S.Ct. 1930, 1943, 26 L.Ed.2d 489 (1970) (Harlan, J., concurring), with a lineage that traces back to the beginning of Western legal culture. There are indications that a right of confrontation existed under Roman law. The Roman Governor Festus, discussing the proper treatment of his prisoner, Paul, stated: "It is not the manner of the Romans to deliver any man up to die before the accused has met his accusers face to face, and has been given a chance to defend himself against the charges." Acts 25:16. It has been argued that a form of the right of confrontation was recognized in England well before the right to jury trial. Pollitt, The Right of Confrontation: Its History and Modern Dress, 8 J.Pub.L. 381, 384–387 (1959).

Most of this Court's encounters with the Confrontation Clause have involved either the admissibility of out-of-court statements, see, e.g., *Ohio v. Roberts*, 448 U.S. 56, 100 S.Ct. 2531, 65 L.Ed.2d 597 (1980); *Dutton v. Evans*, 400 U.S. 74, 91 S.Ct. 210, 27 L.Ed.2d 213 (1970), or restrictions on the scope of cross-examination, *Delaware v. Van Arsdall*, 475 U.S. 673, 106 S.Ct. 1431, 89 L.Ed.2d 674 (1986); *Davis v. Alaska*, 415 U.S. 308, 94 S.Ct. 1105, 39 L.Ed.2d 347 (1974). Cf. *Delaware v. Fensterer*, 474 U.S. 15, 18–19, 106 S.Ct. 292, 294, 88 L.Ed.2d 15 (1985) (*per curiam*) (noting these two categories and finding neither applicable). The reason for that is not, as the State suggests, that these elements are the essence of the Clause's protection—but rather, quite to the contrary, that there is at least some room for doubt (and hence litigation) as to the extent to which the Clause includes those elements, whereas, as Justice Harlan put it, "[s]imply as a matter of English" it confers at least "a right to meet face to face all those who appear and give evidence at trial." *California v. Green, supra*, at 175, 90 S.Ct., at 1943–1944. Simply as a matter of Latin as well, since the word *confront* ultimately derives from the prefix *con* (from *contra* meaning "against" or "opposed") and the noun *frons* (forehead). Shakespeare was thus describing the root meaning of confrontation when he had Richard the Second say: "Then call them to our presence—face to face, and frowning brow to brow, ourselves will hear the accuser and the accused freely speak. . . ." *Richard II*, act 1, sc. 1.

We have never doubted, therefore, that the Confrontation Clause guarantees the defendant a face-to-face meeting with witnesses appearing before the trier of fact. See *Kentucky v. Stincer*, 482 U.S. __ , __ , 107 S.Ct. 2658, 2668, 96 L.Ed.2d 631 (1987) (Marshall, J., dissenting). For example, in *Kirby v. United States*, 174 U.S. 47, 55, 19 S.Ct. 574, 577, 43 L.Ed. 890 (1899), which concerned the admissibility of prior convictions of codefendants to prove an element of the offense of receiving stolen government property, we described the operation of the Clause as follows: "[A] fact which can be primarily established only by witnesses cannot be proved against an accused . . . except by witnesses who confront him at the trial, upon whom he can look while being tried, whom he is entitled to cross-examine, and whose testimony he may impeach in every mode authorized by the established rules governing the trial or conduct of criminal cases." Similarly, in *Dowdell v. United States*, 221 U.S. 325, 330, 31 S.Ct., 590, 592, 55 L.Ed. 753 (1911), we described a provision of the Philippine Bill of Rights as substantially the same as the Sixth Amendment, and proceeded to interpret it as intended "to secure the accused the right to be tried, so far as facts provable by witnesses are concerned, by only such witnesses as meet him face to face at the trial, who give their testimony in his presence, and give to the accused an opportunity of cross-examination." More recently, we have described the "literal right to 'confront' the witness at the time of trial" as forming "the core of the values furthered by the Confrontation Clause." *California v. Green, supra*, at 157, 90 S.Ct., at 1934–1935. Last Term, the plurality opinion in *Pennsylvania v. Ritchie*, 480 U.S. 39, 51, 107 S.Ct. 989, 998, 94 L.Ed.2d 40 (1987), stated that "[t]he Confrontation Clause provides two types of protections for a criminal defendant: the right physically to face those who testify against him, and the right to conduct cross-examination."

The Sixth Amendment's guarantee of face-to-face encounter between witness and accused serves ends related both to appearances and to reality. This opinion is embellished with references to and quotations from antiquity in part to convey that there is something deep in human nature that regards face-to-face confrontation between accused and accuser as "essential to a fair trial in a criminal prosecution." *Pointer v. Texas*, 380 U.S. 400, 404, 85 S.Ct. 1065, 1068, 13 L.Ed.2d 923 (1965). What was true of old is no less true in modern times. President Eisenhower once described face-to-face confrontation as part of the code of his home town of Abilene, Kansas. In Abilene, he said, it was necessary to "[m]eet anyone fact to face with whom you disagree. You could not sneak up on him from behind, or do any damage to him, without suffering the penalty of an outraged citizenry. . . . In this country, if someone dislikes you, or accuses you, he must come up in front. He cannot hide behind the shadow." Press release of remarks given to the B'nai B'rith Anti-Defamation League, November 23, 1953, quoted in Pollitt, *supra*, at 381. The phrase still persists, "Look me in the eye and say that." Given these human feelings of what is necessary for fairness,[2] the right of confrontation "contributes to the establishment of a system of criminal justice in which the perception as well as the reality of fairness prevails." *Lee v. Illinois*, 476 U.S. 530, 540, 106 S.Ct. 2056, 2062, 90 L.Ed.2d 514 (1986).

[1] The perception that confrontation is essential to fairness has persisted over the centuries because there is much truth to it. A witness "may feel quite differently when he has to repeat his story looking at the man whom he will harm greatly by distorting or mistaking the facts. He can now understand what sort of human being that man is." Z. Chafee, The Blessings of Liberty 35 (1956), quoted in *Jay v. Boyd*, 351 U.S. 345, 375–376, 76 S.Ct. 919, 935–936,

100 L.Ed. 1242 (1956) (Douglas, J., dissenting). It is always more difficult to tell a lie about a person "to his face" than "behind his back." In the former context, even if the lie is told, it will often be told less convincingly. The Confrontation Clause does not, of course, compel the witness to fix his eyes upon the defendant; he may studiously look elsewhere, but the trier of fact will draw its own conclusions. Thus the right to face-to-face confrontation serves much the same purpose as a less explicit component of the Confrontation Clause that we have had more frequent occasion to discuss—the right to cross-examine the accuser; both "ensur[e] the integrity of the fact-finding process." *Kentucky v. Stincer*, *supra*, 482 U.S, at ___ , 107 S.Ct., at 2662. The State can hardly gainsay the profound effect upon a witness of standing in the presence of the person the witness accuses, since that is the very phenomenon it relies upon to establish the potential "trauma" that allegedly justified the extraordinary procedure in the present case. That face-to-face presence may, unfortunately, upset the truthful rape victim or abused child; but by the same token it may confound and undo the false accuser, or reveal the child coached by a malevolent adult. It is a truism that constitutional protections have costs.

---

2. The dissent finds Dean Wigmore more persuasive than President Eisenhower or even William Shakespeare. *Post*, at 2807. Surely that must depend upon the proposition that they are cited for. We have cited the latter two merely to illustrate the meaning of "confrontation," and both the antiquity and currency of the human feeling that a criminal trial is not just unless one can confront his accusers. The dissent cites Wigmore for the proposition that confrontation "was not a part of the common law's view of the confrontation requirement." Ibid. To begin with, Wigmore said no such thing. What he said, precisely, was:

"There was never at common law any recognized right to an indispensable thing called confrontation as *distinguished from cross-examination*. There *was* a right to cross-examination as indispensable, and that right was involved in and secured by confrontation; it was the same right under different names." 5 J. Wigmore, Evidence § 1397, p. 158 (J. Chadbourn Rev. 1974) (emphasis in original).

He was saying, in other words, not that the right of confrontation (as we are using the term, i.e., in its natural sense) did not exist, but that its purpose was to enable cross-examination. He then continued:

"It follows that, if the accused has had the benefit of cross-examination, he has had the very privilege secured to him by the Constitution." Ibid.

Of course that does not follow at all, any more than it follows that the right to a jury trial can be dispensed with so long as the accused is justly convicted and publicly known to be justly convicted—the purposes of the right to jury trial. Moreover, contrary to what the dissent asserts, Wigmore did mention (inconsistently with his thesis, it would seem), that a secondary purpose of confrontation is to produce "a certain subjective moral effect . . . upon the witness." *Id.*, § 1395, p. 153. Wigmore grudgingly acknowledged that, in what he called "earlier and more emotional periods," this effect "was supposed (more often than it now is) to be able to unstring the nerves of a false witness," *id.*, § 1395, p. 153, n. 2; but he asserted, without support, that this effect "does not arise from the confrontation of the *opponent* and the witness," but from "the witness' presence before the *tribunal*," *id.*, § 1395, p. 154 (emphasis in original).

We doubt it. In any case, Wigmore was not reciting as a fact that there was no right of confrontation at common law, but was setting forth his thesis that the only essential interest preserved by the right was cross-examination—with the purpose, of course, of vindicating against constitutional attack sensible and traditional exceptions to the hearsay rule (which can be otherwise vindicated). The thesis is on its face implausible, if only because the phrase "be confronted with the witnesses against him" is an exceedingly strange way to express a guarantee of nothing more than cross-examination.

As for the dissent's contention that the importance of the confrontation right is "belied by the simple observation" that "blind witnesses [might have] testified against appellant," *post*, at 2808, that seems to us no more true than that the importance of the right to live, oral cross-examination is belied by the possibility that speech and hearing-impaired witnesses might have testified.

III

[2] The remaining question is whether the right to confrontation was in fact violated in this case. The screen at issue was specifically designed to enable the complaining witnesses to avoid viewing appellant as they gave their testimony, and the record indicates that it was successful in this objective. App. 10–11. It is difficult to imagine a more obvious or damaging violation of the defendant's right to a face-to-face encounter.

The State suggests that the confrontation interest at stake here was outweighed by the necessity of protecting victims of sexual abuse. It is true that we have in the past indicated that rights conferred by the Confrontation Clause are not absolute, and may give way to other important interests. The rights referred to in those cases, however, were not the right narrowly and explicitly set forth in the Clause, but rather rights that are, or were asserted to be, reasonably implicit—namely, the right to cross-examine, see *Chambers v. Mississippi*, 410 U.S. 284, 295, 93 S.Ct. 1038, 1045–1046, 35 L.Ed.2d 297 (1973); the right to exclude out-of-court statements, see *Ohio v. Roberts*, 448 U.S., at 63–65, 100 S.Ct., at 2537–2539; and the asserted right to face-to-face confrontation at some point in the proceedings other than the trial itself, *Kentucky v. Stincer*, 482 U.S. ___ , 107 S.Ct. 2658, 96 L.Ed.2d 631 (1987). To hold that our determination of what implications are reasonable must take into account other important interests is not the same as holding that we can identify exceptions, in light of other important interests, to the irreducible literal meaning of the clause: "a right to *meet face to face* all those who appear and give evidence *at trial*." *California v. Green*, 399 US., at 175, 90 S.Ct., at 1943–1944 (Harlan, J., concurring) (emphasis added). We leave for another day, however, the question whether any exceptions exist. Whatever they may be, they would surely be allowed only when necessary to further an important public policy. Cf. *Ohio v. Roberts*, 448 U.S., at 64, 100 S.Ct., at 2538; *Chambers v. Mississippi*, *supra*, at 295, 93 S.Ct., at 1045–1046. The State maintains that such necessity is established here by the statute, which creates a legislatively imposed presumption of trauma. Our cases suggest, however, that even as to exceptions from the normal implications of the Confrontation Clause, as opposed to its most literal application, something more than the type of generalized finding underlying such a statute is needed when

the exception is not "firmly . . . rooted in our jurisprudence." *Bourjaily v. United States*, 483 U.S. ___ , ___ , 107 S.Ct. 2775, 2783, 97 L.Ed.2d 144 (1987) (citing *Dutton v. Evans*, 400 U.S. 74, 91 S.Ct. 210, 27 L.Ed.2d 213 (1970)). The exception created by the Iowa statute, which was passed in 1985, could hardly be viewed as firmly rooted. (Since there have been no individualized findings that these particular witnesses needed special protection, the judgment here could not be sustained by any conceivable exception.

The State also briefly suggests that any Confrontation Clause error was harmless beyond a reasonable doubt under the standard of *Chapman v. California*, 386 U.S. 18, 24, 87 S.Ct. 824, 828, 17 L.Ed.2d 705 (1967). We have recognized that other types of violations of the Confrontation Clause are subject to that harmless error analysis, see e.g., *Delaware v. Van Arsdall*, 475 U.S., at 679, 684, 106 S.Ct., at 1436, 1437, and see no reason why denial of face-to-face confrontation should not be treated the same. An assessment of harmlessness cannot include consideration of whether the witness's testimony would have been unchanged, or the jury's assessment unaltered, had there been confrontation; such an inquiry would obviously involve pure speculation, and harmlessness must therefore be determined on the basis of the remaining evidence. The Iowa Supreme Court had no occasion to address the harmlessness issue, since it found no constitutional violation. In the circumstances of this case, rather than decide whether the error was harmless beyond a reasonable doubt, we leave the issue for the court below.

We find it unnecessary to reach appellant's due process claim. Since his constitutional right to face-to-face confrontation was violated, we reverse the judgment of the Iowa Supreme Court and remand the case.

It is so ordered.

MARYLAND v. CRAIG

497 U.S. ___ , 1990

Justice O'Connor delivered the opinion of the Court.

This case requires us to decide whether the Confrontation Clause of the Sixth Amendment categorically prohibits a child witness in a child abuse case from testifying against a defendant at trial, outside the defendant's physical presence, by one-way closed circuit television.

I

In October 1986, a Howard County grand jury charged respondent, Sandra Ann Craig, with child abuse, first and second degree sexual offenses, perverted sexual practice, assault, and battery. The named victim in each count was Brooke Etze, a six-year-old child who, from August 1984 to June 1986, had attended a kindergarten and prekindergarten center owned and operated by Craig.

In March 1987, before the case went to trial, the State sought to invoke a Maryland statutory procedure that permits a judge to receive, by one-way closed circuit television, the testimony of a child witness who is alleged to be a victim of child abuse.[1] To invoke the procedure, the trial judge must first "determin[e] that testimony by the child victim in the courtroom will result in the child suffering serious emotional distress such that the child cannot reasonably communicate." Md. Cts. & Jud. Proc. Code Ann. § 9–102(a)(1)(ii) (1989). Once the procedure is invoked, the child witness, prosecutor, and defense counsel withdraw to a separate room; the judge, jury, and defendant remain in the courtroom. The child witness is then examined and cross-examined in the separate room, while a video monitor records and displays the witness' testimony to those in the courtroom. During this time the witness cannot see the defendant. The defendant remains in electronic communication with defense counsel, and objections may be made and ruled on as if the witness were testifying in the courtroom.

In support of its motion invoking the one-way closed circuit television procedure, the State presented expert testimony that Brooke, as well as a number of other children who were alleged to have been sexually abused by Craig, would suffer "serious emotional distress such that [they could not] reasonably communicate," § 9–102(a)(1)(ii), if required to testify in the courtroom. App. 7–59. The Maryland Court of Appeals characterized the evidence as follows:

> The expert testimony in each case suggested that each child would have some or considerable difficulty in testifying in Craig's presence. For example, as to one child, the expert said that what "would cause him the most anxiety would be to testify in front of Mrs. Craig. . . ." The child "wouldn't be able to communicate effectively." As to another, an expert said she "would probably stop talking and she would withdraw and curl up." With respect to two others, the testimony was that one would "become highly agitated, that he may refuse to talk or if he did talk, that he would choose his subject regardless of the questions" while the other would "become extremely timid and unwilling to talk." 316 Md. 551, 568–569, 560 A.2d 1120, 1128–1129 (1989).

---

1. Section 9–102 of the Courts and Judicial Proceedings Article of the Annotated Code of Maryland (1989) provides in full:

(a)(1) In a case of abuse of a child as defined in § 5–701 of the Family Law Article or Article 27, § 35A of the Code, a court may order that the testimony of a child victim be taken outside the courtroom and shown in the courtroom by means of a closed circuit television if:

(i) The testimony is taken during the proceeding; and

(ii) The judge determines that testimony by the child victim in the courtroom will result in the child suffering serious emotional distress such that the child cannot reasonably communicate.

(2) Only the prosecuting attorney, the attorney for the defendant, and the judge may question the child.

(3) The operators of the closed circuit television shall make every effort to be unobtrusive.

(b)(1) Only the following persons may be in the room with the child when the child testifies by closed circuit television:

(i) The prosecuting attorney;

(ii) The attorney for the defendant;

(iii) The operators of the closed circuit television equipment; and

(iv) Unless the defendant objects, any person whose presence, in the opinion of the court, contributes to the well-being of the child, including a person who has dealt with the child in a therapeutic setting concerning the abuse.

(2) During the child's testimony by closed circuit television, the judge and the defendant shall be in the courtroom.

(3) The judge and the defendant shall be allowed to communicate with the persons in the room where the child is testifying by any appropriate electronic method.

(c) The provisions of this section do not apply if the defendant is an attorney pro se.

(d) This section may not be interpreted to preclude, for purposes of identification of a defendant, the presence of both the victim and the defendant in the courtroom at the same time.

For a detailed description of the § 9–102 procedure, see Wildermuth v. State, 310 Md. 496, 503–504, 530 A.2d 275, 278–279 (1987).

Craig objected to the use of the procedure on Confrontation Clause grounds, but the trial court rejected that contention, concluding that although the statute "take[s] away the right of the defendant to be face to face with his or her accuser," the defendant retains the "essence of the right of confrontation," including the right to observe, cross-examine, and have the jury view the demeanor of the witness. App. 65–66. The trial court further found that, "based upon evidence presented . . . the testimony of each of these children in a courtroom will result in each child suffering serious emotional distress . . . such that each of these children cannot reasonably communicate." Id., at 66. The trial court then found Brooke and three other children competent to testify and accordingly permitted them to testify against Craig via the one-way closed circuit television procedure. The jury convicted Craig on all counts, and the Maryland Court of Special Appeals affirmed the convictions, 76 Md. App. 250, 544 A.2d 784 (1988).

The Court of Appeals of Maryland reversed and remanded for a new trial. 316 Md. 551, 560 A.2d 1120 (1989). The Court of Appeals rejected Craig's argument that the Confrontation Clause requires in all cases a face-to-face courtroom encounter between the accused and his accusers, id., at 556–560 A.2d, at 1122–1125, but concluded:

> [U]nder § 9–102(a)(1)(ii), the operative "serious emotional distress" which renders a child victim unable to "reasonably communicate" must be determined to arise, at least primarily, from face-to-face confrontation with the defendant. Thus, we construe the phrase "in the courtroom" as meaning, for sixth amendment and [state constitution] confrontation purposes, "in the courtroom in the presence of the defendant." Unless prevention of "eyeball-to-eyeball" confrontation is necessary to obtain the trial testimony of the child, the defendant cannot be denied that right. Id., at 566, 560 A.2d, t 1127.

Reviewing the trial court's finding and the evidence presented in support of the § 9–102 procedure, the Court of Appeals held that, "as [it] read Coy [v. Iowa, 487 U.S. 1012 (1988)], the showing made by the State was insufficient to reach the high threshold required by that case before § 9–102 may be invoked." Id., at 554–555, 560 A.2d, at 1121 (footnote omitted).

We granted certiorari to resolve the important Confrontation Clause issues raised by this case. 493 U.S. __ 1990.

II

The Confrontation Clause of the Sixth Amendment, made applicable to the States through the Fourteenth Amendment, provides: "In all criminal prosecutions, the accused shall enjoy the right . . . to be confronted with the witnesses against him."

We observed in Coy v. Iowa that "the Confrontation Clause guarantees the defendant a face-to-face meeting with witnesses appearing before the trier of fact." 487 U.S., at 1016 (citing Kentucky v. Stincer, 482 U.S. 730, 748, 749–750 (1987) (Marshall, J., dissenting)); see also Pennsylvania v. Ritchie, 480 U.S. 39, 51 (1987) (plurality opinion); California v. Green, 399 U.S. 149, 157 (1970); Snyder v. Massachusetts, 291 U.S. 97, 106 (1934); Dowdell v. United States, 221 U.S. 325, 330 (1911); Kirby v. United States, 174 U.S. 47, 55 (1899); Mattox v. United States, 156 U.S. 237, 244 (1895). This interpretation derives not only from the literal text of the Clause, but also from our understanding of its historical roots. See Coy, supra, at 1015–1016; Mattox, supra, at 242 (Confrontation Clause intended to prevent conviction by affidavit); Green, supra, at 156 (same); cf. 3 J. Story, Commentaries § 1785, p. 662 (1833).

We have never held, however, that the Confrontation Clause guarantees criminal defendants the absolute right to a face-to-face meeting with witnesses against them at trial. Indeed, in Coy v. Iowa, we expressly "le[ft] for another day . . . the question whether any exceptions exist" to the "irreducible literal meaning of the Clause; 'a right to meet face to face all those who appear and give evidence at trial.'" 487 U.S., at 1021 (quoting Green, supra, at 175 (Harlan, J., concurring)). The procedure challenged in Coy involved the placement of a screen that prevented two child witnesses in a child abuse case from seeing the defendant as they testified against him at trial. See 487 U.S., at 1014–1015. In holding that the use of this procedure violated the defendant's right to confront witnesses against him, we suggested that any exception to the right "would surely be allowed only when necessary to further an important public policy"—i.e., only upon a showing of something more than the generalized, "legislatively imposed presumption of trauma" underlying the statute at issue in that case. Id., at 1021; see also id., at 1025 (concurring opinion). We concluded that "[s]ince there ha[d] been no individualized findings that these particular witnesses needed special protection, the judgment [in the case before us] could not be sustained by any conceivable exception." *Id.*, at 1021. Because the trial court in this case made individualized findings that each of the child witnesses needed special protection, this case requires us to decide the question reserved in *Coy*.

The central concern of the Confrontation Clause is to ensure the reliability of the evidence against a criminal defendant by subjecting it to rigorous testing in the context of an adversary proceeding before the trier of fact. The word "confront," after all, means a clashing of forces or ideas, thus carrying with it the notion of adversariness. As we noted in our earliest case interpreting the Clause:

> The primary object of the constitutional provision in question was to prevent depositions or *ex parte* affidavits, such as were sometimes admitted in civil cases, being used against the prisoner in lieu of a personal examination and cross-examination of the witness in which the accused has an opportunity, not only of testing the recollection and sifting the conscience of the witness, but of compelling him to stand face to face with the jury in order that they may look at him, and judge by his demeanor upon the stand and the manner in which he gives his testimony whether he is worthy of belief. *Mattox, supra*, at 242–243.

As this description indicates, the right guaranteed by the Confrontation Clause includes not only a "personal examination," *id.*, at 242, but also "(1) insures that the witness will give his statements under oath—thus impressing him with the seriousness of the matter and guarding against the lie by the possibility of a penalty for perjury; (2) forces the witness to submit to cross-examination, the 'greatest legal engine ever invented for the discovery of truth'; [and] (3) permits the jury that is to decide the defendant's fate to observe the demeanor of the witness in making his statement, thus aiding the jury in assessing his credibility." *Green*, 399 U.S., at 158 (footnote omitted).

The combined effect of these elements of confrontation—physical presence, oath, cross-examination, and observation of demeanor by the trier of fact— serves the purposes of the Confrontation Clause by ensuring that evidence admitted against an accused is reliable and subject to the rigorous adversarial testing that is the norma of Anglo-American criminal proceedings. See *Stincer, supra*, at 739 ("[T]he right to confrontation is a functional one for the purpose of promoting reliability in a criminal trial"); *Dutton v. Evans*, 400 U.S. 74, 89 (1970) (plurality

opinion) ("[T]he mission of the Confrontation Clause is to advance a practical concern for the accuracy of the truth-determining process in criminal trials by assuring that 'the trier of fact [has] a satisfactory basis for evaluating the truth of the [testimony]' "); *Lee v. Illinois*, 476 U.S. 530, 540 (1986) (confrontation guarantee serves "symbolic goals" and "promotes reliability"); see also *Faretta v. California*, 422 U.S. 806, 818 (1975) (Sixth Amendment "constitutionalizes the right in an adversary criminal trial to make a defense as we know it"); *Strickland v. Washington*, 466 U.S. 668, 684–685 (1984).

We have recognized, for example, that face-to-face confrontation enhances the accuracy of fact-finding by reducing the risk that a witness will wrongfully implicate an innocent person. See *Coy*, 487 U.S., at 1019–1020 ("It is always more difficult to tell a lie about a person 'to his face' than 'behind his back.' . . . That face-to-face presence may, unfortunately, upset the truthful rape victim or abused child; but by the same token it may confound and undo the false accuser, or reveal the child coached by a malevolent adult"); *Ohio v. Roberts*, 448 U.S. 56, 63, no. 6 (1980); see also 3 W. Blackstone, Commentaries *373–*374. We have also noted the strong symbolic purpose served by requiring adverse witnesses at trial to testify in the accused's presence. See *Coy, supra*, at 1017 ("[T]here is something deep in human nature that regards face-to-face confrontation between accused and accuser as 'essential to a fair trial in a criminal prosecution' ") (quoting *Pointer v. Texas*, 380 U.S. 400, 404 (1965)).

Although face-to-face confrontation forms "the core of the values furthered by the Confrontation Clause," *Green, supra*, at 157, we have nevertheless recognized that it is not the *sine qua non* of the confrontation right. See *Delaware v. Fensterer*, 474 U.S. 15, 22 (1985) (*per curiam*) ("[T]he Confrontation Clause is generally satisfied when the defense is given a full and fair opportunity to probe and expose [testimonial] infirmities [such as forgetfulness, confusion, or evasion] through cross-examination, thereby calling to the attention of the factfinder the reasons for giving scant weight to the witness' testimony"); *Roberts, supra*, at 69 (oath, cross-examination, and demeanor provide "all that the Sixth Amendment demands: 'substantial compliance with the purposes behind the confrontation requirement' ") (quoting *Green, supra*, at 166); see also *Stincer, supra*, at 739–744 (confrontation right not violated by exclusion of defendant from competency hearing of child witnesses, where defendant had opportunity for full and effective cross-examination at trial); *Davis v. Alaska*, 415 U.S. 308, 315–316 (1974); *Douglas v. Alabama*, 380 U.S. 415, 418 (1965); *Pointer, supra*, at 406–407; 5 J. Wigmore, Evidence § 1395, p. 150 (J. Chadbourne rev. ed. 1974).

For this reason, we have never insisted on an actual face-to-face encounter at trial in *every* instance in which testimony is admitted against a defendant. Instead, we have repeatedly held that the Clause permits, where necessary, the admission of certain hearsay statements against a defendant despite the defendant's inability to confront the declarant at trial. See, e.g., *Mattox*, 156 U.S., at 243 ("[T]here could be nothing more directly contrary to the letter of the provision in question than the admission of dying declarations"); *Pointer, supra*, at 407 (noting exceptions to the confrontation right for dying declarations and "other analogous situations"). In *Mattox*, for example, we held that the testimony of a government witness was fully cross-examined but had died after the first trial, was admissible in evidence against the defendant at his second trial. See 156 U.S., at 240–244. We explained:

> There is doubtless reason for saying that . . . if notes of [the witness's] testimony are permitted to be read, [the defendant] is deprived of the advantage of that personal presence of the witness before the jury which the law has designed for his protection. But general rules of law of this kind, however beneficient in their operation and valuable to the accused, must occasionally give way to considerations of public policy and the necessities of the case. To say that a criminal, after having once been convicted by the testimony of a certain witness, should go scot free simply because death has closed the mouth of that witness, would be carrying his constitutional protection to an unwarrantable extent. The law in its wisdom declares that the rights of the public shall not be wholly sacrificed in order that an incidental benefit may be preserved to the accused. *Id.*, at 243.

We have accordingly stated that a literal reading of the Confrontation Clause would "abrogate virtually every hearsay exception, a result long rejected as unintended and too extreme." *Roberts*, 448 U.S., at 63. Thus, in certain narrow circumstances, "competing interests, if 'closely examined,' may warrant dispensing with confrontation at trial." *Id.*, at 64 (quoting *Chambers v. Mississippi*, 410 U.S. 284, 295 (1973), and citing *Mattox, supra*). We have

recently held, for example, that hearsay statements of nontestifying co-conspirators may be admitted against a defendant despite the lack of any face-to-face encounter with the accused. See *Bourjaily v. United States*, 483 U.S. 171 (1987); *United States v. Inadi*, 475 U.S. 387 (1986). Given our hearsay cases, the word "confront," as used in the Confrontation Clause, cannot simply mean face-to-face confrontation, for the Clause would then, contrary to our cases, prohibit the admission of any accusatory hearsay statement made by an absent declarant—a declarant who is undoubtedly as much a "witness against" a defendant as one who actually testifies at trial.

In sum, our precedents establish that "the Confrontation Clause reflects a *preference* for face-to-face confrontation at trial," *Roberts, supra*, at 63 (emphasis added; footnote omitted), a preference that "must occasionally give way to considerations of public policy and the necessities of the case," *Mattox, supra*, at 243. "[W]e have attempted to harmonize the goal of the Clause—placing limits on the kind of evidence that may be received against a defendant—with a societal interest in accurate factfinding, which may require consideration of out-of-court statements." *Bourjaily, supra*, at 182. We have accordingly interpreted the Confrontation Clause in a manner sensitive to its purposes and sensitive to the necessities of trial and the adversary process. See, e.g., *Kirby*, 174 U.S., at 61 ("It is scarcely necessary to say that to the rule that an accused is entitled to be confronted with witnesses against him the admission of dying declarations is an exception which arises from the necessity of the case"); *Chambers, supra*, at 295 ("Of course, the right to confront and to cross-examine is not absolute and may, in appropriate cases, bow to accommodate other legitimate interests in the criminal trial process"). Thus, though we reaffirm the importance of face-to-face confrontation with witnesses appearing at trial, we cannot say that such confrontation is an indispensable element of the Sixth Amendment's guarantee of the right to confront one's accusers. Indeed, one commentator has noted that "[i]t is all but universally assumed that there are circumstances that excuse compliance with the right of confrontation." Graham, The Right of Confrontation and the Hearsay Rule: Sir Walter Raleigh Loses Another One, 8 Crim. L. Bull. 99, 107–108 (1972).

This interpretation of the Confrontation Clause is consistent with our cases holding that other Sixth

Amendment rights must also be interpreted in the context of the necessities of trial and the adversary process. See, e.g., *Illinois v. Allen*, 397 U.S. 337, 342–343 (1970) (right to be present at trial not violated where trial judge removed defendant for disruptive behavior); *Ritchie*, 480 U.S., at 51–54 (plurality opinion) (right to cross-examination not violated where State denied defendant access to investigative files); *Taylor v. United States*, 484 U.S. 400, 410–416 (1988) (right to compulsory process not violated where trial judge precluded testimony of a surprise defense witness); *Perry v. Leeke*, 488 U.S. 272, 280–285 (1989) (right to effective assistance of counsel not violated where trial judge prevented testifying defendant from conferring with counsel during a short break in testimony). We see no reason to treat the face-to-face component of the confrontation right any differently, and indeed we think it would be anomalous to do so.

That the face-to-face confrontation requirement is not absolute does not, of course, mean that it may easily be dispensed with. As we suggested in *Coy*, our precedents confirm that a defendant's right to confront accusatory witnesses may be satisfied absent a physical, face-to-face confrontation at trial only where denial of such confrontation is necessary to further an important public policy and only where the reliability of the testimony is otherwise assured. See *Coy*, 487 U.S., at 1021 (citing *Roberts, supra,* at 64; *Chambers, supra,* at 295); *Coy, supra,* at 1025 (concurring opinion).

III

Maryland's statutory procedure, when invoked, prevents a child witness from seeing the defendant as he or she testifies against the defendant at trial. We find it significant, however, that Maryland's procedure preserves all of the other elements of the confrontation right: the child witness must be competent to testify and must testify under oath; the defendant retains full opportunity for contemporaneous cross-examination; and the judge, jury, and defendant are able to view (albeit by video monitor) the demeanor (and body) of the witness as he or she testifies. Although we are mindful of the many subtle effects face-to-face confrontation may have on an adversary criminal proceeding, the presence of these other elements of confrontation—oath, cross-examination, and observation of the witness' demeanor—adequately ensures that the testimony is

both reliable and subject to rigorous adversarial testing in a manner functionally equivalent to that accorded live, in-person testimony. These safeguards of reliability and adversariness render the use of such a procedure a far cry from the undisputed prohibition of the Confrontation Clause: trial by *ex parte* affidavit or inquisition, see *Mattox*, 156 U.S., at 242; see also *Green*, 399 US., at 179 (Harlan, J., concurring) ("[T]he Confrontation Clause was meant to constitutionalize a barrier against flagrant abuses, trials by anonymous accusers, and absentee witnesses"). Rather, we think these elements of effective confrontation not only permit a defendant to "confound and undo the false accuser, or reveal the child coached by a malevolent adult," *Coy*, 487 U.S., at 1020, but may well aid a defendant in eliciting favorable testimony from the child witness. Indeed, to the extent the child witness' testimony may be said to be technically given out-of-court (though we do not so hold), these assurances of reliability and adversariness are far greater than those required for admission of hearsay testimony under the Confrontation Clause. See *Roberts*, 448 U.S., at 66. We are therefore confident that use of the one-way closed-circuit television procedure, where necessary to further an important state interest, does not impinge upon the truth-seeking or symbolic purposes of the Confrontation Clause.

The critical inquiry in this case, therefore, is whether use of the procedure is necessary to further an important state interest. The State contends that it has a substantial interest in protecting children who are allegedly victims of child abuse from the trauma of testifying against the alleged perpetrator and that its statutory procedure for receiving testimony from such witnesses is necessary to further that interest.

We have of course recognized that a State's interest in "the protection of minor victims of sex crimes from further trauma and embarrassment" is a "compelling one." *Globe Newspaper Co. v. Superior Court*, 457 U.S. 596, 607 (1982); see also *New York v. Ferber*, 458 U.S. 747, 756–757 (1982); *FCC v. Pacifica Foundation*, 438 U.S. 726, 749–750 (1978); *Ginsberg v. New York*, 390 U.S. 629, 640 (1968); *Prince v. Massachusetts*, 321 U.S. 158, 168 (1944). "[W]e have sustained legislation aimed at protecting the physical and emotional well-being of youth even when the laws have operated in the sensitive area of constitutionally protected rights." *Ferber, supra,* at 757. In *Globe Newspaper*, for example, we held that a State's interest in the physical and psychological well-being of a minor victim was sufficiently weighty to justify depriving the press and public of their constitutional right to attend criminal trials, where the trial court makes a case-specific finding that closure of the trial is necessary to protect the welfare of the minor. See 457 U.S., at 608–609. This Term, in *Osborne v. Ohio*, 495 U.S. __ (1990), we upheld a state statute that proscribed the possession and viewing of child pornography, reaffirming that " '[i]t is evident beyond the need for elaboration that a State's interest in "safeguarding the physical and psychological well-being of a minor" is "compelling." ' " *Id.*, at __ [slip op. at 4] (quoting *Ferber, supra*, at 756–757).

We likewise conclude today that a State's interest in the physical and psychological well-being of child abuse victims may be sufficiently important to outweigh, at least in some cases, a defendant's right to face his or her accusers in court. That a significant majority of States has enacted statutes to protect child witnesses from the trauma of giving testimony in child abuse cases attests to the widespread belief in the importance of such a public policy. See *Coy*, 487 U.S., at 1022–1023 (concurring opinion) ("Many States have determined that a child victim may suffer trauma from exposure to the harsh atmosphere of the typical courtroom and have undertaken to shield the child through a variety of ameliorative measures"). Thirty-seven States, for example, permit the use of videotaped testimony of sexually abused children;[2] 24 States have authorized the use of one-way closed circuit television testimony in child abuse cases;[3] and 8 States authorize the use of a two-way system in which the child-witness is permitted to see the courtroom and the defendant on a video monitor and in which the jury and judge is permitted to view the child during the testimony.[4]

The statute at issue in this case, for example, was specifically intended "to safeguard the physical and psychological well-being of child victims by avoiding, or at least minimizing, the emotional trauma produced by testifying." *Wildermuth v. State*, 310 Md. 496, 518, 530 A.2d 275, 286 (1987). The *Wildermuth* court noted:

In Maryland, the Governor's Task Force on Child Abuse in its *Interim Report* (Nov. 1984) documented the existence of the [child abuse] problem in our State. *Interim Report* at 1. It brought the picture up to date in its *Final Report* (Dec. 1985). In the first six months of 1985, investigations of child abuse were 12 percent more numerous than during the same period of 1984. In 1979, 4,615 cases of child abuse were investigated; in 1984, 8,321. *Final Report* at iii. In its *Interim Report* at 2, the Commission proposed legislation that, with some changes, became § 9–102. The proposal was "aimed at alleviating the trauma to a child victim in the courtroom atmosphere by allowing the child's testimony to be obtained outside of the courtroom." *Id.*, at 2. This would both protect the child and en-

2. See Ala. Code § 15–25–2 (Supp. 1989); Ariz. Rev. Stat. Ann. §§ 13–4251 and 4253(B), (C) (1989); Ark. Code Ann. § 16–44–203 (1987); Cal. Penal Code Ann. § 1346 (West Supp. 1990); Colo. Rev. Stat. §§ 18–3–413 and 18–6–401.3 (1986); Conn. Gen. Stat. § 54–86g (1989); Del. Code Ann., Tit. 11, § 3511 (1987); Fla. Stat. § 92.53 (1989); Haw. Rev. Stat., ch. 626, Rule Evid. 616 (1985); Ill. Rev. Stat., ch. 38, ¶ 106A–2 (1989); Ind. Code § 35–37–4–8(c), (d), (f), (g) (1988); Iowa Code § 910A.14 (1987); Kan. Stat. Ann. § 38–1558 (1986); Ky. Rev. Stat. Ann. § 421.350(4) (Baldwin Supp. 1989); Mass. Gen. Laws Ann., ch. 278, § 16D (Supp. 1990); Mich. Comp. Laws Ann. § 600.2163(a)(5) (Supp. 1990); Minn. Stat. § 595.02(4) (1988); Miss. Code Ann. § 13–1–407 (Supp. 1989); Mo. Rev. Stat. §§ 491.675–491.690 (1986); Mont. Code Ann. §§ 46–15–401 to 46–15–403 (1989); Neb. Rev. Stat. § 29–1926 (1989); Nev. Rev. Stat. § 174.227 (1989); N. H. Rev. Stat. Ann. § 517:13–1 (Supp. 1989); N. M. Stat. Ann. § 30–9–17 (1984); Ohio Rev. Code Ann. § 2907.41(A), (B), (D), (E) (Baldwin 1986); Okla. Stat., Tit. 22, § 753(c) (Supp. 1988); Ore. Rev. Stat. § 40.460(24) (1989); 42 Pa. Cons. Stat. §§ 5982, 5984 (1988); R. I. Gen. Laws § 11–37–13.2 (Supp. 1989); S. C. Code § 16–3–1530(G) (1985); S. D. Codified Laws § 23A–12–9 (1988); Tenn. Code Ann. § 24–7–116(d), (e), (f) (Supp. 1989); Tex. Crim. Proc. Code Ann., Art. 38.071, § 4 (Vernon Supp. 1990); Utah Rule Crim. Proce. 15.5 (1990); Vt. Rule Evid. 807(d) (Supp. 1989); Wis. Stat. Ann. § 967.04(7) to (10) (West Supp. 1989); Wyo. Stat. § 7–11–408 (1987).

3. See Ala. Code § 15–25–3 (Supp. 1989); Alaska Stat. Ann. § 12.45.046 (Supp. 1989); Ariz. Rev. Stat. Ann. § 13–4253 (1989); Conn. Gen. Stat. § 54–86g (1989); Fla. Stat. § 92.54 (1989); Ga. Code Ann. § 17–8–55 (Supp. 1989); Ill. Rev. Stat., ch. 38, ¶ 106A–3 (1987); Ind. Code § 35–37–4–8 (1988); Iowa Code § 910A–14 (Supp. 1990); Kan. Stat. Ann. § 38–1558 (1986); Ky. Rev. Stat. Ann. § 421–350(1), (3) (Baldwin Supp. 1989); La. Rev. Stat. Ann. § 15:283 (West Supp. 1990); Md. Cts. & Jud. Proc. Code Ann. § 9–102 (1989); Mass. Gen. Laws Ann., ch. 278, § 16D (Supp. 1990); Minn. Stat. § 595.02(4) (1988); Miss. Code Ann. § 13–1–405 (Supp. 1989); N. J. Rev. Stat. § 2A:84A–32.4 (Supp. 1989); Okla. Stat., Tit. 22, § 753(b) (Supp. 1988); Ore. Rev. Stat. § 40.460(24) (1989); 42 Pa. Cons. Stat. §§ 5982, 5985 (1988); R. I. Gen. Laws § 11–37–13.2 (Supp. 1989); Tex. Crim. Proc. Code Ann., Art. 38.071, § 3 (Supp. 1990); Utah Rule Crim. Proc. 15.5 (1990); Vt. Rule Evid. 807(d) (Supp. 1989).

4. See Cal. Penal Code Ann. § 1347 (West Supp. 1990); Haw. Rev. Stat., ch. 626, Rule Evid. 616 (1985); Idaho Code § 19–3024A (Supp. 1989); Minn. Stat. § 595.02(4)(c)(2) (1988); N. Y. Crim. Proc. Law §§ 65.00 to 65.30 (McKinney Supp. 1990); Ohio Rev. Code Ann. § 2907.41(C), (E) (Baldwin 1986); Va. Code § 18.2–67.9 (1988); Vt. Rule Evid. 807(e) (Supp. 1989).

hance the public interest by encouraging effective prosecution of the alleged abuser. *Id.*, at 517, 530 A.2d, at 285.

Given the State's traditional and " 'transcendent interest in protecting the welfare of children,' " *Ginsberg*, 390 U.S., at 640 (citation omitted), and buttressed by the growing body of academic literature documenting the psychological trauma suffered by child abuse victims who must testify in court, see Brief for American Psychological Association as *amicus curiae* 7–13; G. Goodman et al., Emotional Effects of Criminal Court Testimony on Child Sexual Assault Victims, Final Report to the National Institute of Justice (presented as conference paper at annual convention of American Psychological Assn., Aug. 1989), we will not second-guess the considered judgment of the Maryland Legislature regarding the importance of its interest in protecting child abuse victims from the emotional trauma of testifying. Accordingly, we hold that, if the State makes an adequate showing of necessity, the state interest in protecting child witnesses from the trauma of testifying in a child abuse case is sufficiently important to justify the use of a special procedure that permits a child witness in such cases to testify at trial against a defendant in the absence of face-to-face confrontation with the defendant.

The requisite finding of necessity must of course be a case-specific one: the trial court must hear evidence and determine whether use of the one-way closed circuit television procedure is necessary to protect the welfare of the particular child witness who seeks to testify. See *Globe Newspaper Co.*, 457 U.S., at 608–609 (compelling interest in protecting child victims does not justify a *mandatory* trial closure rule); *Coy*, 487 U.S., at 1021; *id.*, at 1025 (concurring opinion); see also *Hochheiser v. Superior Court*, 161 Cal.App.3d 777, 793, 208 Cal.Rptr. 273, 283 (1984). The trial court must also find that the child witness would be traumatized, not by the courtroom generally, but by the presence of the defendant. See, e.g., *State v. Wilhite*, 160 Ariz. 228, 772 P.2d 582 (1989); *State v. Bonello*, 210 Conn. 51, 554 A.2d 277 (1989); *State v. Davidson*, 764 S.W.2d 731 (Mo.App. 1989); *Commonwealth v. Ludwig*, 366 Pa.Super. 361, 531 A.2d 459 (1987). Denial of face-to-face confrontation is not needed to further the state interest in protecting the child witness from trauma unless it is the presence of the defendant that causes the trauma. In other words, if the state interest were merely the interest in pro-

tecting child witnesses from courtroom trauma generally, denial of face-to-face confrontation would be unnecessary because the child could be permitted to testify in less intimidating surroundings, albeit with the defendant present. Finally, the trial court must find that the emotional distress suffered by the child witness in the presence of the defendant is more than *de minimis*, i.e., more than "mere nervousness or excitement or some reluctance to testify," *Wildermuth*, 310 Md., at 524, 530 A.2d, at 289; see also *State v. Mannion*, 19 Utah 505, 511–512, 57 P. 542, 543–544 (1899). We need not decide the minimum showing of emotional trauma required for use of the special procedure, however, because the Maryland statute, which requires a determination that the child witness will suffer "serious emotional distress such that the child cannot reasonably communicate," § 9–102(a)(1)(ii), clearly suffices to meet constitutional standards.

To be sure, face-to-face confrontation may be said to cause trauma for the very purpose of eliciting truth, cf. *Coy, supra*, at 1019–1020, but we think that the use of Maryland's special procedure, where necessary to further the important state interest in preventing trauma to child witnesses in child abuse cases, adequately ensures the accuracy of the testimony and preserves the adversary nature of the trial. See *supra*, at 11–12. Indeed, where face-to-face confrontation causes significant emotional distress in a child witness, there is evidence that such confrontation would in fact *disserve* the Confrontation Clause's truth-seeking goal. See, e.g, *Coy, supra*, at 1032 (Blackmun, J., dissenting) (face-to-face confrontation "may so overwhelm the child as to prevent the possibility of effective testimony, thereby undermining the truth-finding function of the trial itself"); Brief for American Psychological Association as *amicus curiae* 18–24; *State v. Sheppard*, 197 N.J.Super. 411, 416, 484 A.2d 1330, 1332 (1984); Goodman & Helgeson, Child Sexual Assault: Children's Memory and the Law, 40 U. Miami L. Rev. 181, 203–204 (1985); Note, Videotaping Children's Testimony: An Empirical View, 85 Mich.L.Rev. 809, 813–820 (1987).

In sum, we conclude that where necessary to protect a child witness from trauma that would be caused by testifying in the physical presence of the defendant, at least where such trauma would impair the child's ability to communicate, the Confrontation Clause does not prohibit use of a procedure that, despite the absence of face-to-face confrontation, ensures the reliability of the evidence by subjecting it to rigorous adversarial testing and thereby preserves the essence of effective confrontation. Because there is no dispute that the child witnesses in this case testified under oath, were subject to full cross-examination, and were able to be observed by the judge, jury, and defendant as they testified, we conclude that, to the extent that a proper finding of necessity has been made, the admission of such testimony would be consonant with the Confrontation Clause.

IV

The Maryland Court of Appeals held, as we do today, that although face-to-face confrontation is not an absolute constitutional requirement, it may be abridged only where there is a " 'case-specific finding of necessity.' " 316 Md., at 564, 560 A.2d, at 1126 (quoting *Coy, supra*, at 1025 (concurring opinion)). Given this latter requirement, the Court of Appeals reasoned that "[t]he question of whether a child is unavailable to testify . . . should not be asked in terms of inability to testify in the ordinary courtroom setting, but in the much narrower terms of the witness's inability to testify in the presence of the accused." 316 Md., at 564, 560 A.2d, at 1126 (footnote omitted). "[T]he determinative inquiry required to preclude face-to-face confrontation is the effect of the presence of the defendant on the witness or the witness's testimony." *Id.*, at 565, 560 A.2d, at 1127. The Court of Appeals accordingly concluded that, as a prerequisite to use of the § 9–102 procedure, the Confrontation Clause requires the trial court to make a specific finding that testimony by the child in the courtroom *in the presence of the defendant* would result in the child suffering serious emotional distress such that the child could not reasonably communicate. *Id.*, at 566, 560 A.2d, at 1127. This conclusion, of course, is consistent with our holding today.

In addition, however, the Court of Appeals interpreted our decision in *Coy* to impose two subsidiary requirements. First, the court held that "§ 9–102 ordinarily cannot be invoked unless the child witness initially is questioned (either in or outside the courtroom), in the defendant's presence." *Id.*, at 566, 560 A.2d, at 1127; see also *Wildermuth*, 310 Md., at 523–524, 530 A.2d, at 289 (personal observation by the judge should be the rule rather than the exception). Second, the court asserted that, be-

fore using the one-way television procedure, a trial judge must determine whether a child would suffer "severe emotional distress" if he or she were to testify by *two*-way closed circuit television. 316 Md., at 567, 560 A.2d, at 1128.

Reviewing the evidence presented to the trial court in support of the finding required under § 9–102(a)(1)(ii), the Court of Appeals determined that "the finding of necessity required to limit the defendant's right of confrontation through invocation of § 9–102 . . . was not made here." *Id.*, at 570–571, 560 A.2d, at 1129. The Court of Appeals noted that the trial judge "had the benefit only of expert testimony on the ability of the children to communicate; he did not question any of the children himself, nor did he observe any child's behavior on the witness stand before making his ruling. He did not explore any alternatives to the use of one-way closed-circuit television." *Id.*, at 568, 560 A.2d, at 1128 (footnote omitted). The Court of Appeals also observed that "the testimony in this case was not sharply focused on the effect of the defendant's presence on the child witnesses." *Id.*, at 569, 560 A.2d, at 1129. Thus, the Court of Appeals concluded:

> Unable to supplement the expert testimony by responses to questions put by him, or by his own observations of the children's behavior in Craig's presence, the judge made his § 9–102 finding in terms of what the experts had said. He ruled that "the testimony of each of these children *in a courtroom* will [result] in each child suffering serious emotional distress . . . such that each of these children cannot reasonably communicate." He failed to find—indeed, on the evidence before him, *could not have found*—that this result would be the product of testimony in a courtroom in the defendant's presence or outside the courtroom but in the defendant's televised presence. That, however, is the finding of necessity required to limit the defendant's right of confrontation through invocation of § 9–102. Since that finding was not made here, and since the procedures we deem requisite to the valid use of § 9–102 were not followed, the judgment of the Court of Special Appeals must be reversed and the case remanded for a new trial. *Id.*, at 570–571, 560 A.2d, at 1129 (emphasis added).

The Court of Appeals appears to have rested its conclusion at least in part on the trial court's failure to observe the children's behavior in the defendant's presence and its failure to explore less restrictive alternatives to the use of the one-way closed circuit television procedure. See *id.*, at 568–571, 560 A.2d, at 1128–1129. Although we think such evidentiary requirements could strengthen the grounds for use of protective measures, we decline to establish, as a matter of federal constitutional law, any such categorical evidentiary prerequisites for the use of the one-way television procedure. The trial court in this case, for example, could well have found, on the basis of the expert testimony before it, that testimony by the child witnesses in the courtroom in the defendant's presence "will result in [each] child suffering serious emotional distress such that the child cannot reasonably communicate," § 9–102(a)(1)(ii). See *id.*, at 568–569, 560 A.2d, at 1128–1129; see also App. 22–25, 39, 41, 43, 44–45, 54–57. So long as a trial court makes such a case-specific finding of necessity, the Confrontation Clause does not prohibit a State from using a one-way closed circuit television procedure for the receipt of testimony by a child witness in a child abuse case. Because the Court of Appeals held that the trial court had not made the requisite finding of necessity under its interpretation of "the high threshold required by [*Coy*] before § 9–102 may be invoked," 316 Md., at 554–555, 560 A.2d, at 1121 (footnote omitted), we cannot be certain whether the Court of Appeals would reach the same conclusion in light of the legal standard we establish today. We therefore vacate the judgment of the Court of Appeals of Maryland and remand the case for further proceedings not inconsistent with this opinion. It is so ordered.

THE CHILD IN SCHOOL—
PROCEDURAL DUE PROCESS

Case Comment

In *Goss v. Lopez*, the Supreme Court formulated the procedural guidelines for evaluating the constitutionality of school disciplinary procedures. *Goss* was a class action suit by Ohio public school students who had been suspended from school for up to ten days without a hearing. The lower court ruled that the students had been denied due process under the Fourteenth Amendment to the U.S. Constitution, but on appeal, the school officials argued that no due process existed where there was no constitutional right to a public education.

The U.S. Supreme Court, however, affirmed the lower court by concluding that the students had been

deprived of their right to "liberty and property," and thus, minimal due process protection was required. At a minimum, the Court stated that students facing suspension from school require notice and an opportunity to be heard. The hearing does not include a right to counsel or a right to confront or cross-examine witnesses. The Court went on to state in *Goss* that the extent of the due process requirements would be established on a case-by-case basis.[3]

GOSS v. LOPEZ
419 U.S. 565 (1975)

Mr. Justice White delivered the opinion of the Court.

This appeal by various administrators of the Columbus, Ohio, Public School System (CPSS) challenges the judgment of a three-judge federal court, declaring that appellees—various high school students in the CPSS—were denied due process of law contrary to the command of the Fourteenth Amendment in that they were temporarily suspended from their high schools without a hearing either prior to suspension or within a reasonable time thereafter and enjoining the administrators to remove all references to such suspensions from the students' records.

I

Ohio law, Rev. Code Ann. § 3313.64 (1972), provides for free education to all children between the ages of six and 21. Section 3313.66 of the Code empowers the principal of an Ohio public school to suspend a pupil for misconduct for up to 10 days or to expel him. In either case, he must notify the student's parents within 24 hours and state the reasons for his action. A pupil who is expelled, or his parents, may appeal the decision to the Board of Education and in connection therewith shall be permitted to be heard at the board meeting. The Board may reinstate the pupil following the hearing. No similar procedure is provided in § 3313.66 or any other provision of state law for a suspended student. Aside from a regulation tracking the statute, at the time of the imposition of the suspensions in this case the CPSS itself had not issued any written procedure applicable to suspensions.[1] Nor, so far as the record reflects, had any of the individual high schools involved in this case.[2] Each, however, had formally or informally described the conduct for which suspension could be imposed.

The nine named appellees, each of whom alleged that he or she had been suspended from public high school in Columbus for up to 10 days without a hearing pursuant to § 3313.66, filed an action under 42 U.S.C. § 1983 against the Columbus Board of Education and various administrators of the CPSS. The complaint sought a declaration that § 3313.66 was unconstitutional in that it permitted public school administrators to deprive plaintiffs of their rights to an education without a hearing of any kind, in violation of the procedural due process component of the Fourteenth Amendment. It also sought to enjoin the public school officials from issuing future suspensions pursuant to § 3313.66 and to require them to remove references to the past suspensions from the records of the students in question.[3]

The proof below established that the suspensions arose out of a period of widespread student unrest in the CPSS during February and March 1971. Six of the named plaintiffs, Rudolph Sutton, Tyrone Washington, Susan Cooper, Deborah Fox, Clarence Byars, and Bruce Harris, were students at the Marion-Franklin High School and were each suspended for 10 days[4] on account of disruptive or disobedient conduct committed in the presence of the school administrator who ordered the suspension. One of these, Tyrone Washington, was among a group of students demonstrating in the school auditorium while a class was being conducted there. He was ordered by the school principal to leave, refused to do so, and was suspended. Rudolph Sutton, in the presence of the principal, physically attacked a police officer who was attempting to remove Tyrone Washington from the auditorium. He was immediately suspended. The other four Marion-Franklin students were suspended for similar conduct. None was given a hearing to determine the operative facts underlying the suspension, but each, together with his or her parents, was offered the opportunity to attend a conference, subsequent to the effective date of the suspension, to discuss the student's future.

Two named plaintiffs, Dwight Lopez and Betty Crome, were students at Central High School and McGuffey Junior High School, respectively. The former was suspended in connection with a disturbance in the lunchroom which involved some phys-

---

1. At the time of the events involved in this case, the only administrative regulation on this subject was § 1010.04 of the Administrative Guide of the Columbus Public Schools which provided: "Pupils may be suspended or expelled from school in accordance with the provisions of Section 3313.66 of the Revised Code." Subsequent to the events involved in this lawsuit, the Department of Pupil Personnel of the CPSS issued three memoranda relating to suspension procedures, dated August 16, 1971, February 21, 1973, and July 10, 1973, respectively. The first two are substantially similar to each other and require no fact-finding hearing at any time in connection with a suspension. The third, which was apparently in effect when this case was argued, places upon the principal the obligation to "investigate" "before commencing suspension procedures"; and provides as part of the procedures that the principal shall discuss the case with the pupil, so that the pupil may "be heard with respect to the alleged offense," unless the pupil is "unavailable" for such a discussion or "unwilling" to participate in it. The suspensions involved in this case occurred, and records thereof were made, prior to the effective date of these memoranda. The District Court's judgment, including its expunction order, turns on the propriety of the procedures existing at the time the suspensions were ordered and by which they were imposed.

2. According to the testimony of Phillip Fulton, the principal of one of the high schools involved in this case, there was an informal procedure applicable at the Marion-Franklin High School. It provided that in the routine case of misconduct, occurring in the presence of a teacher, the teacher would describe the misconduct on a form provided for that purpose and would send the student, with the form, to the principal's office. There, the principal would obtain the student's version of the story, and, if it conflicted with the teacher's written version, would send for the teacher to obtain the teacher's oral version—apparently in the presence of the student. Mr. Fulton testified that, if a discrepancy still existed, the teacher's version would be believed and the principal would arrive at a disciplinary decision based on it.

3. The plaintiffs sought to bring the action on behalf of all students of the Columbus Public Schools suspended on or after February 1971, and a class action was declared accordingly. Since the complaint sought to restrain the "enforcement" and "operation" of a state statute "by restraining the action of any officer of such state in the enforcement or execution of such statute," a three-judge court was requested pursuant to 28 U.S.C. § 2281 and convened. The students also alleged that the conduct for which they could be suspended was not adequately defined by Ohio laws. This vagueness and overbreadth argument was rejected by the court below and the students have not appealed from this part of the court's decision.

4. Fox was given two separate 10-day suspensions for misconduct occurring on two separate occasions—the second following immediately upon her return to school. In addition to his suspension, Sutton was transferred to another school.

ical damage to school property.[5] Lopez testified that at least 75 other students were suspended from his school on the same day. He also testified below that he was not a party to the destructive conduct but was instead an innocent bystander. Because no one from the school testified with regard to this incident, there is no evidence in the record indicating the official basis for concluding otherwise. Lopez never had a hearing.

Betty Crome was present at a demonstration at a high school other than the one she was attending. There she was arrested together with others, taken to the police station, and released without being formally charged. Before she went to school on the following day, she was notified that she had been suspended for a 10-day period. Because no one from the school testified with respect to this incident, the record does not disclose how the McGuffey Junior High School principal went about making the decision to suspend Crome, nor does it disclose on what information the decision was based. It is clear from the record that no hearing was ever held.

There was no testimony with respect to the suspension of the ninth named plaintiff, Carl Smith. The school files were also silent as to his suspension, although as to some, but not all, of the other named plaintiffs the files contained either direct references to their suspensions or copies of letters sent to their parents advising them of the suspension.

On the basis of this evidence, the three-judge court declared that plaintiffs were denied due process of law because they were "suspended without hearing prior to suspension or within a reasonable time thereafter," and that Ohio Rev. Code Ann. § 3313.66 (1972) and regulations issued pursuant thereto were unconstitutional in permitting such suspensions.[6] It was ordered that all references to plaintiffs' suspensions be removed from school files.

Although not imposing upon the Ohio school administrators any particular disciplinary procedures and leaving them "free to adopt regulations providing for fair suspension procedures which are con-

sonant with the educational goals of their schools and reflective of the characteristics of their school and locality," the District Court declared that there were "minimum requirements of notice and a hearing prior to suspension, except in emergency situations." In explication, the court stated that relevant case authority would: (1) permit "[i]mmediate removal of a student whose conduct disrupts the academic atmosphere of the school, endangers fellow students, teachers or school officials, or damages property"; (2) require notice of suspension proceedings to be sent to the student's parents within 24 hours of the decision to conduct them; and (3) require a hearing to be held, with the student present, within 72 hours of his removal. Finally, the court stated that, with respect to the nature of the hearing, the relevant cases required that statements in support of the charge be produced, that the student and others be permitted to make statements in defense or mitigation, and that the school need not permit attendance by counsel.

The defendant school administrators have appealed the three-judge court's decision. Because the order below granted plaintiffs' request for an injunction—ordering defendants to expunge their records—this Court has jurisdiction of the appeal pursuant to 28 U.S.C. § 1253. We affirm.

II

At the outset, appellants contend that because there is no constitutional right to an education at public expense, the Due Process Clause does not protect against expulsions from the public school system. This position misconceives the nature of the issue and is refuted by prior decisions. The Fourteenth Amendment forbids the State to deprive any person of life, liberty, or property without due process of law. Protected interests in property are normally "not created by the Constitution. Rather, they are created and their dimensions are defined" by an independent source such as state statutes or rules entitling

---

5. Lopez was actually absent from school, following his suspension, for over 20 days. This seems to have occurred because of a misunderstanding as to the length of the suspension. A letter sent to Lopez after he had been out for over 10 days purports to assume that, being over compulsory school age, he was voluntarily staying away. Upon asserting that this was not the case, Lopez was transferred to another school.

6. In its judgment, the court stated that the statute is unconstitutional in that it provides "for suspension . . . without *first* affording the student due process of law." (Emphasis supplied.) However, the language of the judgment must be read in light of the language in the opinion which expressly contemplates that under some circumstances students may properly be removed from school before a hearing is held, so long as the hearing follows promptly.

the citizen to certain benefits. *Board of Regents v. Roth*, 408 U.S. 564, 577 (1972).

Accordingly, a state employee who under state law, or rules promulgated by state officials, has a legitimate claim of entitlement to continued employment absent sufficient cause for discharge may demand the procedural protections of due process. *Connell v. Higginbotham*, 403 U.S. 207 (1971); *Wieman v. Updegraff*, 344 U.S. 183, 191–192 (1952); *Arnett v. Kennedy*, 416 U.S. 134, 164 (Powell, J., concurring), 171 (White, J., concurring and dissenting) (1974). So may welfare recipients who have statutory rights to welfare as long as they maintain the specified qualifications. *Goldberg v. Kelly*, 397 U.S. 254 (1970). *Morrissey v. Brewer*, 408 U.S. 471 (1972), applied the limitations of the Due Process Clause to governmental decisions to revoke parole, although a parolee has no constitutional right to that status. In like vein was *Wolff v. McDonnell*, 418 U.S. 539 (1974), where the procedural protections of the Due Process Clause were triggered by official cancellation of a prisoner's good-time credits accumulated under state law, although those benefits were not mandated by the Constitution.

Here, on the basis of state law, appellees plainly had legitimate claims of entitlement to a public education. Ohio Rev. Code Ann. §§ 3313.48 and 3313.64 (1972 and Supp. 1973) direct local authorities to provide a free education to all residents between five and 21 years of age, and a compulsory-attendance law requires attendance for a school year of not less than 32 weeks. Ohio Rev. Code Ann. § 3321.04 (1972). It is true that § 3313.66 of the Code permits school principals to suspend students for up to 10 days; but suspensions may not be imposed without any grounds whatsoever. All of the schools had their own rules specifying the grounds for expulsion or suspension. Having chosen to extend the right to an education to people of appellees' class generally, Ohio may not withdraw that right on grounds of misconduct, absent fundamentally

fair procedures to determine whether the misconduct has occurred. *Arnett v. Kennedy*, *supra*, at 164 (Powell, J., concurring), 171 (White, J., concurring and dissenting), 206 (Marshall, J., dissenting).

Although Ohio may not be constitutionally obligated to establish and maintain a public school system, it has nevertheless done so and has required its children to attend. Those young people do not "shed their constitutional rights" at the schoolhouse door. *Tinker v. Des Moines School Dist.*, 393 U.S. 503, 506 (1969). "The Fourteenth Amendment, as now applied to the States, protects the citizen against the State itself and all of its creatures—Boards of Education not excepted." *West Virginia Board of Education v. Barnette*, 319 U.S. 624, 637 (1943). The authority possessed by the State to prescribe and enforce standards of conduct in its schools although concededly very broad, must be exercised consistently with constitutional safeguards. Among other things, the State is constrained to recognize a student's legitimate entitlement to a public education as a property interest which is protected by the Due Process Clause and which may not be taken away for misconduct without adherence to the minimum procedures required by that Clause.

The Due Process Clause also forbids arbitrary deprivations of liberty. "Where a person's good name, reputation, honor, or integrity is at stake because of what the government is doing to him," the minimal requirements of the Clause must be satisfied. *Wisconsin v. Constantineau*, 400 U.S. 433, 437 (1971); *Board of Regents v. Roth*, *supra*, at 573. School authorities have suspended appellees from school for periods of up to 10 days based on charges of misconduct. If sustained and recorded, those charges could seriously damage the students' standing with their fellow pupils and their teachers as well as interfere with later opportunities for higher education and employment.[7] It is apparent that the claimed right of the State to determine unilaterally and without process whether that misconduct has occurred

---

7. Appellees assert in their brief that four of 12 randomly selected Ohio colleges specifically inquire of the high school of every applicant for admission whether the applicant has ever been suspended. Brief for Appellees 34–35 and n. 40. Appellees also contend that many employers request similar information. Ibid.

Congress has recently enacted legislation limiting access to information contained in the files of a school receiving federal funds. Section 513 of the Education Amendments of 1974, Pub. L. 93–380, 88 Stat. 571, 20 U.S.C. § 1232g (1970 ed., Supp. IV), adding § 438 to the General Education Provisions Act. That section would preclude release of "verified reports of serious or recurrent behavior patterns" to employers without written consent of the student's parents. While subsection (b)(1)(B) permits release of such information to "other schools . . . in which the student intends to enroll," it does so only upon condition that the parent be advised of the release of the information and be given an opportunity at a hearing to challenge the content of the information to insure against inclusion of inaccurate or misleading information. The statute does not expressly state whether the parent can contest the underlying basis for a suspension, the fact of which is contained in the student's school record.

immediately collides with the requirements of the Constitution.

Appellants proceed to argue that even if there is a right to a public education protected by the Due Process Clause generally, the Clause comes into play only when the State subjects a student to a "severe detriment or grievous loss." The loss of 10 days, it is said, is neither severe nor grievous and the Due Process Clause is therefore of no relevance. Appellants' argument is again refuted by our prior decisions; for in determining "whether due process requirements apply in the first place, we must look not to the 'weight' but to the *nature* of the interest at stake." *Board of Regents v. Roth, supra,* at 570–571. Appellees were excluded from school only temporarily, it is true, but the length and consequent severity of a deprivation, while another factor to weigh in determining the appropriate form of hearing, "is not decisive of the basic right" to a hearing of some kind. *Fuentes v. Shevin,* 407 U.S. 67, 86 (1972). The Court's view has been that as long as a property deprivation is not *de minimis,* its gravity is irrelevant to the question whether account must be taken of the Due Process Clause. *Sniadach v. Family Finance Corp.,* 395 U.S. 337, 342 (1969) (Harlan, J., concurring); *Boddie v. Connecticut,* 401 U.S. 371, 378–379 (1971); *Board of Regents v. Roth, supra,* at 570 n. 8. A 10-day suspension from school is not *de minimis* in our view and may not be imposed in complete disregard of the Due Process Clause.

A short suspension is, of course, a far milder deprivation than expulsion. But, "education is perhaps the most important function of state and local governments," *Brown v. Board of Education,* 347 U.S. 483, 493 (1954), and the total exclusion from the educational process for more than a trivial period, and certainly if the suspension is for 10 days, is a serious event in the life of the suspended child. Neither the property interest in educational benefits temporarily denied nor the liberty interest in reputation, which is also implicated, is so insubstantial that suspensions may constitutionally be imposed by any procedure the school chooses, no matter how arbitrary.[8]

---

8. Since the landmark decision of the Court of Appeals for the Fifth Circuit in *Dixon v. Alabama State Board of Education,* 294 F.2d 150, cert. denied, 368 U.S. 930 (1961), the lower federal courts have uniformly held the Due Process Clause applicable to decisions made by tax-supported educational institutions to remove a student from the institution long enough for the removal to be classified as an expulsion. *Hagopian v. Knowlton,* 470 F.2d 201, 211 (CA2 1972); *Wasson v. Trowbridge,* 382 F.2d 807, 812 (CA2 1967); *Esteban v. Central Missouri State College,* 415 F.2d 1077, 1089 (CA8 1969), cert. denied, 398 U.S. 965 (1970); *Vought v. Van Buren Public Schools,* 306 F.Supp. 1388 (ED Mich. 1969); *Whitfield v. Simpson,* 312 F.Supp. 889 (ED Ill. 1970); *Fielder v. Board of Education of School District of Winnebago, Neb.,* 346 F.Supp. 722, 729 (Neb. 1972); *DeJesus v. Penberthy,* 344 F.Supp. 70, 74 (Conn. 1972); *Soglin v. Kauffman,* 295 F.Supp. 978, 994 (WD Wis. 1968), aff'd, 418 F.2d 163 (CA7 1969); *Stricklin v. Regents of University of Wisconsin,* 297 F.Supp. 416, 420 (WD Wis. 1969), appeal dismissed, 420 F.2d 1257 (CA7 1970); *Buck v. Carter,* 308 F.Supp. 1246 (WD Wis. 1970); General Order on Judicial Standards of Procedure and Substance in Review of Student Discipline in Tax Supported Institutions of Higher Education, 45 F.R.D. 133, 147–148 (WD Mo. 1968) (en banc). The lower courts have been less uniform, however, on the question whether removal from school for some shorter period may ever be so trivial a deprivation as to require no process, and, if so, how short the removal must be to qualify. Courts of Appeals have held or assumed the Due Process Clause applicable to long suspensions, *Pervis v. LaMarque Ind. School Dist.,* 466 F.2d 1054 (CA5 1972); to indefinite suspensions, *Sullivan v. Houston Ind. School Dist.,* 475 F.2d 1071 (CA5), cert. denied, 414 U.S. 1032 (1973); to the addition of a 30-day suspension to a 10-day suspension, *Williams v. Dade County School Board,* 441 F.2d 299 (CA5 1971); to a 10-day suspension, *Black Students of North Fort Myers, Jr.-Sr. High School v. Williams,* 470 F.2d 957 (CA5 1972); to "mild" suspensions, *Farrell v. Joel,* 437 F.2d 160 (CA2 1971), and *Tate v. Board of Education,* 453 F.2d 975 (CA8 1972); and to a three-day suspension, *Shanley v. Northeast Ind. School Dist. Bexar County, Texas,* 462 F.2d 960, 967 n. 4 (CA5 1972); but inapplicable to a seven-day suspension, *Linwood v. Board of Ed. of City of Peoria,* 463 F.2d 763 (CA7), cert. denied, 409 U.S. 1027 (1972); to a three-day suspension, *Dunn v. Tyler Ind. School Dist.,* 460 F.2d 137 (CA5 1972); to a suspension for not "more than a few days," *Murray v. West Baton Rouge Parish School Board,* 472 F.2d 438 (CA5 1973); and to all suspensions no matter how short, *Black Coalition v. Portland School District No. 1,* 484 F.2d 1040 (CA9 1973). The Federal District Courts have held the Due Process Clause applicable to an interim suspension pending expulsion proceedings in *Stricklin v. Regents of University of Wisconsin, supra,* and *Buck v. Carter, supra;* to a 10-day suspension, *Banks v. Board of Public Instruction of Dade County,* 314 F.Supp. 285 (SD Fla. 1970), vacated, 401 U.S. 988 (1971) (for entry of a fresh decree so that a timely appeal might be taken to the Court of Appeals), aff'd, 450 F.2d 1103 (CA5 1971); to suspensions of under five days, *Vail v. Board of Education of Portsmouth School Dist.,* 354 F.Supp. 592 (NH 1973); and to all suspensions, *Mills v. Board of Education of the Dist. of Columbia,* 348 F.Supp. 866 (DC 1972), and *Givens v. Poc,* 346 F.Sup. 202 (WDNC 1972); but inapplicable to suspensions of 25 days, *Hernandez v. School District Number One, Denver, Colorado,* 315 F.Supp. 289 (Colo. 1970); to suspensions of 10 days, *Baker v. Downey City Board of Education,* 307 F.Supp. 517 (CD Cal. 1969); and to suspensions of eight days, *Hatter v. Los Angeles City High School District,* 310 F.Supp. 1309 (CD Cal. 1970), rev'd on other grounds, 452 F.2d 673 (CA9 1971). In the cases holding no process necessary in connection with short suspensions, it is not always clear whether the court viewed the Due Process Clause as inapplicable, or simply felt that the process received was "due" even in the absence of some kind of hearing procedure.

III

"Once it is determined that due process applies, the question remains what process is due." *Morrissey v. Brewer*, 408 U.S., at 481. We turn to that question, fully realizing as our cases regularly do that the interpretation and application of the Due Process Clause are intensely practical matters and that "[t]he very nature of due process negates any concept of inflexible procedures universally applicable to every imaginable situation." *Cafeteria Workers v. McElroy*, 367 U.S. 886, 895 (1961). We are also mindful of our own admonition:

> Judicial interposition in the operation of the public school system of the Nation raises problems requiring care and restraint. . . . By and large, public education in our Nation is committed to the control of state and local authorities. *Epperson v. Arkansas*, 393 U.S. 97, 104 (1968).

There are certain bench marks to guide us, however. *Mullane v. Central Hanover Trust Co.*, 339 U.S. 306 (1950), a case often invoked by later opinions, said that "[m]any controversies have raged about the cryptic and abstract words of the Due Process Clause but there can be no doubt that at a minimum they require that deprivation of life, liberty or property by adjudication be preceded by notice and opportunity for hearing appropriate to the nature of the case." *Id.*, at 313. "The fundamental requisite of due process of law is the opportunity to be heard." *Grannis v. Ordean*, 234 U.S. 385, 394 (1914), a right that "has little reality or worth unless one is informed that the matter is pending and can choose for himself whether to . . . contest." *Mullane v. Central Hanover Trust Co.*, *supra*, at 314. See also *Armstrong v. Manzo*, 380 U.S. 545, 550 (1965); *Anti-Fascist Committee v. McGrath*, 341 U.S. 123, 168–169 (1951) (Frankfurter, J., concurring). At the very minimum, therefore, students facing suspension and the consequent interference with a protected property interest must be given *some* kind of notice and afforded *some* kind of hearing. "Parties whose rights are to be affected are entitled to be heard; and in order that they may enjoy that right they must first be notified." *Baldwin v. Hale*, 1 Wall. 223, 233 (1864).

It also appears from our cases that the timing and content of the notice and the nature of the hearing will depend on appropriate accommodation of the competing interests involved. *Cafeteria Workers v. McElroy*, *supra*, at 895; *Morrissey v. Brewer*, *supra*, at 481. The student's interest is to avoid unfair or mistaken exclusion from the educational process, with all of its unfortunate consequences. The Due Process Clause will not shield him from suspensions properly imposed, but it disserves both his interest and the interest of the State if his suspension is in fact unwarranted. The concern would be mostly academic if the disciplinary process were a totally accurate, unerring process, never mistaken and never unfair. Unfortunately, that is not the case, and no one suggests that it is. Disciplinarians, although proceeding in utmost good faith, frequently act on the reports and advice of others; and the controlling facts and the nature of the conduct under challenge are often disputed. The risk of error is not at all trivial, and it should be guarded against if that may be done without prohibitive cost or interference with the educational process.

The difficulty is that our schools are vast and complex. Some modicum of discipline and order is essential if the educational function is to be performed. Events calling for discipline are frequent occurrences and sometimes require immediate effective action. Suspension is considered not only to be a necessary tool to maintain order but a valuable educational device. The prospect of imposing elaborate hearing requirements in every suspension case is viewed with great concern, and many school authorities may well prefer the untrammeled power to act unilaterally, unhampered by rules about notice and hearing. But it would be a strange disciplinary system in an educational institution if no communication was sought by the disciplinarian with the student in an effort to inform him of his dereliction and to let him tell his side of the story in order to make sure that an injustice is not done. "[F]airness can rarely be obtained by secret, one-sided determination of facts decisive of rights. . . ." "Secrecy is not congenial to truth-seeking and self-righteousness gives too slender an assurance of rightness. No better instrument has been devised for arriving at truth than to give a person in jeopardy of serious loss notice of the case against him and opportunity to meet it." *Anti-Fascist Committee v. McGrath*, *supra*, at 170, 171–172 (Frankfurter, J., concurring).[9]

---

9. The facts involved in this case illustrate the point. Betty Crome was suspended for conduct which did not occur on school grounds, and for which mass arrests were made—hardly guaranteeing careful individualized fact-finding by the police or by the school principal. She claims to have been involved in no misconduct. However, she was suspended for 10 days without ever being told what she was

(continued on next page)

We do not believe that school authorities must be totally free from notice and hearing requirements if their schools are to operate with acceptable efficiency. Students facing temporary suspension have interests qualifying for protection of the Due Process Clause, and due process requires, in connection with a suspension of 10 days or less, that the student be given oral or written notice of the charges against him and, if he denies them, an explanation of the evidence the authorities have and an opportunity to present his side of the story. The Clause requires at least these rudimentary precautions against unfair or mistaken findings of misconduct and arbitrary exclusion from school.[10]

There need be no delay between the time "notice" is given and the time of the hearing. In the great majority of cases the disciplinarian may informally discuss the alleged misconduct with the student minutes after it has occurred. We hold only that, in being given an opportunity to explain his version of the facts at this discussion, the student first be told what he is accused of doing and what the basis of the accusation is. Lower courts which have addressed the question of the *nature* of the procedures required in short suspension cases have reached the same conclusion. *Tate v. Board of Education*, 453 F.2d 975, 979 (CA8 1972); *Vail v. Board of Education*, 354 F.Supp. 592, 603 (NH 1973). Since the hearing may occur almost immediately following the misconduct, it follows that as a general rule notice and hearing should precede removal of the student from school. We agree with the District

Court, however, that there are recurring situations in which prior notice and hearing cannot be insisted upon. Students whose presence poses a continuing danger to persons or property or an ongoing threat of disrupting the academic process may be immediately removed from school. In such cases, the necessary notice and rudimentary hearing should follow as soon as practicable, as the District Court indicated.

In holding as we do, we do not believe that we have imposed procedures on school disciplinarians which are inappropriate in a classroom setting. Instead we have imposed requirements which are, if anything, less than a fair-minded school principal would imposed upon himself in order to avoid unfair suspensions. Indeed, according to the testimony of the principal of Marion-Franklin High School, that school had an informal procedure, remarkably similar to that which we now require, applicable to suspensions generally but which was not followed in this case. Similarly, according to the most recent memorandum applicable to the entire CPSS, see n. 1, *supra*, school principals in the CPSS are now required by local rule to provide at least as much as the constitutional minimum which we have described.

We stop short of construing the Due Process Clause to require, countrywide, that hearings in connection with short suspensions must afford the student the opportunity to secure counsel, to confront and cross-examine witnesses supporting the charge, or to call his own witnesses to verify his version of the incident. Brief disciplinary suspensions are almost

---

accused of doing or being given an opportunity to explain her presence among those arrested. Similarly, Dwight Lopez was suspended, along with many others, in connection with a disturbance in the lunchroom. *Lopez* says he was not one of those in the lunchroom who was involved. However, he was never told the basis for the principal's belief that he was involved, nor was he ever given an opportunity to explain his presence in the lunchroom. The school principals who suspended Crome and Lopez may have been correct on the merits, but it is inconsistent with the Due Process Clause to have made the decision that misconduct had occurred without at some meaningful time giving Crome or Lopez an opportunity to persuade the principals otherwise.

We recognize that both suspensions were imposed during a time of great difficulty for the school administrations involved. At least in Lopez' case there may have been an immediate need to send home everyone in the lunchroom in order to preserve school order and property; and the administrative burden of providing 75 "hearings" of any kind is considerable. However, neither factor justifies a disciplinary suspension without *at any time* gathering facts relating to Lopez specifically, confronting him with them, and giving him an opportunity to explain.

10. Appellants point to the fact that some process is provided under Ohio law by way of judicial review. Ohio Rev. Code Ann. § 2506.01 (Supp. 1973). Appellants do not cite any case in which this general administrative review statute has been used to appeal from a disciplinary decision by a school official. If it be assumed that it could be so used, it is for two reasons insufficient to save inadequate procedures at the school level. First, although new proof may be offered in a § 2501.06 proceeding, *Shaker Coventry Corp. v. Shaker Heights Planning Comm'n*, 18 Ohio Op. 2d 272, 176 N.E.2d 332 (1961), the proceeding is not *de novo*. *In re Locke*, 33 Ohio App.2d 177, 294 N.E.2d 230 (1972). Thus the decision by the school—even if made upon inadequate procedures—is entitled to weight in the court proceeding. Second, without a demonstration to the contrary, we must assume that delay will attend any § 2501.06 proceeding, that the suspension will not be stayed pending hearing, and that the student meanwhile will irreparably lose his educational benefits.

countless. To impose in each such case even truncated trial-type procedures might well overwhelm administrative facilities in many places and by diverting resources, cost more than it would save in educational effectiveness. Moreover, further formalizing the suspension process and escalating its formality and adversary nature may not only make it too costly as a regular disciplinary tool but also destroy its effectiveness as part of the teaching process.

On the other hand, requiring effective notice and informal hearing permitting the student to give his version of the events will provide a meaningful hedge against erroneous action. At least the disciplinarian will be alerted to the existence of disputes about facts and arguments about cause and effect. He may then determine himself to summon the accuser, permit cross-examination, and allow the student to present his own witnesses. In more difficult cases, he may permit counsel. In any event, his discretion will be more informed and we think the risk of error substantially reduced.

Requiring that there be at least an informal give-and-take between student and disciplinarian, preferably prior to the suspension, will add little to the factfinding function where the disciplinarian himself has witnessed the conduct forming the basis for the charge. But things are not always as they seem to be, and the student will at least have the opportunity to characterize his conduct and put it in what he deems the proper context.

We should also make it clear that we have addressed ourselves solely to the short suspension, not exceeding 10 days. Longer suspensions or expulsions for the remainder of the school term, or permanently, may require more formal procedures. Nor do we put aside the possibility that in unusual situations, although involving only a short suspension, something more than the rudimentary procedures will be required.

IV

The District Court found each of the suspensions involved here to have occurred without a hearing, either before or after the suspension, and that each suspension was therefore invalid and the statute unconstitutional insofar as it permits such suspensions without notice or hearing. Accordingly, the judgment is affirmed.

CHILD IN SCHOOL—FREE SPEECH
Case Comment

In addition to school disciplinary matters, the U.S. Supreme Court has also considered the First Amendment rights of children in a school setting. *Tinker v. Des Moines School Dist.* was the first major decision dealing with free speech.[4] It is known as a "passive speech" case because the expression is not associated with the actual speaking of words.

The case involved students who wore black armbands to school to protest the Vietnam War in defiance of a school policy prohibiting such behavior. After being suspended, the students filed a civil rights action that was dismissed by the district court and affirmed by the appellate court. However, the U.S. Supreme Court reversed the decision, stating that neither "students nor teachers shed their constitutional rights to freedom of speech or expression at the schoolhouse gate."

This decision is significant because it recognizes the child's right to free speech in a public school system. *Tinker* established two things: (1) a child is entitled to free speech in school under the First Amendment of the U.S. Constitution and (2) the test used to determine whether the child has gone beyond proper speech is whether he or she materially and substantially interferes with the requirements of appropriate discipline in the operation of the school.

The concept of free speech articulated in *Tinker* can be contrasted with the "active speech" raised in the 1988 case of *Hazelwood School Dist. v. Kuhlmeier*. In *Kuhlmeier*, three student staff members of a high school newspaper filed suit against the local school board contending that their First Amendment rights were violated by the principal's censorship of articles in the student newspaper dealing with divorce and teenage pregnancy. The Supreme Court ruled that the school newspaper was not a public forum and that school officials could act to impose reasonable limitations on what students could print in a school-sponsored publication.

TINKER v. DES MOINES SCHOOL DIST.

393 U.S. 503 (1969)

Mr. Justice Fortas delivered the opinion of the Court.

Petitioner John F. Tinker, 15 years old, and petitioner Christopher Eckhardt, 16 years old, attended high schools in Des Moines, Iowa. Petitioner Mary Beth Tinker, John's sister, was a 13-year-old student in junior high school.

In December 1965, a group of adults and students in Des Moines held a meeting at the Eckhardt home. The group determined to publicize their objections to the hostilities in Vietnam and their support for a truce by wearing black armbands during the holiday season and by fasting on December 16 and New Year's Eve. Petitioners and their parents had previously engaged in similar activities, and they decided to participate in the program.

The principals of the Des Moines schools became aware of the plan to wear armbands. On December 14, 1965, they met and adopted a policy that any student wearing an armband to school would be asked to remove it, and if he refused he would be suspended until he returned without the armband. Petitioners were aware of the regulation that the school authorities adopted.

On December 16, Mary Beth and Christopher wore black armbands to their schools. John Tinker wore his armband the next day. They were all sent home and suspended from school until they would come back without their armbands. They did not return to school until after the planned period for wearing armbands had expired—that is, until after New Year's Day.

This complaint was filed in the United States District Court by petitioners, through their fathers, under § 1983 of Title 42 of the United States Code. It prayed for an injunction restraining the respondent school officials and the respondent members of the board of directors of the school district from disciplining the petitioners, and it sought nominal damages. After an evidentiary hearing the District Court dismissed the complaint. It upheld the constitutionality of the school authorities' action on the ground that it was reasonable in order to prevent disturbance of school discipline. 258 F.Supp. 971 (1966). The court referred to but expressly declined to follow the Fifth Circuit's holding in a similar case that the wearing of symbols like the armbands cannot

be prohibited unless it "materially and substantially interfere[s] with the requirements of appropriate discipline in the operation of the school." *Burnside v. Byars*, 363 F.2d 744, 749 (1966).[1]

On appeal, the Court of Appeals for the Eighth Circuit considered the case *en banc*. The court was equally divided, and the District Court's decision was accordingly affirmed, without opinion. 383 F.2d 988 (1967). We granted certiorari. 390 U.S. 942 (1968).

I

The District Court recognized that the wearing of an armband for the purpose of expressing certain views is the type of symbolic act that is within the Free Speech Clause of the First Amendment. See *West Virginia v. Barnette*, 319 U.S. 624 (1943); *Stromberg v. California*, 283 U.S. 359 (1931). Cf. *Thornhill v. Alabama*, 310 U.S. 88 (1940); *Edwards v. South Carolina*, 372 U.S. 229 (1963); *Brown v. Louisiana*, 383 US. 131 (1966). As we shall discuss, the wearing of armbands in the circumstances of this case was entirely divorced from actually or potentially disruptive conduct by those participating in it. It was closely akin to "pure speech" which, we have repeatedly held, is entitled to comprehensive protection under the First Amendment. Cf. *Cox v. Louisiana*, 379 U.S. 536, 555 (1965); *Adderley v. Florida*, 385 U.S. 39 (1966).

First Amendment rights, applied in light of the special characteristics of the school environment, are available to teachers and students. It can hardly be argued that either students or teachers shed their constitutional rights to freedom of speech or expression at the schoolhouse gate. This has been the unmistakable holding of this Court for almost 50 years. In *Meyer v. Nebraska*, 262 U.S. 390 (1923), and *Bartels v. Iowa*, 262 U.S. 404 (1923), this Court, in opinions by Mr. Justice McReynolds, held that the Due Process Clause of the Fourteenth Amendment prevents States from forbidding the teaching of a foreign language to young students. Statutes to this effect, the Court held, unconstitutionally interfere with the liberty of teacher, student, and par-

---

1. In *Burnside*, the Fifth Circuit ordered that high school authorities be enjoined from enforcing a regulation forbidding students to wear "freedom buttons." It is instructive that in *Blackwell v. Issaquena County Board of Education*, 363 F.2d 749 (1966), the same panel on the same day reached the opposite result on different facts. It declined to enjoin enforcement of such a regulation in another high school where the students wearing freedom buttons harassed students who did not wear them and created much disturbance.

ent.[2] See also *Pierce v. Society of Sisters*, 268 U.S. 510 (1925); *West Virginia v. Barnette*, 319 U.S. 624 (1943); *McCollum v. Board of Education*, 333 U.S. 203 (1948); *Wieman v. Updegraff*, 344 U.S. 183, 195 (1952) (concurring opinion); *Sweezy v. New Hampshire*, 354 U.S. 234 (1957); *Shelton v. Tucker*, 364 U.S. 479, 487 (1960); *Engel v. Vitale*, 370 U.S. 421 (1962); *Keyishian v. Board of Regents*, 385 U.S. 589, 603 (1967); *Epperson v. Arkansas*, *ante*, p. 97 (1968).

In *West Virginia v. Barnette, supra*, this Court held that under the First Amendment, the student in public school may not be compelled to salute the flag. Speaking through Mr. Justice Jackson, the Court said:

> The Fourteenth Amendment, as now applied to the States, protects the citizen against the State itself and all of its creatures—Boards of Education not excepted. These have, of course, important, delicate, and highly discretionary functions, but none that they may not perform within the limits of the Bill of Rights. That they are educating the young for citizenship is reason for scrupulous protection of Constitutional freedoms of the individual, if we are not to strangle the free mind at its source and teach youth to discount important principles of our government as mere platitudes. 319 U.S., at 637.

On the other hand, the Court has repeatedly emphasized the need for affirming the comprehensive authority of the States and of school officials, consistent with fundamental constitutional safeguards, to prescribe and control conduct in the schools. See *Epperson v. Arkansas, supra*, at 104; *Meyer v. Nebraska, supra*, at 402. Our problem lies in the area where students in the exercise of First Amendment rights collide with the rules of the school authorities.

II

The problem posed by the present case does not relate to regulation of the length of skirts or the type of clothing, to hair style, or deportment. Cf. *Ferrell v. Dallas Independent School District*, 392 F.2d 697 (1968); *Pugsley v. Sellmeyer*, 158 Ark. 247, 250 S.W. 538 (1923). It does not concern aggressive, disruptive action or even group demonstrations. Our problem involves direct, primary First Amendment rights akin to "pure speech."

The school officials banned and sought to punish petitioners for a silent, passive expression of opinion, unaccompanied by any disorder or disturbance on the part of petitioners. There is here no evidence whatever of petitioners' interference, actual or nascent, with the schools' work or of collision with the rights of other students to be secure and to be let alone. Accordingly, this case does not concern speech or action that intrudes upon the work of the schools or the rights of other students.

Only a few of the 18,000 students in the school system wore the black armbands. Only five students were suspended for wearing them. There is no indication that the work of the schools or any class was disrupted. Outside the classrooms, a few students made hostile remarks to the children wearing armbands, but there were no threats or acts of violence on school premises.

The District Court concluded that the action of the school authorities was reasonable because it was based upon their fear of a disturbance from the wearing of the armbands. But, in our system, undifferentiated fear or apprehension of disturbance is not enough to overcome the right to freedom of expression. Any departure from absolute regimentation may cause trouble. Any variation from the majority's opinion may inspire fear. Any word spoken, in class, in the lunchroom, or on the campus, that deviates from the views of another person may start an argument or cause a disturbance. But our Constitution says we must take this risk, *Terminiello v. Chicago*, 337 U.S. 1 (1949); and our history says that it is this sort of hazardous freedom—this kind of openness— that is the basis of our national strength and of the independence and vigor of Americans who grow up

---

2. *Hamilton v. Regents of Univ. of Cal.*, 293 U.S. 245 (1934), is sometimes cited for the broad proposition that the State may attach conditions to attendance at a state university that require individuals to violate their religious convictions. The case involved dismissal of members of a religious denomination from a lang grant college for refusal to participate in military training. Narrowly viewed, the case turns upon the Court's conclusion that merely requiring a student to participate in school training in military "science" could not conflict with his constitutionally protected freedom of conscience. The decision cannot be taken as establishing that the State may impose and enforce any conditions that it chooses upon attendance at public institutions of learning, however violative they may be of fundamental constitutional guarantees. See, e.g., *West Virginia v. Barnette*, 319 U.S. 624 (1943); *Dixon v. Alabama State Board of Education*, 294 F.2d 150 (C.A. 5th Cir. 1961); *Knight v. State Board of Education*, 200 F.Supp. 174 (D.C.M.D. Tenn. 1961); *Dickey v. Alabama State Board of Education*, 273 F.Supp. 613 (D.C.M.D. Ala. 1967). See also Note, Unconstitutional Conditions, 73 Harv.L.Rev. 1595 (1960); Note, Academic Freedom, 81 Harv.L.Rev. 1045 (1968).

and live in this relatively permissive, often dispu-tatious, society.

In order for the State in the person of school officials to justify prohibition of a particular expres-sion of opinion, it must be able to show that its action was caused by something more than a mere desire to avoid the discomfort and unpleasantness that always accompany an unpopular viewpoint. Certainly where there is no finding and no showing that engaging in the forbidden conduct would "ma-terially and substantially interfere with the require-ments of appropriate discipline in the operation of the school," the prohibition cannot be sustained. *Burnside v. Byars, supra,* at 749.

In the present case, the District Court made no such finding, and our independent examination of the record fails to yield evidence that the school authorities had reason to anticipate that the wearing of the armbands would substantially interfere with the work of the school or impinge upon the rights of other students. Even an official memorandum prepared after the suspension that listed the reasons for the ban on wearing the armbands made no ref-erence to the anticipation of such disruption.[3]

On the contrary, the action of the school au-thorities appears to have been based upon an urgent wish to avoid the controversy which might result from the expression, even by the silent symbol of armbands, of opposition to this Nation's part in the conflagration in Vietnam.[4] It is revealing, in this respect, that the meeting at which the school prin-cipals decided to issue the contested regulation was called in response to a student's statement to the journalism teacher in one of the schools that he wanted to write an article on Vietnam and have it published in the school paper. (The student was dissuaded.[5])

It is also relevant that the school authorities did not purport to prohibit the wearing of all symbols of political or controversial significance. The record shows that students in some of the schools wore buttons relating to national political campaigns, and some even wore the Iron Cross, traditionally a sym-bol of Nazism. The order prohibiting the wearing of armbands did not extend to these. Instead, a par-ticular symbol—black armbands worn to exhibit op-position to this Nation's involvement in Vietnam—was singled out for prohibition. Clearly, the pro-hibition of expression of one particular opinion, at least without evidence that it is necessary to avoid material and substantial interference with school-work or discipline, is not constitutionally permissible.

In our system, state-operated schools may not be enclaves of totalitarianism. School officials do not possess absolute authority over their students. Stu-dents in school as well as out of school are "persons" under our Constitution. They are possessed of fun-damental rights which the State must respect, just as they themselves must respect their obligations to the State. In our system, students may not be re-garded as closed-circuit recipients of only that which the State chooses to communicate. They may not be confined to the expression of those sentiments that are officially approved. In the absence of a spe-cific showing of constitutionally valid reasons to reg-ulate their speech, students are entitled to freedom of expression of their views. As Judge Gewin, speak-ing for the Fifth Circuit, said, school officials cannot suppress "expressions of feelings with which they do not wish to contend." *Burnside v. Byars, supra,*

---

3. The only suggestions of fear of disorder in the report are these:

"A former student of one of our high schools was killed in Viet Nam. Some of his friends are still in school and it was felt that if any kind of a demonstration existed, it might evolve into something which would be difficult to control."

"Students at one of the high schools were heard to say they would wear arm bands of other colors if the black bands prevailed."

Moreover, the testimony of school authorities at trial indicates that it was not fear of disruption that motivated the regulation prohibiting the armbands; the regulation was directed against "the principle of the demonstration" itself. School authorities simply felt that "the schools are no place for demonstrations," and if the students "don't like the way our elected officials are handling things, it should be handled with the ballot box and not in the halls of our public schools."

4. The District Court found that the school authorities, in prohibiting black armbands, were influenced by the fact that "[t]he Viet Nam war and the involvement of the United States therein has been the subject of a major controversy for some time. When the armband regulation involved herein was promulgated, debate over the Viet Nam war had become vehement in many localities. A protest march against the war had been recently held in Washington, D.C. A wave of draft card burning incidents protesting the war had swept the country. At that time two highly publicized draft card burning cases were pending in this Court. Both individuals supporting the war and those opposing it were quite vocal in expressing their views." 258 F.Supp., at 972–973.

5. After the principals' meeting, the director of secondary education and the principal of the high school informed the student that the principals were opposed to publication of his article. They reported that "we felt that it was a very friendly conversation, although we did not feel that we had convinced the student that our decision was a just one."

at 749.

In *Meyer v. Nebraska, supra,* at 402, Mr. Justice McReynolds expressed this Nation's repudiation of the principle that a State might so conduct its schools as to "foster a homogeneous people." He said:

> In order to submerge the individual and develop ideal citizens, Sparta assembled the males at seven into barracks and intrusted their subsequent education and training to official guardians. Although such measures have been deliberately approved by men of great genius, their ideas touching the relation between individual and State were wholly different from those upon which our institutions rest; and it hardly will be affirmed that any legislature could impose such restrictions upon the people of a State without doing violence to both letter and spirit of the Constitution.

This principle has been repeated by this Court on numerous occasions during the intervening years. In *Keyishian v. Board of Regents,* 385 U.S. 589, 603, Mr. Justice Brennan, speaking for the Court, said:

> The vigilant protection of constitutional freedoms is nowhere more vital than in the community of American schools." *Shelton v. Tucker,* [364 U.S. 479] at 487. The classroom is peculiarly the "marketplace of ideas." The Nation's future depends upon leaders trained through wide exposure to that robust exchange of ideas which discovers truth "out of a multitude of tongues, [rather] than through any kind of authoritative selection."

The principle of these cases is not confined to the supervised and ordained discussion which takes place in the classroom. The principal use to which the schools are dedicated is to accommodate students during prescribed hours for the purpose of certain types of activities. Among those activities is personal intercommunication among the students.[6] This is not only an inevitable part of the process of attending school; it is also an important part of the educational process. A student's rights, therefore, do not embrace merely the classroom hours. When he is in the cafeteria, or on the playing field, or on the campus during the authorized hours, he may express his opinions, even on controversial subjects like the conflict in Vietnam, if he does so without "materially and substantially interfer[ing] with the require-

ments of appropriate discipline in the operation of the school" and without colliding with the rights of others. *Burnside v. Byars, supra,* at 749. But conduct by the student, in class or out of it, which for any reason—whether it stems from time, place, or type of behavior—materially disrupts classwork or involves substantial disorder or invasion of the rights of others is, of course, not immunized by the constitutional guarantee of freedom of speech. Cf. *Blackwell v. Issaquena County Board of Education,* 363 F.2d 749 (C.A. 5th Cir. 1966).

Under our Constitution, free speech is not a right that is given only to be so circumscribed that it exists in principle but not in fact. Freedom of expression would not truly exist if the right could be exercised only in an area that a benevolent government has provided as a safe haven for crackpots. The Constitution says that Congress (and the States) may not abridge the right to free speech. This provision means what it says. We properly read it to permit reasonable regulation of speech-connected activities in carefully restricted circumstances. But we do not confine the permissible exercise of First Amendment rights to a telephone booth or the four corners of a pamphlet, or to supervised and ordained discussion in a school classroom.

If a regulation were adopted by school officials forbidding discussion of the Vietnam conflict, or the expression by any student of opposition to it anywhere on school property except as part of a prescribed classroom exercise, it would be obvious that the regulation would violate the constitutional rights of students, at least if it could not be justified by a showing that the students' activities would materially and substantially disrupt the work and discipline of the school. Cf. *Hammond v. South Carolina State College,* 272 F.Supp. 947 (D.C.S.C. 1967) (orderly protest meeting on state college campus); *Dickey v. Alabama State Board of Education,* 273 F.Supp. 613 (D.C.M.D.Ala. 1967) (expulsion of student editor of college newspaper). In the circumstances of the present case, the prohibition of the silent, passive "witness of the armbands," as one of the children called it, is no less offensive to the Constitution's guarantees.

---

6. In *Hammond v. South Carolina State College,* 272 F.Supp. 947 (D.C.S.C. 1967), District Judge Hemphill had before him a case involving a meeting on campus of 300 students to express their views on school practices. He pointed out that a school is not like a hospital or a jail enclosure. Cf. *Cox v. Louisiana,* 379 U.S. 536 (1965); *Adderley v. Florida,* 385 U.S. 39 (1966). It is a public place, and its dedication to specific uses does not imply that the constitutional rights of persons entitled to be there are to be gauged as if the premises were purely private property. Cf. *Edwards v. South Carolina,* 372 U.S. 229 (1963); *Brown v. Louisiana,* 383 U.S. 131 (1966).

As we have discussed, the record does not demonstrate any facts which might reasonably have led school authorities to forecase substantial disruption of or material interference with school activities, and no disturbances or disorders on the school premises in fact occurred. These petitioners merely went about their ordained rounds in school. Their deviation consisted only in wearing on their sleeve a band of black cloth, not more than two inches wide. They wore it to exhibit their disapproval of the Vietnam hostilities and their advocacy of a truce, to make their views known, and, by their example, to influence others to adopt them. They neither interrupted school activities nor sought to intrude in the school affairs or the lives of others. They caused discussion outside of the classrooms, but no interference with work and no disorder. In the circumstances, our Constitution does not permit officials of the State to deny their form of expression.

We express no opinion as to the form of relief which should be granted, this being a matter for the lower courts to determine. We reverse and remand for further proceedings consistent with this opinion.

Reversed and remanded.

HAZELWOOD SCHOOL DIST. v. KUHLMEIER

Cite as 108 S.Ct. 562 (1988)

Justice White delivered the opinion of the Court.

This case concerns the extent to which educators may exercise editorial control over the contents of a high school newspaper produced as part of the school's journalism curriculum.

I

Petitioners are the Hazelwood School District in St. Louis County, Missouri; various school officials; Robert Eugene Reynolds, the principal of Hazelwood East High School, and Howard Emerson, a teacher in the school district. Respondents are three former Hazelwood East students who were staff members of *Spectrum*, the school newspaper. They contend that school officials violated their First Amendment rights by deleting two pages of articles from the May 13, 1983, issue of *Spectrum*.

Spectrum was written and edited by the Journalism II class at Hazelwood East. The newspaper was published every three weeks or so during the 1982–1983 school year. More than 4,500 copies of the newspaper were distributed during that year to students, school personnel, and members of the community.

The Board of Education allocated funds from its annual budget for the printing of *Spectrum*. These funds were supplemented by proceeds from sales of the newspaper. The printing expenses during the 1982–1983 school year totaled $4,668.50; revenue from sales was $1,166.84. The other costs associated with the newspaper—such as supplies, textbooks, and a portion of the journalism teacher's salary—were borne entirely by the Board.

The Journalism II course was taught by Robert Stergos for most of the 1982–1983 academic year. Stergos left Hazelwood East to take a job in private industry on April 29, 1983, when the May 13 edition of *Spectrum* was nearing completion, and petitioner Emerson took his place as newspaper adviser for the remaining weeks of the term.

The practice at Hazelwood East during the spring 1983 semester was for the journalism teacher to submit page proofs of each *Spectrum* issue to Principal Reynolds for his review prior to publication. On May 10, Emerson delivered the proofs of the May 13 edition to Reynolds, who objected to two of the articles scheduled to appear in that edition. One of the stories described three Hazelwood East students' experiences with pregnancy; the other discussed the impact of divorce on students at the school.

Reynolds was concerned that, although the pregnancy story used false names "to keep the identity of these girls a secret," the pregnant students still might be identifiable from the text. He also believed that the article's references to sexual activity and birth control were inappropriate for some of the younger students at the school. In addition, Reynolds was concerned that a student identified by name in the divorce story had complained that her father "wasn't spending enough time with my mom, my sister and I" prior to the divorce, "was always out of town on business or out late playing cards with the guys," and "always argued about everything" with her mother. App. to Pet. for Cert. 38. Reynolds believed that the student's parents should have been given an opportunity to respond to these remarks or to consent to their publication. He was unaware that Emerson had deleted the student's name from the final version of the article.

Reynolds believed that there was no time to make the necessary changes in the stories before the scheduled press run and that the newspaper would not appear before the end of the school year if printing were delayed to any significant extent. He concluded that his only options under the circumstances were to publish a four-page newspaper instead of the planned six-page newspaper, eliminating the two pages on which the offending stories appeared, or to publish no newspaper at all. Accordingly, he directed Emerson to withhold from publication the two pages containing the stories on pregnancy and divorce.[1] He informed his superiors of the decision, and they concurred.

Respondents subsequently commenced this action in the United States District Court for the Eastern District of Missouri seeking a declaration that their First Amendment rights had been violated, injunctive relief, and monetary damages. After a bench trial, the District Court denied an injunction, holding that no First Amendment violation had occurred. 607 F.Supp. 1450 (1985).

The District Court concluded that school officials may impose restraints on students' speech in activities that are " 'an integral part of the school's educational function' "—including the publication of a school-sponsored newspaper by a journalism class— so long as their decision has " 'a substantial and reasonable basis.' " Id., at 1466 (quoting Frasca v. Andrews, 463 F.Supp. 1043, 1052 (EDNY 1979)). The court found that Principal Reynolds' concern that the pregnant students' anonymity would be lost and their privacy invaded was "legitimate and reasonable," given "the small number of pregnant students at Hazelwood East and several identifying characteristics that were disclosed in the article." 607 F.Supp., at 1466. The court held that Reynolds' action was also justified "to avoid the impression that [the school] endorses the sexual norms of the subjects" and to shield younger students from exposure to unsuitable material. Ibid. The deletion of the article on divorce was seen by the court as a reasonable response to the invasion of privacy concerns raised by the named student's remarks. Because the article did not indicate that the student's parents had been offered an opportunity to respond

to her allegations, said the court, there was cause for "serious doubt that the article complied with the rules of fairness which are standard in the field of journalism and which were covered in the textbook used in the Journalism II class." Id., at 1467. Furthermore, the court concluded that Reynolds was justified in deleting two full pages of the newspaper, instead of deleting only the pregnancy and divorce stories or requiring that those stories be modified to address his concerns, based on his "reasonable belief that he had to make an immediate decision and that there was no time to make modifications to the articles in question." Id., at 1466.

The Court of Appeals for the Eighth Circuit reversed. 795 F.2d 1368 (1986). The court held at outset that Spectrum was not only "a part of the school adopted curriculum," id., at 1373, but also a public forum, because the newspaper was "intended to be and operated as a conduit for student viewpoint." Id., at 1372. The court then concluded that Spectrum's status as a public forum precluded school officials from censoring its contents except when " 'necessary to avoid material and substantial interference with school work or discipline . . . or the rights of others.' " Id., at 1374 (quoting Tinker v. Des Moines Independent Community School Dist., 393 U.S. 503, 511, 89 S.Ct. 733, 739, 21 L.Ed.2d 731 (1969)).

The Court of Appeals found "no evidence in the record that the principal could have reasonably forecast that the censored articles or any materials in the censored articles would have materially disrupted classwork or given rise to substantial disorder in the school." 795 F.2d, at 1375. School officials were entitled to censor the articles on the ground that they invaded the rights of others, according to the court, only if publication of the articles could have resulted in tort liability to the school. The court concluded that no tort action for libel or invasion of privacy could have been maintained against the school by the subjects of the two articles or by their families. Accordingly, the court held that school officials had violated respondents' First Amendment rights by deleting the two pages of the newspaper.

We granted certiorari, 479 U.S. ___ , 107 S.Ct. 926, 93 L.Ed.2d 978 (1987), and we now reverse.

---

1. The two pages deleted from the newspaper also contained articles on teenage marriage, runaways, and juvenile delinquents, as well as a general article on teenage pregnancy. Reynolds testified that he had no objection to these articles and that they were deleted only because they appeared on the same pages as the two objectionable articles.

II

[1] Students in the public schools do not "shed their constitutional rights to freedom of speech or expression at the schoolhouse gate." *Tinker, supra,* 393 U.S., at 506, 89 S.Ct., at 736. They cannot be punished merely for expressing their personal views on the school premises—whether "in the cafeteria, or on the playing field, or on the campus during the authorized hours," *id.,* at 512–513, 89 S.Ct., at 739–740—unless school authorities have reason to believe that such expression will "substantially interfere with the work of the school or impinge upon the rights of other students." *Id.,* at 509, 89 S.Ct., at 738.

[2] We have nonetheless recognized that the First Amendment rights of students in the public schools "are not automatically coextensive with the rights of adults in other settings," *Bethel School District No. 403 v. Fraser,* 478 U.S. __ , __ , 106 S.Ct. 3159, 3164, 92 L.Ed.2d 549 (1986), and must be "applied in light of the special characteristics of the school environment." *Tinker, supra,* 393 U.S., at 506, 89 S.Ct., at 736; cf. *New Jersey v. T.L.O.,* 469 U.S. 325, 341–343, 105 S.Ct. 733, 743–744, 83 L.Ed.2d 720 (1985). A school need not tolerate student speech that is inconsistent with its "basic educational mission," *Fraser, supra,* 478 U.S., at __ , 106 S.Ct., at 3166, even though the government could not censor similar speech outside the school. Accordingly, we held in *Fraser* that a student could be disciplined for having delivered a speech that was "sexually explicit" but not legally obscene at an official school assembly, because the school was entitled to "dissassociate itself" from the speech in a manner that such vulgarity is "wholly inconsistent with the 'fundamental values' of public school education." Ibid. We thus recognized that "[t]he determination of what manner of speech in the classroom or in school assembly is inappropriate properly rests with the school board," *id.,* at __ , 106 S.Ct., at 3165, rather than with the federal courts. It is in this context that respondents' First Amendment claims must be considered.

A

[3] We deal first with the question whether *Spectrum* may appropriately be characterized as a forum for public expression. The public schools do not possess all of the attributes of streets, parks, and other tra-

ditional public forums that "time out of mind, have been used for purposes of assembly, communicating thoughts between citizens, and discussing public questions." *Hague v. CIO,* 307 U.S. 496, 515, 59 S.Ct. 954, 964, 83 L.Ed. 1423 (1939). Cf. *Widmar v. Vincent,* 454 U.S. 263, 267–268, n. 5, 102 S.Ct. 269, 273, n. 5, 70 L.Ed.2d 440 (1981). Hence, school facilities may be deemed to be public forums only if school authorities have "by policy or by practice" opened those facilities "for indiscriminate use by the general public." *Perry Education Assn. v. Perry Local Educators' Assn.,* 460 U.S. 37, 47, 103 S.Ct. 948, 956, 74 L.Ed.2d 794 (1983), or by some segment of the public, such as student organizations. *Id.,* at 46, n. 7, 103 S.Ct., at 955, n. 7 (citing *Widmar v. Vincent*). If the facilities have instead been reserved for other intended purposes, "communicative or otherwise," then no public forum has been created, and school officials may impose reasonable restrictions on the speech of students, teachers, and other members of the school community. Ibid. "The government does not create a public forum by inaction or by permitting limited discourse, but only by intentionally opening a nontraditional forum for public discourse." *Cornelius v. NAACP Legal Defense & Educatonal Fund, Inc.,* 473 U.S. 788, 802, 105 S.Ct. 3439, 3449, 87 L.Ed.2d 567 (1985).

[4] The policy of school officials toward *Spectrum* was reflected in Hazelwood School Board Policy 348.51 and the Hazelwood East Curriculum Guide. Board Policy 348.51 provided that "[s]chool sponsored publications are developed within the adopted curriculum and its educational implications in regular classroom activities." App. 22. The Hazelwood East Curriculum Guide described the Journalism II course as a "laboratory situation in which the students publish the school newspaper applying skills they have learned in Journalism I." *Id.,* at 11. The lessons that were to be learned from the Journalism II course, according to the Curriculum Guide, included development of journalistic skills under deadline pressure, "the legal, moral, and ethical restrictions imposed upon journalists within the school community," and "responsibility and acceptance of criticism for articles of opinion." Ibid. Journalism II was taught by a faculty member during regular class hours. Students received grades and academic credit for their performance in the course.

School officials did not deviate in practice from their policy that production of *Spectrum* was to be part of the educational curriculum and a "regular classroom activit[y]." The District Court found that Robert Stergos, the journalism teacher during most of the 1982–1983 school year, "both had the authority to exercise and in fact exercised a great deal of control over *Spectrum.*" 607 F.Supp., at 1453. For example, Stergos selected the editors of the newspaper, scheduled publication dates, decided the number of pages for each issue, assigned story ideas to class members, advised students on the development of their stories, reviewed the use of quotations, edited stories, selected and edited the letters to the editor, and dealt with the printing company. Many of these decisions were made without consultation with the Journalism II students. The District Court thus found it "clear that Mr. Stergos was the final authority with respect to almost every aspect of the production and publication of *Spectrum,* including its content." Ibid. Moreover, after each *Spectrum* issue had been finally approved by Stergos or his successor, the issue still had to be reviewed by Principal Reynolds prior to publication. Respondents' assertion that they had believed that they could publish "practically anything" in *Spectrum* was therefore dismissed by the District Court as simply "not credible." *Id.,* at 1456. These factual findings are amply supported by the record, and were not rejected as clearly erroneous by the Court of Appeals.

The evidence relied upon by the Court of Appeals in finding *Spectrum* to be a public forum, see 795 F.2d, at 1372–1373, is equivocal at best. For example, Board Policy 348.51, which stated in part that "[s]chool sponsored student publications will not restrict free expression or diverse viewpoints within the rules of responsible journalism," also stated that such publications were "developed within the adopted curriculum and its educational implications." App. 22. One might reasonably infer from the full text of Policy 348.51 that school officials retained ultimate control over what constituted "responsible journalism" in a school-sponsored newspaper. Although the Statement of Policy published in the September 14, 1982, issue of *Spectrum* declared that "*Spectrum,* as a student-press publication, accepts all rights implied by the First Amendment," this statement, understood in the context of the paper's role in the school's curriculum, suggests at most that the administration will not interfere with the students' exercise of those First Amendment rights that attend the publication of a school-sponsored newspaper. It does not reflect an intent to expand those rights by converting a curricular newspaper into a public forum.[2] Finally, that students were permitted to exercise some authority over the contents of *Spectrum* was fully consistent with the Curriculum Guide objective of teaching the Journalism II students "leadership responsibilities as issue and page editors." App. 11. A decision to teach leadership skills in the context of a classroom activity hardly implies a decision to relinquish school control over that activity. In sum, the evidence relied upon by the Court of Appeals fails to demonstrate the "clear intent to create a public forum," *Cornelius,* 473 U.S., at 802, 105 S.Ct., at 3449–3450, that existed in cases in which we found public forums to have been created. See *id.,* at 802–803, 105 S.Ct., at 3449–3450 (citing *Widmar v. Vincent,* 454 U.S., at 267, 102 S.Ct., at 273; *Madison School District v. Wisconsin Employment Relations Comm'n,* 429 U.S. 167, 174, n. 6, 97 S.Ct. 421, 426, n. 6, 50 L.Ed.2d 376 (1976); *Southeastern Promotions, Ltd. v. Conrad,* 420 U.S. 546, 555, 95 S.Ct. 1239, 1245, 43 L.Ed.2d 448 (1975)). School officials did not evince either "by policy or by practice," *Perry Education Assn.,* 460 U.S., at 47, 103 S.Ct., at 956, any intent to open the pages of *Spectrum* to "indiscriminate use," ibid., by its student reporters and editors, or by the student body generally. Instead, they "reserve[d] the forum for its intended purpos[e]," *id.,* at 46, 103 S.Ct., at 955, as a supervised learning experience for journalism students. Accordingly, school officials were entitled to regulate the contents of *Spectrum* in any reasonable manner. Ibid. It is this standard, rather than our decision in *Tinker,* that governs this case.

---

2. The Statement also cited *Tinker v. Des Moines Independent Community School Dist.,* 393 U.S. 503, 89 S.Ct. 733, 21 L.Ed.2d 731 (1969), for the proposition that "[o]nly speech that 'materially and substantially interfers with the requirements of appropriate discipline' can be found unacceptable and therefore be prohibited." App. 26. This portion of the Statement does not, of course, even accurately reflect our holding in *Tinker.* Furthermore, the Statement nowhere expressly extended the *Tinker* standard to the news and feature articles contained in a school-sponsored newspaper. The dissent apparently finds as a fact that the Statement was published annually in *Spectrum;* however, the District Court was unable to conclude that the Statement appeared on more than one occasion. In any event, even if the Statement says what the dissent believes that it says, the evidence that school officials never intended to designate *Spectrum* as a public forum remains overwhelming.

B

The question whether the First Amendment requires a school to tolerate particular student speech—the question that we addressed in *Tinker*—is different from the question whether the First Amendment requires a school affirmatively to promote particular student speech. The former question addresses educators' ability to silence a student's personal expression that happens to occur on the school premises. The latter question concerns educators' authority over school-sponsored publications, theatrical productions, and other expressive activities that students, parents, and members of the public might reasonably perceive to bear the imprimatur of the school. These activities may fairly be characterized as part of the school curriculum, whether or not they occur in a traditional classroom setting, so long as they are supervised by faculty members and designed to impart particular knowledge or skills to student participants and audiences.[3]

[5–8] Educators are entitled to exercise greater control over this second form of student expression to assure that participants learn whatever lessons the activity is designed to teach, that readers or listeners are not exposed to material that may be inappropriate for their level of maturity, and that the views of the individual speaker are not erroneously attributed to the school. Hence, a school may in its capacity as publisher of a school newspaper or producer of a school play "disassociate itself," *Fraser*, 478 U.S., at ___, 106 S.Ct., at 3166, not only from speech that would "substantially interfere with [its] work . . . or impinge upon the rights of other students," *Tinker*, 393 U.S., at 509, 89 S.Ct., at 738, but also from speech that is, for example, ungrammatical, poorly written, inadequately researched,

biased or prejudiced, vulgar or profane, or unsuitable for immature audiences.[4] A school must be able to set high standards for the student speech that is disseminated under its auspices—standards that may be higher than those demanded by some newspaper publishers or theatrical producers in the "real" world— and may refuse to disseminate student speech that does not meet those standards. In addition, a school must be able to take into account the emotional maturity of the intended audience in determining whether to disseminate student speech on potentially sensitive topics, which might range from the existence of Santa Claus in an elementary school setting to the particulars of teenage sexual activity in a high school setting. A school must also retain the authority to refuse to sponsor student speech that might reasonably be perceived to advocate drug or alcohol use, irresponsible sex, or conduct otherwise inconsistent with "the shared values of a civilized social order," *Fraser*, *supra*, 478 US., at ___ , 106 S.Ct., at 3165, or to associate the school with any position other than neutrality on matters of political controversy. Otherwise, the schools would be unduly constrained from fulfilling their role as "a principal instrument in awakening the child to cultural values, in preparing him for later professional training, and in helping him to adjust normally to his environment." *Brown v. Board of Education*, 347 U.S. 483, 493, 74 S.Ct. 686, 691, 98 L.Ed. 873 (1954).

[9] Accordingly, we conclude that the standard articulated in *Tinker* for determining whether a school may punish student expression need not also be the standard for determining when a school may refuse to lend its name and resources to the dissemination of student expression.[5] Instead, we hold that educators do not offend the First Amendment by exercising editorial control over the style and content

---

3. The distinction that we draw between speech that is sponsored by the school and speech that is not is fully consistent with *Papish v. Board of Curators*, 410 U.S. 667, 93 S.Ct. 1197, 35 L.Ed.2d 618 (1973) (*per curiam*), which involved an off-campus "underground" newspaper that school officials merely had allowed to be sold on a state university campus.

4. The dissent perceives no difference between the First Amendment analysis applied in *Tinker* and that applied in *Fraser*. We disagree. The decision in *Fraser* rested on the "vulgar," "lewd," and "plainly offensive" character of a speech delivered at an official school assembly rather than on any propensity of the speech to "materially disrupt[] classwork or involve[] substantial disorder or invasion of the rights of others." 393 U.S., at 513, 89 S.Ct., at 740. Indeed, the *Fraser* Court cited as "especially relevant" a portion of Justice Black's dissenting opinion in *Tinker* "disclaim[ing] any purpose . . . to hold that the Federal Constitution compels the teachers, parents and elected school officials to surrender control of the American public school system to public school students." 478 U.S., at ___ , 106 S.Ct., at 3166 (citing 393 U.S., at 522, 89 S.Ct., at 744). Of course, Justice Black's observations are equally relevant to the instant case.

5. We therefore need not decide whether the Court of Appeals correctly construed *Tinker* as precluding school officials from censoring student speech to avoid "invasion of the rights of others," 393 U.S., at 513, 89 S.Ct., at 740, except where that speech could result in tort liability to the school.

of student speech in school-sponsored expressive activities so long as their actions are reasonably related to legitimate pedagogical concerns.[6]

[10] This standard is consistent with our oft-expressed view that the education of the Nation's youth is primarily the responsibility of parents, teachers, and state and local school officials, and not of federal judges. See, e.g., *Board of Education of Hendrick Hudson Central School Dist. v. Rowley*, 458 U.S. 176, 208, 102 S.Ct. 3034, 3051, 73 L.Ed.2d 690 (1982); *Wood v. Strickland*, 420 U.S. 308, 326, 95 S.Ct. 992, 1003, 43 L.Ed.2d 214 (1975); *Epperson v. Arkansas*, 393 U.S. 97, 104, 89 S.Ct. 266, 270, 21 L.Ed.2d 228 (1968). It is only when the decision to censor a school-sponsored publication, theatrical production, or other vehicle of student expression has no valid educational purpose that the First Amendment is so "directly and sharply implicate[d]," ibid., as to require judicial intervention to protect students' constitutional rights.[7]

III

[11] We also conclude that Principal Reynolds acted reasonably in requiring the deletion from the May 13 issue of *Spectrum* of the pregnancy article, the divorce article, and the remaining articles that were to appear on the same pages of the newspaper.

The initial paragraph of the pregnancy article declared that "[a]ll names have been changed to keep the identity of these girls a secret." The principal concluded that the students' anonymity was not adequately protected, however, given the other identifying information in the article and the small number of pregnant students at the school. Indeed, a teacher at the school credibly testified that she could positively identify at least one of the girls and possibly all three. It is likely that many students at Hazelwood East would have been at least as successful in identifying the girls. Reynolds therefore could reasonably have feared that the article violated whatever pledge of anonymity had been given to the pregnant students. In addition, he could reasonably have been concerned that the article was not sufficiently sensitive to the privacy interests of the students' boyfriends and parents, who were discussed in the article but who were given no opportunity to consent to its publication or to offer a response. The article did not contain graphic accounts of sexual activity. The girls did comment in the article, however, concerning their sexual histories and their use or nonuse of birth control. It was not unreasonable for the principal to have concluded that such frank talk was inappropriate in a school-sponsored publication distributed to 14-year-old freshmen and presumably taken home to be read by students' even younger brothers and sisters.

The student who was quoted by name in the version of the divorce article seen by Principal Reynolds made comments sharply critical of her father. The principal could reasonably have concluded that an individual publicly identified as an inattentive parent—indeed, as one who chose "playing cards with the guys" over home and family—was entitled to an opportunity to defend himself as a matter of journalistic fairness. These concerns were shared by both of *Spectrum*'s faculty advisers for the 1982–1983 school year, who testified that they would not have allowed the article to be printed without deletion of the student's name.[8]

---

6. We reject respondents' suggestion that school officials be permitted to exercise prepublication control over school-sponsored publications only pursuant to specific written regulations. To require such regulations in the context of a curricular activity could unduly constrain the ability of educators to educate. We need not now decide whether such regulations are required before school officials may censor publications not sponsored by the school that students seek to distribute on school grounds. See *Baughman v. Freienmuth*, 478 F.2d 1345 (CA4 1973); *Shanley v. Northwest Independent School Dist., Bexar Cty., Tex.*, 462 F.2d 960 (CA5 1972); *Eisner v. Stamford Board of Education*, 440 F.2d 803 (CA2 1971).

7. A number of lower federal courts have similarly recognized that educators' decisions with regard to the content of school-sponsored newspapers, dramatic productions, and other expressive activities are entitled to substantial deference. See, e.g., *Nicholson v. Board of Education Torrance Unified School Dist.*, 682 F.2d 858 (CA9 1982); *Seyfried v. Walton*, 668 F.2d 214 (CA3 1981); *Trachtman v. Anker*, 563 F.2d 512 (CA2 1977), cert. denied, 435 U.S. 925, 98 S.Ct. 1491, 55 L.Ed.2d 519 (1978); *Frasca v. Andrews*, 463 F.Supp. 1043 (EDNY 1979). We need not now decide whether the same degree of deference is appropriate with respect to school-sponsored expressive activities at the college and university level.

8. The reasonableness of Principal Reynolds' concerns about the two articles was further substantiated by the trial testimony of Martin Duggan, a former editorial page editor of the *St. Louis Globe Democrat* and a former college journalism instructor and newspaper adviser. Duggan testified that the divorce story did not meet journalistic standards of fairness and balance because the father was not given an opportunity to respond, and that the pregnancy story was not appropriate for publication in a high school newspaper because it was unduly intrusive to the privacy of the girls, their parents, and their boyfriends. The District Court found Duggan to be "an objective and independent witness" whose testimony was entitled to significant weight. 607 F.Supp. 1450, 1461 (ED Mo. 1985).

Principal Reynolds testified credibly at trial that, at the time that he reviewed the proofs of the May 13 issue during an extended telephone conversation with Emerson, he believed that there was no time to make any changes in the articles, and that the newspaper had to be printed immediately or not at all. It is true that Reynolds did not verify whether the necessary modifications could still have been made in the articles, and that Emerson did not volunteer the information that printing could be delayed until the changes were made. We nonetheless agree with the District Court that the decision to excise the two pages containing the problematic articles was reasonable given the particular circumstances of this case. These circumstances included the very recent replacement of Stergos by Emerson, who may not have been entirely familiar with *Spectrum* editorial and production procedures, and the pressure felt by Reynolds to make an immediate decision so that students would not be deprived of the newspaper altogether.

In sum, we cannot reject as unreasonable Principal Reynolds' conclusion that neither the pregnancy article nor the divorce article was suitable for publication in *Spectrum*. Reynolds could reasonably have concluded that the students who had written and edited these articles had not sufficiently mastered those portions of the Journalism II curriculum that pertained to the treatment of controversial issues and personal attacks, the need to protect the privacy of individuals whose most intimate concerns are to be revealed in the newspaper, and "the legal, moral, and ethical restrictions imposed upon journalists within [a] school community" that includes adolescent subjects and readers. Finally, we conclude that the principal's decision to delete two pages of *Spectrum*, rather than to delete only the offending articles or to require that they be modified, was reasonable under the circumstances as he understood them. Accordingly, no violation of First Amendment rights occurred.[9]

The judgment of the Court of Appeals for the Eighth Circuit is therefore reversed.

THE CHILD IN THE FAMILY
Case Comment

Whether to terminate parental rights is the difficult question in dependency proceedings. Due process considerations require that the parent-child relationship be governed by constitutional protections. In *Santosky v. Kramer*, the U.S. Supreme Court recognized that before a state may sever the rights of parents with their natural child, "clear and convincing proof" is required. The burden of proof is one of the most critical factors in such proceedings.

Although the Supreme Court has not mandated a right to counsel for parents in termination cases, many states ordinarily provide this right by statute or court rule.[5]

SANTOSKY v. KRAMER
455 U.S. 745 (1981)

Justice Blackmun delivered the opinion of the Court.

Under New York law, the State many terminate, over parental objection, the rights of parents in their natural child upon a finding that the child is "permanently neglected." N.Y. Soc. Serv. Law §§ 384-b.4.(d), 384-b.7.(a) (McKinney Supp. 1981– 1982) (Soc. Serv. Law). The New York Family Court Act § 622 (McKinney 1975 and Supp. 1981–1982) (Fam. Ct. Act) requires that only a "fair preponderance of the evidence" support that finding. Thus, in New York, the factual certainty required to extinguish the parent-child relationship is no greater than that necessary to award money damages in an ordinary civil action.

Today we hold that the Due Process Clause of the Fourteenth Amendment demands more than this. Before a State may sever completely and irrevocably the rights of parents in their natural child, due process requires that the State support its allegations by at least clear and convincing evidence.

---

9. It is likely that the approach urged by the dissent would as a practical matter have far more deleterious consequences for the student press than does the approach that we adopt today. The dissent correctly acknowledges "[t]he State's prerogative to dissolve the student newspaper entirely." *Ante*, at 578. It is likely that many public schools would do just that rather than open their newspapers to all student expression that does not threaten "materia[l] disrup[tion of] classwork" or violation of "rights that are protected by law," *ante*, at 579, regardless of how sexually explicit, racially intemperate, or personally insulting that expression otherwise might be.

I

A

New York authorizes its officials to remove a child temporarily from his or her home if the child appears "neglected," within the meaning of Art. 10 of the Family Court Act. See §§ 1012(f),1021–1029. Once removed, a child under the age of 18 customarily is placed "in the care of an authorized agency," Soc. Serv. Law § 384-b.7.(a), usually a state institution or a foster home. At that point, "the state's first obligation is to help the family with services to . . . reunite it. . . ." § 384-b.1.(a)(iii). But if convinced that "positive, nurturing parent-child relationships no longer exist," § 384-b.1.(b), the State may initiate "permanent neglect" proceedings to free the child for adoption.

The State bifurcates its permanent neglect proceeding into "fact-finding" and "dispositional" hearings. Fam. Ct. Act §§ 622, 623. At the factfinding stage, the State must prove that the child has been "permanently neglected," as defined by Fam. Ct. Act §§ 614.1.(a)-(d) and Soc. Serv. Law § 384-b.7.(a). See Fam. Ct. Act § 622. The Family Court judge then determines at a subsequent dispositional hearing what placement would serve the child's best interests. §§ 623, 631.

At the fact-finding hearing, the State must establish, among other things, that for more than a year after the child entered state custody, the agency "made diligent efforts to encourage and strengthen the pa-

rental relationship." Fam. Ct. Act §§ 614.1.(c), 611. The State must further prove that during that same period, the child's natural parents failed "substantially and continuously or repeatedly to maintain contact with or plan for the future of the child although physically and financially able to do so." § 614.1.(d). Should the State support its allegations by "a fair preponderance of the evidence," § 622, the child may be declared permanently neglected. § 611. That declaration empowers the Family Court judge to terminate permanently the natural parents' rights in the child. §§ 631(c), 634. Termination denies the natural parents physical custody, as well as the rights ever to visit, communicate with, or regain custody of the child.[1]

New York's permanent neglect statute provides natural parents with certain procedural protections.[2] But New York permits its officials to establish "permanent neglect" with less proof than most States require. Thirty-five States, the District of Columbia, and the Virgin Islands currently specify a higher standard of proof, in parental rights termination proceedings, than a "fair preponderance of the evidence."[3] The only analogous federal statute of which we are aware permits termination of parental rights solely upon "evidence beyond a reasonable doubt." Indian Child Welfare Act of 1978, Pub. L. 95-608, § 102(f), 92 Stat. 3072, 25 U.S.C. § 1912(f) (1976 ed., Supp. IV). The question here is whether New York's "fair preponderance of the evidence" standard is constitutionally sufficient.

---

1. At oral argument, counsel for petitioners asserted that, in New York, natural parents have no means of restoring terminated parental rights. Tr. of Oral Arg. 9. Counsel for respondents, citing Fam. Ct. Act § 1061, answered that parents may petition the Family Court to vacate or set aside an earlier order on narrow grounds, such as newly discovered evidence or fraud. Tr. of Oral Arg. 26. Counsel for respondents conceded, however, that this statutory provision has never been invoked to set aside a permanent neglect finding. *Id.*, at 27.

2. Most notably, natural parents have a statutory right to the assistance of counsel and of court-appointed counsel if they are indigent. Fam. Ct. Act § 262.(a)(iii).

3. Fifteen States, by statute, have required "clear and convincing evidence" or its equivalent. See Alaska Stat. Ann. § 47.10.080(c)(3) (1980); Cal. Civ. Code Ann. § 232(a)(7) (West Supp. 1982); Ga. Code §§ 24A-2201(c), 24A-3201 (1979); Iowa Code § 600A.8 (1981) ("clear and convincing proof"); Me. Rev. Stat. Ann., Tit. 22, § 4055.1.B.(2) (Supp. 1981–1982); Mich. Comp. Laws § 722.25 (Supp. 1981–1982); Mo. Rev. Stat. § 211.447.2(2) (Supp. 1981) ("clear, cogent and convincing evidence"); N. M. Stat. Ann. § 40-7-4.J. (Supp. 1981); N. C. Gen. Stat. § 7A-289.30(e) (1981) ("clear, cogent, and convincing evidence"); Ohio Rev. Code Ann. §§ 2151.35, 2151.414(B) (Page Supp. 1982); R. I. Gen. Laws § 15-7-7(d) (Supp. 1980); Tenn. Code Ann. § 37-246(d) (Supp. 1981); Va. Code § 16.1-283.B (Supp. 1981); W. Va. Code § 49-6-2(c) (1980) ("clear and convincing proof"); Wis. Stat. § 48.31(1) (Supp. 1981–1982).

Fifteen States, the District of Columbia, and the Virgin Islands, by court decision, have required "clear and convincing evidence" or its equivalent. See *Dale County Dept. of Pensions & Security v. Robles*, 368 So.2d 39, 42 (Ala. Civ. App. 1979); *Harper v. Caskin*, 265 Ark. 558, 560–561, 580 S.W.2d 176, 178 (1979); *In re J. S. R.*, 374 A.2d 860, 864 (D.C. 1977); *Torres v. Van Eepoel*, 98 So.2d 735, 737 (Fla. 1957); *In re Kerns*, 225 Kan. 746, 753, 594 P.2d 187, 193 (1979); *In re Rosenbloom*, 266 N.W.2d 888, 889 (Minn. 1978) ("clear and convincing proof"); *In re J. L. B.*, 182 Mont. 100, 116–117, 594 P.2d 1127, 1136 (1979); *In re Souza*, 204 Neb.

(continued on next page)

B

Petitioners John Santosky II and Annie Santosky are the natural parents of Tina and John III. In November 1973, after incidents reflecting parental neglect, respondent Kramer, Commissioner of the Ulster County Department of Social Services, initiated a neglect proceeding under Fam. Ct. Act § 1022 and removed Tina from her natural home. About 10 months later, he removed John III and placed him with foster parents. On the day John was taken, Annie Santosky gave birth to a third child, Jed. When Jed was only three days old, respondent transferred him to a foster home on the ground that immediate removal was necessary to avoid imminent danger to his life or health.

In October 1978, respondent petitioned the Ulster County Family Court to terminate petitioners' parental rights in the three children.[4] Petitioners challenged the constitutionality of the "fair preponderance of the evidence" standard specified in Fam. Ct. Act § 622. The Family Court Judge rejected this constitutional challenge, App. 29–30, and

weighed the evidence under the statutory standard. While acknowledging that the Santoskys had maintained contact with their children, the judge found those visits "at best superficial and devoid of any real emotional content." *Id.*, at 21. After deciding that the agency had made " 'diligent efforts' to encourage and strengthen the parental relationship," *id.*, at 30, he concluded that the Santoskys were incapable, even with public assistance, of planning for the future of their children. *Id.*, at 33–37. The judge later held a dispositional hearing and ruled that the best interests of the three children required permanent termination of the Santoskys' custody.[5] *Id.*, at 39.

Petitioners appealed, again contesting the constitutionality of § 622's standard of proof.[6] The New York Supreme Court, Appellate Division, affirmed, holding application of the preponderance-of-the-evidence standard "proper and constitutional." *In re John AA*, 75 App.Div.2d 910, 427 N.Y.S.2d 319, 320 (1980). That standard, the court reasoned, "recognizes and seeks to balance rights possessed by the child . . . with those of the natural parents. . . ." Ibid.

503, 510, 283 N.W.2d 48, 52 (1979); *J. v. M.*, 157 N.J.Super. 478, 489, 385 A.2d 240, 246 (App.Div. 1978); *In re J. A.*, 283 N.W.2d 83, 92, (N.D. 1979); *In re Darren Todd H.*, 615 P.2d 287, 289 (Okla. 1980); *In re William L.*, 477 Pa. 322, 332, 383 A.2d 1228, 1233, *cert. denied sub nom. Lehman v. Lycoming County Children's Services*, 439 U.S. 880 (1978); *In re G. M.*, 596 S.W.2d 846, 847 (Tex. 1980); *In re Pitts*, 535 P.2d 1244, 1248 (Utah 1975); *In re Maria*, 15 V. I. 368, 384 (1978); *In re Sego*, 82 Wash.2d 736, 739, 513 P.2d 831, 833 (1973) ("clear, cogent, and convincing evidence"); *In re X.*, 607 P.2d 911, 919 (Wyo. 1980) ("clear and unequivocal").

South Dakota's Supreme Court has required a "clear preponderance" of the evidence in a dependency proceeding. See *In re B. E.*, 287 N.W.2d 91, 96 (1979). Two States, New Hampshire and Louisiana, have barred parental rights terminations unless the key allegations have been proved beyond a reasonable doubt. See *State v. Robert H.*, 118 N. H. 713, 716, 393 A.2d 1387, 1389 (1978); La. Rev. Stat. Ann. § 13:1603.A (West Supp. 1982). Two States, Illinois and New York, have required clear and convincing evidence, but only in certain types of parental rights termination proceedings. See Ill. Rev. Stat., ch. 37, ¶¶ 705-9(c), (3) (1979), amended by Act of Sept. 11, 1981, 1982 Ill. Laws, P. A. 82–437 (generally requiring a preponderance of the evidence, but requiring clear and convincing evidence to terminate the rights of minor parents and mentally ill or mentally deficient parents); N. Y. Soc. Serv. Law §§ 384-b.3(g), 384-b.4(c), and 384-b.4(e) (Supp. 1981–1982) (requiring "clear and convincing proof" before parental rights may be terminated for reasons of mental illness and mental retardation or severe and repeated child abuse).

So far as we are aware, only two federal courts have addressed the issue. Each has held that allegations supporting parental rights termination must be proved by clear and convincing evidence. *Sims v. State Dept. of Public Welfare*, 483 F.Supp. 1179, 1194 (SD Tex. 1977), *rev'd on other grounds sub nom. Moore v. Sims*, 442 U.S. 415 (1979); *Alsager v. District Court of Polk County*, 406 F.Supp. 10, 25 (SD Iowa 1975), *aff'd on other grounds*, 545 F.2d 1137 (CA8 1976).

4. Respondent had made an earlier and unsuccessful termination effort in September 1976. After a fact-finding hearing, the Family Court Judge dismissed respondent's petition for failure to prove an essential element of Fam. Ct. Act § 614.1.(d). See *In re Santosky*, 89 Misc.2d 730, 393 N.Y.S.2d 486 (1977). The New York Supreme Court, Appellate Division, affirmed, finding that "the record as a whole" revealed that petitioners had "substantially planned for the future of the childen." *In re John W.*, 63 App.Div.2d 750, 751, 404 N.Y.S.2d 717, 719 (1978).

5. Since respondent Kramer took custody of Tina, John III, and Jed, the Santoskys have had two other children, James and Jeremy. The States has taken no action to remove these younger children. At oral argument, counsel for respondents replied affirmatively when asked whether he was asserting that petitioners were "unfit to handle the three older ones but not unfit to handle the two younger ones." Tr. of Oral Arg. 24.

6. Petitioners initially had sought review in the New York Court of Appeals. That court *sua sponte* transferred the appeal to the Appellate Division, Third Department, stating that a direct appeal did not lie because "questions other than the constitutional validity of a statutory provision are involved." App. 50.

The New York Court of Appeals then dismissed petitioners' appeal to that court "upon the ground that no substantial constitutional question is directly involved." App. 55. We granted certiorari to consider petitioners' constitutional claim. 450 U.S. 993 (1981).

II

Last Term, in *Lassiter v. Department of Social Services*, 452 U.S. 18 (1981), this Court, by a 5–4 vote, held that the Fourteenth Amendment's Due Process Clause does not require the appointment of counsel for indigent parents in every parental status termination proceeding. The case casts light, however, on the two central questions here—whether process is constitutionally due a natural parent at a State's parental rights termination proceeding, and, if so, what process is due.

In *Lassiter*, it was "not disputed that state intervention to terminate the relationship between [a parent] and [the] child must be accomplished by procedures meeting the requisites of the Due Process Clause." *Id.*, at 37 (first dissenting opinion); see *id.*, at 24–32 (opinion of the Court); *id.*, at 59–60 (Stevens, J., dissenting). See also *Little v. Streater*, 452 U.S. 1, 13 (1981). The absence of dispute reflected this Court's historical recognition that freedom of personal choice in matters of family life is a fundamental liberty interest protected by the Fourteenth Amendment. *Quilloin v. Walcott*, 434 U.S. 246, 255 (1978); *Smith v. Organization of Foster Families*, 431 U.S. 816, 845 (1977); *Moore v. East Cleveland*, 431 U.S. 494, 499 (1977) (plurality opinion); *Cleveland Board of Education v. LaFleur*, 414 U.S. 632, 639–640 (1974); *Stanley v. Illinois*, 405 U.S. 645, 651–652 (1972); *Prince v. Massachusetts*, 321 U.S. 158, 166 (1944); *Pierce v. Society of Sisters*, 268 U.S. 510, 534–535 (1925); *Meyer v. Nebraska*, 262 U.S. 390, 399 (1923).

The fundamental liberty interest of natural parents in the care, custody, and management of their child does not evaporate simply because they have not been model parents or have lost temporary custody of their child to the State. Even when blood relationships are strained, parents retain a vital interest in preventing the irretrievable destruction of their family life. If anything, persons faced with forced dissolution of their parental rights have a more critical need for procedural protections than do those resisting state intervention into ongoing family affairs. When the State moves to destroy weakened familial bonds, it must provide the parents with fundamentally fair procedures.[7]

In *Lassiter*, the Court and three dissenters agreed that the nature of the process due in parental rights termination proceedings turns on a balancing of the "three distinct factors" specified in *Mathews v. Eldridge*, 424 U.S. 319, 335 (1976): the private interests affected by the proceeding; the risk of error created by the State's chosen procedure; and the countervailing governmental interest supporting use of the challenged procedure. See 452 U.S., at 27–31; *id.*, at 37–48 (first dissenting opinion). But see *id.*, at 59–60 (Stevens, J., dissenting). While the respective *Lassiter* opinions disputed whether those factors should be weighed against a presumption disfavoring appointed counsel for one not threatened with loss of physical liberty, compare 452 U.S., at 31–32, with *id.*, at 41, and n. 8 (first dissenting opinion), that concern is irrelevant here. Unlike the Court's right-to-counsel rulings, its decisions concerning constitutional burdens of proof have not turned on any presumption favoring any particular standard. To the contrary, the Court has engaged in a straightforward consideration of the factors identified in *Eldridge* to determine whether a particular standard of proof in a particular proceeding satisfies due process.

In *Addington v. Texas*, 441 U.S. 418 (1979), the Court, by a unanimous vote of the participating Justices, declared: "The function of a standard of proof, as that concept is embodied in the Due Process Clause and in the realm of fact-finding, is to 'instruct the fact-finder concerning the degree of confidence our society thinks he should have in the correctness of factual conclusions for a particular type of adjudication.'" *Id.*, at 423, quoting *In re Winship*, 397 U.S. 358, 370 (1970) (Harlan, J., concurring). *Addington* teaches that, in any given proceeding, the minimum standard of proof toler-

---

7. We therefore reject respondent Kramer's claim that a parental rights termination proceeding does not interfere with a fundamental liberty interest. See Brief for Respondent Kramer 11–18; Tr. of Oral Arg. 38. The fact that important liberty interests of the child and its foster parents may also be affected by a permanent neglect proceeding does not justify denying the *natural parents* constitutionally adequate procedures. Nor can the State refuse to provide natural parents adequate procedural safeguards on the ground that the family unit already has broken down; that is the very issue the permanent neglect proceeding is meant to decide.

ated by the due process requirements reflects not only the weight of the private and public interests affected, but also a societal judgment about how the risk of error should be distributed between the litigants.

Thus, while private parties may be interested intensely in a civil dispute over money damages, application of a "fair preponderance of the evidence" standard indicates both society's "minimal concern with the outcome," and a conclusion that the litigants should "share the risk of error in roughly equal fashion." 441 U.S., at 423. When the State brings a criminal action to deny a defendant liberty or life, however, "the interests of the defendant are of such magnitude that historically and without any explicit constitutional requirement they have been protected by standards of proof designed to exclude as nearly as possible the likelihood of an erroneous judgment." Ibid. The stringency of the "beyond a reasonable doubt" standard bespeaks the "weight and gravity" of the private interest affected, id., at 427, society's interest in avoiding erroneous convictions, and a judgment that those interests together require that "society impos[e] almost the entire risk of error upon itself." Id., at 424. See also In re Winship, 397 U.S., at 372 (Harlan, J., concurring).

The "minimum requirements [of procedural due process] being a matter of federal law, they are not diminished by the fact that the State may have specified its own procedures that it may deem adequate for determining the preconditions to adverse official action." Vitek v. Jones, 445 U.S. 480, 491 (1980). See also Logan v. Zimmerman Brush Co., ante, at 432. Moreover, the degree of proof required in a particular type of proceeding "is the kind of question which has traditionally been left to the judiciary to resolve." Woodby v. INS, 385 U.S. 276, 284 (1966).[8] "In cases involving individual rights, whether criminal or civil, '[t]he standard of proof [at a minimum] reflects the value society places on individual liberty.' " Addington v. Texas, 441 U.S., at 425, quoting Tippett v. Maryland, 436 F.2d 1153, 1166 (CA4

1971) (opinion concurring in part and dissenting in part), cert. dism'd sub nom. Murel v. Baltimore City Criminal Court, 407 U.S. 355 (1972).

This Court has mandated an intermediate standard of proof—"clear and convincing evidence"—when the individual interests at stake in a state proceeding are both "particularly important" and "more substantial than mere loss of money." Addington v. Texas, 441 U.S., at 424. Notwithstanding "the state's 'civil labels and good intentions,' " id., at 427, quoting In re Winship, 397 U.S., at 365–366, the Court has deemed this level of certainty necessary to preserve fundamental fairness in a variety of government-initiated proceedings that threaten the individual involved with "a significant deprivation of liberty" or "stigma." 441 U.S., at 425, 426. See, e.g., Addington v. Texas, supra (civil commitment); Woodby v. INS, 385 U.S., at 285 (deportation); Chaunt v. United States, 364 U.S. 350, 353 (1960) (denaturalization); Schneiderman v. United States, 320 U.S. 118, 125, 159 (1943) (denaturalization).

In Lassiter, to be sure, the Court held that fundamental fairness may be maintained in parental rights termination proceedings even when some procedures are mandated only on a case-by-case basis, rather than through rules of general application. 452 U.S., at 31–32 (natural parent's right to court-appointed counsel should be determined by the trial court, subject to appellate review). But this Court never has approved case-by-case determination of the proper standard of proof for a given proceeding. Standards of proof, like other "procedural due process rules[,] are shaped by the risk of error inherent in the truth-finding process as applied to the generality of cases, not the rare exceptions." Mathews v. Eldridge, 424 U.S., at 344 (emphasis added). Since the litigants and the fact-finder must know at the outset of a given proceeding how the risk of error will be allocated, the standard of proof necessarily must be calibrated in advance. Retrospective case-by-case review cannot preserve fundamental fairness

---

8. The dissent charges, post, at 772, n. 2, that "this Court simply has no role in establishing the standards of proof that States must follow in the various judicial proceedings they afford to their citizens." As the dissent properly concedes, however, the Court must examine a State's chosen standard to determine whether it satisfies "the constitutional minimum of 'fundamental fairness.' " Ibid. See, e.g., Addington v. Texas, 441 U.S. 418, 427, 433 (1979) (unanimous decision of participating Justices) (Fourteenth Amendment requires at least clear and convincing evidence in a civil proceeding brought under state law to commit an individual involuntarily for an indefinite period to a state mental hospital); In re Winship, 397 U.S. 358, 364 (1970) (Due Process Clause of the Fourteenth Amendment protects the accused in state proceeding against conviction except upon proof beyond a reasonable doubt of every fact necessary to constitute the crime with which he is charged).

when a class of proceedings is governed by a constitutionally defective evidentiary standard.[9]

III

In parental rights termination proceedings, the private interest affected is commanding; the risk of error from using a preponderance standard is substantial; and the contervailing governmental interest favoring that standard is comparatively slight. Evaluation of the three *Eldridge* factors compels the conclusion that use of a "fair preponderance of the evidence" standard in such proceedings is inconsistent with due process.

A

"The extent to which procedural due process must be afforded the recipient is influenced by the extent to which he may be 'condemned to suffer grievous loss.' " *Goldberg v. Kelly*, 397 U.S. 254, 262–263 (1970), quoting *Joint Anti-Fascist Refugee Committee v. McGrath*, 341 U.S. 123, 168 (1951) (Frankfurter, J., concurring). Whether the loss threatened by a particular type of proceeding is sufficiently grave to warrant more than average certainty on the part of the factfinder turns on both the nature of the private interest threatened and the permanency of the threatened loss.

Lassiter declared it "plain beyond the need for multiple citation" that a natural parent's "desire for and right to 'the companionship, care, custody, and management of his or her children' " is an interest far more precious than any property right. 452 U.S., at 27, quoting *Stanley v. Illinois*, 405 U.S., at 651. When the State initiates a parental rights termina-

tion proceeding, it seeks not merely to infringe that fundamental liberty interest, but to end it. "If the State prevails, it will have worked a unique kind of deprivation. . . . A parent's interest in the accuracy and justice of the decision to terminate his or her parental status is, therefore, a commanding one." 452 U.S., at 27.

In government-initiated proceedings to determine juvenile delinquency, *In re Winship, supra*; civil commitment, *Addington v. Texas, supra*; deportation, *Woodby v. INS, supra*; and denaturalization, *Chaunt v. United States, supra*, and *Schneiderman v. United States, supra*, this Court has identified losses of individual liberty sufficiently serious to warrant imposition of an elevated burden of proof. Yet juvenile delinquency adjudications, civil commitment, deportation, and denaturalization, at least to a degree, are all *reversible* official actions. Once affirmed on appeal, a New York decision terminating parental rights is *final* and irrevocable. See n. 1, *supra*. Few forms of state action are both so severe and so irreversible.

Thus, the first *Eldridge* factor—the private interest affected—weighs heavily against use of the preponderance standard at a state-initiated permanent neglect proceeding. We do not deny that the child and his foster parents are also deeply interested in the outcome of that contest. But at the factfinding stage of the New York proceeding, the focus emphatically is on them.

The fact-finding does not purport—and is not intended—to balance the child's interest in a normal family home against the parents' interest in raising the child. Nor does it purport to determine whether the natural parents or the foster parents would provide the better home. Rather, the fact-finding hear-

---

9. For this reason, we reject the suggestions of respondents and the dissent that the constitutionality of New York's statutory procedures must be evaluated as a "package." See Tr. of Oral Arg. 25, 36, 38. Indeed, we would rewrite our precedents were we to excuse a constitutionally defective standard of proof based on an amorphous assessment of the "cumulative effect" of state procedures. In the criminal context, for example, the Court has never assumed that "strict substantive standards or special procedures compensate for a lower burden of proof. . . ." *Post*, at 773. See *In re Winship*, 397 U.S., at 368. Nor has the Court treated appellate review as a curative for an inadequate burden of proof. See *Woodby v. INS*, 385 U.S. 276, 282 (1966) ("judicial review is generally limited to ascertaining whether the evidence relied upon by the trier of fact was of sufficient quality and substantiality to support the rationality of the judgment").

As the dissent points out, "the standard of proof is a crucial component of legal process, the primary function of which is 'to minimize the risk of erroneous decisions.' " *Post*, at 785, quoting *Greenholtz v. Nebraska Penal Inmates*, 442 U.S. 1, 13 (1979). Notice, summons, right to counsel, rules of evidence, and evidentiary hearings are all procedures to place information *before* the factfinder. But only the standard of proof "instruct[s] the factfinder concerning the degree of confidence our society thinks he should have in the correctness of factual conclusions" he draws from that information. *In re Winship*, 397 U.S., at 370 (Harlan, J., concurring). The statutory provision of right to counsel and multiple hearings before termination cannot suffice to protect a natural parent's fundamental liberty interests if the State is willing to tolerate undue uncertainty in the determination of the dispositive facts.

ing pits the state directly against the parents. The State alleges that the natural parents are at fault. Fam. Ct. Act. § 614.1.(d). The questions disputed and decided are what the State did—"made diligent efforts," § 614.1.(c)—and what the natural parents did not do—"maintain contact with or plan for the future of the child." § 614.1.(d). The State marshals an array of public resources to prove its case and disprove the parents' case. Victory by the State not only makes termination of parental rights possible; it entails a judicial determination that the parents are unfit to raise their own children.[10]

At the fact-finding, the State cannot presume that a child and his parents are adversaries. After the State has established parental unfitness at that initial proceeding, the court may assume at the *dispositional* stage that the interests of the child and the natural parents do diverge. See Fam. Ct. Act § 631 (judge shall make his order "solely on the basis of the best interests of the child," and thus has no obligation to consider the natural parents' rights in selecting dispositional alternatives). But until the State proves parental unfitness, the child and his parents share a vital interest in preventing erroneous termination of their natural relationship.[11] Thus, at the fact-finding, the interests of the child and his natural parents coincide to favor use of error-reducing procedures.

However substantial the foster parents' interests may be, cf. *Smith v. Organization of Foster Families*, 431 U.S., at 845–847, they are not implicated directly in the factfinding stage of a state-initiated permanent neglect proceeding against the natural parents. If authorized, the foster parents may pit their interests directly against those of the natural parents by initiating their own permanent neglect proceeding. Fam. Ct. Act § 1055(d); Soc. Serv. Law §§ 384–6.3(b), 392.7.(c). Alternatively, the foster parents can make their case for custody at the dis-

positional stage of a state-initiated proceeding, where the judge already has decided the issue of permanent neglect and is focusing on the placement that would serve the child's best interests. Fam. Ct. Act §§ 623, 631. For the foster parents, the State's failure to prove permanent neglect may prolong the delay and uncertainty until their foster child is freed for adoption. But for the natural parents, a finding of permanent neglect can cut off forever their rights in their child. Given this disparity of consequence, we have no difficulty finding that the balance of private interests strongly favors heightened procedural protections.

B

Under *Mathews v. Eldridge*, we next must consider both the risk of erroneous deprivation of private interests resulting from use of a "fair preponderance" standard and the likelihood that a higher evidentiary standard would reduce that risk. See 424 U.S., at 335. Since the fact-finding phase of a permanent neglect proceeding is an adversary contest between the State and the natural parents, the relevant question is whether a preponderance standard fairly allocates the risk of an erroneous fact-finding between these two parties.

In New York, the fact-finding stage of a state-initiated permanent neglect proceeding bears many of the indicia of a criminal trial. Cf. *Lassiter v. Department of Social Services*, 452 U.S., at 42–44 (first dissenting opinion); *Meltzer v. C. Buck LeCraw & Co.*, 402 U.S. 954, 959 (1971) (Black, J., dissenting from denial of certiorari). See also dissenting opinion, *post*, at 777–779 (describing procedures employed at fact-finding proceeding). The Commissioner of Social Services charges the parents with permanent neglect. They are served by summons. Fam. Ct. Act §§ 614, 616, 617. The fact-finding

---

10. The Family Court Judge in the present case expressly refused to terminate petitioners' parental rights on a "non-statutory, no-fault basis." App. 22–29. Nor is it clear that the State constitutionally could terminate a parent's rights *without* showing parental unfitness. See *Quilloin v. Walcott*, 434 U.S. 246, 255 (1978) ("We have little doubt that the Due Process Clause would be offended '[i]f a State were to attempt to force the breakup of a natural family, over the objections of the parents and their children, without some showing of unfitness and for the sole reason that to do so was thought to be in the children's best interest,' " quoting *Smith v. Organization of Foster Families*, 431 U.S. 816, 862–863 (1977) (Steward, J., concurring in judgment)).

11. For a child, the consequences of termination of his natural parents' rights may well be far-reaching. In Colorado, for example, it has been noted: "The child loses the right of support and maintenance, for which he may therafter be dependent upon society; the right to inherit; and all other rights inherent in the legal parent-child relationship, not just for [a limited] period . . ., but forever." *In re K. S.*, 33 Colo. App. 72, 76, 515 P.2d 130, 133 (1973).

Some losses cannot be measured. In this case, for example, Jed Santosky was removed from his natural parents' custody when he was only three days old; the judge's finding of permanent neglect effectively foreclosed the possibility that Jed would ever know his natural parents.

hearing is conducted pursuant to formal rules of evidence. § 624. The State, the parents, and the child are all represented by counsel. §§ 249, 262. The State seeks to establish a series of historical facts about the intensity of its agency's efforts to reunite the family, the infrequency and insubstantiality of the parents' contacts with their child, and the parents' inability or unwillingness to formulate a plan for the child's future. The attorneys submit documentary evidence, and call witnesses who are subject to cross-examination. Based on all the evidence, the judge then determines whether the State has proved the statutory elements of permanent neglect by a fair preponderance of the evidence. § 622.

At such a proceeding, numerous factors combine to magnify the risk of erroneous fact-finding. Permanent neglect proceedings employ imprecise substantive standards that leave determinations unusually open to the subjective values of the judge. See *Smith v. Organization of Foster Families*, 431 U.S., at 835, n. 36. In appraising the nature and quality of a complex series of encounters among the agency, the parents, and the child, the court possesses unusual discretion to underweigh probative facts that might favor the parent.[12] Because parents subject to termination proceedings are often poor, uneducated, or members of minority groups, *id.*, at 833–835, such proceedings are often vulnerable to judgments based on cultural or class bias.

The State's ability to assemble its case almost inevitably dwarfs the parents' ability to mount a defense. No predetermined limits restrict the sums an agency may spend in prosecuting a given termination proceeding. The State's attorney usually will be expert on the issues contested and the procedures employed at the fact-finding hearing, and enjoys full access to all public records concerning the family. The State may call on experts in family relations, psychology, and medicine to bolster its case. Furthermore, the primary witnesses at the hearing will be the agency's own professional caseworkers whom the State has empowered both to investigate the family situation and to testify against the parents. Indeed, because the child is already in agency custody, the State even has the power to shape the historical events that form the basis for termination.[13]

The disparity between the adversaries' litigation resources is matched by a striking asymmetry in their litigation options. Unlike criminal defendants, natural parents have no "double jeopardy" defense against repeated state termination efforts. If the State initially fails to win termination, as New York did here, see n. 7, *supra*, it always can try once again to cut off the parents' rights after gathering more or better evidence. Yet even when the parents have attained the level of fitness required by the State, they have no similar means by which they can forestall future termination efforts.

Coupled with a "fair preponderance of the evidence" standard, these factors create a significant prospect of erroneous termination. A standard of proof that by its very terms demands consideration of the quantity, rather than the quality, of the evidence may misdirect the fact-finder in the marginal case. See *In re Winship*, 397 U.S., at 371, n. 3 (Harlan, J., concurring). Given the weight of the private interests at stake, the social cost of even occasional error is sizable.

Raising the standard of proof would have both practical and symbolic consequences. Cf. *Addington v. Texas*, 441 U.S., at 426. The Court has long considered the heightened standard of proof used in criminal prosecutions to be "a prime instrument for reducing the risk of convictions resting on factual

---

12. For example, a New York court appraising an agency's "diligent efforts" to provide the parents with social services can excuse efforts *not* made on the grounds that they would have been "detrimental to the best interests of the child." Fam. Ct. Act § 614.1.(c). In determining whether the parent "substantially and continuously or repeatedly" failed to "maintain contact with . . . the child," § 614.1.(d), the judge can discount actual visits or communications on the grounds that they were insubstantial or "overtly demonstrat[ed] a lack of affectionate and concerned parenthood." Soc. Serv. Law § 384-b.7.(b). When determining whether the parent planned for the child's future, the judge can reject as unrealistic plans based on overly optimistic estimates of physical or financial ability. § 384-b.7.(c). See also dissenting opinion, *post*, at 779–780, nn. 8 and 9.

13. In this case, for example, the parents claim that the State sought court orders denying them the right to visit their children, which would have prevented them from maintaining the contact required by Fam. Ct. Act § 614.1.(d). See Brief for Petitioners 9. The parents further claim that the State cited their rejection of social services they found offensive or superfluous as proof of the agency's "diligent efforts" and their own "failure to plan" for the children's future. *Id.*, at 10–11.

We need not accept these statements as true to recognize that the State's unusual ability to structure the evidence increases the risk of an erroneous fact-finding. Of course, the disparity between the litigants' resources will be vastly greater in States where there is no statutory right to court-appointed counsel. See *Lassiter v. Department of Social Services*, 452 U.S. 18, 34 (1981) (only 33 States and the District of Columbia provide that right by statute).

error." *In re Winship*, 397 U.S., at 363. An elevated standard of proof in a parental rights termination proceeding would alleviate "the possible risk that a fact-finder might decide to [deprive] an individual based solely on a few isolated instances of unusual conduct [or] . . . idiosyncratic behavior." *Addington v. Texas*, 441 U.S., at 427. "Increasing the burden of proof is one way to impress the fact-finder with the importance of the decision and thereby perhaps to reduce the chances that inappropriate" terminations will be ordered. Ibid.

The Appellate Division approved New York's preponderance standard on the ground that it properly "balanced rights possessed by the child . . . with those of the natural parents. . . ." 75 App. Div. 2d, at 910, 427 N.Y.S. 2d, at 320. By so saying, the court suggested that a preponderance standard properly allocates the risk of error *between* the parents and the child."[14] That view is fundamentally mistaken.

The court's theory assumes that termination of the natural parents' rights invariably will benefit the child.[15] Yet we have noted above that the parents and the child share an interest in avoiding erroneous termination. Even accepting the court's assumption, we cannot agree with its conclusion that a preponderance standard fairly distributes the risk of error between parent and child. Use of that standard reflects the judgment that society is nearly neutral between erroneous termination of parental rights and erroneous failure to terminate those rights. Cf. *In re Winship*, 397 U.S., at 371 (Harlan, J., concurring). For the child, the likely consequence of an erroneous failure to terminate is preservation of an easy status quo.[16] For the natural parents, however, the consequence of an erroneous termination is the unnecessary destruction of their natural family. A standard that allocates the risk of error nearly equally between those two outcomes does not reflect properly their relative severity.

C

Two state interests are at stake in parental rights termination proceedings—a *parens patriae* interest in preserving and promoting the welfare of the child and a fiscal and administrative interest in reducing the cost and burden of such proceedings. A standard of proof more strict than preponderance of the evidence is consistent with both interests.

"Since the State has an urgent interest in the welfare of the child, it shares the parent's interest in an accurate and just decision" at the *fact-finding* proceeding. *Lassiter v. Department of Social Services*, 452 U.S., at 27. As *parens patriae*, the State's goal is to provide the child with a permanent home. See Soc. Serv. Law § 384-b.1.(a)(i) (statement of legislative findings and intent). Yet while there is still reason to believe that positive, nurturing parent-child relationships exist, the *parens patriae* interest favors preservation, not severance, of natural familial bonds.[17] § 384-b.1.(a)(ii). "[T]he State registers no gain towards its declared goals when it separates children from the custody of fit parents." *Stanley v. Illinois*, 405 U.S., at 652.

The State's interest in finding the child an alternative permanent home arises only "when it is *clear*

---

14. The dissent makes a similar claim. See *post*, at 786–791.

15. This is a hazardous assumption at best. Even when a child's natural home is imperfect, permanent removal from that home will not necessarily improve his welfare. See, e.g., Wald, State Intervention on Behalf of "Neglected" Children: A Search for Realistic Standards, 27 Stan. L. Rev. 985, 993 (1975) ("In fact, under current practice, coercive intervention frequently results in placing a child in a more detrimental situation than he would be in without intervention").

Nor does termination of parental rights necessarily ensure adoption. See Brief for Community Action for Legal Services, Inc., et al. as *amici curiae* 22–23. Even when a child eventually finds an adoptive family, he may spend years moving between state institutions and "temporary" foster placements after his ties to his natural parents have been severed. See *Smith v. Organization of Foster Families*, 431 U.S., at 833–838 (describing the "limbo" of the New York foster care system).

16. When the termination proceeding occurs, the child is not living at his natural home. A child cannot be adjudicated "permanently neglected" until, "for a period of more than one year," he has been in "the care of an authorized agency." Soc. Serv. Law § 384-b.7.(a); Fam. Ct. Act § 614.1.(d). See also dissenting opinion, *post*, at 789–790.

Under New York law, a judge has ample discretion to ensure that, once removed from his natural parents on grounds of neglect, a child will not return to a hostile environment. In this case, when the State's initial termination effort failed for lack of proof, see n. 4, *supra*, the court simply issued orders under Fam. Ct. Act § 1055(b) extending the period of the child's foster home placement. See App. 19–20. See also Fam. Ct. Act § 632(b) (when State's permanent neglect petition is dismissed for insufficient evidence, judge retains jurisdiction to reconsider underlying orders of placement); § 633 (judge may suspend judgment at dispositional hearing for an additional year).

17. Any *parens patriae* interest in terminating the natural parents' rights arises only at the dispositional phase, *after* the parents have been found unfit.

that the natural parent cannot or will not provide a normal family home for the child." Soc. Serv. Law § 384-b.1.(a)(iv) (emphasis added). At the fact-finding, that goal is served by procedures that promote an accurate determination of whether the natural parents can and will provide a normal home.

Unlike a constitutional requirement of hearings, see, e.g., *Mathews v. Eldridge*, 424 U.S., at 347, or court-appointed counsel, a stricter standard of proof would reduce factual error without imposing substantial fiscal burdens upon the State. As we have observed, 35 States already have adopted a higher standard by statute or court decision without apparent effect on the speed, form, or cost of their fact-finding proceedings. See n. 3, *supra*.

Nor would an elevated standard of proof create any real administrative burdens for the State's fact-finders. New York Family Court judges already are familiar with a higher evidentiary standard in other parental rights termination proceedings not involving permanent neglect. See Soc. Serv. Law §§ 384-b.3.(g), 384-b.4.(c), and 384-b.4.(e) (requiring "clear and convincing proof" before parental rights may be terminated for reasons of mental illness and mental retardation or severe and repeated child abuse). New York also demands at least clear and convincing evidence in proceedings of far less moment than parental rights termination proceedings. See, e.g., N.Y. Veh. & Traf. Law § 227.1 (McKinney Supp. 1981) (requiring the State to prove traffic infractions by "clear and convincing evidence") and *In re Rosenthal v. Hartnett*, 36 N.Y.2d 269, 326 N.E.2d 811 (1975); see also *Ross v. Food Specialties, Inc.*, 6 N.Y.2d 336, 341, 160 N.E.2d 618, 620 (1959) (requiring "clear, positive and convincing evidence" for contract reformation). We cannot believe that it would burden the State unduly to require that its fact-finders have the same factual certainty when terminating the parent-child relationship as they must have to suspend a driver's license.

IV

The logical conclusion of this balancing process is that the "fair preponderance of the evidence" stan-

dard prescribed by Fam. Ct. Act § 622 violates the Due Process Clause of the Fourteenth Amendment.[18] The Court noted in *Addington*: "The individual should not be asked to share equally with society the risk or error when the possible injury to the individual is significantly greater than any possible harm to the state." 441 U.S., at 427. Thus, at a parental rights termination proceeding, a near-equal allocation of risk between the parents and the State is constitutionally intolerable. The next question, then, is whether a "beyond a reasonable doubt" or "clear and convincing" standard is constitutionally mandated.

In *Addington*, the Court concluded that application of a reasonable-doubt standard is inappropriate in civil commitment proceedings for two reasons—because of our hesitation to apply that unique standard "too broadly or casually in noncriminal cases," *id.*, at 428, and because the psychiatric evidence ordinarily adduced at commitment proceedings is rarely susceptible to proof beyond a reasonable doubt. *Id.*, at 429–430, 432–433. To be sure, as has been noted above, in the Indian Child Welfare Act of 1978, Pub. L. 95–608, § 102(f), 92 Stat. 3072, 25 U.S.C. § 1912(f) (1976 ed., Supp. IV), Congress requires "evidence beyond a reasonable doubt" for termination of Indian parental rights, reasoning that "the removal of a child from the parents is a penalty as great [as], if not greater, than a criminal penalty. . . ." H. R. Rep. No. 95-1386, p. 22 (1978). Congress did not consider, however, the evidentiary problems that would arise if proof beyond a reasonable doubt were required in all state-initiated parental rights termination hearings.

Like civil commitment hearings, termination proceedings often require the factfinder to evaluate medical and psychiatric testimony, and to decide issues difficult to prove to a level of absolute certainty, such as lack of parental motive, absence of affection between parent and child, and failure of parental foresight and progress. Cf. *Lassiter v. Department of Social Services*, 452 U.S., at 30; *id.*, at 44–46 (first dissenting opinion) (describing issues raised in state termination proceedings). The substantive standards applied vary from State to State.

---

18. The dissent's claim that today's decision "will inevitably lead to the federalization of family law," *post*, at 773, is, of course, vastly overstated. As the dissent properly notes, the Court's duty to "refrai[n] from interfering with state answers to domestic relations questions" has never required "that the Court should blink at clear constitutional violations in state statutes." *Post*, at 771.

19. Unlike the dissent, we carefully refrain from accepting as the "facts of this case" findings that are not part of the record and that have been found only to be more likely true than not.

Although Congress found a "beyond a reasonable doubt" standard proper in one type of parental rights termination case, another legislative body might well conclude that a reasonable-doubt standard would erect an unreasonable barrier to state efforts to free permanently neglected children for adoption.

A majority of the States have concluded that a "clear and convincing evidence" standard of proof strikes a fair balance between the rights of the natural parents and the State's legitimate concerns. See n. 3, *supra*. We hold that such a standard adequately conveys to the factfinder the level of subjective certainty about his factual conclusions necessary to satisfy due process. We further hold that determination of the precise burden equal to or greater than that standard is a matter of state law properly left to state legislatures and state courts. Cf. *Addington v. Texas*, 441 U.S., at 433.

We, of course, express no view on the merits of petitioners' claims.[19] At a hearing conducted under a constitutionally proper standard, they may or may not prevail. Without deciding the outcome under any of the standards we have approved, we vacate

the judgment of the Appellate Division and remand the case for further proceedings not inconsistent with this opinion.

It is so ordered.

END NOTES—CHAPTER VIII

1. Tausha Bradshaw and Alan Marks, "Beyond a Reasonable Doubt: Factors That Influence the Legal Disposition of Child Sexual Abuse Cases," *Crime and Delinquency* 36: 276–85 (1990).

2. Office of Juvenile Justice and Delinquency Prevention, *Using the Law to Improve School Order and Safety* (Washington, D.C.: U.S. Department of Justice, 1989).

3. In addition to issues of school suspension and expulsion, the U.S. Supreme Court has also spoken on corporal punishment in school systems. *Ingraham v. Wright*, 430 U.S. 651 (1977), upheld the right of teachers to use corporal punishment.

4. The concept of free speech articulated in *Tinker* was used again in the 1986 case of *Bethel School District No. 403 v. Fraser*, 478 U.S. 675 (1986). This case upheld a school system's right to suspend or otherwise discipline a student who uses obscene or profane language and gestures.

5. In *Lassiter v. Department of Social Services*, 452 U.S. 18 (1981), the Supreme Court decided that due process does not automatically mandate counsel for parents in termination cases.

Table of Cases

INDEX